Cape Cod

Martha's Vineyard
& Nantucket

Cape Cod
Martha's Vineyard
& Nantucket

Kim Grant

with photographs by the author

The Countryman Press　✳　Woodstock Vermont

DEDICATION

For Lisa M. Otero, to whom I'm deeply grateful

We welcome your comments and suggestions. Please contact Explorer's Guide Editor, The Countryman Press, P.O. Box 748, Woodstock, VT 05091, or e-mail countrymanpress@wwnorton.com.

ISBN: 0-88150-537-4
ISSN: 1533-6875

Cover and text design by Bodenweber Design
Cover photograph and all interior photographs © Kim Grant
Maps by Paul Woodward, © 2003 The Countryman Press
Text composition by PerfecType, Nashville, TN

Published by The Countryman Press,
P.O. Box 748, Woodstock, Vermont 05091

Distributed by W. W. Norton & Company, Inc., 500 Fifth Avenue, New York, NY 10110

Printed in the United States of America

10 9 8 7 6 5 4 3 2 1

EXPLORE WITH US!

Welcome to the fifth edition of the most comprehensive guide to Cape Cod, Martha's Vineyard, and Nantucket. I have been highly selective but broadly inclusive, based on years of repeated visits, cumulative research, and ongoing conversations with locals. All entries—attractions, inns, and restaurants—are chosen on the basis of personal experience, not paid advertising.

I hope you find the organization of this guide easy to read and use. The layout has been kept simple; the following pointers will help you get started.

WHAT'S WHERE

In the beginning of the book you'll find an alphabetical listing of special highlights and important information that you can reference quickly. You'll find advice on everything from where to find the best art galleries, to where to find lighthouses, to where to take a whale-watching excursion.

LODGING

Prices: Please don't hold us or the respective innkeepers responsible for the rates listed as of press time in 2003. Changes are inevitable. At the time of this writing, the state and local room tax was 9.7 percent. Please also see *Lodging* under "What's Where on Cape Cod, Martha's Vineyard, and Nantucket."

RESTAURANTS

In most sections, note the distinction between *Dining Out* and *Eating Out*. Restaurants listed under *Eating Out* are generally inexpensive and more casual; reservations are often suggested for restaurants in *Dining Out*. A range of prices for main dishes is included with each entry.

GREEN SPACE

In addition to trails and walks, "green space" also includes white and blue spaces, that is, beaches and ponds.

KEY TO SYMBOLS

❋ The "off-season" icon appears next to appealing off-season or year-round lodging or attractions.

❧ The "special-value" icon appears next to lodging entries, restaurants, and activities that combine exceptional quality with moderate prices.

🐾 The "pet-friendly" icon appears next to lodgings where pets are welcome.

✎ The "child and family interest" icon appears next to lodging entries, restaurants, activities, and shops of special appeal to youngsters and families.

☂ The "rainy-day" icon appears next to things to do and places of interest that are appropriate for foul-weather days.

Υ The "martini glass" icon appears next to restaurants and entertainment venues with good bars.

♿ The "handicap" symbol indicates lodging and dining establishments that are truly wheelchair accessible.

I appreciate comments and corrections about places you discover or know well. You may e-mail me at cceg@kimgrant.com or write to Explorer's Guide Editor, The Countryman Press, P.O. Box 748, Woodstock, VT 05091.

Please visit my web sites (www.kimgrant.com and www.CapeCodExplorersGuide.com) for up-to-the-minute reviews and to add your voice to the growing chorus of Explorers.

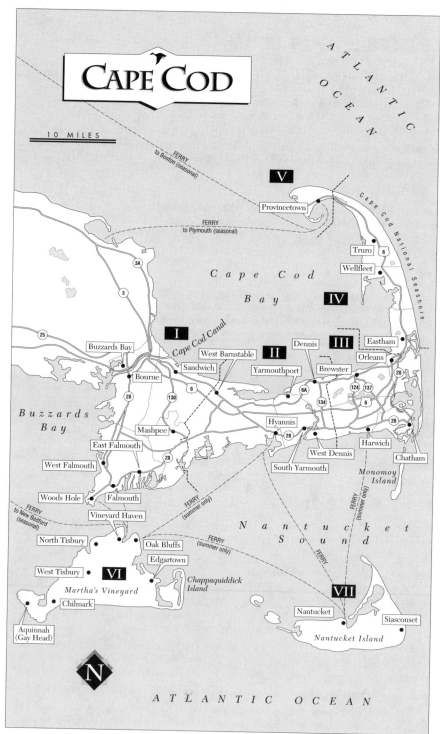

CONTENTS

LIST OF MAPS

INTRODUCTION

Welcome to the fifth edition of *Cape Cod, Martha's Vineyard, and Nantucket: An Explorer's Guide.*

Three big issues have affected this region since the last edition: the economy, September 11, and the Internet. A worsening economy has translated to, quite honestly, area business owners being nicer to and more grateful for their customers. Generally, they aren't so quick to take customers for granted. The attitude of "raise the prices and they will come" has softened. At the same time, low interest rates have sent home prices skyrocketing. Land development for vacation homes is booming, and traffic is at its worst level in years. The Cape's infrastructure is stressed. The 2001 terrorist attacks have made more Americans stay closer to home and taking driving vacations. That bodes well for the Cape's economy, which is within a reasonable drive of many major metropolitan areas.

And of course, there's the Internet. We all know what that's done. It's made my job easier in some respects. I don't have to describe rooms right down to the wallpaper color. Instead, I can spend my precious word count on why you should go one place over another, why one place is right for you and not for your boss. I see my job as providing "decision assistance," as my colleague Tom Brosnahan likes to say. My job has gotten more fun. I've become more of a filter for you.

The Internet has turned many of you into travel experts, or at least your own travel agents. You've never had so much information at your fingertips. All the more power to you if you want to surf the web, finding the best place for your weeklong holiday. What I hope to provide for you is a reasoned assessment of your choices. I have personally visited every place in this guide—and many, many more that don't make it into this guide. I hope it helps you determine where best to spend your hard-earned dollars and precious vacation time.

I am in a position to ferret out the great from the good, to assess those intangible qualities that make a vacation memorable. What I am looking for when I research a place to stay, for instance, is how personable and friendly the innkeepers are; how service-oriented the staff are; how clean the rooms are. Those factors can't be measured by looking at a web page. Proprietors are constantly surprised when I tell them that I rarely consult web sites. I'd rather visit a place. And thankfully, you appreciate the difference, since sales of this guide have increased about 20 percent with each edition. We can tell that you value independent assessment. And we're grateful.

The publishers and I take reader feedback seriously (to comment, please see the *Explore With Us!* page). Some of the comments I've received over the last couple of years are embedded in this edition (after verifying the information). Some of you have mentioned that you want even more restaurant reviews. So I have provided more. But there are dozens and dozens of eateries along Route 28, for instance, that I don't review. You can trust that I've investigated every single one of them, and have chosen the best in each range, from budget to expensive, from family-friendly establishments to places for a romantic rendezvous.

Businesses do not pay to be included in this guide. In fact, I am often asked by restaurateurs and lodging owners, "How much does it cost to take out an ad in your book?" The answer, of course, is: "Nothing. If you do your job well and there is a market for it, I include you." Inevitably they follow up with, "Well, how do you make any money? Other guidebooks charge us for inclusion." The answer is simple. To paraphrase an old Smith-Barney advertisement, "We make money the old-fashioned way: We earn it"—by doing thorough research, and by our readers, in turn, valuing our advice enough to spend 20 bucks on it.

One other significant way this guide differs from the competition is that I alone have researched and written it since 1994. What that means to you, the reader, is that when I say a place is the best clam shack on the Cape, you know that I have visited them all. Many other guidebooks dispatch a team of researchers to various parts of the Cape; when these authors write that a place is the best clam shack on the Cape, what they really mean is, "This is the best clam shack in the territory I was assigned for this edition." Furthermore, because I have written every edition of this book since its inception, you will benefit from insights I have gained over the course of many years of research.

By most accounts and calculations, almost 120,000 cars cross the Cape Cod Canal every day in July and August, and the ferries to Martha's Vineyard and Nantucket transport more than 2.4 million people each summer. So it would be a stretch of the imagination to say that these fragile parcels of prized real estate are undiscovered or unexplored. In fact, sometimes it seems there isn't a grain of sand that hasn't been written about.

But just when I think I've seen it all, a ray of bright, clear sunlight will hit the Provincetown dune shacks in such a way as to make them seem new again. I'll strike up a conversation with a historical society curator, and she'll regale me with stories about town affairs at the turn of the 19th century. I'll walk down a trail in October that I previously walked in May and hear different birds and see different plants. Or I'll take a van tour on Nantucket, and Gail will find just the right anecdote to make history jump off a ship captain's logbook.

There is certainly no lack of information about Cape Cod, Martha's Vineyard, and Nantucket. But the way I see it, there are a few big problems with the material. Some stem from its abundance, and many of the compilations are overwhelming and undiscriminating. (You could fill file cabinets with the stuff—trust me, I have!) Much of what passes for editorial recommendation is actually just paid advertising copy written by the establishments themselves. Catchall web sites are certainly the same. And finally, many of the special-interest brochures—

for antiquing or kids' activities, for instance—cover the entire area. So if you're just visiting one town or concentrating on one region, you must wade through a lot of extraneous information.

This guidebook is intended to be many things to many people. The publishers and I have set our sights to include a wide audience. This book is written for people who live close enough, or are fortunate enough, to be able to make many short trips to the Cape throughout the year—people who know that the region takes on a whole different character from Labor Day weekend to Memorial Day weekend. (It is a common misconception that the region closes down from mid-October to mid-May.) It will prove valuable, as well, to year-rounders who must give advice to a steady stream of summer guests. It's for Cape residents who may live on the Upper Cape, but don't know much about the Lower Cape. It's for people whose only trip to the Cape or the islands is their annual summer holiday—people who have always vacationed in Wellfleet, let's say, but are ready to explore other places. My highest hope, though, is to introduce the "other Cape and islands" to that segment of the traveling public that assumes traffic jams, crowded beaches, and tacky souvenir shops define the region.

This book is the result of years of research, conversation, observation, pleasure reading, and personal exploration. I am a Bostonian who spent youthful summer vacations on Cape Cod, bicycling at the Cape Cod National Seashore, eating saltwater taffy in Provincetown, and camping on Martha's Vineyard. My introduction to Nantucket came later, in the mid-1980s; by then I was old enough to appreciate the island's sophisticated culinary treats and rich history all the more.

Since I am also a professional photographer, I am pleased to supplement my written observations and recommendations with a visual portrait. I have

Kim Grant

intentionally emphasized the region's tranquility, since conventional wisdom already associates the Cape with masses of humanity. But the photos are proof, really, that there are beaches where you can walk alone on a sunny September day.

Traveling, and writing about it, is a nice lifestyle; there's no doubt about that, and I'm grateful for the opportunity to do it. But it is work (as my friends and family, temporarily abandoned in favor of my laptop computer, will attest). The book wouldn't have been possible without the encouragement, guidance, and firsthand experience of many people who appreciate the Cape and the islands from many different perspectives.

As much as I love both four-star dining and a bucket of fried clams from a shack on the pier, I just can't eat everywhere for every edition. I have called upon my innkeeper friends, who benefit from the collective opinions of dozens of guests who eat in dozens of places night after night and then discuss their experiences the next morning over breakfast. Likewise, it is impossible to sleep in every room in every B&B, but I can assure you that I have personally visited and inspected every establishment in this guide.

The folks at The Countryman Press (a division of W. W. Norton) epitomize everything that's good about the publishing industry. I appreciate their responsiveness to and respect for writers, as well as their commitment to providing a quality guidebook to the book-buying public. My special appreciation goes out to managing editor Ann Kraybill, who is both a friend and a pleasure to work with; to superwoman Jennifer Thompson, who worked so hard to put this book together; and to David Corey, the publicity guru who makes sure the books reach you, my readers. And thanks to Norton, for its decision to allow these *Explorer's Guides* to carry on in their great tradition.

As with all editions, this one benefits from the accumulated knowledge that fellow explorers have shared with me, through letters and over breakfast at B&Bs.

For their local expertise and willingness to share it with me, thanks go out to Lynette Molnar and Frank Schaefer in Provincetown; Marla and Buddy Perkel and Eleanor Stefani in Wellfleet; Jean and Gordon Avery in Eastham; the Vessellas and Diane Johnson in Orleans; Kay DeFord in Chatham; Swanee and Sally Swanson in Brewster; Marie Brophy in Dennis; Valerie Butler in Yarmouth; Bill Putman in Hyannis; Ken Traugot and Mary and Bill Kilburn in West Barnstable; Caroline and Jim Lloyd, Renee Ross, and Stu and Jessie Graham in Falmouth; Bob and Caroline Taylor, Sandy Knox-Johnston, Charles and Ann Balas, and Ken Withrow on Nantucket; John Glendon, Claudia Miller, Carl Buder, and Brady Aikens on Martha's Vineyard.

Thanks, especially, to Colby Smith for her unflinching assistance.

I welcome readers' thoughtful comments, criticisms, and suggestions for the next edition of *Cape Cod, Martha's Vineyard, and Nantucket: An Explorer's Guide.*

Feel free to contact me at cceg@kimgrant.com or add your voice to the forum on my web site (www.CapeCodExplorersGuide.com). Please consult it for an ever-changing list of The Best of Cape Cod. You may also purchase black-and-white notecards of Cape Cod through the Bindu Press section of www.kimgrant.com.

SUGGESTED ITINERARIES

IF YOU HAVE 3 DAYS

Thanks, in particular, for buying this book. It contains way more information than you'll ever be able to use. We hope you pass this book along to a friend after it serves you well.

IF YOU HAVE 5 DAYS

You'll need to be efficient. Visit the village of Sandwich, poke around antiques and artisan shops on Route 6A, and drive down scenic bayside roads north of Route 6A, spending 2 nights mid-Cape. On the third morning, pop down to Main Street and the lighthouse in Chatham, and then head to the Outer Cape and the famed Cape Cod National Seashore beaches, stopping at the Salt Pond Visitor Center in Eastham. Spend 2 nights on the Outer Cape (or in Orleans): Visit galleries in Wellfleet, walk the Atlantic beaches and short nature trails, and take a day trip to Provincetown.

IF YOU HAVE 7 DAYS

You'll end up with a very enjoyable trip. Spend 3 nights mid-Cape and 3 on the Outer Cape. Do all of the above, plus linger longer in Sandwich, visiting the Glass Museum and/or Heritage Museums & Gardens. Add a beach walk at Barnstable's Sandy Neck Beach and/or Nauset Beach in Orleans. Visit the Cape Cod Museum of Natural History in Brewster and/or the Wellfleet Bay Wildlife Sanctuary. Spend a day and a half in Provincetown—watching people, walking Commercial Street, ducking into art museums and the informative Provincetown Museum, taking in a sunset from Race Point or Herring Cove, heading out on a whale-watching excursion.

IF YOU HAVE 10 DAYS

You'll be very happy. Allot the entire 3 additional days (from the above plan) to Martha's Vineyard. (Trying to see the Vineyard in a day borders on silliness.) Or add a night or two in the diverse Falmouth/Woods Hole area and a day trip to

Nantucket. Back on the Cape, get out on the water with a trip to Monomoy Island in Chatham or some other boat tour. Add a couple of whistle stops at the Cape's small, sweet historic museums.

IF YOU HAVE 2 WEEKS

You're really lucky. Allot 3 days to one of the islands. Add a quiet canoe or kayak paddle somewhere. Take a leisurely bike ride or an aerial sight-seeing flight. Get tickets to summer stock and cheer on the home team at a free baseball game. Slip into a parking space at the Wellfleet Drive-In. Investigate an old cemetery. Take an art class. Visit Mashpee's Indian sites and South Cape Beach State Park.

IF YOU LIVE ON THE CAPE AND ISLANDS

You're the luckiest of all. Scribble comments in the margins of this book and loan it to visiting friends so you don't have to keep repeating yourself. Explore something new at least once a week. Isn't that one reason you live here?

WHAT'S WHERE ON CAPE COD, MARTHA'S VINEYARD, AND NANTUCKET

AREA CODE The area code for the region of Cape Cod, Martha's Vineyard, and Nantucket is **508**.

AIRPORTS AND AIRLINES There is regularly scheduled air service from Boston to Provincetown. Hyannis is reached by air from Boston, Providence, and New York. Nantucket and Martha's Vineyard enjoy regularly scheduled year-round service; **Cape Air** (800-352-0714; www.flycape-air.com) offers the most flights. Sightseeing by air is best done in Chatham, Barnstable, and Provincetown.

Kim Grant

ANTIQUARIAN BOOKS Among the many shops on Route 6A, three are great: **Titcomb's Book Shop** in Sandwich; **Kings Way Books and Antiques** in Brewster; and **Parnassus Book Service** in Yarmouthport. I also highly recommend **Isaiah Thomas Books & Prints** in Cotuit.

ANTIQUES Antiques shops are located all along Route 6A, on the 32-mile stretch from Sandwich to Orleans, but there is an especially dense concentration in Brewster, often called Antique Alley. You'll also find a good concentration of antiques shops in Barnstable, Dennisport, Chatham,

and Nantucket. (It's never made sense to me to buy antiques on an island, but folks do!) Look for the complete supplement "Arts & Antiques" in the *Cape Cod Times* or the free directory published by the **Cape Cod Antique Dealers Association,** available at on-Cape antiques stores.

AQUARIUMS The **Woods Hole Science Aquarium** is small, but it's an excellent introduction to marine life. There is also the small **Maria Mitchell Association Aquarium** on Nantucket.

ART GALLERIES Wellfleet and Provincetown are the centers of fine art on the Cape. Both established and emerging artists are well represented in dozens of diverse galleries. Artists began flocking to Provincetown at the turn of the 20th century, and the vibrant community continues to nurture creativity. The islands also attract large numbers of artists, some of whom stay to open their own studios and galleries. Chatham, Nantucket, and Martha's Vineyard also have many fine galleries.

ATTIRE The Cape and the islands are casual for the most part; a jacket and tie is only required at one or two places. At the other end of the spectrum, you'll always need shoes and shirts at beachfront restaurants.

AUCTIONS Estate auctions are held throughout the year; check the newspapers. Among the venues are: **Sandwich Auction House; Eldred's Auctions** in East Dennis; and **Rafael Osona** in Nantucket. Just a few of the benefit auctions include: the **Fine Arts Work Center Annual Benefit Silent Auction,** the **AIDS Support Group Annual Silent Auction** in **Provincetown,** and the celebrity-studded **Possible Dreams Auction** on Martha's Vineyard.

Ⴘ BARS Look for the Ⴘ symbol next to restaurants and entertainment venues that have more than a few bar stools.

BASEBALL The 10-team **Cape Cod Baseball League** (www.capecod-baseball.org) was established in 1946. Only players with at least one year of collegiate experience are allowed to participate. Wooden bats are supplied by the major leagues. In exchange for the opportunity to play, team members work part time in the community, live with a community host, and pay rent. Carlton Fisk and the late

Thurman Munson are just two alumni of the Cape Cod League who succeeded in the majors. Currently, about 100 major-league players are former league players. Games are free and played from mid-June to early August; it's great fun. Baseball is listed under *Outdoor Activities.*

BEACHES **Cape Cod National Seashore** (CCNS) beaches are the stuff of dreams: long expanses of dune-backed sand. In fact, you could walk with only a few natural interruptions (breaks in the beach), as Henry David Thoreau did, from Chatham to the tip of Provincetown. My favorites on the Cape include **Sandy Neck Beach** in West Barnstable; Nauset Beach in Orleans; **Old Silver Beach** in North Falmouth; **Chapin Memorial Beach** in Dennis; **West Dennis Beach; Craigville Beach** near Hyannis; and all the **Outer Cape** ocean beaches. Practically all of Nantucket's beaches are public, and although the same cannot be said for Martha's Vineyard, there are plenty of places to lay your towel.

A daily parking fee is enforced from mid-June to early September; many of the smaller beaches are open only to residents and weekly cottage

Kim Grant

renters. CCNS offers a seasonal parking pass for its beaches. There is no overnight parking at beaches. Four-wheel-drive vehicles require a permit, and their use is limited. Open beach fires require a permit. Greenhead biting flies plague non–Outer Cape beaches in mid- to late July; they disappear with the first high tide at the new or full moon in August, when the water level rises, killing the eggs.

Generally, beaches on Nantucket Sound have warmer waters than the Outer Cape Atlantic Ocean beaches, which are also pounded by surf. Cape Cod Bay beaches are shallower and the water a bit cooler than Nantucket Sound beaches. Because of the proximity of the warm Gulf Stream, you can swim in Nantucket Sound waters well into September.

BICYCLING The Cape is generally flat, and there are many paved, off-road bike trails. The 26-mile **Cape Cod Rail Trail** runs along the bed of the Old Colony Railroad from Route 134 in Dennis to Wellfleet; bike trails can be found along both sides of the **Cape Cod Canal;** the **Shining Sea Trail** runs from Falmouth to Woods Hole; and bike trails can be found within the **Cape Cod National Seashore (CCNS)** in Provincetown and Truro. Nantucket is ideal for cycling, with six routes emanating from the center of town and then, circling the island. Bicycling is also great on the Vineyard, but stamina is required for a trip up-island to Aquinnah. For more information, consult *Backroad Bicycling on Cape Cod, Martha's Vineyard, and Nantucket* by Susan Milton and Kevin and Nan Jeffrey (Backcountry Guides).

Rubel Bike Maps (www.bike-maps. com) are simply the best, most detailed maps available for the Cape and islands. Rubel produces a combination Nantucket and Vineyard map ($1.95), as well as another that includes the islands, Cape Cod, and the North Shore ($4.25).

BIRD-WATCHING The **Bird Watcher's General Store** in Orleans is on every birder's list of stops. Natural areas that are known for bird-watching include: **Monomoy National Wildlife Refuge** off the coast of Chatham; **Wellfleet Bay Wildlife Sanctuary; Felix Neck Wildlife Sanctuary** in Vineyard Haven; **Ashumet Holly and Wildlife Sanctuary** in East Falmouth; and on Nantucket, **Coatue–Coskata–Great Point.** The **Maria Mitchell Association** and **Eco Guides,** both in Nantucket, offer bird-watching expeditions, as do **Wellfleet Bay Wildlife Sanctuary** and **Monomoy National Wildlife Refuge.** Scheduled bird walks are also offered from both Cape Cod National Seashore (CCNS) visitors centers: **Salt Pond Visitor Center** in Eastham and

Kim Grant

Province Lands Visitor Center in Provincetown. The **Cape Cod Museum of Natural History** in Brewster is always an excellent source of information for all creatures within the animal kingdom residing on the Cape.

BUS SERVICE The **Plymouth & Brockton** bus line (508-778-9767; www.p-b.com) serves some points along Route 6A and the Outer Cape from Boston. **Bonanza** (800-751-8800; www.bonanzabus.com) serves Bourne, Falmouth, Woods Hole, and Hyannis from Boston, Providence, and New York City.

CAMPING No camping is permitted on Nantucket, but there is still one campground on Martha's Vineyard. The Cape offers dozens of private campgrounds, but only those in natural areas are listed; the best camping is in **Nickerson State Park** in Brewster and in Truro.

Kim Grant

CANOEING AND KAYAKING For guided naturalist trips and lessons there is no better outfitter than **Goose Hummock** in Orleans (508-255-0455; www.goose.com). Also look for the book *Paddling Cape Cod: A Coastal Explorer's Guide* (Backcountry Guides). There are also very good venues and outfitters in Falmouth and Wellfleet, and on Martha's Vineyard and Nantucket.

The **Cape Cod Water Trail,** a burgeoning series of 16 canoe and kayak trails, is being developed by folks at the **Goose Hummock** shop (in Orleans) and others. In recent years, the waterways have gotten so crowded with inexperienced boaters (motorized and not) that life on the water isn't what it used to be. The first trail is slated to run through Orleans and Eastham.

CAPE COD NATIONAL SEASHORE Established on August 7, 1961, through the efforts of President John F. Kennedy, the Cape Cod National Seashore (CCNS) stretches over 40 miles through Eastham, Wellfleet, Truro, and Provincetown. It encompasses more than 43,500 acres of land and seashore. Sites within the CCNS have been identified with "CCNS" at the beginning of the entry. The **Salt Pond Visitor Center** in Eastham and **Province Lands Visitor Center** in Provincetown are excellent resources and offer a variety of exhibits, films, and ranger-led walks and talks. The CCNS is accessible every day of the year, although you must pay to park at the beaches in summer.

✎ **CHILDREN, ESPECIALLY FOR** Within this guide a number of activities and sites that have special "child appeal" are identified by the crayon symbol ✋. When you're on the Cape, look for the free *Kids on the Cape* booklet, which gives a great overview of things to do.

CLASSES AND WORKSHOPS Want to "improve" yourself on vacation, or brush up on some long-lost creative artistic urges? There are more programs in **Provincetown, the Vineyard,** and **Nantucket** than I can list here; see *To Do—Special Programs* under each town or region. Also see the sidebar "Artistic Outlets during Vacation" under "Truro" for hands-on **Cape Cod Photo Workshops** in Eastham (where I teach) and myriad offerings at the **Truro Center for the Arts at Castle Hill.** The other Outer Cape sidebar, "It's Not Just for the Birds" under "Wellfleet," discusses the **Wellfleet Bay Wildlife Sanctuary Adult Field School.**

COUNTRY STORES Old-fashioned country stores still exist on Cape Cod and the islands. Aficionados can seek out **Bournedale Country Store** in Bournedale; **The Brewster Store** in Brewster; and **Alley's General Store** in West Tisbury on the Vineyard.

CRAFTS Craftspeople have made a living on the Cape and the islands since they began making baskets, ships, and furniture 300 years ago. The tradition continues with artists emphasizing the aesthetic as well as the functional. Today's craftspeople are potters, jewelers (particularly in Dennis), scrimshaw and bird carvers, weavers, glassblowers, clothing designers, and barrel makers. Look for the highly coveted (and pricey) lightship baskets in Nantucket, glass objects in Sandwich, Bourne, and Brewster, and barrels (yes, barrels) in

Chatham. A partial list of the particularly noteworthy shops would include **Woods Hole Handworks; Signature Gallery** in Mashpee; **The Spectrum** in Hyannis and Brewster; West Barnstable Tables and **Blacks' Handweaving Shop,** both in Barnstable; **Pewter Crafters** in Harwichport; and the **Orleans Carpenters.** There are too many artisans in Provincetown, Chatham, Nantucket, and Martha's Vineyard to detail here. The **Cape Cod Potters** publishes a small pamphlet that you can pick up in on-Cape shops and studios.

CRANBERRIES The cranberry is one of only three native North American fruits (the other two are Concord grapes and blueberries). Harvesting began in Dennis in 1816 and evolved into a lucrative industry in Harwichport. Harvesting generally runs from

Kim Grant

mid-September to mid-October, when the bogs are flooded and ripe red berries float to the water's surface. Before the berries are ripe, the bogs look like a dense green carpet, separated by 2- to 3-foot dikes. Nantucket has more than 200 acres of bogs, most of which lie fallow these days due to a glut in prices. Harwich, which lays claim to having the first commercial cranberry bog, celebrates with a **Cranberry Harvest Festival** in mid-September. Most on-Cape bogs are located on the mid- and Lower Cape.

DINING Perhaps the biggest surprise to folks is the high quality of cuisine on the Cape these days. Modernity and urbane sophistication are no longer rare breeds once you cross the canal bridges. Indeed, locals are so supportive that many fine restaurants stay open through the winter. During the off-season, many chefs experiment with creative new dishes and offer them at moderate prices. With the exception of July and August (when practically all places are open nightly), restaurants are rarely open every night of the week. The major problem for a travel writer (and a reader relying on the book) is that this schedule is subject to the whims of weather and foot traffic. To avoid disappointment, phone ahead before setting out for a much-anticipated meal.

Expect to wait for a table in July and August, and make reservations whenever possible. Remember that many restaurants are staffed by college students who are just learning the ropes in June and who may depart before Labor Day weekend, leaving the owners shorthanded. Smaller seasonal establishments don't take credit cards.

ECOSYSTEM This narrow peninsula and these isolated islands have a delicate ecosystem. Remember that dunes are fragile, and beaches serve as nesting grounds for the endangered piping plover. Avoid the nesting areas when you see signs directing you to do so. Residents conserve water and recycle, and they hope you will do likewise.

EMERGENCIES Call **911** from anywhere on Cape Cod. Major hospitals are located in Falmouth (508-548-5300) and Hyannis (508-771-1800).

EVENTS The largest annual events are listed within each chapter of this book. Otherwise, invest 50¢ in the *Cape Cod Times* (508-775-1200; www.capecodonline.com), which features a special section about the day's events, and on Friday a calendar supplement for the following week.

The Massachusetts Office of Travel and Tourism (800-227-6277; www.massvacations.com) operates a toll-free events line, **Great Dates in the Bay State,** updated every 2 weeks.

FERRIES There are fast and slow ferries to Provincetown from Boston and a day-tripper from Plymouth. To reach Martha's Vineyard, the car ferry departs from Woods Hole and

Kim Grant

passenger ferries depart from Woods Hole, Falmouth, Hyannis, and New Bedford. There is a seasonal inter-island ferry. There are high-speed and regular ferries to Nantucket from Hyannis (car and passenger) and Harwich (passenger). See the appropriate chapter for details on schedules.

FISHING You don't need a license for saltwater fishing, but you do for fresh-water. Get a state license at any of the various Town Halls.

Charter boats generally take up to six people on 4- or 8-hour trips. Boats leave from the following harbors on Cape Cod Bay: Barnstable Harbor in West Barnstable; Sesuit Harbor in Dennis; Rock Harbor in Orleans; Wellfleet Harbor; and Provincetown. On Nantucket Sound, head to Hyan-nis Harbor, Saquatucket Harbor in Harwichport, and Chatham. You can also fish from the banks of the Cape Cod Canal and surf-fish on the Outer Cape. There are also plenty of oppor-tunities for fishing off the shores of Nantucket and the Vineyard.

Consider taking a course with Con-nie Codner in Eastham; see the side-bar "Casting About" in that chapter. Goose Hummock in Orleans offers lots of very good trips.

FLEA MARKETS Wellfleet Flea Market (at the Drive-In) is the big-gie. **Dick & Ellie's** fate in Mashpee is uncertain but worth investigating.

GOLF There are about 50 courses on the Cape and the islands, and because of relatively mild winters, many stay open all year (although perhaps not every day). **Highland Golf Links** in Truro is the Cape's oldest course; it's also very dramatic.

Kim Grant

&. **HANDICAP ACCESS** Look for the &. icon in the margin to find estab-lishments that are truly wheelchair accessible.

HIGHWAYS Route 6, also called the Mid-Cape Highway, is a speedy, four-lane, divided highway until exit 9½, when it becomes an undivided two-laner. After the Orleans rotary (exit 13), it becomes an undivided four-lane highway most of the way to Provincetown.

Scenic Route 6A, also known as Old King's Highway and Main Street, runs from the Sagamore Bridge to Orleans. It is lined with sea captains' houses, antiques shops, bed & break-fasts, and huge old trees. Develop-ment along Route 6A is strictly regulated by the Historical Commis-sion. Route 6A links up with Route 6 in Orleans. Without stopping, it takes an extra 30 minutes or so to take Route 6A instead of Route 6 from Sandwich to Orleans.

Route 28 can be confusing. It's an elongated, U-shaped highway that runs from the Bourne Bridge south to Falmouth, then east to Hyannis and Chatham, then north to Orleans. The problem lies with the Route 28 directional signs. Although you're actually heading north when you travel from Chatham to Orleans, the signs will say: ROUTE 28 SOUTH. When you drive from Hyannis to Falmouth, you're actually heading west, but the signs will say: ROUTE 28 NORTH. Ignore the north and south indicators, and look for towns that are in the direction you want to go.

HIGH SEASON Memorial Day weekend in late May kicks things off, then there is a slight lull until school lets out in late June. From then on, the Cape is in full swing through Labor Day (early September). There is one exception to this, though, and it's one of the best-kept secrets for planning a Cape Cod vacation: The Cape is relatively quiet during the week following the July 4 weekend. You will find B&B vacancies and no lines at your favorite restaurant. As a rule, traveling to the Cape or the islands without reservations in high season is not recommended. Accommodations—especially cottages, efficiencies, and apartments—are often booked by January for the upcoming summer. The Cape and islands are also quite busy from Labor Day through Columbus Day (mid-October). It's fairly common for B&Bs to be booked solid on every autumn weekend.

Kim Grant

HISTORIC HOUSES Every town has its own historical museum or house, but some are more interesting than others. Among the best are **Hoxie House** in Sandwich; **Centerville Historical Society Museum** and **Osterville Historical Society Museum,** both in Barnstable; **Winslow Crocker House** in Yarmouthport, operated by the Society for the Preservation of New England Antiquities (SPNEA); and the **Truro Historical Museum.** The center of Nantucket has been designated a historic district, so there are notable houses everywhere you turn; the oldest is the **Jethro Coffin House.** The **Nantucket Historical Association** publishes a walking guide to its properties. Don't miss the **Martha's Vineyard Historical Society** on Martha's Vineyard.

HORSEBACK RIDING There are a surprising number of riding facilities and trails on the Cape. Look for them in Falmouth, Brewster, and on Martha's Vineyard.

INFORMATION For those coming from the Boston area, Cape-wide information can be obtained at the tourist office on Route 3 (exit 5) in Plymouth (508-746-1150). If you're coming from the south or west, stop at the information and rest area on Route 25 (508-759-3814), 3 miles east of the Bourne Bridge. Both are open, at a minimum, daily 9–5 year-round.

There is also a year-round **Cape Cod Chamber of Commerce** information booth at exit 6 off Route 6 (508-862-0700; 888-332-2732; www. capecodchamber.org). In addition, a satellite booth located at a mid-Cape rest area on Route 6 is open 9–5 daily (at a minimum) from mid-May through October.

Kim Grant

tucket. (Nobska is certainly more accessible.) But there are also working lighthouses in Chatham, Eastham, Truro, and Provincetown. Nantucket and Martha's Vineyard, too, have their share of working lighthouses. For a really unusual trip, the lighthouses at Race Point in Provincetown and Monomoy Island off Chatham are available for overnights by advance reservation; see *Lodging* under each town.

LODGING There are many choices—from inns and bed & breakfasts to cottages, apartments, and efficiencies. Rates quoted are for two people sharing one room. Cottages are generally rented from Saturday to Saturday. Most inns and bed & breakfasts don't accept children under 10 or 12 years of age. All accept credit cards unless otherwise noted. Pets are not accepted unless otherwise noted by our 🐾 icon in the margin. Practically all establishments restrict smoking to outdoors. So many places require a 2-night minimum stay during the high season that I have not included this information unless it deviates significantly from this. Holiday weekends often require a 3-night minimum stay.

INTERNET AND LIBRARIES The Cape and the islands boast a few libraries with world-class maritime collections and works pertaining to the history of the area: **Sturgis Library** in Barnstable; **William Brewster Nickerson Memorial Room** at Cape Cod Community College in West Barnstable; the Atheneum and **Nantucket Historical Association Research Library,** both in Nantucket; and the **Martha's Vineyard Historical Society** in Edgartown on Martha's Vineyard. I have also included all town and village libraries, most of which provide free Internet access. In addition to being great community resources, libraries also make great rainy-day (🆃) destinations.

LIGHTHOUSES It's a toss-up as to whether the most picturesque lighthouse is **Nobska Light** in Woods Hole or **Great Point Light** on Nan-

Kim Grant

LYME DISEASE Ticks carry this disease, which has flu-like symptoms and may result in death if left untreated. Immediately and carefully remove any ticks that may have migrated from dune grasses to your body. Better yet, wear long pants, tuck pants into socks, and wear long-sleeved shirts whenever possible when hiking. Avoid hiking in grassy and overgrown areas of dense brush.

MAPS *The Cape Cod Street Atlas* by DeLorme ($19.95; www.delorme. com) is the single best map I've ever found to the Cape and islands. Get one right away! I'm forever searching out bodies of water or shorelines that look interesting on the map and always finding scenic roads that I didn't expect.

MOVIES The **Cape Cinema** in Dennis is a special venue, but you can also find art films at the **Gaslight Theatre** in Nantucket. In addition to the standard multiplex cinemas located across the Cape, the **Wellfleet Drive-In** remains a much-loved institution. The **Nantucket Film Festival** and **International Film Festival** in Provincetown, both held in mid-June, are relatively new "must-see" events for independent-film buffs. Because moviegoing is a popular vacation activity, I have also listed mainstream movie theaters under *Entertainment.*

MUSEUMS People who have never uttered the words *museum* and *Cape Cod* in the same breath don't know what they're missing. Don't skip the **Glass Museum** and **Heritage Museums & Gardens,** both in Sandwich; **Museums on the Green** in Falmouth; **Aptucxet Trading Post**

Kim Grant

and **Museum** in Bourne Village; **Cahoon Museum of American Art** in Cotuit; **John F. Kennedy Hyannis Museum; Cape Museum of Fine Arts** in Dennis; **Cape Cod Museum of Natural History** in Brewster; **Provincetown Art Association & Museum,** the **Pilgrim Monument & Provincetown Museum,** and the **Old Harbor Lifesaving Station,** all in Provincetown; **Martha's Vineyard Historical Society** in Edgartown on Martha's Vineyard; and the **Nantucket Whaling Museum** and **Lifesaving Museum** on Nantucket.

Children will particularly enjoy the **Railroad Museum** in Chatham and the **Thornton W. Burgess Museum** in Sandwich.

MUSIC Outdoor summertime band concerts are now offered by most towns, but the biggest and oldest is held in Chatham at **Kate Gould Park.** Sandwich offers a variety of outdoor summer concerts at **Heritage Museums & Gardens.**

Cape & Islands Chamber Music Festival (508-945-8060; 800-229-5739) presents fine classical and contemporary classical music at various venues across the Cape year-round. Founded by a New York City pianist in 1980, the festival includes master classes and top-notch performances. Call for a schedule. The **Nantucket Musical Arts Society** and the Vineyard's **Chamber Music Society** are also excellent, albeit with much shorter seasons.

The 90-member **Cape Symphony Orchestra** (508-362-1111; www.capesymphony.org) performs classical, children's, and pops concerts year-round.

There are a couple of regular venues for folk music, including the **Woods Hole Folk Music Society** and the **First Encounter Coffee House** in Eastham.

This edition lists many more venues with live music; see the *Entertainment* headings under each town.

NATURE PRESERVES There are walking trails—around salt marshes, across beaches, through ancient swamps and hardwood stands—in every town on the Cape and the islands, but some traverse larger areas and are more "developed" than others. For a complete guide, look for the excellent *Walks & Rambles on Cape Cod and the Islands* by Ned Friary and Glenda Bendure (Backcountry Guides). Watch for poison ivy and deer ticks; the latter carry Lyme disease.

To find some Upper Cape green space, head to: **Green Briar Nature Center & Jam Kitchen** in Sandwich; **Lowell Holly Reservation** in Mashpee; and **Ashumet Holly and Wildlife Sanctuary** and **Waquoit Bay National Estuarine Research Reserve,** both in East Falmouth. In the mid-Cape area, you'll find **Sandy Neck Great Salt Marsh Conservation Area** in West Barnstable. The Lower Cape offers **Nickerson State Park** in Brewster and **Monomoy**

National Wildlife Refuge off the coast of Chatham. The **Cape Cod National Seashore** (CCNS) has a number of short interpretive trails on the Outer Cape, while Wellfleet has the **Wellfleet Bay Wildlife Sanctuary** and **Great Island Trail.**

On Martha's Vineyard you can escape the crowds at **Felix Neck Wildlife Sanctuary** in Vineyard Haven; **Cedar Tree Neck Sanctuary** and **Long Point Wildlife Refuge,** both in West Tisbury; and **Cape Pogue Wildlife Refuge** and **Wasque Reservation** on Chappaquiddick.

Nantucket boasts conservation initiatives that have protected one-third of the land from development, including the areas of **Coatue–Coskata–Great Point, Eel Point, Sanford Farm, Ram Pasture,** and the **Woods.**

NEWSPAPERS AND PERIODICALS
The *Cape Cod Times,* with Cape- and islandwide coverage, is published daily. The *Cape Codder,* published on Friday, focuses on the Lower and Outer Cape. The *Falmouth Enterprise* is published every Tuesday and Friday. Provincetown's weekly *Advocate* is noteworthy, as are the *Vineyard Gazette* (508-627-4311; www. mvgazette.com) and Nantucket's

Kim Grant

Inquirer and Mirror (508-228-0001; www.ack.net).

In addition to its bimonthly magazine, *Cape Cod Life* (508-564-4466) publishes an annual guide and a "Best of the Cape & Islands" within its June edition.

❉ **OFF-SEASON** In an attempt to get people thinking about visiting the Cape and the islands off-season, I have put the ❉ symbol next to activities, lodging, and restaurants that are open and appealing in the off-season.

🐾 **PETS** Look for the 🐾 icon to find lodgings where your pet is welcome.

PONDS Supposedly there are 365 freshwater ponds on Cape Cod, one for every day of the year. As glaciers retreated 15,000 years ago and left huge chunks of ice behind, depressions in the earth were created. When the ice melted, "kettle ponds" were born. The ponds are a refreshing treat, especially in August when salty winds kick up beach sand.

POPULATION More than 240,000 people live year-round on the Cape and the islands. No one really has an accurate idea of how many people visit in summer, but it's in the millions.

Kim Grant

RADIO WOMR (92.1 FM) in Provincetown has diverse and great programming. Tune in to National Public Radio with WCCT (90.3 FM), WKKL (90.7 FM), or WSDH (91.5 FM). On the Vineyard tune to WMVY (92.7 FM), on Nantucket tune to WNAN (91.1 FM), and on the Cape try WCOD (106.1 FM), WFCC (107.5 FM), and WQRC (99.9 FM).

☂ **RAINY-DAY ACTIVITIES** Chances are, if it were sunny every day we would start taking the sunshine for granted. So when the clouds move in and the raindrops start falling on your head, be appreciative of the sun and look for the ☂ icon in this book, which tells you where to head indoors.

RECOMMENDED READING ABOUT CAPE COD Henry Beston's classic *The Outermost House: A Year of Life on the Great Beach of Cape Cod* recounts his solitary year in a cabin on the ocean's edge. Cynthia Huntington's marvelous *The Salt House* updates it with a woman's perspective in the late 20th century. Also look for *The House on Nauset Marsh* by Wyman Richardson. Henry David Thoreau's naturalist classic *Cape Cod* meticulously details his mid-1800s walking tours. Josef Berger's 1937 Works Progress Administration (WPA) guide, *Cape Cod Pilot*, is filled with good stories and still-useful information. I devoured the excellent *Nature of Cape Cod* by Beth Schwarzman and anything by poet Mary Oliver. Pick up anything by modern-day naturalists Robert Finch and John Hay. Finch also edited a volume of writings by others about the Cape, *A Place Apart*. Another collection of writings about Cape Cod is *Sand in Their Shoes*, compiled by

Frank and Edith Shay. Look for *Cape Cod, Its People & Their History* by Henry Kittredge (alias Jeremiah Digges) and *The Wampanoags of Mashpee* by Russell Peters. Mary Heaton Vorse, a founder of the Provincetown Players, describes life in Provincetown from the 1900s to the 1950s in *Time and the Town: A Provincetown Chronicle.* And for children, Brian Shortsleeve has written an illustrated history book, *The Story of Cape Cod.* Look for Admont Clark's *Lighthouses of Cape Cod, Martha's Vineyard, and Nantucket: Their History and Lore* and photographer Joel Meyerowitz's *A Summer's Day* and *Cape Light.*

RECOMMENDED READING ABOUT MARTHA'S VINEYARD Start with the *Vineyard Gazette Reader,* a marvelous "best-of" collection edited by Richard Reston and Tom Dunlop; it will give you an immediate sense of the island. *On the Vineyard II* contains essays by celebrity island residents, including Walter Cronkite, William Styron, and Carly Simon, and photographs by Peter Simon (Carly's brother). *Martha's Vineyard* and *Martha's Vineyard, Summer Resort* are both by Henry Beetle Hough, Pulitzer Prize–winning editor of the *Vineyard Gazette.* Photographer Alfred Eisenstaedt, a longtime summer resident of the Vineyard, photographed the island for years. Contemporary *Vineyard Gazette* photographer Alison Shaw has two Vineyard books to her credit: the black-and-white *Remembrance and Light* and the color collection *Vineyard Summer.*

RECOMMENDED READING ABOUT NANTUCKET Edwin P. Hoyt's *Nantucket: The Life of an Island* is a popu-

lar history, and Robert Gambee's *Nantucket* is just plain popular. Architecture buffs will want to take a gander at *Nantucket Style* by Leslie Linsley and Jon Aron and the classic *Early Nantucket and Its Whale Houses* by Henry Chandler Forman. Photography lovers will enjoy *On Nantucket,* with photos by Gregory Spaid.

ROTARIES When you're approaching a rotary, cars already within the rotary have the right-of-way.

SEAL CRUISES A colony of seals lounge around Monomoy, and there is no shortage of outfits willing to take you out to see them. See listings under "Chatham" and "Wellfleet" for detailed information. Chief among the operators is the *Wellfleet Bay Wildlife Sanctuary.*

SHELLFISHING Permits, obtained from local Town Halls, are required

Kim Grant

for the taking of shellfish. Sometimes certain areas are closed to shellfishing due to contamination; it's always best to ask. Consider taking a course with Casey Jones in Orleans; see the sidebar "Clammin' with Casey" in that chapter.

SHOPPING Main Streets in Chatham and Falmouth are well suited to walking and shopping. Commercial Street in Provincetown has the trendiest shops. Mashpee Commons features a very dense and increasingly fine selection of shops. Shopping on the Vineyard and Nantucket is a prime activity.

SMOKING Smoking in bars and restaurants has been banned on Nantucket, the Vineyard, and all Cape Cod towns *except* Falmouth/Woods Hole, Mashpee, Dennis, Eastham, and Wellfleet.

SURFING AND SAILBOARDING Surfers should head to **Nauset Beach** in Orleans, **Coast Guard** and **Nauset Light Beaches** in Eastham, and **Marconi Beach** in Wellfleet. Sailboarders flock to Falmouth. The Vineyard beaches are also good for sailboarding.

SWIMMING POOLS For a small fee, you can swim at the **Willy's Gym** in

Kim Grant

Eastham and the **Nantucket Community Pool.** Swimming at the **Provincetown Inn** is free.

THEATER Among the summer-stock and performing arts venues are **Cape Playhouse** in Dennis; **Cape Repertory Theatre** in Brewster; **Monomoy Theatre** in Chatham; **Academy Playhouse** in Orleans; **Wellfleet Harbor Actors Theater; Provincetown Repertory Theatre** and **Provincetown Theatre Co.; College Light Opera Company** in Falmouth; **Barnstable Comedy Club; Harwich Junior Theatre;** the **Actors Theatre of Nantucket** and **Theatre Workshop of Nantucket;** and the **Vineyard Playhouse** on Martha's Vineyard.

TIDES Tides come in and out twice daily; times differ from day to day and from town to town. At low tide, the sandy shore is hard and easier to walk on; at high tide, what little sand is visible is more difficult to walk on. Since tides vary considerably from one spot to another, it's best to stop in at a local bait-and-tackle shop for a tide chart. For Cape Cod Canal tide information, call 508-759-5991.

TRAFFIC It's bad in July and August no matter how you cut it. It's bumper to bumper on Friday afternoon and evening when cars arrive for the weekend. It's grueling on Sunday afternoon and evening when they return home. And there's no respite on Saturday when all the weekly cottage renters have to vacate their units and a new set of renters arrives to take their places. Call **Smart Traveler** (617-374-1234; *1 on your cell phone) for up-to-the-minute information on traffic. This service uses

Kim Grant

remote cameras and airplanes to report current traffic conditions.

TRAINS The **Cape Cod Central Railroad** runs between Sandwich and Hyannis, alongside cranberry bogs and the Sandy Neck Great Salt Marsh. It turns into a dinner train at night (see *Where to Eat* in "Hyannis").

 VALUE The symbol appears next to entries that represent an exceptional value.

WALKING Cape Cod Pathways (508-362-3828), a growing network of trails linking open space in all 15 Cape Cod towns from Falmouth to Provincetown, is coordinated by the Cape Cod Commission, 3225 Route 6A, Barnstable 02630. They produce quite a comprehensive map that should be stored in the glove compartment of all Explorers' cars.

Also see *Walks & Rambles on Cape Cod and the Islands* by Ned Friary and Glenda Bendure (Backcountry Guides).

WEATHER You really can't trust Boston weather reports to provide accurate forecasts for all the microclimates between Route 28 and 6A, from the canal to Provincetown. If you really want to go to the Cape, just go. There'll be plenty to do even if it's cloudy or rainy. When in doubt, or when it really matters, call the radio station WQRC, 99.9 FM (508-771-5522).

WEB SITES For up-to-the-minute additions and "Best of" selections, please consult my sites www.CapeCodExplorersGuide.com and www.kimgrant.com and post your opinions about places. Web addresses

Kim Grant

for individual chambers of commerce, places to stay, and things to see and do are listed throughout.

WHALE-WATCHING Whale-watching trips leave from Provincetown, including the excellent **Dolphin Fleet Whale Watch** (508-349-1900; 800-826-9300), but you can also catch the **Hyannis Whale Watcher Cruises** (508-362-6088; 888-942-5392) out of Barnstable Harbor.

WINERIES The Cape and islands are not Napa Valley, but you could drop in for tastings at **Truro Vineyards of Cape Cod** in Truro, **Chicama Vineyards** on Martha's Vineyard, and the **Cape Cod Winery** in East Falmouth. The **Nantucket Vineyard** (are you confused?) imports grapes to make wine.

YOUTH HOSTELS Good youth hostels are located on Martha's Vineyard, Nantucket, Eastham, and Truro.

The Upper Cape

BOURNE

SANDWICH

FALMOUTH AND WOODS HOLE

MASHPEE

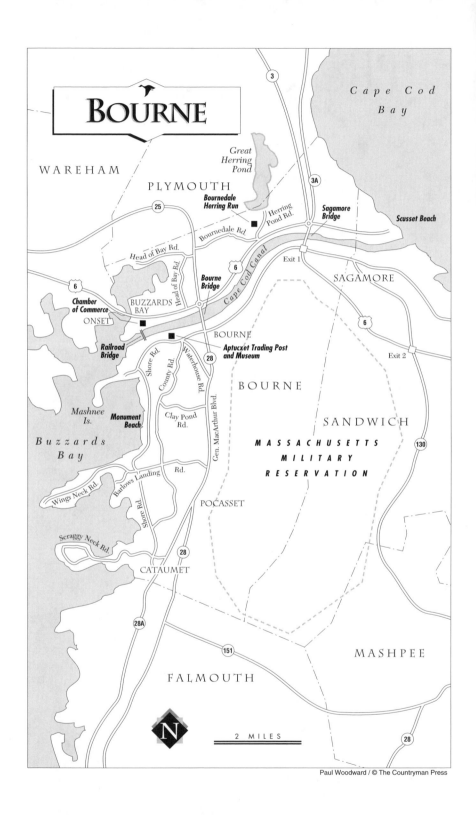

BOURNE

WAREHAM

PLYMOUTH

Cape Cod Bay

Great Herring Pond

3

3A

25

Bournedale Herring Run

Bournedale Rd.

Herring Pond Rd.

Sagamore Bridge

Scusset Beach

Head of Bay Rd.

Head of Bay Rd.

6

Bourne Bridge

Cape Cod Canal

Exit 1

SAGAMORE

Chamber of Commerce

6

ONSET

BUZZARDS BAY

6

Railroad Bridge

Shore Rd.

County Rd.

28

BOURNE

Aptucxet Trading Post and Museum

Waterhouse Rd.

Exit 2

BOURNE

SANDWICH

Mashnee Is.

Monument Beach

Clay Pond Rd.

Gen. MacArthur Blvd.

Buzzards Bay

MASSACHUSETTS MILITARY RESERVATION

130

Wings Neck Rd.

Barlows Landing Rd.

Rd.

Shore Rd.

POCASSET

Scraggy Neck Rd.

28

CATAUMET

28A

151

MASHPEE

FALMOUTH

28

N

2 MILES

Paul Woodward / © The Countryman Press

BOURNE

Despite summertime traffic tie-ups approaching the Sagamore and Bourne Bridges, there's something magical about the first glimpse of them, a sure sign that you're entering a place separate from where you've been. All travelers, except those arriving by plane or boat, must pass through Bourne, over the bridges and the Cape Cod Canal.

Bourne straddles the canal, nips at the heels of Sandwich on the Cape Cod Bay side, and follows the coastline south toward Falmouth along Route 28. (All the land to the immediate east of Route 28 belongs to the Massachusetts Military Reservation.) Bourne is often completely bypassed as travelers head south to catch the Vineyard ferry from Falmouth or Woods Hole. Indeed, there is some justification for not spending a monthlong holiday here. Bourne is predominantly inhabited by year-rounders, who enjoy a quiet, rural, unhurried existence tending their gardens and lives. But perhaps of the entire Cape, Bourne remains the most unexplored. The back roads off County and Shore Roads are lovely for bicycling, as are the peninsulas reached by Scraggy Neck Road and Wings Neck Road. Fishing, walking, and bicycling are prime activities along the Cape Cod Canal. In fact, there are over 1,200 acres of protected land along the canal for your enjoyment.

When Sandwich refused to grant Bourne its independence, the state legislature incorporated it in 1884. Originally known for its fishing wharves, shipbuilding, and factories, Bourne quickly attracted prominent vacationers to its sandy shores. Named for an affluent resident who made his fortune during the whaling heyday, Bourne encompasses 40 square miles and consists of nine tiny villages.

Sagamore, on both sides of the canal and on Cape Cod Bay, has more in common with Sandwich; it even has a renowned glassmaking factory. Bournedale, on the "mainland" wedged between the two bridges, has a handsome country store, a diminutive old red schoolhouse, and a picturesque herring pond. And although Buzzards Bay, north and west of the Bourne Bridge, is the region's commercial center, it also offers some lovely glimpses of Buttermilk Bay. (Buzzards Bay, by the way, was misnamed by inexperienced birders. If the original settlers had gotten it right, it would be called Osprey Bay today.) On the western end of the canal, the Massachusetts Maritime Academy affords nice views of the canal as well as of handsome summer homes on the other side.

Across the 2,384-foot Bourne Bridge (almost twice as long as the Sagamore Bridge), the Cape villages of Monument Beach, Bourne Village, Gray Gables, Pocasset, and Cataumet are tranquil in summer and downright sleepy in winter, although 19,000 people live there year-round. The first Summer White House was in Gray Gables, where President Grover Cleveland spent the season fishing during the 1890s. Monument Beach, Cataumet, and Pocasset are pleasant, residential, seaside towns with old houses, just west of Route 28. Residents don't take much notice of visitors; they just go about their business, fishing, shopping, raising kids, and commuting to work. Cataumet Pier was the site of the nation's first labor strike, when dockworkers demanded a 100 percent pay raise in 1864, from 15¢ per hour to 30¢.

GUIDANCE ❀ **Cape Cod Canal Region Chamber of Commerce** (508-759-6000; www.capecodcanalchamber.org), 70 Main Street, Buzzards Bay 02532. Open 8:30–5 weekdays. Their town booklet has a particularly good map of the canal region. There is also a small booth at the Sagamore rotary (508-888-7839).

Herring Run Visitors Center, Route 6 on the mainland side of the canal, about a mile south of the Sagamore Bridge rotary. Open 9–dusk, year-round; staff dispense canal-related information during the summer. Rest rooms and picnic tables.

The **Cape Cod Canal Recreation Hotline** (508-759-5991) is a 24-hour number with up-to-date tide, weather, and canal recreation information provided by the USACE. See U.S. Army Corps of Engineers under *Guidance* in "Sandwich."

PUBLIC REST ROOMS Stop at the main chamber of commerce office or Herring Run Visitors Center.

PUBLIC LIBRARY ✐ ❀ ☂ **Jonathan Bourne Public Library** (508-759-0644), 19 Sandwich Road, Bourne, is open 9–8 Tuesday through Thursday, 9–5:30 Friday and Saturday. Inquire about story hour and children's programs.

GETTING THERE *By car:* To reach Sagamore, take exit 1 onto Route 6A from the Sagamore Bridge. For Bournedale and Buzzards Bay, take Route 6 west at the Sagamore Bridge rotary. To reach the other villages, take the Bourne Bridge across the canal, and at the rotary take Shore Road. You can also whiz down Route 28 and head west to Pocasset, Cataumet, and Monument Beach.

By bus: **Bonanza** (888-751-8800; www.bonanzabus.com) operates buses from Bourne to Boston as well as Providence, New York City, and other points south and west of the Cape. The bus stops at the Tedeschi Food Shop at the Bourne Bridge rotary.

GETTING AROUND Bourne is quite spread out, so you'll need a car. The Cape Cod Canal has a great bicycle trail (see *Outdoor Activities—Bicycling/Rentals*).

OUR VERY OWN PANAMA CANAL

The Cape Cod Canal (7.5 miles long) separates the mainland from Cape Cod. The canal, between 480 and 700 feet wide at various points, is the world's widest ocean-level canal. In 1623 Capt.ain Myles Standish, eager to facilitate trade between New Amsterdam (New York City) and Plymouth Colonys, was the first to consider creating a canal, which also would eliminate the treacherous 135-nautical-mile voyage around the tip of the Cape. George Washington brought up the idea again in the late 18th century as a means to protect naval ships and commercial vessels during war, but the first serious effort at digging a canal was not attempted until 1880, by the Cape Cod Canal Company.

For a few months, the company's crew of 500 immigrants dug with hand shovels and carted away the dirt in wheelbarrows. Then, in 1899, New York financier Augustus Belmont's Boston, Cape Cod, and New York Canal Company took over the project with more resolve. They began digging in 1909, and the canal opened to shipping five years later, on July 30, 1914. (It beat the Panama Canal opening by a scant 17 days.) On hand at the opening was then Assistant Secretary of the Navy Franklin D. Roosevelt. But the enterprise wasn't a financial success, because the canal was too narrow (it could handle only one-way traffic) and early drawbridges caused too many accidents. In 1928 the federal government purchased the canal, and the U.S. Army Corps of Engineers (USACE) built the canal we know today. The USACE has overseen the canal ever since. The canal provides a north–south shortcut for some 30,000 vessels each year, hundreds daily in summer. Water currents in the 32-foot-deep canal change direction every 6 hours.

The Buzzards Bay Vertical Railroad Bridge (western end of the canal at the **Buzzards Bay Recreation Area**) is the third longest vertical railway bridge in the world. (It stands 270 feet high and 540 feet long, but those in Chicago, Illinois, and Long Island, New York, beat it.) The railroad bridge was completed the same year as the Sagamore and Bourne Bridges. When trains approach, it takes 2 or 3 minutes for the bridge to lower and connect with tracks on either side of it. The most reliable times to witness this event are at 9:30 and 5 (more or less), when trains haul trash off-Cape. Free parking. This is a good place to start the bicycle trail on this side of the canal.

There is great bicycling, fishing, boating, and walking from the canal shores. See the appropriate sections under *Outdoor Activities*.

It's not an "emergency" (the kind you'd expect under this category, anyway), but many area water wells have been closed in recent years. They've been contaminated by years of training with grenades and other live munitions at the Massachusetts Military Reservation. I drink bottled water on the Upper Cape.

✳ To See

Massachusetts Maritime Academy (508-830-5000; www.mma.mass.edu), Taylors Point, off Main Street, Buzzards Bay. The academy's presence explains why you'll see so many young men with close-cropped hair jogging along the canal bicycle trail. Although tours of the 55-acre campus are no longer conducted for the general public, you can arrange to tag along on a tour for prospective merchant-marine cadets. Not only will you see the oldest maritime academy in the country (established in 1891) from an insider's perspective, but you'll also get to tour the cadets' training ship (the *Enterprise*) and eat in the cadets' dining hall overlooking the canal.

Aptucxet Trading Post and Museum (508-759-9487), 24 Aptucxet Road, Bourne. From the Cape-side Bourne Bridge rotary, follow signs for Mashnee Village, then Shore Road and Aptucxet Road; follow the signs. Open 10–4 weekdays, 2–5 Sunday May to mid-October (daily in July and August). Because two rivers converged here before the canal was built, English settlers thought the location was perfect for a post to promote trade with their neighbors, the Wampanoag Indians and the Dutch from New Amsterdam. Furs, sugar and other staples, tools, glass, tobacco, and cloth were bought and sold; wampum (carved quahog shells made into beads) served as currency. Cape Cod commerce was born.

The trading post you see today was built in 1930 by the Bourne Historical Society on the foundations of the original; a few bricks from the fireplace date to the Pilgrims. The hand-hewn beams and wide floor planks came from a 1600s house in Rochester, Massachusetts. On the grounds a small Victorian railroad station was used solely by President Grover Cleveland when he summered at his Gray Gables mansion in Monument Beach. You'll also find a Dutch-style windmill (which was intended merely "to add interest and beauty to the estate"), an 18th-century saltworks, an herb garden, a gift shop, and a shaded picnic area. Curator Eleanor Hammond is a treasure. Adults $4, children $2.

𝒮 **Bournedale Herring Run** (508-759-4431), Route 6, about a mile south of the Sagamore rotary. Mid-April to early June. After the canal destroyed the natural herring run into Herring Pond, local engineers created an elaborate artificial watercourse to allow mature herring to migrate back to their birthplace. Each twice-daily tide brings thousands of the bony fish slithering upstream, navigating the pools created by wooden planks. With the aid of automated fish counters, it's estimated that upwards of 400,000 herring pass through the Bournedale run annually. Kids really get a kick out of this spring ritual. During the season, this is the busiest fishing area in the state, with anglers catching their quota of herring and using them as bait for blues in the canal. Free.

Bournedale Country Store (508-888-8853), 26 Herring Pond Road, off Route 6, Bournedale. Open March through December. This classic red building with wooden floors has been here about 200 years.

⌀ **National Marine Life Center** (508-759-8722; www.nmlc.org), 120 Main Street, Buzzards Bay. Open 10–6 Monday through Saturday; noon–6 Sunday, late May to early September. Plans are afoot here to build a marine-animal rehabilitation hospital for whales, dolphins, sea turtles, and seals that wash ashore on Cape Cod and need medical attention before they can be set free again. It promises saltwater pools, interactive exhibits, and a small science museum where we'll learn about the impact of humankind on the ocean. In the meantime, you can learn about the sea creatures that will eventually be brought here through displays, videos, artifacts, and a kiddie activity table. Free.

Briggs McDermott House & Blacksmith Shop (508-759-6120), 22 Sandwich Road, Bourne. Open 1–4 Tuesday mid-June to early September. This early-19th-century Greek Revival home—complete with period gardens and a granite-walled barn—is maintained by the Bourne Society for Historic Preservation. Docents discuss local architecture and former neighbor Grover Cleveland. And blacksmiths operate the restored forge—complete with artifacts, tools, and a wagon—where President Cleveland's horses were shod. Guided tours, adults $3; children $1.

Mashnee Island. From the Cape-side rotary of the Bourne Bridge, take Shore Road and follow signs for Mashnee Island. From the 2-mile-long causeway, there are lovely views of summer homes dotting the shoreline, sailboats on the still waters, and the distant railroad bridge and Bourne Bridge. Parking is nonexistent in summer, and as the island is private, you'll have to turn around at the end of the causeway.

Mashnee Island's celebrated, homespun Fourth of July parade consists of the current crop of island kids (and their parents) marching or riding their bikes through town.

Massachusetts Military Reservation (Otis Air Force Base) (508-968-4003), off the rotary at Routes 28 and 28A. The 21,000 acres east of Route 28 are a closed installation that contains Camp Edwards Army National Guard Training Site, Otis Air National Guard Base, the U.S. Coast Guard Air Station, the State Army Aviation complex, and the PAVE PAWS radar station. The latter detects nuclear missiles and tracks military satellites (it was established during the Cold War).

Although you won't read about it in most guidebooks, the MMR has long been designated by the Pentagon as a federal environmental "Superfund" site. Most experts agree that it will take decades to clean up the toxic Cold War–era pollutants that are contaminating an estimated 8 million gallons of groundwater a day. Other experts suggest it may be impossible to clean up the underground chemical plumes that resulted from various training exercises, landfill leaks, and oil spills. The EPA (Environmental Protection Agency) has mandated a cleanup, which will cost in the hundreds of millions of dollars.

SCENIC DRIVE See Mashnee Island, above.

✳ Outdoor Activities

BICYCLING/RENTALS **Cape Cod Canal.** The canal is edged by level, well-maintained service roads perfect for biking. The mainland side has almost 8 miles of trail; the Cape side has less than 7 miles. Clearly marked access points along the mainland side of the canal include Scusset State Park off Scusset Beach Road; the Sagamore Recreation Area off Canal Road at the Sagamore rotary; near the Herring Brook Fishway in Bournedale; and beneath the Bourne Bridge. On the Cape side of the canal, there are access points from the U.S. Engineering Observation Station on Freezer Road in Sandwich; from Pleasant Street in Sagamore; and from the Bourne Bridge. If you want to cross the canal with your bike, use the Sagamore Bridge—its sidewalk is safer.

P&M Cycles (508-759-2830), 29 Main Street, Buzzards Bay. Open daily except Monday, March through December. Across from the railroad station and the canal path, this full-service bike shop rents bicycles ($10 for 2 hours or $25 daily) and offers free parking while you ride.

BOAT EXCURSIONS/RENTALS ♂ **Cape Cod Canal Cruises** (508-295-3883), off Routes 6 and 28 at the Onset Bay Town Pier (a few miles west of the mainland-side Bourne Bridge rotary), Onset. Operated by Hy-Line Cruises, these 2- and 3-hour tours—with running commentary—are conducted from May to mid-October. It makes sense to experience the canal by boat; $10–12 adults, $5–6 children 5–12. There are also sunset cocktail cruises, Sunday-afternoon jazz trips, dance cruises, and a discounted family trip (children ride for free) every day at 4 PM.

Maco's Bait and Tackle (508-759-9836), at Routes 6 and 28, Buzzards Bay. Open daily April through October, Maco's rents 16-foot skiffs with motors.

FISHING Freshwater licenses are available from the Bourne Town Hall (508-759-0613) on Perry Avenue. **Flax Pond** and **Red Brook Pond** in Pocasset offer freshwater fishing.

For saltwater fishing, the banks of the Cape Cod Canal provide plenty of opportunities for catching striped bass, bluefish, cod, and pollack. Just bait your hook and cast away; no permits are required if you're fishing with a rod and line from the shore. Lobstermen pull traps from the shoreline. But there is no fishing, lobstering, or boat trolling permitted *in* the canal.

See also Bournedale Herring Run under *To See.*

♂ FOR FAMILIES **Water Wizz Water Park** (508-295-3255; www.waterwizz.com), Routes 6 and 28, 2 miles west of the Bourne Bridge, Wareham. Open 10–6:30 daily, mid-June to early September. Southern New England's largest water park has it all: a 50-foot-high water slide with tunnels, a six-story tube ride, a hanging rope bridge, two more tube rides (one enclosed), a wave pool, two kiddie water parks, a river ride, and more mundane (and dry!)

amusements like an arcade and mini-golf. If you're taller than 4 feet, tickets cost $27, otherwise it's $11; reduced admission after 4 PM.

Thunder Mine Adventure (508-563-7450), Route 28A and County Road, Cataumet. Open daily until 10 PM, late May through September. While this mini-golf park is more attractive than most (thanks to a revolving mill and flower gardens), it's not very challenging. But after battling with motorists at rotaries and bridges, it might be just your speed.

Adventure Isle (508-759-2636), Route 28, 2 miles south of the Bourne Bridge. Open late May through October (daily in summer, Friday through Sunday in September and October). Diversions include go-carts, a bumper boat lagoon, laser tag, a game room, mini-golf, batting cages, a pirate ship in the kiddie area, a superslide, basketball, a little Ferris wheel, and a café after you've worked up an appetite. All-day passes cost $12.

Cartland of Cape Cod (508-295-8360), 3044 Route 6, East Wareham. Open daily in summer, weekends in spring and fall. Bumper boats, go-carts, an air cannon, slip track, game room, and railroad.

❋ **Ryan Family Amusements** (508-759-9892), 200 Main Street, Buzzards Bay. Bowling, a game room, and facilities for birthday parties.

See also Cataumet Arts Center under *Selective Shopping—Art and Artisans.*

HORSEBACK RIDING ❋ **Grazing Fields Farm** (508-759-3763), 201 Bournedale Road, off Head of the Bay Road, Buzzards Bay. Private and semiprivate lessons are offered.

ICE SKATING **Gallo Ice Arena** (508-759-8904), 231 Sandwich Road, Bourne. Call for a highly variable public skating schedule.

KAYAKING **Onset Kayak & Canoe** (508-291-1333; www.onsetkayak.com), 146 Onset Avenue East, Onset. Open June to mid-October for rentals. These folks rent kayaks for exploring miles and miles of shoreline, inlets, and inner bays. They also have a waterside location adjacent to the Town Pier. Singles $15 first hour, doubles $20; each additional hour $10.

SCUBA DIVING **Aquarius Diving Center** (508-759-3483), 3239 Route 28, Buzzards Bay. This full-service dive shop offers rental equipment, instruction, general information, and charters to explore the rocky bottom of Sandwich Town Beach (where you'll see lobsters scurrying about), the "backside" of Chatham, a wreck off Provincetown, and the Plymouth coast ($60–100 per person). Trips are usually scheduled on weekends, but in summer there are Wednesday-night dives.

SPECIAL PROGRAMS ✔ **U.S. Army Corps of Engineers** (508-759-4431), Academy Drive off Main Street, Buzzards Bay. Junior ranger programs (for children 6–12) are usually offered on Wednesday afternoons in July and August.

See also Cataumet Arts Center under *Selective Shopping—Art and Artisans.*

SWIMMING POOL ✐ **Bourne Scenic Park** (508-759-7873), Route 6 on the mainland side of the canal, Buzzards Bay. Open late March to late October. For a $4 day-use fee (free for children up to 18), you can swim in a saltwater swimming hole, fed by canal tides controlled by a system of floodgates. Reeds grow along the edges of the swimming hole, which has a sandy bottom and is surrounded by a chain-link fence. There are also picnic tables, a playground, and camping ($22 daily for tents, $27 with electricity) practically underneath the pylons of the Sagamore Bridge.

TENNIS Public courts are located at **Bourne Memorial Community Building and Town Hall,** Shore Road in Buzzards Bay; the **old schoolhouse,** County Road in Cataumet; **Chester Park,** across from the old railroad station in Monument Beach; and **behind the fire station** on Barlow's Landing Road in Pocasset Village.

✳ Green Space

BEACHES The canal moderates considerable differences in tides between Buzzards Bay (4 feet) and Cape Cod Bay (9½ feet on average). Because of the swift currents caused by tides and because of heavy boat traffic, swimming is prohibited in the Cape Cod Canal.

Scusset and **Sagamore Beaches,** Cape Cod Bay, Sagamore. Both beaches are located off the Sagamore Bridge rotary via Scusset Beach Road. Facilities include changing areas and rest rooms.

Monument Beach, Buzzards Bay, on Emmons Road off Shore Road, Monument Beach. This small beach has rest rooms and a snack bar. The warm waters of Buzzards Bay usually hover around 75 degrees in summer. Free parking.

Town Beach, Buttermilk Bay off Route 28 and Head of the Bay Road, Buzzards Bay. Free parking; no facilities.

THE SIMPLICITY OF SKY AND SAND

Kim Grant

WALKS ❀ **Cape Cod Canal.** The U.S. Army Corps of Engineers (USACE; 508-759-4431), Academy Drive off Main Street, Buzzards Bay, offers numerous and excellent 1- to 2-hour guided programs from early July to mid-October. Look for walks and talks on Sagamore Hill history, managing canal maritime traffic, Bournedale history, astronomy, and dune-beach exploration. There is also biking and hiking along the canal. Call the Cape Cod Canal Recreation Hotline (508-759-5991) for up-to-the-minute recreational offerings and exact days. All free.

Red Brook Pond, Thaxter Road off Shore Road, Cataumet. Forty acres of wooded conservation land.

See also *Outdoor Activities—Bicycling/Rentals* (Cape Cod Canal).

✳ Lodging

There really aren't many places to stay in this quiet corner of Cape Cod.

BED & BREAKFAST ❄ ♪ **Wood Duck Inn** (508-564-6404; www.woodduckinnbb.com), 1050 County Road, Cataumet 02534. This rustic 1848 farmhouse, with a sweeping lawn overlooking a cranberry bog and on a rural road, offers one room and two suites, none of which will suit guests looking for pristine environs. Nonetheless, both suites have a separate sitting room and bedroom and a separate entrance from the rest of the B&B. The Garden Suite features stenciled walls and a king feather bed. Tree Tops, really an efficiency apartment geared to a family, has a little balcony overlooking the cranberry bog. All rooms have TV, telephone, and refrigerator. In the morning innkeepers Dawn Champagne and Phil Duddy deliver a substantial breakfast-in-a-basket. There are miles of conservation paths near the inn, around the cranberry bog. May through October $99–129; off-season $79–99. No credit cards.

CAMPGROUNDS ❀ ♪ **Bayview Campgrounds** (508-759-7610), 260 Route 28 (1 mile south of Bourne), 02532. Open May to mid-October. Since only 50 of 430 sites are reserved for tenters, RVers make up the majority of guests. $31 daily in-season, regardless of your electrical needs.

There is also camping at Bourne Scenic Park (see *Outdoor Activities— Swimming Pool*) and Scusset Beach State Reservation (see *Green Space* in "Sandwich"). Although there is no camping at the Midway Recreation Area (Route 6A on the Cape side of the canal in Bourne), campfire programs led by the Cape Cod Canal Rangers (508-759-4431) are held; call for days and times.

✳ Where to Eat

Despite the region's drive-through feel, there are a number of places to sit down.

𝖸 **Chart Room** (508-563-5350), Shipyard Lane off Shore Road at the Cataumet Marina. Open for lunch and dinner daily, June through September; Thursday through Sunday in May and October. Defining the summertime experience in this neck of the woods, this low-slung building is well positioned on picturesque Red Brook Harbor. If you have to wait for a table—and you might, as the Chart Room packs 'em in—there are a few

Adirondack chairs and tables scattered across a short lawn. For the best sunset views, get a table on the edge of the outer dining room. The Chart Room, bustling and boisterous as it is, serves reliable sandwiches and seafood standards, including lobster salad, bisque, and grilled swordfish. Vinny McGuiness and Tom Gordon have been co-chefs since the early 1980s. Reservations recommended for dinner. Entrées $12–24.

Sagamore Inn (508-888-9707), 1131 Route 6A, Sagamore. Open 11–9 daily except Tuesday, April to mid-November. Shirley and Joseph Pagliarani have served "Yankee Italian" food since 1963, and now their son Joseph Jr., who was practically born in the restaurant, is cooking. Inside the shuttered green-and-white building are signs of "old Cape Cod": shiny wooden floors, captains' chairs at round tables, a white tin ceiling, and wooden booths. The Yankee pot roast has been on the menu from the beginning. There's a lot of fresh seafood on the menu, including broiled, baked, and fried choices. Finish up with traditional Grape-Nut custard, homemade pie, or bread pudding. Take-out. Lunch $5–9, dinner $8–20.

The Beachmoor Inn & Restaurant (508-759-7522), Buttermilk Way Taylor's Point, Buzzard's Bay. Open for brunch in spring and fall, dinner April through December. Although I didn't get a chance to eat here for this edition, the longtime, former, and successful operators of Falmouth's Quarterdeck restaurant own this ocean-view eatery. That sets my mind at ease. Located next to Massachusetts Maritime Academy, they offer traditional seafood dishes like broiled sea scallops and surf and turf. Dine fireside or on the waterside deck. Dinner $13–28.

The Courtyard (508-563-1818), Route 28A and County Road, Cataumet. Open for lunch and dinner. In summer the outdoor bar, raw bar, and courtyard are hopping. And the food is pretty good, too: lunchtime sandwiches and fish-and-chips, whopping prime rib dinner specials (Thursday through Sunday); lighter salads, too. Dishes $11–20.

Lobster Trap (508-759-3992), 290 Shore Road, Bourne. Open for lunch and dinner (weekends only in spring and fall). Every town has one restaurant that overlooks water and has the requisite nautical paraphernalia. This is Bourne's. The menu features fried seafood, seafood rolls, and seafood plates. BYOB; take-out. Dishes $5–18.

Parrot Bar & Grill (508-563-6464), 1356 Route 28A, Cataumet. Open daily except Monday for lunch and dinner. In addition to a few burgers and pizzas, you can also get seafood dishes and prime rib. It has a nice local bar. Lunch $5–8, dinner $7–16.

The Bridge (508-888-8144), 21 Route 6A, Sagamore. Open for lunch and dinner daily. On the Cape side of the Sagamore Bridge, this pleasant and friendly place has been in the Prete family since 1953. You can find something to suit everyone. For lunch the Bridge offers its renowned Yankee pot roast, as well as tuna melts, spaghetti, and burgers. At dinnertime the Italian-influenced menu has seafood and some well-executed Thai dishes to spice things up. Lunch $5–9, dinner $9–18.

FISH MARKET ❈ **Cataumet Fish** (508-564-5956), 1640 Route 28A, Cataumet.

❈ Entertainment

There are a number of **band concerts:** Thursdays at 7 PM in July and August (508-759-6000) at Buzzards Bay Park off Main Street, Buzzards Bay; every other Sunday at 4 PM, July through September (508-291-3677) at Besse Park; and Wednesdays at 7 PM, mid-July through August (508-295-7072) at the Onset Band Shell.

❈ Selective Shopping

❈ Unless otherwise noted, all shops are open year-round.

ART AND ARTISANS **Pairpoint Crystal** (508-888-2344; 800-899-0953; www.pairpoint.com), 851 Route 6A, Sagamore. Retail shop open daily; glassmaking weekdays 9–4:30. This place has existed under one name or another since 1837. Thomas Pairpoint, a glass designer in the 1880s, used techniques created by Deming Jarves. Master craftspeople still employ these techniques here today. Clear or richly colored glass is hand-blown, -sculpted, or -pressed on a 19th-century press. Through large picture windows you can watch the master glassblowers working on faithful period reproductions and cup holders or more modern lamps, paperweights, vases, and candlesticks. (See the introduction and *To See and Do* in "Sandwich" for more about the glass industry.)

✍ **Cataumet Arts Center** (508-563-5434; www.cataumet-arts.org), 76 Scraggy Neck Road, off County Road and Route 28A, Cataumet. This community arts center has ever-changing exhibits; artists' studios to rent; classes for children, printmakers, and others; and an airy gallery showcasing crafts, paintings, wearable art, and whimsical wooden sculptures.

FACTORY OUTLETS AND MALLS

🦃 **Christmas Tree Shops** (508-888-7010), on the Cape side of the Sagamore Bridge, exit 1 off Route 6. This may be the first Christmas Tree Shop you see, but it won't be the last—there are six more on the Cape. This is the main outlet "where everyone loves a bargain," and they've gone all-out to get your attention: You can't miss the revolving windmill and thatched roof. (The thatch is made from Canadian marsh grass and must be groomed every other year.) As for the merchandise, it has absolutely nothing to do with the end-of-the-year holiday. It revolves around inexpensive housewares, random gourmet food items, or miscellaneous clothing accessories—whatever the owners, Doreen and Charles Bilezikian, happen to get in closeout sales that week. Those who turn up their noses at the shops might appreciate knowing that the Bilezikians employ upwards of 2,000 year-round residents.

Cape Cod Factory Outlet Mall (508-888-8417), exit 1 off Route 6, Sagamore. Open daily. Surrounding a food court, 20 or more stores tempt even the most harried: London Fog, Bass, Corning-Revere, Carter's Children's Wear, Van Heusen, Reebok, Samsonite, Oshkosh B'Gosh, and Bannister Shoes.

Tanger Outlet Center (800-482-6437), at the Bourne Bridge rotary. Open daily. Liz Claiborne, Nine West, Izod, and Levi's.

✳ Special Events

Fourth of July: **Mashnee Island's** celebrated, homespun parade. Island kids (and their parents) march or ride their bikes through town.

Mid-September: **Bourne Scallop Festival,** Buzzards Bay and along the canal. A weekend celebration with games, concerts, and restaurants/vendors offering dishes that celebrate—what else?—the scallop. Rain or shine, as the eating takes place under a big tent; since 1969.

Early December: **Christmas in Old Bourne Village.** A traditional holiday celebration with tree lighting.

SANDWICH

Sandwich is calm, even in the height of summer. Many visitors whiz right by it, eager to get farther away from the "mainland." Even people who know about delightful Sandwich Village often hop back onto Route 6 without poking around the rest of Sandwich—the back roads and historic houses off the beaten path. Those who take the time to explore will find that Sandwich is a real gem.

You could spend a day wandering the half-mile radius around the village center, a virtual time capsule spanning the centuries. Antiques shops, attractive homes, and quiet, shady lanes are perfect for strolling. Shawme Duck Pond, as idyllic as they come, is surrounded by historic houses (including one of the Cape's oldest), an old cemetery on the opposite shore, a working gristmill, swans and ducks, and plenty of vantage points from which to take it all in. A museum dedicated to the naturalist Thornton W. Burgess, a town resident and the creator of Peter Cottontail, also sits pondside. Both children and adults delight in the museum and in the Green Briar Nature Center & Jam Kitchen down the road. Sandwich's greatest attraction lies just beyond the town center: Heritage Museums & Gardens, a 76-acre horticulturist's delight with superb collections of Americana and antique automobiles.

Beyond the town center, the Benjamin Nye Homestead is worth a visit; have a look-see, even if it's closed, because it sits in a picturesque spot. East of town on Route 6A, past densely carpeted cranberry bogs (harvested in autumn), you'll find a few farm stands, antiques shops, and artisans' studios. At the town line with Barnstable, you'll find one of the Cape's best beaches and protected areas: Sandy Neck Beach (see the "Barrier Beach Beauty" sidebar in "Barnstable") and Sandy Neck Great Salt Marsh Conservation Area (see *Green Space—Walks* in "Barnstable"). The marina, off Tupper Road, borders the Cape Cod Canal with a recreation area. The often-overlooked town beach is nothing to sneeze at, either, and there are numerous conservation areas and ponds for walking and swimming.

Although a surprising number of Sandwich's 21,000 year-round residents commute to Boston every morning, their community dedication isn't diminished. A perfect example took place after fierce storms in August and October 1991 destroyed the town boardwalk, which had served the community since 1875. To

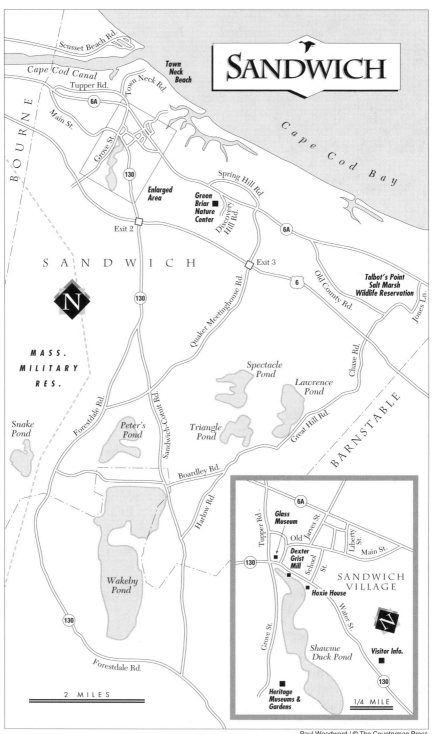

SANDWICH

BOURNE

Scusset Beach Rd.

Cape Cod Canal

Tupper Rd.

6A

Main St.

Town Neck Rd.

Town Neck Beach

Grove St.

130

Enlarged Area

Spring Hill Rd.

Green Briar Nature Center

Discovery Hill Rd.

Cape Cod Bay

6A

Exit 2

SANDWICH

N

Exit 3

6

Old County Rd.

Talbot's Point Salt Marsh Wildlife Reservation

Jones Ln.

130

Quaker Meetinghouse Rd.

MASS. MILITARY RES.

Spectacle Pond

Lawrence Pond

Chase Rd.

BARNSTABLE

Forestdale Rd.

Snake Pond

Peter's Pond

Sandwich-Cotuit Rd.

Triangle Pond

Great Hill Rd.

Boardley Rd.

Harlow Rd.

Wakeby Pond

130

Forestdale Rd.

2 MILES

Tupper Rd.

6A

Glass Museum

James St.

Old School St.

Liberty St.

Main St.

130

Dexter Grist Mill

Hoxie House

SANDWICH VILLAGE

N

Grove St.

Water St.

Shawme Duck Pond

Visitor Info.

130

Heritage Museums & Gardens

1/4 MILE

Paul Woodward / © The Countryman Press

replace it, townspeople purchased more than 1,700 individual boards, each personally inscribed, and a new boardwalk was built within eight months.

The oldest town on the Cape, Sandwich was founded in 1637 by the Cape's first permanent group of English settlers. The governor of Plymouth Colony had given permission to "tenn men from Saugust" (now Lynn, Massachusetts) to settle the area with 60 families. Sandwich was probably chosen for its close proximity to the Manomet (now Aptucxet) Trading Post (see *To See* in "Bourne") and for its abundant salt-marsh hay, which provided ready fodder for the settlers' cows. Agriculture supported the community until the 1820s, when Deming Jarves, a Boston glass merchant, decided to open a glassmaking factory. The location couldn't have been better: There was a good source of sand (although more was shipped in from New Jersey), sea salt was plentiful, salt-marsh hay provided packaging for the fragile goods, and forests were thick with scrub pines to fuel the furnaces. But by the 1880s, Midwestern coal-fueled glassmaking factories and a labor strike shut down Sandwich's factories. The story is told in great detail at the excellent Sandwich Glass Museum. Today, glassblowers work in a few studios in town.

Sandwich was named, by the way, for the English town, not for the sandwich-creator earl, as many think. (That Earl of Sandwich was born 81 years after this town was founded.)

GUIDANCE ❋ **Cape Cod Canal Region Chamber of Commerce** (508-759-6000; www.capecodcanalchamber.org), 70 Main Street, Buzzards Bay 02532. Open 8:30–5 weekdays. The main chamber is housed in an old railroad station in the center of Buzzards Bay, but a more convenient seasonal information booth (508-833-1632) is located on Route 130 as you head into Sandwich from Route 6. You can find a good village walking guide at many shops in town.

U.S. Army Corps of Engineers (USACE) Visitor's Center (508-833-9678), Ed Moffit Drive, Sandwich, east of the Sandwich Marina. Open weekdays June through August, Friday through Sunday in September and October. Staffed by USACE personnel, the office dispenses information about boating, fishing, camping, and other canal activities. Highlights of the center include historic photos, interactive monitors, and a small theater showing films on canal history, critters, and wildflowers. Inquire about their hikes, lectures, and other programs.

PUBLIC REST ROOMS Located in the chamber of commerce office in Buzzards Bay, they are open during business hours.

PUBLIC LIBRARY ✐ ❋ ⊤ **Sandwich Public Library** (508-888-0625), 142 Main Street, is open 9:30–8:30 Tuesday through Thursday, and 9:30–4 Friday and Saturday. From early September to late May, the library is also open 1–5 Sunday. You can borrow toys and videos here; Internet access, too.

GETTING THERE *By car:* Take the Sagamore Bridge to Route 6 east to exit 2 (Route 130 north) and travel 2 miles to Main Street. From exit 1 and Route 6A, you can take Tupper Road or Main Street into the village center.

By bus: There is no bus service to Sandwich proper, but **Plymouth & Brockton** (508-778-9767; www.p-b.com) buses bound for Boston stop at the Sagamore rotary, behind McDonald's in the commuter parking lot. For points south and west, Bonanza (888-751-8800; www.bonanzabus.com) buses stop nearby in Bourne.

GETTING AROUND Sandwich Village is perfect for strolling, but you'll have to get back in your car to reach the marina and Heritage Museums & Gardens (see *To See and Do*).

MEDICAL EMERGENCY Call **911.**

It's not an "emergency" (the kind you'd expect under this category, anyway), but many area water wells have been closed in recent years. They've been contaminated by years of training with grenades and other live munitions at the Massachusetts Military Reservation. I drink bottled water on the Upper Cape.

✳ To See and Do

In Sandwich Village

✎ **Dexter Grist Mill** (508-888-1173), on Shawme Duck Pond, Water Street. Open 10–4:45 Monday through Saturday and 1–4:45 Sunday, mid-June to mid-September; 10–4:45 Saturday, mid-May to mid-June and mid-September to mid-October. The circa-1640 mill has had a multiuse past, and the site wasn't always as quaint as it is now. The mill was turbine powered during Sandwich's glassmaking heyday; it then sat idle until 1920, when it was converted into a tearoom.

> **SAND TRANSFORMED**
> 🔍 🍴 **Sandwich Glass Museum** (508-888-0251; www.sandwichglassmuseum.org), 129 Main Street. Open 9:30–5 daily, May through December; 9:30–4 Wednesday through Sunday, February through April. During the 19th century, Sandwich glassmaking flourished at Deming Jarves's Boston & Sandwich Glass Company (1825–1888) and the Cape Cod Glass Works (1859–1869). Today this internationally known museum, operated by the Sandwich Historical Society, chronologically displays thousands of decorative and functional glass objects, which became increasingly more elaborate and richly colored as the years progressed. The displays are dramatically backlit by natural light streaming through banks of windows. A video describes the rise and crash of the local glass industry, and a diorama displays how the glass was made. If you're in the habit of skipping town historical museums, break the habit this time; you won't be disappointed. After a big renovation, look for a new multimedia theater, interactive exhibits, and glassblowing demonstrations. Adults $3.50, children 6–16, $1; personal guided tours $1 extra.

TRANQUIL SHAWME POND AND THE DEXTER GRIST MILL IN SANDWICH VILLAGE

Kim Grant

After adjacent mills were torn down in the late 1950s, it was opened to tourists in 1961, with the cypress waterwheel you see today. On-site miller and local schoolteacher Leo Manning describes the intricacies of the milling process. You can purchase stone-ground cornmeal—great for muffins, Indian pudding, and polenta. Nominal admission.

✍ **Thornton W. Burgess Museum** (508-888-4668; 508-888-6870; www.thorntonburgess.org), 4 Water Street. Open 10–4 Monday through Saturday and 1–4 Sunday, April through October and the first two weekends in December. This Sandwich native and renowned children's author and naturalist wrote more than 15,000 stories and 170 books, featuring the escapades of Jimmy Skunk, Grandfather Frog, and the beloved Peter Cottontail (not to be confused with Beatrix Potter's Peter Rabbit). The house is crammed with Burgess's books, original Harrison Cady illustrations, a "see-and-touch room," and exhibits honoring Burgess's life and work. Don't miss story time, which takes place on Monday, Thursday, and Saturday mornings at 10:30 on the lawn in July and August; $1 per person. The Thornton Burgess Society was begun by local bookseller Nancy Titcomb (see *Selective Shopping—Bookstore*) in 1974 to celebrate the centennial of Burgess's birth. Adults $2, kids $1. (See also Green Briar Nature Center & Jam Kitchen under *Green Space*.)

🐇 **Hoxie House** (508-888-1173), 18 Water Street. Open 10–5 Monday through Saturday and 1–5 Sunday, mid-June to mid-October. For a long time this circa-1675 structure was thought to be the Cape's oldest saltbox. Although it's impossible to know definitively—the Barnstable County Courthouse deeds were lost in a fire—that claim is now generally thought to be inaccurate. Nonetheless, the house has a rare saltbox roofline, small diamond-shaped leaded windows, and a fine vantage above Shawme Duck Pond. Thanks to loaner furniture from Boston's Museum of Fine Arts, the restored interior looks much as it did during colonial times. One of the most remarkable facts about this house is that it was occupied without electricity or indoor plumbing until the 1950s. The house was named for Abraham Hoxie, who purchased it in 1860 for $400. The Reverend John Smith lived here in 1675 when he came to be minister of the First Parish Church. Adults $2; children 12–16, $1. Combination ticket with Dexter Grist Mill: adults $3; children 12–16, $1.50.

Artesian fountain, between the gristmill and Town Hall. Join residents by filling water jugs with what some consider the Cape's best water.

First Church of Christ, 136 Main Street. This Christopher Wren–inspired church with a tall white spire was built in 1847, but its brass bell, cast in 1675, is thought to be the country's oldest.

Town Hall (508-888-5144), Main Street. Sandwich has certainly gotten its money's worth out of this Greek Revival building. It was constructed at a cost of little more than $4,000 in 1834 and still serves as the center for town government.

Old Town Cemetery, Grove Street, on the shore opposite the Hoxie House and Thornton W. Burgess Museum. You'll recognize the names on many gravestones (including those of Burgess, Bodfish, and Bourne) from historic houses and street signs around town. Although the oldest marker dates to 1683, most are from the 1700s; many are marked with a winged skull, a common Puritan design.

Elsewhere around town

❦ **Heritage Museums & Gardens** (508-888-3300; www.heritageplantation.org), Pine and Grove Streets. Open 9–6 daily (until 8 on Thursday and Friday), early May to late October. Established in 1969 by Josiah Lilly III, a descendant of the founder of the Eli Lilly Pharmaceutical Company, this place is an oasis for garden lovers, antiques and vintage-car buffs, and Americana enthusiasts. These 76 acres are planted with outstanding collections of rhododendrons, including the famous Dexter variety, which bloom from mid-May to mid-June. (Charles O. Dexter was the estate's original owner, and he experimented with hybridizing here.) There are also impressive collections of holly bushes, heathers, hostas, and almost 1,000 daylilies, which bloom from mid-July to early August. The estate is equally pleasant for an autumnal walk.

The **Military Museum** features a collection of 2,000 hand-painted miniatures, while the replica **Shaker Round Barn** houses the museum's outstanding vintage-car collection. A 1981 DeLorean, a 1930 Duesenberg built for Gary Cooper, and President Taft's White Steamer (the first official auto of the White House) are a few mint-condition classics.

The **Art Museum** features folk art, scrimshaw, cigar-store figures, weather vanes, carvings by Elmer Crowell, and Currier & Ives lithographs. Also on the grounds: an 1800 windmill, an operational Coney Island–style 1912 carousel, and the Carousel Café. The alfresco café has a limited but more-than-adequate menu of overstuffed sandwiches, salads, and desserts. A trolley transports people around the grounds, but it is not intended for sight-seeing. Keep your eyes peeled for museum special events, including plant sales and concerts. Adults $9; youths 6–18, $4.50; children 5 and under free.

Benjamin Nye Homestead (508-888-2368), 85 Old County Road, East Sandwich. Open noon–4:30 weekdays, mid-June to mid-October. Off Route 6A, this 1685 homestead belonged to one of Sandwich's first settlers and has undergone many structural changes over the years. It began as a small peaked room with a central chimney. An addition turned it into a saltbox, and then a second floor created the full Colonial you see today. Although the interior is hardly a purist restoration, you'll see some of the original construction, early paneling, 18th-century wallpaper, a spinning wheel, and handwoven sheets. Adults $3, kids $1.

1641 Wing Fort House, 69 Spring Hill Road (off Route 6A), East Sandwich. Open 10–4 Tuesday through Saturday, mid-June to mid-September. The Wing house is the country's oldest home continuously inhabited by the same family. This circa-1646 house began as a one-room cottage when Stephen Wing, descendant of the Reverend John Wing, arrived with his new bride. In the mid-1800s, a second house was added to it to create the current three-quarter Colonial. Adults $2, children $1.

Friends Meeting House (508-888-4181), Quaker Road, off Spring Hill Road (from Route 6A), East Sandwich. Services Sunday at 10 AM. The building standing today was built in 1810, the third Quaker meetinghouse on this site. The congregation has been meeting since 1657, which makes it the oldest continuous meeting in North America. The interior is simple, with pews and a wood-burning stove stoked in winter for 25 or so congregants. Handsome carriage barns flank the meetinghouse.

✑ ❉ **Sandwich Fish Hatchery** (508-888-0008), Route 6A at Old Main Street. Open 9–4 daily. More than 200,000 trout at various stages of development are raised to stock the state's ponds. Throw in pellets of food (bring quarters for the vending machines) and watch 'em swarm.

✑ **Boardwalk,** Harbor Street off Factory Street. The boardwalk crosses marshland, Mill Creek, and low dunes to connect to Town Neck Beach (see *Green Space—Beaches*). Depending on the season, you might see kids jumping into the creek or blue heron poking around the tidal pools and tall grasses. There are expansive views at the end of the 1,350-foot walkway.

✑ **Cape Cod Central Railroad** (508-771-3800; 888-797-7245; www.capetrain. com), 252 Main Street (Main and Center Streets). Weekends in May, June, September, and October; daily except Monday in July and August. The 42-mile trip takes 2 hours and passes cranberry bogs and the Sandy Neck Great Salt Marsh. Since there are two trains daily, you can take the first one, hop off in Hyannis, walk around town (the centrally located station is also close to the harbor), and then catch the next train back to Sandwich. Adults $15; children 11 and under, $11.

❉ Outdoor Activities

BICYCLING/RENTALS Cape Cod Bike Rentals/Sandwich Cycles (508-833-2453), 40 Route 6A. Open seasonally. Bicycles, mopeds, joggers, tandem bikes,

THE BELOVED SANDWICH BOARDWALK, REBUILT BY TOWNSPEOPLE AFTER FIERCE
STORMS DESTROYED IT, LEADS OVER A PICTURESQUE MARSH TO THE TOWN BEACH.

Kim Grant

in-line skates, and emergency repairs to your own bicycle, on-road if needed. On multiday rentals, Sandwich Cycles offers delivery to and pickup from your lodging. The shop is located between Sandwich's shady back roads and the Cape Cod Canal bike path (see *Outdoor Activities* in "Bourne").

BLUEBERRY PICKING **The Blueberry Bog,** Spring Hill off Route 6A. In the 1940s, this former cranberry bog was turned into a blueberry farm. Today there are about 400 bushes on more than 4 acres. The fruit matures from early to mid-July through August; pick your own by the quart or pound.

CANOEING **Shawme Duck Pond,** Water Street (Route 130), is actually linked to two other ponds, so you can do a lot of canoeing here.

Scorton Creek. Head east on Route 6A, turn right onto a gravel road before reaching the Scorton Creek Bridge. This is a good place for picnics, too.

Wakeby Pond, off Cotuit Road, South Sandwich.

FISHING Freshwater fishing licenses and regulations can be procured from the Town Hall Annex (508-888-5144), Main Street.

For saltwater fishing (no permit required), **Sandcastle Recreation Area** (at the Sandwich Marina) and **Scusset Beach State Reservation Pier** (off Scusset Beach Road from the rotary on the mainland side of the canal) are good places to cast a line into the Cape Cod Canal.

FITNESS CLUB ❋ **Sportsite Health & Racquet Club** (508-888-7900), 315 Cotuit Road. Open daily. Two weight rooms, a cardiovascular area, aerobics classes, sauna, steam room, racquetball courts, spinning, and baby-sitting services while you work out. $50 for eight visits, $12 daily, or $25 weekly.

❋ GOLF **Holly Ridge** (508-428-5577), off Route 130, South Sandwich. An 18-hole, 3,000 -yards, par-54 course.

Round Hill Country Club (508-888-3384), exit 3 (off Round Hill Road) off Route 6, East Sandwich. An 18-hole, par-72 course.

✐ MINI-GOLF **Sandwich Minigolf** (508-833-1905), 159 Route 6A. Open weekends mid-May to mid-October and daily in summer. Set on a cranberry bog, this course boasts a floating raft for a green! An honest-to-goodness stream winds around many of the 27 holes.

TENNIS Public courts are located at **Wing Elementary School** on Route 130, **Oak Ridge School** off Quaker Meetinghouse Road, and **Forestdale School** off Route 130.

❋ Green Space

✐ **Green Briar Nature Center & Jam Kitchen** (508-888-6870; www.thorntonburgess.org), 6 Discovery Hill Road off Route 6A, East Sandwich. Trails open year-round; the Jam Kitchen open 10–4 Monday through Saturday and 1–4 Sunday, April through October and the first two weekends in December. Even in an area with so many tranquil spots, Green Briar rises to the top. It's run by the Thornton W. Burgess Society "to re-establish and maintain nature's fine balance among all living things and to hold as a sacred trust the obligation to make only the best use of natural resources." Located on Smiling Pond and adjacent to the famous Briar Patch of Burgess's stories, these 57 acres of conservation land have many short, interpretive nature trails (less than a mile long) and a lovely wildflower garden. The society hosts natural history classes, lectures, nature walks, and other programs. Young children enjoy creeping along marsh creeks in search of hermit crabs, while older children take canoeing expeditions and learn Native American crafts and lore. Fees vary; call for a schedule.

The Jam Kitchen was established in 1903 by Ida Putnam, who used her friend Fanny Farmer's recipes to make jams, jellies, and fruit preserves. Step inside the old-fashioned, aromatic, and homey place to see mason jars filled with apricots and strawberries and watch fruit simmering on vintage-1920 Glenwood gas stoves. Two-hour workshops on preserving fruit and making jams and jellies are also held. About this place, Burgess said to Putnam in 1939, "It is a wonderful thing to sweeten the world which is in a jam and needs preserving."

✐ **Shawme Duck Pond,** Water Street (Route 130), in the village center. Flocks of ducks, geese, and swans know a good thing when they find it. And even though this idyllic spot is one of the most easily accessible on the Cape, it remains a tranquil place for humans and waterfowl alike. Formerly a marshy brook, the willow-lined pond was dammed prior to the gristmill operating in the 1640s. It's a nice spot to canoe.

🦆 ❋ ✐ **Shawme-Crowell State Forest** (508-888-0351; 877-422-6762 reservations; www.reserveamerica.com), Route 130. You can walk, bicycle, and camp ($10–12 nightly) at 285 sites on 742 acres. When the popular Nickerson State

Park (see the sidebar "A Supreme State Park" in "Brewster") is full of campers, there are often dozens of good sites still available here.

🦞 ❄ ✎ **Scusset Beach State Reservation** (508-888-0859; 877-422-6762 reservations; www.reserveamerica.com), on Cape Cod Bay, off Scusset Beach Road from the rotary on the mainland side of the canal. The 380-acre reservation offers about 100 campsites (primarily used by RVers, $12–15 nightly in-season), bicycling, picnicking, and walking opportunities. Cape Cod Canal Rangers (see U.S. Army Corps of Engineers under *Guidance*) hold campfire programs on Thursday evenings. Facilities include in-season lifeguard, rest rooms, changing rooms, and a snack bar. Parking $7.

See also Giving Tree Gallery and Sculpture Gardens under *Selective Shopping— Special Shops.*

BEACHES **Town Neck Beach,** on Cape Cod Bay, off Town Neck Road and Route 6A. This pebble beach extends 1.5 miles from the Cape Cod Canal to Dock Creek. Visit at high tide if you want to swim; at low tide, it's great for walking.

Sandy Neck Beach, off Route 6A on the Sandwich–Barnstable line (see the "Barrier Beach Beauty" sidebar in "Barnstable").

See also Scusset Beach State Reservation, above.

PONDS **Wakeby Pond** (off Cotuit Road), South Sandwich, offers freshwater swimming.

WALKS **Talbot's Point Salt Marsh Wildlife Reservation,** off Old County Road from Route 6A. This little-used, 1.5₂-mile (round trip) hiking trail winds past red pines, beeches, and a large salt marsh.

See also Green Briar Nature Center & Jam Kitchen and Shawme-Crowell State Forest, above.

❄ Lodging

🦞 ❄ Sandwich's historic hostelries provide great diversity, something for everyone—from an incredibly impressive church conversion to a large motor inn. Unless otherwise noted, all lodging is open year-round and in Sandwich 02563.

RESORT MOTOR INN ✎ **Dan'l Webster Inn** (508-888-3622; 800-444-3566; www.danlwebsterinn.com), 149 Main Street. Modeled after an 18th-century hostelry where Revolutionary patriots met, today's motor inn has a

certain colonial charm that's vigilantly maintained by the Catania family, who purchased the property in 1980. They also have a staff horticulturist overseeing the pleasant courtyards and an attractive pool area behind the inn. (Rooms in the Fessenden Wing overlook gardens.) Most of the 54 rooms and suites are of the top-notch motel/hotel variety. A few rooms are more innlike, more distinctive; these are in two separate older houses. Across the board, modern amenities include telephone, cable TV, turndown service, room service, and a daily newspaper at your door. There are four well-regarded dining rooms (see *Dining Out*). Guests have privileges at the nearby Sportsite Health & Racquet Club (see *Outdoor Activities—Fitness Club*). Late May to late October $169–199 rooms, $229–379 suites; off-season $109–279; off-season packages. Children under 12 free.

INN Belfry Inne (508-888-8550; 800-844-4542; www.belfryinn.com), 8 Jarves Street. The central Belfry Inne consists of the circa-1879 Drew House and its adjacent circa-1900 Abbey. All 14 guest rooms have fine antiques and tasteful and comfortable furnishings. While the Drew House rooms are certainly first-rate (I particularly like Kristina Drew), the Abbey rooms are downright spectacular: stained glass, flying buttresses, fancy linens, bold colors, beds made from pews, gas fireplaces, Jacuzzis, and balconies. There isn't one I wouldn't highly recommend. Innkeeper Chris Wilson and his architect deserve awards for this conversion. The Abbey's bistro is open to the public (see *Dining Out*). Drew House $95–165, Abbey $165–195; off-season $95–165 and $165, respectively; continental breakfast included.

BED & BREAKFASTS Captain Ezra Nye House (508-888-6142; 800-388-2278; www.captainezranyehouse.-com), 152 Main Street. Elaine and Harry Dickson have expertly run this 1829 Federal-style B&B since 1986. The four rooms and two suites (one with a working fireplace; one with electric stove; all carpeted and with air-conditioning) are decorated with an eclectic assortment of antiques and objects the Dicksons have collected from around the world. The common

front parlor is a bit formal, but there's a small TV room off the dining room that's more casual. Full breakfast included. Mid-May through October $120–145; off-season $100–120.

The Village Inn at Sandwich (508-833-0363; 800-922-9989; www.capecodinn.com), 4 Jarves Street. Surrounded by perennial gardens and a white picket fence in the middle of town, this 1830s Federal house has a wraparound porch (decked with rocking chairs) and two living rooms for guests to enjoy. Six of eight guest rooms have private bath; third-floor rooms share a bath. All rooms have hardwood floors (some bleached) and down comforters. Full breakfast at individual tables included. May through October $110–200; off-season $100–180.

Summer House (508-888-4991; 800-241-3609; www.summerhousesandwich.com), 158 Main Street. This 1835 Greek Revival Cape has five rooms furnished simply with antiques and quilts; many feature a fireplace, original hardware, and painted hardwood floors. A bountiful breakfast is served in the fanciful living/dining room with Chinese-red walls and a black-and-white checkerboard floor. Take your afternoon tea in the sunroom, in the English-style garden, or (very carefully) in the hammock. Late May through October $95–125; off-season $70–95.

✿ **Windfall House** (508-888-3650; 877-594-6325; www.windfallhouse.com), 108 Route 130 (Main Street). Within walking distance of the village, innkeeper Ted Diggle presides over a snug 1818 hostelry. The cozy gathering room boasts beamed ceilings, wide-pine floors, a working fireplace, cable TV, and beehive oven. Four

Colonial-style rooms and one suite are furnished with homey and impressive antiques like carved cherry four-poster beds and wrought-iron beds. The Burbank Suite features a kitchenette and private entrance (with deck) and can accommodate a family or friends traveling together. A full breakfast, perhaps omelets and home-fries, is included. Late May through October $75–125; off-season $55–110.

☙ **Wingscorton Farm Inn** (508-888-0534), 11 Wing Boulevard, East Sandwich 02537. This circa-1758 working farm, on 13 acres of orchards and woods, is a rare bird. Once a stop on the Underground Railroad, the house has low ceilings, wainscoting, wide-plank floors, rich paneling, and wood-burning fireplaces in the guest rooms. Two living rooms—one with the largest hearth in New England—provide plenty of common space for guests. Accommodations include three suites (each with refrigerator, period antiques, and canopy bed) and a two-story carriage house with a private deck and patio, full kitchen, and woodstove. Innkeeper Sheila Weyers includes a multicourse breakfast, which is served at a long harvest table in front of a working fireplace. Dogs and cats roam around the property, which is also home to pygmy goats, horses, and sheep. You can bring your own well-behaved pets. Free-range chickens and fresh eggs are sold from the barn. You can also walk to the inn's private bay beach. June to mid-October $165–200; off-season $95–165; children $25–45 nightly.

Bay Beach (508-888-8813; 800-475-6398; www.baybeach.com), 3 Bay Beach Lane. Open mid-May to mid-October. Located right smack on a private beach with views of the Cape Cod Canal's east entrance, Emily and Reale Lemieux's contemporary house

A CRUISE SHIP PASSES THROUGH THE CANAL AT THE SANDWICH MARINA.

Kim Grant

has seven luxurious rooms with air-conditioning, refrigerator, telephone, cable TV, and outdoor decks (some have whirlpools). $245–325, including full breakfast.

COTTAGES ✐ **Pine Grove Cottages** (508-888-8179; www.pinegrovecottages.com), 358 Route 6A, East Sandwich 02537. Open May through October. These 10 tidy cottages with kitchens come in various sizes: There are tiny one-room, small one-bedroom, larger one-bedroom, and "deluxe" two-bedroom cottages. (Sandwich bylaws require two-bedroom units to measure 20 feet by 24 feet.) The cottages are freshly painted white. Although guests spend most of their time at the beach, there is also a new pool and play area in the pine grove. Mid-June to early September $345–675 weekly for two to four people; off-season $60–115 nightly.

MOTELS **Spring Garden Inn** (508-888-0710; 800-303-1751; www.springgarden.com), 578 Route 6A, East Sandwich 02537. Open April to mid-November. Reserve early if you can; this is one of the best motels on Route 6A. Although modest from the street, the bilevel motel overlooks a salt marsh and the Scorton River, particularly beautiful at sunset. The backyard is dotted with lawn chairs, grills, and picnic tables. (Owners Stephen and Elizabeth Kauffman pay careful attention to the gardens.) Eight carpeted rooms have knotty-pine paneling, two double beds, TV, air-conditioning, refrigerator, and telephone. In addition, there are two efficiencies and a two-room suite with a private deck. An outdoor pool is nicely shielded from Route 6A. Sandy Neck Beach is a mile from here. July and August $95–135; off-season $79–119.

✐ **Shadynook Inn & Motel** (508-888-0409; 800-338-5208; www.shadynook.com), 14 Route 6A. Sharon and Jim Rinaldi take well-deserved pride in their spiffy, shaded motel with lush landscaping and heated outdoor pool. The large rooms are typically appointed as far as motel rooms go, only a bit nicer. You'll also have a choice of two- and three-room suites, some of which are efficiencies. Children under 12 free; 37 units total. Mid-June to early September $95–200 for two to four people; off-season $65–175.

CAMPGROUND ✐ Peters Pond Park (508-477-1775; www.campcapecod.com), 185 Cotuit Road. Open mid-April to mid-October. The park consists of 450 well-groomed campsites, walking trails, summertime children's activities, and a popular spring-fed lake for trout and bass fishing, boating, and swimming. On-site tepee rentals $250 weekly, $45 daily off-season; $29–42 campsites; two-bedroom cottages $700 weekly, $105 daily off-season. Rental rowboats, paddleboats, kayaks, and tricycles are also available.

See also Shawme-Crowell State Forest and Scusset Beach State Reservation under *Green Space*.

RENTAL HOUSES AND COTTAGES **Real Estate Associates** (508-888-0900), 2 Willow Street, lists seasonal rentals.

✳ Where to Eat

❄ Sandwich eateries run the gamut from fine dining in a former church to casual eating in tiny tea shop. Unless otherwise noted, all entries are open year-round and in Sandwich.

DINING OUT Y **Belfry Bistro** (508-888-8550; 800-844-4542), 8 Jarves Street. Open for dinner. It took Chris Wilson nine months to convert this former church, and it was worth every day of his time. I'm a believer. The setting is divinely dramatic: soaring beadboard ceilings, stained glass, flying buttresses, a confessional that's been converted into a tasteful bar, and a former altar set with tables. It's also elegant: candlelight, damask-linen-covered tables, a wood-burning fireplace. The menu ranges from sautéed duck breast to grilled salmon to bouillabaisse. Off-season, Chris offers wine-tasting dinners on Wednesdays. In-season, look for clambakes on Sunday evenings. Entrées $19–27.

♂ & **Dan'l Webster Inn** (508-888-3622), 149 Main Street. Open for lunch and dinner daily year-round; Sunday brunch; breakfast daily mid-April to mid-November and weekends year-round. Under the direction of chef-owner Vincent Catania, the dining room serves reliable, classic American dishes in four intimate dining rooms. The sunlit conservatory is an indoor oasis, especially for lunch and brunch, while the main dining room is more traditional. The Tavern at the Inn is more casual. Throughout the inn, the dress code is neat but informal. By the way, the inn has an excellent water-filtration system, and its water is perhaps the best tasting on the Cape. Early specials. Brunch and lunch $7–14, dinner $17–26 (half entrées available, too).

EATING OUT & **Bee-Hive Tavern** (508-833-1184), 406 Route 6A, East

Sandwich. Open for lunch and dinner daily and for Sunday breakfast (Saturday, too, in summer). There are benches in front for a reason—there is often a wait due to the tavern's popularity. Low ceilings, barnboard, and booths make this dark, Colonial-style tavern a comfortable choice year-round. If you're tired of eating at picnic tables or in "quaint" clam shacks, try this place. Standard fare includes homemade soups, pasta, sandwiches (including the "roll-up" variety), and burgers. Full-fledged dinner entrées are more substantial: steaks, prime rib, lobster ravioli, and seafood. Part of the reason this place is so consistent is due to chef Mark Fitzpatrick, who's been here since opening day in 1992. Lunch $5–9, dinner $8–16.

Dunbar Tea Room & Shop (508-833-2485), 1 Water Street. Open daily 11 AM–4:30 PM. This tiny English tearoom, in an American-style country setting, has bustled since it opened. Try the authentic ploughman's lunch, or specials like seafood quiche (which sells out fast), or sweets like pies, cakes, scones, and Scottish shortbread. Afternoon English tea ($10 plus the cost of tea) includes scones, finger sandwiches, and desserts. In summer, garden tables are an oasis; in winter, the fireplace makes it cozy indoors. Lunches average about $9.

& ♂ Y **Aqua Grille** (508-888-8889), 14 Gallo Road, at the marina. Open for lunch and dinner mid-April to late October. The Aqua Grille's eclectic regional American menu features the ubiquitous fried seafood and lobster, but also pasta dishes, grilled meats, and fish prepared in a variety of ways. Chef Gert Rausch spent many years in Austin and Aspen, so you'll find some modern interpretations of quesadillas (with cilantro, Vermont goat cheese, and bay shrimp, perhaps) on the menu. It's a spacious, pleasant, and modern place with aqua walls, aqua-colored water glasses, and some Naugahyde, banquette-style booths. The marina and canal are visible from most tables. Specialty drinks are popular. Lunch $7–15, dinner entrées $9–20.

🦞 🔥 🐟 **Seafood Sam's** (508-888-4629), Coast Guard Road. Open for lunch and dinner daily, mid-March to mid-November. This casual spot near the marina serves fried and broiled seafood, seafood sandwiches, and seafood salad plates. Lunch specials $5–7, dinner dishes $7–18.

🦞 🐟 **Marshland Restaurant** (508-888-9824), 109 Route 6A. Open for breakfast and lunch on Monday, all three meals Tuesday through Saturday (6 AM–8 PM), and breakfast Sunday (7 AM–1 PM). It's primarily locals who frequent this small, informal roadside place for coffee and a breakfast muffin—or lunch specials like homemade meat loaf, quiche with great salads, and chicken club sandwiches. They serve real mashed potatoes for dinner, too, along with prime rib. Eat at one of the Formica booths or on a swiveling seat at the U-shaped counter. Breakfast $5, lunch specials $6.25, dinner entrées $7–13. No credit cards.

🐟 **Captain Scott's** (508-888-1675), 71 Tupper Road. Open 11:30–8:30-ish daily. This casual, inexpensive place is hopping with locals who come for the no-frills pasta dishes, fried seafood dinners, and baked or broiled fish. Early specials. Entrées $5–15.

🍸 **Horizons on Cape Cod Bay** (508-888-6166), Town Neck Beach. Open April to late October. Sandwich's only beachfront eatery is a nice place for an afternoon drink on the deck; views are spectacular. Based on a recent experience, the food and service aren't.

See also the Bridge and the Sagamore Inn under *Where to Eat* in "Bourne."

ICE CREAM 🍦 **Twin Acres Ice Cream** (508-888-0566), 21 Route 6A near Bourne. Open April to mid-October. The best in the area. The shop also boasts a lush lawn, little oak grove, and plenty of tables and chairs. (It sure beats standing in a parking lot!) It's lit at night, too. My only complaint: There's so much colorful signage describing the offerings that it's overwhelming. To compensate, I've returned often enough to memorize the menu. Generous servings; banana boats, hot fudge sundaes, and an ample grill menu.

✳ Entertainment

Heritage Museums & Gardens (508-888-3300), Pine and Grove Streets, sponsors outdoor concerts—from big band to jazz, from chamber singers to ethnic ensembles. Mid-June to early September.

🎵 **Band concerts,** at the Wing School off Route 130, are given by the Sandwich Town Band on Thursday evenings at 7 in July and August.

🎵 **Opera New England of Cape Cod** (508-771-3600), a touring company from New York City, performs opera for adults in May and October and for children in November at the Cape Cod Community College in West Barnstable.

✳ Selective Shopping

✳ Unless otherwise noted, all shops are open year-round. (Still, don't expect many to be open (mid-week during the winter).

ANTIQUES Madden & Company (508-888-3663), 16 Jarves Street. Open by chance, as the owner is frequently on buying trips. Set up to resemble a country store (albeit an upscale one), Paul Madden's shop primarily offers antiques and Americana, but he also has decorative country-style household gifts and nautical items.

Sandwich Antiques Center (508-833-3600), 131 Route 6A. Open daily. A multidealer shop worth your time…if you treasure the hunt.

Maypop Lane (508-888-1230), Route 6A at Main Street. Open daily. With many dealers under one roof, you'll find a broad selection: decoys, quilts, clothing, jewelry, sterling, copper, brass, glass, furniture, and other collectibles and antiques.

ARTISAN Glass Studio (508-888-6681), 470 Route 6A, East Sandwich. Open daily except Tuesday, April through December; call for winter hours. Artist Michael Magyar offers a wide selection of glass made with modern and century-old techniques. He's been glassblowing since 1980, and you can watch him work Thursday through Sunday. Choose from graceful Venetian goblets, square vases, bud vases, handblown ornaments (some of which are sold during the Christmas in Sandwich celebration; see *Special Events*), and "sea bubbles" glassware, influenced by the water around him.

See also *Selective Shopping—Art and Artisans* in "Bourne."

AUCTIONS Sandwich Auction House (508-888-1926), 15 Tupper

Road. Consignment estate sales are held Wednesdays in summer and Saturdays off-season. Once a month (call for dates) they hold a superduper Oriental rug auction.

BOOKSTORE Titcomb's Book Shop (508-888-2331), 432 Route 6A, East Sandwich. Open daily. Titcomb's beacon draws you in: It's hard to miss the life-sized statue of a colonist holding a book and walking stick. Book enthusiasts won't be disappointed; rare-book lovers will be even happier. This two-story barn is filled with more than 30,000 new, used, and rare books for adults and children, as well as a good selection of Cape and maritime books. The Titcombs have owned the shop since 1969 and, with the help of their eight children, have made hundreds of yards of shelves. It's a charming place, promoting browsing. By the way, owner Nancy Titcomb helped resurrect interest in Thornton W. Burgess, and, as you might imagine, she offers a great selection of his work.

SPECIAL SHOPS Giving Tree Gallery and Sculpture Gardens (508-888-5446; www.givingtree-gallery.com), 550 Route 6A, East Sandwich. Open April through January. The gallery's motto might as well be "Where Art and Nature Meet." It's a wonderful and aesthetic place. Outdoor sculpture is exhibited on acres of marshland with nature paths, perennial gardens, and a bamboo grove. But don't overlook the indoor gallery, featuring the work of hundreds of artists.

The Weather Store (508-888-1200), 146 Main Street. Open Monday through Saturday, Sunday by chance or appointment, April through December. If it relates to measuring or predicting weather, it's here: weather vanes, sundials, nautical gauges for yachts, "weather sticks" to indicate when a storm is headed your way, even whirligigs *"weather instrument* is broadly defined here).

Home for the Holidays (508-888-4388), 154 Main Street. Open daily from late May through December and on winter weekends. Each room of this 1850 house is filled with decorations and gifts geared to specific holidays or special occasions. Items in one room are changed every month, so there's always a room devoted to the current holiday.

Horsefeathers (508-888-5298), 454 Route 6A, East Sandwich. This small shop sells linens, lace, Victoriana, teacups, and vintage christening gowns.

Collections Unlimited (508-833-0039), 365 Route 6A, East Sandwich. Open daily. Handcrafted items—wood objects, pottery, baskets, stained glass, and the like—from members of the Cape's longest-running cooperative (since 1990).

Crow Farm, Route 6A, East Sandwich. Open seasonally. Killer beach plum jam.

See also Green Briar Nature Center & Jam Kitchen under *Green Space.*

✳ Special Events

Mid-September: **Boardwalk Celebration** (508-923-2733). A road race/walk, a kite festival, and a beachgoers' parade.

Early December: **Christmas in Sandwich** (508-759-6000). A week-long festival with caroling, hot cider served at open houses, trolley tours, and crafts sales.

FALMOUTH

2 MILES

N

WEST FALMOUTH

East Falmouth Hwy.

Sandwich Rd.

28

Waquoit Bay National Estuarine Research Reserve

Central Ave.

South Cape Beach

Menauhant Beach

Daisville Rd.

Acapesket Rd.

Falmouth Heights Beach

Miatavista Ave.

Worcester Ct.

Grand Ave.

Falmouth Heights Rd.

Vineyard Passenger Ferry

Falmouth Inner Harbor

Brick Kiln Rd.

Goodwill Park

Jones Rd.

Gifford St.

FALMOUTH VILLAGE

Main St.

Scranton

Clinton

Shore Dr.

Surf Dr.

Ter Heun Dr.

Palmer Ave.

SIPPEWISSETT

QUISSETT

Locust St.

Enlarged Area

Surf Drive Beach

28

28A

Sippewisset Rd.

The Knob

Quissett Ave.

Quissett Harbor

Woods Hole Rd.

Oyster Pond Rd.

Nobska Rd.

Nobska Light

Church St.

Vineyard Sound

Buzzards Bay

WOODS HOLE

Eel Pond

Vineyard Ferry

FALMOUTH VILLAGE

1/8 MILE

N

Chamber of Commerce

Academy Ln.

Walker St.

Walker St.

Town Hall

Main St.

28

Post Office Rd.

Village Green

Palmer Ave.

W. Main St.

N. Main St.

Locust St.

Depot Ave.

Paul Woodward / © The Countryman Press

FALMOUTH AND WOODS HOLE

The Cape's second largest town, Falmouth has more shore and coastline than any other town on the Cape. In fact, it has 14 harbors, 12 miles of public beaches, and more than 30 ponds. Saltwater inlets reach deep into the southern coastline, like fjords—only without the mountains. Buzzards Bay laps at the western shores of quiet North and West Falmouth and bustling Woods Hole. Falmouth's eight distinctive villages accommodate about 102,000 summer people, more than triple the town's year-round population.

The villages differ widely in character. Quiet, restful lanes and residents who keep to themselves characterize Sippewissett and both North and West Falmouth. The West Falmouth Harbor (off wooded, scenic Route 28A) is tranquil and placid, particularly at sunset. Although Falmouth Heights is known for its opulent, turn-of-the-20th-century shingled houses on Vineyard Sound, its beach is a popular gathering spot for 20-somethings—playing volleyball, sunbathing, flying kites, and enjoying the relatively warm water and seaside condos that line Grand Avenue and Menauhant Road. Falmouth Heights has early ties to the Kennedys: Rose Fitzgerald was vacationing here with her family when Joe Kennedy came calling.

East Falmouth is a largely residential area. There are several motels and grand year-round and summer homes lining the inlets of Green Pond, Bourne's Pond, and Waquoit Bay. Historic Danville was once home to whaling-ship captains and has a strong Portuguese and Cape Verdean fishing community and farming heritage.

The center of Falmouth, with plentiful shops and eateries, is busy year-round. And the village common, picture-perfect with historic houses (converted to beautiful bed & breakfasts) encircling the tidy green space, is well worth a stroll. Falmouth's Inner Harbor is awash with restaurants, boatyards, a colorful marina, and moderate nightlife. Two passenger ferries to Martha's Vineyard operate from here.

Four miles south of Falmouth, Woods Hole is more than just a terminus for the Steamship Authority auto and passenger ferries to the Vineyard. It is also home to three major scientific institutions: the National Marine Fisheries Service ("the Fisheries"), Woods Hole Oceanographic Institution (or WHOI, pronounced "hooey"), and the Marine Biological Laboratory (MBL).

Woods Hole, named for the "hole" or passage between Penzance Point and Nonamessett Island, was the site of the first documented European landing in the New World. Bartholomew Gosnold arrived here from Falmouth, England, in 1602.

GUIDANCE ❄ **Falmouth Chamber of Commerce** (508-548-8500; 508-548-8521 for 24-hour "fax-back" information; 800-526-8532; www.falmouth-capecod.com and www.woodshole.com), Box 582, 20 Academy Lane, Falmouth 02541. Open 8:30–5 weekdays year-round; 9–5 weekends mid-May to mid-October. There is also a seasonal **satellite office,** open mid-May to mid-October, on Palmer Avenue. Both offices also have Woods Hole information, good foldout street maps, and the historical society's walking tour brochure.

MEDIA Pick up the ***Falmouth Enterprise*** (508-548-4700; 800-286-7744), published every Tuesday and Friday at noon, for local news and gossip. On a recent visit, an edition featured photos of actress Julia Roberts "singing" karaoke at the Falmouth Inn on Main Street. (It takes place from 9 PM to 1 AM on Friday and Saturday nights, if you must know.)

THE FIRST CONGREGATIONAL CHURCH ON FAL-MOUTH'S TOWN GREEN

Kim Grant

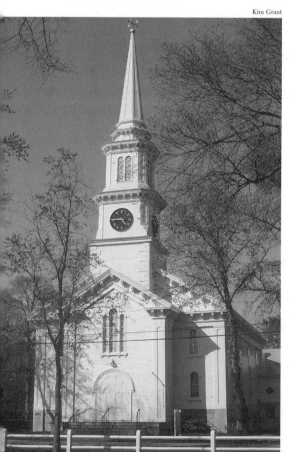

The Falmouth Visitor (508-548-3047; www.falmouthvisitor.com), is great and free publication for visitors who want to get beneath Falmouth's outer shell. It's really best for repeat and long-term visitors.

PUBLIC REST ROOMS Academy Lane; Peg Noonan Park and Town Hall on Main Street; and the harbormaster's Office at Marina Park, Scranton Avenue. In Woods Hole, head to the Steamship Authority.

PUBLIC LIBRARIES ✎ ❄ ☂ The area has five libraries; call each for its hours:

Falmouth Public Library (508-457-2555), 123 Catherine Lee Bates Road, is excellent.

East Falmouth Public Library (508-548-6340), 310 Route 28;

North Falmouth Public Library (508-563-2922), Chester Street.

West Falmouth Library (508-548-4709), 575 Route 28A.

Woods Hole Library (508-548-8961), 581 Woods Hole Road, Woods

Hole. As you might imagine, there are lots of scientists and NPR "Science Friday" types at this branch.

GETTING THERE *By car:* Via Route 28 south, Falmouth is 15 miles from the Bourne Bridge and 20 miles from the Sagamore Bridge. Route 28 turns into Main Street. In northern Falmouth, Route 28A parallels Route 28 and is much more scenic. Route 28 leads directly to Locust Street and Woods Hole Road for Woods Hole.

The directional signposts for Route 28 are a tad confusing from this point on. Although Hyannis and Chatham are east of Falmouth, the signpost from Falmouth to Chatham says ROUTE 28 SOUTH. This is because Route 28 originates in Bourne and does indeed head south to Falmouth before jogging east.

By bus: **Bonanza** (888-751-8800; www.bonanzabus.com) has service to Falmouth (Depot Avenue terminal) and Woods Hole (Steamship Authority) from New York, Providence, Connecticut, western Massachusetts, and Boston. There is direct service to Boston's Logan Airport. Some buses are intended to connect with ferries to Martha's Vineyard, although the ferry won't wait for a late bus. The round-trip fare from Boston's South Station to Woods Hole is $27. (It costs almost twice as much from Logan Airport.)

GETTING AROUND **Whoosh** (508-385-8326; 800-352-7155; www.capecodtransit.org) travels between major points of interest in and between Falmouth and Woods Hole. Tourists can hop on and off downtown and at shops and beaches. Whoosh operates about 9–7 daily, late May to late September; tickets cost $1 adults (50¢ kids 6–17). One-day passes are available from the chamber of commerce (see *Guidance*) or on board for $3 adults (half price for kids). Pick up a schedule and route map at the chamber, Steamship Authority, shops, or any stop along the route. Trolleys are equipped with a bike rack. Parking is extremely limited in Woods Hole, and roads are congested, so take Whoosh if you're just visiting for the afternoon.

Trolley Tours (508-548-4857). Departing from the Julia Wood House on the town green every other Wednesday from July to mid-September. Sponsored by the Falmouth Historical Society, this narrated 2-hour trip covers 10 miles and illuminates Falmouth's almost 350 years of maritime ties and rich history. Tickets $12 adults, $8 children under age 12. Purchase tickets at the chamber of commerce or Museums on the Green.

GETTING TO MARTHA'S VINEYARD There is year-round automobile and passenger ferry service to Martha's Vineyard from Woods Hole; there are two seasonal passenger ferry services to the Vineyard from Falmouth Harbor. For complete information, see *Getting There* in "Martha's Vineyard."

MEDICAL EMERGENCY **Falmouth Hospital** (508-548-5300), 100 Ter Heun Drive (off Route 28), Falmouth. Open 24/7.

Falmouth Walk-In Medical Center (508-540-6790), 309 Route 28, Teaticket Highway. Walk-ins taken 8–5 weekdays.

It's not an "emergency" (the kind you'd expect under this category, anyway), but many area water wells have been closed in recent years. They've been contaminated by years of training with grenades and other live munitions at the Massachusetts Military Reservation. I drink bottled water on the Upper Cape.

✳ To See and Do

In Falmouth

Village green. The green is bordered by Colonial, Federal, Italianate, and Greek Revival homes, many built for wealthy ship captains and then converted to B&Bs. Designated as public land in 1749 and now on the National Register of Historic Places, this large triangle of grass is enclosed by a white fence, surely as pastoral a sight today as it was more than 250 years ago. It's not difficult to imagine local militiamen practicing marches and drills and townspeople grazing horses—in fact, a local militia reenacts maneuvers on July 4.

First Congregational Church, 68 Main Street, on the green. This quintessential New England church—with its high steeple and crisp white lines—is graced by a bell (which still rings) commissioned by Paul Revere. The receipt for the bell—from 1796—is on display; the inscription on the bell reads: THE LIVING TO THE CHURCH I CALL, AND TO THE GRAVE I SUMMON ALL. Today's church was built on the foundations of the 1796 church.

🐚 Museums on the Green (508-548-4857; www.falmouthhistoricalsociety.org), 55–65 Palmer Avenue, just off the village green. Open 10–4 Tuesday through Saturday, July through September; additional weekend hours in June and Octo-

MUSEUMS ON THE GREEN OF THE FALMOUTH HISTORICAL SOCIETY

Kim Grant

ber; archives by appointment year-round. Operated by the Falmouth Historical Society. **The Conant House** (a circa-1730 half house) contains sailors' valentines, scrimshaw, rare glass and china, and old tools. One room honors Katherine Lee Bates, a Wellesley College professor and composer of "America the Beautiful," who was born nearby in 1859 at 16 Main Street (not open to the public). I suspect most Falmouth residents would lend support to the grassroots movement in the United States to change the national anthem from "The Star-Spangled Banner" to Bates's easier-to-sing, less militaristic song.

Next door, look for a formal Colonial-style garden and a Nimrod cannon; the replicated 100-year-old **Dudley Hallett Barn,** with an educational center with hands-on exhibits; and the early-19th-century **Julia Wood House,** home to Dr. Francis Wicks, known for his work with smallpox inoculations. Adults $4; children under 12 free; tours by trained guides are included. See also *Getting Around* for historical society trolley tours.

The Dome (508-548-0800), Woods Hole Road, Woods Hole. When Buckminster Fuller was teaching at MIT, he patented the geodesic dome design in 1954. One of his domes, which "epitomize doing more with less," is just north of town. It's definitely worth a look.

Cape Cod Winery (508-457-5592; www.capecodwinery.com), 681 Sandwich Road, East Falmouth. Open weekends early May to early December; noon–5 Wednesday through Sunday, July and August. Summer weekend tours at 2 PM. Tastings, too, of fruity wines, a Blanc de Blancs blend, Cabernet, Pinot Grigio, and Merlot. During harvesttime in late September and early October, visitors are invited to pick grapes in exchange for a gift certificate redeemable for that particular vintage. Once it's bottled, it includes a custom label that indicates the name of the harvesters.

See also Bourne Farm under *Green Space—Walks.*

In Woods Hole

🦞 ✳ ⌀ **Woods Hole Science Aquarium** (508-495-2001), Water Street. Open 10–4 daily, mid-June to mid-September; 10–4 weekdays the rest of the year. When it opened in 1871, this was the first aquarium in the country. Today it's a fun place to learn about slippery fish, living shellfish (rather than the empty shells we're all accustomed to seeing), and other lesser-known creatures of the deep. Kids are encouraged to use microscopes and interact with lobsters, hermit crabs, and other crawling sea critters in a dozen tanks and shallow pools of icy-cold bubbling seawater. Even when the aquarium is closed, you can see seals in a tank out front. Donations.

🦞 **Woods Hole Oceanographic Institution** (WHOI) Exhibit Center (508-289-2663; 508-289-2252 for tour reservations; www.whoi.edu), 15 School Street. Open 10–4:30 Tuesday through Saturday and noon–4:30 Sunday, May through October; also open 10–4:30 Monday, June through August. Call for irregular weekend hours in March, April, November, and December. A Rockefeller grant of $2.5 million got WHOI off the ground in 1930, and since then its annual budget has grown to about $92 million. It is the largest independent oceanography lab in the country. About 1,000 students and researchers from all over the world are employed year-round. During World War II, WHOI worked on underwater explosives and submarine detection. Today scientists study climate issues, undersea volcanoes, ocean and coastal pollution, deep-sea robotics and acoustics, and large and small marine life. Relatively unpolluted waters and a deep harbor make Woods Hole an ideal location for this work.

WHOI buildings cover 200 acres. One-hour guided walking tours are offered weekdays at 10 AM and 1:30 PM from mid-June to early September. The tour covers a lot of ground and is geared to adults and teenagers. The small exhibit center shows excellent videos and has an interactive display with marine-mammal sounds and a fascinating display of Alvin, the tiny submarine that allowed WHOI researchers to explore and photograph the *Titanic* in 1986. Suggested exhibit donation $2; walking tour free, but reservations required.

✳ **Marine Biological Laboratory** (MBL; 508-289-7623 tour reservations; www.mbl.edu), 127 Water Street. Tours (at 1, 2, and 3 PM only) are very popular and restricted in size, so reservations are required at least a week in advance. Visitors center open 10–4 weekdays June through August, plus 10–3 weekends July and August. Founded in 1888 as "a non-profit institution devoted to research and education in basic biology," the MBL studies more than fish. It studies life at its most basic level, with an eye toward answering the question, "What is life?" And marine creatures tend to be some of the most useful animals in that quest. Scientists (including 37 Nobel laureates over the years) study the problems of infertility, hypertension, Alzheimer's, AIDS, and other diseases. It's not hyperbole to say there's no other institution or academy like it in the world. Guides lead excellent tours that include a video about what goes on at the MBL. History buffs will be interested to note that one of the MBL's granite buildings was a former factory that made candles with spermaceti (whale oil). Free. Not appropriate for children under 10.

St. Joseph's Bell Tower, Millfield Street (north shore of Eel Pond). To encourage his colleagues not to become too caught up in the earthly details of their work and lose their faith in the divine, an MBL student designed this pink-granite Romanesque bell tower in 1929. He arranged for its two bells to ring twice a day to remind the scientists and townspeople of a higher power. (One bell is named for Gregor Mendel, the 19th-century botanist, the other for Louis Pasteur.) Nowadays the bells ring three times, at 7 AM, noon, and 6 PM. Do we need that much more reminding these days? The meticulously maintained **St. Mary's Garden** surrounds the tower with flowers, herbs, a bench, and a few chairs. Right on the harbor, this is one of the most restful places in the entire area.

Church of the Messiah, Church Street. Nine Nobel Prize winners are buried in the churchyard. This 1888 stone Episcopal church is admired by visiting scientists, tourists, and townsfolk alike. The herb meditation garden is a treasure.

✿ ♪ **Woods Hole Historical Museum and Collection** (508-548-7270; www.woodsholemuseum.org), 579 Woods Hole Road. Open 10–4 Tuesday through Saturday, mid-June through October. Archives open Tuesday and Thursday year-round. A treasure. Near the top of the Steamship Authority parking lot, the **Bradley House** historical museum maintains a good library on maritime sub-

WATERFRONT BEAUTIES

Nobska Light, Church Street, off Woods Hole Road. Open for free tours 1–3 some Saturdays and Thursdays, late May to mid-August. Built in 1828, rebuilt in 1876, and automated in 1985, the beacon commands a high vantage point on a bluff. The light is visible from 17 miles out at sea. It's a particularly good place to see the "hole" (for which Woods Hole was named), the Elizabeth Islands, the north shore of Martha's Vineyard, and to watch the sunset. Some 30,000 vessels—ferries, fully rigged sailing ships, and pleasure boats—pass by annually, as does the internationally regarded Falmouth Road Race.

    Spohr Gardens (508-548-0623), Fells Road off Oyster Pond Road from Woods Hole Road or Surf Drive. Thanks to Charles and Margaret Spohr (Charles won the citizen-of-the-year award in 1993), this spectacular 5¼-acre private garden is yours for the touring. Park on Fells Road, or tie up at the dock on Oyster Pond. More than 100,000 daffodils bloom in spring, followed by lilies, azaleas, magnolias, and hydrangeas. (You'll share the wide paths with geese and ducks.)

    Consider bicycling here via the **Shining Sea Bike Path** (see *Outdoor Activities—Bicycling*), which also has great water views.

NOBSKA LIGHTHOUSE—WOODS HOLE

jects, more than 200 local oral histories, a scale model of Woods Hole in the late 1800s, and a replication of Dr. Yale's 1890s workshop. The adjacent Swift Barn exhibits small historic boats that plied these local waters long ago. Try to make time for the staff's free 90-minute walking tour around Eel Pond on Tuesdays at 4 during July and August. Donations.

SCENIC DRIVE Take Route 28A to Old Dock Road to reach placid **West Falmouth Harbor.** Double back and take Route 28A to Palmer Avenue, to Sippewissett Road, to hilly and winding Quissett Avenue, to equally tranquil **Quissett Harbor.** At the far edge of the harbor you'll see a path that goes up over the hill of the Knob, an outcrop that's half wooded bird sanctuary and half rocky beach. Walk out to the Knob along the water and back through the woods. It's a great place for a picnic or to take in the sunset. Sippewissett Road takes you to Eel Pond and Woods Hole the back way. Surf Drive from Falmouth to Nobska Light is also picturesque.

✳ Outdoor Activities

⚓ BASEBALL Fuller Field, just off Main Street, Falmouth. The Commodores, one of 10 teams in the Cape Cod Baseball League, play in July and August. The chamber of commerce has a schedule (see *Guidance*).

BICYCLING/RENTALS **Shining Sea Bike Path.** The easygoing and level 3.3 mile (one way) trail is one of Falmouth's most popular attractions. Following the old Penn Central Railroad line between Falmouth and Woods Hole, the path parallels unspoiled beaches, marshes, and bird sanctuaries. It was named in honor of Katherine Lee Bates, composer of "America the Beautiful." The last line of her song—"from sea to shining sea"—is a fitting description of the trail, which offers lovely views of Vineyard Sound, Martha's Vineyard, and Naushon Island.

The trail connects with several other routes: from Falmouth to Menauhant Beach in East Falmouth; from Woods Hole to Old Silver Beach in North Falmouth; and from Woods Hole to Quissett and Sippewissett. There is a trailhead and parking lot on Locust Street (at Mill Road) in Falmouth, as well as access points at Elm Road and Oyster Pond Road. Park here; it's very difficult to park in Woods Hole.

Holiday Cycles (508-540-3549), 465 Grand Avenue, Falmouth Heights. Along with a wide variety of bikes (including tandems and surreys) and equipment (from child seats to locks), Holiday Cycles offers free parking. Ask for details about the **23-mile Sippewissett route.**

✳ **Corner Cycle** (508-540-4195), 115 Palmer Avenue, Falmouth, also rents bicycles.

BOAT EXCURSIONS/RENTALS ⚓ **Ocean Quest** (508-385-7656; 800-376-2326), Water Street, Woods Hole. Mid-May to mid-October (individuals may be able to tag along on spring and fall group trips). Founder and director Kathy Mullin offers hands-on marine education for the entire family. A science teacher and naturalist, Kathy gives a brief overview of oceanography. The 90-minute trip costs $20 adults, $15 children 3–12. The boat departs four times daily in July and August.

🐟 **Patriot Party Boats** (508-548-2626; www.patriotpartyboats.com), 227 Clinton Avenue at Scranton Avenue, Falmouth. July to early September. This excellent outfit operates 2-hour sails on the *Liberté,* a 1750s schooner replica; adults $20–25; children 12 and under, $15–18; sunset cruise $20 per person. The sunset trip cruises past six lighthouses and four harbors. Bring a picnic; BYOB; soft drinks provided. The Tietje (pronounced "teegee") family has been chartering boats since the mid-1950s, and they know the local waters like the backs of their hands. Patriot also has **ferry shuttle service** to Oak Bluffs on Martha's Vineyard. Although they primarily service commuters, you can catch a ride for $6 one way.

CANOEING AND KAYAKING **Waquoit Kayak at Edward's Boatyard** (508-548-9722; 508-548-2216; www.waquoitkayaks.com), 1209 Route 28, on Waquoit Bay, East Falmouth. From May to mid-October, you can rent canoes ($45 half day, $60 full day) and kayaks ($36 half day, $50 full day) to paddle around Waquoit Bay and over to Washburn Island. Ask about tours, too.

🐟 ✳ **Cape Cod Kayak** (508-563-9377; www.capecodkayak.com). Exploring salt marshes, tidal inlets, freshwater ponds, and the ocean shoreline from the vantage point and speed of a kayak is a great way to experience the Cape. When you rent by the week, delivery is included; one- and two-seaters are available. If you want to go kayaking and don't know where to go, owner Kim Fernandes will recommend spots or locations suited to your interests and level of ability. She also has organized tours with about five people per guide.

See also Waquoit Bay National Estuarine Research Reserve under *Green Space.*

FISHING/SHELLFISHING Contact Town Hall (508-548-7611) or Eastman's Sport & Tackle (508-548-6900), both on Main Street, for fishing and shellfishing licenses and regulations. The Town Hall is open 8–4:30 weekdays. The chamber of commerce (see *Guidance*) publishes a very good (free) fishing map and guide.

Fish for trout, smallmouth bass, chain pickerel, and white perch at the town landing on **Santuit Pond** and on the **Quashnet River.** Surf-casting is great on **Surf Drive.**

🎣 **Patriot Party Boats** (508-548-2626; www.patriotpartyboats.com), 227 Clinton Avenue, Falmouth. Sport- and bottom fishing from late May to mid-October. Bottom fishing aboard the *Patriot II* costs $25 adults; $17 children 6–12; free age 5 and under; rates include bait and tackle. Sportfishing is offered a couple of times weekly aboard the custom-outfitted *Minuteman;* call for exact days of departure.

Shortfin Sport Fishing Charter (508-299-8260; www.shortfin.com), captained by Tom Danforth, is a good charter.

Susan Jean (508-548-6901), Eel Pond, off Water Street, Woods Hole. From late May to mid-October, Captain John Christian's 22-foot Aquasport searches for trophy-sized striped bass. This trip is for the serious angler—John usually departs in the middle of the night (well, more like 4 AM) because of the tides. $450 for an 8-hour trip for one to three people. Reservations necessary.

❋ **Eastman's Sport & Tackle** (508-548-6900), 150 Main Street, Falmouth. A good source for local fishing information; rod and reel rental, too.

FITNESS CLUB ❋ **Falmouth Sports Center** (508-548-7433), Highfield Drive, Falmouth. For $7 a day, you have access to racquetball and a full array of body-building equipment. Massages cost extra.

❋ GOLF **Ballymeade Country Club** (508-540-4005), 125 Falmouth Woods Road, North Falmouth. A tough 18-hole, par-72 semi-private course.

Cape Cod Country Club (508-563-9842), off Route 151, North Falmouth. A scenic 18-hole, par-71 course with great variety.

Paul Harney Golf Club (508-563-3454), off Route 151, East Falmouth. This 18-hole, 3,700-yard, par-59 course offers somewhat narrow fairways but generally within the ability of weekend golfers.

Woodbriar Golf Club (508-495-5500), 339 Gifford Street, Falmouth. Nine holes, 1,285 yards, par 27; quite forgiving.

Falmouth Country Club (508-548-3211), 630 Carriage Shop Road off Route 151, East Falmouth. Open March through November. An 18-hole, par-72 course with a good mix of moderate and difficult pars.

HORSEBACK RIDING ❋ **Haland Stables** (508-540-2552), 878 Route 28A, West Falmouth. Open 9–5 Monday through Saturday; reservations absolutely necessary. Haland offers excellent English instruction, individual and group lessons, and guided trail rides through pine woods, fields, a bird sanctuary, cranberry bogs, and salt-marsh land.

ICE SKATING **Falmouth Ice Arena** (508-548-9083; 508-548-0275 for recorded information), Skating Lane, off Palmer Avenue, Falmouth. Call for variable public skating times. Skating $3; no rentals.

PICK-YOUR-OWN ✍ **Andrew's Farm Stand** (508-548-4717), 394 Old Meeting House Road, East Falmouth. Open daily, mid-June through December, since 1927. Strawberries, strawberries everywhere, and other produce, too, all reasonably priced (especially if you pick your own). From the looks of it, East Falmouth was once the strawberry center of the world! Strawberry season runs from early June to early July, more or less. You can also pick your own peas in June and tomatoes in August, and your own pumpkins in late September and October. Children welcome.

SAILBOARDING **Cape Cod Windsurfing** (508-801-3329; www.capecodwindsurfing.com), 350 Quaker Road, North Falmouth. Open seasonally. Old Silver Beach gets a good, predominantly southwestern wind, so there is good sailboarding here. You can take lessons or rent "nonmotorized" vessels like kayaks, canoes, and Windsurfers in front of the Sea Crest Hotel (off Route 28A, North Falmouth) on Old Silver Beach.

TENNIS The following courts are public: **elementary school,** Davisville Road, East Falmouth; **Lawrence School,** Lakeview Avenue, Falmouth; the **high school,** Gifford Street Extension, Falmouth; **Nye Park,** North Falmouth; **Blacksmith Shop Road,** behind the fire station, West Falmouth; **Taft's Playground,** Bell Tower Lane, Woods Hole.

Ballymeade Country Club (508-540-4005), 125 Falmouth Woods Road, North Falmouth. Six outdoor Har-Tru and four hard courts; lessons and clinics.

Falmouth Sports Center (508-548-7433), Highfield Drive, Falmouth. Six indoor and three outdoor courts; rental rates depend on the time you play and how many people want to participate.

Falmouth Tennis Club (508-548-4370), Dillingham Avenue, off Route 28 heading toward Hyannis. Open late May to early September. Three clay and three Har-Tru outdoor courts.

✳ Green Space

Ashumet Holly and Wildlife Sanctuary (508-362-1426; www.audubon.org), 286 Ashumet Road (off Route 151), East Falmouth. Open daily sunrise to sunset. Local philanthropist Josiah K. Lilly III (of Heritage Museums & Gardens fame; see *To See and Do* in "Sandwich") purchased and donated the land in 1961 after the death of Wilfrid Wheeler, who cultivated most of these plants. Wheeler had been very concerned about holiday overharvesting of holly. Crisscrossed with self-guided nature trails, this 45-acre Massachusetts Audubon Society sanctuary overflows with holly: There are more than eight species, 65 varieties, and 1,000 trees (from America, Europe, and Asia). More than 130 bird species have been sighted here: Since 1935, nesting barn swallows have made their home in the rafters of the barn from mid-April to late August. Other flora and fauna thrive as well. Rhododendrons and dogwoods bloom in spring. Large white franklinia flowers (named for Benjamin Franklin) make a show in autumn, and in summer Grassy Pond is filled with the blossoms of rare wildflowers. The sanctuary offers nature trips to Cuttyhunk Island and guided bird walks. Pick up the informative trail map before setting out. Adults $4; children $3; members free.

Waquoit Bay National Estuarine Research Reserve (508-457-0495; www.waquoitbayreserve.org), 149 Waquoit Highway, East Falmouth. Headquarters open 10–4 Monday through Saturday in summer; 10–4 weekdays off-season. Part of a national system dedicated to research estuaries, there are four components to the reserve: **South Cape Beach** (see also *Green Space—Beach* in "Mashpee"), **Washburn Island, Quashnet River Property,** and the **headquarters** (which houses watershed exhibits). More than 3,000 acres of delicate barrier beaches surround lovely Waquoit Bay. Stop in at the headquarters for a trail map and schedule of guided walks in July and August. In summer look for "Evenings on the Bluff" talks as well as other activities. Within the South Cape

Beach State Park is the little-used, mile-long Great Flat Pond Trail (accessible year-round). It winds past salt marshes, bogs, and wetlands and along coastal pine forests. Guided walks are offered in July and August. The 330-acre, pine-filled Washburn Island is accessible year-round if you have a boat. The 11 primitive island campsites require a permit.

Falmouth Moraine Trail (508-540-0876). These 10 miles of trails are part of **Cape Cod Pathways** (508-362-3828; www.capecodcommission.org), "a growing network of walking paths linking open space in all 15 Cape Cod towns." Pick up the excellent trail map at the chamber of commerce and set out. The lower section of the trail circles Long Pond (3.55 miles) and then heads north along Route 28 (more or less), without doubling back. Park at these spots, which are east off Route 28 (from north to south): Route 151 at the rotary; Thomas Lander's Road; the Service Road off Brick Kiln Road; and Goodwill Park adjacent to Grews Pond (the closest spot for Long Pond).

See also the Knob under *To See and Do—Scenic Drive.*

BEACHES Along Buzzards Bay and Vineyard Sound, 12 miles of Falmouth's 68-mile shoreline are accessible to the public via four beaches. (There are eight additional town beaches.) Generally, waters are a bit warmer off Falmouth than off northside beaches because of the Gulf Stream. Weeklong cottage renters qualify to purchase a beach sticker, obtainable at the Surf Drive Beach Bathhouse 9–4 daily in summer. The permit costs $40 for 1 week, $50 for 2 weeks. Some innkeepers provide beach stickers. Otherwise, you may pay a daily fee to park at the following beaches. (The Town Beach Committee, 508-548-8623, has further details.)

Menauhant Beach, on Vineyard Sound, off Route 28 and Central Avenue, East Falmouth. The best Sound beach, by far. Waters are less choppy on Vineyard Sound than they are on the Atlantic. Parking is $10.

🐚 **Old Silver Beach,** on Buzzards Bay, off Route 28A and Quaker Road, North Falmouth. One of the sandiest beaches in town, this is a good one for children, as an offshore sandbar creates shallow tidal pools. Facilities include a bathhouse, a lifeguard, and a snack bar. Parking is $10.

Surf Drive Beach, on Vineyard Sound, on Surf Drive, off Main and Shore Streets, Falmouth. This beach attracts sea kayakers, walkers, and swimmers who want to escape "downtown" beach crowds. It's accessible via the Shining Sea Bike Path (see *Outdoor Activities—Bicycling/Rentals*); by foot it's 15 minutes from the center of Falmouth. Facilities include a bathhouse. Parking is $10.

Falmouth Heights Beach, on Vineyard Sound, Grand Avenue, Falmouth Heights. Although there is no public parking, the beach is public and popular. Facilities include lots of snack bars.

PONDS 🐚 **Grews Pond,** off Gifford Street at **Goodwill Park,** Route 28A, West Falmouth. Lifeguard in-season, as well as picnic and barbecue facilities and a playground. There are also hiking trails all around the pond.

WALKS ☙ **Beebe Woods,** access from Ter Heun Drive off Route 28 or High-field Drive off Depot Avenue, behind the College Light Opera Company (see *Entertainment*), Falmouth. The Beebes, a wealthy family originally from Boston, lived in Falmouth from the late 1870s to the early 1930s. Generous town bene-factors, they were among the first to purchase land in Falmouth. Highfield Hall (508-495-1878), built in 1878, was the centerpiece of the property, and it's now receiving a much-needed and pricey restoration with the vision of Friends of Highfield. (They are holding an increasing number of concerts, exhibits, and workshops here. The acoustics are great.) The 387 acres around it contain miles of public trails for walking, mountain biking, and bird-watching. Locals often refer to these trails as the Dog Walks because so many of them walk their pets here. In autumn especially, it seems like the whole town takes the trail to the **Punch Bowl** (a kettle pond). It's particularly pretty in May when the lady's slip-pers bloom.

Waterfront Park, Water Street near the MBL, with shaded benches and a sun-dial from which you can tell time to within 30 seconds.

Eel Pond, off Water Street. The harborlike pond has a drawbridge that grants access to Great Harbor for fishing boats, yachts, and research vessels moored here. (The walk around the shore is lovely.) The little bridge goes up and down on the hour and half hour; in summer boats line up to pass through.

Bourne Farm (508-548-8484), Route 28A, North Falmouth. Grounds open year-round; house open by appointment. Owned by the nonprofit Salt Pond Areas Bird Sanctuaries, Inc., this 1775 historic landmark includes a restored and furnished farmhouse, a bunkhouse (now a private residence), a barn, and 49 acres of orchards, fields, and wooded trails. It's a perfectly tranquil spot over-looking **Crocker Pond,** complete with a picnic area under a grape arbor. Donations for trail fees. The property and barn are available for wedding rentals.

See also Spohr Gardens under the sidebar "Waterfront Beauties" and Ashumet Holly and Wildlife Sanctuary, Grews Pond, and Waquoit Bay National Estuarine Research Reserve, above.

✳ Lodging

✳ Falmouth boasts highly sophisti-cated places to stay, lots of B&Bs around the town green, beachfront choices in Falmouth Heights, more secluded B&Bs in West and North Falmouth, and quite a few motels. Unfortunately, many of its family motels have been converted to time-share units. Most people staying in Woods Hole are heading to the Vine-yard. Generally, your lodging dollars will go a long way in this part of the Cape. Unless otherwise noted, all lodgings in Falmouth are open year-round.

BED & BREAKFASTS

In Falmouth Heights 02540
❧ **Inn on the Sound** (508-457-9666; 800-564-9668; www.innonthesound. com), 313 Grand Avenue. Open April through October. Renee Ross, a tal-ented interior designer, has trans-formed this turn-of-the-20th-century inn into an elegantly upscale yet casual oceanfront B&B. She's got a

perfectly attuned sense of what people want. Fabrics are fashionable but not overdone; sitting areas are comfortable and substantial but seaside-breezy. Nine of the 10 bedrooms, each with a tasteful contemporary aesthetic, have great water views. Four have a private deck with water views. A lavish buffet (taken at individual tables) includes an artful array of breads and other tempting epicurean delights. Renee also rents an oh-so-stylish waterfront apartment with private entrance, sitting room, and kitchen for $3,000 weekly in summer. May through October $150–295; otherwise $150–275; $30 additional for a third person.

Scallop Shell Inn (508-495-4900; www.scallopshellinn.com), 16 Massachusetts Avenue. Fifty-two steps from the ocean, the Scallop Shell boasts unusual policies and facilities. There's no check-in or check-out time; there's a complimentary full, top-shelf bar; there are no cancellation policies; there is a 100 percent guarantee policy. I could go on and on. Innkeeper Betsy Cogliani (an interior designer—among other things) poured millions into renovating, installing $1,000 hand-painted sinks, Brazilian mahogany floors, marble bathrooms (some with whirlpool and gas fireplace), a cedar laundry that replicates one at Hammersmith Farm in Newport, and a guest kitchenette where you can cook lobsters. Additional in-room amenities include turndown service, plush robes, French milled toiletries, and hand-cut Belgian chocolates. The four-course breakfast might include a lobster-and-asparagus omelet, fresh-squeezed juice, and crème brûlée. And I shouldn't neglect to mention the bil-

liards table and outdoor shower. Late May through October $285–345; off-season $185–235.

Bailey's by the Sea (508-548-5748; 866-548-5748; www.baileysbythesea.com), 321 Grand Avenue. Open mid-May through October. This newly renovated waterfront B&B boasts a wrap-around porch with a dozen picture windows, plenty of rocking chairs, and very comfortable guest rooms. The accommodating innkeepers, Liz and Jerry Bailey, offer three rooms with fabulous ocean views and TV (some with VCR). Inquire about adjoining rooms at special rates, which are great for families. Third-floor rooms are particularly spacious. Decor ranges from Victorian to Japanese (the Baileys lived in Japan for almost eight years) to traditional. A full breakfast, served on the porch, might include apple cranberry compote, eggs, hams, and scones; Bailey's blended juice drinks are a specialty. And in case you're wondering, Bailey's Irish Cream is available in the evening. Mid-May through October $160–250; call for off-season availability.

On or near the Falmouth green 02540

La Maison Cappellari at Mostly Hall (508-548-3786; 800-682-0565; www.mostlyhall.com), 27 Main Street. Open mid-May to mid-October. This Greek Revival plantation-style house with Italianate features—set back from the road in the heart of the historic district—is quite unusual. Innkeepers Christina and Bogdan Simcic have put a distinctive Euro imprint on the lodging. Christina, a well-known New York trompe l'oeil painter, worked magic on three guest rooms and the common areas. It's impressive. Corsica features seaside murals; Tuscany looks like an indoor garden. Bogdan, a Manhattan antiques consultant, has chosen just the right pieces, too. All six rooms—corner rooms with air-conditioning—are large enough not to be overwhelmed by tall, shuttered casement windows. Parklike gardens, landscaping, and a gazebo are visible from the wraparound porch. A full breakfast might include caviar, octopus salad, biscotti, imported cheeses, pancetta, and French crêpes. Loaner bicycles available. Rooms $185–225.

Palmer House (508-548-1230; 800-472-2632; www.palmerhouseinn.com), 81 Palmer Avenue. Longtime innkeepers Joanne and Ken Baker run a tight ship, complete with an intercom buzzer and a formal portrait of themselves next to the reception desk. The Bakers preside over 16 "bedchambers" and two cottage suites, all with robes, lots of lace, TV, flowers, triple sheeting, turndown service, and telephone. I particularly like rooms, many with gas fireplace, in the adjacent Guesthouse because they afford greater privacy. The main house is a Queen Anne beauty with stained-glass windows, shiny hardwood floors, and front-porch rockers. The upscale Victorian decor is fanciful but tasteful. Breakfast is elaborate and full, served at either individual tables or one long one; it's your choice. Loaner bikes are available. Mid-June to mid-October $125–269; off-season $90–199.

✎ **Captain Tom Lawrence House** (508-540-1445; 800-266-8139; www.captaintomlawrence.com), 75 Locust Street. Open March through December. This 1861 former sea

captain's home with an impressive spiral staircase is a pleasant and friendly B&B operated by Anne Grebert and Jim Cotter. Set back from the road, the inn offers six comfortable rooms with air-conditioning, mini-fridge, and cable TV. A few of the bathrooms are small, so if you are large, inquire. Most rooms have wall-to-wall carpeting to keep down the noise. Families might appreciate the efficiency apartment with private entrance. A full breakfast (perhaps omelets and Irish soda bread) is served at two tables in the combo living/dining room. Mid-May through October $175 rooms, $200 apartment ($30 each additional person); off-season $100–145.

Village Green Inn (508-548-5621; 800-237-1119; www.villagegreeninn. com), 40 Main Street. This pleasant B&B has five Victorian-style guest rooms and one suite, each with some unique feature like a pressed-tin ceiling. I particularly like Tripp, with a gas fireplace and sleigh bed, and Crocker, which has a parquet floor and stained-glass window. Traditionally furnished, the large and bright suite is well suited to longer stays. The friendly innkeepers, Diane and Don Crosby, "strike just the right balance between talking with guests and disappearing," according to one reader. They also provide loaner bikes. Common space includes two open porches and a small formal parlor filled with a collection of Lladros and dolls. Well-behaved children over 12 are welcome. A full breakfast, with blueberry puff pancakes perhaps, is served at 8:30. June through October $160–225; off-season $90–150.

✎ **Elm Arch Inn** (508-548-0133; www.elmarchinn.com), 26 Elm Arch

Way. Open April through October. This classic, old-fashioned hostelry is less than a block from Main Street, but it feels worlds away. Built in 1810 and bombed by the British in 1814 (there are still cannonball "scars" in the former dining room), the friendly inn has several common rooms downstairs and is chock-full of colonial touches, braided rugs, and easy chairs. A large, screened-in flagstone porch overlooks a small pool surrounded by lawn chairs. Half of the 20 guest rooms have private bath; others have an in-room sink; many can accommodate three people. Rooms in the main house are quite modestly furnished, while rooms in the adjacent Richardson House are more modern. The inn has been in the Richardson family since 1926. Mid-June through September $90–150. Inquire about the annex cottage, which sleeps five. No credit cards.

In West Falmouth 02574

✒ **Chapoquoit Inn** (508-540-7232; 800-842-8994; www.chapoquoit.com), 495 Route 28A. This Quaker homestead, one of the first 26 built in Falmouth, is set on 3½ acres a couple of miles from the village center. It features a deep backyard complete with a gazebo and maturing gardens. The helpful innkeepers, Kim and Tim McIntyre (and their young son), offer six rooms and a cottage. The cottage has two cozy suites, each with a queen bed, daybed, sitting area, and gas fireplace. They're great for families. Of those, I like Captain's Quarters, very nautical in design. The inn's guest rooms are spacious and comfortably decorated with quilts and local artwork. A full breakfast—perhaps spiced lemon pancakes stuffed with cream cheese and Kim's grandmother's granola—is served on the deck or in the cheery dining room. The inn is half a mile from Chapoquoit Beach; loaner bikes are available. May through October $140–215 rooms; off-season $95–125.

🦞 🐾 ✒ **The Beach Rose Inn** (508-540-5706; 800-498-5706; www.thebeachroseinn.com), 17 Chase Road (off Route 28A). This 19th-century farmhouse, on a delightfully quiet back road, received a complete and tasteful makeover by David and Donna McIlrath in 2002. Eight rooms in the main inn and carriage house have been freshened with canopy beds, gas fireplaces, and whirlpools. The most intriguing room is off the front porch, with its own dining area. I also like the one with a private entrance and patio (where pet owners stay). A full breakfast is included for all. The housekeeping cottage hasn't been renovated yet, but it's still nice for families since it has a large front yard. June through August $120–185; off-season $110–165. Pets are accepted in some rooms with prior approval.

Inn at West Falmouth (508-540-6503; 800-397-7696; www.innatwestfalmouth.com), 66 Frazar Road (off Route 28A). This secluded turn-of-the-20th-century, shingle-style house features eight guest rooms, many with deck or fireplace. Although the guest room decor hasn't kept up with the Joneses, the common rooms and many quiet nooks are still soothing. The main draws are the privacy, lushly landscaped deck, heated pool, and tennis court. (On my last visit, though, wedding reception paraphernalia lingered on the otherwise lovely deck long after the party had departed.)

The beach is a 10-minute walk away. May through October $195–345; off-season $130–225, with continental buffet breakfast.

In Woods Hole 02543

✒ **Woods Hole Passage** (508-548-9575; 800-790-8976; www.woods-holepassage.com), 186 Woods Hole Road. On the road connecting Woods Hole and Falmouth, this quiet B&B (with 2 acres of gardens enjoyed from a hammock and plenty of lounge chairs) has a welcoming feel, thanks to innkeeper Deb Pruitt. The attached barn has five renovated guest rooms; second-floor rooms are more spacious, with vaulted ceilings and exposed beams. Decor is crisp country modern, and each room has a bold splash of color. Full breakfast is included, as are loaner bikes, beach chairs, beach towels, and use of the outdoor shower. Children are accommodated by advance arrangement. Mid-May to mid-September $125–165; otherwise $100–120.

✒ **Capeside Cottage** (508-548-6218; 800-320-2322; www.capesidecottage.com), 320 Woods Hole Road. This snug and simple Cape-style B&B has five guest rooms that are warmly presided over by innkeepers Gabriel and Jennifer Roggiolani. Behind the inn sits a lovely pool and a little path that leads to the ocean and Shining Sea Bike Path. You might wish to inquire about the cottage (which I was unable to see). Full breakfast included. June to mid-October $150–180; off-season $100–150.

MOTOR INN ✒ **Coonamessett Inn** (508-548-2300), Jones Road and Gifford Street, Falmouth 02540. Although billed as an inn, complete with a foyer-style living room, the 28 units with outside entrances more closely resemble motel rooms. Choose between suites overlooking picturesque Jones Pond and two-bedroom apartment-style accommodations. There is one self-contained cottage. With 7 acres of meticulously landscaped lawns, the Coonamessett hosts its share of weddings and conferences. The inn is filled with the late Cotuit artist Ralph Cahoon's whimsical, neoprimitive paintings. Late June to early September $180 rooms, $230 two-bedroom suite, $260 cottage; expanded continental breakfast included.

MOTELS ⊻ ✒ **Seaside Inn** (508-540-4120; 800-827-1976; www.seasideinn-falmouth.com), 263 Grand Avenue, Falmouth Heights 02540. Across from Falmouth Heights Beach (see *Green Space—Beaches*), this family-oriented 23-room motel is right next to a park, another plus for families. Rates vary widely and are based on the degree of water view; whether the room has access to a deck, full kitchen, or kitchenette; and if the deck is shared or private. Rooms in the back building are the nicest, but the reservation folks won't guarantee a particular room. Too bad, since the third-floor rooms are the best. Late May through September $115–250; off-season $54–129.

By the way, the **British Beer Company** (508-540-9600) is on the premises. It's a fine (if commercial) place for an authentic stout or ale on tap. If you're not in a hurry, wait for some fish-and-chips or a burger for lunch or dinner.

Ġ **Sands of Time** (508-548-6300; 800-841-0114; www.sandsof-time.com), 549 Woods Hole Road,

Woods Hole 02543. Open April to mid-November. Some of the guests here missed the last ferry; others know this is a convenient place for exploring Woods Hole. There are 20 air-conditioned motel rooms (most with a delightful view of Little Harbor), an apartment with a kitchen, and 15 nice and large innlike rooms in the adjacent 1870s Victorian Harbor House. Many of these enjoy a harbor view and working fireplace. Fresh flowers, lovely gardens, a small heated pool, and a morning newspaper set this place apart. June through September $140–200; otherwise $100–170.

EFFICIENCIES Ideal Spot Motel (508-548-2257; www.idealspotmotel. net), Route 28A at Old Dock Road, West Falmouth 02540. Open April through late December. In a quiet part of town, this nicely landscaped motel has two simple rooms (which can accommodate four people) and 12 efficiencies. Grill available for barbecuing. Mid-June to mid-September $98–120; spring and fall $65–75; inquire about weekly rates.

Mariner's Point Resort (508-457-0300; www.marinerspointresort.com), 425 Grand Avenue, Falmouth 02540. Open April to late November. This bilevel time-share offers 37 efficiency studios and apartments within a short stroll of Falmouth Heights Beach. Most units overlook the pool area; a few have unobstructed views of Vineyard Sound and a town-owned park popular with kite fliers. Some units sleep up to six people, provided they're all very good friends. April through September $130 studio, $225 up to six people; off-season $95–150.

See also Captain Tom Lawrence House under *Bed & Breakfasts.*

RENTAL HOUSES AND COTTAGES
Real Estate Associates (www.real-estateassociates.com), with four offices, has the local market covered. Depending on where you want to be, call the office in North Falmouth (508-563-7173), West Falmouth (508-540-3005), Falmouth (508-540-1500), or Pocasset (508-563-5266). Although first priority is given to monthly and seasonal rentals, they fill schedule holes in April or early May.

See also Coonamessett Inn under *Motor Inn* and Elm Arch Inn under *Bed & Breakfasts.*

CAMPGROUNDS Sippewissett Campground and Cabins (508-548-2542; 508-548-1971; 800-957-2267; www.sippewissett.com), 836 Palmer Avenue, Falmouth 02540. Open mid-May to mid-October. This well-run private campground has 11 cabins and 100 large campsites for tents, trailers, and RVs; clean, large bathrooms and showers; and free shuttles to Chapoquoit Beach, the ferry to Martha's Vineyard, and other Falmouth-area locations. In-season camping $32 daily, cabins $330–650 weekly; off-season camping $25 daily, cabins $225–450 weekly. Pets permitted prior to Memorial Day and after Labor Day, but not in cabins.

See also Waquoit Bay National Estuarine Research Reserve under *Green Space.*

✴ Where to Eat
✳ Falmouth and Woods Hole restaurants satisfy all palates and budgets — through upscale bistro dining, waterfront fish houses, taverns, and

diners. Unless otherwise noted, all establishments are open year-round.

DINING OUT

In Falmouth

☿ **RooBar City Bistro** (508-548-8600), 285 Main Street. Open for dinner daily. As they say in their advertising, "Life is too short to eat boring food." I couldn't agree more. Following in the footsteps of its Hyannis predecessor, this vibrant and buzzy space (which gets quite loud in-season) has an open kitchen that churns out a world-influenced menu of contemporary coastal cuisine. Look for dishes like pan-seared nori-wrapped salmon or scallops Marsala with prosciutto and asparagus. Pizzas $10–15, dinner entrées $17–25.

🌸 ☿ & **Chapoquoit Grill** (508-540-7794), 410 Route 28A, West Falmouth. Open for dinner daily at 5 PM. From the moment this eclectic New American bistro opened in mid-1993, it was a success. (Readers from Mississauga, Ontario, suggest a double value symbol!) No longer did locals have to drive 45 minutes to get innovative cooking in a low-key atmosphere. You can spot the regulars: They order from the nightly specials menu. Swordfish and seafood dishes are always superb. The popular wood-fired, thin-crust, garlicky pizzas are also excellent. No reservations are taken, so get there when it opens or be prepared for a wait in the convivial bar. Entrées $8–20.

La Cucina Sul Mare (508-548-5600), 237 Main Street. Open for lunch and dinner. Northern Italian and Mediterranean cuisine has never been so good in Falmouth. Intimate and villa-like, this newcomer made an immediate splash in 2002 by offering fresh pasta and seafood specials. Lunch mains $5–12, dinner mains $14–20, specials more.

Coonamessett Inn/Eli's (508-548-2300), Jones Road and Gifford Street. Open for lunch and dinner. The inn features traditional regional American fare with an emphasis on seafood—baked stuffed lobster, seafood Newburg, and lobster bisque. Each dining room has something to recommend it: hot-air-balloon paintings by the late Ralph Cahoon or a view of secluded Jones Pond from an outdoor mahogany deck. Eli's, a tavern-style room, is known for traditional New England fare. Check out the daily specials (like chicken Parmesan) or scallop dishes. Reservations recommended at the inn. Tavern dishes $11–14, inn entrées $18–29.

EATING OUT

In Falmouth

The Quarterdeck (508-548-9900), 164 Main Street. Probably open for lunch and dinner daily. At press time, this popular place had just been purchased by the longtime owner of the Chart Room (see *Where to Eat* in "Bourne"). Ask around.

🌸 **TraBiCa** (508-548-2076), 327 Gifford Street, Falmouth. Open nightly (except Monday off-season). Locals know a good thing when they find it. TraBiCa, derived from combining the first letters of *trattoria, bistro,* and *café,* takes its cues from the subtle differences among those types of eateries. You can get conventional family-style Italian dishes like shrimp scampi over linguine from the trattoria menu. unpretentious burgers from the café menu, and down-to-earth seasonal offerings from the bistro menu. (Rich seafood crêpes, anyone?)

It's not high cuisine, but the combination of moderate prices, comfortable surroundings, consistent preparation, and friendly service is rarely beatable. Reservations recommended on weekends. Entrées $8–15.

Laureen's (508-540-9104), 170 Main Street. Open 8:30–5 Monday through Saturday. Even without considering its prime downtown location, Laureen's would be a fine choice for casual lunches, homemade desserts, and good coffee. Busy sister-and-brother caterers Diane Harvey and John Marderosian offer eclectic dishes like a Middle East sampler plate, a vegetarian burrito plate, a few fancy feta pizzas, and sandwiches. There's table service as well as take-out.

The Chickadee (508-548-4006), 881 Old Palmer Avenue, West Falmouth. Open daily April through December. On a quiet country road, the Chickadee at Peach Tree Circle Farm is surrounded by 6 acres of apple and peach orchards, and flower and vegetable gardens. You can dine alfresco or at a few tables inside. Light lunches of quiche, sandwiches, soups (the chowder is delicious), and seafood salads are recommended. Vegetables are particularly fresh. (Remember, this is a farm.) Or simply come for tea and sweets from the bakery. Lunch $3–10.

*⚓ **Clam Shack** (508-540-7758), 227 Clinton Avenue. Open 11:30–8 daily, late May to early September. Since 1962, chef-owner Jim Limberakis has operated this tiny and busy clam shack. There is rarely enough room inside. But it's just as well—head to the back deck to munch on fried clams, scallops, and fish while watching pleasure boats and fishermen come and go. Dishes $8–17.

♧ **Peking Palace** (508-540-8204), 452 Main Street. Open from "lunchtime until late" daily. If you're tired of fried seafood platters or grilled fish and wishing for take-out from your favorite Chinese restaurant at home, the Peking Palace won't disappoint. If anything, it will make you think twice about your Chinese back home! It's definitely the best on the Upper or mid-Cape. There must be 200 Mandarin, Szechuan, and Cantonese dishes on the menu. All furnishings and decor, by the way, have been imported from Taiwan. Lunch $5–6, dinner entrées $8–15.

*⚓ **Betsy's Diner** (508-540-0060), 457 Main Street, East Falmouth. Open for all three meals daily. This old-fashioned 1957 Mountain View Diner was transported in 1992 from Pennsylvania to Main Street, and placed on the site of another diner. The boxy addition isn't historic, just functional. The place is packed with locals and families who come for the inexpensive fare: club sandwiches, breakfast specials, or perhaps the famous roast turkey dinner. Specials are generally excellent and portions large. Breakfast is served all day to tunes from the '60s. Dishes $2–14.

*⚓ **Moonakis Cafe** (508-457-9630), 460 Route 28, Waquoit. Open for breakfast and lunch daily. Paul Rifkin and Ellen Mycock run a great breakfast joint. Specialties include homemade sausage, corned beef hash, and chowder, as well as fresh fruit waffles, crabcakes, and Reubens. Ellen is family-friendly: Upon request, she'll make simple, small dishes for kids. Dishes $3–9.

♧ ♟ *⚓ **Flying Bridge** (508-548-2700), 220 Scranton Avenue (west side of Inner Harbor). Open 11:30–9 daily, mid-April through November; until 11 PM in summer. This enormous, 600-seat restaurant overlooks the *Island Queen* dock and the busiest area of Falmouth's Inner Harbor. The view is the main attraction, so ask for a table on the deck. I nosh on appetizers or get a salad and sandwich. The same menu is served all day; dishes $15–25.

❦ ♿ ♪ **Seafood Sam's** (508-540-7877), Route 28/Palmer Avenue. Open daily March through November. Ignore the plastic silverware and focus on the crispy, crunchy fried fish. Lunch specials $5–7, dinner dishes $7–18.

See also Nimrod, Liam Maguire's, and Boathouse under *Entertainment—Nightlife* and the British Beer Company at the Seaside Inn under *Lodging—Motels.*

In Woods Hole

♿ ❦ ♪ ♈ **Fishmonger Cafe** (508-548-9148), 56 Water Street. Open for all three meals daily, mid-February to mid-December (except closed Tuesday off-season, and no breakfast is served on Tuesday in summer). The 'Monger has been the most consistent place in town since Frances Buehler opened it in 1974. The eclectic, international menu features Thai spring rolls, tuna satay, and fried calamari, as well as fisherman's stew, tofu and veggies, and rice and refried beans. Savvy patrons order off the specials menu. Specials change throughout the day and sometimes during a meal as well—keep an eye on the blackboard. The location and atmosphere couldn't be better, overlooking the Eel Pond Bridge. And even though the 'Monger is always bustling, the friendly staff keep it comfortable. Evenings sparkle,

thanks to candlelight, shiny wooden tables, and lots of little windowpanes. Friendly bar. Lunch $6–18, dinner $10–24.

❦ ♪ **Shuckers World Famous Raw Bar & Cafe** (508-540-3850), 91A Water Street. Open for lunch and dinner May through October. Sit on the deck overlooking Eel Pond and enjoy twin lobsters (on Tuesday evening), lobster bisque, lobster rolls, stuffed tomatoes with lobster, and lobster ravioli. Do you get the idea that lobster is a specialty? Of course, there is also raw and steamed seafood, and even mesquite-grilled fish and chicken. It's a fun place, kept consistent by the vision of a longtime chef-owner. The dockside patio is heated on cool spring and fall evenings. Dishes $12–20.

♈ **Captain Kidd** (508-548-8563), 77 Water Street. The tavern is open for lunch and dinner daily; the fancier waterfront section overlooking Eel Pond is open for dinner daily, mid-June to early September. This local watering hole is named for the pirate who supposedly spent a short time in the environs of Woods Hole on the way to his execution in England. A playful pirate mural hangs above barrel-style tables across from the long, hand-carved mahogany bar. The Kidd, as it's affectionately called, offers specialty pizzas, burgers, sandwiches, fish-and-chips, scrod, steaks, and blackboard fish specials. It's all very good. The glassed-in patio with a woodstove is a cozy place to be in winter. The only drawback here: The staff are at times more attentive to the TV at the bar than they are to patrons. Tavern lunch and dinner $7–15, waterfront dining entrées $15–25.

✧ ♿ ⅄ **Landfall** (508-548-1758), Luscombe Avenue. Open 11–10 daily, mid-April through November. The Landfall, in the Estes family since 1946, is one of the best Upper Cape places to soak up local atmosphere: Both preppies and weather-beaten fishermen are regulars here. Bedecked with seafaring paraphernalia and built with salvaged materials, the large dining room is also cozy with hurricane lamps. The waterfront location is excellent: Ask for a table overlooking the ferry dock. Fare is Cape Cod traditional: lobster and seafood like swordfish, cod, and scallops. Reservations recommended. Lunch $8–12, dinner $20–26.

Pie in the Sky (508-540-5475), 10 Water Street. Open 363 days a year (6 AM–9 PM in summer, 6–6 in winter). This funky—in a good way—institution has strong coffee, good pastries, hearty sandwiches, and homemade soups. There are a few tables inside and garden/streetside.

COFFEE, ICE CREAM, & MARKETS

Coffee Obsession (508-540-2233), 119 Palmer Avenue, Falmouth. Open at least 7 AM–8 PM daily. Caffeine addicts flock to the bohemian "Coffee O" for bracing espressos, a slice of coffee cake, and a smidgen of counterculture à la Falmouth. Eggnog, apple cider, and other seasonal beverages, too. A retail shop serves all your chai- and coffee-related needs.

Bass River Baking Co (508-540-8572), 281 Main Street. Open daily. For baked treats, sandwiches, homebrewed teas, and flavorful espresso, this storefront café is a fine place to watch the street traffic.

Windfall Market (508-548-0099), 77 Scranton Avenue. Open daily. Prepared foods, a deli section, trout, lobsters, homemade breads, and a fine wine selection with knowledgeable staff.

See also Ben & Bill's Chocolate Emporium under *Selective Shopping—Special Shops.*

✳ Entertainment

✧ **Band concerts,** July and August. The Falmouth Town Band performs at Marina Park, on the west side of the Inner Harbor, on Thursday evenings at 7:30 or 8. Bring a chair or a blanket and watch the kids dance to simple marches and big-band numbers. Or wander around and look at the moored boats. There are also free Friday concerts at 6:30 PM at Peg Noonan Park on Main Street in July and August.

College Light Opera Company (508-548-0668; www.collegelight-opera.com), Highfield Theatre, Depot Avenue, Falmouth. Open late June to late August. Performances Tuesday through Saturday at 8 PM and Thursday at 2 PM. Founded in 1969, this talented and energetic company includes music majors and theater arts students from across the country. They perform 9 shows in nine weeks; tickets cost $25 for those age 5 and older.

Woods Hole Folk Music Society (508-540-0320), Community Hall, Water Street, Woods Hole. Well-known touring folkies generally play on the first and third Sunday of each month, October to early May. Tickets $10.

Cape Cod Theatre Project (508-457-4242; www.tcctp.com), Community Hall, Water Street, Woods Hole. Established by two New York actors who were vacationing in Woods Hole in 1994, they "stage" low-production readings of new American plays in July.

See also Highfield Hall under Beebe Woods in *Green Space—Walks.*

🦞 ❄ ⚓ MOVIES **Hoyts Cinema Nickelodeon** (508-563-6510), Route 151, North Falmouth.

Hoyts Cinema Falmouth Mall (508-540-2169), Route 28 (Teaticket Highway).

🍸 NIGHTLIFE **Liam Maguire's Irish Pub & Restaurant** (508-548-0285), 273 Main Street, Falmouth. Open for lunch and dinner. It doesn't get any more "real" or more fun than this unless you go to South Boston or Dublin. Irish students serve shepherd's pie, Irish beef stew, corned beef and cabbage, or fish-and-chips in beer batter for $8–10. Food is average, the sandwiches a bit better. Come for beer (Guinness on draft) and live entertainment nightly (including sing-alongs). Liam himself plays some nights.

The Nimrod (508-540-4132), 100 Dillingham Avenue, Falmouth. Open for lunch and dinner. Listen to jazz—piano, trios, and piano bar sing-alongs—nightly except Monday. Grab a seat at the bar or order traditional fare like shrimp scampi or a grilled chicken club sandwich. Off-season, you'll probably appreciate one of the nine working fireplaces. Luncheon specials at this "townie" place are a good deal at $6–10. Dinner entrées $15–30.

The Boathouse (508-548-7800), 88 Scranton Avenue, Falmouth. Open late May through December. An attractive and decent restaurant by day, the Boathouse jumps with live music and lively crowds nightly in summer (on weekends in spring and fall).

✳ **Selective Shopping**
❋ In recent years, the quality of Main Street stores in Falmouth has risen, sidewalks have been repaved, benches added, and flower beds and boxes are overflowing. Unless otherwise noted, all shops are open year-round and in Falmouth proper.

ARTISANS **Woods Hole Handworks** (508-540-5291), 68 Water Street, Woods Hole. Open late June to mid-October and late November to late December. This tiny artisans' cooperative, perched over the water near the drawbridge to Eel Pond, has a selection of fine handmade jewelry, scarves, weaving, beadwork, and tiles.

Under the Sun (508-540-3603), 22 Water Street, Woods Hole. An eclectic selection of handcrafted jewelry, pottery, glass, wood, and furniture. Although the quality is somewhat uneven, the "very good" far outweighs the "all right."

ART GALLERIES **Gallery 333** (508-564-4467; www.gallery333.com), 333 Old Main Road (near the intersection of Routes 151 and 28A), North Falmouth. Open afternoons Wednesday through Sunday, mid-May to mid-September. Arlene Hecht's gallery is housed in a wonderful 19th-century home that has been expanded many times over the last 200 years. Once the site of an asparagus farm, the house now showcases a medley of works by 40 local, regional, and national artists (both abstract and representational). Look for paintings, drawings, photography, ceramics, and limited-edition prints. Don't miss the sculpture garden. On many Saturdays in summer, the gallery holds meet-the-artists receptions.

Woods Hole Gallery (508-548-4329), 14 School Street, Woods Hole. Open late June through September. Owner, curator, and all-around arbiter of fine art Edie Bruce has operated this gallery since 1963. It's hardly a pristine environment; the old house has low ceilings, walls are in need of a paint job, and the shag rug is worn. But amid the general feeling of clutter, with paintings stacked everywhere, you will find some real gems. Some are inexpensive; some are pricey. But any way you look at it, you can trust Edith's expertise about area artists.

Falmouth Artist Guild (508-540-3304; www.arts-cape.com/falag), 311 (rear) Main Street. Open 10–3 Tuesday through Saturday, noon–5 Sunday. This nonprofit guild (active since the 1950s) holds 8 to 10 exhibitions annually, four of which are juried. They have a fund-raising auction in June and a big "Arts Alive Festival" in early August (see *Special Events*). Since these digs are temporary, you'll want to call for class and exhibition information.

BOOKSTORES ♪ **Eight Cousins Children's Books** (508-548-5548; www.eightcousins.com), 189 Main Street. Long before it won the equivalent of the Pulitzer Prize for children's bookstores in 2002, this excellent shop enjoyed broad and deep roots in the community. Named for one of Louisa May Alcott's lesser-known works, Eight Cousins stocks more than 17,000 titles and is a great

resource, whether you're a teacher, a gift buyer, or entertaining a child on a rainy afternoon. It continues to excel with kids' programs, regular story times, and great service.

Booksmith (508-540-6064), Falmouth Plaza, Route 28. This fine general (independent) bookstore should win a most-improved award.

CLOTHING Maxwell & Co. (508-540-8752), 200 Main Street. Absolutely fine men's and women's clothing.

Liberty House (508-548-7568), 89 Water Street, Woods Hole. Open mid-April through December. Good taste and reasonable prices for linen shorts and slacks, sundresses, and stacks of cotton T-shirts.

MALL Falmouth Mall (508-540-8329), Route 28. A smaller version of the nearby Cape Cod Mall in Hyannis.

SPECIAL SHOPS Oolala (508-495-2888), 104 Palmer Avenue. A hip and funky store with great gifts: fun greeting cards, candles, soaps, journals, jewelry, bags, and home accessories.

Rosie Cheeks (508-548-4572), 233 Main Street. Women's clothing and home accents.

Twigs (508-540-0767), 178 Main Street. Practical, decorative, and functional accessories for the home and garden. (Do gardens need accessorizing? Think wind chimes.)

Bojangles (508-548-9888), 239 Main Street. This is a wonderfully tactile shop; in fact, it appeals to all the senses. It has a nostalgic feel, but the goods are modern, funky, and contemporary. Stop in for high-end gifts: scarves, perfume bottles, hats, throws, candles, glassware, loose-hanging women's clothing, specialty place settings, unusual utensils.

Ben & Bill's Chocolate Emporium (508-548-7878), 209 Main Street. This old-fashioned sweets shop is lined with walls of confections, some made on the premises. The excellent store-made ice cream is tasty, cheap, and served in abundant quantities.

✳ Special Events

Early June: **Illumination Weekend,** Woods Hole. Illuminated boats moored in Eel Pond, crafts demonstrations, open houses, a concert, cruises, a bagpipe jamboree, casino night, and more.

July 4: **Blessing of the Fleet** off Falmouth Heights Beach (at noon). Spectacular evening fireworks over Vineyard Sound; militia reenactment on the village green.

Early–mid-July: **Arts and Crafts Street Fair.** A fund-raising auction for Falmouth Artists' Guild. Beginning at 10 AM, Main Street fills with crafts, artisans, and food stalls.

Late July–early August: **Woods Hole Film Festival** (508-495-3456; www.woodsholefilmfestival.com). About 50 films by established and new filmmakers have been screened at various locations since the early 1990s.

Early August: **Arts Alive Festival** (508-540-3304; www.arts-cape.com/falag), at the marina. Artists' demonstrations and a "wet auction" of paintings made around town by local artists that morning.

Mid-August: **Annual Antiques Show,** Falmouth Historical Society. Sponsored by the society since 1970; $3.50.

♂ FAIRS AND POWWOWS

Early July: **Powwow** (508-477-0208, Wampanoag Tribal Council), Barnstable County Fairgrounds, Route 151, East Falmouth. The People of the First Light's Mashpee Wampanoag Powwow has been open to the public since 1924, and the Mashpee Wampanoag Tribal Council has sponsored it since 1974. The powwow attracts Native Americans in full regalia from nearly every state as well as from Canada, Mexico, and some Central and South American countries. These traditional gatherings provide an opportunity for tribes to exchange stories and to discuss common problems and goals. Dancing, crafts demonstrations, storytelling, pony rides, a "fire ball," clambake, and vendor booths. Kids are encouraged to join in the dancing and nearly constant percussive music. Adults $7; children 6–12, $4.

Late July: **Barnstable County Fair** (508-563-3200), Route 151, East Falmouth. A popular weeklong family tradition. Local and national musical acts, a midway, livestock shows, and horticulture, cooking, and crafts exhibits and contests. Over age 12, $8; otherwise free.

Falmouth Road Race (508-540-7000; www.falmouthroadrace.com). The event of the year in Falmouth: an internationally renowned 7-mile seaside footrace, limited to 9,500 participants. Get your registration in before April 15 or you won't have a chance of running (Falmouth Road Race, Box 732, Falmouth 02541). Reserve your lodging before May; places usually fill up by then.

Late October: **The Cape Cod Marathon** (508-540-6959; www.cape-codmarathon.com). A high-spirited event, beginning and ending on Fal-mouth's village green, and attracting several thousand long-distance run-ners and relay teams. Commit by Sep-tember or you'll be disappointed.

Mid-December: **Christmas by the Sea.** Tree lighting, caroling at the lighthouse and town green, and a sig-nificant Christmas parade. Popular house tours are operated by the West Falmouth Library (508-548-4709).

MASHPEE

Just east of Falmouth, fast-growing Mashpee (which means "land near the great cove") is one of two Massachusetts towns administered by Native Americans (the other is Aquinnah, or Gay Head, on Martha's Vineyard). For 1,000 years prior to the colonists' arrival, native Wampanoag Indians had established summer camps in the area, but with the settlement of Plymouth Colony, they saw larger and larger pieces of their homeland taken away from them and their numbers decimated by imported disease. In 1617, three years after Captain John Smith explored the area, six Native Americans were kidnapped and forced into slavery. By 1665, the missionary Reverend Richard Bourne appealed to the Massachusetts legislature to reserve about 25 square miles for the Native Americans. The area was called Mashpee Plantation (or Massapee or Massipee, depending on who's doing the translating), in essence the first Native American reservation in the United States. In 1870, the plantation was incorporated as the town of Mashpee. When the *Mayflower* arrived at Plymouth, the Wampanoag population was an estimated 30,000; there are a about 400 Wampanoag in Mashpee today.

Mashpee wasn't popular with wealthy 19th-century settlers, so there are few stately old homes here. The Wampanoag maintain a museum and church, both staffed by knowledgeable tribespeople. In the 1930s classic *Cape Cod Ahoy!*, Wilson Tarbel observed something about Mashpee that could still be said today: It's "retiring, elusive, scattered, a thing hidden among the trees."

The largest developed area of Mashpee is New Seabury, a 2,300-acre resort of homes, condos, restaurants, golf courses, shops, and beaches. When developers won their lengthy legal battle with the Wampanoag, the tribe—and the town—lost much of its prettiest oceanfront property. The only noteworthy beach is South Cape Beach, a relatively pristine barrier beach with several miles of marked nature trails and steady winds that attract sailboarders. Compared with its neighbors, Mashpee is a quiet place, with a year-round population of 13,000, plenty of commuters (into Boston), and an upscale outdoor mall, Mashpee Commons.

GUIDANCE ❖ **Mashpee Chamber of Commerce** (508-477-0792; 800-423-6274; www.mashpeechamber.com), in the Cape Cod Five Cents Savings Bank off the Mashpee rotary (Routes 28 and 151). Open 9:30–4:30 weekdays.

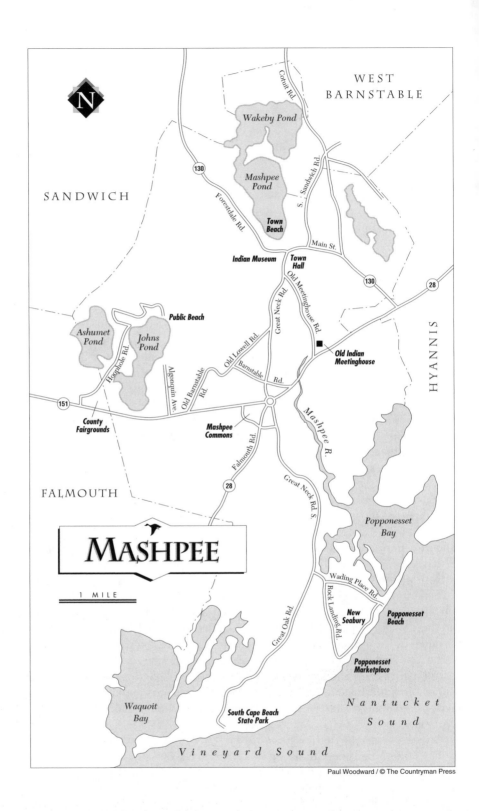

N

WEST
BARNSTABLE

SANDWICH

Wakeby Pond

Cotuit Rd.

130

S. Sandwich Rd.

Forestdale Rd.

Mashpee
Pond

Town
Beach

Main St.

Indian Museum

Town
Hall

130

28

HYANNIS

Public Beach

Ashumet
Pond

Johns
Pond

Great Neck Rd.

Old Meetinghouse Rd.

Old Indian
Meetinghouse

Hoophole Rd.

Old Lowell Rd.

Barnstable Rd.

151

Algonquin Ave.

Old Barnstable Rd.

Mashpee R.

County
Fairgrounds

Mashpee
Commons

Falmouth Rd.

FALMOUTH

28

Great Neck Rd. S.

Popponesset
Bay

MASHPEE

1 MILE

Wading Place Rd.

Rock Landing Rd.

New
Seabury

Popponesset
Beach

Great Oak Rd.

Popponesset
Marketplace

Waquoit
Bay

South Cape Beach
State Park

Nantucket
Sound

Vineyard Sound

Paul Woodward / © The Countryman Press

PUBLIC REST ROOMS Year-round rest rooms are available at Mashpee Commons (see *Selective Shopping—Mall*). Seasonal ones are located at South Cape Beach (at the end of Great Oak Road), and Johns Pond, a town park off Hoophole Road.

PUBLIC LIBRARY ✎ ❋ ♀ **Mashpee Public Library** (508-539-1435), Route 151 across from Mashpee Commons, is open 9–5 Monday and Wednesday, Noon–8 Tuesday and Thursday, Noon–5 Friday, and 9–1 Saturday.

GETTING THERE *By car:* From the Sagamore Bridge, take Route 6 east to Route 130 south to North Great Neck Road to the Routes 151/28 Mashpee rotary. The Mashpee Commons shopping area at the rotary acts as Mashpee's hub.

MEDICAL EMERGENCY **Mashpee Family Medicine** (508-477-4282), Mashpee Health Center, 5 Industrial Drive at Route 28, accepts walk-ins 9–11 weekdays, 9–1 Saturday.

It's not an "emergency" (the kind you'd expect under this category, anyway), but many area water wells have been closed in recent years. They've been contaminated by years of training with grenades and other live munitions at the Massachusetts Military Reservation. I drink bottled water on the Upper Cape.

❋ To See and Do

HISTORIC HOUSES **Old Indian Meetinghouse** (508-477-0208, Wampanoag Tribal Council), Meetinghouse Way off Route 28. Open 10–2 Wednesday and

OLD INDIAN MEETINGHOUSE

Kim Grant

Friday, July and August. Located on the edge of what was once a Wampanoag-only cemetery ("They even took our burial ground away from us and made it theirs," laments a volunteer guide), this is the Cape's oldest surviving meeting-house. It was built in 1684 and moved to its present spot in 1717. Inside, quilts commemorate the "glorious dead" tribe members; in the choir loft look for accomplished carvings of multimasted ships whittled during lengthy 19th-century Baptist sermons.

⚘ ❄ **Mashpee Wampanoag Indian Museum** (508-477-1536), on Route 130 across from Lake Avenue. Hours uncertain due to renovation; call 508-477-0208 for up-to-date information. This small, early-19th-century house was built by Richard Bourne, minister and missionary to the Mashpee Wampanoag. Exhibits (again, subject to renovation) include tools, baskets, traditional clothing, arrowheads, a reconstructed wigwam, and a model of a pre-European-invasion tribal village. Although the displays aren't particularly enlightening, explanatory literature is available and the Wampanoag staff are happy to answer questions. (Check out the herring run at the end of the parking lot.) Donations.

FISHING/SHELLFISHING Obtain freshwater fishing and shellfishing licenses from the town clerk. The office (508-539-1416), at Town Hall, 16 Great Neck Road North, is open 8:30–4:30 weekdays year-round, 9–noon on Saturdays in summer.

Fish for trout, smallmouth bass, chain pickerel, and white perch at **Mashpee-Wakeby Pond** and the **Mashpee River** (access from Quinnaquissett Avenue). Surf-casting is great at **South Cape Beach State Park** (see *Green Space— Beach*).

⚘ **FOR FAMILIES** ❄ ⚐ **Cape Cod Children's Museum** (508-539-8788; www.capecodchildrensmuseum.pair.com), 577 Great Neck Road South. Open 10–5 Monday through Saturday, noon–5 Sunday (shorter daily hours September through April). Toddlers love the castle, puppet theater, and 30-foot pirate ship; kids of all ages love arts and crafts; check out the Starlab Planetarium, too. $4 age 5 and over, $3 age 1–4. Memberships, providing unlimited visits, cost $55 for a family of four, $5 each additional person.

GOLF ❄ **Quashnet Valley Country Club** (508-477-4412), Lowell Road, off Great Neck Road from Route 130. This semiprivate course winds around woods and cranberry bogs; ponds and marshes surround 12 of 18 holes; par 72.

New Seabury Country Club (508-477-9400), Shore Drive, New Seabury. Open to the public on weekdays from September to May. This semiprivate club has two excellent 18-hole courses.

TENNIS Mashpee High School, 500 Old Barnstable Road (off Route 151), has public courts.

❋ Green Space

BEACH South Cape Beach State Park (508-457-0495), on Vineyard Sound, Great Neck Road. Open 9–6 daily late May to early September, daily off-season.

The 432-acre state park boasts a lovely mile-long, dune-backed barrier beach, boardwalks, and nature trails. In-season facilities include a concession stand, rest rooms, handicap ramp onto the beach, and lifeguards. Parking $7 daily in-season, free off-season (but you'll have to access through the Mashpee Town Beach parking lot).

PONDS Mashpee and **Wakeby Ponds,** off Route 130. Combined, these ponds create the Cape's largest freshwater body, wonderful for swimming, fishing, and boating. This area was a favorite fishing spot of both patriot Daniel Webster and President Grover Cleveland.

WALKS Lowell Holly Reservation (781-821-2977), off Sandwich Road from Route 130. Open year-round. Ranger on duty 9–5 PM daily, late May to early September. Donated by Harvard University's President Abbott Lawrence Lowell to the Trustees of Reservations in 1943, this tranquil 130-acre preserve contains an untouched forest of native American beeches and more than 500 hollies, as well as white pines, rhododendrons, and wildflowers. The Wheeler Trail circles the peninsula that separates Wakeby and Mashpee Ponds. There is a small bathing beach (no lifeguard).

Mashpee River Woodlands/South Mashpee Pine Barrens. Parking on Quinnaquissett Avenue (off Route 28 just east of the rotary) and at the end of River Road off Great Neck Road South. The 8-mile hiking trail winds along the Mashpee River, through a quiet forest, and along marshes and cranberry bogs. Put in your canoe at the public landing on Mashpee Neck Road. Free.

Jehu Pond Conservation Area. Established in 1997, there are almost 5 miles of trails here on almost 80 acres encompassing woodlands, marshes, an abandoned cranberry bog, two islands, and Atlantic white cedar swamp. Take Great Neck Road South toward South Cape Beach and follow the CONSERVATION AREA signs.

Mashpee National Wildlife Refuge (508-495-1702). A partnership of nine groups has banded together to protect 3,000 acres from development, and they expect to procure another 2,800 adjacent acres. Plans are in the works for a visitors center and trail guide. Stop in at the chamber of commerce for current details.

See also South Cape Beach State Park under *Beach.*

* Lodging

*Family-style accommodations are the rule in Mashpee.

RESORTS New Seabury Resort (508-477-9400; 800-999-9033; www.newseabury.com), Rock Landing Road, New Seabury 02649. Open March through December. This self-contained resort, purchased by corporate raider Carl Icahn in 1998, is scattered across 2,300 acres fronting Nantucket Sound. The 13 "villages" of small, gray-shingled buildings offer a variety of rental accommodations (numbering about 130). Sea Quarters consists of one- and two-bedroom town houses; Maushop Village resembles Nantucket, with its lanes of crushed shells and weathered buildings; Tidewatch is a

1960s-style hotel near the golf course; Mews consists of contemporary California-influenced units. All villas have fully equipped kitchens. Some units overlook golf courses; some are ocean-front; others have more distant water views. Facilities include two restaurants (see Popponessett Inn under *Dining Out*), 16 tennis courts, two golf courses, a well-equipped health club, two outdoor pools, 3 miles of private beach on Nantucket Sound, bike rentals and trails, a small shopping mall, mini-golf, and kids' activities. You needn't leave the grounds. Late June through August $255 one-bedroom, $355–385 two-bedroom, 3-night minimum in summer; rates less off-season. Golf packages in spring and fall.

❄ **Cape Cod Holiday Estates** (508-477-3377; 800-228-2968; www.vrivacations.com), 97 Four Seasons Drive, Mashpee 02649. These 33 upscale time-share houses are operated by Vacation Resorts International. The airy two-bedroom and two-bath units have a full modern kitchen, Jacuzzi, central air-conditioning, separate living and family room, and private patio. On-premise activities and facilities include an indoor pool, shuffleboard, playground, tennis, basketball, and a nine-hole putting green. Late June to early September $245 nightly, $1,550 weekly; off-season $90–125 nightly, $600–750 weekly.

❄ **Sea Mist Resort** (508-477-0549; 800-228-2968; www.vriresorts.com), Great Neck Road South, Mashpee 02649. Yes, they are time-share condos, but these 90 one- and two-bedroom suites and town houses are a good value for families. Facilities include tennis, an outdoor pool, mini-golf, and volleyball. Golf packages available. Late June to early September $130–220 nightly and $875–1425 weekly for a one-bedroom, $210 nightly and $1,350 weekly for a two-bedroom; off-season $90–125 nightly, $525–750 weekly.

RENTAL HOUSES AND COTTAGES
Century 21 Regan Realtors (508-539-2121), and **Real Estate Associates** (508-477-7771), both in Mashpee Commons, Routes 151 and 28, rent seasonal cottages and houses.

❋ **Where to Eat**

There aren't many choices in Mashpee, but the ones listed here are good. If you're not satisfied with these, stop at Mashpee Commons shopping area to see if there are any new restaurants.

DINING OUT ✎ ❋ ♿ **Popponessett Inn** (508-477-8258; 508-477-1100), Shore Drive, New Seabury. Open for dinner late May to mid-October; call for mealtimes. Within 50 feet of the ocean and with sweeping views of Nantucket Sound, this is the area's only choice for elegant dining. The Cape's largest resort village offers traditional New England seafood served in romantic dining rooms. Live entertainment throughout the summer under a big function tent. (This is a popular wedding location.) Reservations required; jackets preferred. Entrées $17–25.

❋ ♈ **Contrast @ the Commons** (508-477-1299), Mashpee Commons. Open for lunch and dinner. After opening the successful Contrast Bistro and Espresso Bar in Dennis (and then selling it), Christian Soderstom thankfully came to Mashpee. He opened an urban-style bistro, a tad edgy and bold. At midday, the salads, creative sandwiches, and chicken pot-pie are deservedly popular. Seasonal dinners get more creative with signature codcakes, lavish pizzas, good pasta dishes, and daily specials. There is also a convivial bar, heated patio, and a concert series. Lunch $7–12, dinner entrées $14–26.

& **The Flume** (508-477-1456), Lake Avenue, off Route 130. Open for dinner April through November. Wampanoag and Mashpee native chef-owner Earl Mills trained at the Popponessett and Coonamessett Inns before opening The Flume in the early 1970s. His rendering of traditional recipes attracts a diverse clientele to this small, casual, novelty restaurant built over a herring run. Fish figures prominently on the menu. Dishes include salt codfish cakes; marinated herring garnished with sour cream, red onion, and apple; and chowder. In spring, when the herring are running (along with Brewster, this is one of the oldest herring runs in the state), try the herring roe and bacon. For dessert, try Indian pudding, made with cornmeal, molasses, and ginger. Dishes $11–24.

EATING OUT The Raw Bar (508-539-4858), Popponessett Marketplace, New Seabury. Open May to late October (weekends only in spring and fall). You know this tiny place has something going for it when locals outnumber tourists. Part Cape Cod, part Caribbean, the raw bar boasts loyal staff and fresh seafood. Their lobster salad may be the best on Cape Cod!

♂ ❀ **Cooke's Seafood** (508-477-9595), 7 Ryan's Way, off Great Neck Road. Open for lunch and dinner seasonally. The best fried clams in the area, along with other seafood, of course, and lighter fare. Lunch specials from $5, dishes $9–17.

✳ Entertainment

Boch Center for the Performing Arts (508-477-2580; www.bochcenterarts.com), Mashpee Commons, Routes 151 and 28. The center is still in the capital fund-raising stages, but until it breaks ground, it sponsors performances at area venues.

Mashpee Commons (508-477-5400), Routes 151 and 28, Mashpee. Dozens of performances, including some free musical concerts, take place here. Keep your eyes peeled for current listings.

🦞 ❀ ↑ **Hoyts Cinema** (508-477-7333), Mashpee Commons, Routes 151 and 28.

✳ Selective Shopping

MALL ❀ Mashpee Commons (508-477-5400), Routes 151 and 28. Open daily. If you're familiar with Seaside, the planned community of architectural note in Florida, you may recognize elements of this 30-acre outdoor shopping mall–cum–new town center. It's located at what Wampanoags used to call "pine tree corner," back when Mashpee was quieter than it is today. The Commons is pleasant and the layout is better than at most malls, but it still looks a bit contrived. (Developers went so far as to measure the sidewalk widths in an old, quintessential Vermont town and duplicate the dimensions here.) Having said that, it's won numerous awards for transforming a strip mall into a veritable downtown commercial district. It's one of the most concentrated shopping venues on the Cape, boasting several good clothing stores, specialty boutiques, a movie theater, restaurants, cafés, and free outdoor entertainment in summer. Shops range from the **Gap** and **Starbuck's** to more interesting shops like **Paper Palette, Booksmith,** and **M Brann.**

FLEA MARKET **Dick & Ellie's Flea Market** (508-477-3550), Route 28 across from Deer Crossing Shopping Center. Open summer weekends (possibly, since this Market's fate was uncertain at press time). More than 100 antiques and collectibles dealers peddle their wares here. Don't be afraid to bring the kids along—there's mini-golf.

SPECIAL SHOP ❊ ❧ **Signature Gallery** (508-539-0029; www.signaturecraftgallery.com), 10 Steeple Street, Mashpee Commons, Routes 151 and 28. This exceptional gallery carries work by more than 600 distinguished American craftspeople. The acclaimed inventory includes jewelry, art glass, furniture, ceramics, wood, and wearable art.

✳ Special Events

See the "Fairs and Powwows" sidebar in "Falmouth."

Late July: **Mashpee Night at the Pops** (508-539-0635), Mashpee Commons. Hosted by the Mashpee Community Concert Committee (MCCC) since 1992, an outdoor concert by the Cape Symphony Orchestra, capped off by spectacular fireworks. Over 15,000 people pack this free event, but you can also purchase reserved seats; just make sure you do it by March, as they sell out out quickly. Good job!

Mid-Cape

BARNSTABLE

HYANNIS

YARMOUTH

DENNIS

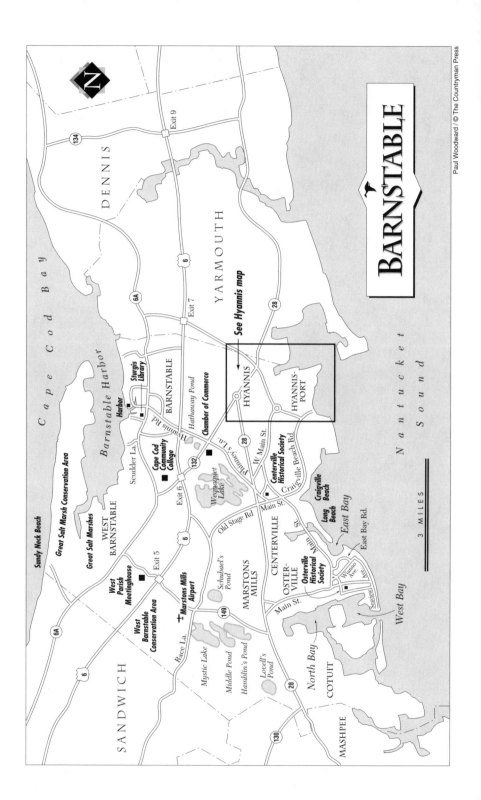

BARNSTABLE

The Cape's largest town covers 60 square miles and is home to 48,000 year-round souls. It's also the Cape's second oldest town, incorporated two years after Sandwich, in 1639. Barnstable actually comprises seven distinct villages—Cotuit, Marstons Mills, Osterville, Centerville, and Hyannis along Route 28, and West Barnstable and Barnstable along Route 6A. (Barnstable is sometimes referred to as Barnstable Village to distinguish it from Barnstable County, which embraces the whole of the Cape.)

On the bayside, Route 6A (also called Old King's Highway and Main Street) winds through West Barnstable and Barnstable Village. Development—or lack thereof—is rigidly controlled by the Old King's Highway Historical Commission, which regulates signage and does not allow gas stations, chain stores, or unconventional restorations within sight of the road. Sandy Neck, a haven for naturalists and beachgoers, is located off Route 6A, as are stately homes now converted into B&Bs.

On the southside, off Route 28, you'll find Centerville, Osterville, and Cotuit—parts of which front Nantucket Sound. Centerville's Main Street is full of handsome old homes built during the 19th century by affluent sea captains and businessmen. Osterville boasts some of the Cape's largest summer mansions, all with Nantucket Sound as their front yard. Osterville's Main Street is lined with upscale shops. At the turn of the 20th century, Cotuit was dubbed Little Harvard, as it was home to many academicians. Cotuit's Main Street is lined with impressive Federal, Greek Revival, and Queen Anne houses, with American flags and Adirondack chairs dotting the lawns. The popular Craigville Beach dominates this side of Barnstable.

Landlocked and wedged between Routes 28 and 6, Marstons Mills is tiny, quiet, and residentially developed. It was founded by the Marston family, who built and ran the mills driven by the Goodspeed River.

Barnstable was founded by English Congregationalist minister John Lothrop and a small band of religious renegades who felt that Plymouth Colony was a bit too settled for them. The neighborhood of Oysterville, as it was called, was purchased from the Native Americans in 1648 for "two copper kettles and some fencing." The area then was called Mattakeese, which translates as "plowed fields"—indeed, the land had already been cleared—but the settlers eventually named it for a similar harbor in Barnstaple, England.

GUIDANCE ❄ **Hyannis Area Chamber of Commerce** (508-362-5230; 800-449-6647 for 24-hour information; www.hyannischamber.com), 1481 Route 132, Hyannis 02601. Open 9–4:30 or 5 Monday through Saturday year-round; open 10–2 Sunday, late May to early September. A mile south of Route 6, the chamber has information about all Barnstable villages.

MEDIA Pick up the weekly *Barnstable Patriot* (508-771-1427) to check the local news and gossip.

PUBLIC LIBRARY See Sturgis Library under *To See and Do.*

GETTING THERE *By car:* Barnstable is 15 miles from the Cape Cod Canal. Take Route 6 to exit 5 for West Barnstable (Route 149 north) and Marstons Mills, Cotuit, and Osterville (Route 149 south). Take exit 6 for Barnstable Village (Route 132 west) and Centerville (Route 132 east).

By bus: The **Plymouth & Brockton** bus line (508-778-9767; www.p-b.com) connects Barnstable with other Cape towns, as well as with Boston's Logan Airport. The bus stops at the big commuter parking lot at Burger King, exit 6 off Route 6 at Route 132.

GETTING AROUND **The Villager** (508-385-8326; 800-352-7155; www.capecodtransit.org) connects Barnstable's Route 6A (at the courthouse) with the malls in Hyannis on Route 132, the new Hyannis Transportation Center bus terminal in the center of Hyannis, the West End Rotary, and Star Market. Schedules are available from the chamber of commerce (see *Guidance*). Purchase tickets on board. Fares: $1 over age 5.

MEDICAL EMERGENCY **Cape Cod Hospital** (508-771-1800), 27 Park Street, Hyannis. Open 24/7.

✷ To See and Do

Along or near Route 6A

West Parish Meetinghouse, Route 149 at Meeting House Way, West Barnstable. Open 10–4 daily, late May to mid-October; Sunday services at 10. This majestic example of early Colonial architecture is the second oldest surviving meetinghouse on Cape Cod. (The oldest, the 1684 Old Indian Meetinghouse, is in Mashpee.) Its members belong to the oldest Congregationalist church fellowship in America, established in 1639 and descended from London's First Congregationalist Church. Founding pastor John Lothrop and his small band of followers erected their first meetinghouse in 1646. By 1715 the Congregational church had become so popular that Barnstable split into two parishes; the building you see today was constructed in 1717. Its bell tower, topped by a gilded rooster, holds a bell cast by Paul Revere in 1806; it still rings. Until 1834 the meetinghouse doubled as a town hall—so much for separation of church and state! In the 1950s, the meetinghouse was fully restored to its original modest, neoclassical beauty. Donations.

⫙ ❄ **William Brewster Nickerson Memorial Room at Cape Cod Community College** (508-362-2131), Route 132, West Barnstable. Open 9–3 Tuesday and 8:30–4 Monday, Wednesday, and Friday. Rainy day or not, visitors with more than a passing interest in the social history, literature, institutions, and people of the Cape and islands owe it to themselves to stop here. Students voted in 1966 to set up this collection to honor the college's second president, a Vietnam War hero and *Mayflower* descendant. The significant collection contains more than 5,000 documents: religious treatises, biographies, autobiographies, oral histories, letters by dune poet Harry Kemp, scrimshaw, ship registers and logs, early diaries, U.S. Lifesaving Service reports, telephone directories from 1886 on, and aerial photographs. The place is a treasure trove for researchers; several excellent books have been written using solely these materials.

✐ ⫙ ❄ **Sturgis Library** (508-362-6636; www.sturgislibrary.org), 3090 Route 6A, Barnstable Village. Open 10–5 Monday, Wednesday, and Friday; 1–8 Tuesday; 1–5 Thursday; 10–4 Saturday. Researchers from all over the country (including entrepreneurs looking for information about shipwrecks) visit the country's oldest public library. It boasts one of the finest collections of genealogical records, dating to the area's first European settlers; an original 1605 Lothrop Bible; more than 1,500 maps and charts; and archives filled with other maritime material. $5 fee for the genealogy and research collection; otherwise, free. The library has a very good children's corner. William Sturgis, by the way, was born in the original part of the building, went off to sea at age 15 when his father died, and returned four years later as a ship's captain. Although he received no formal education, this self-made man obtained reading lists from a Harvard-educated friend and deeded the building to the town as a library.

Barnstable County Courthouse (508-362-2511), 3195 Route 6A, Barnstable Village. Open 8–4:30 weekdays. Built in 1831–1832, this imposing, granite, Greek Revival building is one of few reminders that tranquil Barnstable is the county seat for the Cape. (It's been the county seat since 1685.) Look for original murals and a pewter codfish in the main courtroom. On the side lawn, a bronze sculpture commemorates James Otis Jr., a West Barnstable "patriot" who wrote the famous 1761 Writs of Assistance speech. President John Adams said that Otis was the "spark by which the child of Independence was born."

Lothrop Hill Cemetery, Route 6A, just east of Barnstable Village. Slate headstones are scattered across this little hillock, where John Lothrop and other Barnstable founders rest. Near the stone wall along Route 6A, look for a large granite memorial bearing the following inscription: "In this cemetery lie the mortal remains of Capt. John Percival known as 'Mad Jack.' Born April 3, 1779. Died September 17, 1862 in command of Old Ironsides around the world 1844–1846."

Barnstable Harbor, Mill Way Road off Route 6A. Fishing charters and whale-watching trips depart from this small harbor.

♿ ✐ ⫙ **Donald G. Trayser Memorial Museum Complex (Old Customs House)** (508-362-2092), 3353 Route 6A, Barnstable Village. Open 1:30–4:30 Thursday through Sunday, mid-June to mid-October. Before Barnstable Harbor filled with silt around 1900, it was the Cape's busiest port. The Old Customs House was built in 1856 to oversee the enormous stream of goods passing through the harbor. When harbor activity diminished, the brick Italian Renaissance Revival building served as a post office, until the Barnstable Historical Commission made it their headquarters in 1959. The commission restored the beautiful building, painted it deep red, and opened this museum complex. It contains a second-floor custom keeper's office (with a harbor view), Native American arrowheads, Sandwich glass, ivory, and children's toys. Adjacent is a shed with a horse-drawn hearse, an 1869 velocipede, and a 1900 wooden-frame bicycle. Also on the grounds is a circa-1690 jail cell, complete with colonial "graffiti." Donation $2.

Off Route 28

🍴 🐾 ❄ **Cahoon Museum of American Art** (508-428-7581; www.cahoon-musuem.org), 4676 Route 28, Cotuit. Open 10–4 Tuesday through Saturday, February through December. This magnificent 1775 Georgian Colonial farmhouse was once a stagecoach stop on the Hyannis-to-Sandwich route. Today it houses a permanent collection of 19th- and early-20th-century American art and features the whimsical and often humorous paintings of the late neoprimitive artists Martha and Ralph Cahoon. The building's low ceilings, wide floorboards, fireplaces, and wall stenciling provide an intimate backdrop for the artwork. Don't miss it. The museum also offers summer classes in watercolor and other fine and applied arts. Gallery talks are held on many Friday mornings at 11. Adults $3, children under 12 free.

✏ 🍴 **Centerville Historical Society Museum** (508-775-0331), 513 Main Street, Centerville. Open 12:30–4:30 Wednesday through Saturday, mid-June to mid-September. The 1840s Mary Lincoln House (no relation to Abraham) was built by Mary's father, Clark, a local tinsmith. Charles Ayling, a wealthy Cape businessman and philanthropist, endowed much of the museum, although many of the mid-19th-century furnishings were donated by townspeople. Ayling also assembled an entire Cape Cod colonial kitchen, complete with large open fireplace and dozens of iron utensils. The 14 rooms are filled with rare Sandwich glass, Civil War artifacts, maritime artifacts, historic quilts, costumes from 1750 to 1950, children's toys and games, perfume bottles, and A. E. Crowell's miniature duck carvings. Adults $3, children under 12 free.

❄ **The 1856 Country Store** (508-775-1856), 555 Main Street, Centerville. Beyond a selection of cutesy country and perfumed things, you'll find large pickles in a barrel of brine and wheels of cheddar cheese. The store is more picturesque outside than inside, although the original wood floors have been preserved.

Osterville Historical Society Museum (508-428-5861; www.osterville.org), 155 West Bay Road, Osterville. Open 1:30–4:30 Thursday through Sunday, mid-June to mid-September. The society maintains three properties, well worth a visit. The **Captain Jonathan Parker House,** built circa 1824, contains period art, antiques, furniture, and dolls, as well as paintings and porcelain from the China trade. The one-room-deep **Cammett House,** a simple Cape Cod farmhouse built circa 1790, is furnished with period pieces. And the **Boat Shop Museum** showcases the famous Crosby-designed catboat *Cayuga*, built in 1928, and the *Wianno Senior* and *Junior*. Half models, tools, and historic Osterville waterfront photographs are also displayed. Don't miss the period Colonial gardens maintained by the Osterville Garden Club. Adults $3, children free.

Samuel B. Dottridge House (508-428-0461), 1148 Main Street, Cotuit. Open noon–5 Thursday through Sunday, June to early September; Saturday until mid-October. Owned by the Sansuit and Cotuit Historical Society, this 1790 house contains historical but otherwise fairly unremarkable objects pertaining to daily 19th-century life. Adults $1, children 50¢.

SPECIAL PROGRAMS ❦ **Tales of Cape Cod** (508-362-8927; www.capehistory. com), 3018 Route 6A at Rendezvous Lane, Barnstable Village. This simple, white-clapboard building served as the Barnstable County Courthouse from 1772 to 1832, when the "new" granite structure down the road was built. The secular Old King's Colonial Courthouse then became a Baptist church until it was purchased in 1949 by Tales of Cape Cod, a nonprofit organization that preserves Cape folklore and oral histories. The organization sponsors an excellent lecture series Tuesday evenings at 7:30 in July and August. Subjects range from "Inventors, Entrepreneurs, and Opportunists of Cape Cod" to "Cape Cod Attics:

THE OSTERVILLE HISTORICAL SOCIETY MUSEUM

Kim Grant

Antique Appraisal Evening," "Whale Rescues," "Shipwrecks," and "Growing Up on Cape Cod in the 1930s." Talks are delivered by knowledgeable townspeople. $5 per person. (Refreshments alone are worth the price of admission.)

See also Barnstable Comedy Club under *Entertainment*.

SCENIC DRIVES These village back roads are quite lovely. From the center of Centerville, take South Main Street toward Osterville. Turn left on East Bay, which will wind around and become Seaview; follow that to the end. Double back and turn left on Eel River, then turn left onto Bridge. You will not be able to go very far on this road (it empties into a gated community), but it does cross a lovely waterway. After turning around, follow West Bay back to Main Street.

You can also take Main Street off Route 28 in Santuit (as you head toward Falmouth on Route 28, turn left onto Main Street just before the Mashpee town line). Follow Main Street through Cotuit center, jog left onto Ocean View overlooking Nantucket Sound, then jump back on Main Street and follow it to the end for more pond and sound views.

✳ Outdoor Activities

AIRPLANE RIDES ✳ **Cape Cod Soaring Adventures** (508-420-4201; 800-660-4563; www.capecodsoaring.com), Marstons Mills Airport, Route 149, Marstons Mills. Open 10–5 daily, weather permitting; reservations highly recommended. Flying aboard Randy Charlton's glider at 5,000 feet and 40 mph, you'll see butterflies, seagulls, and hawks. The unrestricted views and the quietness are like nothing you've probably ever experienced. Fall is perhaps the best time to fly, with spring a close second. On a sunny winter day, you can see for 80 miles, far better than on an average hazy summer day, when visibility peaks at about 5 miles. The key is low humidity and seasonally cool days. Randy takes one person at a time and charges $75–125 for 20 to 40 minutes.

✳ **Cape Cod Flying Service** (508-428-8732; 888-247-5263), Marstons Mills Airport, Route 149, Marstons Mills. These scenic and glider rides, from the Cape's only grass-strip airport, can go virtually anywhere on the Cape. A trip for up to three people for 30 minutes costs $69. For twice the price and time ($120 for an hour) you can head up to Wellfleet.

🖋 **BASEBALL** The Cotuit Kettlers play at Lowell Park in Cotuit from mid-June to mid-August.

BICYCLING If you don't have a friend with a summer place in the exclusive Wianno section of town, the best way to enjoy the village of Osterville is to cycle or drive along Wianno Avenue to Seaview Avenue, then turn right onto Eel River Road to West Bay Road and back into town.

FISHING/SHELLFISHING Get freshwater fishing licenses from the town clerk's office (508-790-6240) in Town Hall, 367 Main Street, Hyannis. Shellfishing permits are required and may be obtained from the Department of Natural

Resources (508-790-6272), 1189 Phinney's Lane (which runs between Routes 28 and 132), Centerville. You can also get freshwater fishing permits here.

Wequaquet Lake in Centerville has plenty of largemouth bass, sunfish, and tiger muskies to go around. Park along Shoot Flying Hill Road. Marstons Mills has three pretty ponds stocked with smallmouth bass, trout, and perch: **Middle Pond,** Race Lane; **Hamblin's Pond,** Route 149; and **Schubael's Pond,** Schubael Pond Road off Race Lane.

Barnstable Harbor Charter Fleet (508-362-3908; www.aquariussportsfishing.com), 186 Millway, off Route 6A. Late May to mid-October. A fleet of seven boats takes up to six passengers each for 4-, 6-, and 8-hour fishing expeditions in Cape Cod Bay.

Sea Witch (508-776-1336; 413-283-8375 off-season; www.seawitchcharters.com), Barnstable Harbor. May through September. Captain Bob Singleton, who's been fishing these waters since 1960, pilots a custom-built, 32-foot sportfishing boat. Captain Bob supplies the tackle and a money-back guarantee: If you don't return with fish, you get your money back. Up to six people for 4-, 6-, and 8-hour trips.

✔ **FOR FAMILIES** ❋ **Cape Cod YMCA** (508-362-6500; www.ymcacapecod.com), Route 132, West Barnstable. In addition to a fitness and cardiovascular center, the YMCA offers a number of programs where short-term visitors are welcome: open swims, Saturday-evening "Teen Nights," and Friday "Kids' Night Out." Drop off the kids and go out to dinner while they do arts and crafts. The Y also has a summer camp with weekly sessions, for which fees vary.

Main Street Playground, adjacent to the recreation building, Centerville. Built by local volunteers in 1994, there are swings slides, a fancy jungle gym, sand for digging and building, climbing rings, and picnic tables.

❋ **GOLF** **Cotuit Highground Country Club** (508-428-9863), 31 Crocker Neck Road, Cotuit. A popular nine-hole, 1,500-yard, par-28 course.

Olde Barnstable Fairgrounds Golf Course (508-420-1142), 1460 Route 149, Marstons Mills. An 18-hole course (par 70) so close to the airport that you can see the underbellies of approaching planes from the driving range.

TENNIS Public courts are located at the **Centerville Elementary School** on Bay Lane; at the **Cotuit Elementary School** on Highland Avenue; at the **Osterville Bay School** off West Bay Road between Eel River Road and Main Street; at the **Marstons Mills East Elementary School** on the Osterville–West Barnstable Road; and at the Barnstable–West Barnstable Elementary School on Route 6A.

WHALE-WATCHING ✔ **Hyannis Whale Watcher Cruises** (508-362-6088; 888-942-5392; www.whales.net), Mill Way off Route 6A, Barnstable Harbor. Daily departures, mid-May through October. A convenient mid-Cape location and a new, fast boat make this a good choice for whale-watching. An onboard naturalist provides commentary. There are also sunset cruises in summer. Adults $26; children 4–12, $16.

❋ Green Space

BEACHES Millway Beach, just beyond Barnstable Harbor. Although a resident parking sticker is needed in summer, you can park and look across to Sandy Neck Beach in the off-season.

✎ **Craigville Beach,** on Nantucket Sound, Centerville. This crescent-shaped beach—long and wide—is popular with college crowds and families. Facilities include rest rooms, changing rooms, and outdoor showers. Parking $15 weekday, $20 weekend, $40 weekly.

Long Beach, on Nantucket Sound, Centerville. Centerville residents favor Long Beach, at the western end of Craigville Beach; walk along the water until you reach a finger of land between the sound and the Centerville River. Long Beach is uncrowded, edged by large summer shore homes and a bird sanctuary on the western end. Although a resident sticker is required, I include it anyway because it's the nicest beach.

PONDS Hathaway Pond, Phinney's Lane, Barnstable Village, is a popular freshwater spot with a bathhouse and lifeguard. The following freshwater locations require a resident sticker: **Lovell's Pond,** off Newtown Road from Route 28, Marstons Mills; **Burgess Park,** off Route 149 in Marstons Mills; **Hamblin's Pond,** off Route 149 from Route 28, Marstons Mills; and **Wequaquet Lake,** off Shoot Flying Hill Road from Route 132 (Iyanough Road), Centerville.

WALKS Sandy Neck Great Salt Marsh Conservation Area (508-362-8300), West Barnstable; trailhead from parking lot off Sandy Neck Road. First things

BARRIER BEACH BEAUTY

Sandy Neck Beach, on Cape Cod Bay, off Route 6A, West Barnstable. One of the Cape's most stunning beaches. The entrance to this 6-mile-long barrier beach is in Sandwich. Encompassing almost 9,000 acres, the area is rich with marshes, shellfish, and bird life. Sandy Neck dunes protect Barnstable Harbor from the winds and currents of Cape Cod Bay. Sandy Neck was the site of a Native American summer encampment before the colonists purchased it in 1644 for three axes and four coats. Then they proceeded to harvest salt-marsh hay and boil whale oil in tryworks on the beach. Today a private summertime cottage community occupies the far eastern end of the beach. Known locally as the Neck, the former hunting and fishing camps, built in the late 19th century and early 20th, still rely on water pumps and propane lights.

Beach facilities include rest rooms, changing rooms, and a snack bar. Parking costs $10. You can purchase four-wheel0drive permits at the gatehouse (508-362-8300). But six items must be in your car when the permit is issued: a spare tire, jack, jack pad, shovel, low-pressure tire gauge, and something to tow the car. If you live outside Barnstable, the cost is $40 from early September to mid-April or $80 per calendar year.

first: Hike off-season when it's not so hot. It takes about 4 hours to do the whole circuit. The 9-mile (round trip) trail to Beach Point winds past pine groves, wide marshes, low blueberry bushes, and 50- to 100-foot dunes. This 4,000-acre marsh is the East Coast's largest. Be on the lookout for endangered piping plovers nesting in the sand. Eggs are very difficult to see and, therefore, easily crushed. Parking $10.

St. Mary's Church Gardens, 3005 Route 6A (across from the library), Barnstable Village. Locals come to these peaceful, old-fashioned gardens to escape summer traffic swells on Route 6A. In spring, the gardens are full of crocuses, tulips, and daffodils. A small stream, crisscrossed with tiny wooden bridges, flows through the property; the effect is rather like an anglicized Japanese garden.

Tidal flats, Scudder Lane, off Route 6A, West Barnstable. At low tide you can walk onto the flats and almost across to the neck of Sandy Neck.

West Barnstable Conservation Area, Popple Bottom Road, off Route 149 (near Route 6), West Barnstable. Park at the corner for wooded trails.

Armstrong-Kelley Park, Route 28 near East Bay Road, Osterville. This lovely 8½-acre park has shaded picnic tables, wooded walking trails with identified specimens, and a wetland walkway.

✳ Lodging

✤ While a number of historic B&Bs line Route 6A, I've only included a selective selection; Barnstable's only beachfront option is a motel. To get off the beaten path, head "inland" to Cotuit or Centerville. Unless otherwise noted, all lodgings are open year-round.

BED & BREAKFASTS Honeysuckle Hill (508-362-8418; 866-444-5522; www.honeysucklehill.com), 591 Route 6A, West Barnstable 02668. Seasoned and welcoming innkeepers Mary and Bill Kilburn have applied their considerable talents to making this 1810 cottage a favorite. Their four rooms and two-bedroom suite (an extremely good value) have feather bedding, air-conditioning, robes, fine toiletries, and marble baths. Comfortably elegant and modestly furnished with a mix of white wicker and antiques, they're a breath of fresh air. I particularly like Magnolia with a pineapple poster bed, but Wisteria is the largest

and boasts its own entrance. Common space includes a living room with fireplace and a screened-in porch where you'll find lots of extra amenities. A full breakfast might include "Dutch Babies" (small puffy pancakes) and citrus salad, served at a common table. May through October $130–160 rooms, $210 suite (for two to four—kids must be over age 12); off-season $100–130 and $180, respectively.

Beechwood (508-362-6618; 800-609-6618; www.beechwoodinn.com), 2839 Route 6A, Barnstable Village 02630. This 1853 Queen Anne–style house, named for copper beeches flanking it, offers six romantic guest rooms furnished with high Victorian charm and modern air-conditioning. Rooms are all very different from one another; it's up to you to decide whether you're more interested in a canopy bed, marble fireplace, or steeply angled walls. (The Garret Room is tucked under third-floor eaves.) A wide veranda overlooks the beeches, and a privacy hedge separates the inn from Route

6A. The dining room—where a full breakfast (big on sweet carbs) and afternoon tea are served—features tongue-and-groove paneling and a pressed-tin ceiling. Accommodating innkeepers Ken and Debra Traugot enjoy talking with guests. May through October $150–180; off-season $95–130.

🌿 **Josiah Sampson House** (508-428-8383; 877-574-6873; www.josiahsampson.com), 40 Old King's Road, Cotuit 02635. The most fun part of my job is discovering new places and sharing them. Well, here it is: Carol and Leonard Carter's Federal-style manse is a treat. And it's made more so by the Carter's graciousness. You get the impression they've opened up the house because they really want to share it. They rent six comfortable and spacious rooms, some with fireplace, all with updated bathroom. As for the equally spacious common space, the living room is elegant without being stuffy; the dining room, handsome and inviting. In the deep backyard (perfect for small weddings) you'll find a gazebo for reading, a hot tub for soaking, and a deck for enjoying full breakfast in warm weather. Loaner bikes; adjacent tennis courts. Late May to mid-October $135; off-season $95–115.

🐾 ✎ **Lamb and Lion Inn** (508-362-6823; 800-909-6923; www.lambandlion.com), 2504 Route 6A, Barnstable 02630. Proprietors Alice Pitcher and Tom Dott have nicely upgraded this property, which consists of 10 rooms (including a cottage and "barn-stable" that can accommodate families) surrounding a heated swimming pool. Although the physical setup is rather like a U-shaped motel, the diverse rooms are quite pleasant with wicker

and antiques. Long hallways have been delightfully brightened with sky murals. I particularly like room 9, which gets great afternoon sun. Although rooms are quite different from one another, they all have TV and phone; most have a fireplace, more than half have a kitchenette, and most have a spiffy motel-style bathroom. Before leaving, ask to see the rare, triple-sided fireplace in the original 1740 house. Expanded continental breakfast included. Mid-May through October $145–210 rooms, $180–250 cottage/suite/barn; off-season $125–160 and $125–180, respectively; $15 per pet; children over 8 welcome.

✎ 🌿 **Adam's Terrace Gardens Inn** (508-775-4707; www.adamsterrace.com), 539 Main Street, Centerville 02632. If you're looking for an unpretentious place off the beaten path (and just a 10-minute walk from Craigville Beach), host Louise Pritchard's circa-1830s sea captain's house fits the bill. All five guest rooms with private bath have TV, homey furnishings, and include a full breakfast. Off-season, Louise also has three rooms, which share a bath. These are an even better value (especially when you consider that you'll probably have the bath to yourself anyway). Late May to mid-September $95–125; off-season $65–95, less for shared bath; $45 for a single with shared bath; children $20 additional.

MOTEL ✎ **Trade Winds Inn** (508-775-0365; 877-444-7966; www.twicapecod.com), Craigville Beach, Centerville 02632. Open May through October. The raison d'être for this four-building, 6-acre, 46-room complex: Craigville Beach is across the street. (The motel maintains its own private stretch of this beach.) Ocean-view rooms and efficiencies have sliding glass doors that open onto balconies. Less expensive non-ocean-view rooms (some with kitchen) are also available, as are suites. Adults will like the putting green; kids will flock to the small lake with swans, geese, and ducks. Of all your area lodging choices, this motel is the best, about 2 miles from downtown Hyannis. Mid-June to early September $129–250; off-season $119–139; discounts for longer stays.

RENTAL HOUSES AND COTTAGES

Craigville Realty (508-775-3174), 648 Craigville Beach Road, West Hyannisport 02672. This agency specializes in two- to four-bedroom rental houses. They're usually in quiet neighborhoods within a mile of Craigville Beach. At any given time there are about 125 houses in the rental pool; $725–5,000 weekly in-season.

See also Lamb and Lion Inn under *Bed & Breakfasts.*

CAMPGROUND 🦞 🛶 **Sandy Terraces Nudist Family Campground** (508-428-9209), Box 98, Marstons Mills 02648. Open mid-May to mid-October. Geared toward couples and families, this 10-acre campground has 12 wooded sites, a sandy beach on a mile-long lake, a redwood sauna, and lots of activities and cookouts. Call or write in advance of your visit.

✳ Where to Eat

Barnstable doesn't have a plethora of restaurants, but it does boast one of the best restaurants on the Cape, a waterfront restaurant, an excellent

local tavern, and the best homemade ice cream on the Cape. What else do you want?

DINING OUT 🦞 ✳ ♿ **The Regatta of Cotuit** (508-428-5715), 4613 Route 28, Cotuit. Open for dinner. Dollar for dollar, this is one of the Cape's top two or three restaurants—at once elegant and relaxed. Brantz and Wendy Bryan's superb restaurant, housed in a 200-year-old Federal mansion—a former stagecoach stop—is quite romantic, with eight intimate dining rooms. Chef Heather Allen's seasonal menus feature Asian- and European-inspired pairings of traditional New England meats and seafood. For those with a lighter appetite, a bistro menu is offered all evening. Plan on ending your gastronomic romp with Chocolate Seduction with *sauce framboise.* Or get the sampler plate of three desserts (a bargain at $14.50). While you might fear haughty service in such surroundings this is not the case whatsoever. A pianist performs in the tavern most evenings. Entrées $28–36, including a sorbet course and scrumptious side dishes. Reservations suggested.

✳ 🍷 🛶 **Dolphin** (508-362-6610), 3250 Route 6A, Barnstable. Open for lunch and dinner. This friendly watering hole, which has been in chef-owner Nancy Jean Smith's family for three generations, features extensive seafood selections. At midday you'll find everything from crabcakes and oysters to salads, specialty sandwiches, and baked and fried seafood. At dinner it's a bit more elaborate, with grilled swordfish, braised salmon, and good shrimp dishes. The Dolphin, complete with a long bar separated from the main dining room, is heavily patronized by locals who know a good thing when they see it. It's also staffed by folks just as loyal. Lunch $5–11, dinner entrées $15–22.

❋ **Five Bays Bistro** (508-420-5559), 825 Main Street, Osterville. Open for dinner. Named for the five bodies of water that surround Osterville, this little place is (thankfully) a tad urban and stylish—especially for the neighborhood. And my thanks continue: Thanks for making sophisticated dishes with high-quality, fresh ingredients. Thanks for preparing fusion cuisine that regular folks can understand. Local seafood and fish are always a good bet, perhaps done with an Oriental twist. Reservations recommended (otherwise dine early or late). Entrées $17–27.

See also Mattakeese Wharf under *Eating Out.*

EATING OUT Mattakeese Wharf (508-362-4511), 271 Mill Way, Barnstable Harbor. Open 11:30–9 daily, May through October. Few places beat this quintessential harborside location for $64 million water views. Get a table an hour before sunset so you can watch the fishermen and pleasure craft come and go in this quiet harbor. Prices are high relative to the quality, but you're here for the views, aren't you? Tried-and-true entrées include bouillabaisse, large burgers, scrod, and boiled lobster. Keep it simple. Bob Venditti has owned Mattakeese since 1968, and chef Ken La Casse has run the kitchen since the early 1980s. Reservations suggested. Lunch $6–12, dinner entrées $14–25.

🦞 **Mill Way Fish and Lobster Market** (508-362-2760; www.millwayfish. com), 275 Mill Way, Barnstable Vil-

lage. Open March through December. Culinary Institute of America–trained chef Ralph Binder puts his heart into this special market. He does a booming business in prepared foods for seafood lovers and vegetarians, as well as take-out fried seafood and grilled fish. His specialty is "shellfish sausage," designed for the grill and made with shrimp, lobster, and scallops. He mails it all over the country; you'll know why when you taste it.

❋ 🍷 **Breaking Grounds** (508-420-1311), 791 Main Street, Osterville. Open for breakfast and lunch daily. This pleasant place serves omelets, pancakes, and a limited menu of soups, salads, and hot sandwiches. There is also a large selection of flavored coffee and espresso drinks. Check out the patio dining in warm weather. Michael Tuffias, the chief owner/cook/bottle washer, has a fun spirit that rubs off on the place. Dishes $3–10.

❋ **Craigville Pizza & Mexican** (508-775-2267), Craigville Beach Road, West Hyannisport. Open for lunch and dinner. A favorite of readers Dan and Judie Dunham Spiritus, it's a no-frills place, but you can't beat it for these parts. Pies from $9.

❋ **Osterville Cheese Shop** (508-428-9085), 29 Wianno Avenue, Osterville. Open daily. Osterville residents and summer folks order imported and domestic cheeses and other gourmet goodies for their cocktail parties here. Enjoy a thick sandwich, soup, breakfast pastries and breads, a slice of chicken pie, or a pint of pasta salad, all wrapped up to take away.

❋ 🍸 **Barnstable Tavern** (508-362-2355), 3176 Route 6A, Barnstable Village. Open for lunch and dinner, but I only recommend you stop for a drink on the front patio at this old tavern in Barnstable's historic district.

❋ **Cotuit Grocery/Cotuit Pizza Factory** (508-428-6936; 508-420-1994), 737 Main Street, Cotuit. This old multiuse building would go unnoticed in Vermont, but on the Cape it's an anomaly. It's a convenience store–cum–wine shop–cum–pizza parlor.

❋ Entertainment

Barnstable Comedy Club (508-362-6333; www.barnstablecomedy club.com), 3171 Route 6A, across from the Barnstable Tavern, Barnstable Village. Performances November through June. First things first: This is not a comedy club! Founded in 1922, the country's oldest amateur theater group performs more than comedies—look for musicals and straight (though not heavy or provocative) theater. Since 1922 its motto has been "To Produce Good Plays and Remain Amateurs." (Kurt Vonnegut got his feet wet here.) A 200-seat theater; tickets $12–14; discounts for students and seniors.

❋ Selective Shopping

❊ All shops are open year-round unless otherwise noted. Osterville center, with a number of upscale shops, is good for a short stroll.

ANTIQUES **Harden Studios** (508-362-7711), 3264 Route 6A, Barnstable Village. This late-17th-century house was beautifully restored by Charles M. Harden in 1993 and now functions as an antiques shop and gallery. It's a true family affair: Harden's son Charles operates an etching press and art gallery in the adjacent shed, and son Justin researches the fine antiques collection. The collection includes American antiques from the early 1700s to the 1840s; Empire and Federal pieces; Oriental rugs, lamps, and chandeliers.

Sow's Ear Antiques (508-428-4931), Route 28 at Route 130, Cotuit. Open daily except Monday. Americana and primitive folk art and furniture sold from an 18th-century house; some garden antiques, too.

Cotuit Antiques (508-420-1234), 70 Industry Road, behind Cotuit Landing off Route 28, Cotuit. Henry Frongillo enjoys people and keeping

---

SINFUL SCOOPS

♪ ❀ ♿ **Four Seas** (508-775-1394), 360 South Main Street, at Centerville Four Corners. Open 9 AM–10:30 PM daily, mid-May to mid-September; sandwiches served 10–2:30. Founded in 1934, Four Seas has been owned by Dick Warren since 1960, when he bought the place from the folks who had given him a summer job as a college student. It's named for the four "seas" that surround the Cape: Buzzards Bay, Cape Cod Bay, the Atlantic Ocean, and Nantucket Sound. The Cape's absolute best ice cream is made every day, using the freshest ingredients. For instance, Dick makes beach plum ice cream only once a year—when the beach plums are ripe. The walls of this funky place, a former garage, are lined with photos of preppy summer crews, newspaper articles about Four Seas (it wins national ice cream awards every year), and poems written for Four Seas' 60th anniversary. Lobster salad sandwiches are great, too.

his shop folksy. Since he buys estates, you never know what you'll find. Primarily, though, he offers fine furniture, collectibles, some art, pottery, and lots of great old signage and advertising memorabilia.

Samuel Day Gallery (508-362-0175), 4039 Route 6A, Barnstable. This contemporary gallery has distinctive, artistic glass pieces like earrings and sculptures. As one Explorer says, there's "no crummy, touristy stuff" here.

ART GALLERIES **Cape Cod Art Association** (508-362-2909), 3480 Route 6A, Barnstable Village. This nonprofit was founded in 1948 and displays a fine range of juried art and artists in a beautiful and airy gallery. Shows change monthly. Indoor and outdoor classes and workshops are offered.

Tao Water Art Gallery (508-375-0428), 1989 Route 6A, West Barnstable. This contemporary Asian gallery, representing over 20 artists from post–Cultural Revolution China and the States, runs the gamut from exceptional abstract painting to landscapes and sculpture. One of the largest galleries on the Cape, with over 5,600 square feet, Tao Water also offers Chinese tea ceremonies and calligraphy classes in the off-season. Also look for antique furniture and handmade crafts and gifts from all over Asia.

Cummaquid Fine Arts (508-362-2593), 4275 Route 6A, Cummaquid. Gallery owners Jim Hinkle and Roy Hammer promote work by living, resident Cape Cod artists. You'll find landscapes, still lifes, coastal scenes, and figure studies within their 18th-century house.

See also Harden Studios under *Antiques.*

ARTISANS **The Blacks' Handweaving Shop** (508-362-3955), 597 Route 6A (about half a mile west of Route 149), West Barnstable. The Blacks create beautiful woven pieces with a variety of textures, colors, and materials: chenille, mohair, wool, and cotton. Bob Black—who's been weaving since he was 14 and studied at the Rhode Island School of Design—and his wife, Gabrielle, have been working at their looms in this post-and-beam shop since 1954. They are quite well known for custom, one-of-a-kind jacquard coverlets and throws, signed and dated.

Oak and Ivory (508-428-9425; www.oakandivory.com), 1112 Main Street, Osterville. If you've always wanted a Nantucket lightship basket but haven't made it to Nantucket, this is the off-island place for you. The baskets are expensive (from about $700 to several thousand dollars), reflecting the fine craftsmanship and 35–45 hours of work that go into each delicate piece. Basket makers Bob and Karen Marks (he a Nantucketer, she a wash-ashore) also offer traditional 18th-century coastal New England artwork and gifts like scrimshaw, Wedgwood china with lightship basket patterns, sailors' valentines, and hand-carved shorebirds. Reproduction furniture, too.

BOOKSTORES **Isaiah Thomas Books & Prints** (508-428-2752), 4632 Falmouth Road, at Routes 28 and 130, Cotuit. Open year-round (weekends January through March). Jim Visbeck offers a selection of more than 60,000 antiquarian, first-edition, and slightly used books, as well as books for children. They're divided by age group and interest. He also offers appraisals, search services, archival materials, and lectures on book collecting. This place is marvelous; you could easily spend an afternoon here. (Well, I have.)

SPECIAL SHOPS **West Barnstable Tables** (508-362-2676; www.west-barnstables.com), Route 149, West Barnstable. Open daily. This showroom features the work of a dozen master craftsmen and artists, including that of Dick Kiusalas. Since it's difficult (not to mention prohibitively expensive) to find antique tables anymore, Dick makes tables using 18th- and 19th-century wood scavenged from houses about to be demolished. His creations are exquisite and worth admiring even if you don't have a couple of thousand dollars to spare. Less expensive pieces include windowpane mirrors, primitive cupboards made with old painted wood and found objects, and Windsor and thumbback chairs. Furniture maker Stephen Whittlesey's whimsical, primitive folk art pieces are also noteworthy.

Tern Studio (508-362-6077), Route 149, West Barnstable. Wood turner Albert Barbour creates artful bowls and vases using local woods, including driftwood that washes ashore during hurricanes. His work is very organic. Call before visiting in the off-season, though.

Maps of Antiquity (508-362-7169; www.mapsofantiquity.com), 1022 Route 6A, West Barnstable. These folks carry rare antique and reproduction maps of the 19th century and earlier, from around the world. If you want to know what the Cape or a spe-

cific town looked like 100 years ago, this shop will have a reproduction map that will tell you. It's a treasure trove.

Margo's Practically Unusual (508-428-5664), 27 Wianno Avenue, Osterville. The name dictates the buying: "unusual" picture frames, serving pieces, hand-painted furniture and home accessories, handmade lamps with "unusual" finials, bed linens, jewelry, scarves, and sweaters.

✳ Special Events

Late April: **Osterville Village Daff-O'Ville Day** (talk to Gail at 508-428-6327). Hayrides, musical entertainment, some crafts, a dog show, and daffodil flower arrangements made by the garden club and gracing shop windows.

Mid-July: **Osterville Village Day** (talk to Gail at 508-428-6327). Always on the third Saturday in July, and held since 1976, this event includes a crafts and antiques fair, road race, children's events, and a parade.

✒ Late-July: **Barnstable County Fair** (508-563-3200), Route 151, East Falmouth. Local and national music acts, a midway, livestock shows (including horse, ox, and pony pulls), and horticulture, cooking, and crafts exhibits and contests. A popular weeklong tradition, especially for teens and families with young children. Over age 12, $8; otherwise free.

Mid-August: **Centerville Old Home Week.** Main Street open houses; until 1994 this event hadn't been held for 90 years.

Late September: **Osterville Village Fall Festival Day** (talk to Gail at 508-428-6327). Wine tasting, an arts and crafts show, entertainment, antiques show, dog show, and food. Always held on the Saturday before Columbus Day weekend.

Mid-December: **Osterville Christmas Open House and Stroll** (talk to Gail at 508-428-6327). Since 1972, the village has gussied itself up with traditional decorations. This is New England's second oldest stroll. Upwards of 2,000 to 3,000 participate in Friday-evening festivities, which include hayrides, trolley rides, wine tastings, and more. Bell ringers, too.

HYANNIS

Hyannis is the Cape's commercial and transportation hub: An astonishing 1 million people take the ferry from Hyannis to Nantucket every year. Most Cape visitors end up in Hyannis at some point, whether by choice or by necessity.

Among Cape visitors, Hyannis seems to be everyone's favorite whipping post: A sigh of sympathy is heard when someone mentions he "has" to go into Hyannis in July or August. Yes, traffic is gnarly and Route 28 is overbuilt, but those same Cape residents and off-Cape visitors who moan about congestion in Hyannis couldn't live as easily without its services, including many fine restaurants. They come to buy new cars, embark to the islands, visit doctors, shop at malls. Thus, because it is so distinct from the rest of Barnstable, I have given it its own chapter even though Hyannis is technically one of Barnstable's seven villages.

Hyannis's harborfront and Main Street were somewhat revitalized in the 1990s, thanks in part to the encouragement of the late Ben Thompson, architect of Boston's Quincy Market shopping complex and other successful urban waterfront development projects. Boating activity on Lewis Bay is active. Main Street is a study in contrasts: lined with benches and hanging flower baskets, in a an attempt to attract strollers, it also has lots of T-shirt shops, some vacant storefronts, and a growing crop of congregating youth and shops geared to them. (Hyannis is, after all, the closest thing to a "city" that the Cape has.) Look for a nice, spiffy link between Main Street and the waterfront, to be called Walkway to the Sea, that will cut through the own green. It was in the works at press time.

Hyannis has a bit of everything: discount outlets, upwards of 60 eating establishments in the waterfront district alone, some quiet cottages and guesthouses, plenty of motels geared to overnight visitors waiting for the morning ferry, harbor tours, and lots of lively bars and nightlife.

Then there's the Kennedy mystique. Hyannisport—a neighborhood within Hyannis but quite distinct from Hyannis—will forever be remembered as the place where, in the early 1960s, President John F. Kennedy and Jacqueline sailed offshore and played with Caroline and John. Visitors who come in search of the "Kennedy compound," or in hopes of somehow experiencing the Kennedy aura, will find only an inaccessible, residential, Yankee-style community of posh estates.

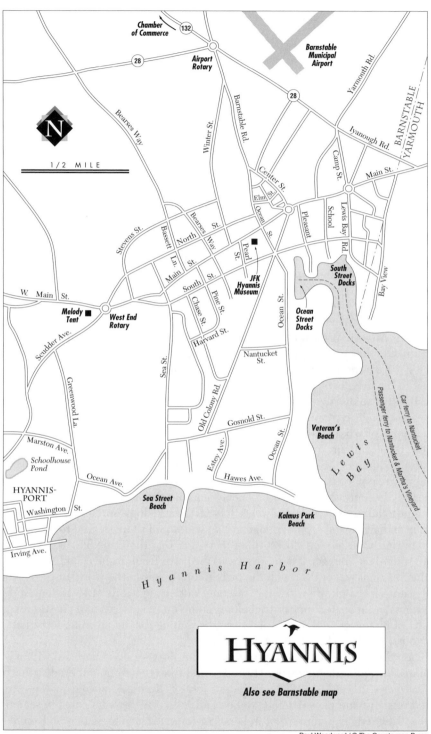

Chamber of Commerce

132

28

Airport Rotary

Barnstable Municipal Airport

Yarmouth Rd.

28

Bearses Way

Winter St.

Barnstable Rd.

Iyanough Rd.

BARNSTABLE
YARMOUTH

N

1/2 MILE

Center St.

Camp St.

Main St.

Elm

Ocean St.

Pleasant

Lewis Bay
School

Stevens St.

Bassett

Bearses Way

North St.

Main St.

Lewis Bay Rd.

Bay View

Bassett Ln.

Pearl St.

JFK
Hyannis
Museum

South
Street
Docks

W. Main St.

Melody
Tent

West End
Rotary

South St.

Pine St.

Ocean St.

Ocean
Street
Docks

Scudder Ave.

Chase St.

Harvard St.

Nantucket
St.

Sea St.

Greenwood La.

Old Colony Rd.

Gosnold St.

Veteran's
Beach

Passenger ferry to Nantucket & Martha's Vineyard

Car ferry to Nantucket

L e w i s   B a y

Marston Ave.

Schoolhouse
Pond

Estey Ave.

Ocean St.

HYANNIS-
PORT

Ocean Ave.

Hawes Ave.

Washington St.

Sea Street
Beach

Kalmus Park
Beach

Irving Ave.

H y a n n i s   H a r b o r

HYANNIS

Also see Barnstable map

Paul Woodward / © The Countryman Press

Hyannis's harbor area was inhabited about 1,000 years ago by ancestors of the Eastern Algonquian Indians, who set up summer campsites south of what is now Ocean Street. The first European to reach Cape Cod, Bartholomew Gosnold, anchored in the harbor in 1602. Shortly thereafter, settlers persuaded Native American sachem Yanno to sell them what is now known as Hyannis and Centerville for £20 and two pairs of pants.

Main Street was laid out in 1750, and by the early 1800s Hyannis was already known as the Cape's transportation hub. The harbor bustled with two- and three-masted schooners. When the steam-train line was extended from Barnstable in 1854, land-based trade and commerce supplanted the marine-based economy. Tourists began arriving in much greater numbers by the end of the century. Yachts filled the harbor by the 1930s, until John Kennedy (who tied up at the Hyannisport Yacht Club) renewed interest in traditional local sailboats, known as catboats, in the 1950s. More and more big boats return as the economy improves.

GUIDANCE ❋ **Hyannis Area Chamber of Commerce** (508-362-5230; 800-449-6647 for 24-hour information; www.hyannischamber.com), 1481 Route 132, Hyannis 02601. Open 9–4:30 or 5 Monday through Saturday year-round; open 10–2 Sunday, late May to early September. A mile south of Route 6, the chamber has information about all Barnstable villages. There is also a small visitors booth at the JFK Hyannis Museum on Main Street, staffed in summer only.

MEDIA The Cape's paper of record, the daily *Cape Cod Times* (508-775-1200), is published in Hyannis (319 Main Street).

PUBLIC REST ROOMS Public rest rooms are located at the beaches (see *Green Space—Beaches*), behind the JFK Hyannis Museum on Main Street, and at the Ocean Street Docks (Bismore Park).

PUBLIC LIBRARY ❋ ✐ ☂ **Hyannis Public Library** (508-775-2280), 401 Main Street. This charming little house has a much larger facility tacked onto the rear. It's open 11–5 weekdays (until 8 PM on Tuesday and Wednesday) from early June to mid-September. Off-season hours are 11–8 Tuesday and Wednesday, 11–5 Thursday through Saturday. Buy your paperbacks here to benefit the library.

GETTING THERE *By car:* To reach Hyannis, about 30 minutes from the Cape Cod Canal, take exit 6 off Route 6; follow Route 132 south to the airport rotary (at the junction of Routes 28 and 132). Take the second right off the rotary onto Barnstable Road, which intersects with Main, Ocean, and South Streets (for the harbor).

By bus: The **Plymouth & Brockton** bus line (508-778-9767; www.p-b.com) connects Hyannis with other Cape towns, as well as with Boston's Logan Airport. **Bonanza Bus** (508-775-6502; 800-751-8800; www.bonanzabus.com) connects Hyannis to Providence, T. F. Green Airport, and New York City. Both buses operate out of the new Hyannis Transportation Center (at Center and Main

Streets). In-season there are six daily trips to and from New York City. The trip takes about 6 hours, and coaches are equipped with movies.

By air: **Barnstable Municipal Airport** (508-775-2020), at the rotary junction of Route 28 and Route 132, Hyannis. Small carriers flying in and out of Hyannis include **Colgan Air** (which partners with US Airways; 888-265-4267), offering year-round service to New York's La Guardia Airport, Boston, and Providence. **Cape Air** and **Nantucket Air** (508-790-1980; 800-352-0714; www.flycapeair.com) have year-round service from Boston to Hyannis; Cape Air provides year-round service from Providence, too. Cape Air and Nantucket Air have grown considerably in recent years; they currently fly more than a quarter of a million people to the Cape and islands each year. Service is excellent.

GETTING AROUND *By car:* Hyannis suffers from serious summer traffic problems. Parking on Main Street is free if you can get a space. If not, try North Street, one block north of Main Street and parallel to it. Main Street (one way) is geared to strolling, but it's a long walk from end to end.

For **rentals,** call the big agencies based at the airport: **Hertz** (800-654-3131), **National** (800-227-7368), **Avis** (800-331-1212), **Budget** (800-527-0700), and **Thrifty** (508-771-0450; 800-367-2277). Or try **Trek** (508-771-2459)—near the bus terminal, but they'll pick you up from the airport.

By shuttle: The H$_2$O (508-385-8326; 800-352-7155; www.capecodtransit.org) bus line, used by more locals than visitors, travels along Route 28 between Hyannis

THE STEAMSHIP AUTHORITY FERRY FROM NANTUCKET DOCKS IN HYANNIS.

Kim Grant

and Orleans daily except Sunday year-round. In Hyannis it stops at the Hyannis Transportation Center.

Yarmouth Shuttle (508-385-8326; 800-352-7155; www.capecodtransit.org) operates late June to early September. Funded by a state grant, the shuttle begins at the Hyannis Transportation Center and runs along Route 28 to various family-oriented points (including beaches) in Yarmouth. Flag down the driver, who will pull over to pick you up. (It sure beats sitting in traffic.) Adults $1 one way; kids age 6–17, 50¢. One-day passes ($3) and tickets are purchased aboard the trolley or at the chamber of commerce (see *Guidance*).

The Breeze (508-385-8326; 800-352-7155; www.capecodtransit.org). Operating daily year-round, The Breeze operates two popular routes. The summertime shuttle (also called the Wave) makes a loop down Main Street to Sea Street, the beaches, and South Street. It operates daily, every half hour, from late June to early September. Fare $1.

The other route connects Hyannis to Barnstable, Mashpee, Falmouth, and Woods Hole. The fare depends on the distance traveled; children 5 and under ride free. Pick up a schedule at the chamber of commerce (see *Guidance*) or Hyannis Transportation Center for complete details.

The Villager (508-385-8326; 800-352-7155; www.capecodtransit.org) connects Barnstable's Route 6A (at the courthouse) with the malls in Hyannis on Route 132, the Hyannis Transportation Center, the West End Rotary, and Star Market. Schedules are available from the chamber of commerce (see *Guidance*). Purchase tickets on board. Fares: $1 over age 5.

GETTING TO THE ISLANDS From Hyannis, there is year-round auto and passenger service to Nantucket from Hyannis and seasonal passenger service to Martha's Vineyard. For complete information, see *Getting There* in "Martha's Vineyard" and "Nantucket." *Note:* You can also fly to the islands.

MEDICAL EMERGENCY Cape Cod Hospital (508-771-1800), 27 Park Street. Open 24/7.

✳ To See

⬆ **John F. Kennedy Hyannis Museum** (508-790-3077), 397 Main Street. Open 9–5 Monday through Saturday, noon–5 Sunday, mid-April through October (with slightly shorter hours November, December, and mid-February to mid-April). This museum opened in 1992 to meet the demands of visitors making the pilgrimage to Hyannis in search of JFK. People wanted to see "something," so the chamber gave them a museum that focuses on JFK's time in Hyannisport and on Cape Cod. The museum features more than 100 photographs of Kennedy from 1934 to 1963, arranged in themes: JFK's friends, his family, JFK the man. JFK said, "I always go to Hyannisport to be revived, to know the power of the sea and the master who rules over it and all of us." (If you want to learn something about the president and his administration, head to the JFK Museum in Boston.) Adults $5; children 11–16, $2.50.

JFK Memorial, Ocean Street. The fountain, behind a large presidential seal mounted on a high stone wall, is inscribed: I BELIEVE IT IS IMPORTANT THAT THIS COUNTRY SAIL AND NOT SIT STILL IN THE HARBOR. There is a nice view of Lewis Bay from here.

Kennedy compound. Joe and Rose Kennedy rented the Malcolm Cottage in Hyannisport from 1926 to 1929 before purchasing and remodeling it to include 14 rooms, nine baths, and a private movie theater in the basement. (It was the first private theater in New England.) By 1932 there were nine children scampering around the house and grounds, which included a private beach, dock, tennis court, and pool. In 1956, then Senator John Kennedy purchased an adjacent house (at the corner of Scudder and Irving Avenues), which came to be known as the Summer White House. Bobby bought the house next door, which now belongs to his widow, Ethel. Senator Edward Kennedy's former house (it now belongs to his ex-wife, Joan) is on private Squaw Island. Eunice (Kennedy) and Sargent Shriver purchased a nearby home on Atlantic Avenue.

It was at Malcolm Cottage that JFK learned he'd been elected president, at Malcolm Cottage that Jacqueline and the president mourned the loss of their infant son, at Malcolm Cottage that the family mourned the deaths of the president and Bobby Kennedy, at Malcolm Cottage that Senator Edward Kennedy would annually present his mother with a rose for each of her years, and at Malcolm Cottage that matriarch Rose Kennedy died in 1995 at the age of 104. Regardless of the fact that Kennedy sightings are rare, the Kennedys are still Hyannis's number one "attraction."

If you drive or walk around this stately area, you'll see nothing but high hedges and fences. Those who can't resist a look-see will be far better off taking a boat tour (see *Outdoor Activities—Boat Excursions/Rentals*); some boats come quite close to the shoreline and the white frame houses.

St. Francis Xavier Church, 347 South Street. When Rose Kennedy's clan was in town, they worshiped here. The pew used by JFK is marked with a plaque, while the altar is a memorial to JFK's brother, Lieutenant Joe Kennedy Jr., killed during World War II. More recently, Maria Shriver and Arnold Schwarzenegger were wed here.

❋ ✍ ⊤ **Cape Cod Potato Chip Factory** (508-775-7253; www.capecodchips.com), Breed's Hill Road, Independence Park, off Route 132. Open 9–5 weekdays year-round. After Chatham resident Steve Bernard began the company in 1980 and parlayed it into a multimillion-dollar business, he sold it to corporate giant Anheuser-Busch in 1986, and moved on to the business of purveying Chatham Village Croutons. But in late 1995, when Anheuser-Busch wanted to sell or close it, Bernard bought the company back, saving about 100 year-round jobs. Take the 15-minute self-guided tour of the potato-chip-making process, then sample the rich flavor and high crunchability resulting from all-natural ingredients cooked in small kettles. You, too, will be glad Bernard saved the company. Free.

✍ **Cape Cod Central Railroad** (508-771-3800; 888-797-7245; www.capetrain.com), Main and Center Streets. Narrated trips daily except Monday, July and August; weekends in May, June, September, and October. The 42-mile trip takes 2 hours and passes cranberry bogs and the Sandy Neck Great Salt Marsh. Since there are two trains daily, you take the first one, hop off in Sandwich, walk into the picturesque village (it's about a 10-minute walk), and then catch the next train back to Hyannis. Adults $15; children 3–11, $11.

Town green, adjacent to the JFK Hyannis Museum. Note the life-sized bronze of the sachem Iyanough, chief of the Mattakeese tribe of Cummaquid and friend to the Pilgrims, created in 1995 by Osterville sculptor David Lewis.

Weeping beech tree, in the courtyard behind Plush & Plunder (605 Main Street). To the town's knowledge, this is one of seven remaining weeping beeches in the entire country. (Another is in Yarmouth.) It's an awesome, magnificent 200-plus-year-old specimen.

SCENIC DRIVE Hyannisport is by far the loveliest section of Hyannis, but don't come expecting to see the Kennedys. The "compound" is wedged between Scudder and Irving Avenues. From Main Street, turn left onto Sea Street, right onto Ocean Avenue, left onto Hyannis Avenue, left onto Iyanough Avenue, right onto Wachusett Avenue, and left onto Scudder Avenue.

✳ Outdoor Activities

BASEBALL The Hyannis Mets play mid-June to early August at McKeon Field. (Take South Street to High School Road and turn right.)

BICYCLING/RENTALS ✳ **Cascade Motor Lodge** (508-775-9717), 201 Main Street. One block north of the harbor and 1½ blocks east of the bus and train stations, Cascade rents mountain and threespeed bikes daily April to mid-November (year-round, weather permitting).

BOAT EXCURSIONS/RENTALS Hyannisport Harbor Cruises (508-778-2600; www.hy-linecruises.com), Ocean Street Docks. Mid-April to late October. Lewis Bay and Hyannis Harbor are beautiful, and the best way to appreciate them is by water. Also, if you're like 85,000 other visitors each season and you want the best possible view of the Kennedy compound, take this hour-long Hy-Line excursion. The boat comes within 500 feet of the shoreline. Hy-Line also offers a special deal for families: From late June to early September, children ride free on early-morning and late-afternoon boats. During the height of summer, there are also two sunset trips; a Sunday-afternoon family cruise with Ben & Jerry's ice cream sundaes; Thursday-evening jazz cruise; Friday blues cruise; and Saturday-evening cocktail cruise. Adults $12–21; children 5–12, $6–15.

Cat Boat (508-775-0222; www.catboat.com), Ocean Street Docks. Mid-April to late November. Look for the big cat on the sail. *Eventide* has a full complement of trips; head down to the dock to see what they offer.

Cape Cod Duckmobiles (508-790-2111; 888-225-3825; www.capecodduckmobile.com), 437 Main Street. Mid-April through May, weekends; to mid-October daily. These amphibious tours last 45 minutes and go splashing around Hyannis

Harbor, then roll along the street, rather like a duck out of water. Adults $14; children over 5, $11.

FISHING/SHELLFISHING Freshwater fishing licenses are obtained from the town clerk's office (508-790-6240) in Town Hall, 367 Main Street, Hyannis. Shellfishing permits are required and may be obtained from the Department of Natural Resources (508-790-6272), 1189 Phinney's Lane (which runs between Routes 28 and 132), Centerville. You can also get freshwater fishing permits here.

❄ **Sports Port** (508-775-3096), 149 West Main Street. Surely you've seen the statue of a yellow guy in a red rowboat? That means the store is open—which it has been since Karen Hill unlocked the doors in 1958. References for charters and tours; supplies for freshwater, saltwater, and fly-fishing; ice fishing, too.

Hy-Line Fishing Trips (508-790-0696; www.hy-linecruisers.com), Ocean Street Docks. Bottom fishing and deep-sea fishing for fluke and blues from late April to late September. Half-day trips cost $23 adults, $18 children. Inquire about full-day trips and night trips.

❄ **The supercruiser *Helen-H*** (508-790-0660), Pleasant Street Docks, goes in search of big fish, too. You'll find cod all year long, bottom fish in the spring, and blues in summer.

FITNESS CLUB ❄ **Barnstable Athletic Club** (508-771-7734), 55 Attucks Way, Independence Park, off Route 132. Racquetball, basketball, squash, aerobics classes, fitness machines, tanning booths, and day care for $10 daily, $25 weekly. Fees permit access to pools at the Ramada Inn and Comfort Inn, too. Both are on Route 132.

❄ **GOLF** **Hyannis Golf Club** (508-362-2606), Route 132. An 18-hole, par-71 course.

Twin Brook Golf Course (508-775-7775), West End Circle. Sheraton's par-54 course is 18 holes and 2,621 yards.

ICE SKATING **Kennedy Memorial Skating Rink** (508-790-6346), Bearses Way. Public skating mid-October through March. Skate rentals $2.

MINI-GOLF **Storyland Miniature Golf** (508-778-4339), 70 Center Street. April to mid-October. Bumper boats and a 2-acre mini-golf course. Adults might take this opportunity to teach their kids a little about regional architecture and history, as some holes are modeled after local landmarks. Adults $7, children $6.

Carousel & Funhouse Arcade (508-790-0167), 541 Main Street, offers a break from walking around.

SPECIAL PROGRAMS **Eastern Mountain Sports (EMS)** (508-362-8690; www.ems.com), 1513 Iyanough Road (Route 132). In addition to renting kayaks (great for navigating herring rivers, creeks, and inlets), the Cape's largest purveyor of outdoor gear offers free instructional clinics every couple of weeks throughout the year. Topics range from outdoor cooking to mastering compass skills. Check the bulletin board for a schedule.

TENNIS Public courts are located at **Barnstable High School** on Route 28 and at **Barnstable Middle School** on West Bay Road.

✳ Green Space

BEACHES Weekly cottage renters can purchase beach stickers at the Kennedy Memorial Skating Rink (508-790-6346), Bearses Way.

Kalmus Park Beach, on Nantucket Sound, at the end of Ocean Street. This beach is good for sailboarding. The land, by the way, was donated by Technicolor inventor Herbert Kalmus, who also owned the Fernbrook estate in Centerville. Facilities include a rest room, snack bar, and bathhouse. Parking $10.

⟡ **Veteran's Beach,** on Hyannis Harbor (Lewis Bay), off Ocean Street. This is a good beach for children because the waters are fairly shallow and calm, and it's a good place to watch harbor sailboats (the Hyannis Yacht Club is next door). Facilities include a rest room, bathhouse, snack bar, swings, grills, and a big wooded area with picnic tables. Parking $10.

Sea Street Beach, on Nantucket Sound, off Sea Street. Facilities include a rest room and bathhouse. Parking $10.

✳ Lodging

✾ Hyannis has hordes of nondescript motels, a small but good selection of B&Bs, and many good family-oriented cottages. All properties are located in Hyannis unless otherwise noted. The zip code for Hyannis is 02601. Unless otherwise noted, they're all open year-round.

⟡ RESORT MOTOR INNS ♿ **Cape Codder Resort & Spa** (508-771-3000; 888-297-2200; www.capecodderresort.com), Route 132 at Bearses Way. About 3 miles from the center of town, this two-story destination property was recently purchased and upgraded by the Catania family, who poured about $7 million into it. (The Catanias have long owned the venerable Dan'l Webster Inn in Sandwich and the Cape-wide, family-style Hearth & Kettle restaurants.) Now the ultra-family-friendly resort has

260 rooms, an indoor Cape Cod theme pool (complete with 2½-foot waves and water slides), a full-service spa, two restaurants, a wine bar, fitness center, game room, tennis court, and volleyball court. Mid-May to mid-October $159–229; off-season $99–159; children under age 17 free; inquire about packages.

Sheraton Hyannis Resort (508-775-7775; 800-325-3535, West End Circle. These 224 standard-issue rooms, equipped with a king bed or two doubles and cable TV, are pleasant enough. The bilevel motel has plenty of facilities, including a large indoor pool overlooking an 18-hole golf course, heated outdoor pool, tennis courts, health club, massage and treatments at the spa, a bar, and a dining room. Ask for a garden- or golf-course-view room. Late June through August $169–209; spring and fall $109–159; winter $79–99; kids under age 17 free. Rates seem to fluctuate hour to hour, based on tourist traffic.

BED & BREAKFASTS 🍴 **Inn on Sea Street** (508-775-8030; www.innon-seastreet.com), 358 Sea Street. Open May through October. Innkeepers Sylvia and Fred LaSelva rent nine pristine and lovely rooms, most with private bath, air-conditioning, and TV. Some are furnished with Victorian antiques, including the Garden Room, which has a private entrance. The most popular rooms, completely refurbished and decorated with English country antiques and canopy beds, are across the street. One has a particularly large bathroom; another has a private porch. The inn also boasts one of the sweetest places to stay on the Cape—a small but airy, all-white cottage with peaked ceiling, kitchen, separate bedroom, and sitting room. Other pluses: There's plenty of common space; it's located a 2-minute walk from the beach; and the inn never has a minimum-night stay. Breakfasts are rich—crab scramble, cream cheese coffee cake, and buttery

oatmeal bread on lacy-clothed tables set with china. $150 cottage, $85–125 rooms. Inquire about golf packages.

Sea Breeze Inn (508-771-7213; www.seabreezeinn.com), 270 Ocean Avenue. These 14 rooms (some with two beds) are within a stone's throw of the beach. Although the old-fashioned rooms aren't fancy or filled with antiques, they are certainly comfortable, clean, and pleasant. Expanded continental breakfast included. Mid-June to mid-September $80–120; off-season $60–95.

🐚 **Memories by the Sea** (508-775-9300; 877-737-9300; www.memories-bythesea.com), 162 Sea Street. For families weary of motels and cottages, hosts Debbie and Eric Hubler offer three fine guest rooms in their 1880s house. Each room has a cable TV, sitting area, air-conditioning, and a fireplace; VCRs are available. The inn is half a mile from the beach, with a convenience store in between them for picnic lunches and drinks. Since the Hublers can supply beach chairs and towels, you'll be all set for a

FENCING AND DEEP ROOTS KEEP SANDS FROM RETREATING.

Kim Grant

beach vacation. Afterward, relax on the front porch with a drink or in the spacious living room. Expanded continental breakfast included. May through September $120; off-season $90; each additional person $15; inquire about various packages.

🐾 🌿 **Simmons Homestead Inn** (508-778-4999; 800-637-1649; www.simmonshomesteadinn.com), 288 Scudder Avenue. Innkeeper Bill Putman relishes his quirkiness and has furnished this 1820s sea captain's home to reflect his offbeat tastes. The basics: There are two suites and 12 antiques-appointed guest rooms, some with fireplace and canopy bed; outdoor space includes porch rockers, well-placed hammocks, and a hot tub. The idiosyncrasies: It's been taken over by carved, painted animals; the living room is chock-full of bric-a-brac; hoods from Bill's old racing cars guard the hallway. (Bill has a mini-museum with over 50 cars.) The adjacent annex, with family-appropriate accommodations, has its own living room and billiards room. You might indulge in wintertime single-malt Scotch tastings from Bill's collection. Full breakfast included. May through October $220–260 rooms, $350 suites; off-season $120–160 rooms, $200 suites; $10–20 per additional child, depending on age. Non-smokers take note: Bill smokes, as do many guests.

🌿 COTTAGES AND EFFICIENCIES

🐾 **Harbor Village** (508-775-7581; www.harborvillage.com), 160 Marstons Avenue, Hyannisport 02647. Open April through October. Delightfully off the beaten path but still centrally located, Tim Fuller's one- to four-bedroom cottages can sleep 3 to 12 people. Each of the 14 cottages has a living room, dining area, fully equipped kitchen, individual heat, a fireplace, deck or patio with grill, cable TV, and VCR. You'll need to bring your own beach towels and chairs, though. On a private, wooded, 17-acre compound, Harbor Village is within a 2-minute walk of Quahog Beach. Late June to early September from $1,450 weekly for a two-bedroom, $1,600 for a three-bedroom. Cottages have a 3-night minimum off-season: from $125 for a two-bedroom, $135 for a three-bedroom. Service charge of $30 weekly added; no credit cards; pets with prior approval (for an additional fee).

🐾 **The Breakwaters** (508-775-6831), Sea Street Beach. Open May to mid-October. Within a sandal shuffle of Sea Street Beach, these 18 well-maintained cottages accommodate two to six people. Kitchens are small but complete and updated. All cottages have a private deck or patio; some have ocean views. Even though it's on the beach, Breakwaters also has a heated pool with a lifeguard; swimming lessons are sometimes offered. Late June through August $975–1,050 weekly for a one-bedroom, $1,525 for a two-bedroom, $2,100 for a three-bedroom; off-season $560–725, $900, and $1,200, respectively; spring and fall $68–160 daily, depending on unit size. No credit cards.

Capt. Gosnold Village (508-775-9111; www.captaingosnold.com), 230 Gosnold Street. In a residential area near the harbor, the family-friendly Gosnold's is a short walk to the beach. And children will enjoy the wooded and grassy grounds with a fenced-in pool and lifeguard, lawn games, and a play area. Although some motel rooms are a tad dull, most of the 31 knotty-pine-paneled cottages are spacious and have a private deck and gas grills. Request a newer cottage with three bedrooms, and you'll also get three bathrooms and three TVs. While you can expect daily maid service and fully equipped kitchens, you'll have to bring your own beach towels. Mid-June to early September $90 rooms, $105 studios, $170 one-bedroom cottages, $240–280 two- and three-bedroom cottages; off-season $55 rooms, $65 studios, $100 one-bedroom cottages, $140–160 two- and three-bedroom cottages. Three-night minimum in cottages, 2 nights for other lodging. Gosnold's adds a $6–12 nightly gratuity.

See also Inn on Sea Street under *Bed & Breakfasts.*

TOWN HOUSES ♂ **The Yachtsman** (508-771-5454; 800-695-5454; www.yachtsman.com), rental office at 500 Ocean Street, Apt. 14. These privately owned townhouse condominiums, with their own private stretch of beach between Kalmus and Veteran's Beaches (see *Green Space*), are right on Lewis Bay. During the summer, about 50 of the 125 units are available for rent. Although the decor varies from one unit to another, all meet certain standards. Multilevel units have a full kitchen, 2½ baths, private sundeck, sunken living room, and two to four bedrooms. About half have water views; half overlook the heated pool. Late June to early September $1,500–2,800 weekly; about 25–40 percent less off-season.

MOTOR INN See Tidewater under *Lodging—Motor Inns* in "Yarmouth."

❋ Where to Eat

❋ With more than 60 eateries, Hyannis offers everything from fine Continental to Tex-Mex. Reservations are recommended at all the establishments under *Dining Out.* Unless otherwise noted, all restaurants are open year-round.

DINING OUT ♀ **Naked Oyster** (508-778-6500), 20 Independence Drive, off Route 132. Open for lunch and dinner. My favorite area eatery, this cosmopolitan and sophisticated bistro is thankfully (slightly) off the beaten path. Its seafood menu is exciting to the palate and complemented by a wonderful selection of wines by the glass. In addition to enjoying the excellent raw bar, try appetizers like Thai shrimp, tuna sashimi, Caesar salads, lobster salad, and the oyster sampler plate. Dishes like halibut with lobster meat, swordfish chops, and filet mignon take center stage at night. On a recent visit, I was tipped off to their silk chocolate martini (it's a hip bar) and crème brûlée (arguably the best on the Cape) by Kristian, our excellent waiter. Reservations recommended. Lunch $8–14, dinner entrées $14–30.

♀ **RooBar City Bistro** (508-778-6515), 586 Main Street. Open for dinner. This is one happening place, especially when the bar crowd reappears. Along with an exposed kitchen, high ceilings, and steel-based art (does a car grille hanging on the wall constitute art?), the innovative bistro offers internationally influenced New American fusion. Think along the lines of Wellfleet oysters, grilled swordfish with roasted corn and cilantro salsa, and fire-roasted chicken rubbed with toasted fennel and cumin seed marinade. Check it out. Fancy and fabulous brick-oven pizzas ($10), too. Entrées range from $14 for vegetarian rigatoni to $20 for steak *au poivre* with herbed mashed potatoes and a nice brandy sauce. Reservations needed Thursday through Saturday.

Penguins SeaGrill & Steakhouse (508-775-2023), 331 Main Street. Open for dinner February through December. Penguins serves the best seafood in town. The menu (and a winning execution) sails the globe, from French to Italian to Asian; from char-grilled aged steaks and chops (a specialty) to Szechuan salmon (excellent); from tuna tartare to a seafood hot pot feast. There are usually half a dozen daily fish specials, while pastas and risottos make regular menu appearances. Kudos to chef-owners Bobby and Portia Gold, who've been at the helm since 1980. Oh, two last things: The wine list is lengthy and well chosen, and save room for flourless chocolate cake at dessert. The large dining room manages to be subdued and family-friendly. Early specials; reservations highly recommended. Entrées $18–22.

Sweetwater's Grille & Bar (508-775-3323), 644 Main Street. Open daily for lunch and dinner. Sure as coyotes howl and adobe is made of mud and straw, southwestern cuisine has come to Hyannis. Although the menu has its share of sizzling fajitas and burritos, the kitchen is really much more creative than that. Nightly specials are always a good bet, as are the Thai-, Caribbean-, and Cuban-influenced dishes. I would order every dish from my last visit again: vegetarian ravioli, Baja-grilled shrimp, and "seafood salina." A screened-in porch opens for summer dining. There are always lots of families here

in the early evening. Reservations requested. Sunday brunch $9–11, lunch $7–10, dinner entrées $10–20.

Fazio's Trattoria (508-775-9400), 294 Main Street. Open for dinner. Chef-owners Tom and Eileen Fazio hail from San Francisco's Italian North Beach neighborhood. And while Hyannis is not North Beach, you'd never know it inside this trattoria. The mod storefront bistro space has high ceilings, pale yellow walls, and exposed air ducts. The menu features excellent homemade pasta dishes (like *fettuccine rosmarino con pollo*) and a few chicken and veal specialties. Thin-crust, brick-oven pizzas and homemade bread have no equal. On my last visit, service was a tad slow and off. Dinner $11–17.

Alberto's Ristorante (508-778-1770), 360 Main Street. Open for dinner daily, lunch on Sunday. Catering to a loyal following since 1984, chef-owners Felis and Donna Barreiro's popular restaurant is elegant and romantic, all done up in pink and off-white. While it may look formal, the service is professional but not stuffy at all. The extensive menu features large portions of homemade pasta and northern Italian specialties. Look for eggplant parmigiana, lobster diavolo, seafood ravioli, and veal Sienese, a mushroom lover's delight. Alberto's, deserving of their fine reputation, does an excellent job. Top off your meal with a rich cappuccino. Early-dinner specials 4–5:45; reservations recommended. Entrées $13–26.

Roadhouse Cafe (508-775-2386), 488 South Street. Open for dinner nightly. This pleasant place—with polished floors, Oriental carpets, hanging plants, tongue-and-groove ceilings with paddle fans, candlelight, and two fireplaces—is also very dependable, thanks to the long tenure of owners Dave and Melissa Colombo and chef Tim Souza. Come for a romantic interlude or with a group for some fun. The extensive Italian and seafood menu features large portions. Consider splitting an entrée and pairing it with a couple of appetizers. Creative, thin-crust pizzas are offered in the **Back Door Bistro** (see *Entertainment—Nightlife*), which has a clubby feel with dark paneling and a mahogany bar. It also has a large selection of wine by the glass and 40 brands of beer. Early specials from 4 to 6 PM. Reservations suggested. Entrées $16–26.

The Paddock (508-775-7677), West End rotary. Open for lunch and dinner April to mid-November. If you're in the mood for traditional seafood and Continental cuisine, the main dining room's Victorian airs provide the requisite backdrop. It sports dark beams, upholstered armchairs, frosted glass, linen-covered tables, and fresh-cut flowers. For lunch, stick to salads, chowder, and sandwiches. For dinner, try the spicy peppercorn steak, pistachio-encrusted halibut, roast rack of lamb, or maple-glazed pork tenderloin. When there's an event at the Melody Tent, stay away until after 9 PM. The Zartarian family has operated this institution since 1970, and John Anderson has been the chef since 1973. The wine list is excellent; early specials 30 percent off. Lunch $7–11, dinner entrées $17–28.

EATING OUT *Baxter's Boat House Club and Fish 'n Chips* (508-775-4490), 177 Pleasant Street. Open for lunch and dinner, mid-April to mid-October. It's as much about location as it is food here, and even though they serve they same menu throughout the day, I prefer going at lunchtime. Built on an old fish-packing dock near the Steamship Authority terminal, Baxter's has attracted a crowd since 1956, from beautiful people tying up at the dock to singles meeting at the bar, from families to folks who just purchase a soda and go through the side door to a harborfront picnic table. It's really the best waterfront table in town. The fried and broiled seafood is consistent, too, if not exemplary. Dishes $10–17.

Chef Sigmund's (508-775-7125), 561 Main Street. This low-key seafood take-out place (with popular summertime patio seating) provides value for the bucks. Dishes $5–10.

Brazilian Grille (508-771-0109), 680 Main Street. Open for lunch and dinner. You'd have to fly to Rio for more authentic *churrascaria rodizio,* a traditional, elaborate all-you-can-eat barbecue buffet of skewered meats. Buffet $16.

Back Yard Buffet (508-775-0251), 572 Main Street. Open for lunch and dinner. Originally opened to serve a local Brazilian population active in the service sector, this small spot offers a hearty alternative to American seafood. Buffet, featuring lots of meat and beans, sold by the pound.

Tugboats (508-775-6433), 21 Arlington Street, behind the hospital off Willow Street. Open for lunch and dinner mid-April to mid-October. This casual place overlooking the harbor—with an outdoor deck—has lots of food, especially fried seafood, but beyond that, the salmon is very good and the lobster specials are reasonably priced. Dishes $6–26.

Perry's (508-775-9711), 546 Main Street. Open for 5 AM–3 PM. This-well priced diner opens very early in the morning to feed local fishermen. Try their outstanding honey oatmeal bread. Philadelphia residents and longtime Explorers Neil and Sandy Scheinin highly recommend it—and I'm not going to argue, since we agree on almost everything.

✓ **Ying's Sushi Bar** (508-790-2432), 59 Center Street. Open for lunch and dinner. Ying's boasts very good pad Thai, Japanese and Korean dishes, noodles, and sushi. The atmosphere here is tranquil, rather like an indoor garden, and all dishes are available for take-out. Lunch specials $7–9, dinner $10–16.

Ying's sister restaurant, **Blue Anchor Cafe and Sushi** (508-771-9464), 453 Main Street), open for dinner only, serves sushi and some Asian dishes (like tasty sweet-and-sour duck), but they have more lobster, steaks, and traditional seafood dishes (like very good Portuguese-style scrod). They're working hard to bring in nightly entertainment (jazz, reggae, and Latin). Entrées $11–19.

🍴 **La Petite France** (508-771-4445), 349 Main Street. Open daily (except Sunday off-season) April through December. This informal café serves fresh salads, sandwiches, and soups. Chef-owner Lucien (Lu) Degioanni hails from the south of France, so many homemade offerings are distinctly French—like the onion soup and cold tomato, feta, and basil salad. Baguettes and pastries are baked daily. In a nod to his current home, Lu also makes great clam chowder and roasts his own beef, turkey, and ham for sandwiches. As might be expected, the café also serves a

respectable cup of coffee. There are half a dozen tables; otherwise, take a picnic to the park. Dishes $4–6.

🍴 **Common Ground Cafe** (508-778-8390), 420 Main Street. Open for lunch and dinner Monday through Thursday and 10–3 Friday. When you step inside, let your eyes adjust to the darkness for a minute: You'll find hand-hewn booths resembling hobbit houses and an old-fashioned community (a religious collective actually) of folks serving honest food. The menu includes a few wholesome sandwiches, salads, and "south-of-the-border" dishes like burritos. Everything is made from scratch. Note that the restaurant is closed on weekends, when members prefer to spend time with their families rather than pursue the almighty buck. There's also a juice bar upstairs. Dishes $5–10.

Black Cat (508-778-1233), 165 Ocean Street. Open for lunch and dinner year-round except January to mid-February. Noisy and pubby, the Black Cat offers an upscale American menu with an emphasis on seafood. And while it's not a fry joint, they happen to serve the best fried scallops and clams in town. Dine alfresco surrounded by a white picket fence and flowering baskets (across the street from the harbor) or indoors. Lunch $7–15; dinner entrées average $19.

✓ **Sam Diego's** (508-771-8816), 950 Iyanough Road. Open 11:30 AM–1 AM; dinner (and take-out) until midnight. Decorated with little white lights, colorful serapes, toucans, and sombreros, this huge and hopping place is often full of families. They come for reliable southwestern- and Mexican-inspired fare like chicken fajitas, barbecued ribs, burritos, and enchiladas. In warm weather, there is a large outdoor patio for dining. For weekday lunches (year-round), try the all-you-can eat chili, soup, and taco bar for a mere $6.25 ($3 for kids 8 and under). Dishes $5–13.

Υ ✎ **Starbuck's** (508-778-6767), Route 132. Open 11:30 AM–1 AM daily. Part bar, part family restaurant, part roomy barn with bric-a-brac (and no relation to the ubiquitous coffee chain), Starbuck's opened in 1985 with a diverse menu: pastas, Tex-Mex, Thai hot-peppered shrimp, burgers, and chicken sandwiches. Many people come just for the frozen drinks and 20-ounce cocktails, though. Live entertainment in the bar (nightly except Monday). Dishes $7–20.

Υ **Harry's** (508-778-4188), 700 Main Street. Open for lunch and dinner daily. This small, local bar/hangout features Cajun dishes, BBQ, seafood (including popular stuffed quahogs), and homemade soups. Lunch leans heavily toward New Orleans with "hoppin' John" (rice with black-eyed peas), jambalaya, and blackened chicken. The joint jumps with live blues and jazz nightly. Lunch $5–8, dinner $9–20.

🦞 ✎ ♿ **The Egg & I** (508-771-1596), 521 Main Street. Open 6–1 for breakfast March through November, weekends year-round. This charming half-timber house is not your run-of-the-mill breakfast joint. It's a Hyannis institution, dishing up crabcakes, fancy pancakes, waffles, and French toast creations along with corned beef hash, since 1971. Dishes $4–10.

COFFEE Spiritus (508-775-2955), 500 Main Street. Open daily. If you can make your way past the loitering

teens and Gen-Xers, you'll be rewarded with strong coffee; hot slices of pizza decked with broccoli, eggplant, and sun-dried tomatoes; tasty focaccia sandwiches; and buttery ice cream. After 10 PM the congregation of kids out front swells to a "wild" level for Cape Cod.

Caffe e Dolci (508-790-6900), 430 Main Street. Open for pastries and sandwiches until 11 in summer, until about 5 the rest of the year. All you 40-somethings who aren't interested in the vibe at Spiritus or The Prodigal Son have an alternative. Strong espresso and flavored coffee drinks share the stage with focaccia sandwiches and pastries. There's some indoor seating.

The Prodigal Son (508-771-1337), 10 Ocean Street. Open 9:30 AM–6 (or midnight, depending on the day) daily except Tuesday. This coffeehouse and bar, decorated with offbeat art and popular with a 20-something crowd, features microbrews, wine by the glass, espresso drinks, and specialty sandwiches. There's a full calendar of live entertainment scheduled: acoustic folk, blues, jazz, open-mike nights on Wednesday. Dishes $6–8.

See also La Petite France under *Eating Out*.

ICE CREAM The contest is basically local versus regional: **Maggie's Ice Cream** (508-778-8118), 570 Main Street; **Ben & Jerry's** (508-790-0910), 352 Main Street; and **Emack & Bolio's** (508-775-2955), within Spiritus, 500 Main Street (open year-round).

DINNER TRAIN ✎ **Cape Cod Dinner Train** (508-771-3800; 888-797-7245; www.capetrain.com), 252 Main

Street. June through January. Most Thursday, Friday, and Saturday evenings and Sunday afternoons from May to October; Saturday evenings and Sunday afternoons in November and December. These vintage-1920s cars run at "soup speed" for a 3-hour trip to the canal and back. The train gets good reviews from diners, who appreciate that the food is cooked on board, and who enjoy fancy white linens, candlelight, crystal, and china. Tables are set for four, so if you want dine alone as a couple when it's crowded, you'll have to purchase an additional ticket. Here's another tip: If you care about seeing scenery during the latter part of the trip, schedule a train ride in summer, when the days are longer. $57 per person; alcohol and tipping additional. For the summertime family supper train, linens and china are replaced by high chairs and paper plates. Reservations required.

✴ Entertainment

MUSIC ♪ **Cape Symphony Orchestra** (508-362-1111; www.capesymphony.org). September through May. The orchestra performs about 15 concerts for children and adults at the 1,400-seat Barnstable Performing Arts Center, at Barnstable High School, West Main Street in Hyannis.

🍸 🌴 ✴ MOVIES **Hoyts Cinema Center** (508-771-7460), Routes 132 and 28, at the Cape Cod Mall. The Cape's only stadium-seating megacomplex, with 12 screens.

🍸 ✴ NIGHTLIFE **The Beechtree Bar** (508-771-3272), 599 Main Street. Open seasonally. Come for outdoor cocktails under a magnificent weeping beech tree.

Back Door Bistro at the Roadhouse Cafe (508-775-2386), 488 South Street. Jazz on Monday night year-round, jazz by Lou Colombo nightly in summer, and piano on Friday and Saturday off-season.

Hyport Brewing Company (508-775-8289), 720 Main Street. If you consider a sampler rack of beer to be "entertainment," this is the place for you. Unfortunately, the food isn't as entertaining. Nightly entertainment in-season.

See also Naked Oyster and RooBar City Bistro under *Dining Out;* Blue Anchor Cafe and Sushi, Starbuck's, and Harry's under *Eating Out;* and the Prodigal Son under *Coffee.*

STAR STRUCK
Cape Cod Melody Tent (508-775-5630; www.melodytent.com), West Main Street. Shows June through September. When this big white tent was erected in 1950, entertainment was limited to Broadway musicals. Today it's the Cape's biggest and best venue for top-name comics and musicians. Look for the likes of Shawn Colvin, Natalie Merchant, Tony Bennett, Julio Iglesias, Lyle Lovett, Bill Cosby, and Kenny Rogers. It's only "big" by Cape standards; you'll be surprised at how close you are to your favorite stars here. There are **children's shows** ($6) Wednesday morning in July and August. Profits are poured into arts programs and education on the Cape and Boston's South Shore.

✹ Selective Shopping

❋ Unless otherwise noted, all shops are open year-round.

ART GALLERY AND CRAFTS Spectrum (508-771-4554; www.spectrum-america.com), 342 Main Street. Textiles, jewelry, lamps, glass objects, wooden boxes and business-card holders, musical instruments, and ceramics—all creatively handcrafted by contemporary American artists.

Artistic Appetites (508-771-4084), 645 Main Street. Part of the attraction at this beautiful art gallery is Gregory, the friendly owner, who enjoys both his work and visitors. He shows some realistic work, some impressionistic oils on paper, some dry-point etchings.

Red Fish Blue Fish (508-775-8700), 374 Main Street. The most fun and whimsical "gallery" in town carries unusual gifts and crafts. When it's not too busy, you can watch owner Jane Walsh making hand-blown jewelry in the store. When the shop is closed, a video runs in the front window.

Guyer Barn Gallery (508-790-6370), 250 South Street. Weekly shows are hung from mid-June through October; Sunday openings. The Barnstable Arts and Humanities Council established this art gallery in 1986.

BOOKSTORES Barnes & Noble (508-862-6310; www.bn.com), Route 132, north of the airport rotary. Although there are a few independent new- and used-book stores on Main Street, if you want a particular book, it's probably here.

Borders (508-862-6363; www.borders.com), Route 132, north of the airport rotary. The superstore with a café.

Rodney's Bookstore (508-790-3448), 580 Main Street, is just one of a few bookstores on Main Street. Rodney's deals in used hardcovers and nonfiction; I've always found the staff very helpful.

CLOTHING Plush & Plunder (508-775-4467; www.plushandplunder.com), 605 Main Street. Vintage and eccentric used clothing adorns those marching to an offbeat drummer, including fabled customers like Cyndi Lauper, Joan Baez, and Demi Moore. You don't have to be an entertainer to stop here, although you'll end up entertained and entertaining (if you purchase something). Thousands of hats hang from the rafters like bats in the Carlsbad Caverns. Need gold lamé, a boa, or other retro accessories? Don't miss this great place.

Europa (508-790-0877), 37 Barnstable Road at North Street. Fine and fun clothing, in a full range of sizes, made of natural fibers from around the world…plus a really great selection of accessories, including sterling jewelry and scarves.

FACTORY OUTLETS Christmas Tree Shops (508-778-5521), between Route 28 and Route 132, next to the Cape Cod Mall. Of the seven Christmas Tree Shops on the Cape, this Victorian-style one is the largest.

Dansk Factory Outlet (508-775-3118), Route 132, across from the Cape Cod Mall. Contemporary designs for the kitchen and table.

MALL ✍ Cape Cod Mall (508-771-0200; www.shopsimon.com), Routes 132 and 28. Open daily. The Cape's only "real" mall—as distinguished from a plethora of strip malls—has been updated and expanded. Anchored by big retailers and supplemented by more than 100 other stores, it has a huge food court and ultramodern movie theater. To keep kids occupied, there is an arcade and Venetian carousel, too.

SPECIAL SHOPS Cellar Leather (508-771-5458), 592 Main Street. Quality coats, vests, shoes, clogs, sandals, briefcases, hats, and wallets—if you have any money left over.

Play It Again Sports (508-771-6979), 25 Route 28. Whether it's new or used equipment you're after, this shop has it all.

All Cape Cook's Supply (508-790-8908), 237 Main Street. Useful gadgets for pros and amateurs.

Kandy Korner Gifts (508-771-5313), 474 Main Street. Closed January. Watch the saltwater taffy and fudge being made in the front windows before heading in to indulge your sweet tooth.

✳ Special Events

May: **Annual Figawi Sailboat Race Weekend.** The largest sailboat race in New England goes from Hyannis to Nantucket.

Late July: **Regatta.** At the Hyannis Yacht Club since the early 1940s.

Early August: **Pops by the Sea.** Boston Pops Esplanade Orchestra on the town green. In the past, guest conductors have included Mike Wallace, Julia Child, Olympia Dukakis, and Walter Cronkite. Reserved-seating and general-admission tickets.

Early December: **Harbor Lighting.** Parade of boats includes the arrival of Santa; entertainment with a holiday theme.

YARMOUTH

Yarmouth, like neighboring Dennis, stretches from Cape Cod Bay to Nantucket Sound; it unfolds along quiet Route 6A and congested Route 28. It's a family-oriented town, with many golf courses, tennis courts, and town-sponsored sailing lessons, as well as quite a few southside oceanfront resorts. There are almost 4,000 beds to rent in Yarmouth.

Although Yarmouth's 5.3-mile section of Route 28 was planted with more than 350 trees in 1989 (on its 350th birthday), the road is still a wall-to-wall sea of mini-golf courses, shops, fast-food places, and family-style attractions like a combination zoo-aquarium, a billiards emporium, and boating on the Bass River. A larger-than-life plastic polar bear, lunging shark, and elephant epitomize the Cape's kitschier side. They're alternately viewed as icons and eyesores.

It's difficult to imagine that Route 28 was once open land dotted with small farms and that Yarmouth's ports bustled in the 19th century: Packets sailed to New York and Newark from South Yarmouth at Bass River. Today the scenic Bass River and South Yarmouth Historic District provide a delightful detour south of Route 28.

On the northside, Route 6A was settled in the 1600s, was traveled by stagecoaches in the 1700s, and reached its height of prosperity in the 1800s, when it was lined with houses built for and by rope makers, sea captains, bankers, and shipbuilders. At one time, a mile-long section of Yarmouthport was referred to as Captain's Row, as it was home to almost 50 sea captains. Many former sea captains' houses are now attractive B&Bs.

Stephen Hopkins, a *Mayflower* passenger, built the first house in Yarmouth in 1638 (off Mill Lane) and the town was incorporated just one year later. Today Yarmouth is the third most populous town on the Cape, with 25,000 year-round residents. Meander along tranquil Route 6A and you'll find crafts and antiques shops, a former apothecary with a working soda fountain, a quiet village green, a couple of fine historic houses open to the public, walking trails, and an antiquarian bookstore. Take any lane off Route 6A to the north, and you'll find picturesque residential areas.

GUIDANCE ✤ **Yarmouth Area Chamber of Commerce** (508-778-1008; 800-732-1008; www.yarmouthcapecod.com), 424 Route 28, West Yarmouth 02673.

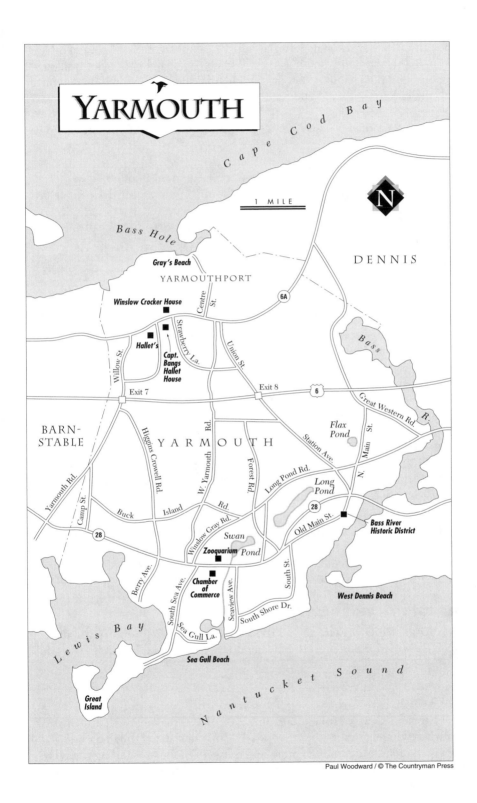

YARMOUTH

Cape Cod Bay

1 MILE

N

Bass Hole

DENNIS

Gray's Beach

YARMOUTHPORT

Winslow Crocker House

Centre St.

6A

Hallet's

Strawberry La.

Union St.

Bass

Capt. Bangs Hallet House

Willow St.

Exit 7

Exit 8

6

Great Western Rd.

R.

BARN-STABLE

Higgins Crowell Rd.

YARMOUTH

W. Yarmouth Rd.

Flax Pond

N. Main St.

Station Ave.

Yarmouth Rd.

Camp St.

Buck Island Rd.

Forest Rd.

Long Pond Rd.

Long Pond

28

Old Main St.

Bass River Historic District

28

Berry Ave.

Winslow Gray Rd.

Swan Pond

Zooquarium

South Sea Ave.

Chamber of Commerce

Seaview Ave.

South St.

South Shore Dr.

West Dennis Beach

Lewis Bay

Sea Gull La.

Sea Gull Beach

Nantucket Sound

Great Island

Open 9–5 Monday through Saturday and 10–3 Sunday, early May to mid-October; 9–5 weekdays mid-October to early May. The chamber booklet is filled with coupons, and the chamber staff are very helpful. Pick up two self-guided historical tours of Yarmouth and Old South Yarmouth here.

MEDIA Pick up the weekly paper, *The Register* (508-375-4900), to catch up on local happenings.

PUBLIC REST ROOMS Public rest rooms are located on Route 6 between exits 6 and 7, and at Gray's Beach (open seasonally, off Centre Street from Route 6A).

PUBLIC LIBRARIES ❋ ✐ ☂ With such variable hours, it's best to call ahead:
South Yarmouth Library (508-760-4820), 312 Old Main Street.
West Yarmouth Library (508-775-5206), 391 Route 28.
Yarmouthport Library (508-362-3717), 297 Route 6A.

GETTING THERE *By car:* Yarmouth is 26 miles from Cape Cod Canal; take Route 6 to exit 7 for the northside (Yarmouthport and points along Route 6A). For points along Route 28 on the southside, take exit 7 south to Higgins Crowell Road for West Yarmouth, or exit 8 south for South Yarmouth and the Bass River.

GETTING AROUND Yarmouth Shuttle (508-385-8326; 800-352-7155; www.capecodtransit.org) operates late June to early September. Funded by a state grant, the shuttle begins at the Hyannis Transportation Center and runs along Route 28 to various family-oriented points (including beaches) in Yarmouth. Flag down the driver, who will pull over to pick you up. (It sure beats traffic.) Adults $1 one way; kids age 6–17, 50¢. One-day passes ($3) and tickets are purchased aboard the trolley or at the chamber of commerce (see *Guidance*).

❋ The H$_2$O (508-385-8326; 800-352-7155; www.capecodtransit.org) bus, primarily used by residents, travels along Route 28 between Hyannis and Orleans daily except Sunday year-round. It stops in South Yarmouth on Main Street, Star Market, and Stop & Shop; in West Yarmouth it stops at Higgins Crowell Road.

MEDICAL EMERGENCY Call **911.**

Bass River Chiropractic (508-394-1353), 833 Route 28, South Yarmouth. Open daily except Sunday. Dr. Reida and Dr. Allen are both health savers, full of quiet wisdom.

❋ To See

❋ ✐ **Edward Gorey House** (508-362-3909; www.edwardgoreyhouse.org), 8 Strawberry Lane, Yarmouthport. Open 10–5 Wednesday through Saturday and noon–5 Sunday, May through September; noon–5 Thursday through Sunday, October through April. *Curious, surreal, bizarre, whimsical,* and *quirky:* These have all been used to describe Gorey. His masterful pen-and-ink illustrations, as well as his offbeat sense of humor, endeared him to a wide audience. And the reputation he earned by doing the introductory credit for PBS's *Mystery* propelled him even farther. So did the Tony Award he won for costume design for the Broadway production of *Dracula*. Closer to home, when Gorey moved to the Cape full time in the early 1980s, he contributed greatly to local theater productions. New in 2002, the restored house contains three exhibits celebrating this marvelous artist, who lived here and died in 2000. Adults $5; children 6–12, $2.

☂ ❀ **Hallet's** (508-362-3362; www.hallets.com), 139 Route 6A, Yarmouthport. Open April through December. Hallet's has been a community fixture since it was built as an apothecary in 1889 by Thacher Taylor Hallet. T. T. Hallet's great-grandson Charles owns and operates the store, which boasts an old-fashioned oak counter and a marble-topped soda fountain. As time stands still, sit on a swivel stool or in one of the wrought-iron, heart-shaped chairs beneath the tin ceiling, and relax over a ice cream soda (the food's not much to write home about). The second floor has been turned into something of a museum, documenting Yarmouth's history as seen through one family's annals and attic treasures. In addition to being a pharmacist (old medicine bottles are on display), T. T. Hallet was a postmaster (during his tenure, only 15 families had mail slots), selectman (the second floor was used as a meeting room from 1889 to the early 1900s), and justice of the peace. The charming displays include store posters from the last 100 years and historical photographs. Donation for the museum.

Village pump, Route 6A near Summer Street, Yarmouthport. This wrought-iron pump has served the community since 1886. It's located just west of the Old Yarmouth Inn, the oldest inn (and stagecoach stop) on the Cape, dating from 1696. The pump's iron frame, decorated with birds, animals, and a lantern, is supported by a stone trough from which horses drank. Horse-drawn carriages traveling from Boston to Provincetown stopped here.

☂ **Captain Bangs Hallet House** (508-362-3021), 2 Strawberry Lane (park behind the post office on Route 6A), Yarmouthport. Open for tours at 1, 2, and 3 Thursday through Sunday, June to mid-October. The original section of this Greek Revival house was built in 1740 by town founder Thomas Thacher, but it was substantially enlarged by Captain Henry Thacher in 1840. Captain Hallet and his wife, Anna, lived here from 1863 until 1893. The house, maintained by the Historical Society of Old Yarmouth, is decorated in a manner befitting a prosperous sea captain who traded with China and India. Note the original 1740 kitchen, and don't miss the lovely weeping beech behind the house. Adults $3; children 12 and under, 50¢.

❀ ☂ **Winslow Crocker House** (508-362-4385; www.spnea.org), 250 Route 6A, Yarmouthport. Tours hourly 11–4 on weekends, June through August. Set back from Route 6A, this two-story Georgian home was built in 1780 with 12-over-12 small-paned windows and rich interior paneling. The house was constructed for a wealthy 18th-century trader and land speculator and moved to its present location in 1936 by Mary Thacher. Thacher, a descendant of Yarmouth's original land grantee, was an avid collector of 17th-, 18th-, and 19th-century furniture, and she used the house as a backdrop for her magnificent collection. The house was donated to the Society for the Preservation of New England Antiquities (SPNEA) and is the only SPNEA property on Cape Cod. Sara Porter and Jim McGuinness administer the house and will regale you with stories. Adults $4; children 5–12, $2; members and Cape Cod residents free.

✐ **Baxter Grist Mill,** Route 28, West Yarmouth. Call Town Hall (508-398-2231, ext. 221) for opening hours. The original mill was built in 1710 with an exterior waterwheel. But in 1860, when water levels in Mill Pond became so low that the wheel froze, an inside water turbine was added. (This is the Cape's only mill with an inside water turbine.) Kids can help grind corn with "the Mill Man." Free.

Windmill Park, off River Street from Old Main Street, South Yarmouth. This eight-sided windmill on the Bass River was built in 1791 and moved here in 1866. This scenic spot also has a small swimming beach.

☀ Outdoor Activities

✐ **BASEBALL** The Cape League sponsors the Yarmouth-Dennis Red Sox. Games are held from mid-June to early August at 5 PM at the Dennis-Yarmouth High School, Station Avenue, South Yarmouth.

BILLIARDS, BOWLING, AND ARCHERY *✐* **Classical Billiards** (508-771-5872), 657B Route 28, West Yarmouth. Open daily. This family-oriented billiards room has lots of tables, darts, foosball, video games, and table tennis.

☀ ⊤ *✐* **Ryan Family Amusement Center** (508-394-5644), 1067 Route 28, South Yarmouth. Open daily. When rain strikes, head indoors to bowl away the blues. Ten-pin and candlepin.

Riverview Bait & Tackle (508-394-1036), 1273 Route 28, South Yarmouth, has an indoor archery range.

SCENIC DRIVES

South Yarmouth and the Bass River Historic District, on and around Old Main Street (off Route 28), South Yarmouth. The Pawkannawkut Indians (a branch of the Wampanoag tribe) lived, fished, and hunted on a tract of land Yarmouth set aside for them along Long Pond and the Bass River in 1713. But by the 1770s, a smallpox epidemic wiped out most of the Native population. In 1790 David Kelley (a Quaker) acquired the last remaining Pawkannawkut land from the last surviving Pawkannawkut, Thomas Greenough. Quakers then settled the side streets off Old Main Street near Route 28 and built handsome homes. The Historical Society of Old Yarmouth publishes a walking tour to Old South Yarmouth, which you can purchase at the chamber of commerce (see *Guidance*). Note the simple traffic rotary at River and Pleasant Streets; it's thought to be the oldest in the country.

Yarmouthport. From Route 6A, turn onto Church Street across from the village green. Follow it around to Thacher Shore Drive and Water Street. When Water Street turns left, head right down a dirt road for a wide-open view of marshland. Continue on Water Street across Keveney Bridge, which crosses Mill Creek; Keveney Lane takes you back to Route 6A. Turn left to head east, back into Yarmouthport. This scenic loop is nice for a quiet walk, a bicycle ride, or an early-morning jog.

✐ **Soccer.** The Cape Cod Crusaders (508-394-1171; www.capecodcrusaders. com), the Cape's only pro team, play from late April to early August on many Saturdays at 7:30 PM at Dennis-Yarmouth High School. Adults $8; children 14 and under, $5.

❋ **FISHING/SHELLFISHING** Shellfishing permits and freshwater fishing licenses are required. Obtain them from Town Hall (508-398-2231), Route 28, South Yarmouth.

Truman's Bait & Tackle (508-771-3470), 608 Route 28, West Yarmouth. A great resource: one-stop shopping for rod rentals, repairs, freshwater licenses, and local maps and charts.

Riverview Bait & Tackle (508-394-1036), 1273 Route 28, South Yarmouth. Among other services, the staff will direct you to local fishing spots, including the Bass River and High Bank Bridges, Sea Gull Beach at Parker's River, and Smugglers Beach off South Shore Drive.

FITNESS CLUB ❋ **Mid-Cape Racquet Club** (508-394-3511), 193 White's Path (off South Yarmouth Road), South Yarmouth. For a day-use fee of $10, you'll get access to racquetball and squash courts, basketball, Nautilus, free weights, and kick boxing. There's an additional fee for the nine indoor courts, Pilates, spinning, and child care. It's obviously a full-service kind of place.

✐ **FOR FAMILIES** **Zooquarium of Cape Cod** (508-775-8883; www.zooquarium-capecod.net), Route 28, West Yarmouth. Open 9:30–5 daily, February to late November; until 6 PM in summer. Part zoo (with a petting area), part aquarium (with performing sea lions), Zooquarium is packed on cloudy days, but if you come at the beginning or end of a sunny beach day, you can avoid the crowds. Although the place may conjure up thoughts of the movie *Free Willy,* keep in mind that many of these animals would have died if they hadn't been brought here. Some arrive injured or blind. With the exception of the farm animals, all land and sea creatures are native. Small endangered animals will educate small children at the **Zoorific Theater.** Children 10 and older $9; children 2–9, $6.

Jump On Us (508-775-3304), Route 28, West Yarmouth. This trampoline center is open late May to mid-October.

Flax Playground is on Center Street in South Yarmouth; another is on Route 6A at Church Street in Yarmouthport.

GOLF **King's Way** (508-362-8870), off Route 6A, Yarmouthport. Open March to early December. A challenging 18-hole, 4,100-yard, par-59 course designed by Cornish and Silva.

Bayberry Hills (508-394-5597), off West Yarmouth Road, West Yarmouth. Open early April to late November. A town-owned, 18-hole, par-72 course with driving range.

❋ **Bass River Golf Course** (508-398-9079), off Highbank Road, South Yarmouth. Open year-round, weather permitting. A town-owned, 18-hole, par-72 course with great views of the Bass River.

✳ **Blue Rock Golf Course** (508-398-9295), off Highbank Road, South Yarmouth. Open year-round, weather permitting. A short 18-hole, par-54 course.

✐ **MINI-GOLF Pirate's Cove Adventure Golf** (508-394-6200), 728 Route 28, South Yarmouth. Open daily mid-April to late October. At the granddaddy of all Cape mini-golf courses, kids have their choice of two 18-hole courses complete with lavish pirate-themed landscaping, extravagant waterfalls, and dark caves. Kids receive eye patches, flags, and tattoos.

Bass River Sports World (508-398-6070), 928 Route 28 at Long Pond Road, South Yarmouth. Open weekends March to mid-May and daily mid-May to late September. In addition to a "Swiss Family Treehouse" adventure mini-golf, Bass River lures families with baseball and softball batting cages, soccer cages, a game room, and a driving range.

TENNIS The public can play at **Flax Pond,** which has 4 courts (off North Main Street from Route 28 in South Yarmouth); at **Sandy Pond,** which has 4 courts (from Route 28 in West Yarmouth, take Higgins Crowell Road to Buck Island Road); and at **Dennis-Yarmouth High School,** which has 10 courts (from Route 28, take Station Avenue to Regional Avenue in South Yarmouth). All are free.

SOME MINI-GOLF COURSES TOWER ABOVE THE COMPETITION.

Kim Grant

✳ Green Space

BEACHES Some lodging places offer discounted daily beach stickers; don't forget to ask. Weekly stickers for cottage renters are available for $40 at Town Hall (508-398-2231), 1146 Route 28, South Yarmouth. If you take the Yarmouth Shuttle (see *Getting Around*), there is no fee to walk onto the beach.

Sea Gull Beach, off South Sea Avenue from Route 28, West Yarmouth. This is the longest, widest, and nicest of Yarmouth's southside beaches, which generally tend to be small, narrow, and plagued by seaweed. The approach to the beach is lovely, with views of the tidal river. (The blue boxes you see, by the way, are fly traps—filled with musk oil, they attract the dreaded biting greenhead flies that terrorize sunbathers in July.) Parking $10; facilities include a bathhouse, rest rooms, and food service.

WALKS **Botanical Trails of the Historical Society of Old Yarmouth,** behind the post office and Captain Bangs Hallet House, off Route 6A, Yarmouthport. This 1.5-mile trail, dotted with benches and skirting 60 acres of pines, oaks, and a pond, leads past rhododendrons, holly, lady's slippers, and other delights. The trail begins at the gatehouse, which has a lovely herb garden. A spur trail leads to the profoundly simple **Kelley Chapel,** built in 1873 as a seaman's bethel by a father for his daughter, who was mourning the untimely death of her son. The interior contains a few pews, an old woodstove, and a small organ. It may be rented (508-375-6424) for small weddings and special events.

Bray Farm, Bray Farm Road South, off Route 6A near the Dennis town line. The Bray brothers purchased this land in the late 1700s and created a successful shipyard and farm. Now town-owned conservation land, this working farm offers a short walking trail and tidal-marsh views. It's a nice place for a picnic. You can't help but take a deep breath of fresh air here.

Meadowbrook Road Conservation Area, off Route 28. This recommendation originally came from Joseph Molinari, a longtime Explorer from New Jersey. It's a 310-foot boardwalk with an observation deck that overlooks a swamp and salt marsh. It's a peaceful place to relax. Take Winslow Gray Road north from Route 28 in West Yarmouth. After a few miles, take Meadowbrook Lane to the right and park at the end.

> **BOARDWALK, NOT PARK PLACE**
> **Bass Hole (or Gray's) Beach,** off Centre Street from Route 6A. The small, protected beach is good for children, but the real appeal lies in the **Bass Hole Boardwalk,** which extends across a marsh and a creek. From the benches at the end of the boardwalk, you can see across to Chapin Memorial Beach in Dennis. It's a great place to be at sunset, although you won't be alone. The 2.5-mile **Callery-Darling Trail** starts from the parking lot and crosses conservation lands to the salt marsh. As you walk out into the bay, a mile or so at low tide, recall that this former harbor used to be deep enough to accommodate a schooner shipyard in the 18th century. Free parking; handicap ramp.

See also Bass Hole (or Gray's) Beach in the "Boardwalk, Not Park Place" sidebar. And, don't forget about the walking tour brochure published by the Historical Society of Old Yarmouth (see *Guidance*).

✳ Lodging

Route 6A is lined with lovely B&Bs, while the southside generally appeals to families (with a couple of notable exceptions).

RESORT ♂ **Red Jacket Beach Resort** (508-398-6941; 800-672-0500; www.redjacketinns.com/redjacket), South Shore Drive, South Yarmouth 02664. Open early April through October. Occupying 7 acres wedged between Nantucket Sound and the Parker's River, this extensive complex courts families. In fact, two-room family suites cost just $30 more than a single room. Amenities include a large private beach, indoor and outdoor pools, a supervised children's program, tennis, parasailing, boat rentals, and a putting green. A family-style restaurant serves all three meals. All accommodations (150 rooms and 13 cottages) have their own deck or patio and in-room fridge. Rates vary considerably, according to view: near the hotel entrance, riverside or poolside, ocean view, and oceanfront (from least to most expensive). July to late August $195–265; off-season $90–145; two children under age 8 free in parent's room. Inquire about myriad packages as well as weekly rates in the two- and three-bedroom town houses and cottages.

BED & BREAKFASTS ✳ ❀ **Wedgewood Inn** (508-362-5157; www. wedgewood-inn.com), 83 Route 6A, Yarmouthport 02675. An elegant and sophisticated 1812 B&B with helpful hosts, the Grahams, who are neither fussy nor overbearing, the Wedgewood Inn is arguably the top inn on Route 6A. Within the main inn, the antiques-filled rooms are furnished with pencil-post beds, quilts, and wing chairs. Most have a fireplace and hardwood floors covered with Oriental carpets or hooked rugs. Two rooms have their own screened-in porch. The expertly renovated two-story carriage house/barn is more private, great for romantic getaways and off-season jaunts. The dramatic and lofty entry boasts original wainscoting, barnboard, and a sliding barn door. Rooms are lovely, with custom-made tiger maple bureaus, sculpted mantels, wood-burning fireplaces, four-poster beds, quilts, TV, and luxurious bathrooms. Two of the three rooms have private decks overlooking the shaded back lawn. Back in the main inn, Gerrie cooks and Milt serves a full breakfast on fine china at individual tables. June through October $135–205; off-season $115–165.

&. ✳ **Liberty Hill Inn** (508-362-3976; 800-821-3977; www.libertyhillinn. com), 77 Route 6A, Yarmouthport 02675. Innkeepers Ann and John Cartwright tend this former 1825 whaling tycoon's home as a labor of love. On a knoll set back from Route 6A, the Cartwrights have nine comfortable rooms in the main house and adjacent modern carriage house. Light and airy rooms in the main inn benefit from lofty ceilings, floor-to-ceiling windows, a dramatic spiral staircase, and restored bathrooms. Next door, rooms might have a whirlpool, fireplace, or canopy bed. Afternoon tea on the wraparound porch (overlooking the ever-more-landscaped grounds)

BASS HOLE BOARDWALK AT GRAY'S BEACH IN YARMOUTHPORT

and sumptuous breakfasts (served at individual tables) are included. Mid-June to mid-September $125–200; off-season $80–190.

❄ **Captain Farris House** (508-760-2818; 800-350-9477; www.captainfarris.com), 308 Old Main Street, South Yarmouth 02664. Located within a small pocket of historic homes off Route 28, the 1845 Captain Farris House offers understated elegance and luxurious modern amenities. Lovely window treatments and fine antiques fill the guest rooms. Other nice touches include fine linens, damask duvets, down comforters, thick white towels, and Jacuzzi tubs. Of the 10 rooms, 4 are suites, a few have private deck, and most have a private entrance. A fancy three-course breakfast is served at individual tables in the courtyard or at one long, formal dining room table. Afternoon tea is set out year-round. The lovely gardens are enticing in-season, while five rooms with fireplace are well suited to off-season cocooning. May through September $125–175 rooms, $185–250 suites; off-season $95–160

and $130–210, respectively.

🐾 🐾 ❄ **Lane's End Cottage** (508-362-5298), 268 Route 6A, Yarmouthport 02675. Open April through February. Down a quiet lane off Route 6A, this circa-1740 Cape cottage is a dear place, one of a dying breed of authentic B&Bs; enjoy it while you can. It's surrounded by flowers and woods, and its back patio is encircled by potted geraniums. Host Valerie Butler (along with Chloe, an adorable Rescue League cocker spaniel) has been whipping up full breakfasts and attending to guests' needs since 1984. Her three guest rooms are simply furnished; my favorite has a fireplace and French doors leading to its own cobblestone terrace. The living room is "lived-in comfortable," with American, English, and country antiques and a fireplace. $120–135 (no room tax is charged). No credit cards.

❄ 🐾 **Inn at Lewis Bay** (508-771-3433; 800-962-6679; www.innatlewisbay.com), 57 Maine Avenue, West Yarmouth 02673. In a seaside residential neighborhood near a small, protected beach, this Dutch Colonial has six nice guest rooms (two with ocean view). Innkeepers Janet and Dave Vaughn include a full breakfast, afternoon refreshments, beach towels, and beach chairs. May through October $128; off-season $88.

🦞 🐚 **Village Inn** (508-362-3182; www.thevillageinncapecod.com), 92 Route 6A, Yarmouthport 02675. Open May through December. In keeping with the delightfully old-fashioned idea of providing a place for travelers to relax and interact, the Village Inn has two comfortable living rooms that fit like an old shoe. There's also a wicker-filled, screened-in porch overlooking the backyard. A full breakfast, served on Cape Cod place mats, is included. They don't make 'em like this anymore—this historic, colonial landmark has been operated by the Hickey family since 1952. The 10 guest rooms (some smaller than others) are modestly furnished with prices to match: $89–119 private bath, $50–75 shared bath.

COTTAGES 🐚 **Seaside** (508-398-2533; www.seasidecapecod.com), 135 South Shore Drive, South Yarmouth 02664. Open May to late October. These 42 one- and two-room cottages, built in the 1930s but nicely upgraded and well maintained, are very popular for their oceanfront location. Reserve by mid-March if possible; otherwise, cross your fingers. Sheltered among pine trees, the shingled and weathered units are clustered around a sandy barbecue area and sit above a 500-foot stretch of private beach. (A playground is next door.) Kitchens are fully equipped, and linens are provided, as is daily maid service. Many of the tidy units have a working fire-

place. The least expensive units (without views) are decorated in 1950s style. One-room studio units sleep two to four; one-bedroom efficiencies sleep four to six. Don't bother with the motel efficiencies. Mid-June to early September $900–1,125 weekly for one-room units, $1,195–1,525 weekly for two-room units; off-season $75–120 and $110–160 daily, respectively.

See also Red Jacket Beach Resort under *Resorts*.

🐚 **MOTOR INNS** 🦞 **Beach House at Bass River** (508-394-6501; 800-345-6065), 73 South Shore Drive, Bass River (South Yarmouth) 02664. Open late March through October. This tasteful bilevel motor inn sits on a 110-foot stretch of private Nantucket Sound beach. Each of the 26 rooms is decorated differently (some with antiques), but generally the ocean-front rooms are a bit spiffier, with country-pine furnishings. Most rooms have private balcony; all have a refrigerator. Cliff Hagberg built the tidy complex in the 1970s and still operates it. An expansive buffet breakfast is included. July to early September $140–185; off-season $90–120; discounts for early bookings; children under 10 free in parent's room; free cribs and use of microwave for heating baby bottles and such.

Ocean Mist (508-398-2633; 800-248-6478), 97 South Shore Drive, South Yarmouth 02664. Open early February through early December. This shingled three-story complex fronting a 300-foot private Nantucket Sound beach offers 32 rooms and 32 loft suites. Each of the contemporary rooms has a wet bar or full efficiency kitchen, two double beds, and air-conditioning. Loft suites feature an open, second-floor sitting area—many of the rooms have ocean views, all have a sofa bed; many of these have skylights and two private balconies. There's a small indoor pool on the premises. July to early September $179–289; June and mid-September to mid-November $79–239; off-season $59–209; three children up to age 15 stay free in parent's room.

🦞 ❄ ♿ **Tidewater Motor Lodge** (508-775-6322; 800-338-6322; www.tidewaterml.com), 135 Route 28, West Yarmouth 02673. For inexpensive accommodations close to the Nantucket ferry, this is the best of the lot. There are about 100 rooms, as well as indoor and outdoor pools. July and August $99–125; off-season $69–90; two children under 12 free with adult.

RENTAL HOUSES AND COTTAGES
🐚 **Great Island Ocean Club** (508-775-0985; www.greatislandocean-club.com), South Sea Avenue, West Yarmouth 02673. Open April through November. This gated residential community has about 30 rental homes, fully equipped houses with one to six bedrooms. Best of all, they're located on or within a quarter mile of a private Nantucket Sound beach. Off by itself, it's a real find, perfect for families. Send for the detailed list of where each house is located and its particulars. Shared facilities include tennis courts and pool. Reservations by mail only, until mid-March. Mid-June to early September $1,150–2,100 weekly for two bedrooms, $1,700–3,700 for three bedrooms; about 40 percent lower off-season.

Crocker & Flinksterom (508-362-3953; www.crockerflinksterom.com),

Cranberry Court, 947 Route 6A, Yarmouthport 02675. Nancy and Charlie Flinksterom rent 30 to 40 houses each season (weekly, monthly, or longer). For the best pick, call in January.

Century 21–Sam Ingram Real Estate (508-362-8844; 800-697-3340; www.summerrentalcapecod.com), 938 Route 6A, Yarmouthport 02675. This agency rents 100 or so private homes that go for as little as $650 weekly for a one-bedroom to as much as $9,000 weekly for a spectacular six-bedroom waterfront perch. Call in January or February. Rentals are shown throughout the winter by appointment.

❋ Where to Eat

❄ Route 6A has a couple of excellent restaurants, and while Route 28 is lined with dozens, most are not discernible from one another. I have only reviewed the few that are. If you're staying on the southside, and want more choice, check the entries under "Dennis." Unless otherwise noted, all restaurants are open year-round.

DINING OUT 🦞 **Inaho** (508-362-5522), 157 Route 6A, Yarmouthport. Open for dinner nightly except Monday. Alda and Yuji Watanabe continue to give patrons plenty of reason to remain loyal. They offer some of the most sophisticated and authentic Japanese cuisine east of Tokyo. Yaki-Nasu, a broiled eggplant appetizer topped with a delicate blend of miso and sesame, is particularly savory. While fearless diners are handsomely rewarded, the less adventurous revel in traditional tofu, teriyaki, bento box combinations, and miso soup. Then there is tempura, an exemplary metaphor for life: Wait too long to partake, and the fleeting, perfect moment passes by. Meanwhile, over at the sushi bar, intense concentration is focused on the Zen of sushi preparation. Don't miss the beautiful back garden or bananas tempura for dessert. If you feel like switching palates, Alda's flourless chocolate cake is great, too. Take-out; reservations highly recommended in-season. Dishes $12–23.

🌺 **Abbicci** (508-362-3501), 43 Route 6A, Yarmouthport. Open for lunch weekdays, dinner nightly, and Sunday brunch. If you're filled to the gills with seafood served in nautically challenged surroundings, this mod bistro will delight you. Housed in a mustard-yellow 1775 cottage, its style is more apropos of New York's SoHo than of conservative Route 6A. Check out the stunning trompe l'oeil floors, track lighting, sleek bar, and hip but friendly waitstaff. Sophisticated and contemporary Italian dishes, infused with olive oil and garlic, might include seafood stew with saffron broth, or roasted duck with sweet-and-sour sauce and apricots. Marietta Hickey's menu changes seasonally. Early, three-course dinner specials for $15–20 are a great value. Reservations recommended. Lunch $9–15, dinner entrées $15–28.

✿ ᴴ **Old Yarmouth Inn** (508-362-9962), 223 Route 6A, Yarmouthport. Open for lunch, dinner, and a very popular and extensive Sunday buffet brunch. You have a choice to make at this 1696 inn, the oldest on the Cape: casual pub dining or fine dining in one of three dining rooms. The fireplaces and white linens in the main dining rooms create a cozy elegance, but I often end up at the low-key tav-

ern, a former stagecoach stop. It's just the perfect place for a grilled chicken Caesar, cup of clam chowder, or great burger. In addition to lighter fare, you can get serious with lobster ravioli with a fresh tomato and cream sauce or a broiled seafood platter. All entrées are served with wonderfully dense bread. Lunch $7–15, brunch $14 per person, dinner entrées $10–25.

✿ **Black Rock Grille** (508-771-1001), 633 Route 28, West Yarmouth. Open 4 PM to "late." This handsome grill specializes in wild game. And for the red-meat lovers in your party who like red wine and béarnaise sauces, this place is a winner. Try their specialty seasonal ales, too, while you're at it. Early specials. Entrées $10–28.

Ardeo Mediterranean Tavern (508-760-1500), Union Station Plaza (exit 8 off Route 6), 23V Whites Path, South Yarmouth. Open for lunch and dinner. A fun place for noshing with friends, this sleek eatery has creative woodstove pizzas, excellent Middle Eastern appetizers (based on recipes from the owner's grandmother), sandwich wraps, panini, homemade pastas, and creative mains (but I go for the former rather than the latter). Ignore its strip-mall location. Dishes $9–17.

EATING OUT 🌺 ✿ **Keltic Kitchen** (508-771-4835), 415 Route 28, West Yarmouth. Open for breakfast all day (6 or 7 AM–2 PM). Chef-owner and Irishman Dave Dempsey and his staff still sport thick brogues from the old country when they take your orders. How about an Irish farmhouse breakfast with rashers and black and white pudding or Keltic Bennys with poached eggs on an English muffin and corned beef hash? And despite having no ties to Ireland, the cranberry French toast, made with Portuguese bread, is a favorite. This friendly and cozy place is a family operation—Dave's father did trompe l'oeil artwork on walls. Come once and I bet you'll come back again. Try the beef and barley soup for lunch. And dine outside in fine weather. Dishes $3–7. No credit cards.

Stefani's Restaurant (508-760-2929), at the Bayberry Hills Golf Course, 635 West Yarmouth Road. Open 6–6 daily April through November. Longtime caterer and restaurateur Stefani Wright offers baked goodies that are gobbled up quickly, great clam chowder, turkey Reubens, chicken BLT roll-ups, burgers, and grilled roast beef with horseradish mayo. While the pleasant concessionaire overlooks the course, this place isn't just for golfers. Sandwiches about $5.

&. *♪* **Oliver's** (508-362-6062), Route 6A, Yarmouthport. Open for lunch and dinner daily. Serving generous portions in cozy, tavernlike surroundings, the wide-ranging menu also features reduced portions. Chef-owner Dale Ormon attracts an older crowd at lunchtime, longtime Cape residents who like to keep things simple, and families who need to satisfy everyone. Specialties include broiled seafood, but hearty sandwiches, burgers, and veal parmigiana are also quite popular. Thankfully, specials come in two portion sizes and two prices. Early specials as well. At press time, there were plans afoot to build an outdoor dining deck. Live entertainment on weekends. Dishes $10–18.

♣ *♪* **Jack's Outback** (508-362-6690), 161 Route 6A, Yarmouthport. Open for breakfast and lunch daily. Classic American down-home cooking is served from an exposed, dinerlike kitchen that revels in a no-nonsense attitude. A local institution for years, patrons help themselves to coffee, write their own orders after looking at the wall menu, and take their plates back to the pine-paneled dining room. Dishes $2–6.

♪ **Clancy's** (508-775-3332), 175 Route 28, West Yarmouth. Open for lunch and dinner. This is the kind of no-surprises place that appeals to a variety of palates and budgets: chicken fingers and shrimp cocktail appetizers; Reubens and smoked turkey sandwiches; burgers; eggplant Parmesan and chicken cordon bleu for dinner. The pleasant decor is classic Victorian, with wainscoting and the portions are generous. With its older clientele, the place clears out after 8 PM on weekends off-season. Lunch $5–11, dinner entrées $14–20.

♣ *♪* **Seafood Sam's** (508-432-1422), 1006 Route 28, South Yarmouth. Open for lunch and dinner, February through October. You can always count on Sam's for reliable, informally presented, reasonably priced fried or broiled seafood. Lunch specials $5–7, dinner dishes $7–18.

See also Hallet's under *To See.*

✳ Entertainment

♪ **Band concerts** (508-778-1008), Mattachesse Middle School band shell, Higgins Crowell Road, West Yarmouth. Since 1970, concerts have been held on Monday nights at 7 in July and August.

♣ ꭲ ✳ MOVIES **Hoyts Entertainment Cinemas** (508-394-1100), Patriot Square Mall, Route 134, South Dennis.

✳ Selective Shopping

❋ Unless otherwise noted, all shops are open year-round.

SPECIAL SHOPS Parnassus Book Service (508-362-6420; www.parnassusbooks.com), 220 Route 6A, Yarmouthport. Deliberately avoiding signs and categories, proprietor Ben Muse wants people to browse and dig around, perhaps finding a first edition James or Melville among the stacks. Specializing in maritime, Cape Cod, and ornithology, Muse has been selling new, used, and rare books since 1950. Bookshelves line the wall outside (under a little roof), where the books are available for browsing or purchase on a 24/7 honor system. In its former incarnations, this 1840 building served as a general store and as a church; it was once home to the Yarmouth Society of the New Jerusalem. This really is one unique shop with one unique guy running it.

Bass River Boatworks (508-398-4883), 1361 Route 28, South Yarmouth. Barely west of the Bass River, these two crammed shops will satisfy nautical fanatics. Look for copper weather vanes, lightship baskets, marine antiques, custom-made glass display cases, lighthouse models, and the largest number of ship-model kits on the Cape. They also do lots of ship-model restoration.

Design Works (508-362-9698), 159 Route 6A, Yarmouthport. Open daily.

Festive and fanciful Mackenzie-Childs pottery, Scandinavian country antiques, home furnishings, and accessories like throws, pillows, and linens.

Peach Tree Designs (508-362-8317), 173 Route 6A, Yarmouthport. Open daily. Homebodies will delight in this two-floor shop filled to the brim with an assortment of decorative accessories for gracious living.

Town Crier (508-362-3138), 153 Route 6A, Yarmouthport. Open May to mid-October. Five dealers share this space, where you can find plates, glassware, collectibles, silver, brass, and small furniture.

✳ Special Events

Late May–late September: **Art shows.** The Yarmouth Art Guild sponsors outdoor shows at the Cape Cod Cooperative Bank (Route 6A in Yarmouthport) on many Sundays (10–5).

Mid-October: **Seaside Festival.** Begun in 1979, this festival features jugglers, clowns, fireworks, field games, a parade, sand-castle competitions, arts and crafts, and bicycle, kayak, and road races.

✐ *Early December:* **Yarmouthport Christmas Stroll.** Tree lighting on the village common, caroling, and special children's activities; wreaths for sale.

DENNIS

L ocated at the Cape's geographic center, Dennis is a convenient base for day trips. Some visitors are drawn to Dennis for fine summer theater; others come for family-style attractions along Route 28. Indeed, to outsiders (including the 45,000 or so summer visitors), Dennis suffers from a split personality. Luckily, the 15,000 year-round residents have long since reconciled the village's conflicting natures.

On the north side of town, Route 6A continues along its scenic way, governed by a historical commission. Skirting Dennis and East Dennis, Route 6A is lined with a smattering of antiques shops, crafters, and sea captains' gracious homes. (During the 19th century, more than 400 sea captains called Dennis home.) Colonial side roads off Route 6A lead to beach communities, Quivett Neck (settled in 1639), and Sesuit Marsh and Sesuit Harbor, where the fishing industry once flourished and fishing charters now depart. Note the streets in this area, named for methods of preserving fish: Cold Storage Road and Salt Works Road.

The oldest cranberry bog is also off Route 6A; Dennis resident Henry Hall cultivated the first cranberries in 1807. He discovered that the berries grow much better when covered with a light layer of sand. His brother, Isaiah, a cooper, patented the barrels used to transport the harvest. It wasn't until the 1840s, when sugar became more readily available, that anyone could do much with these tart berries, though.

The center of Dennis has a quintessential white steeple church, town green, and bandstand.

On the southern side of town, the 6-mile-long Bass River is the largest tidal river on the eastern seaboard. It serves as a natural boundary between Yarmouth and Dennis, offering numerous possibilities for exploration, fishing, and birding. Although it's never been proved, it's widely believed that Viking explorer Leif Eriksson sailed up the Bass River about 1,000 years ago, built a camp, and stayed awhile. Follow Cove Road off Route 28 and Main Street for nice views of the Bass River and sheltered Grand Cove. (The villages of South Dennis and West Dennis were once connected by a bridge here.) In Dennisport, kids will enjoy the smaller Swan River in a paddleboat.

Each side of Dennis has its own nice, long beach: Chapin Memorial Beach on

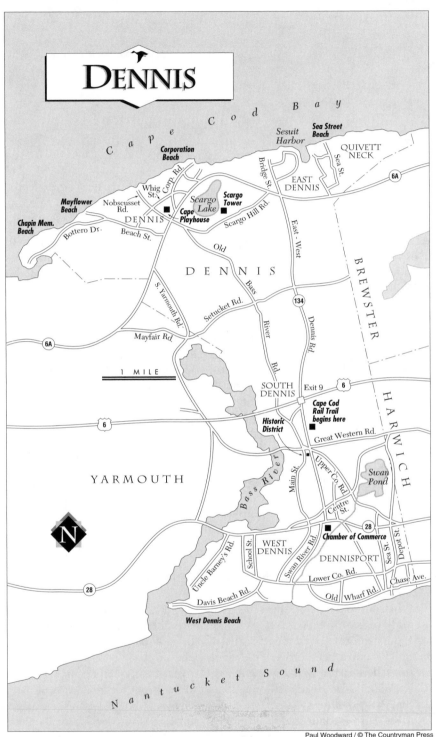

DENNIS

Cape Cod Bay

Cape Cod

Corporation
Beach

Sesuit
Harbor

Sea Street
Beach

QUIVETT
NECK

Bridge St.

Sea St.

EAST
DENNIS

6A

Whig
St.

Corp. Rd.

Mayflower
Beach

Nobscusset
Rd.

Scargo
Lake

Scargo
Tower

DENNIS

Cape
Playhouse

Scargo Hill Rd.

East - West

BREWSTER

Chapin Mem.
Beach

Bottero Dr.

Beach St.

Old

D E N N I S

Bass

River

134

Dennis Rd.

S. Yarmouth Rd.

Setucket Rd.

6A

Mayfair Rd.

Rd.

1 MILE

SOUTH
DENNIS

Exit 9

6

HARWICH

6

Cape Cod
Rail Trail
begins here

Historic
District

Great Western Rd.

YARMOUTH

Bass River

Main St.

Upper Co. Rd.

Swan
Pond

N

Uncle Barney's Rd.

School St.

WEST
DENNIS

Swan River Rd.

Centre
St.

28

Chamber of Commerce

Sea St.

Depot St.

DENNISPORT

Davis Beach Rd.

Lower Co. Rd.

28

Old

Wharf Rd.

Chase Ave.

West Dennis Beach

N a n t u c k e t   S o u n d

Paul Woodward / © The Countryman Press

Cape Cod Bay and West Dennis Beach on Nantucket Sound. Head to Scargo Tower for an expansive view.

GUIDANCE ❋ **Dennis Chamber of Commerce** (508-398-3568; 800-243-9920; www.dennischamber.com), 242 Swan River Road (near the intersection of Routes 134 and 28), West Dennis. Open 10–4 daily. Chamber members are knowledgeable and proud of the long hours they staff their booth. There is also an unstaffed satellite outlet at 821 "Rear" Route 6A, Dennis, just east of the Scargo Cafe, that's open 9–5 daily year-round.

PUBLIC REST ROOMS Public rest rooms are located at Sesuit Harbor in East Dennis and at Town Hall, Main Street, South Dennis.

✂ ❋ ♟ PUBLIC LIBRARIES There are five village libraries; it's best to call each for their hours.
Dennis Memorial Library (508-385-2255), 1020 Old Bass River Road, Dennis.
Dennis Public Library (508-760-6219), 673 Route 28.
Jacob Sears Memorial Library (508-385-8151), Center Street, East Dennis.
South Dennis Free Public Library (508-394-8954), 389 Main Street.
West Dennis Village Library (508-398-2050), 272 Route 28.

GETTING THERE *By car:* From the Cape Cod Canal, take exit 9 off the Mid-Cape Highway (Route 6). Head north on Route 134 to Route 6A for Dennis and East Dennis. Head south on Route 134 to Route 28 for West Dennis and Dennisport. The tiny historic district of South Dennis is just west of Route 134 as you head south. Depending on traffic, it takes 20 to 30 minutes to get to various points in Dennis from the canal.

GETTING AROUND As the crow flies, Dennis is only about 7 miles wide from Cape Cod Bay to Nantucket Sound; it's 2 to 5 miles wide. When navigating, keep a couple of things in mind: South Dennis is actually the geographic center of Dennis, and Dennisport (the southeastern portion of town) doesn't have a harbor on the ocean as you might expect it to (given its name!). In general, there isn't much to interest travelers between Routes 6A and 28. Year-rounders make their homes here, visit doctors' and lawyers' offices, and buy food and gardening supplies. Concentrate your meandering north off Route 6A and around the tiny historic district on Main Street in South Dennis.

The **H₂O** (508-385-8326; 800-352-7155; www.capecodtransit.org) bus, generally used by locals, travels along Route 28 between Hyannis and Orleans daily except Sunday year-round. It stops at the central shopping area in Dennisport, Patriot Square in South Dennis, and School Street in West Dennis.

MEDICAL EMERGENCY Call **911.**

✴ To See

♂ ❀ ⇞ **Cape Museum of Fine Arts** (508-385-4477; www.cmfa.org), Route 6A, Dennis. Open 10–5 Monday through Saturday, until 8 on Wednesday and Thursday, 1–5 Sunday and holidays (except closed Monday mid-October to late May). The CMFA underwent a $1.5 million renovation from 1997 to 2001, and it's never been better. There are five exhibition spaces, a glassed-in sculpture court, and a new Education Wing. On the grounds of the Cape Playhouse, Cape Cod's important artists—both living and dead—are represented by more than 1,000 works on paper and canvas as well as sculpture. It should definitely be on your top list of things to do. The museum also sponsors lectures and art classes for adults and children, and features first-run independent and foreign films in their Reel Art cinema. One of the most popular events is a Secret Garden Tour in late June, which features local artists painting scenes inspired by Dennis's most lovely gardens; tickets $75 (see *Special Events*). Adults $7, children under 18 free.

♂ **Scargo Tower,** Bass Hill Road, Dennis. (Bass Hill Road is just off Scargo Hill Road from Route 6A.) The 28-foot stone tower sits 160 feet above sea level atop the area's tallest hill, and on a clear day the panoramic view extends all the way to Provincetown. Even on a hazy day you can view the width of the Cape: from Nantucket Sound to Cape Cod Bay. Scargo Lake (see *Green Space—Ponds/Lakes*), a glacial kettle pond, is directly below the tower.

♂ **Josiah Dennis Manse Museum** and **Old West Schoolhouse** (508-385-2232), 77 Nobscusset Road at Whig Street, Dennis. Open 10–noon Tuesday and 2–4 Thursday, late June through September, and 2–4 Saturday in September. This 1736 saltbox was home to the Reverend Mr. Dennis, for whom the town is named. Today it's set up much as it would have been during the reverend's time, with a keeping room, child's room, maritime wing, and spinning exhibit in the attic. Costumed interpreters are on hand to answer questions. The 1770 one-room schoolhouse, filled with wooden and wrought-iron desks, was moved to its present location in the mid-1970s. Children's program. Donations.

Congregational Church of South Dennis (508-394-5992), 234 Main Street, South Dennis. The 1835 church itself is not open, but the office is (9–noon Monday, Tuesday, and Thursday), and staff are happy to let folks inside. What's there? The chapel features a chandelier made with Sandwich glass and a 1762 Snetzler pipe organ, the country's oldest, which still in use every Sunday morning. The church is also called the Sea Captain's Church because more than 100 of its founding members were sea captains.

♂ **Jericho House and Barn Museum** (508-398-6736), Trotting Park Road and Old Main Street, West Dennis. Open 2–4 Wednesday and 10–noon Friday, July and August, and by appointment. The 1801 full-Cape-style house contains period furnishings, and the 1810 barn is filled with antique tools, carriages, and a fanciful collection of folk art animals (a veritable "driftwood zoo") crafted in the 1950s by Sherman Woodward. Donations.

SCENIC DRIVES The **South Dennis Historic District,** on and around Main Street from Route 134, gets wonderful afternoon light and relatively little traffic.

Escape the crowds and head for this little gem; it's worth a short drive or quiet walk. Note the South Dennis Free Public Library (circa 1858) on Main Street, a cottage-style building covered with wooden gingerbread trim. Liberty Hall is also noteworthy; it was used for concerts, fairs, lectures, and balls when the second story was added in 1865. Edmond Nickerson, founder of the Old South Dennis Village Association, deserves much of the credit for initiating fund-raising drives and overseeing restoration projects.

For a pleasant alternative to Route 134, which also connects the north- and southsides, take Old Bass River Road, which turns into Main Street in the South Dennis Historic District.

✳ Outdoor Activities

BICYCLING/RENTALS The Cape Cod Rail Trail is a well-maintained asphalt bikeway that follows the Old Colony Railroad tracks for 26 miles from Dennis to Wellfleet. The trail begins off Route 134 in South Dennis across from Hall Oil.

Parking and bike rentals are available at the trailhead from **Barbara's Bike and Sports Equipment** (508-760-4723), 430 Route 134. Bikes are about $10 for 2 hours, $20–25 daily. The shop also rents in-line skates and stays open from late March to late October. On the southside, you can rent from the even more seasonal Pizazz (508-760-3888), 633 Route 28, Dennisport, about 1.5 miles from the Rail Trail.

BOAT EXCURSIONS/RENTALS **The Schooner *Freya*** (508-385-4399), Town Marina, Dennis. Take a 2-hour Cape Cod Bay sail aboard a 63-foot ship captained by Frank and Elaine Meigs. The 11 AM sail usually costs a bit less ($15) than the 2 PM one ($17); the sunset trips cost a bit more ($20). Children always pay less.

✎ **Water Safari's *Starfish*** (508-362-5555), Bass River Bridge, Route 28, West Dennis. These 90-minute narrated trips of the Bass River, the largest tidal river on the East Coast, operate late May to mid-October. Along the shoreline you'll see windmills, luxurious riverfront estates, sea captains' homes, and lots of birds. The flat-bottomed aluminum boat (which has an awning) accommodates almost 50 people. Adults $12; children age 1–11, $7.

✎ **Cape Cod Waterways** (508-398-0080), Route 28 near Route 134, Dennisport. Open May to mid-October. The small and winding Swan River heads about 0.75 mile north to the 200-acre Swan Pond and 2 miles south to Nantucket Sound. Cape Cod Waterways rents electric and manual paddleboats, canoes, and kayaks that can accommodate a family with two small children.

FISHING/SHELLFISHING Freshwater fishing is good at **Scargo Lake,** stocked with smallmouth bass and trout. Obtain a state fishing license at Town Hall (508-394-8300), Main Street, South Dennis. Shellfishing permits are required and can also be obtained at Town Hall.

Bass River Bridge, Route 28, West Dennis. Park on one side and try your luck; or just stop and watch.

A number of competitively priced, seasonal fishing charters depart from Sesuit Harbor, off Route 6A in East Dennis. Contact **Blue Fish** (508-385-7265), offering half-day charters for $390 for 4 hours (one to six people).

FITNESS Lifecourse, South Dennis, is a 1.5-mile trail through the woods with 20 exercise stations along the way. Take Route 28 to Route 134 north; turn left onto Bob Crowell Road to the pavilion.

∂ FOR FAMILIES Cartwheels (508-394-6755), 11 South Gages Way, across from Tony Kent Arena, South Dennis. Open 10–10 daily in the summer. "Indy-style" go-carts; batting cages.

❋ GOLF Dennis Highlands (508-385-8347), Old Bass River Road, Dennis. An 18-hole, par-71 course that's wider and more forgiving; great driving range and practice putting greens.
Dennis Pines (508-385-8347), off Route 134, East Dennis. A tight and flat 18-hole, par-72 course that's more competitive than Highlands.
The Longest Drive (508-398-5555), 131 Great Western Road, South Dennis. A driving range with covered enclosures, lessons, and clinics.

ICE SKATING ❋ Tony Kent Arena (508-760-2400; 508-760-2415 for a human being), 8 South Gages Way, South Dennis. Off Route 134, this rink served as Olympic silver medalist Nancy Kerrigan's training ground. Public skating hours vary, so it's best to call. They have rental skates, too.

IN-LINE SKATING See Barbara's Bike and Sports Equipment under *Bicycling/Rentals.*

KAYAKING ❋ Sesuit Creek Outfitters (508-385-1912), 22 Bridge Street. Kayak rentals, demos, and guided tours.

∂ MINI-GOLF Holiday Hill (508-398-8857), Route 28, Dennisport. Open late April to mid-October. Route 28 is lined with mini-golf courses similar in quality, but can others claim that they plant more than 12,000 flowers annually, as Holiday Hill can?

SAILING ∂ West Dennis Yacht Club (508-398-9757), 259 Loring Way. Sailing school for kids 5–14. The 3-hour morning and afternoon classes are geared to "pre-sailors," beginners, and advanced students.

TENNIS ❋ Sesuit Tennis Centre (508-385-2200), 1389 Route 6A, East Dennis. Open year-round, depending on weather. The center offers three Har-Tru clay courts (rented hourly), a ball machine, open tournaments, and instruction. There is another location at Signal Hill that features a heated pool (508-385-2211).

BEACHES Cottage renters may purchase a weekly parking pass for $39 at Town Hall (508-394-8300), Main Street, South Dennis. Day-trippers can pay a daily fee of $10 to park at the following beaches:

⅃ ✍ **West Dennis Beach** (off Davis Beach Road) on Nantucket Sound is the town's finest and longest beach (it's more than a mile long). Like many Nantucket Sound beaches, though, it's also rather narrow. While there's parking for more than 1,000 cars, the lot rarely fills. If you drive to the western end, you can usually find a few yards of beach for yourself. The eastern end is for residents only. Facilities include 10 lifeguard stations and a snack bar at the eastern end. It's difficult to imagine that fishing shanties, fish weirs, and dories once lined the shores of West Dennis Beach. But they did. Facilities include a concession stand, showers, and rest rooms.

Chapin Memorial Beach, off Chapin Beach Road on Cape Cod Bay, is open to four-wheel-drive vehicles. It's a nice, long, dune-backed beach. As you drive up to Chapin, you'll probably notice an incongruous-looking building plunked down in the marshes and dunes. In fact, it's the headquarters for the Aquaculture Research Corporation (known as the Cultured Clam Corp.), the only state-certified seller of shellfish seed. Begun in 1960, the company is a pioneer in the field of aquaculture. There's no better place to study shellfish.

⅃ **Corporation Beach,** off Corporation Road on Cape Cod Bay, is also backed by low dunes and was once used as a packet-ship landing by a group of town

TIDAL FLATS AT CHAPIN MEMORIAL BEACH STRETCH INTO CAPE COD BAY FOR MORE THAN A MILE.

Kim Grant

residents who formed the Nobscusset Pier Corporation (hence its name). The crescent-shaped beach has concession stands, a play area, and rest rooms.

 ♿ ✎ **Mayflower Beach,** off Beach Street on Cape Cod Bay, has a boardwalk, rest rooms, and a concession stand. **Sea Street Beach,** off Sea Street, and **Howes Street Beach,** off Howes Street and backed by low dunes; both have boardwalks. The Sea Street parking lot fills up by noon. These three beaches are relatively small and good for families with young children because the water is shallow. As at Corporation and Chapin Memorial Beaches, at low tide you can walk a mile out into the bay.

There are about eight other public beaches on Nantucket Sound, but all are quite small.

PONDS/LAKES **Scargo Lake,** a deep, freshwater kettle hole left behind by retreating glaciers, has two beaches: **Scargo Beach** (off Route 6A) and **Princess Beach** (off Scargo Hill Road). Princess Beach has a picnic area; bathers at Scargo Beach tend to put their beach chairs in the shallow water or on the narrow, tree-lined shore. There are two legends concerning the lake's creation—you decide which you prefer: Did an Indian princess have the lake dug for fish that she received as a present? Or did a giant named Maushop dig the hole as a remembrance of himself to the local Native Americans?

Swan Pond Overlook, off Centre Street from Searsville Road and Route 134. Beach, picnic area, and bird-watching area.

WALKS **Indian Lands Conservation Area,** South Dennis. This easy, 2-mile round-trip walk skirts the banks of the upper Bass River. In winter you'll see blue herons and kingfishers; lady's slippers bloom in May. From the northern end of the Town Hall parking lot on Main Street, follow the power-line right-of-way path for half a mile to the trailhead.

✴ Lodging

 ✿ Almost to a place, Dennis lodging establishments represent very good values. Only one place off Route 6A really stands out on the northside, while the southside is loaded with family places (with one noteworthy exception). Most southside places are on or quite close to the beach.

RESORT ✎ ♿ **Lighthouse Inn** (508-398-2244; www.lighthouseinn.com), off Lower County Road, West Dennis 02670. Open mid-May to mid-October. On Nantucket Sound, this old-fashioned, family-friendly resort has 68 rooms and tidy cottages set on 9 grassy acres of waterfront property. Its Bass River Lighthouse is the only privately owned working lighthouse in the country. The resort, expertly operated by the Stones since 1938, has lots of amenities: supervised children's activities, special children's dinners, a heated pool, tennis, shuffleboard, mini-golf, volleyball, and the Sand Bar Club and Lounge. On rainy days guests gather in the common rooms of the lodge-style main building, stocked with games, books, and a TV. Lunch is served on the deck or poolside (see *Eating Out*). A full breakfast is included. July and August $230–300; off-season $160–230. Children sharing a room with a parent cost an additional $35–55 daily, depending on age. Rates including dinner are an additional $25 nightly per adult, $10 per child.

BED & BREAKFASTS Isaiah Hall Bed and Breakfast Inn (508-385-9928; 800-736-0160; www.isaiah-hallinn.com), 152 Whig Street, Dennis 02638. Open May to late October. On a quiet street off Route 6A, this rambling 1857 farmhouse is one of the most comfortable places mid-Cape. Innkeeper Marie Brophy's enthusiasm is infectious, and her garden a delight. With each visit, I'm reminded how much I really like this place. Rooms in the main house are comfortably furnished with country-style antiques. Rooms in the attached carriage house are newer, each decorated with stenciling, white wicker, and knotty-pine paneling. All rooms are air-conditioned and equipped with TV, VCR, and phone. There is plenty of indoor and outdoor common space, including a cathedral-ceilinged great room (with a DSL line) and a deep lawn that leads to the Cape's oldest cranberry bog. An expanded continental breakfast is served at one long table. Mid-June to mid-September $110–180, $190 for the king-bedded suite with balcony; off-season rates slightly lower.

English Garden B&B (508-398-2915; 888-788-1908; www.theenglish-gardenbandb.com), 32 Inman Road, Dennisport 02639. Open mid-April through October. This is a very good, comfortable, contemporary choice. Within a 2-minute walk of the beach, this completely renovated guesthouse has eight tasteful rooms outfitted with quilts. Each boasts hardwood floors and a deck or small balcony; some have a whirlpool and ocean view. As for common space, both airy living rooms are the kind of places where you could easily spend a rainy afternoon, reading in front of the fireplace. A full breakfast is included (always with a choice of eggs any style) and served at individual tables in a spacious, bright, and contemporary breakfast room. July to early September $129–144 nightly rooms, $1,300–1,400 weekly for one-bedroom suites; off-season $80–95 rooms, $975–925 weekly or $150 nightly for suites (with a 3-night minimum).

By The Sea Guests B&B (508-398-8685; 800-447-9202; www.bythe-seaguests.com), Chase Avenue at Inman Road, Dennisport 02639. Open May through November. You can't get closer to Inman Beach than this. Each of the 12 large rooms, with refrigerator and cable TV, is basically but pleasantly outfitted. Look for well-maintained 1950s-style cottage furniture, white cotton bedspreads, and white curtains. It's all very summery, charming, and breezy. On rainy days, B&B guests can head to the enclosed porch overlooking the private beach (just steps away) or to the large living room with books, games, and a ready supply of fruit and cookies. There are also five contemporary, fully equipped one- and two-bedroom suites that can accommodate four to six people for weekly stays. Mid-June to mid-September (3-night minimum stay) $105–175, $30 each additional person. Off-season $80–120 (2-night minimum), $30 each additional person. Continental breakfast included for B&B rooms. Suites: late June to early September $1,800–2,450 weekly; otherwise, $1,200–1,700.

❋ **Shady Hollow Inn** (508-394-7474; www.shadyhollowinn.com), 370 Main Street, South Dennis 02660. This off-the-beaten path B&B, with a tranquil side garden for reading and watching the birds, is a graciously renovated sea captain's house that dates to 1839. The four guest rooms (two with shared bath), with mission-style furnishings and quilts, are also outfitted with TV/VCRs and a hefty dose of attention. Hearty vegetarian breakfasts, with organic ingredients as often as possible, are included. The ever-considerate hosts—Ann Hart and David Dennis—also offer use of two loaner bicycles, two kayaks (both on a first-come, first-served basis), and the divine outdoor shower. Join them, on the occasional cool summer evening, as they enjoy their outdoor chimenia. It's always a treat to find places like this. Late May to mid-October $100–125, off-season $80–100.

✎ ❋ **Beach House Inn Bed & Breakfast** (508-398-4575), 61 Uncle Stephen's Road, West Dennis 02670. Off a sandy lane in a residential area (well off Route 28), the Beach House is well suited to families who want to be right on the beach. Parents can watch their kids from the glassed-in breakfast porch or from the deck overlooking the private beach. Although the living room has a beach-worn appearance, the seven guest rooms with wood floors (each with TV and private deck) are nicely decorated. Each room can accommodate two adults and two children, who sleep in sleeping bags on futons. Although guests have access to the fully equipped kitchen, an expanded continental breakfast buffet is included in-season. There are also picnic, barbecue, and play areas on the premises. Mid-June to mid-September $500–700 weekly (with a few nightly slots available); mid-October to mid-May $79 for 3 nights or $500 for the whole house for a whole weekend. No credit cards.

COTTAGES ✎ **Dennis Seashores** (508-398-8512; 508-432-5465 for advance inquiries), 20 Chase Avenue, Dennisport 02639. Open May through October. These 33 house-keeping cottages are some of the best on Nantucket Sound; make reservations a year in advance. The two-, three-, and four-bedroom shingled cottages, with knotty-pine paneling and fireplaces, are decorated and furnished in a "Cape Cod Colonial" style. Cottages, with fully equipped kitchens, towels, and linens, are either beachfront or nestled among pine trees; each has a grill and picnic table. The resort's private stretch of beach is well tended. Early July to early September $1,060–1,415 weekly for a two-bedroom, $1,695–3,695 for a three- or four-bedroom; off-season $455–610 weekly for a two-bedroom. Three-night rentals are available in May, June, September, and October. No credit cards.

RENTAL HOUSES AND COTTAGES For summer rentals, try the helpful **Peter McDowell Associates** (508-385-9114; www.capecodrentals.com), 585 Route 6A in Dennis. They have over 150 houses ranging from $3,200 weekly for a two-bedroom on the water to $2,200 off the water. You can spend as little as $800, though, or as much as $7,000 for a weekly rental.

See also Century 21–Sam Ingram Real Estate in "Yarmouth."

✳ Where to Eat

Dennis has plenty of restaurants to satisfy every budget and whim.

DINING OUT ✳ ♿ **Red Pheasant Inn** (508-385-2133), Route 6A, Dennis. Open for dinner (except during March). Low ceilings, wood floors, exposed beams, and linen-draped tables set a rustic and romantic tone. Located in a 200-year-old renovated barn (actually, a former ship chandlery on Corporation Beach), the restaurant appreciates its local connections: Look for glassware from Sydenstricker and earthenware from Scargo Pottery. The Red Pheasant enjoys a fine reputation for attentive service, first-rate cuisine, and a well-chosen (and a very well-priced) wine list. Prime cuts of lamb, beef, and game with regional American influences are offered. Lobster and other seafood are always popular, and their rack of lamb could compete head to head with anyone's! Chef-owner Bill Atwood and his wife, Denise, have been hosting return patrons since 1980. Reservations highly recommended; off-season early-evening specials. Entrées $18–30.

♈ 🦞 **Ocean House** (508-394-0700, Depot Street, Dennisport. Open for dinner mid-February through December. Don't let appearances deceive you: The boxy brick building belies the ocean views within. Go before sunset to enjoy the water views. Artful chef Tim Miller prepares seasonal, contemporary, world-influenced dishes. Depending on what's available, you might find bouillabaisse, salmon with lobster-mashed potatoes, swordfish Provençal, or short ribs with potato puree. If you don't want to wait for a table, you can get full meals at the bar (off-season), which also serves gourmet pizzas and appetizers. Definitely save room for distinctive desserts. And consider starting with an ice-cold martini. Entrées $17–29.

♿ ♈ **Gina's By The Sea** (508-385-3213), 134 Taunton Avenue, Dennis. Open for dinner Thursday through Sunday, April through November; nightly June through September. Gina's is a very friendly place, with a low-key bar, knotty-pine walls, a fireplace, and exposed beams. A fixture in this beachside enclave since 1938 (chef Chris Lemmer has been cooking since 1990), Gina's really is as consistently good as everyone says. Its northern Italian menu features signature dishes like garlicky shrimp scampi, mussels marinara, and chicken "gizmondo." Because the restaurant is small, very popular, and doesn't take reservations, arrive early or wait until after 9 PM. Otherwise, put your name on the waiting list and take a walk on nearby Chapin Memorial Beach or have a drink and watch the sunset. Entrées $9–22.

✳ **Gerardi's Café** (508-394-3111), 702 Route 28, West Dennis. Open for dinner. New in 2001, this tiny and casual place packs a big punch relative to its size. Look for authentic Italian dishes like chicken Marsala, veal scallopini, and fettuccine Alfredo. You gotta love a place that knows what it is, doesn't overreach, and executes with aplomb. Gerardi's accepts reservations. Entrées $12–19.

🦞 ✳ ✎ ♿ **Scargo Cafe** (508-385-8200), Route 6A, Dennis. Open for lunch and dinner. The friendly staff here are particularly adept at getting patrons to Cape Playhouse shows (see *Entertainment*) on time without hurrying them. If you're *really* late, light bites and finger foods such as "Arizona" shrimp and pesto bruschetta are served in the pleasant bar. Otherwise, always dependable specials include "wildcat chicken" with Italian sausage and mushrooms, a vegetable-and-Brie sandwich, and seafood strudel. As for the atmosphere, the bustling, renovated former sea captain's house is awash in wood: paneling, wainscoting, and floors. Brothers Peter and David Troutman have presided over the extensive and well-executed menu since 1987. Off-season early specials. Lunch $6–14, dinner $7–22.

✆ **Ebb Tide** (508-398-8733), 94 Chase Avenue, Dennisport. Open for dinner early May to mid-October. The McCormick family, serving classic New England meals since 1959, takes great pride in what they do, including teaching at the Cape Cod Community College's culinary arts and management program. Their restaurant offers fine dining without the customary formality. It's the kind of place that serves sorbet between courses but that also has a children's menu. Specialties include baked stuffed scrod with lobster stuffing, broiled swordfish with béarnaise sauce, prime rib, lobster, and seafood Newburg. Extensive early menu 4:30–5:30. Entrées $14–26.

EATING OUT ✳ **Contrast Bistro and Espresso Bar** (508-385-9100), 605 Route 6A, Dennis. Open for lunch and dinner. For a quick lunch (or strong take-out cappuccino) in refreshingly untraditional surroundings, Contrast offers salads, frittatas, quiche, chili, and sandwiches. The decor screams hip and artsy: bright

blue ceilings, red walls, and oversized modern paintings. At dinner, stick to specials or comfort foods like chicken potpie or Caesar salad with chicken. Lunch $7–9, dinner entrées $10–22.

🦞 ✳ ✆ **Marshside** (508-385-4010), 25 Bridge Street, East Dennis. Open for all three meals and Sunday brunch. A local favorite, Marshside is noted for its casual atmosphere (with country-floral tablecloths, for instance), good food (shrimp scampi, lobster, salads, sandwiches, and veggie melts), and reasonable prices (you can get a teriyaki chicken salad for $8.50). It's a family-oriented restaurant that provides coloring books, toys, and contests for children. Some tables overlook the namesake marsh, with a view of Sesuit Harbor. Lunch $5–16, dinner $7–17.

🦞 ✆ **Sesuit Harbor Café** (508-385-6134; 508-385-2442), on Sesuit Harbor. Open seasonally. Drive through the marina and boatyard to get to this simple harborfront shack. It's nothing to look at, but the raised herb beds augur well for quality ingredients and attention to detail. Order off the blackboard menu and eat at picnic tables, inside or outside, with mismatched umbrellas. Dishes $5–15.

✳ **Lost Dog Pub** (508-385-6177), 1374 Route 134, East Dennis. Open daily for lunch and dinner. I wouldn't waste good daylight hours here at lunchtime, but this place makes a cozy spot after dark—when you just want something homey and decent, with good service. Their burgers are good; seafood is a specialty, of course. Entrées $9–14.

✆ ♿ **Lighthouse Inn** (508-398-2244), off Lower County Road, on the road to West Dennis Beach. Open for breakfast and dinner, mid-

May to mid-October, and for lunch in July and August. The decor here, as well as the cuisine, is decidedly old-fashioned. Indoor tables are draped with white linen, and the service is professional; it's the kind of place you might expect in the Catskills, à la 1950. Except this is seaside. Along with peaked ceilings and knotty-pine paneling, the large and open dining room features a full wall of windows overlooking the ocean. I prefer their casual lunch-eons, served on the oceanfront deck; the seaside setting is a treat. Keep it simple with sandwiches, broiled or fried fish, burgers, and light salads. Cocktails are served on the deck after 4 PM. The extensive dinner menu is reasonably priced, and steamed lobster is always a popular choice. Breakfast is a hot or cold buf-fet ($11 and $7, respectively). Lunch $7–13, dinner entrées $17–26.

🐾 ♂ **Bob Briggs' "Wee Packet"** (508-398-2181), Depot Street, Den-nisport. Open 11:30–8:30 daily, May through September; open for break-fast late June to early September. This spiffy little restaurant, regarded with great affection by hordes of repeat customers, was opened in 1949 by Bob Briggs. (In case you're wonder-ing, a *wee packet* is a small ship.) Today Bob's son Rob and daughter Sheila carry on the tradition. An exposed kitchen, counter-style seat-ing, and a dining room with shiny yel-low tables and bright yellow walls lend the place a homespun feel. As for the food, specialties include Cape Cod Bay scallops, onion rings, fried lobster, and Sheila's homemade desserts, including blueberry short-cake. Dishes $3–16. Look for the old-fashioned doughnut shop and bakery

next door. Opened in 1997, it's already become a local tradition.

♂ ❄ **The Breakfast Room** (508-398-0581), 675 Route 28, West Dennis. Open for breakfast 7–2 daily, April through November; weekends year-round. This place is classic, a local fix-ture. In addition to griddle cakes, you can order no-nonsense egg dishes or go whole hog and chow down on steak, eggs, and potatoes. They have cran-nut pancakes, eggs Benedict, and French toast, too. In high season, you can wait 40 minutes for a table. Dishes $4–10.

♿ 🐾 ♂ **Captain Frosty's** (508-385-8548), 219 Route 6A, Dennis. Open 11–8 or 9 early April through Septem-ber; closed Monday off-season. Since 1976, Mike and Pat Henderson have run one of the Cape's best roadside clam shacks. The Hendersons use only premium ingredients, including hooked (not gillnetted) Chatham cod, Gulf shrimp, native clams, lobster, and small sea scallops. Daily specials are always fresh. You can also rest assured that the seafood and onion rings are deep-fried in 100 percent canola oil. You can choose among the casual dining room, outdoor seating at a brick patio surrounded by rhodo-dendrons, and take-out. Frosty's is also Route 6A's original soft-serve dairy bar, established in the 1950s. Dishes $3–14. No credit cards.

🐾 ❄ ♂ **Bob's Best Sandwiches** (508-394-8450), 613 Route 28, Dennisport. Open for breakfast and lunch year-round, and dinner in summer. There really is a Bob, and his sandwiches are made with thick slices of homemade bread and thick slices of home-smoked turkey or roast beef. If you're a Texas chili fan, Bob's rules. For breakfast, you have a choice of veggie omelets, homemade French toast, and the like. Early specials; dishes $4–7.

Ø **Swan River Seafood** (508-394-4466), 5 Lower County Road, Dennisport. Open for lunch and dinner, late May to late September; take-out, too. This casual restaurant's appeal is fresh, fresh, hook-caught fish, thanks to the attached fish market. Cynthia Ahern, chef-owner since the mid-1970s, keeps it simple with lobster, clams, oysters, and the catch of the day. Arrive early to secure a table overlooking a river, marsh, Nantucket Sound, and windmill. Lunch $5–10, dinner $12–18.

Ŷ **Clancy's Fish 'n Chips and Beach Bar** (508-394-6900), 228 Lower County Road, Dennisport. Open for lunch and dinner mid-May to early September. You can count on reliable seafood in pleasant and casual surroundings here. Food arrives in plastic baskets at outdoor tables under canvas umbrellas, within the screened-in porch, or at shiny wooden tables with directors' chairs. Try the boneless Buffalo wings. Or belly up to the convivial bar. Dishes $6–19.

Ø **Kream 'n' Kone** (508-394-0808), Route 28, Dennisport. Open February through October. Honest-to-goodness kitsch, not imported from any consultant who says kitsch is cool. Self-serve fried seafood, ice cream, and clams. Booth seating. Although it's campy, it is not necessarily cheap; a family can easily spend $60 here.

& ● **The Dog House** (508-398-7774), 189 Lower County Road, Dennisport. Open 11–7 seasonally. This old-fashioned hot dog stand dispenses dogs with sauerkraut or bacon and cheese or lots of other combinations for $2–6. After you've ordered from the take-out window, have a seat at one of a few covered picnic tables. Green Mountain coffee, too.

See also Woolfies Home Bakery under *Coffee and Sweets.*

COFFEE AND SWEETS ❊ **Buckies Biscotti & Co** (508-385-4700; 877-247-2688), 780 Route 6A. Open 6:30–6:30 daily. On the grounds of the playhouse and behind the post office, this tiny ground-level place has excellent espresso and authentic Italian cookies, biscotti, and cannoli. Long live entrepreneurs like baker Alyson Bucchiere, who does a brisk mail-order business.

❊ **Stage Coach Candy** (508-394-1791), 411 Main Street, Dennisport. Ray and Donna Hebert originated the ultimate chocolate-covered cranberry. You gotta try it. They'll make chocolates in any shape, including computer boards and TV remote controls.

Sundae School Ice Cream Parlor (508-394-9122), 387 Lower County Road, Dennisport. Open mid-April to mid-October, until 11 PM in summer for that late-night fix. This old-fashioned parlor is replete with a marble soda fountain, marble tables, tin signage, and a nickelodeon. Some confections are delightfully modern, though: Frozen yogurt and ice cream are made with two-thirds less fat. Fruit sundaes are very good, too.

Woolfies Home Bakery, 279 Lower County Road, Dennisport. Open daily, May through September. Terri Moretti whips up honey wheat bread for the morning and walnut Danish rings and éclairs for the afternoon. It's frankly not so much *what* she whips up as it is having an inviting and low-key place to enjoy it. Typical breakfast selections and lunch items like focaccia and pizza are also offered.

GO FLY A KITE!

Kim Grant

Wednesday through Saturday
Woolfies stays open until 10 PM, when
indoor tables and the outside patio
furniture are candlelit. Otherwise, the
shaded front lawn has rocking chairs
and benches.

P&D Fruit, Lower County Road,
Dennisport. Open mid-May to mid-
September. Who says the southside of
Cape Cod is so commercialized that
you can't find a decent farm stand?
Look no further.

&. **Ice Cream Smuggler** (508-385-5307), 716 Route 6A, Dennis. Open late March to late October. Homemade ice cream—including a great mocha chip—and frozen yogurt.

See also Bob Briggs' "Wee Packet" and Contrast Bistro and Espresso Bar under *Eating Out*.

✴ Entertainment

&. ✾ ✎ ☂ **Cape Playhouse** (508-385-3838; 508-385-3911 box office; www.capeplayhouse.com), Route 6A, Dennis. Shows daily but with a limited Sunday schedule, mid-June to early September. The Cape Playhouse was established in 1927 by Californian Raymond Moore, who initially went to Provincetown to start a theater company but found it too remote. Moore's attitude when he purchased this former 1830s Unitarian meetinghouse for $200 was, "If we fix it up, they will come." Sure enough, the playhouse proudly claims the title of the country's oldest continuously operating professional summer theater and the Cape's only full Equity

theater. Basil Rathbone starred in the company's first production, *The Guardsman*. Over the years, the playhouse has featured the likes of Helen Hayes, Julie Harris, Olivia de Havilland, and Jessica Tandy, when they were already "stars." Henry Fonda, Bette Davis, Humphrey Bogart, and Gregory Peck acted here before they were "discovered." On Friday mornings in July and August there is **children's theater.** If you make it to only one summer production, let it be here. Tickets $20–38; children's theater $6.

✎ **Band concerts,** whether the music be country or American classics, are held on both town greens in July and August. Head to Dennis on Route 6A every other Monday and Dennisport off Route 28 on Wednesday. Check with the chamber (see *Guidance*) for an exact schedule of places and times.

✴ ♈ **The Olde Inn of West Dennis** (508-760-2627), 348 Route 28. This Irish pub is packed with locals.

✴ ♈ **Michael Patrick's Publick** (508-398-1620), 435 Route 28, Den-

---

HEAVENLY SCREENINGS

Cape Cinema (508-385-2503; www.capecinema.com), Route 6A, Dennis. Screenings daily, mid-April through October. Built in 1930 as a movie theater, Cape Cinema continues to bring fine art films, foreign films, and independent productions to Cape audiences. The exterior was designed after the Congregational church in Centerville, while the interior ceiling was designed by Rockwell Kent to represent his view of heaven, filled with comets and constellations. When Kent refused to set foot in Massachusetts because he was protesting the 1921 verdict in the Sacco and Vanzetti trial, Jo Mielziner supervised the painting and installation of the 6,400-square-foot art deco mural, which was done by the Art Students League in a New York theater and shipped by train to the Cape. There are about 300 seats in this theater, which was chosen to premiere *The Wizard of Oz* in 1940. Don't miss catching a flick here; screening times are usually 4:30, 7, and 9. Tickets $7.50 adults, $4 children.

nisport. Open daily. Another local favorite. You decide which you like better; I'm not going to wade into that one.

Christine's (508-394-7333), 581 Route 28, West Dennis. This restaurant and show club features a full lineup of jazz, cabaret, comedy, dance, and party bands—groups you've heard of—nightly in summer.

🐾 ☂ ❄ MOVIES **Hoyts Cinemas** (508-394-1100), Patriot Square Mall, South Dennis. Take exit 9 off Route 6.

See also Cape Museum of Fine Arts under *To See*.

❋ Selective Shopping

❋ Unless otherwise noted, all shops are open year-round.

ANTIQUES Dennisport center is becoming a quiet place for year-round antiques browsers. There are more than half a dozen shops within a block, chief among them **Main Street Antique Center** (508-760-5700), 691 Main. With more than 100 dealers, it's just one of many retailers trying to revitalize the little district. Also, stop into **Antiques at 671 Main** (508-398-0100) and **South Side Antique Center** (508-394-8601).

Mrs. Mugs (508-362-6462), 680 Route 6A, East Sandwich. Reader Janet Grant (no relation) and my mother (relation) write passionately about this place, which has mugs (of course) but also specialty foods and unique watches. The owner, Lori Simon, is very beloved by her customers.

Webfoot Farm Antiques (508-385-

2334), 1475 Route 6A, East Dennis. Each of the four tasteful rooms in this 1845 captain's house is crammed with impressive Continental, American, and English decorative arts and fine antiques. The sterling collection is strong, as are the Oriental porcelains and pottery.

Gloria Swanson Antiques (508-385-4166), 608 Route 6A, Dennis. This shop is brimming with Flow Blue, Mulberry, and Staffordshire china, early glass and bottles, teapots, and tins. It's a treasure.

Antiques Center of Cape Cod (508-385-6400), 243 Route 6A, Dennis. With more than 150 dealers, this two-story (former) building supply store is the Cape's largest cooperative, offering curios large and small. Don't miss it or the giant warehouse next door. Most objects sell for under $200 and are classified as "old," "vintage," or "collectible" rather than "antique."

Antiques 608 (508-385-2755, 385-4166), 608 Route 6A, Dennis. This multidealer shop deals more in what owner Marcia Cardaropoli calls "junque," but if you hunt through the stuff you'll find antiquarian books, Flow Blue, Staffordshire, daguerreotypes, and ephemera.

Finders Keepers (508-760-3440), 257 Lower County Road, Dennisport. Antiques, nautical items, glass, toys, even fishing poles: This shop has a little of everything and is great fun.

ART GALLERIES **Grose Gallery** (508-385-3434), 524 Route 6A, Dennis. This barn-gallery features the work of illustrator and printmaker David Grose, who created the wood engravings and pen drawings for three of John Hay's books: *The Great Beach, Nature's Year,* and *The Run.*

He also has produced serigraphs of Dennis landmarks.

The Artists Gallery (508-385-4600), 593 Route 6A, Dennis. While the art may be a bit uneven, you do have the opportunity to buy direct from the artists at this cooperative.

Wilson Gallery (508-385-0856), 800 Route 6A, Dennis. The directors here, a father-and-son team, thankfully see no reason to traffic in Cape Cod landscapes and scenics. Their gallery on Newbury Street was quite sophisticated and the art here speaks for itself, too. It's refreshing.

Kate Nelson (at **Ross Coppelman**) (508-385-7900), 1439 Route 6A, East Dennis. Open April through December. Kate's work is some of the most sophisticated abstraction I've seen on the Cape. Her nonrepresentational paintings and prints are extraordinary and, as she says, "ever-changing, like the path to the outgoing tide on the Brewster flats." She continues to fuse the experience of exterior landscape with the "inscape," the inner landscape of psyche and spirit.

ARTISANS **Fritz Glass** (508-394-0441; www.fritzglass.com), 36 Upper County Road, Dennisport. Open 11–4 Monday, Wednesday, and Friday in summer, and by appointment. Although this is primarily a wholesale glassblowing operation, the colorful and striking showroom is filled with extraordinarily decorative, functional creations. You can watch Fritz Lauenstein work and check out the inventory of fun and intricate marbles (sold in museums around the country) and sand dollars, honey pots and bud vases. Chances are that Fritz's wife, June, and daughter Coco will be in the shop, too.

Scargo Pottery (508-385-3894; www.scargopottery.com), 30 Dr. Lord Road South, off Route 6A, Dennis. Down a path through the woods, potter Harry Holl, his four daughters (Tina, Kim, Mary, and Sarah), and son-in-law (Kevin) make whimsical and decidedly untraditional birdhouses, fountains, and architectural sculptures, among other things. The "gallery" is a magical world that you won't want to miss: Pieces hang from tree branches and sit on tree stumps. The work isn't cheap, but it isn't run-of-the-mill, either. There's no question that this is pottery as art. Harry has been working here since 1952.

A Touch of Glass (508-398-3850), 711 Route 28, West Dennis. These stained-glass lamps and lamp shades have been created using the same techniques employed by Tiffany.

AUCTIONS **Eldred's Auctions** (508-385-3116), 1483 Route 6A, East Dennis. This high-end auction house—the Cape's largest—moves magnificent collections. In July the weekly auctions concentrate on books, collectibles, marine items, and paintings. During August there is an Americana auction the first week; a fine and decorative arts auction the second week; and a weeklong Oriental auction late in the month. In spring and fall, call about the monthly specialty auctions.

BOOKSTORES **Arm Chair Bookstore** (508-385-0900; www.armchairbookstore.com), 619 Route 6A, Dennis. Open 9:30 AM–9 PM in summer; shorter hours off-season. This fantastic, family-owned and -operated shop has a devoted following, with obvious reason. There simply isn't a more inviting bookstore on the Cape.

Patty Barnes began the shop, and now her family helps her run it.

Paperback Cottage (508-760-2101), 927 Route 28 at Route 134, next to the chamber of commerce booth, South Dennis. Open daily in summer; Thursday through Monday in spring and fall; Saturday through Monday in winter. In addition to selling books the old-fashioned way, Joan Sullivan rents books by the week. She has a good children's section, too.

JEWELERS **Michael Baksa Studio** (508-385-5733), 766 Route 6A, Dennis, and **Ross Coppelman** (508-385-7900), 1439 Route 6A, East Dennis, have fashioned stunning designs as goldsmiths for more than 20 years. Both men work on the premises. Ross's shop is a special-occasion kind of place; his creations have lots of zeros on the price tags. If you're serious about having a stone set or buying something in gold or silver, don't overlook **Jewelry by Etta** (508-394-8964), 530 Route 28, West Dennis. Many people who don't venture to the southside are unaware of Etta and unwittingly bypass this fine, singular shop.

SPECIAL SHOPS **Arm Chair Cottage** (508-385-4808; www.armchair-cottage.com), 611 Route 6A, Dennis. Search no more for that distinctive summery cottage look. Loaded with Maine cottage furniture and Cape Cod gifts, this fun store appeals to all budgets. Offerings are built around colors, which makes shopping all that much easier and harder to resist.

Wee Cottage Baby (508-385-2929), 623 Route 6A, Dennis. This small shop is devoted to baby gifts and items.

Grandma Daisy's (508-394-3373), 444 Lower County Road. Open early May to mid-December. This former blacksmith's barn is loaded with tasteful gifts for any occasion, books, and distinctive home accessories. It's great browsing *and* buying.

Tobey Farm, Route 6A, Dennis. This colorful farm has been in the same family since 1678, when it was given to Thomas Tobey for his service during King Philip's War.

✑ **Pizazz** (508-760-3888), 633 Route 28, Dennisport. Giant blowup beach toys and summer novelties. There are dozens of other similar shops, but they just don't have pizzazz, so to speak.

✻ Special Events

Mid- to late June: **Secret Garden Tour,** sponsored by the Cape Museum of Fine Arts (508-385-4477, ext. 19). Tour gardens and watch artists paint their inspiration.

✑ *Mid- to late August:* **Dennis Festival Days.** Billed as the Cape's oldest festival (since 1958), this 5-day celebration includes a crafts fair, an antique-auto parade, kite-flying and sand-castle-building contests, puppet shows, fireworks, and band concerts.

The Lower Cape

BREWSTER

HARWICH

CHATHAM

ORLEANS

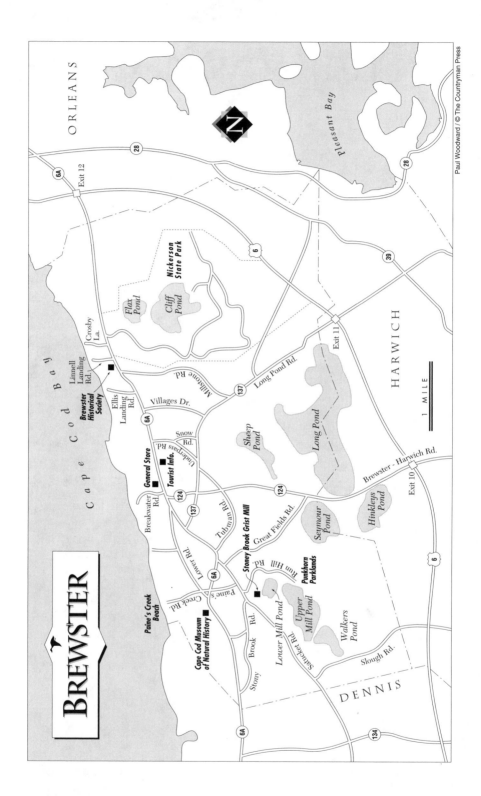

BREWSTER

ORLEANS

Cape Cod Bay

Pleasant Bay

Nickerson State Park

Flax Pond

Cliff Pond

Crosby La.

Linnell Landing Rd.

Brewster Historical Society

Ellis Landing Rd.

Villages Dr.

Millstone Rd.

Long Pond Rd.

Snow Rd.

Underpass Rd.

General Store

Tourist Info.

Sheep Pond

Long Pond

HARWICH

1 MILE

Breakwater Rd.

Tubman Rd.

Great Fields Rd.

Stoney Brook Grist Mill

Seymour Pond

Hinkleys Pond

Brewster - Harwich Rd.

Exit 10

Exit 11

Paine's Creek Beach

Lower Rd.

Paine's Creek Rd.

Run Hill Rd.

Punkhorn Parklands

Cape Cod Museum of Natural History

Stony Brook Rd.

Lower Mill Pond

Upper Mill Pond

Setucket Rd.

Walkers Pond

Slough Rd.

DENNIS

Exit 12

6A

28

6

39

137

124

137

124

6A

6A

6

134

Paul Woodward / © The Countryman Press

BREWSTER

Y ou could spend a charmed week in Brewster with plenty to occupy you. While the 2,000-acre Nickerson State Park boasts facilities for a dozen outdoor activities, there is also Punkhorn Parklands, an undeveloped, 800-acre parcel of conservation land in town. Although Brewster has only 8,700 year-round residents, it has more than its share of attractions, including two good golf courses, horseback-riding trails, an outstanding museum of natural history, a few smaller museums, and exceptional dining choices.

Brewster's section of Route 6A is a vital link in the 80-square-mile Old King's Highway Historic District. Known for its selection of fine antiques shops, Brewster also attracts contemporary artists, who are drawn to a landscape more evocative of the countryside than the seaside—the land south of Route 6A is dotted with ponds, hills, and dales.

Brewster, settled in 1659 and named for *Mayflower* passenger Elder William Brewster, wasn't incorporated until 1803, when it split from Harwich. By then the prosperous sea captains who'd built their homes on the bay side wanted to distance themselves from their less-well-off neighbors to the south. Between 1780 and 1870, 99 sea captains called Brewster home (although they sailed their clipper ships out of Boston and New York), a fact that even Henry David Thoreau commented on during his 1849 trip. Many of these beautiful houses on Route 6A have been converted to B&Bs and inns.

In the early 1800s, Breakwater Beach was a popular landing for packet ships, which transported salt and vegetables to Boston and New York markets and brought tourists to the area. Salt making was big business in 1837, when more than 60 saltworks dotted Brewster beaches. Windmills pumped seawater into 36-by-18-foot vats, where it was left to evaporate (this process was developed in Dennis). During the late 18th and early 19th centuries, Brewster's Factory Village sold cloth, boots, and food to people all over the Cape.

GUIDANCE Brewster Visitor Information Center (508-896-3500; www.brewstercapecod.org), 2198 Route 6A (P.O. Box 1241), about half a mile east of Route 124, in the rear of the town offices. Open 9–3 daily June to early September; 9–1 Tuesday through Saturday from late April through May and early September to mid-October. Jan Moore and the staff here are very friendly and quite knowledgeable.

PUBLIC REST ROOMS Public rest rooms are located at Nickerson State Park and the Visitor Information Center, both on Route 6A.

PUBLIC LIBRARY See Brewster Ladies' Library under *To See*.

GETTING THERE *By car:* Brewster is 30 minutes from the Cape Cod Canal (take Route 6 east to exit 9, to Route 134, to Route 6A); it is 45 minutes from Provincetown, at the tip of the peninsula.

GETTING AROUND Brewster is very easy to get around. There's no real "center" to the town; places of interest are strung along Route 6A.

MEDICAL EMERGENCY **Call 911.**

✳ To See

☂ ✳ ✇ **Cape Cod Museum of Natural History** (508-896-3867; www.ccmnh. org), 869 Route 6A. Open 9:30–4:30 Monday through Saturday, 11–4:30 Sunday. Founded by naturalist John Hay (along with seven local educators) in 1954, this is one of the best resources for learning about the Cape's natural world. The museum takes its mission seriously: to "inspire and foster an understanding and appreciation of our environment through education, and a means to sustain it." You can check out marine tanks (containing crabs, lobsters, mollusks, turtles, eels, and frogs), whale displays, a natural history library, as well as many interactive, hands-on exhibits for kids. The gift shop is packed with fun and educational toys, books, and games. The John Wing Trail—just one trail traversing the museum's 80 acres of marshes, beaches, and woodland—begins from here (see *Green Space—Walks*). Adults $5; children 5–12, $2; fee for some programs. (Also see Summer camps under *For Families*.)

Stoney Brook Grist Mill and Herring Run (508-896-1734), Stony Brook Road. This millside pond is one of the Cape's most picturesque places, especially during the spring migration (mid-April to early May), when the herring are "running" and the natural "ladders" are packed with the silver-backed fish. In 1663 America's first water-powered mill stood on this location. The present gristmill, constructed on 1873 woolen mill foundations (part of the 19th-century Factory Village), contains old milling equipment and a 100-year-old loom on which age-old techniques are demonstrated by special request (508-896-6194). Donations.

✳ **The Brewster Store** (508-896-3744), 1935 Route 6A at Route 124. Open daily. Purveying groceries and general merchandise since 1866, this quintessentially Cape Cod store was built in 1852 as a Universalist church. Since then, four generations of families have relied on the store. As always, locals and visitors sit outside on old church pews, sip coffee, read the morning newspaper, eat penny candy and ice cream, and watch the world go by. Upstairs has been re-created with memorabilia from the mid-1800s to the mid-1900s; downstairs has a working antique nickelodeon and oft-used peanut roaster.

✳ ✇ ☂ **Brewster Ladies' Library** (508-896-3913), 1822 Route 6A. Open 10–8 Tuesday and Wednesday, 10–6 Thursday, and 10–4 Friday and Saturday. In 1852

LOCALS AND VISITORS ENJOY COFFEE AND THE MORNING PAPER AT THE 1866
BREWSTER STORE.

two teenage Brewster girls established this "library," which began as a shelf of books lent from the girls' houses. After local sea captains donated funds in 1868, the ever-expanding library moved to a handsome red Victorian building. The two original front-parlor rooms—each with a fireplace, stained-glass windows, and armchairs—are still filled with portraits of sea captains and ships. Not just for ladies, the modern library has a large children's area, videos, CDs, periodicals, newspapers, Internet access, and word processing equipment. Call for current information about musicals, lectures, and art exhibits.

✍ New England Fire & History Museum

(508-896-5711), 1439 Route 6A. Open 10–4 weekdays and noon–4 weekends, late May through August; open noon–4 weekends, September to mid-October. Surrounding a 19th-century New England–style town common, this complex includes an apothecary's shop, a blacksmith shop, antique fire-fighting equipment, a diorama of the 1871 Chicago Fire, a "Boston Burns 1872" exhibit, 10 life-sized figures of firefighters through the centuries, and 35 working fire engines. Some exhibits are on loan from the Smithsonian. Picnic area. Adults $5; children 5–12, $2.50.

Brewster Historical Society Museum

(508-896-9521), 3341 Route 6A. Open 1–4 weekends in mid- to late

TIDAL FLATS

At low tide, you can walk 2 miles out onto the tidal flats of Cape Cod Bay. During Prohibition, townspeople walking on the flats would often stumble onto cases of liquor thrown overboard by rumrunners. But encounters are tamer these days: Kids discover tidal pools, play in channels left by receding tides, and marvel at streaked "garnet" sand. On a clear day you can gaze from the Provincetown Monument to Sandwich. You can reach the flats from any of the bay beaches.

June and early to mid-September; 1–4 Tuesday through Friday in July and August. Free. Highlighting Brewster's rich heritage, this small museum has an 1884 barbershop, an 1830s sea captain's room, dolls and toys, the old East Brewster Post Office, and antique gowns. A walking trail originates from the house (see Spruce Hill Conservation Area under *Green Space—Walks*).

Crosby Mansion (508-896-1744), Crosby Lane off Route 6A. This Colonial Revival, once the elegant home of Albert and Matilda Crosby, sits on 19 acres of bayside property. Massachusetts acquired the land (and the house by default) by eminent domain in 1985 so that the public could access Cape Cod Bay from Nickerson State Park. Because the state couldn't afford to maintain it (the 28-room mansion requires millions in repairs), a volunteer group, the Friends of Crosby Mansion, stepped in. They've done an impressive job repairing the worst structural damage and much of the interior.

Once upon a time, Albert Crosby owned the Chicago Opera House and fell in love with one of the showgirls, Matilda. When she came to live in Albert's modest turn-of-the-20th-century house, she was so unhappy that Albert had a mansion built for her—around his original four-room house! (Kids compare stepping into the smaller house to what Alice must have felt like in Wonderland.) Matilda is said to have entertained in the larger mansion while Albert stayed in his interior boyhood home. The mansion is open 5 days per season—the first and third Sunday in July and August and during the weekend of Brewster in Bloom (see *Special Events*)—but you can always peek in the oversized windows.

✔ **First Parish Church** (508-896-5577), 1969 Route 6A, on the town green, which is also nicknamed the Egg because of its shape and natural depression. Gothic windows and a bell tower mark the church's 1834 clapboard exterior, while interior pews are marked with names of prominent Brewster sea captains. Wander around the graveyard behind the church, too. On summertime Wednesday mornings at 10 AM), marionette shows are held ($6).

Higgins Farm Windmill and **Harris-Black House** (508-896-9521), 785 Route 6A, Drummer Boy Park. Hours unavailable at press time. These two structures are operated by the Brewster Historical Society. Members are on hand to tell you that a family raised 10 children in the one-room house (possibly the "last remaining primitive one-room house on the Cape"), and that the 1795 windmill is known for its octagonal design, while its top resembles a boat's hull. Free.

✴ Outdoor Activities

✔ **BASEBALL** The Brewster Whitecaps (508-896-3424), who joined the Cape Cod Baseball League in 1988 as an expansion team, play at the Cape Cod Technical High School, Route 124, Harwich. From mid-June to early August, games begin at 5 PM.

The Whitecaps also sponsor weeklong, weekday clinics from mid-June to early August for boys and girls age 6–13. Pick up registration forms at the Visitor Information Center, then meet at the Cape Cod Tech High School on Route 124 in Harwich.

BICYCLING/RENTALS Because the Cape Cod Rail Trail runs through Brewster, and Nickerson State Park (see the "Supreme State Park" sidebar) has its own network of bicycle trails linked to the trail, there are many places to rent bicycles in town. Look for **Rail Trail Bike & Blades** (508-896-8200), 302 Underpass Road. It rents and sells bikes year-round. **Brewster Bike** (508-896-8149), 442 Underpass Road, is open seasonally. Both shops offer plenty of parking. In-season rates are about $10 for 2 hours, $15 for 4 hours, $22 for 24 hours, $48 for 3 days, $70 weekly. Pick up the excellent, free Nickerson trail map.

If you brought your own bikes, there is rail-trail parking on Route 137, on Underpass Road off Route 137, and at Nickerson State Park on Route 6A.

✔ Trailers and alleycats (rented above) for hauling kids are great for this stretch because it's shady and fairly flat. Nickerson trails are a bit hillier.

BOATING/RENTALS See the sidebar "A Supreme State Park" under *Green Space*.

FISHING/SHELLFISHING Brewster has almost 50 freshwater ponds; required state fishing licenses are obtained from the town clerk's offices (508-896-3701), 2198 Route 6A. The following ponds are stocked: **Sheep Pond,** off Route 124, and **Flax, Little Cliff,** and **Higgins Ponds** within Nickerson State Park.

For shellfishing permits, head to the Visitor Information Center in summer; head to the town offices weekdays off-season. In July and August shellfishing is permitted only on Thursday and Sunday. (In June, it's AOK daily.) Shellfish beds at **Saint's Landing Beach** (off Lower Road from Route 6A) are seeded in summer. Quahogs and sea clams are harvested June to mid-September; steamers are harvested October to mid-April. Nonresident permits cost $15 weekly.

✔ **FOR FAMILIES Summer camps** (508-896-3867; www.ccmnh.org), 869 Route 6A, at the Cape Cod Museum of Natural History (see *To See*). Got an extra 2 hours or 5 days? Got children age 3–15? These classes explore "incredible insects," "marine mania," tidal flats, archaeology, and Monomoy's barrier beach. The emphasis is on fun, outdoor adventure, and education. Adults are catered to with canoe trips, birding trips, walking tours, Cape Cod Bay ecology trips, and excursions to Monomoy (see *Outdoor Activities—Boat Excursions/Rentals* in "Chatham"). Call for a schedule of programs.

Playground by the Bay, Drummer Boy Park, Route 6A. Shaped like a packet ship to honor Brewster's seafaring history, this play structure has separate areas for toddlers and older kids. Picnic tables.

See also Cape Repertory Theatre under *Entertainment* and First Parish Church under *To See*.

❋ **GOLF Captain's Golf Course** (508-896-5100; 508-896-1716 pro shop), 1000 Freeman's Way off Route 6A. Rated among the top 25 public courses by *Golf Digest,* you'll find 36 holes (named for Brewster sea captains) at the Port and Starboard Courses. The adjacent practice center is quite extensive.

Ocean Edge Golf Club (508-896-5911), Villages Drive off Route 6A. This 18-hole, tournament-caliber course designed by Cornish and Silva has Scottish-style bunkers and one hole that crosses a cranberry bog.

HORSEBACK RIDING ❋ ♘ **Woodsong Farm Equestrian Center** (508-896-5800), 121 Lund Farm Way. Open daily by appointment. Established in 1967, Woodsong offers riding instruction, boarding, training, coaching for competitive riders, children's day programs (Horsemasters for experienced riders age 8–18 and Pony Kids, an introductory program, for kids 5–13), horse shows, two-phase events, and an on-premises tack shop.

IN-LINE SKATING ❋ **Rail Trail Bike & Blades** (508-896-8200), 302 Underpass Road. Skate rentals, including pads and helmets, daily.

SAILING **Cape Sail** (508-896-2730; www.c4.net/capesail), out of Brewster and Harwich Harbors. Late May to mid-October. Captain Bob Rice has been offering customized sailing lessons and an overnight sailing school since 1983. The price for two people for instruction and an overnight to Nantucket (accommodations on board) is $850; $1,150 for four. Otherwise, the 6-hour basic course takes place over 3 days and costs $360 for one person, $540 for two. Bob also leads custom charters ($750 for two to Nantucket without lessons, for example) and sunset and moonlight cruises. He doesn't have any set schedule, so call him to discuss your interests.

TENNIS There are four public courts located **behind the Fire and Police Department** near the town offices, Route 6A. Free.

Ocean Edge Resort (508-896-4880) has five Har-Tru and six hard courts, which are open from mid-April through October. Non–resort guests pay $15 for the court and then $5 per person per hour.

❋ Green Space

BEACHES Brewster has 8 miles of waterfront on Cape Cod Bay and eight public beaches, none of which is particularly spacious and all of which are located off Route 6A. Daily ($8), weekly ($25), and seasonal parking permits are purchased at the Visitor Information Center (508-896-4511), 2198 Route 6A, 9–3 daily from mid-June to early September. (In other words, you cannot pay at the beach.) No permit is required at any town beach after 3 PM.

Paine's Creek Beach, Paine's Creek Road off Route 6A. This is one of Brewster's most picturesque beaches because of the creek that feeds into it. Parking fee.

PONDS **Long Pond** and **Sheep Pond,** both off Route 124, have freshwater swimming and sandy beaches. Long Pond has a lifeguard. Long and Sheep Ponds are among the best of Brewster's more than 50 ponds. Parking permits are required for residents and visitors.

See also the sidebar "A Supreme State Park."

A SUPREME STATE PARK

Nickerson State Park (508-896-3491; www.state.ma.us/dem), 3488 Route 6A. Open dawn to dusk daily. This former estate of Chatham native Roland Nickerson, a multimillionaire who founded the First National Bank of Chicago, contains more than 2,000 acres of pine, hemlock, and spruce and includes eight kettle ponds. Nickerson and his wife, Addie, who entertained such notables as President Grover Cleveland, had a fairly self-sufficient estate, with their own electric generator, ponds teeming with fish, vegetable gardens, and game that roamed the land. When the mansion that Roland's father, Samuel, built for him burned down in 1906, a disconsolate Roland died two weeks later. (The "replacement" is now the Ocean Edge Conference Center.) Addie ultimately donated the land in 1934 to honor their son, who died in the 1918 influenza epidemic.

Nickerson State Park has been developed with walking trails, bicycling trails, jogging paths, picnic sites, boat launches, and sandy beaches. Winter conditions often provide for ice skating and ice fishing and occasionally for cross-country skiing. (Snow rarely stays on the ground for more than a few days, though.) If you're at all interested in the out-of-doors, don't bypass Nickerson, one of the Cape's real treasures. Almost 300,000 people visit each year. Day use is free.

Within the park you'll find:

Jack's Boat Rentals (508-896-8556), open mid-June to early September. Jack's rents canoes, kayaks, Sunfish, surf bikes, sea cycles, and pedal–boats on Flax Pond. Rates $20-28 hourly, depending on what you rent; each additional hour about 40 percent less.

Flax Pond and **Cliff Pond**. Flax has Nickerson's best public beach, picnic tables, and a bathhouse, but no lifeguard. Cliff Pond is ringed with little beaches, but bathers share the pond with motorized boats. (It's not really a problem, though.)

🦌 💧 ⛺ **Camping** (877-422-6762 reservations; www.reserveamerica.com; 508-896-3491 for general, in-season information), mid-April to mid-October. Since Nickerson is very popular, summer reservations are absolutely essential. They're also accepted six months in advance for 80 percent of the 418 available sites. In summer, other sites are first come, first served—sometimes, even after waiting in line at 6 AM for 4 or 5 days, you might not even get one. (You'd think you were waiting in line for Bruce Springsteen tickets.) There is a 14-day limit in summer. Fees $12–15; pets permitted; inquire about four- and six-person yurts.

See also *Bicycling/Rentals* and *Fishing/Shellfishing* under *Outdoor Activities*.

WALKS Famed nature writer John Hay lives in Brewster. He's got plenty of places nearby to enjoy Mother Nature. You can follow in his footsteps.

John Wing Trail, South Trail, and **North Trail,** at the Cape Cod Museum of Natural History (see *To See*), 869 Route 6A. Named for Brewster's first settler, a Quaker forced to leave Sandwich due to religious persecution, the John Wing Trail (about 1.5 miles round trip) meanders past sassafras groves and salt marshes, which provide habitat for diverse plants and animals. Traversing a tidal island, it ends on the dunes with a panoramic bay view. South Trail is on the opposite side of Route 6A and extends for about a mile past Stony Brook, a beech grove, and the remnants of a cranberry bog. The short North Trail wends around the museum's immediate grounds, crossing a salt marsh. Naturalist-led walks depart from the museum daily in summer and on weekends off-season. Call 508-896-3867 for times.

Punkhorn Parklands, Run Hill Road, off Stony Brook Road. Miles of scenic trails on more than 800 acres—some overlooking kettle ponds—traverse oak and pine forests, meadows, and marshes. Trails are used by birders and mountain bikers, even coyotes and foxes. Pick up a detailed trail and off-road map from the Visitor Information Center (see *Guidance*).

Spruce Hill Conservation Area, behind the Brewster Historical Society Museum, 3341 Route 6A. This trail, and the uncrowded little beach at the end of it, is a secret treasure. The 30-minute, round-trip trail follows a wide old carriage road—probably used for off-loading fish and lumber and rumored to have been used by bootleggers during Prohibition—which runs from the museum to the bay and a private stretch of sandy beach. The Conservation Commission manages the 25-acre area.

See also the sidebar "A Supreme State Park."

✳ Lodging

Brewster has it all, from first-class inns and homey B&Bs to resort condos and family cottages. The zip code for Brewster is 02631.

RESORT ✳ ✍ Ocean Edge Resort (Great Vacations booking agent: 508-896-2090, 800-626-9984; resort: 508-896-9000, 800-343-6074; www. oceanedge.com), 2660 Route 6A. Open year-round if booking through the resort; town houses available seasonally through Great Vacations. Once part of the vast Roland Nickerson estate (see the "Supreme State Park" sidebar), this 380-acre complex includes a Gothic and Renaissance Revival stucco mansion (now a resort hotel and conference center) and 17 private, contemporary condominium "villages." If you want to stay at the hotel/mansion, book directly through the resort.

Units are configured as apartments, two-story town houses (with one, two, and three bedrooms), and Cape cottages. Some units are bayside; others overlook the golf course. All have "real" backyards, and most are within walking distance of resort facilities. Resort facilities include indoor and outdoor pools, a private 1,000-foot bayside beach (for bayside rentals only), four restaurants, a fitness center, a playground, and organized programs for kids age 4–10 (for a fee). Golf and tennis packages, with and

Kim Grant

BREWSTER'S STONY BROOK GRIST MILL

without instruction, are available through the resort on a "pay-as-you-play" basis. Condo prices vary widely; it's best to call.

INNS Bramble Inn (508-896-7644; www.brambleinn.com), 2019 Route 6A. Open April through December. Innkeepers Cliff and Ruth Manchester opened the historic Bramble Inn in 1985 and offer five comfortable rooms in their mid-19th-century building. The country -traditional rooms—featuring wide sanded floors, antiques, Oriental carpets, and a lacy four-poster canopy beds — are Cliff's domain. He has meticulously high standards. All have air-conditioning. Ruth, a very talented chef (see *Dining Out*), prepares a full breakfast of, perhaps, strata, bacon, and breads. $138–148.

Chillingsworth (508-896-3640; 800-430-3640; www.chillingsworth.com), 2449 Route 6A. Open late May to late November. This 1689 house, believed to be Brewster's second oldest, rents three European-style guest rooms above the restaurant (see *Dining Out*). The antiques-filled Stevenson Room boasts a private entrance and four-poster bed—it's the largest and nicest of the rooms. The Foster Room has views of the back gardens and gazebo. Although the Ten Eyck Room is small and without a view, it's charming nonetheless. All have private bath, TV, and air-conditioning. Rates include afternoon wine and cheese, a full breakfast, access to a private beach at the end of the street, and privileges at a private club with an indoor/outdoor pool, tennis courts, and golf. $120–165.

✳ ⚓ ♪ ✿ **Old Sea Pines Inn** (508-896-6114; www.oldseapinesinn.com),

2553 Route 6A. In 1907 the building housed the Sea Pines School of Charm and Personality for Young Women. Today longtime hosts Michele and Steve Rowan combine 1920s and '30s nostalgia with modern comforts. All 21 rooms and three suites are pleasant, furnished with old brass or iron beds and antiques. The less expensive "classrooms" are small and share baths—it will be easy to imagine yourself as a young girl at boarding school. The rear annex has less charm, while the family suites are quite economical. The Inn is set on 3½ acres, and there's plenty of space to relax inside, too, including a large, comfy living room with fireplace that leads onto the wraparound porch set with rockers. On Sunday evenings in summer, the Cape Repertory Theatre holds a Broadway musical dinner revue here (see *Entertainment*). Full breakfast included. July and August $75–150 double, $140–165 family suite; $10–40 less off-season.

BED & BREAKFASTS ✳ **Captain Freeman Inn** (508-896-7481; 800-843-4664; www.captainfreeman-inn.com), 15 Breakwater Road. This fine 1866 inn has been gussied up with four-poster canopy beds, sanded hardwood floors, designer window treatments, and air-conditioning. A private pool and decadent, yet healthy breakfasts are also big draws. Of the 12 rooms, 6 are upscale suites with TV, VCR, mini-fridge, fireplace, and whirlpool bath on a private enclosed porch. One particularly secluded room (off the dining area) overlooks the garden. Some traditional quarters, many of which are large corner rooms, boast inlaid floors and over-sized windows. All rooms have sitting areas, but there are also two living rooms, the cozier one with a working wood fireplace. The very personable innkeepers, Carol and Tom Edmondson, set out excellent full breakfasts and also offer free loaner bikes in season. June through October $150–250; off-season $130–190.

Ruddy Turnstone (508-385-9871; 800-654-1995; www.theruddyturnstone.com), 463 Route 6A. Open April to mid-October. This is one of only two B&Bs on Route 6A with a view of Cape Cod Bay and the salt marsh. And what a view it is! If the weather is good, you'll enjoy it from the garden, under the fruit trees, or from a hammock. If it's cold or rainy, a second-floor common room has a large picture window with an unobstructed view. This early-19th-century Cape-style house has four guest rooms and one large suite (which boasts a fireplace and view) appointed with antiques, Oriental carpets, and luxurious feather beds. The adjacent barn, recently restored and furnished with pencil-post canopy beds and quilts, offers a bit more privacy. It's rustic—in a good way. Hosts Swanee and Sally Swanson offer a full breakfast. June to mid-October $125–175; off-season $95–150.

❧ **The Blue Cedar Bed & Breakfast** (508-896-4353; 866-896-4353; www.thebluecedar.com), 699 Route 6A. Open May through October. This completely renovated 1840 farmhouse still retains wide-pine flooring, latch doors, and some exposed post-and-beam construction. Innkeepers Diane and Clyde Mosher have three guest rooms, devoid of knickknacks, and awash in tranquil colors. Room 1 was the original Brewster farmhouse and boasts a large bathroom and pencil-post bed. Room 2 is also quite large,

with a spiffy bathroom; room 3 is even larger. An expanded continental breakfast is served on the screened-in, wicker-filled patio. But there's a nice side patio, too. July to early September $110–135; off-season $95–110.

❧ **Old Manse Inn** (508-896-3149; www.oldmanseinn.com), 1861 Route 6A. Open late May to mid-October. David and Suzanne Plum's historic 1801 inn has nine guest rooms with period wallpapers, antique beds, air-conditioning, cable TV, and newly refurbished bathrooms. I particularly like room 4, the largest, with hardwood floors and a spacious bathroom, and room 3, completely redecorated with a four-poster pencil-post bed. Third-floor rooms benefit from high, mansard-ceilinged rooflines. A full buffet breakfast, with delectable pastries and baked goods, is included. On my last visit offerings included a wonderfully simple crustless quiche and apple cinnamon scones. Rooms $120–145.

❊ **Brewster Farmhouse Inn** (508-896-3910; 800-892-3910; www.brewsterfarmhouseinn.com), 716 Route 6A. Carol and Gary Concors pamper guests at their Greek Revival farmhouse. Personally, the main draw is the heated pool and hot-tub area (where afternoon tea is served), which is nicely landscaped with big blue hydrangeas. For you, it may be three luxurious suites within the new carriage house, each with a gas fireplace and whirlpool tub. Of these, the upstairs suites feel more spacious. Four stylish guest rooms and a two-bedroom suite (rented as separate rooms with shared bath off-season) in the main house also feature luxurious amenities like thick towels, fine bedding, and nightly turndown with chocolates. One room has a private deck; another has a fireplace. Full breakfast included. Late May to mid-October $165–225; off-season $145–175.

🐾 **The Painted Antique Guest House** (508-240-6744), 3736 Main Street. Open late May to mid-October. Dianne and Joe Paolucci's little place, adjacent to their retail shop, only has three rooms but they're sweetly filled with painted antiques and other whimsical objects. I haven't seen the new room on the first floor, but the two rooms upstairs share a bath. (These two rooms are only rented to folks who know each other.) An expanded continental breakfast is left in a basket for guests to pick up when it suits them. Rooms $85–95.

🐾 **COTTAGES AND APARTMENTS**
🐾 ❄ **Michael's Cottages** (508-896-4025; 800-399-2967; www.sunsol.com/michaels/), 618 Route 6A. Set back from the road in a pine grove, these five tidy cottages are a 15-minute walk from a bayside beach. They're a bargain, and proprietor Michael DiVito maintains them nicely. One is actually a small house that sleeps six and features a full living room. Most others have a screened-in porch and fireplace; all have air-conditioning and include linen service. Michael also rents two B&B rooms, but I didn't get a chance to see them for this edition. July and August $695–775 weekly for two, $15 each additional person; large cottage $1,175 weekly for four; off-season $75–105 nightly. Rooms $130 nightly in summer, $90–120 off-season.

Linger Longer By The Sea (508-240-2211; www.capecodtravel.com/lingerlonger), 261 Linnell Landing Road. Open April to late November. Off a quiet lane and within a

sandal shuffle of a private stretch of Linnell Landing Beach, this place is perfect for couples and families who appreciate not having to pile into a car or cross a busy street to get to the beach. Most of the 10 cottages have been completely remodeled, and all of the six apartments overlook Cape Cod Bay. All have deck, barbecue grill, linens, and picnic table. Some have a fireplace. Late June through August $800–1,175 weekly for a studio or one-bedroom unit, $960–1,850 weekly for a two-, three-, or four-bedroom; off-season rentals have a 2-night minimum.

Ellis Landing Cottages (508-896-5072), Ellis Landing. Open late May to mid-October. Only dune grasses and sandy lanes separate these 15 cozy waterfront and water-view cottages from the bay. In Gil Ellis's family since the 1930s, most of the refurbished and simply furnished housekeeping cottages were built by Gil's father in the 1940s and 1950s. Some of the pine-paneled cottages are more rustic than others. All have complete kitchens, and many have fireplace. My favorite is the cozy Rest Haven Cottage, once the East Brewster railroad station, which now features a private garden, screened-in porch, and three bedrooms. Late June to early September $2,000 weekly for a three-bedroom waterfront cottage, $1,200–1,800 weekly for a two-bedroom. Off-season, cottages go for $700–1,000 weekly or can be rented for a 3-night minimum. No credit cards.

RENTAL HOUSES AND COTTAGES
Stonecroft-Abbott Real Estate (508-896-2290), Foster Square, 2655 Route 6A. A friendly agency with good listings.

Vacation Cape Cod/Kinlin-Grover GMAC (508-896-7004; www.vacationcapecod.com), 1900 Route 6A. This agency has upwards of 240 listings, from studios to two-bedroom knotty-pine cottages to homes with four bedrooms. The bulk of rentals are booked October through March (for the following summer), but if you wait until July, they can still probably find something for you.

See also Ocean Edge Resort under Resort.

CAMPGROUNDS See the sidebar "A Supreme State Park" under *Green Space.*

Alternatives to Nickerson State Park include **Shady Knoll Campground** (508-896-3002), Route 6A at Route 137, which is open mid-May to mid-October, and **Sweetwater Forest** (508-896-3773), off Route 124, which is open year-round and set on 60 acres abutting a freshwater lake. Both accept reservations, but I like Sweetwater's 250 wooded sites a bit better. They also cost less: Expect to pay about $25 in-season, $20 off-season.

✳ Where to Eat

Brewster has a wide variety of really great restaurants.

DINING OUT ✿ **Bramble Inn** (508-896-7644), 2019 Route 6A. Open for dinner on weekends April through December and nightly in summer. Chef-owner Ruth Manchester's creative talents extend to exceptional New American and internationally inspired cuisine. Longtime house specialties include veal with shiitake mushrooms, parchment-roasted chicken with grilled lobster, rack of lamb, and seafood curry. Along with

gracious service and intimate dining rooms, you'll find elegantly casual mix-and-match antique place settings. The broad, prix fixe menu changes every few weeks. There's no entertainment in the dining room, unless you consider Ruth's husband Cliff; they've presided over the place since 1984. Ruth's son-in-law, David Plumb (of Old Manse fame), helps out on weekends. October through December (on Wednesday and Thursday), the "club night" three-course prix fixe menu is a bargain at $28 per person. Otherwise, four-course dinners $42–68, by reservation only.

🍸 ✿ **Brewster Fish House** (508-896-7867), 2208 Route 6A. Open daily (almost) for lunch and dinner April to early December. This small roadside bistro doesn't look like much from the outside, but inside, owner Vernon Smith has created a pleasant atmosphere with white table linens, Windsor chairs, fresh flowers, high ceilings, and a small bar. Alongside creative luncheon specials, you'll find grilled and broiled seafood and fish served on mod plates. Try the chowder or lobster bisque, which has a nice spicy kick to it. For dinner, try innovative specials like grilled sea scallops with roasted tomatoes, garlic, olives and artichokes. Save room for the crème brûlée. Arrive before 7 PM or expect to wait at least an hour. Put your name on the list and walk across the street to the beach; they'll honor your position on the list when you return. Lunch $8–13, dinner entrées $15–26.

Chillingsworth (508-896-3640; 800-430-3640), 2449 Route 6A. Open for lunch and dinner, late May to late November; off-season schedule varies. Seven-course, prix fixe

French/California-style haute cuisine is served at two seatings (one off-season). Choose the early seating, unless you want to be eating until 11:30 or midnight. The small, candlelit dining rooms, filled with antiques, feel rather like salons. Service is well paced and discreet. For those with less of an appetite (and wallet), a bistro menu is served in the airy greenhouse or alfresco. À la carte luncheons in the greenhouse (or on the terrace) are relaxing. Chef "Nitzi" Rabin and his wife, Pat, proudly preside. Bistro lunch $8–14, dinner $15–25; fine dining $55–65. Reservations required for fine dining, suggested for the bistro; jacket or tie suggested for dinner.

EATING OUT ❄ **Peddler's Restaurant** (508-896-9300), 67 Thad Ellis Road. Open for dinner. Off Route 6A (turn at the Brewster Bookstore), this small roadhouse is an unlikely suspect in the restaurant wars. Ignore its drab location across from an automotive shop. Peddler's offers Italian and French dishes like seared scallops Provençal or pasta Bolognese. A side of angel hair accompanies each entrée, but you might also consider ordering two appetizers. Entrées $14–19.

❄ 🌺 **Brewster Teapot** (508-896-9534), 1360 Route 6A. Open 11–4 Tuesday through Sunday (11:30–5 in summer). At the Beechcroft Inn, hosts Jan and Paul Campbell offer authentic ploughman's lunches (with Stilton cheese or baked ham), shepherd's pie, and afternoon teas (with an assortment of finger sandwiches, scones with jam, and clotted cream). The building might be tired looking, but the lunches are a treat. Dishes $8–13.

❄ 🐟 **Cafe Alfresco** (508-896-1741), Lemon Tree Village, 1097 Route 6A. Open for breakfast and lunch. This modest café offers breakfast (eggs any style, omelets, and croissants), lunch sandwiches (very good lobster rolls as well as smoked salmon), great soups and homemade bread, and nightly specials like fish-and-chips, scallop rolls, and chicken salad. The grilled portobello mushroom sandwich is particularly good. There are a few outdoor tables where you hear trickling water fountains, but most people sit inside. Dishes $4–10.

Breakwater Fish (508-896-7080), 235 Underpass Road. Open mid-March through December. Cyclists on the rail-trail can get serious eats at this fish market: oysters, clamcakes, smoked salmon rolls. If you're renting a cottage, these folks have excellent fish and lobster, too. They'll also steam the lobster for you.

🐟 **Cobie's** (508-896-7021), 3260 Route 6A. Open 10:30–9 late May through August. I like this seafood shack for its charbroiled burgers and covered picnic tables near the pine trees. Serving northside patrons since 1948, Cobie's is convenient for rail-trail cyclists (see *Outdoor Activities—Bicycling/Rentals*). Lunch $4–7, dinner $8–14.

PICNICS, COFFEE, & ICE CREAM
Satucket Farm Stand (508-896-5540), Route 124 just off Route 6A. Open April through September. An old-fashioned open-air stand with farm-fresh produce including fantastic corn, pies, soups, salads, baked goods, jams, honey, and cheeses. It's a popular spot for local chefs.

Brewster Scoop (508-896-7824),

Route 6A. Open noon–10 mid-June to early September. Behind the Brewster Store, this small shop is a purveyor of Bliss Dairy's sugar-free ice cream and nonfat frozen yogurt.

❋ **Brewster Express** (508-896-6682) and **Box Lunch** (508-896-1234), both on the bike trail on Underpass Road, offer ice cream and sandwiches to hungry cyclists. Box Lunch has Four Seas ice cream (imported all the way from Centerville), but Brewster Express has picnic tables under scrub oaks. It boils down to this: Do you like your sandwich meats and cheeses rolled up in pita bread or between two slices?

Also see Great Cape Cod Herb, Spice & Tea Co. under *Selective Shopping—Special Shops*.

❋ Entertainment

♈ **The Woodshed** (508-896-7771), Route 6A near The Brewster Store. Open nightly for live acoustic rock, late May to late November. This answers the question: Where do all the summer workers go on their night off? With wooden rafters and well-worn wooden floors (reeking of stale beer), this dark joint jumps with locals.

♪ **Band concerts,** Drummer Boy Park, Route 6A, 2.5 miles west of Route 124. July and August concerts on Sunday at 6 PM at the gazebo. Bring a blanket and lawn chairs.

❋ ♪ **Cape Repertory Theatre** (508-896-1888 for schedule information; www.caperep.org), 3397 Route 6A. Under the longtime directorship of Bob Troie, the company presents engaging open-air theater in the woods (on the former Crosby estate), performances at its new 140-seat indoor theater, and a musical dinner revue at the Old Sea Pines Inn (see *Lodging—Inns*) on Sunday nights from mid-June to mid-September. Indoor shows Tuesday through Saturday, May through November. Tickets $20 adults, $8 for age 21 and under. Children's productions $6 on Tuesday and Friday mornings at 10 and free contemporary plays on Mondays.

❋ Selective Shopping
❋ Unless otherwise noted, all shops are open year-round.

ANTIQUES Dozens of antiques shops line Route 6A; only a sampling follows.
Wysteria Antiques, Etc. (508-896-8650), 1199 Route 6A. Open May through October. The purple exterior, the overwhelming scent of wisteria as you cross the threshold, and three rooms filled top to bottom with purple glassware and porcelain, adds up to one unusual establishment. The owners have a good eye, even if the presentation is over the top.
Spyglass Antiques (508-896-4423), 2257 Route 6A. Eighteenth- and 19th-century American furniture and accessories.

ARTISANS Brewster Pottery (508-896-3587), 437 Harwich Road. Open May through December. Potter Marion Eckhardt moved to this house/studio in 1947, and according to her, she's the first and oldest potter in town. Since opening in 1960, she's mentored young apprentices from all over the country. One young man came to learn the craft when he was 15 and is still here (and now in his 40s). Marion's functional and whimsical porcelain and stoneware (birdbaths, birdhouses, fountains) are lovely, made all the more so by watching her work.

Heart Pottery (508-896-6189), 1145 Route 6A. Open daily except Sunday. Specializing in functional and decorative porcelain, raku, and stoneware, Diane Heart spends most days at her wheel here in the shop. Her raku, using an ancient Japanese firing technique, is particularly fine.

Clayworks (508-255-4937), 3820 Route 6A. Open daily, except Sunday off-season. A bit more unconventional than other Cape potters, Clayton Calderwood works in porcelain, stoneware, and terra-cotta and creates interesting abstract sculptures, large fish platters, and mammoth urns.

Kemp Pottery (508-385-5782), 258 Route 6A. Open daily May through September. Stoneware and porcelain: fountains, garden sculpture, abstract pieces, stained glass, and decorative and functional forms made with sand from Nauset Beach. Steven Kemp also has a bigger shop in Orleans.

The Woodwright (508-896-3393), 2091 Route 6A. Open weekdays, and Saturday by appointment. Before you leave home, measure your needy window casings or door frames and have Leonard Courchesne replace them for you. He's an expert in restoration, reproduction, custom design, and millwork.

ART GALLERIES Underground Art Gallery (508-896-3757), 673 Satucket Road. Open Wednesday through Sunday. Amazingly, this working studio sits beneath 100 tons of soil and is supported by 10 tree trunks. The gallery features the work of watercolorist Karen North Wells, who also

uses oil and acrylic for her seascapes and landscape florals. Her husband, Malcolm Wells, who is also a painter, designs earth-covered solar buildings like this one.

Maddocks Gallery (508-896-6223), 1283 Route 6A. Open March through December and by appointment off-season. James Maddocks paints nostalgic traditional and representational Cape Cod scenes. His gallery, where you'll often find him painting and where he happily talks with visitors, is an 1840s carriage house attached to his home. He also offers less expensive limited-edition prints.

Ruddeforth Gallery (508-255-1056), 3753 Route 6A. Watercolors, oils, and lithographs of Cape Cod scenes, florals, and still lifes by Debra Ruddeforth (a signature member of the Copley Society in Boston). Husband Tom Ruddeforth's color and black-and-white photographs are also displayed.

Franny Golden (508-896-6353; www.frannygolden.com), 502 Harwich Road. Franny's gallery defies easy interpretation. There are some portraits, some landscapes (sort of), some expressionist abstracts, many visual journals that have to do with experience. She works a lot with process. Franny teaches part time at Cape Cod Community College (the "4Cs") and does a local public TV cable show. Thankfully, this is not your standard Cape fare.

Struna Galleries (508-255-6618), 3873 Route 6A. Working from copper plates to make dry-point engravings, artist Tim Struna creates sweet little renderings of Cape Cod scenes. They're a nice (and affordable) reminder of why life on the Cape is so special. Since his studio is here, you'll often find Tim hard at work. He also sells larger watercolors.

BOOKSTORES ✐ **Brewster Book Store** (508-896-6543), 2648 Route 6A. One of the Cape's better bookstores, this one features a large and excellent selection of children's books within a small space. Also Cape Cod titles, games, toys, story time (Tuesdays and Fridays at 10), and book signings.

Kings Way Books and Antiques (508-896-3639), 774 Route 6A. Open April through December; by appointment January through March. Specializing in out-of-print and rare books, Proprietor Dick Socky's collection includes medieval and military history, book arts, biography, architecture, archaeology, and nature books. His antique cherrywood shelves were salvaged from the New Haven, Connecticut, public library. As for the select small antiques, most are book-related items.

SPECIAL SHOPS **Eve's Place** (508-896-4914), 564 Route 6A. Eve Roulier learned all about pearls in Hawaii where she lived for eight years. She buys directly from growers; she strings and sells pearls; and she's an authority on rare black Tahitian pearls, pearls from Kobe, Japan, and freshwater pearls from China. She'll tell you that injecting an irritant into an oyster's shell creates cultured pearls and that about 40 percent of the oysters die as a result of the injection. Those that don't die secrete a substance (nacre, the basis of the pearl) in reaction to the irritant. It then takes about three or four years for the pearl to mature. Whether you're ready to buy, just want to learn about pearls, or need some pearls restrung, Eve is your woman.

Spectrum (508-385-3322), 369 Route 6A. This two-story shop, which opened in 1966, represents more than 500 high-quality craftspeople from all over the country. I hesitate to itemize even a few of their pieces, because I don't want to limit your imagination.

Sydenstricker Galleries (508-385-3272), 490 Route 6A. Glass-fusing demonstrations, using a technique developed by Brewster native Bill Sydenstricker (who died in 1994), are given 9:30–2:30 daily except Sunday. Sydenstricker glass is used in two American embassies and displayed in museum collections around the country.

Spyglass (508-896-4423), 2257 Route 6A. Although this exceptional shop is best known for its telescope collection, there are all sorts of nautical antiques like barometers, sextants, maps, charts, and even a few paintings and sea captains' portraits. It's great to poke around and recapture a sense of the Cape's maritime glories.

Great Cape Cod Herb, Spice & Tea Co. (508-896-5900; 800-427-7144; www.greatcape.com), 2628 Route 6A. Open daily. With more than 170 varieties of Western and Chinese herbs in stock, this herbal apothecary may well be the largest retailer of its kind in New England. Proprietor Stephan Brown (who opened the rustic shop in 1991) also stocks a selection of New Age literature on health and well-being. The herb farm is certified organic for medicinal herbs. Weekly herb-identification "weed walks" May through September. Before leaving, revive yourself with a cup of strong espresso.

✳ Special Events

April–early May: **Herring Run.**
Hundreds of thousands of alewives
(herring) return from the salt water to
lay their eggs in the same freshwater
ponds where they were born (see
Stoney Brook Grist Mill and Herring
Run under *To See*).

Last weekend in April: **Brewster in
Bloom** (508-896-2670; www.brew-
sterinbloom.com). Faith Dibble pro-
posed the idea to plant 100,000

daffodils in 1983. Today there's an
annual festival celebrating the bright
yellow flowers that line the already
picturesque streets. Events include an
arts and crafts festival, food festival,
and parade.

Mid-September: **Bird Carvers
Exhibit,** at the Cape Cod Museum of
Natural History (Route 6A; see *To
See*). One of the premier exhibits of
its kind in the country boasts carving
and painting demonstrations.

HARWICH

Harwich isn't nearly as developed as its westerly neighbors, although its stretch of Route 28 does have its share of bumper boats, mini-golf courses, and go-carts. In fact, the town exudes a somewhat nonchalant air. It's as if the 12,000 year-rounders are collectively saying, "This is what we have and you're welcome to come and enjoy it with us if you wish"—which is not to say that Harwich doesn't attract visitors. It boasts a wide range of places to stay and eat, from the fanciest Victorian inn to the most humble B&B, from exceptional New American fare to roasted chicken-on-a-spit. At the same time, while Harwich has more saltwater and freshwater beaches than any other town on the Cape, only a few have parking for day-use visitors.

Harwich, mostly blue collar and middle class, comprises seven distinct villages and is blessed with one of the most picturesque harbors on the Cape, Wychmere Harbor. Nearby, lovely Saquatucket Harbor is reserved for fishing charters and ferry service to Nantucket. It's worth poking around the quiet center of Harwich, with its historic homes standing in marked contrast to the heavily developed areas just a mile or so away. Harwich, which bills its annual Cranberry Harvest Festival as "the biggest small-town celebration in the country," lays claims to cultivating the first commercial cranberry bog.

GUIDANCE Harwich Chamber of Commerce (508-432-1600; 800-441-3199; www.harwichcc.com), Route 28, P.O. Box 34, Harwichport 02646. Open 9–5 daily late May to mid-September; 9–5 Friday through Sunday, mid-September to mid-October. An informed chamber staff and a well-organized, townwide publication make Harwich an easy place to navigate. Pick up their biking and walking trail maps, as well as their very helpful (free) street map. For off-season info, head four doors down to the Cape Cod Five Cents Savings Bank (508-430-1165; open 9–1 weekdays). You can park for free in the booth's large parking lot and walk to Bank Street Beach.

PUBLIC REST ROOMS Public rest rooms are located at the chamber parking lot (see *Guidance*).

PUBLIC LIBRARY ❋ ✍ ☂ **Brooks Free Library** (508-430-7562), 739 Main Street, Harwich. The main renovated and expanded branch has free Internet

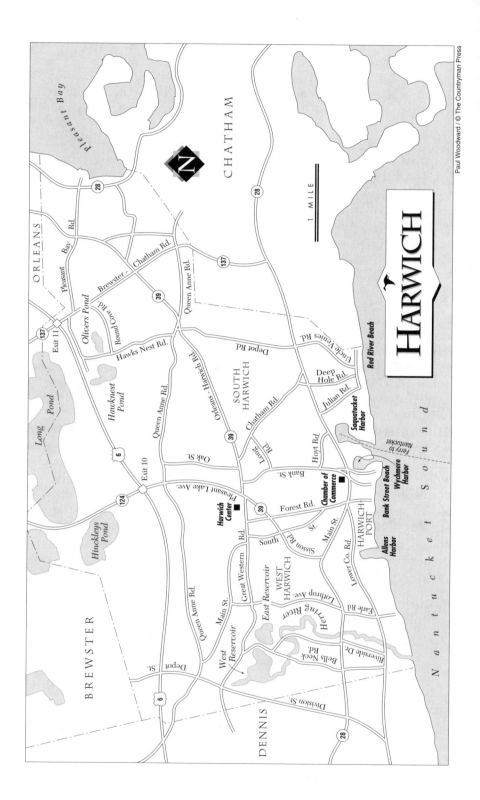

PLEASANT BAY

ORLEANS

CHATHAM

N

1 MILE

BREWSTER

DENNIS

Long Pond

Hawknest Pond

Hinckleys Pond

Olivers Pond

Pleasant Bay Rd.

Brewster - Chatham Rd.

Round Cove Rd.

Hawks Nest Rd.

Queen Anne Rd.

Depot Rd.

Uncle Venies Rd.

SOUTH HARWICH

Deep Hole Rd.

Julian Rd.

Saquatucket Harbor

Red River Beach

Ferry to Nantucket

Bank Street Beach

Wychmere Harbor

Allens Harbor

HARWICH PORT

Lower Co. Rd.

Main St.

Sisson Rd.

Earle Rd.

Lothrop Ave.

WEST HARWICH

Bells Neck Rd.

Riverside Dr.

Herring River

Division St.

East Reservoir

West Reservoir

Great Western Rd.

Main St.

Queen Anne Rd.

Depot St.

South St.

Pleasant Lake Ave.

Forest Rd.

Harwich Center

Chamber of Commerce

Bank St.

Hoyt Rd.

Long Rd.

Chatham Rd.

Oak St.

Queen Anne Rd.

Orleans - Harwich Rd.

Exit 10

Exit 11

Chatham Rd.

Queen Anne Rd.

137

28

39

137

28

6

124

6

39

39

28

Nantucket Sound

HARWICH

Paul Woodward / © The Countryman Press

access. It's open 10–6 Monday and Wednesday; 10–4 Thursday through Sunday; noon–8 Tuesday.

GETTING THERE *By car:* From the Cape Cod Canal, take Route 6 to exit 10 (Route 124 south and Route 39 south) to Route 28, or take exit 11 to Route 137 for East Harwich. It takes 35 to 40 minutes to reach Harwich from the canal.

By bus: The **Plymouth & Brockton** bus line (508-778-9767; www.p-b.com) connects Harwich with Hyannis and other Cape towns, as well as with Boston's Logan Airport. The bus stops at the Park & Ride commuter lot near the intersection of Routes 6 and 124.

GETTING AROUND *By car:* Route 28 is also called Main Street. (This is not to be confused with the Main Street—aka Route 39—in the center of Harwich, which is inland.) Although most points of interest are located along or off the developed Route 28, head inland to explore Harwich's ponds and conservation areas.

By bus: The **H₂O** (508-385-8326; 800-352-7155; www.capecodtransit.org) bus line, used by more locals than visitors, travels along Route 28 between the Hyannis Transportation Center and Orleans weekdays year-round and on weekends in summer. It stops at the chamber of commerce, but you can flag it down anywhere along Route 28.

GETTING TO NANTUCKET There is seasonal passenger ferry service to Nantucket from Harwichport. For many people, this service is more convenient than going into Hyannis to catch a boat. For complete information, see *Getting There* in "Nantucket."

MEDICAL EMERGENCY **Long Pond Medical Center** (508-432-4100), off Route 137, Harwich. Walk-ins 8–5 weekdays and 9–1 Saturday.

✳ To See and Do

⚓ **Brooks Academy Museum** (508-432-8089; www.capecodhistory.org/harwich), Routes 124 and 39 at Main Street. Open 1–4 Thursday and Friday, mid-June to mid-October. This imposing 1844 Greek Revival schoolhouse was home to the country's first vocational school of navigation, established by Sidney Brooks. Now operated by the Harwich Historical Society, the museum exhibits a history of cranberry farming, historical photographs, and Native American and maritime artifacts. There are also collections of glass, furniture, decorative art objects, textiles, and art by C. D. Cahoon. Genealogical resources and a significant manuscript collection round out the research facility. Also on the premises: a gunpowder house used from 1770 to 1864 and a restored 1872 outhouse. Donations.

First Congregational Church, Routes 124 and 39, Harwich Center. Built in the mid-1700s, this church is surrounded by a white picket fence and anchors the tiny town center.

Bird Carvings (508-430-0400), at the Cape Cod Five Cents Savings Bank,

Route 28 in the center of Harwichport. Check out a fine collection of carved miniature shore- and songbirds by hometown artist Elmer Crowell.

⚓ ✳ **Harwich Junior Theatre** (508-432-2002; 508-432-0934; www.hjtcapecod. org), Division and Willow Streets, West Harwich. This semiprofessional theater—the country's oldest children's theater, established in 1952—produces four shows in summer and another four off-season. In summer children age 7–15 star in kids' roles, manage the sound and lighting, and sell refreshments. Whether your child is considering acting or you want to introduce him or her to theater, this is an imaginative alternative to another round of mini-golf. Classes or workshops are offered year-round. Tickets $12–16.

✳ Outdoor Activities

All listings are in Harwich Center unless otherwise noted.

⚓ **BASEBALL** The Harwich Mariners (508-432-2000; www.harwichmariners.org) play baseball at Whitehouse Field behind the high school in Harwich Center, off Oak Street from Route 39. Most games begin at 7 PM and are played from mid-June to mid-August. Free.

They also host weekly clinics (9–noon) for kids age 6–18 from late June to early August; $50–90. Sign up on Monday morning at the field.

BICYCLING/RENTALS About 5 miles of the Cape Cod Rail Trail run through Harwich; you can pick up the trail near the Pleasant Lake General Store on

HARWICH CULTIVATED THE COUNTRY'S FIRST COMMERCIAL CRANBERRY BOG; IT CELEBRATES WITH A CRANBERRY HARVEST FESTIVAL IN MID-SEPTEMBER.

Kim Grant

Route 124 and off Great Western Road near Herring Run Road. The chamber of commerce publishes a good biking map. **Harwichport Bike Company Inc.** (508-430-0200), 431 Route 28, rents bicycles year-round. **The Bike Depot** (508-430-4375), 500 Depot Street on the rail-trail, is open May through October.

BOATING AND CANOEING Saquatucket Harbor, Route 28. With 200 berths, this is the largest municipal marina on the Cape; about 10 slips are reserved for transient visitors. A ramp pass costs $7.

Wychmere Harbor, Harbor Road off Route 28. A fleet of sloops is often moored here, making it one of the Cape's most scenic (albeit human-made) harbors. In the late 1800s, Wychmere Harbor was simply a salt pond, around which a racetrack was laid. But locals, disapproving of horse racing, convinced the town to cut an opening from the pond into Nantucket Sound. A harbor was born.

Allens Harbor, on Lower County Road, is the town's other picturesque, well-protected, and human-made harbor; it has a docking ramp ($7).

See also Herring River/Sand Pond Conservation Area/Bells Neck under *Green Space—Walks.*

FISHING/SHELLFISHING Shellfishing permits ($15 daily for nonresident families, $30 seasonally) are obtained from Town Hall (508-430-7513) on Route 39 on weekdays 8:30–4 off-season, and from the harbormaster (508-430-7532) at Saquatucket Harbor on weekends 8:30–4, June through September.

A number of charter fishing boats depart from Saquatucket Harbor, including the *Yankee* (508-432-2520), which departs twice daily and costs $25 for 4 hours. From Wychmere Harbor, the *Golden Eagle* (508-432-5611) offers deep-sea-fishing trips from mid-May to mid-October ($24 adults, $20 children, for a 4-hour trip). Rod, reel, bait, and fish bag included.

Try your luck casting from a jetty at **Red River Beach** (see *Green Space—Beaches*) or the **Herring River Bridge** in West Harwich. Rent equipment from **Kildee Bait & Tackle** (508-430-1590), 390 Route 28.

❄ Fishing the Cape (508-432-1200), Routes 137 and 39, Harwich commons. From May through August, the king of fly-fishing—Orvis—offers a 2½-day saltwater fly-fishing course for $430. (The price includes equipment, lunch, and fish food.) Guided fishing trips, too. A full line of Orvis supplies, flies, and tackle is sold at the shop.

✐ **FOR FAMILIES Grand Slam Entertainment** (508-430-1155), 322 Route 28. Open weekends in April, then late May to mid-September (9 AM–10 PM daily in summer). Batting cages with varying degrees of difficulty and bumper boats for toddlers to teens. Also a radar pitching cage and one of the world's only (purportedly) Wiffle ball cages for kids.

Trampoline Center (508-432-8717), 296 Route 28. Open weekends only, late May to late June and early September to mid-October; 9 AM–11 PM daily, late June to early September. There are no age or height restrictions; the only limit at this outdoor center is that kids can't do flips.

Bud's Go-Karts (508-432-4964), 9 Sisson Road, at Route 28. Open 9 AM–11 PM daily, mid-June to early September, and weekends only from mid-April to mid-June and early September to mid-October. Kids have to be more than 54 inches tall and at least 8 years old to ride without parents at this busy track. Five minutes cost $5.

Castle in the Clouds, behind the Harwich Elementary School, South Street. A fun playground. There are also picnic tables and a playground at Brooks Park, Route 39, Harwich.

GOLF **Cranberry Valley Golf Course** (508-430-7560; 508-430-5234), Oak Street, off Main Street, which turns into Route 39. Open March through December. An 18-hole, par-72 course with driving range and practice putting green.

❇ **Harwichport Golf Club** (508-432-0250), South and Forest Streets. A nine-hole, par-34 course.

IN-LINE SKATING ✄ **Harwich Skate Park** (508-430-7554), Brooks Park at Route 39, Harwich. Full protective gear required. Ostensibly open 2–4 during the school year; longer hours and night skating in summer. Call before going, as it's supervised by volunteers and might not be open.

KAYAKING ❇ **Cape Water Sports** (508-432-5996; www.capewatersports.com), at the junction of Routes 28 and 124. The Herring River, which runs north to a reservoir and south to Nantucket Sound, is great for kayaking. This shop rents singles ($70) and doubles ($85) daily or weekly ($300 and $350, respectively); you can also rent Sunfish.

✄ MINI-GOLF **Harbor Glen Miniature Golf** (508-432-8240), Route 28, West Harwich. Open April to mid-October. With fountains and imitation rocky waterfalls, this place packs 'em in, especially at night. Perhaps it's due to the adjacent restaurant, which offers kids' meals and ice cream. Adults $6, children $2–4.

Club House Mini Golf (508-432-4820), Route 39 near Route 137. Open daily, mid-June to early September. Adults $7, children $3–5.

SAILING See Cape Sail under *Sailing* in "Brewster."

TENNIS Three public courts are located at **Brooks Park** (508-430-7553), Route 39 and Oak Street. Free. In summer there are morning programs for kids, adult lessons on Wednesday and Thursday evenings, and free adult round-robins.

Wychmere Harbor Tennis Club (508-430-7012; 508-394-3511), 792 Route 28. Open mid-May to early September. Primarily for members, this full-service facility offers nine clay and two hard courts, instruction, a pro shop, and clinics to nonmembers only when members haven't booked up all the time slots. It's still worth calling.

✴ Green Space

BEACHES Weekly beach stickers ($25) are required for all but one of Harwich's 16 public saltwater beaches. If you're renting a cottage, purchase a parking sticker at the Community Center (508-430-7568), Oak Street; open 8:30–5 daily, June to early September.

Red River Beach, off Depot Road or Uncle Venies Road from Route 28, is the only beach with parking for day visitors. Parking $5 weekdays, $10 weekends. Facilities include rest rooms, concessions, and a lifeguard.

Pleasant Bay, off Route 28, is salt water, but calm, like a pond. It's open to nonresidents, but parking is quite limited

PONDS **Hinckleys Pond** and **Seymour Pond,** both off Route 124, are open to nonresidents. You can also swim at **Bucks Pond,** off Route 39, where there is a lifeguard.

Long Pond has two beaches, although both require parking stickers. One is located off Long Pond Drive from Route 124, the other off Cahoons Road from Long Pond Drive from Route 137.

Sand Pond is off Great Western Road.

WALKS The chamber of commerce (see *Guidance*) publishes a good walking trail map.

Herring River/Sand Pond Conservation Area/Bells Neck (park off Bell's Neck Road from Great Western Road) in West Harwich. These 200-plus acres of marshland, tidal creeks, reservoir, and riverway are great for birding and canoeing. You may see cormorants, ospreys, and swans.

🐾 **Thompson's Field,** Chatham Road, south of Route 39. This 57-acre preserve, with dirt-road trails for you and your canine friends, is full of wildflowers in springtime. This gives you an idea of what the Cape probably looked like 100 years ago.

✴ Lodging

❋ Unless otherwise noted, all lodgings are open year-round.

BED & BREAKFASTS **Augustus Snow House** (508-430-0528; 800-320-0528; www.augustussnow.com), 528 Route 28, Harwichport 02646. This 1901 Queen Anne Victorian mansion—complete with turrets, gabled dormers, a gazebo, and a wraparound porch—has six large guest rooms furnished in authentic Victorian style to complement the luxuriously outfitted bathrooms. I've seen a lot of bathrooms in my day, and the ones here are reason enough to stay here! The spacious Carriage House suite, with a deck overlooking the gardens, has a private entrance. All rooms have gas fireplace and TV; some have a Jacuzzi. Innkeepers Joyce and Steve Roth serve a full breakfast at individual tables in the elegant breakfast room. Mid-May to mid-October $160–210 rooms, $275–395 suite; off-season $105–170 and $195–330, respectively; ask about off-season packages.

🦢 **Blue Heron Bed & Breakfast** (508-430-0219; www.theblue-heronbb.com), 464 Pleasant Lake

Avenue, Harwich 02645. The main draw for Susan Horvath's pleasant and homey 19th-century B&B is its proximity to the Cape's largest freshwater lake and to the rail-trail: Both are across the street. (The beach is private.) Off the beaten path, these three simple rooms (one with private bath, all with air-conditioning) rent for $75–90, including an expanded continental breakfast.

❧ **Lion's Head Inn** (508-432-7766; 800-321-3155; www.capecodinns. com), 186 Belmont Road, West Harwich 02671. On a quiet residential street within walking distance of a beach, this modest B&B has some nice attributes. Four of the six guest rooms can accommodate three people; one room has a private deck and original pine floors. The Huntington Suite is large, with a sitting area, TV, and private entrance to the pool. Nineteenth-century common rooms include two comfortable parlors, one with fireplace. The sunny breakfast room/terrace overlooks the nicely landscaped pool. Enough said? Inquire about the two moderately priced cottages; they're a bit more rustic than the B&B, but fully equipped for family stays. Expanded continental breakfast included. June through September $125–175; off-season $75–125. Cottages $700–850 weekly in-season.

🐾 **Barnaby Inn** (508-432-6789; 800-439-4764; www.barnabyinn.com), 36 Route 28, West Harwich 02671. Although this rambling farmhouse is on busy Route 28, it's set back from the road. Innkeepers Bill and Eileen Ormond purchased this formerly ramshackle place in 1995 and set about gutting and refurbishing it. (Bill grew up 300 yards from the inn.) Most of the four rooms and two suites (really deluxe rooms) are modest, each with new carpeting and private bathroom. Two have a fireplace and Jacuzzi. A brand-new two-bedroom cottage, with complete kitchen, is a bargain at $800 weekly in summer, $600 weekly off-season. Breakfast is delivered to all inn rooms. Well-behaved pets are accepted. Late May through September $110–150; off-season $65–100.

GUESTHOUSES **Winstead Inn & Beach Resort** (508-432-4444; 800-870-4405; www.winsteadinn.com), 4 Braddock Lane, Harwichport 02646. You'll pay dearly for this privileged perch, just a few toe lengths from the beach, but it's a rare bird. There's nothing between the decks and the ocean except a private beach. Owners Gregg Winston and David Plunkett have transformed this modest beachfront house into an upscale establishment with 14 simple but deluxe rooms and three suites. All rooms are off a central hallway; two offer a beach view; some have a private deck and Jacuzzi. All rooms have air-conditioning, TV, and refrigerator. The back porch, sheltered by *Rosa rugosa*, leads to multilevel decks set with lounge chairs. Extensive continental breakfast buffet included. Mid-June to mid-September $215–375 (3-night minimum); off-season $145–275.

🐚 **Cape Winds By-The-Sea** (508-432-1418; www.capewinds.com), 28 Shore Road, West Harwich 02671. Innkeeper Judi Shank has four quiet and airy rooms with across-the-street views of Nantucket Sound; a studio that can accommodate three people; and a two-room efficiency apartment. In the off-season only two rooms are rented. The beach is just a 5-minute

WYCHMERE HARBOR IN HARWICHPORT

walk away. Continental breakfast and coffee are best enjoyed in a front-porch rocker. Late May to early September $100–150; off-season $80–120; $16 each additional person. No credit cards.

Seadar Inn By-The-Sea (508-432-0264; 800-888-5250; 508-842-4525 off-season; www.seadarinn.com), Braddock Lane, Harwichport 02646. Open May through October. In a quiet neighborhood, just a short shuffle from Bank Street Beach the rambling and shingled Seadar Inn has 23 air-conditioned rooms decorated in early American style. Bill Collins's family has proudly hosted guests at this old-fashioned hostelry since 1970; his is only the fourth family to own the Seadar since it opened in 1946. A buffet breakfast, served in the Colonial-style dining room, is included. Summer $115–205; off-season

$75–115; each additional person $20.

COTTAGES ✍ **Tern Inn** (508-432-3714; 800-432-3718; www.theterninn.com), 91 Chase Street, West Harwich 02671. Open mid-April to late February. A 10-minute walk from the beach, these six nicely maintained and recently renovated cottages and efficiencies (one of which is shaped like a gazebo) are set on a 2-acre wooded lot. The Tern Inn also rents eight rooms in a half-Cape house. A pool, swings and basketball court are on the premises, perfectly oriented toward family stays. Mid-June to early September $119 rooms, $600–975 weekly cottages; off-season $69 nightly for rooms.

See also Cape Winds By-The-Sea under *Guesthouses* and Barnaby Inn and Lion's Head Inn under *Bed & Breakfasts*.

MOTELS **Wychmere Village Lodging** (508-432-1434; 800-432-1434; www.wychmere.com), 767 Route 28, Harwichport 02646. Open April through October. This motor inn complex, set on 3 piney acres, is so tidy that I can't help but recommend it even though it's on Route 28. It's a mere half a mile from the beach or the Nantucket ferry. The 24 traditional motel-style rooms and four suites are configured with either one or two double beds or a king; cribs and cots are available for families. Some rooms have a kitchenette; all have cable TV, air-conditioning, and refrigerator. One cottage sleeps a family of five. After the beach, kids will enjoy the large pool, shuffleboard, table tennis, volleyball, and a playground with swings and games. Mid-June to mid-September $104–140 rooms, $155–170 two-bedroom unit, $1,050 weekly cottage. Off-season $55–85, $95–110, and $800, respectively.

Sandpiper Beach Inn (508-432-0485; www.sandpiperbeachinn.com), 16 Bank Street, Harwichport 02646. Open mid-April through October. Fronting its own private beach, this U-shaped building is constructed around a well-tended grassy courtyard. All 20 renovated and redecorated rooms have TV, refrigerator, telephone, and air-conditioning. Some can sleep three to five people; most have a private patio. The duplex cottage that opens directly onto the beach is stunning, but it's often booked a year in advance for July and August. Innkeeper Barbara Talley also provides a continental breakfast. Mid-June to mid-September $140–365 rooms; off-season $105–240; each additional person $25.

Commodore Inn (508-432-1180; 800-368-1180; www.commodoreinn.com), 30 Earle Road, West Harwich 02671. Open April through October. At first glance, Dick and Flora Jones's complex looks like just another cluster of motel rooms set around a pool. But on closer inspection, it's quite a large (heated) pool, a full breakfast buffet is included, and the 27 rooms are nicely outfitted with wicker furniture and white cotton bedspreads. Some have a Jacuzzi, gas fireplace, wet bar, and microwave. Many can sleep four in two double beds. Ask for a room with a vaulted ceiling; they feel much more spacious. Located in a residential area, the Commodore is a 1-minute walk to the beach, and there's a play area. Mid-June to mid-September $165–245 (3-night minimum); off-season $65–175; additional person $35. Full buffet breakfast included in summer; otherwise it's continental.

RENTAL HOUSES AND COTTAGES The Real Estate Place (508-430-4606; 866-760-6606; www.capecodrealty.com), 72 Route 28, West Harwich. Talk to Pam Reida-Allen; she's friendly and knowledgeable about the local market.

✳ Where to Eat

Harwich has one of the Cape's best restaurants, a great hole-in-the-wall, and a bunch of places in between: You won't go hungry here.

DINING OUT &. **Cape Sea Grille** (508-432-4745; www.seagrille.com), 31 Sea Street, Harwichport. Open for dinner mid-April to mid-November. This contemporary bistro still makes my top-10 list of places to eat on the Cape. It's a mightily undersung place. Chef-owners Doug and Jennifer Ramler, who came on board in 2002, offer exceptionally well-prepared French Mediterranean dishes. They're served by candlelight in a lovely old sea captain's home. Outstanding signature dishes include pan-seared lobster with pancetta and asparagus. Or try the grilled salmon with caramelized onions. (Despite those suggestions, pasta dishes are always popular.) Dishes change seasonally, but preparations always play with the classics. You'd better save room for pastry chef Cheryl Matteson's lemon-lime soufflé tart or silky ginger crème brûlée. There is a three-course sunset menu 5–5:45. Reservations suggested. Entrées $18–30.

Y 🦞 ♿ **New Moon** (508-432-9911), 551 Route 28, Harwichport. Open for lunch (weekends) and dinner (nightly). This eclectic bar and grill offers a healthy selection of salads (a favorite has spinach, Vermont cheddar, spiced pecans, and smoked bacon); homemade soups (or chili); thin and crispy pizzas (one with spinach, broccoli, feta, and plum tomatoes); a few pasta dishes (like Thai rice noodles with chicken); and some traditional entrées like grilled salmon. Applewoodsmoked baby back ribs are an "awesome" specialty. You're bound to find something to suit your taste buds and wallet at this nice neighborhood place. How long will it take for everyone to know your name here? Not long, if fourth-generation Harwich proprietor Karen Thornton has anything to say about it. Catch a Sox game at the bar. Lunch $5–13, dinner $12–23.

EATING OUT ✳ All entries under *Eating Out* are open year-round unless otherwise noted.

199

HARWICH

🦞 ♿ **Ay! Caramba Cafe** (508-432-9800), 703 Main Street, Harwich Center. Open 11–9 daily (closed Sunday off-season). With outdoor seating overlooking the town green and church, Ralph and Ira Mendoza's cheery eatery has authentic and fresh Mexican dishes: carne asada, combo plates with chiles rellenos or flautas, burritos and tacos, tortas and tostadas. Mole and enchiladas are a specialty. It's a tasty alternative to the usual fast food. In summer (when the wait may be 45 minutes), the patio is pleasant. Dishes $2–13.

Y **Brax Landing** (508-432-5515), 705 Route 28, Harwich. Open for lunch, dinner, and Sunday brunch April through December. Bar open yearround. Overlooking Saquatucket Harbor, this popular and casual tavernlike restaurant has a varied menu. Look for fish and chicken sandwiches, fried seafood, seafood stew, and sautéed lobster. Their steamers are particularly good. A few indoor seats have choice views, but the real draw is outdoor seating on the tranquil harbor. A bountiful buffet packs 'em in on Sundays. Entrées $13–20, brunch $13.

🦞 ♿ **Bonatt's Restaurant & Bakery** (508-432-7199), 537 Route 28 at Sea Street, Harwichport. Open for breakfast and lunch daily, late May to early September; closed Tuesday offseason. A Harwich landmark since they created the melt-a-way sweet bun in 1939, Bonatt's is still very well known for excellent breakfasts. The short-order kitchen specializes in lobster Benedict and raspberry-stuffed French toast. Fortunately, breakfast is served all day on Sunday. Although I didn't get a chance to try lunch for this edition (and there was a change in ownership, but not chefs), look for specials like fish-and-chips, fisherman's platters, and open steak sandwiches. They also provide box lunches for the beach (call an hour in advance in summer or be prepared to wait). Dishes $4–10.

✿ **Luscious Louie's** (508-430-4131), 600 Route 28, Harwichport. Open for all three meals, mid-May to mid-October. This pleasant place, owned by a pastry chef and the former executive chef at the Chatham Bars Inn, has a wide variety of offerings. From dinnertime pasta, fried seafood, and baked stuffed lobster to lunchtime sandwiches to morning burritos and omelets, you'll find something for everyone in your party. Or go all-out and order a clambake with lobster, mussels, steamers, corn, potatoes, and chorizo ($26). There's also patio dining on Route 28 in warm weather. Lunch $5–9, dinner dishes $10–22.

The Mason Jar (508-430-7600), 544 Route 28, Harwichport. Open daily in-season and closed Sunday off-season. Chef-owner Guy Winialski has fine specialty sandwiches, homemade soups, prepared meals-to-go, rotisserie chicken and desserts. Patio seating. Dishes $5–7.

🦞 ✿ **Seafood Sam's** (508-432-1422), 302 Route 28, Harwichport. Open for lunch and dinner, February through October. You can always count on Sam's for reliable, informally presented, reasonably priced fried or broiled seafood. Outdoor seating, chicken, burgers, and ice cream, too. Lunch specials $5–7, dinner dishes $7–18.

SNACKS **Lambert's** (508-432-5415), 710 Route 28, Harwichport. Open

daily except Monday in winter. This upscale market and deli is an appealing place to gather picnic fixings. Café seating, where you can enjoy baked goods and coffee in an air-conditioned setting, is also an option.

Sundae School Ice Cream Parlor (508-430-2444), 606 Route 28, Harwichport. Open late May to mid-October. This "olde" fashioned "shoppe" is the place to go for homemade ice cream concoctions.

❋ **Pleasant Lake General Store** (508-432-5305), Route 124. Open daily. A good old-fashioned store, perfectly situated for cyclists on the rail-trail (see *To Do—Bicycling/Rentals*).

❋ **Entertainment**

✿ Band concerts are held Tuesday evening at 7:30 in Brooks Park, at Route 39 and Oak Street.

✿ See also Harwich Junior Theatre under *To See and Do*.

❋ **Selective Shopping**

❋ All establishments are open year-round unless otherwise noted.

ANTIQUES **The Barn at Windsong** (508-432-8281), 245 Bank Street, Harwichport. Open May through October. Seven dealers offer a variety of goods: quilts, silver, china, glassware, and furniture.

ARTISANS AND CRAFTS **Pamela Black/Paradise Pottery** (508-432-1713), 928 Route 28, South Harwich. Black creates and displays her whimsical and functional stoneware and raku (as well as hand-cut paper designs) in an old barn next to her house. This is a self-serve kind of place; don't be shy.

Pewter Crafter of Cape Cod (508-432-5858; www.pewtercraftercape-cod.com), 719 Route 28, Harwichport. Open Tuesday through Saturday. Ron Kusins has been toiling at this ancient craft, creating traditional and contemporary designs, since the late 1970s. Finishes are either satin or shiny; forms are functional. This is one of only half a dozen pewter studios in the country (and the only one on the Cape), so now is the time to get an up-close view of pewter making.

BOOKSTORES Wychmere Book & Coffee (508-432-7868), 521 Route 28, Harwichport. This fine shop stocks a great selection of books, cards, and specialty toys. Author events, book club, and reading hour, too.

SPECIAL SHOPS Monahan & Co. Jewelers (508-432-3302; 800-237-4602), 540 Route 28, Harwichport. Prices for high-end jewelry (purchased from estate auctions and left on consignment) range from the double digits to six digits. The largest jewelry shop on the Cape and America's oldest family-owned jewelry store (established in 1815), it's been in Michael Monahan's family for generations.

Cape Cod Tileworks (508-432-7346), 705 Main Street, Harwich Center. Open weekdays and 9–1 Saturday. This colorful shop sells nothing but tile: ceramic, marble, limestone, and hand-painted. They do custom designs and installation, too.

Cape Cod Bonsai Studio (508-432-8400; www.capecodbonsai.com), 1012 Route 28, Harwich. Closed January. In addition to selling more bonsai

trees than you've ever seen, they also sell all the paraphernalia to go along with it. Classes and workshops are offered on creating miniature bonsai and on rock planting.

Cape Cod Braided Rug Co. (508-432-3133), 537 Route 28, Harwichport. In 1910 Romeo Paulus, great-grandfather of the current generation of rugmakers, was the first American to make these old-fashioned braided rugs on a machine. All sizes and shapes and color combinations are available—the in-store inventory is large, but you can also have them custom-make a rug in 6 weeks for about the same price.

Rose Cottage Shop (508-430-4610), 105 Route 137, East Harwich. Richard Morris, an expert at restoring and renovating old houses, also has a talent for decorating their interiors. This expansive showroom offers mostly larger pieces, tasteful country-pine antiques, fine reproductions, and unique home accessories. Richard travels to England several times a year, where he finds most of his pieces.

✴ Special Events

July and August: **Guild of Harwich** Artists sponsors Monday "Art in the Park" at Doane Park, off Lower County Road. (Rain date is Wednesday.)

Early September: **A Taste of Harwich** (508-432-1600), a 1-day food-tasting event at the Cape Cod Technical High School on Route 124, features almost 20 participating restaurants.

Mid-September: **Cranberry Festival.** Community spirit prevails at this popular celebration, which boasts an attendance of almost 40,000 people. Events include fireworks, a parade, and hundreds of top-notch craft displays.

Late October: **Antiques on the Road** (508-430-1165). Representatives from Klinger & Co. appraise your antiques and collectibles at 500 Depot Street.

Early December: **Christmas Weekend in the Harwiches.** Hayrides, strolling minstrels, a choral group, and B&B tours.

CHATHAM

Although Chatham is less accessible from Route 6 than are its neighbors, even the most hurried Cape visitors stop here. Occupying the tip of Cape Cod's elbow, the town offers a good mix of archetypal Cape Cod architecture, a classic Main Street, a refined sensibility, plenty of excellent beaches and shops, and a rich seafaring history.

When Samuel de Champlain and his party tried to land at Stage Harbor in 1606, they were met with stalwart resistance from the Native inhabitants. Fifty years later, though, Yarmouth's William Nickerson purchased a great deal of land from Chief Mattaquason. By 1712, the permanent "settlers" had incorporated the town.

Today Chatham is known for its calm, genteel, independent spirit. The town's vigilant zoning commission has kept tourist-trap activity to a minimum. Bordered on three sides by water, the town is populated by descendants of its oceangoing founders, many of whom continue in their ancestors' footsteps. Despite the difficulty in navigating the surrounding waters, Chatham sustains an active fleet of fishermen and leisure-time sailors. Sailors, fishermen, shop owners, and an increasing number of retirees live quietly in this delightfully traditional village.

Chatham, along with the spectacularly desolate Monomoy National Wildlife Refuge, boasts 65 miles of shoreline. As such, Chatham's beaches are varied: Some are hit by pounding surf, sandbars shelter others; some are good for shell collecting, others are wide and sandy. A walk along the shore reveals gentle inlets and beautiful seafront homes. An inland drive or bicycle ride takes you past elegant shingled cottages and stately white houses surrounded by picket fences and boasting primroses and tidy lawns.

In the center of Chatham, Main Street is chock-full of upscale shops, offering everything from tony antiques and nautically inspired gifts to jewelry, clothing, and culinary supplies. This central part of town has excellent restaurants and inns, and some of the Cape's finest bow-shaped roof houses (so named because they're shaped like the bow of a ship turned upside down). North Chatham, primarily residential, is dotted with several picturesque inlets. West and South Chatham border the beaches; you'll find lots of rental houses, summer cottages, and piney woods here.

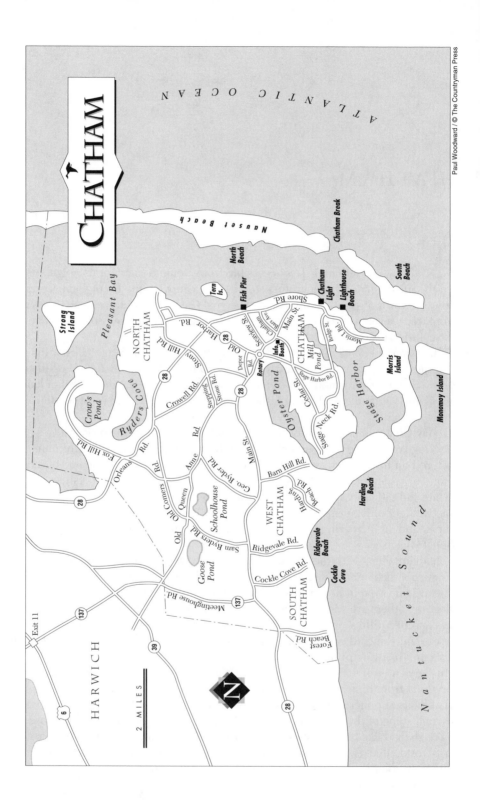

CHATHAM

ATLANTIC OCEAN

Nauset Beach

North Beach

Chatham Break

South Beach

Pleasant Bay

Strong Island

Tern Is.

Fish Pier

Chatham Light

Lighthouse Beach

NORTH CHATHAM

Hill Rd.

Stony Rd.

Harbor Rd.

Old

Depot Rd.

Rotary

Seaview St.

Chatham

Bar's Ave

Main St.

Shore Rd.

Info. Booth

Bridge St.

Morris I. Rd.

CHATHAM

Mill Pond

Cedar St.

Stage Harbor Rd.

Stage Neck Rd.

Stage Harbor

Morris Island

Monomoy Island

Crow's Pond

Ryder's Cove

Fox Hill Rd.

Orleans Rd.

Crowell Rd.

Stepping Stone Rd.

Main St.

Barn Hill Rd.

WEST CHATHAM

Harding Rd.

Harding Beach

Rd.

Anne Rd.

Geo. Ryder Rd.

Queen

Old Comers Rd.

Old

Schoolhouse Pond

Sam Ryders Rd.

Ridgevale Rd.

Ridgevale Beach

Goose Pond

Cockle Cove Rd.

Cockle Cove

Meetinghouse Rd.

SOUTH CHATHAM

Forest Beach Rd.

Exit 11

HARWICH

2 MILES

N

Nantucket Sound

GUIDANCE Information booth (508-945-5199; 800-715-5567 for recorded information year-round; www.chathamcapecod.org), 533 Main Street, Chatham 02633. Open 10–5 daily mid-May to mid-October. The map-lined walls come in handy when you're planning an itinerary or looking for a specific place—as does the walking guide.

There is also a **seasonal welcome center** with the same hours at the historic Bassett House, Routes 137 and 28, South Chatham. Even if you don't need information, this is a great old house.

PUBLIC REST ROOMS Year-round public rest rooms are located at the town offices on Main Street and at the Fish Pier on Shore Road. Additional summertime facilities are located behind Kate Gould Park (off Main Street) and the welcome center (see *Guidance*) at Routes 137 and 28.

PUBLIC LIBRARY ❊ ✿ ♟ **Eldredge Public Library** (508-945-5170), 564 Main Street. Open Monday, Wednesday, Friday, and Saturday 10–5; Tuesday and Thursday 1–9. One of the Cape's best libraries houses modern literature, genealogical records, books on tape, free Internet access, and newspapers and magazines.

GETTING THERE *By car:* From the Cape Cod Canal, take Route 6 east to exit 11 (Route 137 south) to Route 28 south. The center of Chatham is 3 miles from this intersection, about 45 minutes from either bridge.

By bus: There is no bus service to Chatham; you'll have to catch the **Plymouth & Brockton** bus line (508-778-9767; www.p-b.com) in Orleans to reach other Cape towns or Boston's Logan Airport. If you have to do this, you'll need a **cab** (508-945-0068).

GETTING AROUND Chatham is crowded in July and August, and you'll be happiest exploring Main Street on foot. It's about a 15-minute walk from mid–Main Street to the lighthouse and another 15 minutes from the light to the pier (one way). There is free parking at Town Hall (off Main Street), the Colonial Building (off Stage Harbor Road), one block west of the rotary at the elementary school, and on Chatham Bars Avenue behind the Impudent Oyster restaurant off Main Street.

Chatham Area Transit (CAT; 508-385-8326; 800-352-7155; www.thebreeze. info) operates mini-buses on one route around town from late June to early August. It runs every 20 minutes 9:30–9 daily. Since Main Street is extremely crowded in summer, you should really consider this option. Park at the West Chatham Park & Ride lot of Route 28 and George Ryder Road, or the A&P at Route 28 and Queen Anne Road, or the elementary school on Depot Road. Fares 50¢ adult.

The **H₂O** (508-385-8326; 800-352-7155; www.capecodtransit.org) bus line, used by more locals than visitors, travels along Route 28 between the Hyannis Transportation Center and Orleans daily except Sunday year-round. It stops on Shore Road in North Chatham, at the rotary in the center of Chatham, and on Morton's Road in South Chatham.

CHATHAM BREAK

Coin-operated telescopes across from the lighthouse allow visitors to take a closer look at the famous Chatham Break, the result of a ferocious nor'easter on January 2, 1987. During that historic storm, the barrier beach (the lower portion of Nauset Beach) that had previously protected Chatham Harbor from the open ocean was breached. As a result, low dunes were flattened, tidal waters rose, and waves and high winds forced a channel through Nauset Beach. Over the next few years, nine expensive waterfront homes were destroyed by the ensuing, unrestrained pounding of the fierce Atlantic Ocean. Although fishermen now have a more direct passage through the (formerly) long barrier beach, boating around the harbor's strong currents is more difficult than ever.

In a matter of hours in 1987 (rather than over the natural course of 50 years), the break altered the Chatham's way of life. The effects are still felt and debated today. But ocean currents have a mind of their own; in 1846 a previous break in South Beach repaired itself. That hasn't happened to this breach yet. But some beachfront is returning, and some of it belongs to folks who saw their lots washed away in the late 1980s. Sand, like birds, migrates south; Wellfleet's and Eastham's beach losses are Chatham's gain. Lighthouse Beach is directly below the lookout area; South and North Beaches are visible across the harbor (see *Green Space— Beaches*). Enjoy the view; it's a work in progress.

VIEWING CHATHAM BREAK   Kim Grant

✳ To See

Chatham Light (508-430-0628), Main Street and Bridge Street. Built in 1828 and rebuilt in 1876, the lighthouse has a beacon visible 23 miles out to sea. The U.S. Coast Guard–operated lighthouse is open during July and August on Wednesdays 1–3:30; no kids under age 5 allowed. Parking limit of 30 minutes during the summer.

Fish Pier, Shore Road at Bar Cliff Avenue. Chatham's fleet of fishing boats returns—from as far away as 100 miles—to the pier daily about 2–4. From the pier's second-floor observation deck you can watch fishermen unloading their catch of haddock, lobster, cod, halibut, flounder, and pollack. While you're at the pier, take a gander at the **Fisherman's Monument.** A 1992 call for designs attracted nearly 100 applicants from around the world. The committee chose Sig Purwin, a Woods Hole sculptor, to memorialize the town's fishermen.

In recent years, as stocks have begun to dwindle, fishermen have increasingly turned to shellfish harvesting. (Local scallops harvested in late fall are like nothing you've ever tasted.) In fact, more commercial licenses are purchased yearly in Chatham than anywhere else on the Cape. And while Chatham has particularly rich, natural beds, many fishermen are turning to organized aquaculture farming.

🐾 ↑ **Railroad Museum** (508-945-0342), 153 Depot Road. Open 10–4 Tuesday through Saturday, mid-June to mid-September. This carefully restored 1887 depot—on the National Register of Historic Places—is chock-full of Victorian details, from a turret to its gingerbread trim. Inside you'll find treasures such as a 1910 New York Central train caboose and photos, models, and equipment pertaining to the Cape's railroad history. Donations.

↑ 🐾 **Old Atwood House** (508-945-2493; www.atwoodhouse.org), 347 Stage Harbor Road. Open 1–4 Tuesday through Friday and 9:30–noon Saturday, mid-June through September. This gambrel-roofed house, built by a sea captain in 1752, has been maintained by the Chatham Historical Society since 1926. (Note the low doorways and how much we've grown over the last two centuries by eating our vegetables!) The museum houses antique dolls, tools, toys, portraits of sea captains, seashells from around the world, Sandwich glass, and other Chatham seafaring artifacts. The adjoining train barn features a three-panel mural by Alice Wright that depicts more than 130 townspeople with a "modern Christ." Adults $3, children under 12 free.

Mayo House (508-945-6098, 945-4084), 540 Main Street. Open 11–4 Tuesday through Thursday, late June through September. Built in 1818 by Josiah Mayo (who served for 40 years as Chatham's first postmaster) and filled with period antiques, the Mayo House is the headquarters of the Chatham Conservation Foundation. The tiny, yellow three-quarter Cape isn't the "best this" or the "oldest that;" it's just a nice little old house. Donations.

SCENIC DRIVES Chatham is one of the most scenic Cape towns. Route 28 toward Orleans provides, with views of Pleasant Bay to the east. Shore Road passes handsome cedar-shingled houses. The causeway to Morris Island affords harbor views as well as views of the open ocean beyond tall grasses and sandy shores. And the road to Cockle Cove Beach from Route 28 in South Chatham runs along a picturesque salt marsh and tidal river.

✳ Outdoor Activities

AIRPLANE RIDES 🐾 ✳ **Cape Cod Flying Circus** (508-945-9000; 508-945-2363), Chatham Municipal Airport, George Ryder Road. To really appreciate Chatham's shoreline and the fragility of the Outer Cape landscape, head 900 feet above it in a three-seater Cessna. These wonderful sight-seeing rides are a bargain (25 minutes, $85; 55 minutes, $155). Prices are per ride, whether it's one person or three (max). Reserve a day in advance in summer.

✐ **BASEBALL** The Chatham Athletics, one of 10 teams in the Cape Cod Baseball League, usually play ball at 7 PM from mid-June to early August at Veterans Park, Route 28, just west of the rotary. The information booth (see *Guidance*) has schedules.

The A's (508-945-5511) sponsor weekly clinics for youngsters from mid-June through July. The cost is $50 for age 6–12, $90 for age 13 and over. Register at Veterans Park on Monday morning at 8. And bring your own glove.

BICYCLING/RENTALS With gentle inclines, quiet lanes, and a well-marked 2.75-mile route around town, Chatham is nice for bicycling. **Bert & Carol's Lawnmower and Bicycle Shop** (508-945-0137), 347 Route 28, North Chatham, offers rentals and makes personalized routes and recommendations based on your level and needs. They also carry a full line of accessories like roof racks, baby seats, and trail-a-bikes. For extensive cycling, look for the $2.99 Chatham bike trail maps. Open from April through November, with parking on the premises.

See also Bikes & Blades under *In-Line Skating*.

BOAT EXCURSIONS/RENTALS **Outermost Adventures** (508-945-5858; www. outermostharbor.com), Outermost Harbor Marine, off Morris Island Road. Late June to mid-September. This outfit offers seal cruises and continuous shuttles to pristine South Beach and Monomoy Island. Round-trip South Beach shuttles costs $10 for adults, $5 children under 12; Monomoy is $15 per person; both run 8–5 daily. Hour-long seal trips are by reservation; the minimum cost is $70, or $16 adults, $8 children under 12.

Rip Ryder (508-945-5450; www.monomoyislandferry.com), off Morris Island Road. Boats run April through October; make reservations the night before. Regular launches to North Monomoy and South Beach. When the captain drops you off, tell him what time you want to be picked up. Inquire about fly-fishing, birding, and seal trips. You'll get a better deal when combining a seal trip with a beach trip.

Beachcomber (508-945-5265; www.sealwatch.com), from the Fish Pier, Seal Harbor, and Stage Harbor. Beach and fishing shuttles to North Beach. Like most other outfits, they also offer 90-minute seal trips, but they use a faster boat so you spend more time watching seals and less time traveling. In this case it's the destination, not the journey.

Cape Water Sports/Nauti Jane's Boat Rentals, at the Wequassett Inn Resort (508-432-5400; 508-430-6893), Route 28. You can rent daysailers, kayaks, catamarans, surf bikes, powerboats, and Sunfish at this beachfront location from May through October. Make reservations for lessons. Their Ridgevale Beach location (508-432-4339) has sailboats from mid-June to early September.

Rent boats at **Oyster River Boatyard** (508-945-0736), Barn Hill Lane extension, off Route 28, West Chatham.

FISHING/SHELLFISHING Goose Hummock (508-255-0455) at the Orleans rotary sells freshwater fishing licenses. For shellfishing licenses, contact the Permit Department (508-945-5180) on George Ryder Road in West Chatham.

✿ **The Fishin' Bridge.** Follow Stage Harbor Road to Bridge Street, where Mill Pond empties into Stage Harbor. You'll probably haul in several crabs, small flounders, eels, and perhaps even a bluefish. Locals will certainly be there with long rakes, harvesting shellfish. Stop even if you don't fish; it's picturesque.

South Beach offers the best opportunity for surf-casting for striped bass, but **North Beach** is a close second.

Schoolhouse Pond (reached via Sam Ryders Road) and **Goose Pond** (off Fisherman's Landing) offer freshwater fishing for rainbow trout. In-season there is resident-only parking at Schoolhouse.

For sportfishing charters (May through November), try Bob Miller's ***Booby***

DIGGING FOR CLAMS AT LOW TIDE IN PLEASANT BAY

Kim Grant

Hatch (508-430-2312) and Ron McVickar's **Banshee** (508-945-0403), both out of Stage Harbor Marine.

Captain Jack Wesley Randall (508-432-4630) leads guided charter fly-fishing trips. For custom tackle, supplies, rod rentals, and more charter information, stop in at **Top Rod Fly & Surf Fish Shop** (508-945-2256), 1082 Route 28, next to Ryders Cove in North Chatham.

See also Beachcomber under *Boat Excursions/Rentals.*

✐ ⴟ **FOR FAMILIES Play-a-Round Playground,** on Depot Road behind Chatham Elementary School. This wonderful, multilevel wooden structure includes an area for disabled children and a fenced-in area for toddlers.

GOLF ❄ **Chatham Seaside Links** (508-945-4774), Seaview Street, next to the Chatham Bars Inn. Open year-round, weather permitting; a nine-hole, par-34 course.

✐ ❄ **IN-LINE SKATING/SKATEBOARDING Bikes & Blades** (508-945-7600), 195 Crowell Road. Rentals of just what the name implies: bicycles and in-line skates. Bikes cost $16; skates $20. Half-day, 3-day, and weekly rates, too. There is free parking and direct access to the Cape Cod Rail Trail from here.

Skateboard park, at the Chatham Municipal Airport. Ramps, half-pipes, and grinds; open 10–dark.

KAYAKING For rentals see Monomoy Sail & Cycle under *Sailboarding,* and Cape Water Sports under *Boat Excursions/Rentals.*

SAILBOARDING Monomoy Sail & Cycle (508-945-0811), 275 Route 28, North

FROM CHATHAM'S FISH PIER

Kim Grant

Chatham, rents sailboards and kayaks. Pleasant Bay enjoys easterly and north-easterly winds, while Forest Beach receives southwesterly winds.

SEAL CRUISES See the sidebar "Monomoy National Wildlife Refuge" under *Green Space.*

TENNIS Public courts are located on **Depot Road** by the Railroad Museum and at **Chatham High School** on Crowell Road. Free.

Chatham Bars Inn (508-945-0096), Shore Road. Mid-April to mid-November. CBI has three waterfront courts made of synthetic "classic-clay" (which play like clay but are much easier to maintain) that rent to nonguests for $30 an hour ($20 off-season). Lessons are $60–70 per hour plus the court fee.

✳ Even More Things to Do

ART CLASSES ✳ **Creative Arts Center** (508-945-3583; www.capecodcre-ativearts.org), 154 Crowell Road. The center offers classes in pottery, drawing, photography, painting, jewelry making, and other fine arts. Work is shown at the center's on-site **Edward A. Bigelow Gallery.** Since 1971, the center has held an annual art festival in August (see *Special Events*), where you may meet the artists and purchase their work.

FITNESS CLUB ✳ **Chatham Health & Swim Club** (508-945-3555), 251 Crowell Road. A full-service place with a five-lane lap pool and weekly fee of $75.

GENEALOGY Nickerson Family Association (508-945-6086), 1107 Orleans Road. Chatham's founder, William Nickerson, has over 350,000 descendants. Think you're one of them? This genealogical research center will help you find out. In addition to mapping the Nickerson family tree Nickersons, the volunteer association casts a wide net, compiling information on folks associated the Nickersons and original settlers of Cape Cod and Nova Scotia.

✳ Green Space

Chase Park, on Cross Street, is a tranquil vest pocket of parkland just a couple of blocks from the summertime madness on Main Street. It's perfect for a picnic lunch and overlooks a tranquil gristmill built in 1797. The mill is open 10–3 weekdays, July to early September.

Hydrangea Walkway. Heading north on Shore Road from Main Street, the road is lined with stately private homes overlooking the ocean. One house on the left, in particular, is really eye-catching from mid-June through September, when its front walkway is awash with more than 25 blooming hydrangea plants.

BEACHES Cottage renters purchase weekly beach stickers for Hardings, Ridgevale, and Cockle Cove Beaches (see below). Otherwise, from late June to early September, parking (508-945-5158) is $10 daily, weekly $40.

Hardings Beach, on Nantucket Sound. From Route 28, take Barn Hill Road to

MONOMOY NATIONAL WILDLIFE REFUGE

North and South Monomoy Islands, acquired by the federal government as part of a wildlife refuge in 1944, comprise a 2,700-acre habitat for more than 285 species of birds. Birds and seaside animals rule the roost; there are no human residents, no paved roads, no vehicles, and no electricity. (Long ago the island did support a fishing community, though.) It's a quiet, solitary place. Monomoy, one of four remaining "wilderness" areas between Maine and New Jersey, is an important stop for shorebirds on the Atlantic Flyway—between breeding grounds in the Arctic and wintering grounds in South America. Conditions here may well determine whether the birds will survive the journey. Some beaches are closed from April to mid-August to protect threatened nesting areas for piping plovers and terns. The lovely old lighthouse, built in 1823 and not used since 1923, was restored in 1988.

In the mid-1990s, the U.S. Fish and Wildlife Service embarked on a long-term management project to restore avian nesting diversity to Monomoy NWR by creating habitat for terns, which historically numbered in the thousands. Restoring the nesting space was controversial because the government considered it necessary to "remove" (with bread chunks laced with poison) about 10 percent of the aggressive seagulls that also nested here. As a result, by the late 1990s, the number of nesting terns, including 18 pairs of roseate terns, increased dramatically. Some protesters still maintain that the Fish and Wildlife Service took this action under pressure from off-road-vehicle drivers, who are often banned from driving on mainland beaches because of nesting endangered birds. But by the late 1990s, Monomoy had become the second largest tern nesting site on the East Coast, and the biggest between here and the Canadian Maritimes. In 1998, the refuge was dogged by another controversy: dens of coyotes (and their pups) were feasting on newborn chicks. Management "removed" them as well. These days commercial clammers and crabbers are sparring with the refuge over the issuance (or lack thereof) of permits.

Monomoy was attached to the mainland until a 1958 storm severed the connection; a storm in 1978 divided the island in two. The islands are accessible only by boat (see *Outdoor Activities—Boat Excursions/Rentals*), and only under favorable weather conditions. Guided tours are available from the Cape Cod Museum of Natural History (508-896-3867 for reservations; see *To See* in "Brewster") and the Wellfleet Bay Wildlife Sanctuary (508-349-2615 for reservations; see the "It's Not Just For the Birds" sidebar in "Wellfleet").

Groups of six or more must obtain a permit from the refuge headquarters on Morris Island (508-945-0594). The 40-acre Morris Island is accessible by car and foot: Head south from Chatham Light and turn left onto Morris Island Road, then take your first right and continue on Morris Island Road to the end.

About 300 gray and harbor seals summer off the shores of Chatham, and about 3,000 seals rally here in winter. While the Chatham shores have attracted seals since the early 1980s, Monomoy has been a haven only since the 1991 hurricane created a break in the barrier beach.

Hardings Beach Road. One Explorer e-mails: "Hardings Beach is great mostly because it has a channel into a salt pond and marsh. You can tube or float in the channel depending on the tide, and the water's warm." Small dunes. Rest rooms and concession stand.

Ridgevale Beach, on Nantucket Sound. Take Ridgevale Road off Route 28. Rest rooms and snack bar.

🔊 **Cockle Cove Beach,** protected from Nantucket Sound by Ridgevale Beach. Take Cockle Cove Road off Route 28. Gentle waves and soft sand make this a good choice for families.

🔊 **Pleasant Bay Beach,** Route 28, North Chatham. The 7,000-acre inlet and bay has been called breathtakingly beautiful, and it is. It's also on the state's list of 25 areas of "critical environmental concern." This beach is narrow but great for children because the water is so shallow.

CHATHAM LIGHT BEACH

Kim Grant

North Beach, on the Atlantic Ocean. North Beach, which is actually the southern end of Nauset Beach, is accessible only by boat (see *Outdoor Activities—Boat Excursions/Rentals* for water-taxi services). It's well worth the effort and expense to get here.

Lighthouse Beach or **South Beach,** below the lighthouse, on the Atlantic Ocean. Parking is limited to 30 minutes, but you can bicycle or walk to the lane off Morris Island Road just beyond the lighthouse; a sign points the way to South Beach. If you're day-tripping to Chatham, pay to park at the Eldredge Taxi parking lot, 365 Main Street, and take its taxi to the beach. The most desolate part of the beach requires quite a long walk, but the early sections are very nice, too. Many ferries (see *Outdoor Activities—Boat Excursions/Rentals*) take passengers to the farthest, most remote reaches of the beach. One of the best aspects of this beach is that you've got surf on the east side and calm bay waters on the west.

POND **Oyster Pond Beach,** off Stage Harbor Road, near the rotary. This inland saltwater pond is connected to Nantucket Sound by way of Oyster Creek and Stage Harbor. Good for families, its shores are calm and its waters are the warmest in town. Free parking; lifeguard.

WALKS **Chatham Conservation Commission** (508-945-4084). With the over 550 acres, the commission has created three distinct walking areas traversing marshes, wetlands, and meadows. Contact the town information booth on Main Street (see *Guidance*) for directions.

❀ **The Dog Runs,** as it's known locally. Walk 10 minutes along Bridge Street from the lighthouse to find this forested coastal trail along Stage Harbor. Enjoy a picnic in the cattail marshes.

See also the sidebar "Monomoy National Wildlife Refuge."

❈ Lodging

Generally, Chatham is one of the more expensive places to stay on Cape Cod. Two-night minimum stays in July and August are normal, and many of Chatham's most notable places are booked for July and August well before July 4. Unless otherwise noted, all lodging is in Chatham 02633.

🖋 RESORTS ❈ ♿ **Chatham Bars Inn** (508-945-0096; 800-527-4884; www.chathambarsinn.com), Shore Road. This grande dame's gracious elegance is rivaled by only a handful of places in New England. Built in 1914 as a hunting lodge, it's now the quintessential seaside resort. And after extensive, multimillion-dollar renovations, it's better than ever. Grounds are lushly landscaped, and the seaside setting nearly perfect. Scattered over 25 acres, the main inn and cottages have a total of 205 rooms and suites comfortably decorated with wicker, hand-painted furniture, and understated florals. Some ocean-view rooms have private balconies or decks.

The complex includes: a private beach, heated outdoor pool, four tennis courts, croquet, health and wellness center, nine-hole golf course, launch service to Nauset Beach, and a full and complimentary children's programs. Although prices don't include meals, a lavish buffet is available every morning. A 10-minute walk from town, the hotel also has an expansive veranda and very comfortable, grand living rooms. Mid-June to mid-September $310–550; off-season $150–480 (serious minimum stays required in summer). Rates considerably higher for ocean-view rooms and suites; off-season packages.

& **Wequassett Inn Resort** (508-432-5400; 800-225-7125; www.wequassett.com), 2673 Route 28. Open April through November. If CBI (see above) appeals to a "new money" set, then the Wequassett (10 minutes north of Chatham on picturesque Pleasant Bay) appeals to "old money." Renowned for an attentive staff, exceptional service, and understated elegance, the complex consists of 18 buildings set on 23 beautifully landscaped acres. It also boasts an excellent restaurant (see *Dining Out*), four tennis courts, sailing, and a pool. (There isn't a more perfectly situated

pool on the Cape.) Other resort amenities include a fitness center, boat rentals, ferries to an uncrowded section of the National Seashore, baby-sitting, and summertime children's programs. The resort also offers guests playing privileges on the otherwise private Cape Cod National Golf Course, a challenging Cornish and Silva course (golf packages available).

As for the rooms, most cottages have cathedral ceilings and their own decks, though not all have views of boat-studded Round Cove. Triple sheeting, morning delivery of the newspaper, and turndown service are standard. Rooms are in the process of being upgraded, but most have lovely country-pine furnishings. Light lunches are served poolside; nightcaps are soothing at the charming Thoreau's. June through September $340–425 non-water-view rooms, $535–665 water views, suites more; off-season $125–355 rooms, $215–405.

HOTEL ❋ **Chatham Wayside Inn** (508-945-5550; 800-391-5734; www.

A HIDDEN POOL AT THE CHATHAM BARS INN

Kim Grant

waysideinn.com), 512 Main Street. This historic 1860 hostelry (which now looks brand new) was completely renovated and expanded in the mid-1990s. Disgruntled locals think it lacks soul these days; it certainly dominates Main Street. Nonetheless, the 53 guest rooms and three suites are furnished with flair and a decorator's sure touch. Triple sheeting, thick towels, and top-notch bathroom amenities are standard. Each room has a canopy or four-poster bed and reproduction period furniture. Some rooms have a fireplace, whirlpool tub, or a private patio or balcony. Views are of the town green, golf course, or parking lot. Summer and winter, cocktails are served fireside in the pub. Outdoor swimming pool and tennis courts. Mid-June to early September $185–375 rooms and suites; otherwise $95–295; inquire about off-season packages.

BED & BREAKFASTS 🏵 🎗 The Moorings

(508-945-0848; 800-320-0848; www.mooringscapecod.com), 326 Main Street. Open mid-February through December. It's hard to say what I like best about this B&B: the large landscaped backyard (a riot of color), central location, comfortably elegant guest rooms, or relaxed atmosphere. When Roberta and Frank Schultz renovated this fine old house, they thankfully retained its "old-house feel." The soothing living room boasts high wainscoting and Oriental carpets. Five of the 16 rooms are in the main house. Of these, the yellow room is the best and brightest, although all are lovely. Rooms in the adjacent building are quite large and feature private deck, gas fireplace, and fresh bathroom (some with whirlpool). The charming hideaway cottage is completely renovated, too. There's more: A full breakfast served in the cheery dining room; the beach

THE LAUNCH TO THE SEASHORE AT THE WEQUASSET INN

Kim Grant

is a 10-minute walk; and the B&B loans beach chairs. Mid-June to mid-September $142–235 rooms, $300 nightly or $2,100 weekly for cottage; off-season $80–138 rooms, $165 nightly or $950 weekly for cottage.

❋ **Port Fortune Inn** (508-945-0792; 800-750-0792; www.portfortune-inn.com), 201 Main Street. Open April to mid-October. This B&B has a most enviable location, a couple of hundred yards from Lighthouse Beach (see *Green Space—Beaches*). Since innkeepers Renee and Mike Kahl completely renovated their 11 rooms and one suite, each has a tasteful, modern feel, with air-conditioning, telephone, and reproduction furnishings. Most rooms have four-poster beds, refrigerator, and TV; room 9 has a warming southern exposure. The front building boasts two ocean-view rooms. On rainy days, there are two comfortable common rooms, one with a gas fireplace. Beach towels and chairs are provided. The action on Main Street is a 10-minute walk away. Mid-June to mid-September $150–210, $260 suite; spring and fall $95–165 and $210, respectively; includes breakfast buffet.

❋ **Captain's House Inn of Chatham** (508-945-0127; 800-315-0728; www.captainshouseinn.com), 369–377 Old Harbor Road. This traditional Greek Revival inn enjoys a privileged position. Jan and Dave McMaster, innkeepers since 1993, preside over an enthusiastic British hotel management staff, 2 acres of well-tended gardens, 12 handsome rooms, and four sumptuous suites in adjacent buildings. The Captain's Cottage contains one particularly historic room with wood-burning fireplace, walnut-paneled walls, and pumpkin-pine flooring; a hideaway attic suite; and a honeymoon-style room with a double whirlpool. Antiques-filled inn rooms are more traditional, but all have triple sheeting, air-conditioning, telephone, fireplace, and TV/VCR. Full breakfasts are served on linen, china, and silver in a wonderfully airy room. Smoked salmon graces the sideboard every morning, and an authentic English tea is offered every afternoon. Always upgrading the property and staying ahead of the innkeeping curve, the McMasters added a swimming pool and fitness room in 2002. Loaner bikes are available. Mid-May through October $175–400; off-season $145–295.

🦞 ❋ ✿ **Bow Roof House** (508-945-1346), 59 Queen Anne Road. A 5-minute walk from town—and a 2-minute walk from the town beach—Vera Mazulis's late-18th-century B&B is a real find. After seeing so many fancied-up inns, decorated with designer this and that, the Bow Roof House is a breath of fresh air. It feels authentic. Of the six guest rooms, I prefer the first-floor ones. Room 1 features an old beehive oven, antiques, and two double beds. The comfy living room, with woodstove, leads to a deck. A continental breakfast is served at one table in the plant-filled dining room. Vera has owned this B&B since 1975 and welcomes children. $75–85.

🦞 ✿ **Blowin' A Gale Guest House** (508-945-9716), 219 Old Harbor Road. Open mid-June to mid-October. This snug and weathered 1888 house is operated by Nancy Petrus (who grew up across the street) and husband Bob. They rent only one room (or two rooms to a family), but it's very comfy and well looked after.

The first-floor sitting room is separate from the owners' quarters, and the back porch overlooks conservation land. Expanded continental breakfast. $125 double, $200 as a two-room suite; $10 surcharge for 1-night stays; 10 percent discount for weeklong stays.

❋ **Cranberry Inn** (508-945-9232; 800-332-4667; www.cranberryinn. com), 359 Main Street. A 10-minute walk from Chatham Light and the beach, this completely renovated two-story inn has 18 traditional rooms off a long hallway. In attitude and decor, it more closely resembles an elegant small hotel than a B&B. Common space includes a traditional living room that also serves as a reception area and a small, handsome bar. Upscale guest room furnishings—mixing period antiques with reproductions—might have a fireplace, private balcony, and wet bar. All have air-conditioning. Behind the inn a little nature trail and an unharvested cranberry bog beckon, but most guest enjoy rocking in chairs on the long veranda. The innkeepers, Kay and Bill DeFord, include a full breakfast, which is enjoyed at individual tables. Early May to late October $150–260; off-season $100–180.

COTTAGES **Metter's Cottages** (508-432-3535), Chatham Harbor Lane, West Chatham 02669. Open May through October. These three water-view cottages are more like homes than cottages. Talk with George and Donna Metter about your needs when reserving; there's probably a cottage with your name on it. July to early September $1,200–1,800 weekly for a water-view three-bedroom; off-season $800–1,000. Reservations are

taken after January 1 for the upcoming summer.

See also The Moorings under *Bed & Breakfasts.*

EFFICIENCIES AND MOTELS

🦜 🐾 ♿ **Chatham Highlander I and II** (508-945-9038; www.realmass. com/highlander), 946 Route 28. Open April through November. An excellent choice for budget-minded travelers, this favored motel has friendly and hands-on proprietors, Mike and Pauline Holly, who are always upgrading their place. Just a stone's throw from the center of town, the two adjacent motels sit on a little knoll above a well-traveled road. Each of the 28 rooms has a TV, small refrigerator, tiled bathroom, and air-conditioning; most have two double beds. Decor is quite cheery, albeit old-fashioned; aspects are charmingly retro. Rooms are sparkling white, freshened with new mattresses and spreads. I'm partial to units at the Highlander II. There are also two heated pools. Mid-June to early September $115–145; off-season $65–110; additional child $10, additional adult $20.

♿ 🦜 **Chatham Tides Waterfront Motel** (508-432-0379; www.chatham-tides.com), 394 Pleasant Street, South Chatham 02659. Open mid-May to mid-October. Delightfully off the well-trodden path, this quiet beachfront complex of 24 rooms and suites is a real find. Fronted by dunes and ocean, the view alone is worth the price. It's been in Ellen and Ed Handel's family since 1966 and is still maintained with impressive care. After staying here once, you'll probably return again and again. Try booking in February after the repeat guests get their pick of the litter in

January. Rooms with kitchenette, air-conditioning, decks. Late June through August $160–185 daily, $1,050–1,200 weekly; off-season $125–150 daily, $800–975 weekly. Town houses in-season $1,350–1,900 weekly.

Hawthorne Motel (508-945-0372; www.thehawthorne.com), 196 Shore Road. Open mid-May to mid-October. A 10-minute walk from Main Street, this motel is popular because nothing stands between it and the ocean except grass and a path to their private beach. The 10 efficiencies are "summer campish," but who cares—you're coming for the easy access to sunning, swimming, and lazing on the beach. A few more particulars: The 16 motel rooms received new furnishings in 2002; corner rooms are much larger; some rooms have a kitchenette. Late June to early September $150–170 nightly for rooms/efficiencies, $3,500 weekly for cottage; off-season $110–130 for rooms/efficiencies, $2,450 weekly for cottage. Four-night minimum in-season.

✔ **Pleasant Bay Village Resort Motel** (508-945-1133; 800-547-1011; www.pleasantbayvillage.com), Route 28. Open May through October. Three miles from town, this place will forever change your opinion of a motel complex. The 6 acres of lush, Japanese-style landscaping and tasteful pool are reason enough to recommend it, and the assortment of 58 well-maintained rooms is extensive. Some have a sundeck, others overlook a cascading waterfall; some are spacious, others are snug; some have grills, some have fully equipped kitchens. Walk across the street and down Route 28 to Pleasant Bay Beach (see *Green Space—Beaches*). Late

June to early September $165–255 rooms, $185–275 efficiencies, $295–455 suites for four. (The lower end of these ranges is for late June to late July.) Inquire about weekly rates; children $15–20 additional per day.

LIGHTHOUSE South Monomoy Lighthouse (508-896-3867; www.ccmnh.org). Overnights permitted late May to early October. Administered by the Cape Cod Museum of Natural History, this 30-hour Monomoy Island overnight includes transportation to and from the island and time with a naturalist, who will cook your dinner by kerosene lamp. Breakfast and a substantial lunchtime snack are also included. The rustic keeper's house has three bedrooms with air mattresses and cots. This overnight is very popular; you'd be well advised to make reservations after mid-February, if you can. $200 per person.

RENTAL HOUSES AND COTTAGES
Sylvan Vacation Rentals (508-432-2344; www.sylvanrentals.com), 1715 Route 28, South Chatham 02659, has listings ranging from basic beach cottages to luxury homes.

Chatham Home Rentals (508-945-9444; www.chathamhomerentals.com), 1402 Route 28. Expect to spend $800–2,000 weekly.

✳ Where to Eat

Dining options in Chatham run the gamut from elegant to child-friendly places. Reserve ahead in summer (especially at *Dining Out* eateries) or be prepared for a lengthy wait.

DINING OUT ☿ **28 Atlantic** (508-432-5400), Route 28, North Chatham (just over the Harwich town line, actually). Open for all three meals, April through November. At the Wequassett Inn Resort's signature restaurant, is it the water view or the food that reigns supreme? Hard to say, since they both rise above lofty expectations. Executive chef Bill Brodsky oversees the regional American and Continental menu, full of artfully presented dishes packed with great flourishes and flavors. The seasonal menu is served ever-so-graciously on Limoges china in a genteel, understated, open, and elegant dining room. Lengthy recitations by the waitstaff about the ingredients and preparations accompany and elevate each course. Seafood is a specialty, of course, and everything we tried was spirited and ambitious. Dinner entrées $17–38.

🦪 **Le Petit Cafe** (508-945-0028), 155 Crowell Road. Open for dinner April to mid-January. Chef-owner Michael Marciezyk and his wife, Pam, preside over this unpretentious, intimate, 12-table café. The sweet, well-kept secret gets rave reviews from those in the know (including me!). Their menu features creative specials (like my recent seafood risotto) as well as signature dishes like bouillabaisse, rack of lamb, sea scallops with exotic mushrooms, and steak *frites* in a red wine shallot sauce. Don't be fooled by the modest surroundings; they belie high quality preparations. Save room for a rich dose of Chocolate Revenge. Entrées $15–28.

❊ **Sosumi Asian Bistro & Sushi Bar** (508-945-0300), 14 Chatham Bars Avenue. Open daily for dinner. Exciting and exotic, the adventurous menu is best treated like tapas: order assorted appetizers, soups, and salads as you go along. I haven't never met a dish I didn't like. Try the grilled egg-

CHATHAM SQUIRE RESTAURANT

Kim Grant

plant with plum paste, lobster bisque, spicy seaweed salad, house-made parsnip chips, or pungent purple pickles. If you don't want to stretch that far, stick to sushi, tuna teriyaki, or scallops tempura. The tuna burger with wasabi mayo is also a treat. Live big and order a sake sampler with five varied rice wines. Appetizers $5–12, entrées $15–22.

Vining's Bistro (508-945-5033), 595 Main Street (on the second floor). Open for dinner April through November (often closed Sunday and Monday off-season). This bistro, one of the more adventurous and creative restaurants in the area, specializes in wood grilling. Try the spit-roasted grilled pork loin. While the menu roams the world, it is strongly influenced by the West Coast. Look for seasonal staples like warm lobster tacos and Thai crabcakes. Given its inauspicious location, it's surprisingly romantic and quiet. No reservations taken. Entrées $16–24.

✿ **The Chatham Café** (508-945-5225), 1448 Route 28. Open for breakfast and dinner mid-May to mid-October. This unpretentious place gets an unqualified thumbs-up. The renovated house, with an upbeat contemporary feel, has a warm and welcoming vibe. Although it's owned by a former pilot and his wife (Tom and Mimi Skilling), rest assured that the cuisine in no way resembles airplane food! In fact, since 2000, their Jamaican chefs have garnered praise for consistent, flavorful preparations. At dinnertime, settle into rich lobster bisque, sautéed scallops, or arguably the best swordfish on the Cape. Or join the morning mob for sweet French toast or an herb breakfast wrap of scrambled eggs and sausage.

Make reservations! Breakfast $5–9, dinner entrées $15–24.

❈ ✿ ⊺ **Chatham Bars Inn** (508-945-0096; 800-527-4884), Shore Road. Open for breakfast year-round; dinner, mid-May to mid-October. The grand hotel's terrace, overlooking the ocean, also makes a picture-perfect setting for a late-afternoon drink. As for the other draws, panoramic ocean views and a grand Sunday-night buffet are legendary. If you normally avoid buffets, break that rule here. Breakfast buffet $17 adults, $10 children; dinner entrées $18–34. Jacket and tie requested at dinner; reservations highly recommended.

❈ ✿ **Impudent Oyster** (508-945-3545), 15 Chatham Bars Avenue. Open for lunch and dinner nightly. The atmosphere is pleasant enough: peaked ceiling with exposed beams, skylights, and hanging plants. And the extensive menu highlights internationally inspired fish and shellfish dishes. Try the deservedly popular spicy Portuguese mussels, Nantucket scallop sandwich, or beer-battered fish and chips for lunch. If those don't appeal to you, follow the lead of the regulars and order from the daily specials. Lunch $8–13, dinner entrées $18–24.

EATING OUT ⊺ ✿ ❈ ✿ ♿ **Chatham Squire** (508-945-0945 restaurant; 508-945-0942 tavern), 487 Main Street. Open for lunch and dinner daily. A friendly place, Chatham's best family restaurant offers something for everyone—from burgers and moderately priced daily seafood specials to a raw bar, multi-ethnic dishes, and excellent chowder. Paisley carpeting, low booths, captains' chairs at wooden tables, exposed beams, and pool tables (off-season only) add to the family-den feel of the place. Drop in for a drink in the busy and colorful tavern (a watering-hole haven for 20-somethings in summer until locals take it back for the off-season). One reader called it "the perfect lunch place for what it is" and I couldn't agree more. Lunch $5–14, dinner entrées double that.

☥ **Outer Bar & Grille** (508-432-5400), Route 28, North Chatham (just over the Harwich town line, actually). Open for lunch and dinner, mid-June to mid-September. At the Wequassett Inn Resort, this "smart casual" eatery overlooks the pool and bay. One of the Cape's few oceanside eateries, the grille's porch is a great place to enjoy a lunchtime lobster roll, salad, grilled pizza or panini, or sandwich. They also have a few more serious seafood choices. Dishes $7–19.

🍴 **Marion's Pie Shop** (508-432-9439), 2022 Route 28. Open 7–6 Tuesday through Saturday and 7–2 Sunday, March through December. Joe Zelich and Bob Messina's pies are a delicious alternative. (Marion's gone, but the recipes are better than ever!) You can't go wrong with the savory potpies (chock-full of chicken), clam pies, beefsteak pies, sweet fruit pies (the bumbleberry knocks my socks off), or any of the breakfast baked goods. This humble but humming little house only has take-out. Come once and you'll come often. I'm a convert. Careful with the kids; misbehaving ones "will be made into pies."

🖊 **Beach House Grill** (508-945-0096; 800-527-4884), Shore Road. Open for breakfast, lunch, and theme dinners mid-June to mid-September. One of the Cape's few alfresco ocean-side eateries, the grill's deck is anchored in the sand, overlooking a wide, golden beach. The overpriced menu features upscale seaside standards: burgers, summer salads, lobster rolls ($17), peel-and-eat shrimp, and fried seafood platters. Lunch $10–18.

❋ **Local Bites** (508-945-5700), 1603 Route 28, West Chatham. Open for all three meals. Luckily, for those of us without summer homes in Chatham, well-respected caterer Jenn Mentzer has a retail shop. If you want to avoid in-town crowds, this is a great place for take-out sandwiches, chilled gourmet salads, and hot prepared foods. You can put together one heck of a picnic here, which you can take away or enjoy at one of the tables out back. Sandwiches about $6.

❋ **Chatham Wayside Inn** (508-945-

NOSTALGIA REIGNS
🖊 Band concerts at Kate Gould Park, off Main Street. Every Friday night at 8, early July to early September, this brass-band concert is the place to be. Upwards of 6,000 lighthearted visitors enjoy music and people-watching as they have for the past 60 years. Dance and swing to Sousa marches, big-band selections, and other standards. The bandstand, balloons tied to strollers, bags of popcorn, blankets on the grass (set yours out at 10 AM for the best position), and the Star-Spangled Banner finale—it hasn't changed a "whit" since it began. (Except that beloved Whit Tileston, who led the band for almost 50 years, passed away in 1995.)

5550), 512 Main Street. Open daily for all three meals, except closed Monday off-season. Because of its prominent in-town location and a constant parade of strollers-by, this pleasant room really packs visitors in at lunch. Sandwiches and salads dominate the midday menu. Breakfast $5–8, lunch $5–14, dinner entrées $15–18.

🖊 **Carmine's** (508-945-5300), 595 Main Street. Open for lunch and dinner April through December (weekends only in fall and spring). Quick and inexpensive, Carmine's offers very good traditional and gourmet pizzas (slices and whole pies).

🍸 ❄ 🖊 ♿ **Christian's** (508-945-3362), 443 Main Street. "Upstairs" open for dinner nightly year-round; "downstairs" open for dinner nightly in-season. Owned by the Chatham Wayside Inn, Christian's serves traditional (read: uninspired) Yankee cuisine downstairs and burgers upstairs. The pub-style second floor is more boisterous and casual, with a piano bar. Expect piano nightly in summer and on off-season weekends. Entrées $9–23.

Chatham Village Cafe (508-945-2525), 400 Main Street. Open for breakfast and lunch. This upscale deli beckons with creative sandwiches for $6. There are a couple of picnic tables in front.

❄ **Chatham Provisions** (508-432-7126), 1403 Old Queen Ann Road. Open daily. At the corner of Route 137, this picnic place has breakfast goodies and lunchtime treats like sesame snap peas, pesto tortellini, and tuna salad with practically no filler.

See also Concerts (lobster roll suppers) under *Entertainment*.

at The **Captain's House Inn of Chatham** (508-945-0127), 369–377 Old Harbor Road. This inn serves an exceptional afternoon tea to non–inn guests by reservation. With a vast assortment of savories and sweets, all beautifully presented, it's well worth $12 per person.

Farmer's Market (508-945-5199), Veterans Park (Route 28, just west of the rotary), is usually held late May to early September, 8–noon on Tuesday.

❄ **Clambake Celebrations** (508-945-7771; 877-792-7771; www.clambake-to-go.com), 1223 Route 28. Lobsters and steamers are air-shipped in a cooking pot layered with seaweed. Just add water and steam for 30 minutes. Packages also include mussels, corn on the cob, new potatoes, onions, and sweet Italian sausage, as well as claw crackers, bibs, forks, and moist towelettes. Clambake for four people is $228 (including FedEx delivery); for two, $146; combinations priced accordingly. Local pickup prices are lower ($70 for four people, $40 for two).

Chatham Fish Market/Lobster Pound, at the Fish Pier on Shore Road. Open seasonally. Without going out on the day boats yourself, it's hard to get fresher fish!

❄ **Chatham Fish & Lobster Company** (508-945-1178), Route 28, Cornfield Market Place. For those of you with cooking facilities: They hook 'em, you cook 'em.

✳ Entertainment

Monomoy Theatre (508-945-1589), 776 Main Street. Performances mid-June through August. Operated by Ohio University, the Monomoy is among the Cape's better-known and oldest (1930) playhouses. A new production—anything from a Rodgers and Hammerstein musical to Shakespeare—is staged every week. There isn't a bad choice among the 263 seats. Evening curtain at 8 or 8:30 (Tuesday through Saturday), matinees at 2 (Thursday).

♨ ♪ Concerts (lobster roll suppers), First United Methodist Church (508-945-0474), 16 Cross Street. The church sponsors free choral, jazz, big-band, light classical, and a cappella concerts Sunday summer evenings at 8. Since the mid-1960s, the church has also held popular Friday lobster roll suppers at 4 PM prior to the concerts in Kate Gould Park. Adults $10, children $4.

Bands. Locals flock to the Chatham Squire (see *Eating Out*) to hear live music off-season.

❋ Selective Shopping

❋ Although merchants and visitors loyal to Provincetown's Commercial Street may have something to say about it, Chatham's Main Street might be the Cape's best shopping street. Instead of organizing shops by category like I usually do, I list them here in the order you'll encounter them while strolling. Unless otherwise noted, all shops are open year-round. Note, though, that many places listed as open year-round are open only on weekends in winter.

West of the rotary

Chatham Glass Company (508-945-5547), 758 Main Street. Open daily except Sunday. James Holmes designs and creates unique, colorful glass items—candlesticks, goblets, platters, bud vases, and marbles—which are sold at Barneys, Neiman-Marcus, and Gump's. The working studio is just behind the brilliantly lit displays, so you can watch the creative process of glassblowing.

Munson Gallery (508-945-2888), 880 Main Street. Open April through December. Munson's has been showing fine paintings and sculpture by

THERE'S PLENTY OF TIME FOR REFLECTION AT THE BEACH.

Kim Grant

contemporary artists since 1955. The collection, with something for everyone in both price and taste, is housed in a wonderfully restored barn. Even the horse stalls are hung with art.

Ivy Cottage Shop (508-945-1809), 894 Main Street, Munson Meeting Complex. Buyer Peggy DeHan has a good eye for both vintage and new stuff—linens, place settings, decorative home accessories, framed prints, painted furniture—that would look perfect in a country cottage or summerhouse. Pieces are generally affordable (unlike at many shops in Chatham), in the $40–100 range. She haunts flea markets and scours the countryside so you don't have to.

Kingsley Brown Galleries (508-945-6408), 902 Main Street. You probably didn't come to the Cape looking for African art, but this gallery has a great selection of masks, sculptures, textiles, and other art. There is another location on the other side of the rotary at 499 Main Street.

The Cooperage at the 1736 House (508-945-5690), 1731 Route 28, West Chatham. It's worth stopping here simply to walk through the oldest house in Chatham. But watch out: It's tantalizingly easy to spend money on period antiques shown in a period house! Anthony and Barbara Bridgewater, a lovely English couple, have also filled a series of barns behind the house with antiques and items from their Cape Cod Cooperage (see below). Check out the sturdy lobster-pot chairs, a truly unique marriage of form and function invented by a Chatham commercial fisherperson.

Chatham Pottery (508-430-2191), 2058 Route 28, South Chatham. Open daily. Gill Willson and Margaret Willson-Grey's large studio offers a wide array of functional, decorative stoneware—hand-thrown pots, pitchers, sinks, plates, bowls, tiles, and tables.

Chatham Jam and Jelly Shop (508-945-3052), Route 28, West Chatham. Two miles east of Routes 28 and 137, this colorful shop sells dozens of varieties of homemade jams and jellies. Feel free to taste them before committing. Try the wild beach plum, elderberry, or damson plum.

Cape Cod Cooperage (508-432-0788), 1150 Queen Anne Road at Route 137. Within a rambling barn, floors covered in sawdust, the state's only remaining cooperage has been making barrels to hold fish and cranberries for shipment to Boston and New York since the late 1800s. Coopers here still use the 100-year-old methods. The cooperage also has well-priced furniture to paint yourself, primitive folk-style painted furniture, and slate WELCOME signs. Painting and stenciling classes are offered throughout the year.

See also Creative Arts Center under *Even More Things to Do—Art Classes.*

East of the rotary

Main Street Pottery (508-945-0128), 645C Main Street. Barbara Parent works here, so you can watch her making pots similar to the one you're purchasing.

Cabbages and Kings (508-945-1603), 628 Main Street. New hardcovers, paperbacks, and many children's books and toys in a light-filled shop. Long live the independents!

Spyglass (508-945-9686), 618 Main Street. Although this exceptional shop is best known for telescopes, you'll also find nautical antiques like barometers, sextants, maps, charts, and some sea captains' portraits. It's great to poke around when you begin to lose sight of the Cape's maritime paste.

Yankee Ingenuity (508-945-1288), 525 Main Street. This eclectic assortment of "cool things" extends from glass and jewelry to clocks and lamps. Prices run $2–1,500. If you don't get something here the day you see it, it may be gone tomorrow.

Yellow Umbrella Books (508-945-0144), 501 Main Street. Owner Eric Linder has gathered a fine selection of Cape Cod titles and some used books, too, for all ages and interests. Ditto on the earlier "long-live-the-independents" remark.

Falconer's (508-945-2867), 492 Main Street. Get your limited-edition Friday-night band concert lithographs here. Actually, there are many different Cape scenes available in lithograph, and original oil paintings, too.

Mark August Designs (508-945-2600), 490 Main Street. Functional and fun, creative and artsy decorative items for your house. Jewelry, too. If you don't like the background music, you're probably too old to be shopping here.

Regatta Shop (508-945-4999), 483 Main Street. Open April through December. Seaside motifs and sailing-oriented gifts for your favorite sailor or sailor wannabe. Prints of ships, lighthouses, and beach scenes; hand-painted furniture; sterling pendants and charms; foul-weather gear; and colorful blankets to ward off chills aboard your yacht or sofa.

Chatham Candy Manor (508-945-0825; 800-221-6497), 484 Main Street. Open daily. They've been making hand-dipped chocolate, fudge, and liqueur-flavored truffles since 1955.

♪ **The Mayflower** (508-945-0065), 475 Main Street. Established in 1885, this venerable, old-time general store has joined the modern era (almost) on swanky Main Street.

The Patten Gallery (508-945-5313), 459A Main Street. Many of Nick Patten's hand-colored lithographs and oil paintings are brooding, spare interiors, and still lifes that create a sense of quiet. He works in the front of the gallery and enjoys discussing the work.

Demos Antiques, Ltd. (508-945-1939), 447 Main Street. You can't miss this place; items spill out onto the front lawn. A trove of funky treasures, as well as Victorian and estate jewelry; miniature gold Nantucket lightship baskets; Tiffany lamps; Sandwich whale oil lamps; and fine glass, china, coins, sterling, and antique prints. Run by Peter and Cynthia Demos, the shop has been a family-owned business since 1956. If they don't have it, you don't need it.

Odell's Studio and Gallery (508-945-3239), 423 Main Street. Open daily except Sunday, and evenings by chance in summer. Tom and Carol Odell, metalsmith and painter, respectively, have lived and worked in their lovely old home since 1975. They've turned it into a bright and airy gallery space. Carol does colorful nonobjective, multimedia paintings, monotypes, and gouaches. Her work complements Tom's jewelry and sculpture, which he fashions from precious metals and alloys. Tom's recent work shows evidence of a Japanese aesthetic. I confess: This is my favorite shop in town.

✎ **Mermaids on Main** (508-945-3179), 410 Main Street. Open late May through December. Kids love this colorful place, bursting at the seams with purple- and aquamarine-colored playthings. Hold on to your wallets. (Actually, items are well priced.) Books, bubble bath, candles, mobiles, mermaids, and stuffed and rubber creatures.

✴ Special Events

✎ *Early May:* **Spring Fling** opens the summer season. Bake sales, a crazy-hat contest, jugglers and clowns, and a treasure hunt for children.

July 4: **Independence Day Parade** from Main Street to Veterans Park; strawberry festival with shortcake at the First United Methodist Church (16 Cross Street) postparade.

Early August: **Antique Show.** Since the mid-1950s; held at the Chatham Elementary School, Depot Road.

Mid-August: **Chatham Festival of the Arts,** Chase Park. Since 1970. On the third weekend in August, the Creative Arts Center sponsors more than 100 exhibitors, from painters to quilters to sculptors (see *Even More Things to Do—Art Classes*).

Mid-October: **Seafest,** an annual tribute to Chatham's maritime industry. There are exhibits and demonstrations on net mending, casting techniques, quahog raking, the proper way to eat a lobster, fishing skills, boating, filleting fish, and rigging.

Late November–December: **Christmas by the Sea and Christmas Stroll.** This annual event includes a tree-lighting ceremony, candy-cane-making demonstrations, caroling, mulled cider served at the Mayo House (see *To See*), hayrides, open houses, and much more.

New Year's Eve: **First Night Celebration.** Fireworks over Oyster Pond. Chatham limits the number of buttons sold to residents and visitors so the town won't be overrun.

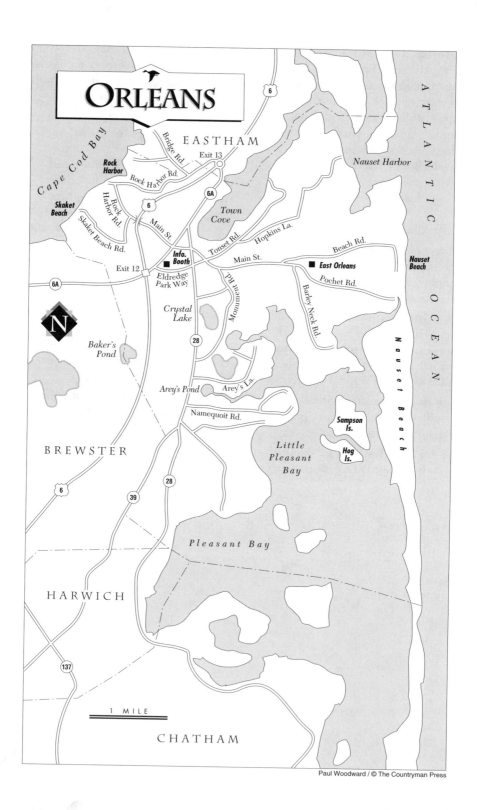

ORLEANS

ATLANTIC

EASTHAM

6

Exit 13

Nauset Harbor

Cape Cod Bay

Rock
Harbor

Rock Harbor Rd.

6A

Skaket
Beach

Rock Harbor Rd.

6

Town
Cove

Skaket Beach Rd.

Main St.

Tonset Rd.

Hopkins La.

Beach Rd.

Nauset
Beach

Info.
Booth

Exit 12

Main St.

East Orleans

OCEAN

6A

Eldredge
Park Way

Monument Rd.

Pochet Rd.

Barley Neck Rd.

N

Crystal
Lake

28

Nauset Beach

Baker's
Pond

Arey's Pond

Arey's La.

Namequoit Rd.

Sampson
Is.

BREWSTER

Little
Pleasant
Bay

Hog
Is.

28

6

39

Pleasant Bay

HARWICH

137

1 MILE

CHATHAM

Paul Woodward / © The Countryman Press

ORLEANS

Many could argue, with some success, that Orleans's biggest draw is Nauset Beach, an Atlantic Ocean barrier beach more than 9 miles long. It can accommodate hundreds of sun seekers and sand-castle builders in summer. But in the off-season, you'll be practically alone, walking in quiet reflection, observing shorebirds and natural rhythms. It's a beautifully haunting place during a storm—so long as it's not a huge storm. Nauset Beach also has historical significance. Gosnold explored it in 1602 and Champlain in 1605. It was the location of the first recorded shipwreck on the eastern seaboard, in 1626, when the *Sparrow Hawk* ran aground near Pochet. It is the only place in the continental United States to be fired upon in the War of 1812 (by the British) and in World War I (in 1918 it was shelled by a German submarine). More recently, two Englishmen set off from nearby Nauset Harbor to row successfully across the Atlantic Ocean.

The real charm of Orleans, which has few historical sights, lies not in the sand but in the waters that surround the town. A large number of fingerlike inlets creep into the eastern shoreline from aptly named Pleasant Bay, dotted with tiny islands. And most of these quiet inlets are accessible via back roads and town landings. Excursion boats explore the rich habitat of Nauset Marsh to the north, while bayside, Rock Harbor is home to the Cape's most active charter fishing fleet.

Because Routes 6, 6A, and 28 converge in Orleans, traffic is heavy in summer; getting anywhere takes time. But Orleans straddles the two distinct worlds of the Outer and Lower Cape. On the one hand, Orleans serves as a year-round commercial and retail center for the area. It offers plenty of activities and a variety of dining and lodging options. On the other hand, Orleans has its share of exclusive residential areas and plenty of quiet, waterside spots.

Orleans is the only Cape town without a Native American or English name. Incorporated in 1797 after separating from Eastham, Orleans was named for Louis Philippe de Bourbon, duke of Orléans (and later king of France), who sojourned here in 1797 during his exile.

GUIDANCE Orleans Chamber of Commerce Information Booth (508-255-1386; www.capecod-orleans.com), P.O. Box 153, Orleans 02653. Booth open 9–5 Monday through Saturday and 11–3 Sunday, late May to mid-October. The booth is on Eldredge Parkway (just off Route 6A), south of the Orleans rotary. The administrative office, at 44 Main Street, is open 10–2 weekdays year-round. Orleans publishes a helpful booklet and excellent free map.

PUBLIC REST ROOMS Public rest rooms are located at the information booth and 44 Main Street.

PUBLIC LIBRARY ❋ ✍ ⊤ **Snow Library** (508-240-3760), Main Street at Route 28. Open 10–5 Monday, 10–8 Tuesday and Wednesday, 10–5 Thursday and Friday, 10–4 Saturday. It's open only Sunday 2–4 from November through March.

GETTING THERE *By car:* Take Route 6 east from the Cape Cod Canal for about 48 miles to exit 12. Route 6A east takes you directly into town.

By bus: The **Plymouth & Brockton** bus line (508-778-9767; www.p-b.com) connects Orleans with Hyannis and other Cape towns, as well as with Boston's Logan Airport. It only stops at the CVS on Main Street.

GETTING AROUND East Orleans Village and Nauset Beach are 3 miles east of Orleans center (which stretches along Route 6A); Rock Harbor and Skaket Beach are 1.5 miles west of the center.

The **H₂O** (508-385-8326; 800-352-7155; www.capecodtransit.org) bus, used more by locals than visitors, travels Route 28 between the Hyannis Transportation Center and Orleans daily except Sunday year-round. It makes about five stops in Orleans, so it's best to call them for locations. It'll take about an hour to get from Orleans to Hyannis.

MEDICAL EMERGENCY **Orleans Medical Center** (508-255-9577), Route 6A or exit 12 off Route 6. Walk-ins accepted 8–4 weekdays year-round. Outside these hours call **911**.

❋ To See

⊤ **Meeting House Museum** (508-255-1386), at Main Street and River Road. Open 10–1 Thursday through Saturday, July and August. Built in 1833 as a Universalist meetinghouse, and now operated by the Orleans Historical Society, the museum contains artifacts documenting Orleans's early history. Among the items are an assessor's map of Orleans homes in 1858, photographs, Native American artifacts, and a bicentennial quilt. The building itself is a fine example of Greek Revival Doric architecture. Down at Rock Harbor, the museum also has a Coast Guard rescue boat that was used during a 1952 shipwreck off the Chatham coast. How 30 people piled into this tiny boat is beyond belief. You can board the boat; a tour schedule is posted on site. Free.

⊤ **French Cable Station Museum** (508-240-1735), Route 28 at Cove Road. Open 1–4 Monday through Saturday, July and August; 1–4 Friday through Sunday, June and September; otherwise, by appointment. Before the advent of the "information superhighway" and wireless communications, there was the French Cable Station. Direct transmissions from Brest, France (via a 3,000-mile underwater cable), were made from this station between 1890 and 1941, at which time transmissions were automated. Among the relayed news items: Charles Lindbergh's successful crossing of the Atlantic and his 1927 Paris landing, and Germany's invasion of France. Much of the original equipment and instruments are still set up and in working order. (Alas, the cable is no longer operational.) The displays, put together with the help of the Smithsonian Institution, are a bit intimidating, but someone is on hand to unravel the mysteries. Free.

Jonathan Young Windmill (508-240-3700, ext. 425), Route 6A at Town Cove Park; park at the Orleans Inn. Open 11–4 daily, late June to early September. This circa-1720 gristmill was built in East Orleans, transported to the center of town in 1839, moved to Hyannisport in 1897, and returned to Orleans in 1983. Although it's no longer operational, the windmill is significant because of its intact milling machinery. Inside, you'll find interpretive exhibits including a display of a 19th-century miller's handiwork, as well as a guide who might explain the origins of "keep your nose to the grindstone." (Because grain is highly combustible when it's ground, a miller who wasn't paying close attention to his grain might not live to see the end of the day.) The setting, overlooking Town Cove, provides a nice backdrop for a picnic. Free.

Rock Harbor, on Cape Cod Bay, at the end of Rock Harbor Road from Main Street. This protected harbor, the town's first commercial and maritime center, served as a packet landing for ships transporting goods to Plymouth, Boston, and Maine. When the harbor filled with silt, several old houses in the area were built from the lumber of dismantled saltworks. During the War of 1812, Orleans militiamen turned back Britain's HMS *Newcastle* from Rock Harbor. As for the dead trees in the water, they mark the harbor channel that is dredged annually for the charter fishing fleet. This is a popular sunset spot for watching the boats come in, if you can tolerate the bugs.

SCENIC DRIVES Pleasant Bay, Little Pleasant Bay, Nauset Harbor, and Town Cove creep deep into the Orleans coastline at about a dozen named inlets, ponds, and coves. With the detailed centerfold map from the Orleans Chamber of Commerce guide in hand (see *Guidance*), head down the side roads off Tonset Road, Hopkins Lane, Nauset Heights Road, and Barley Neck Road to the town landings. After passing beautifully landscaped residences, you'll be rewarded with serene, pastoral scenes of beach grass and sailboats. Directly off Route 28 heading toward Chatham there are two particularly lovely ponds with saltwater outlets: **Arey's Pond** (off Arey's Lane from Route 28) and **Kescayogansett Pond** (off Monument Road from Route 28). There's a little picnic area with limited parking at **Kent's Point** near here, off Frost Fish Lane from Monument Road.

✳ Outdoor Activities

⚓ BASEBALL The Orleans Cardinals (508-255-0793; www.capecodbaseball.org) play ball at Eldredge Park Field, off Route 28 at Eldredge Parkway, from mid-June to early August.

Their 7-week clinics for boys and girls age 6–13 begin in late June. As many as

EARLY MORNING AND LOW TIDE ON NAUSET MARSH

Kim Grant

60 or 70 kids might show up, but there is always a good ratio of player-instructors to kids. The cost is $55 for the first week.

BICYCLING/RENTALS ✈ The Cape Cod Rail Trail runs near the center of town, right past **Orleans Cycle** (508-255-9115), 26 Main Street, which is open April through December. Expect to spend about $14 for 3 hours, $24 daily, $44 for 3 days; less for kids' bikes.

BOAT EXCURSIONS 🦆 ✈ **Nauset Marsh Cruise** (508-349-2615; www.wellfleet-bay.org), Town Cove, behind Goose Hummock, off Route 6A. Mid-June to mid-October. Sponsored by the Wellfleet Bay Wildlife Sanctuary, these 2-hour catamaran voyages do not depart daily, so it's best to call for departure times and days. Adult trips are heavily weighted toward birding and depart with high tides; kids' trips are synced with low tide, all the better for interactive exploration. Along with informative onboard narration, kids haul traps, unearth worms and steamers, and participate in scavenger hunts. Adults $30; children 12 and under, $25.

FISHING/SHELLFISHING Pick up freshwater fishing permits at Goose Hummock (508-255-2620), off Route 6A on Town Cove, or the town clerk's office (508-240-3700), 19 School Road, off Main Street. Then head to **Crystal Lake,** off Monument Road (see *Green Space—Ponds*), which has perch, trout, and bass. There are also a dozen fresh- and saltwater town landings in Orleans. Contact the har-

bormaster (508-240-3755), Route 28, Orleans, about a shellfishing permit and
regulations before you head out with your shovel, rake, and bucket.

❋ **Goose Hummock** (508-255-2620), Town Cove, Route 6A at the rotary,
Orleans. This outfitter fulfills all fishing-related needs, including rod rentals, fishing trips, instruction, and wintertime fly-tying seminars. Shellfishing equipment,
too. The great staff offers lots of free advice and information.

❡ **Rock Harbor Charter Fleet** (508-255-9757; 800-287-1771 within Massachusetts), Rock Harbor. Trips daily mid-May to mid-October; harbor booth
staffed from June through September. These 18 boats make up the largest charter fleet in New England. U.S. Coast Guard–licensed captains offer 4- and 8-
hour trips for groups in search of bluefish and striped bass. Children welcome.
$110 per person for a 4-hour trip,
$120 per person for an 8-hour trip. If
you round up six people, it costs $425
for a half day, $650 for a full day.

❡ MINI-GOLF **Cape Escape** (508-
240-1791), Canal Road, off Route 6A
near the Orleans rotary. Open seasonally.

SAILING ❡ **Arey's Pond Boat Yard**
(508-255-0994, 255-7900), Arey's
Lane off Route 28, South Orleans.
Late May to early September. They
offer 10 hours of beginning and intermediate sailing instruction over the
course of 5 weekdays for $186. Group
and private lessons by appointment.

❡ SKATEBOARDING A bona fide
skateboard park is located on the
middle school fields.

SURFING **Nauset Sports** (508-255-
4742), Jeremiah Square, Route 6A at
the Orleans rotary. Open year-round,
but rentals are only provided in-season: surfboards, kayaks, skimboards,
boogie boards, kayaks, and wet suits.

TENNIS You'll find three public
courts at **Eldredge Park** (off Route
28 at Eldredge Parkway) and three at
the **elementary school** (off
Eldredge Parkway). Seasonal fees.

CANOEING AND KAYAKING
The protected, calm waters of
northern **Pleasant Bay** offer
delightful paddling opportunities.
And the folks at Goose Hummock
(508-255-2620; www.goose.com),
off Route 6A on Town Cove, are the
experts in this neck of the bay. Talk
to them about Southern Pleasant
Bay, for instance; it can be tricky
for the uninitiated. Pick up the
Nauset Harbor tide chart and rent
a canoe or recreational kayak ($25
for 4 hours, $45 daily, $100–120 for
3 days; more for big touring sea
kayaks). For 24-hour rentals, the
center throws in a loaner roof rack.
(Parking is limited at the town landings, but it's free.) If you're new to
kayaking, take their 3-hour intro
flatwater course ($75) to learn
basic paddle strokes and skills.
Otherwise, they have a huge array
of other courses and specialty
tours: saltwater safety, tidal currents and navigation, open-water
kayaking, sunrise tours, women on
water, kids in kayaks, and more.

See also the Recreational Department under *Even More Things to Do—For Families.*

✳ Even More Things to Do

BOWLING ✳ ⚲ ↑ **Orleans Bowling Center** (508-255-0636), 191 Route 6A. Okay, so you didn't come to the Cape to go bowling, but if it's raining and you've got kids in the car, it's an idea.

FITNESS CENTER ✳ ⚲ **Willy's Gym and Fitness Center** (508-255-6826), 21 Old Colony Way, off West Road from Route 6A, Orleans Marketplace. Open daily. One of the Cape's best fitness centers, Willy's has an extensive array of cardiovascular machines, free weights, sauna and steam rooms, classes, juice bar, and supervised child care. $15 daily, $35 for a 3-day weekend, $44 weekly.

⚲ FOR FAMILIES **Recreational Department** (508-240-3785), 44 Main Street, offers instructional tennis for adults and kids; softball and aerobics; a playground program; and swimming lessons. Call for schedule details and registration.

Pirate Adventure (508-430-0202; www.pirateadventurescapecod.com), Town Cove near Goose Hummock. Trips daily except Sunday mid-June to early September. Particularly fun for kids 3–11, this swashbuckling trip begins with face painting on the dock. Then kids sign onto the pirate ship as crew, take a pirate oath, search for sunken treasure, and fire water cannons against the invading Spanish. On the return voyage, the booty is shared and pirates celebrate with song and dance. Age 3 and older $16, age 2 and under $12. Reservations required.

See also *Outdoor Activities—Boat Excursions.*

SKATING ✳ ⚲ **Charles Moore Arena** (508-255-2971), O'Connor Way; look for signs near the information booth (see *Guidance*). Although this big arena is reserved most of the year, public skating times are set aside; call them. Every Friday 8–10 PM year-round is Rock Night, when the strobe-lit rink is reserved for 9- to 14-year-olds.

CLAMMIN' WITH CASEY

⚲ **Casey Jones** (508-896-4048) offers an unusual service. In fact she's the only one on the East Coast (and probably the West Coast, though I haven't researched it thoroughly) to offer it. If you've always wondered how people find clams and dig with those shovels and rakes you've seen, Casey will teach you how and where. She has a commercial permit; she's been clamming all her life; and she's been offering these trips since 1993. This tide-dependent activity isn't as easy as it looks, but after searching out littlenecks, cherrystones, and mussels with Casey, you'll be a pro. $35 per person for a 2½- to 4-hour adventure, plus an inexpensive seasonal shellfish permit (per family). Children's rates; all equipment provided.

SPECIAL PROGRAMS ✳ ✧ **Academy of Performing Arts** (508-255-5510 for the school), 5 Giddiah Hill Road. The academy offers instruction (to all ages) in jazz, tap, and ballet; visual arts; music; and drama and creative writing. Their 2-week sessions (concentrating on musical theater, ballet, and drama production) in July and August end with a public performance. Children's summer matinees are held Fridays at 10.

✳ Green Space

BEACHES ✧ **Nauset Beach** (508-240-3780), on the Atlantic Ocean, off Beach Road, beyond the center of East Orleans. It doesn't get much better than this: good bodysurfing waves and 9 miles of sandy Atlantic shoreline, backed by a low dune. (Only about a half-mile stretch is covered by lifeguards; much of the rest is deserted.) A gently sloping grade makes this a good beach for children. Facilities include an in-season lifeguard, rest rooms, a snack bar, chairs and umbrellas for rent, and plenty of parking (parking is rarely a problem). Parking costs $10 daily ($40 weekly), mid-June to early September; $5 on late-May, early-June, and off-season holiday weekends. Free after 4:30.

Four-wheel-drive vehicles with permit are allowed onto Nauset Beach. Certain areas, though, may be restricted during bird breeding and nesting periods. Obtain permits at the beach in-season. Off-season, by appointment only, head to the Parks and Beaches Department (508-240-3775), 18 Bay Ridge Lane.

✧ **Skaket Beach** (508-255-0572), on Cape Cod Bay, off West Road. Popular with families, as you can walk a mile out into the bay at low tide; at high tide the beach grass is covered. The parking lot often fills up early, creating a 30-minute wait for a space. Parking $10 daily from mid-June to early September. (The parking fee is transferable to Nauset Beach on the same day; free after 4:30.) Facilities include an in-season lifeguard, bike rack, rest rooms, and a snack bar.

NAUSET BEACH, THE 9-MILE-LONG BARRIER BEACH IN ORLEANS

Kim Grant

Pleasant Bay Beach, Route 28, South Orleans. A saltwater bayside inlet beach with limited roadside parking.

PONDS Crystal Lake (off Monument Road and Route 28) and **Pilgrim Lake** (off Monument Road from Route 28) are both good for swimming. Pilgrim Lake has an in-season lifeguard, rest rooms, changing rooms, picnic tables, a dock, and a small beach; parking stickers only. At Crystal Lake, parking is free but limited.

WALKS AND PICNICS Paw Wah Point Conservation Area, off Namequoit Road from Eldredge Parkway, has one trail leading to a nice little beach with picnic tables.

Rhododendron Display Garden, Route 28 and Main Street. A nice place for a picnic.

Sea Call Farm, Tonset Road, just north of the intersection with Main Street. Overlooking Town Cove, is another fine picnic spot.

✳ Lodging

🦞 All in all, lodging in Orleans is a very good value. You'll find everything from contemporary studios to friendly B&Bs, from almost-beachfront motels to family motor inns.

RESORT MOTOR INN ✳ ♪ **The Cove** (508-255-1203; 800-343-2233; www.thecoveorleans.com), 13 Route 28, Orleans 02653. This modest complex of 47 rooms and suites is situated on 300 feet of shorefront along Town Cove. Pluses include a free boat tour of Town Cove and Nauset Beach; an outdoor heated pool; a dock for sunning and fishing; and picnic tables and grills that are well situated to exploit the view. Deluxe rooms have a sitting area and sofa bed; waterfront rooms have a shared deck overlooking the water; two-room suites have a kitchen (some with a fireplace and private deck); and inn rooms have a bit more decor (some also have a fireplace and private deck). Late June to early September $109–199; off-season $65–128. Children under 18 free in parent's room.

BED & BREAKFASTS Nauset House Inn (508-255-2195; www.nauset-houseinn.com), Beach Road, East Orleans 02643. Open April through October. These 14 rooms (8 with private bath) are the best in the area for many reasons. The inn has genuinely hospitable hosts; it's half a mile from Nauset Beach; guest rooms are thoughtfully and tastefully appointed; a greenhouse conservatory is just one of the many quiet places to relax. You'll have Diane Johnson, her daughter Cindy, and son-in-law John to thank: They've owned and constantly upgraded the 1810 farmhouse since 1982. Rooms in the carriage house are generally larger than inn rooms, while the rustic cottage, with peaked ceiling, is quite private and cozy. Rooms $75–160; full breakfast, of perhaps crab scramble, included. One single room rents for $60.

A Little Inn on Pleasant Bay (508-255-0780; www.alittleinnonpleasant-bay.com), 654 Route 28, South Orleans 02662. Open May to early January. Well, well, well. This completely renovated place could easily be dubbed "A Little Slice of Heaven on High." The new European innkeepers (Sandra, Pamela, and Bernd) have transformed this 1798 house into a priceless diamond with commanding views of Pleasant Bay and a thoroughly contemporary aesthetic. Formerly a stop on the Underground Railroad, the main house has plenty of common space, including a big living room with windows all around. It's all quite conducive to luxuriating. Guest rooms feature white-washed barnboard, lovely bathroom tilework, and private decks or patios. Blue stone patios grace the front and backyards, which are beautifully landscaped. Knowing what's already been done here, I suspect the three motel-style rooms in the former paddock, and the rustic carriage house (which sleeps four), are soon to be renovated. A full European breakfast, late-afternoon sherry, and access to a private beach and dock are all included. Children over 10 welcome. Late May to early September $150–175 rooms, $850 weekly for carriage house; otherwise, $100–150 rooms, $675 weekly carriage house.

❊ **Morgan's Way** (508-255-0831; www.capecodaccess.com/morgans-sway/), Morgan's Way, Orleans 02653. This is a quiet find, off the beaten path. Page McMahan and Will Joy opened their contemporary home, about a mile south of town, to guests in 1990. Lush landscaping extends across 5 acres, and a multilevel deck wraps around a 20-by-40-foot heated pool. The delightful poolside guesthouse is bright and modern, with a full kitchen and private deck. Inside the main house, one of the two guest rooms has a small, attached green-

house, but both rooms share the second-floor living room, complete with TV, VCR, and wood-burning stove. Rooms: $140 May through October, $95 off-season, including a full breakfast. Cottage: $1,100 weekly June through September; $900 May and October; $700 off-season. No credit cards.

Parsonage Inn (508-255-8217; 888-422-8217; www.parsonageinn.com), 202 Main Street, East Orleans 02643. Open February through December. This very pleasant, rambling, late-18th-century house has eight guest rooms comfortably furnished with country antiques. (Only two rooms have adjoining walls, so there is plenty of privacy.) Wide-pine floors, canopy beds, and newly redone bathrooms are common. The studio apartment Willow has a kitchenette and private entrance, while the roomy Barn, recently renovated with exposed beams and eaves, has a sitting area and sofa bed. Longtime innkeepers Elizabeth and Ian Browne, who hail from England, serve a full breakfast at individual tables or on the brick patio. Maybe it'll be cheese soufflé or ginger pancakes. Mid-May to mid-October $115–145; otherwise $95–105.

Bay Cottage Bed & Breakfast (508-240-5640; www.baycottage-capecod.com), 44 Captain Linnell Road, Orleans 02653. Open mid-May to mid-October; Nest open through December. On a quiet road delightfully off the beaten path, host Judy Hunt offers a charming cottage with two guest rooms (and a full breakfast). Each room has a private bath, but they share a living room and patio. It's perfect for two couples traveling together. The adjacent "Nest," which

I didn't get a chance to see, is rented weekly ($785) and nightly ($130). Based on my impressions of the cottage, I have every confidence that the Nest is great. Cottage rooms $118–120. No credit cards.

MOTELS & **Nauset Knoll Motor Lodge** (508-255-2364), Nauset Beach, East Orleans 02643. Open mid-April to mid-October. Nauset Knoll, a few steps from Nauset Beach, is often booked long before other places because of the expansive views of dune and ocean. You can watch the sun as it rises over the ocean from lawn chairs atop the lodge's namesake knoll. The 12 simply furnished rooms (à la 1950s) with large picture windows are in three separate units, distinctively modeled after a barn, shed, and Cape-style cottage. Mid-June to early September $150; off-season $90–110.

☞ **Barley Neck Inn** (508-255-0212; 800-281-7505; www.barleyneck.com), Beach Road, East Orleans 02643. Open May through November. After purchasing this neglected 18-room, bilevel motel in mid-1994, Joe and Kathi Lewis completely rehabbed it, much to the appreciation of area residents. It offers a good value for families: There is no charge for up to two children under age 12. Rooms are tastefully appointed, albeit with hotel/motel-style furnishings. There is a fenced-in swimming pool, but, alas, without any landscaping per se. The Barley Neck is well positioned between Orleans and Nauset Beach, about a mile from the beach. Prices fluctuate with the market, but use this as a benchmark: late June to mid-September $129–159; off-season $79–109.

COTTAGES AND ROOMS ☙ **Rive Gauche** (508-255-2676), 9 Herring-brook Way, Orleans 02653. Open mid-May to mid-October. This light and airy studio, located in a carriage house in a residential neighborhood about a mile south of town, is also situated above a saltwater pond and just 100 feet from a freshwater lake. Guests are welcome to use the dock and canoe. With a complete kitchen and a deck overlooking the pond, it's easy to settle into this treehouse hideaway for a week. $875 weekly.

☞ **Ridgewood Motel & Cottages** (508-255-0473), junction of Routes 28 and 39, South Orleans 02662. Cottages open May to late October. These six tidy housekeeping cottages, upgraded since 1980 by the Knowles family, are a couple of miles south of Orleans center and one mile from the saltwater Pleasant Bay Beach. I like units 12, 17, and 18—all very comfortable in an "olde" Cape Cod way. A large pool, grill and picnic area, lawn games, and playground are set within the wooded compound. Weekly cottage rates, early June to early September, are $530–640 for three to six people. Shoulder-season rates go as low as $320 and $390, respectively.

EFFICIENCIES ❊ **Kadee's Gray Elephant** (508-255-7608), 216 Main Street, East Orleans 02643. Every surface of woodwork and furniture here has been whimsically painted lavender, sea green, and bright pink. Beyond that, each of the six efficiencies has a cable TV, phone, air-conditioning, and kitchen (the refrigerator is stocked the first morning). Don't come here if you're looking for a touchy-feely B&B experience; these studios are for independent travelers who want to come and go as they please. Kris Kavanagh renovated in 1992. Before that, the 200-year-old sea captain's house belonged to her grandmother. July and August $140; off-season $95; three people max per room; cots $20 nightly.

See also Morgan's Way under *Bed & Breakfasts*.

RENTAL HOUSES AND COTTAGES

The Real Estate Company (508-255-5100; www.capecodvacation.com), 207 Main Street, East Orleans. Over 350 listings.

✳ Where to Eat

✳ Orleans has an excellent variety of restaurants, the great majority of which are open year-round (unless otherwise noted).

DINING OUT ♈ ABBA (508-255-8144), 89 Old Colony Way. Open for dinner nightly except Monday. This ultracontemporary Thai-Mediterranean bistro would be perfectly at home in Boston's South End or New York's SoHo. It's taken this part of the Cape by storm. Chef-owner Erez Pinhas and his front-of-the-house partner Christina Bratberg have a flair for creating mod spaces and inviting plates. The urbane menu changes quite often, but look for the likes of seeded salmon with cauliflower potato puree and stir-fried greens, or grilled tuna with a vegetable spring roll and Chinese black mushroom risotto. Dishes $23–30.

Academy Ocean Grille (508-240-1585), 2 Academy Place at Route 28. Open for dinner, mid-April through December. Chef Christian Schultz's menu changes constantly, but look for sole Française (dipped in egg batter

and topped with lobster and orange-mustard-dill beurre blanc); "clams Christian" (broiled with macadamia nuts, apricots, Black Forest ham, garlic, and Parmesan cheese); swordfish with a basil glaze; and rich roast duckling with plum, port wine, and peppercorn sauce. All entrées include salad and veggies. (Christian probably showcases 10 to 15 different vegetables daily.) Reservations suggested. Entrées $22–26.

🌂 **Captain Linnell House** (508-255-3400), 137 Skaket Beach Road. Open for dinner; closed March. For a truly lovely dining experience, let chef-owner Bill Conway's fine fare match the gracious ease of this former sea captain's mansion. Dining is romantic, with candles, fine china, and linens. One dining room overlooks a small water garden; the salon overlooks the side garden. Start with chowder and move to rack of lamb or scallops and shrimp sautéed in a tarragon lobster sauce. Prime rib specials are always popular. Chef Conway will also dish out small portions for children with refined palates. If you're seated by 5:30, you'll receive a complimentary lobster bisque or chowder and dessert. Bill and his wife, Shelly, have owned and been restoring this gem since 1988. Reservations strongly suggested. Entrées $19–30.

🌂 **The Beacon Room** (508-255-2211), 23 West Road. Open for lunch and dinner. For casual fine dining on the way to Skaket Beach, this intimate bistro offers sizable portions of well-presented dishes at reasonable prices. Dishes range from stuffed portobello caps as a starter to pasta, halibut, lamb (quite popular), and chicken saltimbocca for dinner. Sandwiches and burgers are offered at lunch

($8–14) on the deck. Dinner entrées $14–23.

Nauset Beach Club (508-255-8547), 222 Main Street, East Orleans. Open for dinner. This restaurant changed ownership at press time and the jury (that's me) hadn't heard the case yet, much less begun deliberation.

Y **Mahoney's Atlantic Bar & Grill** (508-255-5505), 28 Main Street. Open for dinner. This cozy storefront bistro serves a surprisingly sophisticated menu. You can expect contemporary American dishes like pan-roasted lobster, tuna sashimi, and roasted chicken. Their lively and upscale bar (where you can get lighter dishes) also sports a few satellite TVs, all the better to catch a Sox game. And not to be outdone, Mahoney's hosts live jazz on Thursday evenings (7 PM); bands on weekends (10 PM). On a personal note, my innkeeper friend Al Johnson enjoyed this place, and I'm including it in his memory. Bar menu $5–10, dinner entrées $17–24.

Y 🦞 **Rosina's Cafe** (508-240-5513), 15 Cove Road off Route 6A near Main Street. Open for dinner. Since the chef was a fisherman in Sicily, you can trust him to know something about handling seafood. Devoted patrons flock here for Italian food that's not outrageously priced and that's served with a friendly attitude. I always enjoy the sole, scallop scampi, and shrimp diavolo. The dining room is understated with etched glass and lots of wood. If you have to wait, there's a nice bar. Early specials, outside dining, and take-out too. Dinner entrées $12–26.

EATING OUT Y & 🦞 **Joe's Beach Road Bar & Grille** (508-255-0212), Beach Road, East Orleans. Open for dinner weekends, late April through December; nightly, early May to mid-October. Joe's has a split personality: One side has smaller, quieter dining rooms and the other is a hopping joint, a lively, bar-happy place with barnboard walls and a large fieldstone fireplace. Your choice merely depends on your mood since both sides offer the same well-executed menu. I've eaten here often (on both sides) and always enjoyed it. As Joe himself works the room with great ease (as does wife Kathi), locals continue to flock here even as the summer crowds swell. Look for lobster prepared five different ways, New American dishes prepared with flair and French accents, as well as a revolving selection of Asian dishes. Braised lamb shank with garlic mashed potatoes is always terrific. For lighter appetites and thinner wallets, there's pizza, pasta, soup, and main-course salads. While the crème brûlée is deservedly popular, the dessert quesadilla is really special. Entrées $10–24.

Cap't Cass Rock Harbor Seafood, Rock Harbor. Open 11–2 and 5–9 daily except Monday in July and August; 11–2 and 5–8 on Friday and Saturday, 11–2 on Sunday, from mid-April through June and September to mid-October. This classic harborside lobster shack, adorned with colorful buoys on the outside and checkered tables on the inside, is as good as they come. The food is a cut above: The lobster roll ($14) hasn't a shred of lettuce in it, and the homemade chowder and clam dinners are great, too. The menu is posted on cardboard, as it's been done since 1958. There really is a Captain Cass, by the way: George Cass, his wife, Betty, and their daughter Sue run the place. Lunch

$8–13, dinner $14–30. BYOB. No credit cards.

Ⓨ 🐾 ✎ **Land Ho!** (508-255-5165), Route 6A. Open noon–10 daily. A favorite local hangout since 1969, John Murphy's place is very colorful (literally), from red-and-white-checked tablecloths, to old business signs hanging from the ceiling, to a large blackboard menu. Newspapers hang on a wire to separate the long bar from the dining area. Beyond club sandwiches, fried seafood dishes, and great burgers, look for specialties like fish-and-chips, barbecued ribs, stuffed clams, clam pie, and kale soup. With the addition of sashimi and grilled tuna, the menu is also going a bit upscale these days. But they'll always have draft beer. You'll find lots of families, college students, and old-time locals here. Dishes $8–16.

🐾 **Binnacle Tavern** (508-255-7901), 20 Route 28. Open nightly for dinner, May to mid-October; Wednesday through Sunday the rest of the year. Barnboard walls, low lighting, "oldies" top-40 music, and a ubiquitous nautical motif pervade the interior of this cozy, popular tavern. An enclosed outdoor patio is heated in the shoulder seasons. The Binnacle—always lively, even in the dead of winter—is known for its appetizers and designer pizzas, but it also serves seafood and homemade pasta. Entrées $8–17.

♿ ✎ **Kadee's Lobster & Clam Bar** (508-255-6184), 212 Main Street, East Orleans. Open for lunch and dinner, mid-May to early September. A summer tradition since 1975 because of its location (on the way to Nauset Beach), Kadee's serves fresh local seafood. The setting is casual, at shellacked picnic tables under an open-air structure or on the deck at umbrella-covered tables. Choose from oysters on the half shell; broiled, steamed, or fried seafood; special kale soup; or a rich "seafood simmer" with lobster, shrimp, and scallops in a sherry wine sauce. Lighter salad plates are a good lunch idea. Portions are large, but there is a hefty plate charge if you

A CLAM SHACK ON THE CAPE COD RAIL TRAIL

Kim Grant

share. Frozen drinks are quite popular, as is the single dessert choice: chocolate-marbled cheesecake. Be careful, or expect the prices to add up. Lunch $6–14, dinner entrées $10–18.

♿ ✏ **The Lobster Claw** (508-255-1800), Route 6A, near the Orleans rotary. Open 11:30–9 daily, April through October. Since 1970 the Berig family has been dishing up seafood at their large, convenient, family-style restaurant. Proudly maintained and decorated with the requisite nautical motif, The Lobster Claw serves straightforward and consistent preparations like delicately broiled fisherman's platters, Marylou's home-made crabcakes, and fried clams. Lobster sandwiches and salads are popular at lunch. Early specials from 4 to 5:30, and a "waiting lounge" upstairs. Grape-Nut custard flies off the dessert menu. Lunch $4–15, dinner entrées $10–19.

🍸 ✏ **Old Jailhouse Tavern** (508-255-5245), 28 West Road. Open 11:30–11 daily. Slightly boisterous by night, more sedate by day, the tavern is a good choice when everyone in your party wants something different: nachos, soup and salad, fish-and-chips, or a broiled seafood sampler. Or when you have late-night munchies. Eat in one of the booths, on the atriumlike terrace overlooking the garden, at the long oak bar, or within the rock walls of the old jail. In the early 1800s the town constable offered the use of his front bedroom, complete with bars on the windows, as an overnight lockup facility. Dishes $10–21.

🦞 ✏ **Sir Cricket's Fish 'n Chips** (508-255-4453), Route 6A. Open daily. This tidy hole-in-the-wall dishes

out pints of fried seafood, fish sandwiches, and mixed platters (scallops, oysters, and clams are the most popular). Kids might prefer chicken tenders and hot dogs. Plan on take-out, as there are only a couple of tables. Dishes $10–16.

🦞 ✏ **The Hole** (508-255-3740), Route 6A within Main Street Square. Open 5 AM–2 PM (until noon on Sunday). The Hole is a pleasant and airy place, a real local hangout. It's packed at breakfast time and friendly all day. $2–6.

SNACKS, ICE CREAM, & COFFEE

The Hot Chocolate Sparrow (508-240-2230), Old Colony Way, behind CVS on Route 6A. Open 7 AM–late night daily. On the rail-trail (with a convenient window for ice cream), this place makes the best cappuccino, lattes, and hot chocolate between Beantown and Provincetown. Proprietor Marje Sparrow sends her staff to "espresso lab" to make sure they know the hows and whys of making a consistent cup. In addition to a blackboard menu of drinks like frozen "hot" chocolate, caffe mocha Sparrow (espresso with "real" hot chocolate), and chai, they also make luscious hand-dipped chocolates and sweet treats. Marje's big new space is a terrific place to hang out.

Cottage St. Bakery (508-255-2821), Cottage Street near Routes 6A and 28. Open 6–6. This European-style bakery, buttering up the community since 1984, has a number of oddly named specialties, including "dirt bombs," an old-fashioned French doughnut recipe that requires baking, not frying, and "fly cemeteries," puff-pastry squares, knotted on top and filled with currants and nuts. Their breads are also great. Knead I say more? Okay, I will: You can get homemade soups, lasagna, chicken pies, and sandwiches here, too. There are a few indoor and outdoor tables.

Fancy's Farm (508-255-1949), 199 Main Street, East Orleans. Open daily mid-March through December. Fancy's is not your average farm stand. You can assemble a gourmand's feast with cold pastas, roasted chicken, sesame noodles, baked goods, and deli sandwiches. There's a salad bar, too.

Jo Mama's (508-255-0255), 125 Route 6A. Open 6:30–2 daily. Bagel sandwiches, smoothies, health tonics, and fair trade coffee. This mod little space has a few tables.

Phoenix Fruit & Vegetable (508-255-5306), Orleans Marketplace, Route 6A. Open daily. This tiny shop, tucked into the corner of a strip mall, is a delight for foodies. If you have cooking facilities, you'll appreciate organic greens, locally grown shiitake mushrooms, locally made clam pies, and hearty *pain d'Avignon*.

Choose your ice cream parlor based on location, as both shops offer sublime flavors. **Emack & Bolio's** (508-255-5844) is on Route 6A (check out revitalizing smoothies and energizing drinks), and the **Sundae School** (508-255-5473) is at 210 Main Street in East Orleans (try the black raspberry and Grape-Nut ice cream).

See also Orleans Whole Food Store under *Selective Shopping—Special Shops.*

FISH MARKETS **Young's Fish Market** (508-255-3366), Rock Harbor. Open mid-June to mid-September. If you don't like to cook lobster, place your order here by 5 PM (the earlier, the better) and they'll do it for you. Their lobster rolls are also good. The market, by the way, has been in the Harrison family since 1962, when they bought it from the Youngs.

✳ Entertainment

✲ **Academy Playhouse** (508-255-1963 box office; www.apa1.org), 120 Main Street. This 162-seat playhouse, in the 1873 Old Town Hall, and its resident theater company (established in 1975) host 10 to 12 dramas, comedies, and musicals each year. Since 1986, they've kicked the season off with a literary cabaret, *A Night of New Works.* The eagerly awaited April event brings established and unknown Cape writers (who have been holed up working all winter) together with audiences. Tickets $14–20.

☖ See also Mahoney's Atlantic Bar & Grill, under *Dining Out.*

✳ Selective Shopping

✲ Unless otherwise noted, all shops are open year-round.

ANTIQUES **Pleasant Bay Antiques** (508-255-0930), 540 Route 28, South Orleans. Most of these high-quality, 18th- and 19th-century American antiques come from area residents rather than auctions. They're displayed in a lovely old barn.

Continuum (508-255-8513), 7 Route 28. Open daily except Sunday in the off-season. Dan Johnson sells expertly restored antique lamps and textures from the Victorian to the art deco period.

Countryside Antiques (508-240-0525), 6 Lewis Road, behind the Box

Lunch on Main Street, East Orleans. Open March through December. Deborah Rita has been traveling the world since 1984 in order to fill these eight rooms with English, Irish, Scandinavian, European, and Chinese antiques and fine reproductions.

ART GALLERIES Left Bank Gallery (508-247-9172), 8 Cove Road. Open daily. One of the best galleries on the Cape, with ceramics, glass, jewelry and furniture. The owner, Audrey Parent, has a good eye.

Addison Art Gallery (508-255-6200), 43 Route 28. Helen Addison represents both new and established artists working in realistic and traditional realms. Look for oils, watercolors, limited-edition prints, egg tempuras, and sculpture. It's comfortable for browsing and buying, for serious collectors and novices. Saturday openings throughout the summer.

Tree's Place (508-255-1330; 888-255-1330), Route 6A at Route 28. Open daily year-round, except closed Sunday early January to mid-April. When Elaine and Julian Baird bought this place in 1981, they put the Lower Cape on the art map. Tree's offers a vast collection of unusual gifts (like kaleidoscopes and antique jewelry) displayed throughout nine small rooms; an excellent collection of representational New England painters; and a tile shop. Meet-the-artist champagne receptions 5–7 Saturdays in summer.

Hogan Art Gallery (508-240-3655), 39 Main Street. Open 10–5 Monday through Saturday in summer; hours vary off-season. Ruth Hogan has amassed a fine body of work: primitive white-line woodblock prints, impressionistic landscape paintings, and lovely pastels. Husband Frank offers a collection of 20th-century regional paintings.

ARTISANS Orleans Carpenters (508-255-2646), Commerce Drive. These folks make magnificent reproduction Shaker nesting oval boxes, oval trays, oval carriers, and music boxes from cherry and bird's-eye maple. These traditional oval boxes are so expertly made and durable that you could put your full weight on one and it would feel more sturdy than a stepladder. Although this is primarily a wholesale shop with museum customers, the front of the unprepossessing shop has a small display of goods. The "seconds," which look perfect to all but the most expert eyes, go very quickly in summer. Orleans Carpenters is hard to find, off Finlay Road (from Route 28), behind Brewster Welding.

Nauset Lantern Shop (508-255-1009; 800-899-2660), 52 Route 6A. Ken Alman expertly handcrafts copper and brass colonial- and early American–style lanterns. Most of the nautical and onion lanterns are for exterior use, but he also makes sconces and indoor accessories. Watch him work.

Kemp Pottery (508-255-5853), Route 6A near the Orleans rotary. Open daily, except Sunday off-season. Steven Kemp creates unusual designs utilizing Nauset Beach sand. He has functional porcelain and stoneware pieces like bird feeders and bathroom sinks, as well as less common decorative objects for the garden, like pagodas, torsos, and moated castles. He also works with stained glass.

BOOKSTORES Booksmith/Musicsmith of Orleans (508-255-4590),

Skaket Corners, Route 6A. Paperbacks and best-sellers.

CLOTHING Karol Richardson (508-
255-3944), 47 Main Street, and **Hannah** (508-255-8234), 47 Main Street,
both sell stylish women's clothing and
are open year-round. Across the
street, **XO Clothing Store** (508-255-
4407), 50 Main Street, offers loose-fitting styles made of natural fabrics and
sold at refreshing prices.

**FARMER'S MARKET Orleans
Farmer's Market,** Old Colony Way
near Depot Square. Pick up local produce 8–noon every Saturday from
mid-June through October.

**SPECIAL SHOPS Bird Watcher's
General Store** (508-255-6974; 800-
562-1512; www.birdwatchersgeneral-
store.com), Route 6A near the
Orleans rotary. Open daily. If it per-
tains to birds or watchers-of-birds,
this store has it: bird feeders in every
size and shape, birdseed in barrels (a
ton of seed is sold daily), fountains,
bird notecards, bird kitchen magnets,
bird playing cards. As important as
commerce is, though, this place is an
invaluable resource for news of where
and when birds have been sighted or
will be sighted. (This place isn't just
for the birds!)

Oceana (508-240-1414), 1 Main
Street Square. Carol Wright stocks

lovely household items, watercolors,
glass, and jewelry inspired by the sea
and nature.

Orleans Whole Food Store (508-
255-6540), 46 Main Street, Orleans.
Open daily. Healthy foods, pizza on
Tuesday and Thursday, lunches-to-go,
vitamins, books, and items that promote holistic living.

Baseball Shop (508-240-1063), 26
Main Street. The shop carries more
than 1,000 caps, as well as trading
cards, clothing, and other baseball
paraphernalia.

Cape Cod Photo & Art Supply
(508-255-0476), 38 Main Street.
Open daily except Sunday. One-hour
film processing, and painting supplies
if the wonderful Cape Cod light
inspires you.

✴ Special Events

Late May through November: **Fine
Art and Craft Shows.** At a few locations on various days; check at the
information booth.

Late August: **Pops in the Park.** The
Cape Cod Symphony performs a con-
cert in Eldredge Park, off Route 28 at
Eldredge Parkway.

Late September/early October: **Fall
for Orleans Festival.** Activities
include a car show, pet parade, and
pancake breakfast.

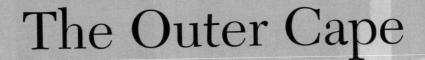

The Outer Cape

EASTHAM

WELLFLEET

TRURO

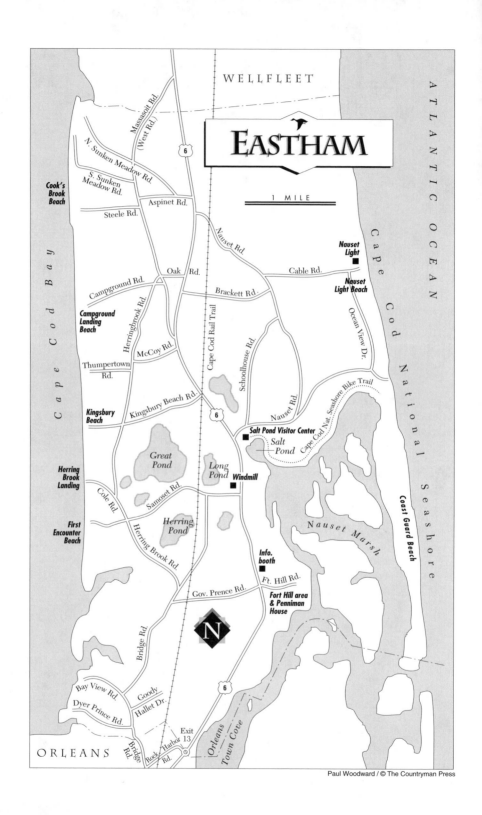

WELLFLEET

EASTHAM

1 MILE

ATLANTIC OCEAN

Cape Cod Bay

Cook's Brook Beach

Massasoit Rd.

(West Rd.)

N. Sunken Meadow Rd.

S. Sunken Meadow Rd.

Aspinet Rd.

Steele Rd.

6

Nauset Rd.

Nauset Light

Oak Rd.

Cable Rd.

Nauset Light Beach

Campground Rd.

Brackett Rd.

Campground Landing Beach

Herringbrook Rd.

McCoy Rd.

Ocean View Dr.

Cape Cod Rail Trail

Schoolhouse Rd.

Thumpertown Rd.

Kingsbury Beach Rd.

Kingsbury Beach

6

Nauset Rd.

Cape Cod Nat. Seashore Bike Trail

Salt Pond Visitor Center

Salt Pond

Great Pond

Long Pond

Windmill

Herring Brook Landing

Cole Rd.

Samoset Rd.

Nauset Marsh

Coast Guard Beach

Cape Cod National Seashore

First Encounter Beach

Herring Pond

Herring Brook Rd.

Info. booth

Ft. Hill Rd.

N

Gov. Prence Rd.

Fort Hill area & Penniman House

Bridge Rd.

6

Bay View Rd.

Goody Hallet Dr.

Dyer Prince Rd.

Exit 13

Bridge Rd.

Rock Harbor Rd.

Orleans Town Cove

ORLEANS

Paul Woodward / © The Countryman Press

EASTHAM

Settled by the Pilgrims in 1644, Eastham is content to remain relatively undiscovered by 21st-century tourists. In fact, year-round residents (fewer than 4,500) seem perfectly happy that any semblance of major tourism development has passed them by. There isn't even a Main Street or town center per se.

What Eastham does boast, as gateway to the Cape Cod National Seashore (CCNS), is plenty of natural diversions. There are four things you should do, by all means. Stop in at Salt Pond Visitor Center, one of two CCNS headquarters, which dispenses a wealth of information and offers ranger-guided activities and outstanding nature programs. Consider taking a boat trip onto Nauset Marsh, a fragile ecosystem that typifies much of the Cape. Hop on a bike or walking trail; a marvelous network of paths traverses this part of the seashore, including the Fort Hill area. And of course, head to the beach. The Cape's renowned, uninterrupted stretches of sandy beach, backed by high dunes, begin in earnest in Eastham and extend all the way up to Provincetown. One of them, Coast Guard Beach, is also where exalted naturalist Henry Beston spent 1928 observing nature's minute changes from a little cottage and recording his experiences in *The Outermost House.*

Eastham is best known as the site where the *Mayflower's* Myles Standish and a Pilgrim scouting party met the Nauset Indians in 1620 at First Encounter Beach. The "encounter," in which a few arrows were slung (without injury), served as sufficient warning to the Pilgrims: They left and didn't return for 24 years. When the Pilgrim settlers, then firmly entrenched at Plymouth, went looking for room to expand, they returned to Eastham. Led by Thomas Prence, they purchased most of the land from Native Americans for an unknown quantity of hatchets.

Although the history books cite these encounters as the beginning of Eastham's recorded history, the 1990 discovery of a 4,000-year-old settlement (see the sidebar "Coast Guard Beach") is keeping archaeologists and anthropologists on their toes.

GUIDANCE **Eastham Information Booth** (508-255-3444; 508-240-7211 year-round; www.easthamchamber.com), near Fort Hill on Route 6 (P.O. Box 1329, Eastham 02642). Open 9–7 daily, July to mid-September; 10–5 Friday and Saturday, mid-June to mid-October. You might get lucky with additional Sunday hours off-season.

   ♿ ⚘ ☂ ✳ **Salt Pond Visitor Center** (508-255-3421; www.nps.gov/caco), off Route 6. Open daily 9–5 in summer and daily 9–4:30 the rest of the year. Expect temporary facilities in the parking lot during 2003. In 1961, newly elected President John F. Kennedy, Senator Leverett Saltonstall, and Representative Hastings Keith championed a bill to turn more than 43,000 acres into the **Cape Cod National Seashore** (CCNS), protected forever from further development. (About 500 private homes remain within the park.) Today, over 5 million people visit the CCNS annually. The excellent center shows short films on Thoreau's Cape Cod, Marconi, and the ever-changing natural landscape. And the fine museum includes displays on the salt and whaling industries and the diaries of Captain Penniman's wife, Augusta, who accompanied him on several voyages. In addition to nightly presentations during the summer, rangers lead lots of activities, from sunset campfires on the beach to talks on tidal flats and bird walks. I learn something every time I participate. Free.

PUBLIC REST ROOMS Public rest rooms are located in the Salt Pond Visitor Center.

PUBLIC LIBRARY ✳ ☂ ✒ **Eastham Library** (508-240-5950), west of the windmill, 190 Samoset Road. Open Monday, Friday, and Saturday 10–4, Tuesday and Thursday 10–8 in summer. Call for off-season hours. Story time and summer events for children, plus audio books and Internet access.

GETTING THERE *By car:* Eastham is 40 miles from Cape Cod Canal via Route 6.

By bus: The **Plymouth & Brockton** bus line (508-778-9767; www.p-b.com) connects Eastham with Hyannis and other Cape towns, as well as with Boston's Logan Airport. The bus stops across from Town Hall on Route 6 and at the Village Green Plaza at Bracket Road on Route 6 in North Eastham.

GETTING AROUND Eastham is only a few miles wide and 6 miles long. Most points of interest are well marked along or off Route 6. The CCNS is to the east of Route 6.

MEDICAL EMERGENCY Call **911.**

✳ To See

Edward Penniman House (508-255-3421), off Route 6 in the Fort Hill area, CCNS. In summer, open for tours at 10 on Monday and Saturday; house open without tours 1–4 Tuesday through Friday. At age 11, Penniman left Eastham for the open sea. When he returned as a captain 26 years later, he had this 1868 house built for him. Rumor has it that he used ships' carpenters because he didn't trust landlubber architects. Boasting indoor plumbing and a kerosene chandelier, this French Second Empire–style house has Corinthian columns, a mansard roof, and a cupola that once afforded views of the bay and ocean. Ever-helpful National Park Service guides dispense lots of historical information. Even if it's closed, peek in the windows. Free.

Swift-Daley House and **Tool Museum** (508-240-1247), next to the post office on Route 6. Open 1–4 weekdays, July and August; 1–4 Saturday, September. In 1998 one of the seashore dune shacks (see Dune shacks under *To See* in "Provincetown") was moved to this site. Although it's difficult to imagine what dune-shack life might have been like, this helps. As for the Swift-Daley House, it's a completely furnished full-Cape Colonial built by ship's carpenters in 1741. It has wide floorboards, pumpkin-pine woodwork, narrow stairways, and a fireplace in every room on the first floor. The Tool Museum behind the house displays hundreds of old tools for use in the home and in the field. Free.

Old Schoolhouse Museum (508-255-0788), off Route 6 across from the Salt Pond Visitor Center. Open 1–4 weekdays, July and August; 1–4 Saturday, September. During the time when this former one-room schoolhouse served the town (1869 until 1936), there were separate entrances for boys and girls. Inside you'll learn about Henry Beston's year of solitude spent observing natural rhythms on nearby Coast Guard Beach. Thanks to the Eastham Historical Society, you can also learn about the town's farming history, daily domestic life, Native Americans, offshore shipwrecks, and the impressive Lifesaving Service. Free.

Oldest windmill, on Route 6 at Samoset Road. Open 10–5 daily, July and August. Across from Town Hall, the Cape's oldest working windmill was built in Plymouth in the 1680s and moved to Eastham in the early 1800s.

THE NATIONAL SEASHORE'S EDWARD PENNIMAN HOUSE IS GRACED BY THE JAWBONE OF A WHALE.

Kim Grant

First Encounter Beach, off Samoset Road and Route 6. A bronze marker commemorates where the Pilgrims, led by Captain Myles Standish, first met the Native Americans. The exchange was not friendly. Although arrows flew, no one was injured. The site goes down in history as the place where the Native Americans first began their decline at the hands of European settlers. On a more modern note of warfare history, for 25 years the U.S. Navy used an offshore ship for target practice. Until recently, it was still visible on a sandbar about a mile offshore. The beach, with its westward vista, is a great place to catch a sunset.

Doane Homestead Site, between the Salt Pond Visitor Center and Coast Guard Beach, CCNS. Only a marker remains to identify the spot where Doane, one of Eastham's first English settlers, made his home.

Old Cove Cemetery, Route 6. Many of these graves date back to the 1700s, but, look for the memorial to the three *Mayflower* Pilgrims who were buried here in the 1600s.

Nauset Light (508-240-2612), at the corner of Cable Road and Ocean View Drive, CCNS. Open 4–7:30 Sunday, May through September. This light was originally built in Chatham in the 1870s, one of twins, but was moved here shortly thereafter. In 1996, when Nauset Light was just 37 feet from cliff's edge, the large red-and-white steel lighthouse was moved—via flatbed truck over the course of 3 days—from the eroding shoreline. In 1998, the keeper's house (which dates to 1875) was also moved back. For now, the cast-iron behemoth sits a respectable 250 feet from the shoreline, its beacon still stretching 17 miles to sea. Free, but you may have to pay to park at the Nauset Light Beach (see *Green Space—Beaches*).

Three Sisters Lighthouses (508-255-3421), inland from Nauset Light, CCNS. Open 3–7 Sunday, May through September. In 1838 this coastal cliff was home to three brick lighthouses that provided beacons for sailors. They collapsed from erosion in 1892 and were replaced with three wooden ones. When erosion threatened those in 1918, two were moved away; the third was moved in 1923. Eventually the National Park Service acquired all three and moved them to their present location, nestled in the woods far back from today's coastline. (It's a rather incongruous sight, lighthouses, surrounded by trees, unable to reach the water.) Head inland from the beach parking lot along the paved walkway. Free, but you may have to pay to park at the Nauset Light Beach (see *Green Space—Beaches*).

✳ Outdoor Activities

BICYCLING/RENTALS Cape Cod Rail Trail. This scenic, well-maintained, 26-mile (one way) paved path winds from Dennis to Wellfleet. Park at the Salt Pond Visitor Center (see *Guidance*).

Nauset Bike Trail, CCNS. This 2.25-mile (one way) trail connects with the Cape Cod Rail Trail and runs from the Salt Pond Visitor Center, across Nauset Marsh via a boardwalk, to Coast Guard Beach. The trail passes large stands of thin, tall black locust trees not native to the area—they were introduced to return nitrogen to the soil after overfarming.

Rent at the "conglomerate" **Idle Times Bike Shop** (508-255-8281; open year-round), on Route 6 about 2 miles north of the Salt Pond Visitor Center, or the family-owned **Little Capistrano Bike Shop** (508-255-6515; open April through December), across from the Salt Pond Visitor Center behind the Lobster Shanty. Rentals are a bit cheaper at Little Cap: $20 a day for a mountain bike or hybrid, $65 weekly, $16 for 8 hours; less for children's bikes. Both shops do repairs; Little Cap also sells bikes.

FISHING/SHELLFISHING Purchase your required freshwater fishing license at Goose Hummock (508-255-0455; Route 6 at the rotary) and then head to the stocked, spring-fed **Herring Pond** (see *Green Space—Ponds*). Contact the Department of Public Works (508-240-5972), 555 Old Orchard Road (off Route 6 or Brackett Road), for shellfishing permits and regulations. Annual permits cost $30. The office is open 9–4 Monday through Saturday (except 9–noon on Wednesday) in summer. Shellfishing is permitted at Salt Pond (Route 6) and Salt Pond River only on Sunday.

FITNESS CLUB ❋ **Willy's Gym** (508-255-6370), Route 6. Open daily. Facilities include racquetball and squash courts, Nautilus and free weights, a lap pool, saunas and steam rooms, a whirlpool, six indoor tennis courts, and aerobics, yoga, Pilates, and spinning classes. Daily $15.

✑ **FOR FAMILIES** **Recreational programs** (508-240-5974) are held 9–noon weekdays, late June to mid-August. Visitors and summer residents are encouraged to bring their children (age 6–18) to the playground at Nauset Regional High School (on Cable Road, North Eastham) to participate in various programs including archery, arts and crafts, and soccer. Supervised swimming and instruction are offered at Wiley Park (see *Green Space—Ponds*) for children age 1–16 on weekday mornings. Fees for specific programs vary.

Poit's Place (508-255-6321), Route 6. Open mid-May to early September. Families have stopped here since 1954 for mini-golf, ice cream, onion rings, hot dogs, and fish-and-chips. Will yours?

T-Time Family Sports Center (508-255-5697), Route 6, North Eastham. Open daily in summer, weekends mid-May to mid-October. If you're desperately in need of a bucket of balls to belt out, this will suffice. The mini-golf is a bit run-down, but the Outer Cape has slim pickings.

CASTING ABOUT
Connie Codner (508-255-1308), the women's world line record holder for striped bass, teaches novices how to cast from shore from June through October. The informative and fun 3-hour sessions cost $50 per person. Demonstrations and discussions include knot tying, when to use which bait, and where you'll have the best luck. Shorts and sneakers are the order of the day, unless it's chilly, when waders and boots are de rigueur. (You'll have to bring your own; otherwise, Connie provides all the equipment.)

TENNIS **Nauset Regional High School,** Cable Road, North Eastham. The public can use the six courts after school gets out for free.
See also *Fitness Club.*

✳ Green Space

BEACHES **Nauset Light Beach,** CCNS, on the Atlantic Ocean. An idyllic, long, broad, dune-backed beach. Facilities include changing rooms, rest rooms, and a lifeguard in-season. Parking $10 daily in-season (transferable to any CCNS beach); the lot fills by 10 AM in summer.

First Encounter Beach, Campground Landing Beach, and **Cook's Brook Beach.** These bayside town beaches are well suited to kite flying and shelling. Because of the shallow water and gradual slope, they are safe for children. At low tide, vibrant green sea grasses and rippled sand patterns are compelling. Parking is $10 daily in-season. Weekly stickers ($40) are available from the Department of Natural Resources (508-240-5972), 555 Old Orchard Road (off Route 6 or Brackett Road). The office is open 9–4 Monday through Saturday (except it closes at noon on Wednesday), but you should call ahead to avoid waiting in line.

Town beach, between Nauset Light and Coast Guard Beach. In 2002 Eastham residents grew frustrated at not being able to park at the two National Seashore beaches (as was their right under the original terms with the seashore), so they decided to take matters into their own hands. They're trying to create a new town beach and if successful, they'll charge $10–15 to park.

PONDS **Herring Pond** and **Great Pond,** both west of Eastham center off Samoset, Great Pond, and Herring Brook Roads. Parking $10 daily in-season. Great Pond has more parking, a bigger beach, and two swimming areas (including Wiley Park, with a beach, playground, and new bathhouse).

THE NAUSET LIGHT TRAIL BOARDWALK CROSSES BELOW THE COAST GUARD STATION.

Kim Grant

COAST GUARD BEACH

This long National Seashore beach, backed by grasses and heathland, is perfect for walking and sunning. Facilities include changing rooms, rest rooms, and in-season lifeguards. In summer a shuttle bus ferries visitors from a well-marked parking lot on Doane Road. It fills by 10 AM. (Don't bother trying to drop off passengers at the beach before park:. The seashore banned it to control traffic.) Parking $10 daily (good all day on any CCNS beach); seasonal pass $30; walkers and bicyclists $3; fees in effect late June to early September and on weekends from late May to mid-October.

At times during the winter, you might be lucky enough to spot gray seals and small brown harbor seals congregating at the southern tip of Coast Guard Beach. They feed on the ever-present sand eels. Take the walk at low tide and allow an hour to cover the 2 miles.

Henry Beston wrote his 1928 classic, *The Outermost House,* during the year he lived in a two-room bungalow on Coast Guard Beach. The book chronicles Beston's interaction with the natural environment and records seasonal changes. The cottage was designated a national literary landmark in 1964, but the blizzard of 1978 washed it into the ocean. Bundled up (tightly!) against the off-season winds, you'll get a glimpse of the haunting isolation Beston experienced.

After a brutal 1990 storm washed away a large chunk of beach, an amateur archaeologist discovered evidence of a prehistoric dwelling on Coast Guard Beach. (Watch the video at the Salt Pond Visitor Center.) It is one of the oldest undisturbed archaeological sites in New England, dating back 4,000 years to the Early Archaic and Woodland cultures. Because Coast Guard Beach was then 5 miles inland, the site provided a safe encampment for hunters and gatherers.

The Coast Guard Station at the top of the cliff was decommissioned in 1958 and now serves as the Environmental Educational Center for the CCNS. The U.S. Coast Guard evolved from the Lifesaving Service established in 1872 in response to the thousands of ships that were wrecked off the treacherous coast. When the Cape Cod Canal was built in 1914, and ships could pass through instead of going around the Cape, fatalities decreased dramatically.

WALKS **Fort Hill area,** CCNS; trailhead and parking off Route 6. The trail—one of my all-Cape favorites—is about 1.5 miles round trip with a partial boardwalk, some log steps, and some hills. It offers lovely views of Nauset Marsh, especially from Skiff Hill, but also winds through the dense Red Maple Swamp and past the Edward Penniman House (see *To See*). Birders enjoy this walk year-round, but it is particularly beautiful in autumn when the maples turn color.

Pastoral Fort Hill was farmed until the 1940s, and rock walls still mark boundaries.

Nauset Marsh Trail, CCNS; trailhead behind the Salt Pond Visitor Center (see *Guidance*). About 1 mile round trip; some log steps. This trail runs along Salt Pond and yields expansive vistas of Nauset Marsh, which was actually Nauset Bay when French explorer Samuel de Champlain charted it in 1605. As the barrier beach developed, so did the marsh. Along those same lines, Salt Pond was a freshwater pond until the ocean broke through from Nauset Marsh. This complex ecosystem sustains all manner of ocean creatures and shorebirds.

Buttonbush Trail, CCNS, trailhead at the Salt Pond Visitor Center. The trail is half a mile, with some boardwalk, some log steps. It was specially designed with Braille markers for the blind and visually impaired.

✳ **Eastham Hiking Club** (508-255-3021). The club meets at 9 AM on Wednesday for a vigorous 2-hour walk somewhere between Yarmouth and Provincetown. Generally about 45 or 50 people gather for the 5- to 6-mile hike. Call for the meeting place.

✳ Lodging

Route 6 is lined with cottage colonies, but there are a few notable alternatives. Unless otherwise noted, all lodging is in Eastham 02642.

HOTEL ✳ ✿ & **Four Points Hotel** (508-255-5000; 800-533-3986), Route 6, Eastham 02642. This bilevel Sheraton hotel has all the amenities you'd expect: an indoor and an outdoor pool, a whirlpool, a fitness center, and two tennis courts. The odd thing is that you just don't expect to see a Sheraton on the Outer Cape. About half of the 107 nicely appointed rooms and two suites overlook the tasteful indoor pool area, which resembles an inverted ship's hull. The other rooms overlook woods; these are slightly larger and brighter and have small refrigerators. July and August $219–245; off-season $89–149. Children under 17 free in parent's room.

BED & BREAKFASTS ✳ **Fort Hill Bed and Breakfast at Sylvanus Knowles House** (508-240-2870; www.forthillbedandbreakfast.com), 75 Fort Hill Road, Eastham 02642. Perched on a little knoll overlooking Nauset Marsh, Jean and Gordon Avery's three-suite B&B enjoys one of the Cape's best locations. The casual, yet refined 19th-century Greek Revival farmhouse is a charmer—with wonderful hosts, separate guest quarters, and a common room with a working fireplace. As for the guest rooms, Lucille is sweet with slanted eaves, wide-pine floors, and a separate dressing room. The two-room Emma Suite features a library, piano, and oversized tub. The adjacent, ever-so-private Nantucket Suite boasts a secluded garden, distant marsh views, cathedral ceilings, and a sitting room with gas fireplace. (All suites have TV and AC.) A delectable full breakfast—perhaps zucchini quiche or piping-hot baked apples with "jammy" muffins—is included. July through September $165–225; off-season $145–200. No credit cards.

✿ ✿ 700 **Samoset** (508-255-8748), 700 Samoset Road. Open May through October. The ever-resourceful Sarah Blackwell moved this abandoned 1870 Greek Revival farmhouse to its present location on the bay side of Route 6, on a quiet road near the bike trail. She also did a wonderful job restoring it, sanding floors and woodwork, and blending period pieces with contemporary accents like a painted checkerboard floor and tin lamps. There's only one downside: There are only two guest rooms (each with a private bath). From the open country kitchen, guests enjoy an expanded continental breakfast of muffins, bagels, cereal, yogurt, and fruit. Plan your day from the front-porch rocking chairs. July and August $95–110 ($10 additional per child nightly); off-season $70–85. No credit cards.

♿ **Whalewalk Inn** (508-255-0617; www.whalewalkinn.com), 220 Bridge Road. Open mid-January through November. Off the beaten path, this 19th-century whaling captain's home is run like a tight ship by Elaine and Kevin Conlin. Expect a range of accommodations, including a romantic cottage, three stand-alone suites, and a luxurious new carriage house. Rooms in the latter are outfitted with four-poster beds and gas fireplace; most have a small private deck or balcony, and some have a large whirlpool. The four inn rooms are decorated with country sophistication, a smattering of fine antiques, and breezy floral fabrics. I particularly like the brick patio where a full breakfast (of perhaps granola pizza) and afternoon drinks and hors d'oeuvres are served. The inn also has loaner bikes. Late May to mid-October $175–300; off-season $150–250.

❄ ✎ **Over Look Inn** (508-255-1886; www.overlookinn.com), 3085 Route 6.

Pam and Don Andersen's big yellow Victorian house on the rail-trail is delightfully hidden from Route 6 and across from the Salt Pond Visitor Center. Guests enjoy relaxing on the wide wraparound veranda or in the billiards room or parlor with velveteen curtains. All 14 guest rooms have lacy curtains and a smattering of antiques; most have TV and AC; some have cathedral ceiling and skylight. The Garden Room, my favorite, has a private porch and fireplace. An adjacent carriage house, which the family-oriented owners have been trying to fix up, has three rooms geared toward families. A full breakfast of Parmesan baked eggs or "ableskivers" (Danish pancakes) is included. June through October $145–200; off-season $95–160.

❄ ✎ **Penny House Bed & Breakfast** (508-255-6632; 800-554-1751;

NAUSET MARSH

Kim Grant

www.pennyhouseinn.com), 4885 Route 6, North Eastham 02651. From the street, this shingled and bow-roofed Cape doesn't look nearly as old as it is; sections date back to the mid-1700s, though. The dining room (where a full breakfast is served) has wide floorboards, original beams, and barnboard walls. The rest of the house has a newer feel: Each of the 10 guest rooms (of varying sizes and styles) has comfortable furnishings, AC, and telephone; most have TV. Newly added suites boast two-person whirlpool tub, gas fireplace, and balcony. The mother-and-daughter innkeeping team of Margaret and Becky Keith, presiding over the place since 1988, have created lots of common space, including a "great room," 2 acres of lawns, and a garden-style brick patio. June through September $165–315; off-season $140–290.

COTTAGES ✿ 🐾 Cottage Grove

(508-255-0500; 877-521-5522; www.grovecape.com), 1875 Route 6. Open May through October. You can tell this is not your average cottage colony just by the unusually aesthetic fence that fronts Route 6. Hosts Greg Wolfe and Chris Nagle have nicely renovated eight cozy cottages and a "meeting house," all on 3 acres set back from the road. Cottages are rustic, with knotty-pine walls, but they have upgraded bathrooms and kitchens, firm new mattresses with cotton sheets, phones, and a smattering of antiques. In-season planned activities include massage, beach bonfires, and clambakes. Off-season, you might consider this a perfect retreat for a group get-together. Continental breakfast included. Mid-June to mid-September $100–180 studio or one-bedroom, $260 two-bedroom;

off-season $70–110 and $185, respectively; weekly rates in-season; 3-night minimum otherwise.

🐾 ❄ ✿ **Cranberry Cottages** (508-255-0602; 800-292-6631; www.sun-sol.com/cranberrycottages), 785 Route 6. This tidy cottage colony has been in Lisa Grant's family since 1964, when her grandparents began operating it. Since the mid-1990s, Lisa and her husband, Guy, have set about refurbishing the 14 two-bed-room housekeeping cottages, all set back from the highway. For longer stays, you'll definitely want one of the significantly bigger units with fully equipped kitchen. Cottages without kitchen, which can accommodate two adults and a child, and are rented on a nightly basis (May and November $50–72; June through October $95–100). In-season $750–850 weekly.

🐾 ❀ ✿ **Gibson Cottages** (508-255-0882), off Samoset Road from Route 6 Eastham 02642. Open April through November. Some of the Cape's best lakeside cottages are down a little dirt road marked only with GIBSON. Jerry and Mary Jane Gibson have owned these seven neat-and-tidy cottages since 1966 and take great pride in maintaining them. Each of the well-spaced one-, two-, and three-bedroom cottages (all freshly painted white) has a screened porch or deck and fully equipped kitchen. A swimming dock, sailboat, rowboats, and barbecue area are shared by all. There are also two bike trails on the other side of the pristine lake, which boasts a private, sandy beach. This is a gem; call early. Late June to early September $800–1,000 weekly; off-season $500–700 weekly (3-night minimum off-season). The Gibsons also rent their former five-bedroom house for $2,400 in-season. No credit cards.

Marsh View Cottage (508-247-9408), 2170 Route 6. Open June through October. David Angelica's two-story barn commands a beautiful, distant view of Nauset Marsh—and a screened-in porch keeps the bugs at bay so you can enjoy it. Two bedrooms upstairs have twin beds, while the first floor consists of a good-sized kitchen and separate living room. David is constantly updating the place. June and October $775 weekly; July through September $875 weekly.

⌧ **Midway Motel & Cottages** (508-255-3117; 800-755-3117; www.midwaymotel.com), Route 6, North Eastham 02651. Open April through October. Pine and oak trees shield this reasonably priced complex from the road. The tidy grounds, over which Ron and Sally Knisely have presided since 1983, feature a nice children's play area, shuffleboard, badminton, horseshoes, picnic tables, grills, and direct access to the Cape Cod Rail Trail (see *Outdoor Activities—Bicycling/Rentals*). In-season $86–92 rooms (each additional person $10), $760–880 weekly cottages; off-season $56–94 rooms, $450–590 weekly cottages. Children under 16 are free, as is the morning coffee and tea.

RENTAL HOUSES AND COTTAGES
Anchor Real Estate (508-255-4949; www.anchor-realestate.net), 4761 Route 6, North Eastham 02651.

HOSTEL ⌧ ⌧ **Hostelling International Mid-Cape** (508-255-2785; www.usahostels.org; 888-901-2085 for in-season reservations; 617-531-0459 for reservations prior to high season), 75 Goody Hallet Drive, off Bridge

Road. Open mid-May to mid-September. Located in a quiet residential neighborhood off the Orleans rotary, this hostel has about 50 beds in seven coed, same-sex, and family cabins. The hostel boasts no lockout times, movie nights in summer, bike rentals ($5 daily), and dial-up Internet access ($1 for 15 minutes). Further facilities include a fully equipped common kitchen, bike shelter, outdoor shower, volleyball, table tennis, and a barbecue area. It's about a mile to the nearest bay beach. Reservations are essential in July and August. $19 for AYH members; $22 for nonmembers; children under 14 are half price; entire cabin $95.

✳ **Where to Eat**

There aren't many restaurants—good or bad—in Eastham.

⌧ ⌧ **Arnold's Lobster & Clam Bar** (508-255-2575), 3580 Route 6. Open 11:30–8 daily (until 10 in summer), mid-May to mid-September. Arnold's, under the same stewardship for years, offers a raw bar, lobster clambake dinners, excellent local clams (without the sand!), homemade ice cream, colorful salads, and the normal array of fried seafood baskets. Onion rings are excellent, too; during the summer of 2002 they sold 4,000 pounds of them! Weekday lunch specials are an incredible bargain at $3. Abutting the rail-trail, the neat-and-tidy Arnold's has a nice fenced-off area with tables under pine trees and open-air patio. Dishes $7–34. No credit cards.

Eastham Lobster Pool (508-255-9706; 508-255-3314 for take-out), 4360 Route 6, North Eastham. Open 11:30–9 daily, April through October. Besides the requisite fried fish and seafood platters, you can order fish poached, broiled, or grilled ($14–18). The choices and combinations are practically endless. Weekly and daily specials (like a lobster shore dinner for $21) are usually a good bet, as are the no-filler lobster rolls. The indoor dining room is pleasant, with wooden tables and chairs. There's outdoor dining and less expensive take-out, too. Although the Pool offers burgers and steaks, stick to the fish.

✳ ✑ **Box Lunch** (508-255-0799), Route 6, North Eastham. Open daily year-round, until 4 PM off-season. If you've got a hungry family or have had enough fried food, stop at this inconspicuous strip mall. (In case you didn't know, they roll their sandwich meats in pita bread at this ubiquitous Cape franchise.) Sandwiches $5–10.

🌭 **Big Al's Hot Dogs,** Route 6, Eastham. Open 11–4 daily, seasonally. Across from Willy's Gym, this overgrown doghouse has inexpensive and great wieners when a quick fix is all you need. They're the same dogs that are sold at New York City pushcarts, except Big Al's has about 30 condiments available. Will you join their cultish following?

SNACKS **Ben & Jerry's** (508-255-2817), Route 6 at Brackett Road. Open mid-March to mid-November. The trademark black-and-white cows of Vermont have migrated to the warmer pastures of Cape Cod. The Bluesberry frozen yogurt, with blueberries, strawberries, and raspberries, can't be beat; or choose from dozens of creamy, crunchy, and chunky ice cream offerings.

✳ Entertainment

First Encounter Coffee House (508-255-5438), Samoset Road.

Open year-round except December and May. Performances on the second and fourth Saturday of each month. Acoustic, folk, blues, and bluegrass reign here, attracting musicians with national reputations—including Wellfleet's Patty Larkin and Vineyarder Livingston Taylor. Home to the 1899 Unitarian Universalist church (aka Chapel in the Pines) since 1974, the intimate venue has only 100 seats, beneath stained-glass windows. Off-season, it's a very local affair, where everybody knows your name and knows to arrive early to get a good seat. Tickets $10–15; children free.

✳ Selective Shopping

✳ Unless otherwise noted, all shops are open year-round.

The Chocolate Sparrow (508-240-0606), 4205 Route 6. Marjorie Sparrow opened this shop in 1989 to sell her luscious hand-dipped chocolates and homemade fudge. It's for the chocoholics among us who aren't trying to overcome the affliction. She also has a nice selection of notecards for the communicators among us who haven't completely succumbed to e-mail.

Sunken Meadow Basketworks & Pottery (508-255-8962), North Sunken Meadow Road, North Eastham. Open year-round, but call first in winter. Hugh and Paulette Penney craft well-executed handwoven baskets, wall panels, stoneware, and jewelry in a newly constructed barn.

Collector's World (508-255-3616), Route 6. Since 1974, Chris Alex has been selling an eclectic lineup of antiques, gifts, and collectibles like Russian lacquer boxes, scrimshaw, pewter, and wooden nutcracker soldiers. It's one of the wackiest collections on the Cape.

Exposure (508-255-6808; www.capecodphotoworkshops.com), 135 Oak Leaf Road, North Eastham. Linda McCausland's lab is one of the few Cape places that process black-and-white film. In fact, she does such a fantastic job that I even mail them my 4-by-5-sheet film from Boston and beyond when I'm traveling! (See also the "Artistic Outlets During Vacation" sidebar in "Truro."

Eastham Pottery & Loomworks (508-255-1556), 105 Gigi Lane, North Eastham. Just south of the Wellfleet town line, Brian Brader's studio and showroom barn contains pots, platters, sculpture, and stoneware that reflect his interest in the natural world.

Four Winds Leather (508-240-7998), 5130 Route 6, North Eastham. You probably didn't come to the Cape in search of sheepskins and moccasins, but these are the real things. The store is piled high with Native American art, leather coats, wallets, and the like.

✳ Special Events

July–August: **Eastham Painters' Guild,** at the Old Schoolhouse Museum, Route 6 at the Salt Pond Visitor Center. Outdoor art shows are held here most Thursdays and Fridays, as well as over the Memorial Day, Labor Day, and Columbus Day weekends.

Mid-September: **Windmill Weekend.** This 3-day community festival is staged for locals and features a road race, band concert, arts and crafts show, square dancing, and a parade.

WELLFLEET

Although a whopping 70 percent of Wellfleet is conservation land, the town is perhaps best known as an art stronghold. Wellfleet's two principal thoroughfares, Main Street and Commercial Street, are dotted with 20 or so galleries representing a wide gamut of art: from souvenir works to images that transcend their media. Many artists and artisans who exhibit here call Wellfleet home, at least for a short time each year, gaining inspiration from pristine landscapes and an unrelenting ocean.

After art, Wellfleet's other main draw is its natural environment. The outstanding Wellfleet Bay Wildlife Sanctuary offers practically unparalleled opportunities for observing marine and bird life through guided activities and self-guided walks. A mostly sandy, 8-mile-long National Seashore trail on Great Island yields solitude and commanding views of Wellfleet Bay. On the Atlantic side, dunes and cliffs back broad and uninterrupted beaches. Any of Wellfleet's meandering roads are perfect for cycling, leading you past ponds, salt marshes, heathlands, and scrub pines.

Wellfleet appeals to a distinct crowd, many of whom have returned year after year for decades. In fact, many nonnative families—wash-ashores—rent houses here for the entire summer. (The *Boston Globe* reports that two-thirds of Wellfleet's houses are unoccupied off-season.) When shopkeepers and restaurateurs begin dusting off the shelves in early to mid-June, it feels like a real homecoming—old friends catching up over a coffee in a café, neighbors renewing relationships as they tend their gardens. And although Wellfleet is very popular with vacationing Freudian analysts, there's also a notable seasonal contingent of lawyers, professors, and writers—most of whom you'll find purchasing the morning's *New York Times* with a bagel. They've all come for the same purpose: to commune with their thoughts, recharge batteries, and lead a simpler life (albeit only temporarily). Summer folks also venture out of their cocoons to dine on wonderful food in laid-back settings, to square dance outdoors, and to engage in lively conversation after a particularly spirited performance by the Wellfleet Harbor Actors Theater.

Wellfleetians are an independent bunch. Almost 30 percent of the 2,700 year-rounders are self-employed (proverbial Jacks and Jills of all trades), more than in any other Cape town, and almost 20 percent are unemployed in winter. (If you

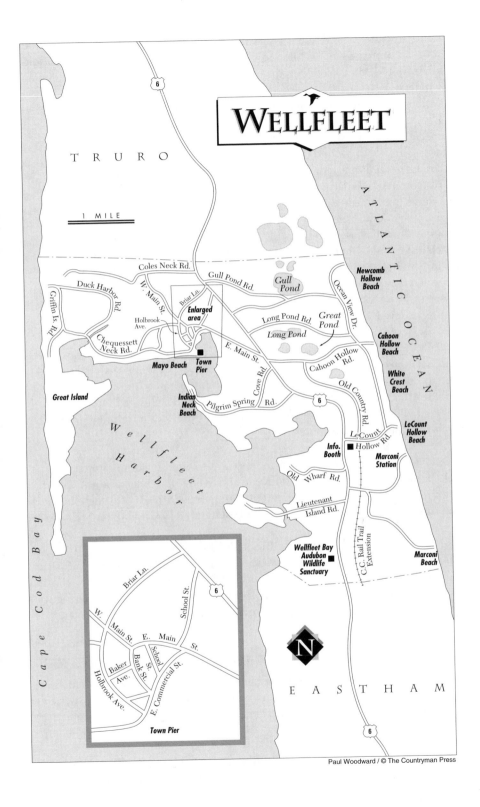

WELLFLEET

TRURO

1 MILE

6

Coles Neck Rd.
Gull Pond Rd.
Gull Pond
Newcomb Hollow Beach
Ocean View Dr.
Duck Harbor Rd.
W. Main St.
Briar Ln.
Griffin Is. Rd.
Enlarged area
Long Pond Rd.
Great Pond
Holbrook Ave.
Long Pond
Cahoon Hollow Beach
Chequessett Neck Rd.
E. Main St.
Mayo Beach
Town Pier
Cahoon Hollow Rd.
White Crest Beach
Great Island
Cove Rd.
Old Country Rd.
Indian Neck Beach
Pilgrim Spring Rd.
6
Wellfleet Harbor
LeCount Hollow Rd.
LeCount Hollow Beach
Info. Booth
Marconi Station
Old Wharf Rd.
Lieutenant Island Rd.
Cape Cod Bay
Wellfleet Bay Audubon Wildlife Sanctuary
C.C. Rail Trail Extension
Marconi Beach

N

EASTHAM

6

Briar Ln.
W. Main St.
School St.
6
E. Main St.
School St.
Baker Ave.
Bank St.
E. Commercial St.
Holbrook Ave.
Town Pier

do visit midwinter, you'll find a few warm beds and the frozen bay—a romantic sight on an overcast day.) While most of the town rolls up its shutters from mid-October to mid-May, Wellfleet may also feel like a ghost town on a weekday in mid-June.

Wellfleet was most likely named for a town in England, which, like "our" Wellfleet, was also renowned for its oyster beds. As early as the 17th century, when Wellfleet was still a part of Eastham known as Billingsgate, the primary industries revolved around oyster and cranberry harvesting. Whaling, fishing, and other related industries also flourished until the mid-1800s. And by the 1870s, commercial markets had really opened up for littlenecks, cherrystones, and clams for chowder. Today, with the depletion of natural fish and shellfish stocks, year-round fishermen have turned to aquaculture. Currently about 50 or so aquaculturists lease 120 acres of Wellfleet Harbor; you'll see them off Mayo Beach at low tide. Shellfish like quahogs and oysters are raised from "seed," put out in "protected racks," and tended for two to three years while they mature. Since as many as 2 million seeds can be put on an acre of land, this is big business. For those looking for fishing charters, though, the harbor and pier are still centers of activity.

GUIDANCE Wellfleet Chamber of Commerce (508-349-2510; www.wellfleet-chamber.com), Route 6, P.O. Box 571, Wellfleet 02667. Open 9–6 daily, mid-June to mid-September, with additional but limited hours for one month prior to and after that. The information booth is well marked right off Route 6 in South Wellfleet. The frequently overworked chamber publishes a rudimentary foldout map of Wellfleet bicycle routes.

PUBLIC REST ROOMS Public rest rooms can be found in summer at Bakers Field across from Mayo Beach (on Kendrick Avenue), as well as at the Town Pier and the marina (both at the end of Commercial Street). Throughout the year, during business hours, head to the basement of Town Hall on Main Street.

PUBLIC LIBRARY ✳ ✎ ☂ **The Wellfleet Public Library** (508-349-0310), West Main Street. Open Monday, Wednesday, and Thursday 2–8; Tuesday and Friday 10–5; and Saturday noon–5. Housed within the former Candle Factory, this outstanding library is available to all Wellfleet vacationers; call for children's story hour times. They sponsor an impressive lineup of readings, screenings, and speakers; Internet access.

GETTING THERE *By car:* Wellfleet is 50 miles beyond Cape Cod Canal via Route 6. *By bus:* The **Plymouth & Brockton** bus line (508-778-9767; www.p-b.com) connects Wellfleet and South Wellfleet with Hyannis and other Cape towns, as well as with Boston's Logan Airport. The bus stops in front of Town Hall on Main Street in Wellfleet, and at D&D Market on Route 6 in South Wellfleet.

GETTING AROUND *By car:* From Route 6, take Main Street to the town center or veer from Main to Commercial Street to the colorful harbor. There is free parking at the Town Pier (at the end of Commercial Street) and behind Town Hall on Main Street. As the seagull flies, the town is anywhere from 2 to 5 miles wide.

MEDICAL EMERGENCY Outer Cape Health Services (508-349-3131), Route 6, Wellfleet. Not an urgent-care facility; call them if it's anything less than a 911 emergency.

✳ To See

Marconi Wireless Station, CCNS, off Route 6 at the Marconi Area. In 1901 Guglielmo Marconi began construction of the first wireless station on the U.S. mainland, in little old Wellfleet. Two years later the first U.S. wireless transatlantic message was transmitted between this station and England: President Roosevelt sent King Edward VII "most cordial greetings and good wishes." (Canada beat the United States in sending a wireless transatlantic message by one month.) A mere 15 years later, the station was closed for wartime security reasons; it was dismantled and abandoned in 1920 because of erosion and the development of alternative technologies. There are few remains today, save the concrete foundation of the transmitter house (which required 25,000 volts to send a message) and sand anchors that held guy wires to the 210-foot towers.

The Cape Cod peninsula is at its narrowest here, and from a well-positioned observation platform you can scan the width of it—from Cape Cod Bay, along Blackfish Creek, to the Atlantic Ocean. (See the Atlantic White Cedar Swamp Trail under *Green Space—Walks.*)

WELLFLEET'S WINTER "SKYLINE" FROM ACROSS DUCK CREEK AT LOW TIDE

Kim Grant

Wellfleet Historical Society Museum (508-349-9157), 266 Main Street. Open 10–4 Tuesday and Friday and 1–4 Wednesday and Thursday, late June to early September. The society has collected photographs, toys, shipwreck detritus, marine artifacts, displays on Marconi and oystering, and household items to illustrate and preserve Wellfleet's past. Adults $1, children under 12 free. Inquire about the 75-minute walks around town on Tuesday and Friday during the summer ($3).

First Congregational Church of the United Church of Christ (508-349-6877), 200 Main Street. Although the church was organized in 1721, this Greek Revival meetinghouse dates to 1850. The interior is graced with a brass chandelier, pale blue walls, curved pews, and a Tiffany-style stained-glass window depicting a 17th-century ship similar to the *Mayflower*. (The church office is open 9–noon Wednesday through Friday year-round; they'll let you in.) On Sunday evenings at 8 in July and August, try to catch a concert featuring the restored Hook and Hastings pipe organ. The bell-shaped cupola, by the way, was added in 1879 after a storm destroyed the traditional one. (It was thought that a bell-shaped tower would be sturdier—perhaps it has been.)

Town clock, First Congregational Church, Main Street. According to the arbiter of strange superlatives, *Ripley's Believe It or Not,* this is the "only town clock in the world that strikes ship's time." Listen for the following chimes and try to figure out what time it is for yourself: Two bells distinguish 1, 5, and 9 o'clock; six bells signify 3, 7, and 11 o'clock; eight bells toll for 4, 8, and 12 o'clock. To make matters even more interesting, adding one chime to the corresponding even hours signifies the half hours. (After all these years of hanging out in Wellfleet, I still double-check my "newfangled" wristwatch!)

Our Lady of Lourdes Church (508-349-2222), Main Street. On the occasion of the country's 1976 bicentennial, two troubadours expressed their thanks to the town after a long celebration by donating the handsome painted carvings attached to the doors, which are thankfully kept open for all to see.

Samuel Rider House, Gull Pond Road. Although the house is not open to the public, it's a fine early-1700s Outer Cape farmstead.

Atwood Higgins House (508-255-3421), Bound Brook Island Road, off Pamet Point Road. Open Thursdays 1–4 from late May to mid-October; bona fide tours on Wednesdays at 1 require a reservation. The pastoral 5-acre homestead, under the auspices of the CCNS, has a little store and post office. The tour only discusses the architecture and versatility of the 18th-century full Cape that was restored by its early-20th-century owners. Free.

SCENIC DRIVES Ocean View Drive. Take LeCount Hollow Road to Ocean View (despite its name, it has only limited views) and head back to Route 6 via Gull Pond Road or Long Pond Road. You'll pass heathlands, cliffs, and scrub pines.

Chequessett Neck Road. Cross the dike at Herring River and head to the end of the road for magnificent sunset views. Although there is room for only a few cars at the very end of the road, you can park near the Great Island Trailhead and walk down to the beach (about 15 minutes).

Pilgrim Spring Road. Not to be confused with the Pilgrim Spring Trail in Truro, where the Pilgrims got their first taste of fresh water, this quiet road offers lovely inlet and cove views; at the end of the road, look back toward Wellfleet Harbor.

✳ Outdoor Activities

BICYCLING/RENTALS **Cape Cod Rail Trail.** Extended in the mid-1990s, the trail now terminates in Wellfleet at LeCount Hollow Road (where there is parking), just east of Route 6.

Idle Times Bike Shop (508-349-9161), Route 6. Open mid-May to early September. A full line of bicycles for the whole family.

See also Black Duck Sports Shop under *Fishing/Shellfishing.*

BOAT EXCURSIONS/RENTALS **Jack's Boat Rentals** (508-349-7553), Gull Pond. Open late June to early September. This friendly outfit rents canoes, boogie boards, pedal boats, sea cycles, surf bikes, kayaks, and Sunfish. If you want to paddle somewhere besides Gull Pond, pick up a boat at the shop (508-349-9808) on Route 6. More interestingly, though, they offer guided kayak and canoe tours (about twice daily) through estuary marshes, along the tidal Pamet and Herring Rivers, and out to Great Island. Departure times vary with the tides; call Eric at 508-349-1429 in the evenings.

Wellfleet Marine Corp. (508-349-2233), Town Pier. From mid-June to mid-September, you can rent Stur-Dee Cat sailboats, sloops, and fishing skiffs by the hour or by the day.

FISHING/SHELLFISHING Obtain a freshwater fishing permit at Town Hall (508-349-0301) on Main Street. Freshwater fishing holes include **Great Pond, Gull Pond,** and **Long Pond** (see *Green Space—Ponds*).

Shellfishing permits are required for the taking of oysters, clams, and quahogs. Expect to pay $40 for a four-month nonresident permit (valid June through September). Wellfleet's tidal flats are wondrous places at low tide. Contact the **Beach Sticker Booth** (508-349-9818) on the pier in July and August or Town Hall (508-349-0300) off-season. Try your luck surf-casting early in the morning or at night at the following Atlantic beaches: **Newcomb Hollow, White Crest, LeCount Hollow** or at **Duck Harbor** on the bayside.

Black Duck Sports Shop (508-349-9801), off Route 6, South Wellfleet. Open May to mid-October. One-stop shopping for rod rentals, tide charts, live eels, squid, worms, sand eels, outdoor maps, and camping equipment. Bike rentals, coolers, and beach chairs, too. Like I said: one-stop shopping.

For half- and full-day bass and blues charters, contact *Snoop* (508-349-6113) and *Jac's Mate* (508-255-2978; 508-237-3289 mobile). Both are friendly, docked at the Wellfleet Harbor Marina, and offer charters mid-May to mid-October. Book a week or two in advance in season. Prices are $425 and $550, respectively, for up to six people.

Navigator (508-349-6003), also at the Wellfleet Harbor Marina. With more than

30 years of experience plying Cape Cod waters, Captain Rick Merrill offers morning and afternoon fishing trips in July and August; $25 adults, $17 kids.

GOLF **Chequessett Yacht & Country Club** (508-349-3704), Chequessett Neck Road. Open March through November, weather permitting. This nine-hole, par-35 course offers beautiful views of Wellfleet Harbor.

⚓ **MINI-GOLF** **At the Wellfleet Drive-In** (508-349-2520), Route 6. Open late April through September. The only game in town is conveniently located next to the flea market, drive-in, and a classic dairy bar.

SAILING ⚓ **Chequessett Yacht & Country Club** (508-349-0198), Chequessett Neck Road, offers sailing lessons. Junior and adult sailing programs run from early July to late August. Group instruction by the week for youths; individual instruction (for one to five adults) by the hour.

SEAL CRUISES See the "It's Not Just for the Birds" sidebar.

SPECIAL PROGRAMS See the "It's Not Just for the Birds" sidebar.
⚓ **Summer recreation programs** (508-349-0330), Bakers Field and Gull Pond. Weekdays 9–noon, early July to mid-August. Sports, arts and crafts, and swimming lessons. Nonresidents $50 weekly for the first child, $20 each additional.

TENNIS Town courts are on **Mayo Beach,** Kendrick Avenue. **Chequessett Yacht & Country Club** (508-349-3704), Chequessett Neck Road. Open March through November, weather permitting. Five hard courts are available to the public for a fee.

A BOARDWALK CROSSES THE DUNES TO THE NATIONAL SEASHORE.

Kim Grant

TRAILS, BIRDS, SEALS, & CLASSES

Wellfleet Bay Wildlife Sanctuary (508-349-2615; www.wellfleetbay.org), off Route 6, South Wellfleet. Trails open daily sunrise to sunset; center open daily 8:30–5, year-round, except closed Monday from November through April. With almost 1,000 acres of pine, moors, freshwater ponds, tidal creeks, salt marsh, and beach, the Audubon sanctuary is one of New England's most active. Despite that, you'll appreciate the relative lack of human presence after a day of gallery hopping and sunbathing.

Three **trails** total more than 5 miles: Silver Spring Trail, a lovely, wooded walking trail alongside a long pond; Goose Pond Trail, past ponds, woodlands, a marsh, and heathland (a boardwalk leads to the bay from here); and Bay View Trail.

The sanctuary also offers a steady stream of **activities** throughout the summer (plenty year-round, for that matter): canoe trips, sunset walks, night hikes, evening natural history talks, marine-life cruises in Pleasant Bay and Cape Cod Bay, birding expeditions, and trips to Monomoy Island (see the sidebar under *Green Space* in "Chatham").

The popular year-round **seal cruises** to Monomoy Island and South Beach (in Chatham) last 90 minutes. Trips depart most weekends and some weekdays; call for the tide-dependent schedule. They also have a 2-hour Sea Bird and Seal Cruise in late fall, which goes out on an open commercial fishing vessel. Onboard naturalists will educate you about the habits and habitats of harbor and gray seals. Tickets: $25–35 for nonmembers, $5 less for members.

Wellfleet Bay Wildlife Sanctuary **Natural History Day Camps** are offered in July and August. Geared toward children 4–14, these excellent weeklong programs are designed to "expand curiosity about and respect for the environment through hands-on outdoor experiences . . . and to develop skill in discovering the natural world using the principles of scientific inquiry." Indeed. $165–275 for nonmembers, $115–225 members.

The sanctuary's summertime **Adult Field School** incorporates multiday, hands-on courses. Topics include Cape Cod natural history, ornithology, marine life, nature photography, field archaeology, geology, local endangered habitats, and sketching in the field. Instruction is expert. Shared accommodations are available onsite for an additional fee.

Before departing, check out the visitors center's environmentally friendly composting toilets, which save 100,000 gallons of water per season. Trails are free to members, $5 for adult nonmembers, $3 for children nonmembers. Members may tent in the wooded, natural setting (call for fees and reservations).

✴ Green Space

BEACHES Marconi Beach, CCNS, on the Atlantic. A boardwalk and steep staircase lead to the long, narrow beach backed by dramatic dunes. In-season amenities include lifeguards, outdoor showers, and changing facilities. Parking $10 (permit valid all day at any CCNS beach); seasonal pass $30. The cost to enter on foot or bicycle is $3.

Cahoon Hollow Beach and **White Crest Beach,** town beaches on the Atlantic Ocean. Sandy shoals create shallow, warmish (i.e. not frigid) pools of water here. Although each beach is wide and sandy, local townsfolk favor the sea grass and dunes of White Crest, and hang gliders and surfers appreciate the surf. (Hang gliders are allowed only before 9 AM and after 5 PM.) White Crest has more parking. Amenities include lifeguards and rest rooms. Parking $10 daily.

Mayo Beach, Kendrick Avenue. Parking is free, but the beach is nothing to e-mail home about. From here you can see some of the offshore areas—marked by yellow buoys—where modern aquaculture thrives in the form of constructed shellfish farms.

The following beaches require a town sticker: **Maquire Landing** and **Newcomb Hollow Beach,** both off Ocean View Drive on the Atlantic Ocean; **Burton Baker Beach** (the only place in town where sailboarding is permitted) and **Indian Neck Beach,** both off Pilgrim Spring Road on the bayside; **Powers Landing** and **Duck Harbor,** both off Chequessett Neck Road on the bay side. Cottage renters may purchase a sticker at the well-marked Beach Sticker Booth (508-349-9818) on the Town Pier from July to early September, the only time you'll need a sticker. It's open 8:30–4 daily (until 8 PM on Friday and Saturday). $40 weekly, $150 seasonally.

PONDS Great Pond, Long Pond, and **Gull Pond** offer freshwater swimming. If you're staying at an inn or cottage, you'll be eligible for the requisite parking

UNCLE TIM'S BRIDGE

Kim Grant

Kim Grant

GREAT ISLAND TRAIL

sticker. Purchase them at the Beach Sticker Booth, (508-349-9818), on the Town Pier. All ponds have lifeguards.

WALKS See the "It's Not Just for the Birds" sidebar.

Great Island Trail, CCNS, off Chequessett Neck Road. About 8 miles round trip, this trail is relatively flat, but soft sand makes for a challenging trek. Walk at low tide when the sand is more firm. (Besides, Jeremy Point, the tip of land farthest out to sea, is covered at high tide.) During the 4-hour round-trip hike, you'll be rewarded with scant human presence and stunning scenery. It's great for birders, and it's best on a sunny spring day or a crisp autumn one. No matter the season, bring plenty of water and sunscreen.

This area was once an island, hence its name. Over time Cape Cod Bay currents deposited sandbars that eventually connected it to the mainland. Long ago, Great Island was home to various commercial enterprises—oystering, cranberry harvesting, and shore whaling—and the land was dotted with lookout towers used to spot whales. There was even a local watering hole and overnight hostelry, the Great Island Tavern, built in 1690 and used until about 1740. But as shore whaling died, so did the Great Island community. By 1800 the island was deserted and deforested. (Pines have been planted in an effort to keep erosion under control.)

Atlantic White Cedar Swamp Trail, CCNS, Marconi Area. One of the best Outer Cape trails, this swamp, navigable via a boardwalk, has a primordial feel. A dense overhead cover also keeps it cool even on the most stifling of days. Nonetheless, the early and latter parts of this 1.5-mile round-trip trail traverse steep stairs and soft sand. As for what you'll see, this trail features one of the few remaining stands of white cedar on the Cape. Because white cedar was prized by the settlers for its light weight and ease of handling, a century of overuse took its toll. While the swamp (in places, 24 feet deep with peat) has begun to recover, nature has its own cycles; however: Red maples will eventually choke the white cedars out of existence. In August, wild trailside blueberries are ripe for the picking.

Uncle Tim's Bridge, East Commercial Street. The often-photographed wooden footbridge connects Commercial Street to a small wooded island, crossing a tidal creek (Duck Creek) and marshland. Short, sandy trails circle the island.

✳ Lodging

Most summer visitors to Wellfleet stay in cottages and houses, rented by the week or, most probably, longer, but there are plenty of places for short-term guests. Unless otherwise noted, all lodging is in Wellfleet 02667.

INN 🐾 ✿ **Inn at Duck Creeke** (508-349-9333; www.innatduckcreeke. com), 70 Main Street. Open early May to mid-October. Half a mile from the town center, this rambling, old-fashioned 1800s inn is situated between an idyllic duck pond and a salt marsh (ask for one of the rooms overlooking it). Owners Bob "Moo" Morrill and Judy Pihl (and their long-time assistant Nancy) describe it as "friendly but not fussy." And that's just about right. Fine for active explorers who won't be spending mornings lying around their rooms, the simple guest rooms serve both families and budget-conscious travelers. My favorite rooms are in the Salt-works Cottage (they share a homey living room) and the carriage house (they have a spiffed-up, romantic cabin feel). Continental breakfast included. In-season $85–95 private bath, $70–85 shared bath; off-season $50–85.

BED & BREAKFASTS ✿ **Aunt Sukie's Bayside Bed & Breakfast** (508-349-2804; 800-420-9999; www.auntsukies.com), 525 Chequessett Neck Road. Open mid-May to mid-October. Hidden by a fence from a road less traveled, Sue and Dan Hamar's bayfront B&B is full of westward-facing picture windows. It takes just 30 seconds to walk from the shingled house, with a contemporary addition, across a boardwalk marsh to the inn's private bay beach. As for the rooms, two contemporary ones boast private decks and splendid westward bay views. The suite features wide-pine floors, Oriental carpets, a private patio, and a separate sitting room in the original 1830 section of the house. The common room, dotted with antiques, overflows with "Aunt Sukie's" history. An expanded continental breakfast is served on the bayside deck, weather permitting. $210.

🐾 **Holbrook House** (508-349-6706; www.holbroookwellfleet.com), 223 Main Street. Open late April to late October. This place is a gem. Completely gutted by Brailsford Nixon and Jean Nelson in 1999, the house retains all that's classic in an 1820s Greek Revival inn. Sophisticated but relaxed, urbane but tranquil, the inn straddles both worlds. It juxtaposes polished wood floors with abstract paintings; antiques coexist with artist-transformed hand-me-downs. The three guest rooms have all the modern conveniences like telephone, refrigerator, and cable TV. Fresh flowers are a nice touch. A full breakfast is included, and first-floor guests may enjoy it on their private patio; others chose between their rooms and the spacious living room. Inquire about the lovely apartment, rented weekly or monthly. Mid-June to early September $125–140; off-season $90–120.

🍃 **Blue Gateways** (508-349-7530; www.bluegateways.com), 252 Main Street. Open mid-April through October. Bonnie and Richard Robicheau operate a comfortable, cheery, completely refurbished B&B in the center of town. Since Richard is a builder, the house has been expertly renovated, right down to latch doors and sanded floors. And Bonnie obviously enjoys taking care of guests; homemade granola and the continual addition of little touches are just two examples of how she does it. The three crisp and comfy guest rooms share an upstairs reading room and a downstairs TV room, complete with one of the house's three working fireplaces. An expanded continental breakfast (with perhaps yummy almond honey orange bread) is served on the light sunporch, overlooking the little reflecting pool (a great place for a second cup of coffee). Late May to early September $120–130; off-season $100–110.

COTTAGES 🍃 **The Colony** (508-349-3761), 640 Chequessett Neck Road. Open late May to mid-September. This is not your average cottage colony. In fact, no place on the Cape remotely resembles it. If I were going to spend a week or two anywhere, it'd be in one of these Bauhaus treasures, 1949 low-slung duplexes. Well-traveled guests flock here for quietude (you'll be speaking in hushed tones before you know it), communing with nature, and excellent service—including turndown and daily maid service. Eleanor Stefani purchased the low-key place in 1963, but Ned Saltonstall (a trustee of Boston's Institute for Contemporary Arts) built it as a private club in 1949. Scads of original artwork grace the cottages, which are furnished in mod 1950s style. Cottages also feature galley kitchens and enclosed dining porches. Each of the 10 charming units has decks and lots of picture windows, which bring the natural surroundings indoors.

LOW-TIDE ABSTRACTIONS

Kim Grant

$1,050–2,100 weekly, $165–300 daily (3-night minimum). No credit cards.

☙ **Surf Side Cottages** (508-349-3959; www.surfsidevacation.com), Ocean View Drive, South Wellfleet 02663. Open April through November. The 1950s-style housekeeping cottages aren't much to look at. But they're within a minute's walk of the dunes and ocean. Nothing separates them from the ocean except other Surf Side cottages and scrub pines; a few of the 18 units have ocean views. Most larger cottages have a roof deck; each has a screened-in porch and wood-burning fireplace and a private outdoor shower. Modern kitchens, knotty-pine paneling, and tasteful rattan furnishings are the norm. Bring sheets and towels and leave the cottage clean and ready for the next tenants. Reserve early. Pets accepted off-season. Mid-June through August $825 for a one-bedroom, $1,250–1,500 for a two- or three-bedroom, weekly; off-season $80–130 daily, $560–910 weekly.

🖉 **The Even'tide** (508-349-3410; 800-368-0007; www.eventidemotel.com), Route 6, South Wellfleet 02663. Open April through October. These nine cottages are a cut above. Wooded and set back from Route 6, the complex has a nice children's play area, a big heated indoor pool, direct access to the rail-trail, and a walking trail to Marconi Beach. All cottages have TV, telephone, fully tiled bathroom, and full kitchen (except Tern). There are also above-average motel rooms and suites that rent for $98–140 nightly mid-June to early September. July and August $900-1,400 for four to six people weekly; off-season $515–925 for four to six people weekly (or $75–120 nightly for

two people). Summertime minimum stay is 3 to 6 nights; add $8 per child nightly.

See also Maurice's Campground under *Campgrounds*.

MOTELS ♿ ❄ **Wellfleet Motel & Lodge** (508-349-3535; 800-852-2900; www.wellfleetmotel.com), Route 6, South Wellfleet 02663. The bilevel, 1960s-style motel has 65 rooms and suites across from the Wellfleet Bay Wildlife Sanctuary. Rooms in the nicely landscaped lodge, built in 1986, are generally more spacious than the motel rooms. In addition to direct access to the Cape Cod Rail Trail, you'll find a gas grill, whirlpool, and indoor and outdoor pools. July and August $145–270, $10 each additional person; off-season $70–135.

See also the Even'tide under *Cottages*.

CAMPGROUNDS 🐾 🖉 **Paine's Campground** (508-349-3007; 800-479-3017; www.campingcapecod.com), off Old County Road from Route 6, South Wellfleet 02663. Open mid-May to mid-September. At this tenters' haven there are designated areas for "quiet" campers, youth groups, and families, as well as sites to which you must lug your tent. Of the 150 sites, only 6 are reserved for big RVs. You can walk from the campground to the National Seashore. Freshwater swimming is found in nearby kettle ponds. Sites $26 for two ($12 additional adult, $5 additional children 6–18).

🐾 🖉 **Maurice's Campground** (508-349-2029; www.mauricescampground.com), Route 6. Open late May to mid-October. You'll find 180 wooded sites for tents and trailers. There are also a few cottages that can sleep four and cabins that can sleep three with a cot. Direct access to the Cape Cod Rail Trail. $25 for two; additional adults $6, additional children $3. Cottages $500 weekly for two, $550 for four. Cabins $75 nightly.

See also the "It's Not Just for the Birds" sidebar.

RENTAL HOUSES AND COTTAGES
Thomas Brown Real Estate Associates (508-349-8072; www.capevaca-tionrentals.com), 2700 Route 6.

✳ Where to Eat

Wellfleet oysters are renowned: Legend has it that England's Queen Victoria served them at her state dinners (no others would do). According to aficionados, Wellfleet oysters taste better when harvested from the cooler waters in the off-season, but you'll have little choice if you vacation in July or August; order them anyway. Wellfleet is also known for its hardshell quahog and steamer clams. In fact, these waters yield millions of dollars' worth of shellfish annually.

Although there are many restaurants reviewed here, most are closed offseason. Furthermore, most opening and closing dates wholly dependent on weather and tourist traffic.

DINING OUT ⅋ **Aesop's Tables** (508-349-6450), 316 Main Street, next to Town Hall. Open for lunch in July and August and dinner mid-May to mid-October. For some patrons, no summer is complete without a trip to Aesop's; for others, there are better places to spend your fine-dining dollars. On my last visit, service was a bit disappointing. Nonetheless, Aesop's is known for local seafood, coastal cui-

sine influenced by other places that are also influenced by the sea: Italy, France, Japan, Thailand, and New Zealand. You might simply head upstairs to the converted attic space with occasional entertainment. It's a comfortable place for an aperitif or coffee with your Death by Chocolate, a dense chocolate mousse with a brownie crust. There's no better way to go. Lunch $7–15, dinner entrées $14–26.

Sweet Seasons (508-349-6535), 70 Main Street. Open for dinner mid-June to mid-September. Longtime chef-owner Judy Pihl has a knack for sauces. Try the house specialties of osso buco with orzo risotto or lamb chops with pears stuffed with roasted shallots. The tables are thankfully well spaced. If you don't want to drive to Provincetown this may be your best bet. Entrées $19–25.

EATING OUT ♿ ✎ 🐚 **Moby Dick's** (508-349-9795), Route 6. Open 11:30–9 or 10 daily, early May to mid-October. Pride of ownership has its rewards. Although the place is always packed, would you really want to patronize an establishment that wasn't? Since 1983 Todd Barry and his team have provided the best and largest portions of area seafood. Order off the blackboard menu, and then take a seat surrounded by weathered nautical paraphernalia or at a picnic table on the open upper level. You know the fare (it's just not normally this fresh and tasty)—Chatham steamers (clams) caught off Monomoy Island, lobsters, Wellfleet oysters, seafood rolls (with barely a hint of mayo), "dayboat" scallops, and unusually presented onion rings. The chowder, loaded with big chunks of clams, really tastes like clam chowder should. BYOB. Lunch $6–10, dinner $8–25.

✳ ✦ **Finely JP's** (508-349-7500), 554 Route 6, South Wellfleet. Open for dinner Wednesday or Thursday through Sunday year-round, nightly in July and August. Despite the lack of atmosphere (think pine paneling), this nondescript roadside offers very good food. Many loyal vacationers return multiple nights over a 14-day vacation. Chef-owner John Pontius has been reelin' 'em in since 1991 with large portions of grilled scallops on linguine, poached salmon with ginger, and baked Wellfleet oysters. No reservations are taken, but try calling ahead and putting your name on the waiting list. If you arrive after 6 PM, you'll be waiting. Entrées $12–16; off-season specials are usually $11.

✦ **Flying Fish Cafe** (508-349-3100), 29 Briar Lane, between Route 6 and Main Street. Open early April through October. Breakfast and dinner daily (except Monday) mid-June to early September; more limited days off-season. As the owner says, this is a "funky little place to eat," with modest tables, local art, and a partially visible kitchen. The café's vegetarian and ethnic menu is much more interesting than the simple decor suggests. For breakfast, try great omelets or scrambled tofu with veggies or green eggs and ham (even if you can't proclaim, "Sam I am"). Keep dinner simple with a vegetable stir-fry or local seafood, but don't pass up appetizers like sun-dried tomato quesadillas and Eastham mussels. Vegetarians depart very satisfied here. Breakfast $4–8, dinner $14–22.

✐ ✳ **High Toss Pizza & Cafe** (508-349-0005), 50 Main Street. Open for breakfast and dinner. A friendly and low-key place, this café serves omelets (with ingredients like avocado, goat cheese, and pesto, for instance) and other specialties (like poached eggs over clamcakes) until noon. It's also the kind of place you want to hang out in until noon, too. At night I gravitate toward their pizzas (available for take-out) and simple pasta dishes rather than more elaborate dishes. The coffee bar turns out rich espresso and baked goods. Mexican is featured on Wednesday. Mains $9–23.

✳ **The Blue Willow** (508-349-0900), 1426 Route 6, South Wellfleet. Open daily 7–7. Across from the visitors center and steps from the rail-trail, this tiny place has everything you need for a picnic or sunset hors d'oeuvres. You can expect gourmet sandwiches, cold tuna or curried chicken salads, daily frittata and quiche specials, baked goods, crabcakes, and prepared meals (for you cottage dwellers and house renters).

✦ **Christine's Oasis** (508-349-0000), Route 6, near the post office. Open April to mid-October. I make a beeline for Christine's sour cream and walnut coffee cake, as well as the cranberry-blueberry scones, but I know the shop sells other deli items and "real" dinners. Trouble is, I'm always so single-minded in my pursuit of the above-mentioned sweet treats that my ever-reasonable research methods fly out the window when I pull into the parking lot.

♿ ☿ **Duck Creeke Tavern Room** (508-349-7369), 70 Main Street. Open for dinner and late-night appetizers mid-May to mid-October. Under the watchful eye of chef-owner Judy Pihl since 1974, Wellfleet's oldest tavern is cozy, lively, friendly, and fun. It offers well-priced, less formal dishes like steak and ale, burgers, seafood stew, and—in a nod to "bistro fare"—roasted eggplant on basil focaccia. A fireplace, beamed ceilings, greenery, and a bar fashioned from old doors set the tone for live entertainment Thursday through Sunday. Melodies range from jazz to folk, piano, pop, and blues. Entrées $12–17.

✺ **On the Creek Cafe** (508-349-9841), 55 Commercial Street. Open for breakfast and lunch mid-June to mid-October (only weekends in fall). Because of the tranquil location and outdoor seating on the edge of Duck Creek, you might find yourself here despite the "laid-back" service. This depot-style place is simple and cheery, and the offerings are simple, too: eggs, bagels, and pancakes for breakfast; sandwiches, seafood stew, Greek salads, and PB&J or fluffernutter for the kids at lunch. Blackboard specials are always a good choice. Dishes $4–9.

✿ ✻ ✺ **Box Lunch** (508-349-2178), 50 Briar Lane. Proprietor Owen Macnutt's original branch of the ever-expanding chain is open for breakfast and lunch daily. "Rollwiches" (sandwich meats rolled up tight in pita bread) are perfect for the beach or to take on a Great Island hike. P.S.: Folks swear by "Porky's Nightmare." Dishes $3–7.

Mac's Seafood and Harbor Grill (508-349-0404), Town Pier. Open late May to mid-October. Mac, who buys seafood direct from boats throughout the day, offers a raw bar, sushi, smoked pâté, and mussels or littlenecks with linguine in white wine sauce. You'll also find decent fried seafood, burritos, clambakes-to-go,

and vegetarian dishes. Regardless of whether you eat in or take out, it's the harborside location and casual outdoor patio at sunset that draw folks; BYOB. Entrées $10–15.

Bookstore Restaurant (508-349-3154), Kendrick Avenue. Open mid-February to mid-December. Since owner Michael Parlante raises oysters from his harbor shellfish beds, I recommend you come simply for oyster appetizers, preferably raw, as they're so fresh. Lobsters are okay, too.

✿ **The Juice** (no phone), Commercial Street. Open for lunch and dinner mid-May to mid-October (Thursday through Sunday in shoulder season). This funky, archetypal Wellfleetian eatery (which looks like it's falling down but isn't) serves strong morning java, midday falafel and veggie burgers, and nighttime Mexican food (including a cross between burritos and quesadillas). Although the service is slow, the 20-something clientele typically has time on their hands. Ask proprietor Chad Williams to blend you a specialty organic smoothie. Dishes $6–9.

✿ ✻ ✺ **The Lighthouse** (508-349-3681), 317 Main Street. Open for breakfast, lunch, and dinner daily year-round (except closed in March). Nothing else open? This fixture in the center of town since 1930 offers no-nonsense omelets, waffles, and two eggs any style (until noon). Try to get a table in the quieter, glassed-in dining room to the side. Guinness on tap.

Wellfleet Oyster & Clam Co./Fish Market, across from Marconi Station, has fresh fish, shellfish, and lobsters for all you cottage renters.

See also Beachcomber under *Entertainment.*

COFFEE See The Juice and High Toss Pizza under *Eating Out*.

❋ Entertainment

Ꮭ **Wellfleet Harbor Actors Theater** (508-349-6835; www.what.org), 1 Kendrick Avenue, Wellfleet. Performances mid-May to mid-October (8 PM nightly in July and August, Thursday through Sunday off-season; matinees and kids' shows); 90 seats. Known locally as WHAT, it's clear why this serious theater company doesn't receive federal government funding from the current National Endowment for the Arts: You'd never see John Ashcroft at one of its experimental, new-wave, and sometimes misunderstood shows. WHAT produces plays by new writers and directors, established folks like David Mamet, and radical interpretations of Chekhov, too. A fixture in the community since 1985, WHAT can always be counted on to be provocative. Founder Gip Hoppe (a marvelous actor) writes some of the plays himself (he is perhaps best known for *Jackie: An American Life*) and shares the co–artistic director title with Jeff Zinn, son of historian Howard Zinn. Tickets $21; half-price "student rush" just prior to curtain time.

✐ ❀ **Cape Cod Tales from Past and Present** (508-349-0103). In July and August (Wednesday through Friday at 7:30 PM) at the Wellfleet United Methodist Church on Main Street, master storyteller Jim Wolf does very dramatic (read: loud and highly interpretive) storytelling that's entertaining for both adults and children. Stories are related to the Cape, of course. Adults $7, kids $4.

❀ **Square dancing,** Town Pier. On Wednesday evenings in July and August, the pier takes on a different tone. Dancing begins at 7:30, and the steps get progressively more difficult until 10 or so.

❀ ❋ ↑ **Wellfleet Cinemas** (508-349-7176; 800-696-3532), Route 6. Adjacent to the drive-in, the only cinema on the Outer Cape that's open year-round. First-run movies on four screens.

♈ **Beachcomber** (508-349-6055; www.thebeachcomber.com), off

---

AN OPEN-AIR SCREEN WITH STARS

Wellfleet Drive-In (508-349-7176; 508-349-2450 for a human being; 800-696-3532), Route 6. Shows late April through September. One of the last holdouts of a vanishing American pastime, this drive-in has lured patrons since 1957, when the number of U.S. drive-ins peaked at 4,000. Today there are fewer than 800 left, only a handful in New England, no others on the Cape. Hence, it remains a treasured local institution. Late owner John Jentz, a former engineering professor at MIT, designed the screen with his MIT pals; perhaps that's why it's withstood hurricanes with winds up to 135 mph. Double features are shown nightly at dusk (about 8 PM in summer). Movies change up to three times a week, and there's a play area behind the reasonably priced **Intermission Bar & Grill.** The box office opens at 7. Films are generally family-oriented. Tickets: $6.50 adults, $4 kids 5–11.

Ocean View Drive on Cahoon Hollow Beach. Open daily noon–1 AM from late May to early September. In its former incarnation, this 1850 structure was one of the Outer Cape's nine lifesaving stations. Today, perched on a bluff right above the beach, it's better known as a bar and club, but it also serves surprisingly good food. By day, shuffle from the beach to hang out with a 20-something crowd on the outdoor deck, complete with a 40-foot-long, cabana-style raw bar. Burgers, seafood plates, and boneless Buffalo wings also offered. Inside is dark, with wooden booths. Only appetizers and pizza are available after 9 PM. There's nothing else like it on the Cape and it's simply amazing that it's survived this long, as a college-age bar surrounded by National Park Service land. Be careful about wandering out onto the beach after a couple of drinks; the first step is a doozy! Hip Boston bands and national blues artists perform in the evenings, but the club is perhaps best known for its Sunday-afternoon concerts and reggae-filled happy hours (frozen mudslides are very popular). Dishes $5–15.

✳ Selective Shopping

Arts and crafts shows are held on many Mondays and Tuesdays in July and August at the Wellfleet Drive-In on Route 6. This is generally high-quality stuff, from oils and watercolors to pottery, jewelry, and objets de wood or glass. Free.

Wellfleet Flea Market (508-349-2520; 800-696-3532), at the Wellfleet Drive-In, Route 6. Open Saturday, Sunday, and Monday holidays mid-April through October; also Wednesday and Thursday in July and August.

With more than 300 stalls, there's more junk than treasure, but you never know what you'll find: name-brand clothing, a hat to ward off the summer sun, used and antique furniture, and trinkets, tea sets, and colored glasses. Wander in with the intention of spending a few minutes and a few dollars and you'll probably find that hours have passed and you've bought more than you bargained for! It's the Cape's biggest and best. Admission $2 per car.

ART GALLERIES Wellfleet is an art town. The **Art Gallery Association** (508-349-9546) publishes a complete list of galleries, some of which are excellent, others of which peddle to souvenir art. In July and August, many galleries host wine-and-cheese openings on Saturday evening.

Cherry Stone Gallery (508-349-3026), 70 East Commercial Street. Open June to mid-September. Sally Nerber has collected and sold works by Abbott and Atget, Motherwell and Rauschenberg (and emerging artists) since 1971. Unpretentious and friendly, this small place is for the serious collector.

✳ **Left Bank Gallery** (508-349-9451; www.leftbankgallery.com), 25 Commercial Street. Open April to mid-October, Thursday through Monday off-season. Audrey and Gerald Parent's gallery is arguably the most interesting in town. Don't miss the crafts-filled potter's room behind the wonderfully diverse main exhibition area.

The Nicholas Harrison Gallery (508-349-7799), 275 Main Street. Open May through December. Owner-artists Anna Besciak and Laura and Mark Evangelista have catapulted contemporary crafts into the fine art category with this collection. In addition to excellent ceramics (their forte), they're have amassed an outstanding assortment of glass objects, metalwork, lighting, woodworking, jewelry, and other wearable art. Don't miss it, really.

❄ **Left Bank Small Works & Jewelry** (508-349-7939), 3 West Main Street. Same hours as above. Works on paper and contemporary jewelry are highlighted.

Kendall Art Gallery (508-349-2482), Main Street. Open May through October. These folks probably carry more sculpture in more media—bronze, aluminum, and marble—than any other gallery on the Cape. The sculpture garden is tranquil. In all, Walter and Myra Dorrell carry the work of about 30 artists and craftspeople, in addition to selling Walter's paintings. And they've been doing it since 1983.

Blue Heron Gallery (508-349-6724), 20 Bank Street. Open mid-May to mid-October. Royal and Jocelyn Thurston pack a lot of art and crafts (Cape scenes, jewelry, and pottery) into a seemingly endless series of small rooms. More than 30 representational contemporary artists and artisans are shown.

Cove Gallery (508-349-2530), 15 Commercial Street. Open mid-June to mid-October. This gallery has featured oils and pastels since 1968; it also has a lively sculpture garden overlooking Duck Creek.

The Davis Gallery (508-349-0549), 2766 Route 6. Open mid-May to mid-October. It's worth stopping at this unusual assortment of contemporary sculpture, crafts, and painting.

ARTISANS ❄ **Salty Duck Pottery** (508-349-3342), 115 Main Street. Katherine Stillman was attracted to Wellfleet because of its reputation as a community of tolerant eccentrics. Now she's one of them, living and shaping her clay beside a salt marsh. Her lead-free vessels gracefully combine simple lines with utilitarian purposes. Fellow potter Maria Juster makes blue-green stoneware pottery, tiles, mirrors, and tables.

Wellfleet Pottery (508-349-6679), Commercial Street. Open June through September. Trevor and Kathleen Glucksman have been making pottery in Wellfleet since 1970. He designs and crafts the small-scale china, employing all methods of casting, throwing, and pressing to achieve the desired results. Kathleen glazes and hand-paints them with simple depictions of wildflowers and grasses. The umber country china (very strong china good for daily use) is decorated and displayed without flourish.

Narrow Land Pottery (508-349-6308), 3 West Main Street. Open April through December. Joe McCaffery, who studied at the School of the Museum of Fine Arts Boston, throws pots, vases, mugs, lamp bases, and plates. His glazes, porcelain, and stoneware come in a variety of colors.

BOOKSTORES **Herridge Books** (508-349-1323), 11 East Main Street. Open late May to late September. Used books covering a wide range of subjects.

CLOTHING Style-conscious women are in luck (in-season) in Wellfleet. Loose-fitting designs in cotton, linen, rayon, and earth tones reign. Try **Hannah** (508-349-9884), 234 Main

Street; Eccentricity (508-349-7554), 361 Main Street (beautiful kimonos and ethnic designs featuring tactile fabrics); **Eccentricity's Off Center** (508-349-3634), across the street; and **Karol Richardson** (508-349-6378), nearby at 11 West Main Street.

FARM STAND **Hatch's Fish Market/Hatch's Produce** (508-349-2810), behind Town Hall on Main Street. Open 9–6 daily late May to mid-September. Although you might find better prices at the supermarket, the fish and produce here are fresh and beautifully displayed, and the location can't be beat. Hatch's smokes its own fish, pâté, and mussels.

SPECIAL SHOPS ❋ **Jules Besch Stationers** (508-349-1231), 15 Bank Street. Open May to mid-October; weekends mid-October to late December and April. This shop features products that will make you want to take pen (perhaps an antique 1880s pen or a quill) to paper (perhaps some handmade paper or a bound journal). It also sells unique wrapping paper, collectible postcards, artsy boxed notecards, specialty albums, and blank books. Parts of the shop resembles a study, set up with writing tables, leather blotters, and stylish desk lamps. Buy a blank card and ask Michael Tuck (aka Jules) to personalize it; he's known for his calligraphy and verse.

The Chocolate Sparrow (508-349-1333), Main Street. Open late June to early September. As long as anyone can remember, Wellfleet has had a penny-candy store. The Chocolate Sparrow opened in 1990 to continue the tradition, and added rich, hand-dipped chocolates.

❋ Special Events

July 4: **Independence Day parade.**

Mid-October: **Oyster Festival.** A tradition since 2001 (!), this "aw shucks" weekend celebrates the famed local delicacy (and the men and women who make their livelihoods farming it) with oyster-shucking demonstrations, live music, a scholarship auction (a local event since the mid-1980s), and more. Keep it simple with food and games, or get serious with shellfish education talks and demonstrations.

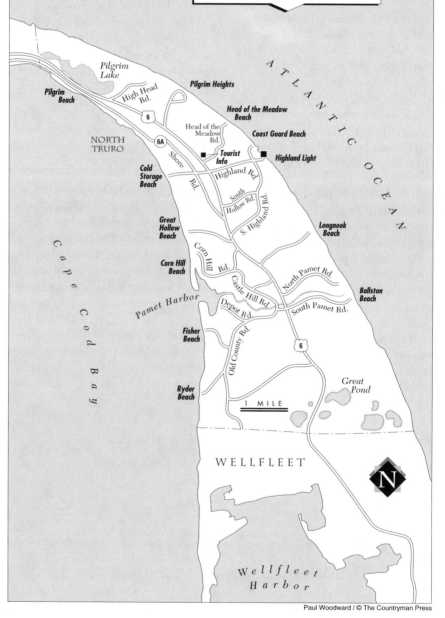

TRURO

Pilgrim Lake

Pilgrim Heights

ATLANTIC

Pilgrim Beach

High Head Rd.

6

Head of the Meadow Beach

NORTH TRURO

6A

Head of the Meadow Rd.

Coast Guard Beach

OCEAN

Shore Rd.

■ **Tourist Info**

Highland Rd.

■ *Highland Light*

Cold Storage Beach

South Hollow Rd.

S. Highland Rd.

Great Hollow Beach

Longnook Beach

Corn Hill Rd.

Corn Hill Beach

North Pamet Rd.

Ballston Beach

Cape Cod Bay

Pamet Harbor

Castle Hill Rd.

Depot Rd.

South Pamet Rd.

6

Fisher Beach

Old County Rd.

Great Pond

Ryder Beach

1 MILE

WELLFLEET

N

Wellfleet Harbor

TRURO

C onsidered to be the last vestige of "old Cape Cod," Truro has no stop-
lights, no fast-food outlets, no supermarket. It does have, though, the last working farm on the Outer Cape. Truro center consists of a tiny ramshackle strip mall
and a nearby gourmet food shop. That's it. And local folks and summer people
(vacationing writers and urban professionals who have built large houses in the
rolling hills and dunes) are determined to keep it that way.

North Truro is also tiny but has blue-collar ties to Provincetown. Compare
Dutra's Market (an institution) to Jams (a fancy food shop born in the '80s) and
the differences are readily apparent. As you head toward Provincetown, the only
real development—in a nod to the tourist industry—consists of hundreds of tiny
cottages, motels, and houses lining a narrow strip of shore wedged between
Cape Cod Bay and the dramatic parabolic dunes on Pilgrim Lake. It's an odd
juxtaposition, but one I always look forward to.

There aren't many human-made sites to explore, except for Highland Light
and the Truro Historical Museum, but there are plenty of natural ones. Almost
70 percent of Truro's 42 square miles (one of the largest towns on the Cape, in
acreage) falls within the boundaries of the Cape Cod National Seashore (CCNS).
There are hiking and biking trails as well as expanses of beach. Rolling moors
and hidden valleys characterize the tranquil back roads east and west of Route 6.
Windswept dunes, lighthouses, beach grass, and austere shorelines will inspire
you, as they did Edward Hopper. The painter built a summer home in Truro in
the 1930s and worked there until 1967.

Truro, established in 1697, has endured many name changes. Originally it was
called Payomet or Pamet, after the Native American tribe that inhabited the
area before the Pilgrims. In 1705 it was known as Dangerfield because of the
large number of offshore sailing disasters. Eventually it was named Truro, for a
Cornish coastal town in England.

Although today Truro is sleepy and rural, it has been, at times during the last
few centuries, a hotbed of activity. The *Mayflower*'s Myles Standish spent his
second night ashore in Truro. His band of 16 fellow Pilgrims found their first
fresh water in Truro, as well as a stash of corn (which belonged to the Native
Americans) from which they harvested their first crop. And although you would-
n't know it today, since Pamet Harbor choked up with sand in the mid-1850s,

Truro's harbor once rivaled neighboring Provincetown as a whaling and cod-fishing center. By the late 1700s, shipbuilding was thriving and the harbor bustling. Vessels bound for the Grand Banks were built here, and a packet boat sailed from Truro to Boston. The whaling industry also owes a debt to early Truro residents, one of whom (Ichabod Paddock) taught Nantucketers how to catch whales from shore.

In 1851 the population soared to a rousing 2,000 souls. But in 1860 the Union Company of Truro went bankrupt due to declining harbor conditions, and townspeople's fortunes and livelihoods sank with it. Commercially, Truro never rebounded. Today, the year-round population is about 1,800 (despite a recent housing boom); the summer influx raises that number tenfold.

GUIDANCE Truro Chamber of Commerce (508-487-1288), Route 6, P.O. Box 26, North Truro 02652. Open 10–4 daily, late June to early September; 10–4 Friday and Saturday, noon–4 Sunday, late May to late June and early September to mid-October.

PUBLIC REST ROOMS Stop at the Pilgrim Heights area in summer.

PUBLIC LIBRARIES ❋ ☂ ✐ **Truro Public Library** (508-487-1125), off Standish Way, north of North Truro. Open 9:30–8 Tuesday and Wednesday, 9:30–6 Thursday, 9:30–4 Friday, and 9:30–2 Saturday; a spanking new library with Internet access and programs for adults and kids.

GETTING THERE *By car:* The center of Truro is about 60 miles from the Cape Cod Canal via Route 6. Route 6A and Shore Road are synonymous.

By bus: The **Plymouth & Brockton** bus line (508-778-9767; www.p-b.com) connects Truro with Hyannis and other Cape towns, as well as with Boston's Logan Airport. The bus stops at Dutra's in North Truro and at Jams in Truro center.

GETTING AROUND *By car:* Beaches, sites, and roads are well marked off Route 6. Generally, the CCNS is east of Route 6. The Shore Road exit in North Truro takes you into North Truro and eventually to Beach Point, choked with motels as it approaches Provincetown. At its narrowist, Truro is only a mile wide, while it stretches for 10 miles north to south.

By bus: The excellent **Summer Shuttle** (508-385-8326; 800-352-7155; www.capecodtransit.org) operates daily late May to early September. The bus runs from Dutra's Market in North Truro along Route 6A and up to Provincetown, with stops in Provincetown on Bradford Street, MacMillan Wharf, the A&P grocery store, Pilgrims Park, and Herring Cove Beach. Buses run every 20 to 30 minutes 7:15 AM–12:15 AM (until 8 PM in spring and fall). Fares are $1 one way (kids 50¢ up to age 17).

MEDICAL EMERGENCY Call 911.

Cape Cod Light or **Highland Light,** CCNS, Highland Light Road, off South Highland Road, North Truro. The original lighthouse that guarded these treacherous shores was erected in 1798. It was the first on Cape Cod and had to be rebuilt in 1853, the year that a whopping 1,200 ships passed by within a 10-day period. Almost as important to landlubbers as mariners, the lighthouse provided shelter to Henry David Thoreau during one of his famous Outer Cape walks. The spot where he once stood and proclaimed that here a man could "put all America behind him" is thought to be 150 feet offshore now, thanks to erosion. One of only four working lighthouses on the Outer Cape, it was the last to become automated, in 1986. The original light shone with whale oil from 24 lamps, while later lamps were fueled with lard and kerosene. The modern light has a 110-watt halogen bulb. Visible 23 miles out to sea, it's the brightest lighthouse on the New England coast. And at 120 feet above sea level, it's aptly named Highland.

In mid-1996 the National Park Service, Coast Guard, Truro Historical Society, and the state joined forces to avert a looming disaster. Engineers cautioned that the lighthouse would crumble into the ocean. Erosion, at the rate of 3 to 4 feet per year, had chewed away the cliff upon which the lighthouse was built. (Thanks to ferocious storms in 1990, some 40 feet were lost in one year alone!) And when cliffs erode to within 100 feet of a lighthouse, it is too dangerous to bring in the heavy equipment needed to move it. So at a cost of $1.6 million, and over a period of 18 days, the 430-ton historic lighthouse and keeper's house was jacked up onto steel beams and pushed along steel tracks by hydraulic rams. At a rate of 25 feet per day, it was moved 450 feet west and 12 feet south (that is, inland), to a spot on the golf course. It should be safe for another 150 years, unless we get a lot of nor'easters.

Lighthouse tours (508-487-1121; www.trurohistorical.org), which include a short video and exhibit in the keeper's house, are offered daily May through October, 10–5:30, for $3 per person. Combination tickets ($5) include a visit to the Highland House Museum (see below). No children allowed under 51 inches. An observation deck, where the lighthouse recently stood, overlooks the ocean.

🕯 **Highland House Museum** (508-487-3397; www.trurohistorical.org), 6 Highland Light Road, North Truro. Open 10–4:30 daily, June through September. Operated expertly by the Truro Historical Society and housed in the circa-1907 Highland House, this museum is wholly dedicated to preserving Truro's maritime and agricultural past. Permanent items on display include a pirate's chest, fishing and whaling gear, 17th-century firearms, photos of Truro residents and places, toys, and ship models. Upstairs is reserved for rotating exhibits. One room is dedicated to Courtney Allen, the Truro Historical Society founder, artist, model maker, and wood carver. The building is a fine example of the fashionable, once prominent, turn-of-the-20th-century summer hotels. Adults $3, children under 12 free; combination ticket with lighthouse $5.

Truro Vineyards of Cape Cod (508-487-6200), South Hollow Vineyards, Route 6A, North Truro. Tastings noon–5 daily, late May through November;

noon–5 Friday through Sunday, April and May. Tastings $3, include four of seven wines and a souvenir wineglass. Free tours at 1, 2, and 3 PM daily. Feel free to bring lunch, buy a bottle of wine, and enjoy a picnic amid the huge antique wine casks. Look for notices of special events and festivals held on the grounds.

Jenny Lind Tower, CCNS, off Highland Light Road, North Truro. Between the Highland Golf Links and the former **North Truro Air Force Base,** this 55-foot tower of granite seems out of place. In fact, it is. The short story goes like this: In 1850, P. T. Barnum brought Swedish singing legend Jenny Lind to America. When Barnum oversold tickets to her Boston concert, and when Lind heard the crowds were going to riot, she performed a free concert from the roof tower for the people in the street. When the building was to be destroyed in 1927, a Boston attorney purchased the tower and brought it here (he owned the land at that time). The CCNS owns the property now and the entrance is blocked, but the granite tower still stands 150 feet above sea level, visible to passing ships and those of us on the ground.

Congregational church and **cemetery,** off Bridge Road, Truro. A marble memorial commemorates the terrible tragedy of the 1841 October Gale, when seven ships were destroyed and 57 crewmembers died. Renowned glassmakers of Sandwich made the church windows, and Paul Revere cast the steeple bell. Take Route 6 to Snow's Field to Meetinghouse Road to Bridge Road.

Payomet Performing Arts Center (508-487-5400), Noons Height Road, Route 6. Seasonal. That's a big name for this temporary tent structure! Nonetheless, it hosts worthy alternatives (comics, plays, and readings) to reading trashy novels. Tickets $15–20.

TRURO'S FIRST CONGREGATIONAL CHURCH AND CEMETERY

Kim Grant

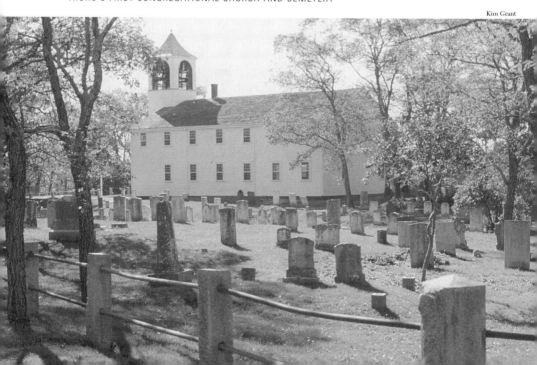

Truro Center for the Arts at Castle Hill (see the sidebar "Artistic Outlets During Vacation").

SCENIC DRIVES It's difficult to find an unpicturesque Truro road. Both North and South Pamet Roads, connected prior to a breach at Ballston Beach, wind past bayberry, beach plums, and groves of locust trees. From Truro center, Castle Road to Corn Hill Beach is lovely. In North Truro, take Priest Road to Bay View Road to the bayside Cold Storage Beach for great bay views.

✸ Outdoor Activities

BICYCLING/RENTALS **High Head Road,** CCNS, off Route 6, North Truro. Just south of Pilgrim Lake, this 4-mile bikeway runs from High Head Road, past salt marshes and dunes, to Head of the Meadow Beach (see *Green Space—Beaches*). Four-wheel-drive vehicles with proper stickers can enter the dunes here, too.

Bayside Bikes (508-487-5735), 102 Shore Road (Route 6A), North Truro, rents and repairs cycles; free parking and easy access to Head of the Meadow bike trail, Provincetown, and three of Truro's bayside beaches.

BOATING **Pamet Harbor,** off Depot Road, Truro. If you have your own boat, contact the harbormaster (508-349-2555) for launching information.

FISHING/SHELLFISHING Permits for freshwater fishing and shellfishing are available from Town Hall (508-349-3635), off Bridge Road from Route 6, Truro. Kids love fishing from the grassy shores off **Pond Road** (which leads to Cold **Storage Beach**); it's tranquil for picnicking and watching the sun set, too. Surf-fishing is good all along the Atlantic coastline. For freshwater fishing, try **Great Pond,** off Savage Road from Route 6 in southern Truro.

GOLF ❊ **Highland Golf Links** (508-487-9201), Highland Light Road, off South Highland Road, North Truro. Open 7–5 year-round (6 AM–7 PM mid-May to mid-September). Perched on a high windswept bluff, the Cape's oldest course (founded in 1892) is one of the country's oldest, too. At the turn of the 20th century, the course was part of the Highland House resort (now a museum; see *To See and Do*), which drew Boston visitors by train. Today the museum sits between the eighth and ninth holes. The course exemplifies the Scottish tradition, with deep natural roughs, Scotch broom, heath, unirrigated open fairways, occasional fog, and spectacular ocean views. That's why golfers come to this nine-hole, par-35 course. That, and dime-sized greens, whale sightings from the sixth tee in summer, and the view of Highland Light adjacent to the seventh hole. Avoid the crowds by playing on Sunday. It's the only public course between Orleans and Provincetown. $24 for nine holes, regardless of age; annual passes $500; clubs $10; power ($12) and hand ($2) carts.

TENNIS Pamet Harbor Yacht & Tennis Club (508-349-3772), 7 Yacht Club Road, on the harbor. When not reserved for club members, these three courts are available for rental to the public.

❊ Green Space

BEACHES Town parking stickers are required from July through August. Weekly cottage renters may purchase parking stickers ($20 weekly) at the Beach Program Office (508-349-3635) behind the Truro center post office.

Head of the Meadow Beach, on the Atlantic Ocean. Half the beach is maintained by the town, half by the CCNS; both have lifeguards. The only difference is that the latter half has changing rooms and rest rooms; otherwise it's the same wide, dune-backed beach. Parking $10 in-season.

Corn Hill Beach, off Corn Hill Road, on Cape Cod Bay. This is the only other town-managed beach where nonresidents can pay a daily parking fee ($10). Facilities include portable toilets and a large parking area. Backed by a long, low dune. The width of Corn Hill Beach decreases measurably as the tide comes in. There's good sailboarding too.

Long Nook Beach, off Long Nook Road, on the Atlantic Ocean. Although this wonderful beach requires a town parking sticker, in the off-season anyone can park here.

Coast Guard Beach, off Highland Road, and **Ballston Beach,** off South Pamet Road; both on the Atlantic Ocean. Each is owned by the town and requires a resident sticker, but anyone can bicycle in for free. (This Coast Guard

Kim Grant

CORN HILL COTTAGES OVERLOOKING CAPE COD BAY

Beach is not to be confused with Henry Beston's Coast Guard Beach in East-ham, under the auspices of CCNS.) Lifeguard, no; portable toilets, yes. *Note:* Use caution because of the tricky undertow.

WALKS Pilgrim Heights Area, CCNS, off Route 6, North Truro. Two short walks yield open vistas of distant dunes, ocean, and salt marsh. As the name implies, the easy three-quarter-mile round-trip **Pilgrim Spring Trail** leads to the spot where the Pilgrims reportedly tasted their first New England water. One subsequently penned: "We . . . sat us downe and drunke our first New England water with as much delight as ever we drunke in all our lives." A small plaque marks the spot.

Small Swamp Trail (about the same distance) was named not for the size of the swamp or trail but rather for the farmer (Mr. Small) who grew asparagus and corn on this former 200-acre farm. By August, blueberries are ripe for the pick-ing. In spring, look for migrating hawks. There's a wooded picnic area.

Cranberry Bog Trail, North Pamet Road, Truro. You won't want to pick this tangy and sour fruit come late September, but take the lovely walk—partially over a boardwalk—around the bog. The trailhead is located at the parking lot below the youth hostel.

✴ Lodging

BED & BREAKFAST ✴ ✎ 🐾 🐾 The Moorlands Inn (508-487-0663), 11 Hughes Road, North Truro 02652.

Laid-back and welcoming, this inn is a rarity in the modern world of commercial innkeeping. You'll be selecting books from the shelves and getting ice from the kitchen before you know it. On a back road, the massive sea captain's house is a great place for family reunions, children of any age, and a game of croquet (wearing whites and drinking champagne, of course). The house has two brightly colored suites and one room — each with phone and antiques, most with TV. The third-floor aerie has its own deck. Innkeepers Skipper and Bill Evaul have filled the house with Bill's art and music (anyone up for a spur-of-the-moment jam session?). An adjacent two-story carriage house has a kitchen and private courtyard hot tub. Two adjacent cottages sleep three

and have a full kitchen, TV, and phone. An apartment, which occupies the inn's third floor, has a private entrance. Expanded continental breakfast included for inn guests. July and August $119–159 rooms, $129–149 apartment, $775–1,295 weekly carriage house, $695–775 weekly cottages. Call for off-season nightly rates.

COTTAGES AND EFFICIENCIES
✎ **Kalmar Village** (508-487-0585; 617-247-0211 in winter; www.kalmar-village.com), Route 6A, North Truro 02652. Open mid-May to mid-October. On a strip chock-full of cottage colonies, Kalmar stands out. It's particularly great for families, since Kalmar sits on 400 feet of private bay beach. The Prelacks have owned the place since 1968, and you can spot their care and attention in the details: well-tended lawns around the pool, freshly-painted chimneys atop the

IDENTICAL COTTAGES FACE WESTWARD AND LINE THE BAYSIDE OF ROUTE 6A.

Kim Grant

shingled cottages, and six new waterfront cottages. All 45 cottages are delightfully roomy inside, with modern kitchens. Other perks include daily housekeeping; each unit has its own picnic table and grill. There are also small, large, and two-room efficiencies and three motel rooms. July and August $1,140–1,425 weekly for one- and two-bedroom cottages, $1,865–2,050 for newer two-bedroom units, $720–920 weekly for efficiencies ($120–165 nightly); off-season cottages $550–1,180 weekly, $100–210 nightly; efficiencies $72.50 nightly.

✔ **East Harbour** (508-487-0505; www.eastharbour.com), 618 Route 6A (Shore Road), North Truro 02652. Open April through October. Although Truro has dozens of small cottage colonies, Sonja Soderberg's is among the best. The tidy, paneled two-bedroom beachfront cottages (some are "mere" water-view units) enjoy daily maid service and manicured lawns and gardens. In total, there are seven cottages (fully equipped), nine motel rooms (with microwaves and refrigerators), and one suite. Grills, deck chairs, and umbrellas are available. Although some guests have been coming for five generations, Sonja's kept up with the times. Late June to early September $950–1,000 weekly; $100 per additional child, $200 per additional adult; cottages rent nightly off-season, or $650–700 weekly. Motel rooms $120–135 in-season, $72–92 off-season. Make reservations in January if you can.

Day's Cottages (508-487-1062), Route 6A (Shore Road), North Truro 02652. Open May to late October. These little green-and-white cottages,

all 23 of them lined up like ducks in a row, are something of a local icon. When you see them, you know you're just about to the tip of the Cape. Although each is only a few feet from the next, people love them. Perhaps because there's nothing between them and the ocean, except for a couple of lawn chairs (albeit on a cement slab). And perhaps because they face due west, toward the setting sun. Late June to early September $920 weekly; fall $570 weekly; May $540 weekly, $80 nightly.

MOTEL **Top Mast** (508-487-1189; www.capecodtravel.com/topmast), Route 6A, North Truro 02652. Open May to mid-October. Owned by the Silva family since 1971, this nicely maintained two-story motel flanks Route 6A well before the congestion begins. Beachfront units are built right on sandy Cape Cod Bay, and each opens onto an individual balcony with lawn chairs. Poolside garden rooms rent by the night, even in high season. There are 31 rooms and two 2-bedroom apartments. Swimming pool. Mid-June to early September $900 weekly for beachfront efficiencies, $1,200 weekly for apartment for four people, $85 nightly for poolside room; spring and fall $80–85 nightly, $580 weekly.

RENTAL HOUSES AND COTTAGES **Duarte/Downey Real Estate** (508-349-7588; www.ddre.com), 12 Truro Center Road, in the center of town, is the place for house and cottage rentals.

CAMPGROUNDS 🦞 ✔ **North of Highland Camping Area** (508-487-1191; www.capecodcamping.com), Head of the Meadow Road, North

Truro 02652. Open mid-May to mid-September. On 60 acres of scrub pine forest within the CCNS, these 237 sites are suitable for tents and tent trailers only (no hook-ups, though) and are a 10-minute walk from Head of the Meadow Beach (see *Green Space—Beaches*). There are strict quiet hours. From mid-July to mid-August, reservations must begin and end on a Saturday or Sunday. $20 for two people with one car.

✿ ☃ **North Truro Camping Area** (508-487-1847; www.ntcacamping. com), Highland Road, North Truro 02652. Open mid-April through December. Within the CCNS, these 22 acres of wooded sites can accommodate 350 tents and RVs. It's less than a mile to Coast Guard Beach (see *Green Space—Beaches*), and only 7 miles to Provincetown. $20 daily for two, $27 for hookups.

HOSTEL ✿ **Hostelling International, Truro** (508-349-3889; www.usa-hostels.org; 888-901-2086 for in-season reservations), North Pamet Road, Truro 02666. Open mid-June to early September. Originally a U.S. Coast Guard station, the hostel commands a dramatic location—amid dunes, marshes, and a cranberry bog. The hostel is within the CCNS and just a 7-minute walk from Ballston Beach (see *Green Space—Beaches*). National Park Service interpreters host special programs each week; they're free to all and not to be missed. Each of 42 dormitory beds rents for $22–24 nightly to members, $25–27 to nonmembers.

✴ **Where to Eat**

EATING OUT ♿ ✿ ⚓ **Adrian's** (508-487-4360), Route 6, North Truro.

Open for breakfast and dinner daily, mid-June to early September; breakfast on weekends and dinner Thursday through Monday from mid-May to mid-June and early September to mid-October. Chef Adrian Cyr and his wife, Annette, have wooed and won a decidedly loyal and ever-growing following since they opened their first area restaurant in 1985. There are so many fine, well-priced regional Italian choices: brick-oven pizzas, *linguine alle vongale,* a generous cold insalate and mixed antipasto, and specials like cayenne-crusted salmon with grilled polenta. Sole and ginger-infused swordfish are always good. For breakfast, try huevos rancheros, specialty omelets, and cranberry pancakes. In addition to an accommodating waitstaff, the restaurant has an outdoor deck up on a bluff. Inside, candlelight and large picture windows light the well-spaced tables. Breakfast $3–8, pizzas $12–13, dinner entrées $8–23.

⚓ **Terra Luna** (508-487-1019), Route 6A, North Truro. Open for dinner, mid-May to mid-October. All in all, this is one of the Outer Cape's best values. Peaked ceilings, large canvases, shellacked wooden tables, and candlelight transform this otherwise unassuming roadside eatery with barnboard walls into a very desirable place to spend a couple of hours (except when it's really hot, since there's no air-conditioning). Chef-owner Raina Stefani (at the helm since 1990) deftly executes New American and Italian dishes like shrimp linguine with kalamata olives, spinach, capers, feta, and plum tomatoes. On my last visit, the pan-seared salmon with a rock salt crust and roasted corn salsa was simple but sublime. And the wild mushroom ragout was rich, rich, rich. I dare you to finish it. Dipping oil infused with basil accompanying hearty bread sets an early tone, and the house specialty of polenta bread pudding caps it off nicely. Dinner $17–20.

& ❀ **Village Cafe** (508-487-5800), in the center of North Truro. Open 7 AM–10 PM daily in July and August, 7–5 daily May through June and September to mid-October. This pleasant and friendly sandwich place has a big brick courtyard where you can eat your Portuguese kale soup (a specialty) or H&H bagels. The extensive blackboard menu features hearty and creative sandwich combinations, pastries, espresso, desserts, and ice cream, too. Lunch $5–9. No credit cards.

❊ ✿ **Montano's** (508-487-2026), Route 6, North Truro. Open nightly. This family restaurant serves dependable Italian favorites like seafood fra diavolo and steak umbriago, with unlimited refills on the garden salads, and early specials (4:30–6) for about $11–14. Montano's gets big points in my book for serving hungry Explorers in the dead of winter. Entrées $10–24.

SEAFOOD MARKETS **Pamet Seafood** (508-349-7044), 14 Truro Center Road, behind the post office in Truro center; **Nana Molly's** (508-487-2164), on Route 6 next to the Hillside Farm Stand. Both open mid-May to mid-October. Fish, steamed lobsters, and clambakes-to-go.

SNACKS AND COFFEE ✿ **Jams** (508-349-1616), off Route 6 in Truro center. Open 7:30 AM–"closing" daily, late May to early September. Jams caters to those attached to their *New York Times*, tonic water, truffles, pesto pizzas, and fine art notecards (by yours truly). Coffee aficionados take note: Jams serves rich espresso and lattes. Basic groceries share the stage with sun-dried tomatoes, rotisserie-roasted chicken, and Port Salut cheese. For those of you who don't live nearby, carry your picnic fixings to the small field across the street, perfect for bicyclists and the car-weary. Jams also makes PB&J and bologna sandwiches for the kids. Sandwiches $5–8; salads by the pound.

Highland Creamery (508-487-3435), 316 Route 6. Open seasonally. Explorers (and readers) Dan and Judie Dunham consider the Creamery to have the Cape's best ice cream. As they say, it sure makes a good evening stop on the way out of Provincetown. I couldn't agree more.

❊ Selective Shopping

Susan Baker Memorial Museum (508-487-2557), Route 6A, Truro. Open late May to early September and by appointment. One of the most irreverent painters on the Cape, Baker is a humorist at heart. She has a great body of work exploring the history of Provincetown and a more recent one from Italy.

❊ **Atlantic Spice Co.** (508-487-6100), Route 6 at 6A, North Truro. Open daily except Sunday. Culinary herbs and spices, botanicals, make-your-own potpourri, teas, spice blends, nuts, and seeds. They're here, they're fresh, and they're in a cavernous warehouse. Although this is primarily a wholesaler, you can purchase small quantities (less than the usual 1-pound increments) of most products. At the very least, pick up the mail-order form.

Whitman House Quilt Shop (508-487-3204), Route 6, North Truro. Open mid-May to mid-October, daily in summer and weekends off-season. This former schoolhouse is packed with Amish quilts.

Trifles and Treasures (508-349-9509), Truro center. Open May to mid-October. A little bit of art, a few quilts, some pine furniture, and a few collectibles.

✳ Special Events

Mid-September: **Truro Treasures.** Since 1992, this folksy 2-day weekend has featured a craft fair, parade, beach bash, road race, pancake breakfast, and parade. The highlight, attended by more than 300 townsfolk, is the dump dance—held at the recycling center (aka the town dump).

Provincetown

PROVINCETOWN

ATLANTIC OCEAN

Race Point Beach

■ Race Point Lighthouse

Hatches Harbor

Herring Cove Beach

✈ Provincetown Municipal Airport

Province Lands Rd.

Race Point Rd.

■ Lifesaving Museum
■ Province Lands Visitor Center

■ Dune Shacks

Conwell St.

6A

6

Snail Rd.

Enlarged Area

Bradford St.

Commercial St.

Shank Painter Rd.

6A

Provincetown Harbor

■ Breakwater

■ Long Point Lighthouse

Cape Cod Bay

1 MILE

N

Paul Woodward / © The Countryman Press

1/4 MILE

West End

6

6A

6A

Bradford St.

Atwood St.
W.
Vine St.
Tremont St.
Franklin St.
Conant St.
Central St.
Court St.
Shank Painter Rd.

Commercial St.

Commercial St.

Masonic Pl.
Gosnold St.
Ryder St.
Alden St.
Standish St.
Winslow St.
Center St.
Arch St.
Pearl St.
Dyer St.
Lovetts Ct.
Kiley Ct.
Bangs St.
Cook St.
Daggett Ln.
Howland St.

■ Pilgrim Monument

Harry Kemp Way

Conwell St.

6

East End

Snail Rd.

Bradford St.

Commercial St.

Kendall St.
Allerton St.

6A

Town Hall ■

Info. Booth

MacMillan Wharf

Freeman St.

Art Assoc. & Museum ■

N

PROVINCETOWN

As you cross into Provincetown, where high dunes drift onto Route 6, you begin to sense that this is a different place. This outpost on the tip of the Cape, where glaciers deposited their last grains of sand, attracts a varied population. Whether seeking solitude or freedom of expression in the company of like-minded souls, visitors relish Provincetown's fringe status. P-town, as it's often referred to by nonlocals but not by locals, is perhaps best known as a community of tolerant individuals. Gay men and lesbians, artists, Portuguese fishermen, and families all call it home and welcome those who are equally tolerant.

Visitors parade up and down Commercial Street, the main drag, ducking in and out of hundreds of shops and galleries. The town has a carnival-like atmosphere, especially in July and August, testing the limits of acceptability. As you might imagine, people-watching is a prime activity. On any given Saturday, the cast of characters might include cross-dressers, leather-clad motorcyclists, barely clad in-line skaters, children eating saltwater taffy, and tourists from "Anytown, USA," who can't quite figure out what they've stumbled into.

Provincetown's history began long before the *Mayflower* arrived. It's said that Leif Eriksson's brother, Thorvald, stopped here in 1004 to repair the keel of his boat. Wampanoag Indians fished and summered here—the tiny strip of land was too vulnerable to sustain a year-round settlement. In 1620 the Pilgrims first set foot on American soil in Provincetown, anchoring in the harbor for five weeks, making forays down-Cape in search of an agreeable spot to settle. By the late 1600s and early 1700s, only 200 fishermen lived here.

But from the mid–18th to the mid–19th century, Provincetown was a bustling whaling community and seaport. After the industry peaked, Portuguese sailors from the Azores and Cape Verde Islands, who had signed on with whaling and fishing ships, settled here to fish the local waters. The Old Colony Railroad was extended to Provincetown in 1873, transporting iced fish to New York and Boston. Upwards of four trains a day departed from the two-room station, located where Duarte Motors parking lot is today, two blocks from MacMillan Wharf. But by the early 1900s, Provincetown's sea-driven economy had slowed. Trains stopped running in 1950. Today, although a small fishing industry still exists, tourism is the steam that drives the economy's train.

In 1899 painter Charles W. Hawthorne founded the Cape Cod School of Art.

He encouraged his Greenwich Village peers to come north and take advantage of the Mediterranean-like light. By 1916 there were six art schools in town. By the 1920s, Provincetown had become as distinguished an art colony as Taos, East Hampton, and Carmel. Hawthorne encouraged his students to flee the studio and set up easels on the beach, incorporating the ever-changing light into their work. By the time Hawthorne died in 1930, the art scene had a life of its own, and it continues to thrive today.

Artistic expression in Provincetown wasn't limited to painting, though. In 1915 the Provincetown Players, a group of playwrights and actors, staged their works in a small waterfront fish house. In their second season they premiered Eugene O'Neill's *Bound East for Cardiff* before moving to New York, where they are still based.

Provincetown's natural beauty isn't overshadowed by its colorful population. Province Lands, the name given to the Cape Cod National Seashore (CCNS) within Provincetown's borders, offers bike trails and three remote beaches, where, if you walk far enough, you can find real isolation. Most summertime visitors venture onto the water—to whale-watch or sail and sailboard in the protected harbor. A different perspective comes with a dune or aerial tour.

Provincetown is a delight in late spring and fall, when upwards of 40,000 summer visitors return home. Commercial Street is navigable once again, and most shops and restaurants remain open. Tiny gardens bloom profusely, well into October. From January to March, though, the town is given back to the almost 3,000 hardy year-rounders—almost half of whom are unemployed during this time. Although about 80 percent of the businesses close during January and February, there are still enough guesthouses (and a handful of restaurants, especially on the weekends) open all winter, luring intrepid visitors with great prices and stark natural beauty. Steel yourself against the wind and take a walk on the beach, attend a reading at the Fine Arts Work Center, or curl up with a good book.

GUIDANCE ❈ **Provincetown Chamber of Commerce** (508-487-3424; www.ptownchamber.com), 307 Commercial Street at MacMillan Wharf, P.O. Box 1017, Provincetown 02657. Open 10–5 daily mid-May to mid-October; 10–4 off-season, when it's closed Wednesday and Sunday. I've always found this chamber to be the most informative and helpful on the Cape.

❈ **Provincetown Business Guild** (508-487-2313; 800-637-8696; www. ptown.org), 3 Freeman Street #2, Provincetown 02657. The guild, established in 1978 to support gay tourism, promotes about 275 gay-owned businesses.

❈ Women travellers: check out www.GirlPowerEvents.com; www.Provincetown-ForWomen.com; and www.womeninnkeepers.com.

🐾 ✒ ♿ **Province Lands Visitor Center** (508-487-1256; www.nps.gov/caco), Race Point Road, Cape Cod National Seashore (CCNS). Open daily 9–5, early May to late October. First things first: Climb atop the observation deck for a 360-degree view of the outermost dunes and ocean. The center offers informative exhibits on Cape history, local flora and fauna, and dune ecology, along with frequent short films. Organized summer activities include sunset campfires and storytelling, birding trips, dune tours, and a junior ranger hour for children age 8–12.

MEDIA Pick up the ***Provincetown Banner*** (508-487-7400) to get a sense of the town's local, juicy, and fascinating politics.

Tune in to 92.1 FM (508-487-2619), the homegrown radio station.

PUBLIC REST ROOMS Public rest rooms are located behind the chamber of commerce at the MacMillan Wharf parking lot (open daily in-season and Friday through Sunday off-season) and in the Provincetown Town Hall at 260 Commercial Street (open weekdays year-round).

PUBLIC LIBRARY ❄ ✎ ✝ **Provincetown Public Library** (508-487-7094; www.ptownlib.com), 330 Commercial Street (at Freeman Street). Open Monday 10–5, Tuesday and Thursday noon–8, Wednesday 10–8, Friday 10–5, Saturday 10–2; Sunday (off-season only) 1–5. Internet access for a requested minimal donation. The library is moving to the old Heritage Museum location at Commercial and Center Streets, but I bet this takes a while.

INTERNET ACCESS **Cyber Cove** (508-487-7778), 237 Commercial Street, second floor. Blazing-fast Internet and e-mail services. (See also Public Library.)

GETTING THERE *By car:* Provincetown is the eastern terminus of Cape Cod, 63 miles via Route 6 from the Cape Cod Canal and 128 miles from Boston and Providence. It takes almost 2½ hours to drive from Boston.

By boat from Boston: **Bay State Cruise Company, Inc.** (508-487-9284 seasonally on MacMillan Wharf; 617-748-1428 on Boston's Commonwealth Pier, Northern Avenue; www.baystatecruisecompany.com). There are two boats, a fast one and a slow one. The **Provincetown Express** takes 90 minutes and operates three times daily from late May to mid-October. You could conceivably take the first boat to Provincetown in the morning, have 6 hours in town and at the beach, and be back in Boston by around 8:30 PM. The fare is the same for adults and kids: $49 return ($28 one way). Bike fare is $10 return.

As for the regular ferry, ***Provincetown II,*** there are weekend departures late May to late June and early September to mid-October; daily departures late June to early September. Boats leave Boston at 9 AM and return at 3:30 for the 3-hour voyage. Return tickets cost $30 adults, $21 children, $10 bicycles. The schedule doesn't permit much of a day trip to Boston from Provincetown, but you could spend the night in Boston and take the morning boat back to Provincetown.

Boston Harbor Cruises (617-227-4321; 877-733-9425; www.bostonharborcruises.com) operates one or two daily fast boats from Boston's Long Wharf to Provincetown from early May to mid-October. The 90-minute trip aboard a catamaran costs $49 adults, $35 children, $10 bikes (all prices are round trip).

By boat from Plymouth: **Cape Cod Cruises (Capt. John's Boats)** (508-747-

2400), State Pier (next to the *Mayflower*) in Plymouth and Fisherman's Wharf in Provincetown. The ferry schedule is designed so that you leave Plymouth at 10 AM, spend about 5 hours in Provincetown, and are back in Plymouth by 6 PM. You even get a narrated history of Plymouth Harbor as the boat pulls away from shore. Weekends late May to late September; daily mid-June to early September. Round trip: $28 adults; $18 children under 12; $3 bicycles. Free parking on the waterfront.

By bus: The **Plymouth & Brockton** bus line (508-778-9767; www.p-b.com) connects Provincetown with Hyannis and other Cape towns, as well as with Boston's Logan Airport. The bus stops behind the chamber of commerce. Purchase tickets on board. There are five buses a day in summer, two from early September to early May; travel time is 3½ hours and requires a bus change in Hyannis; $27 one way, $52 return.

By air: **Cape Air** (508-487-0241; 508-771-6944; 800-352-0714 reservations; www.flycapeair.com) provides extensive daily, year-round service from Boston to Provincetown Municipal Airport. The flight takes 25 minutes, and the airport is 3 miles north of town. It can be pesky getting a taxi from the airport. Summer fares $140–200 round trip; $780 for a book of 10 one-way tickets.

GETTING AROUND *By car:* The first exit off Route 6 (Snail Road) leads to the East End. (Street numbers in the East End are higher than in the West End.) Take the second exit for MacMillan Wharf and Town Hall, where street numbers are in the 300s. Shank Painter Road, the third exit, leads to the West End. Follow Route 6 to its end for Herring Cove Beach. A right off Route 6 takes you to the Province Lands section of the CCNS.

ART'S DUNE TOURS WILL GIVE YOU A DIFFERENT PERSPECTIVE OF PROVINCETOWN

Kim Grant

Provincetown's principal thoroughfare, Commercial Street, is narrow, one way, and 3 miles long. When you want to drive from one end of town to another quickly, use Bradford Street, parallel to Commercial. There are no sidewalks on Bradford, known as Back Street in the days when Provincetown had only a front and a back street. About 40 narrow cross-streets connect Commercial and Bradford.

Finding free on-street parking is a problem. Meters require feeding from 8 AM to midnight daily (with 3-hour limits), and meter maids are ruthless. There are municipal lots next to the Pilgrim Monument off Bradford Street; on MacMillan Wharf; off Commercial Street; off Bradford Street; and one at the end of Commercial Street near the Breakwater.

❧ *By bus:* The excellent **Summer Shuttle** (508-385-8326; 800-352-7155; www.capecodtransit.org) operates daily late May to mid-October. The bus runs from Herring Cove Beach to Pilgrims Park and the A&P grocery store, with a detour at MacMillan Wharf, and down Route 6A to Dutra's Market in North Truro. Flag down the bus anywhere along the route. Buses run every 20 to 30 minutes 7:15 AM–12:15 AM (until 8 PM in spring and fall). Fares are $1 one way (kids 50¢ up to age 17).

❧ *By boat:* **Flyer's Shuttle** (508-487-0898; www.flyersboats.com), 131A Commercial Street. From mid-June to early October, an hourly shuttle takes bathers and picnickers to and from remote, unspoiled Long Point (see *Green Space—Beaches*). Fare is $8 one way, $12 round trip; children under 7 free. The boat runs from about 10 to 5:30-ish, when the last pickup is made at Long Point.

Provincetown Trolley, Inc. (508-487-9483), Commercial Street at Town Hall. These 40-minute, narrated sight-seeing trips depart approximately every half hour 10–4 and hourly 5–8 (daily), May through October. You can get on and off at the Provincetown Art Association & Museum (see *To See*); the Provincetown Inn next to the breakwater (see *Green Space—Walks*), at the western end of Commercial Street; and the Province Lands Visitor Center (see *Guidance*). Adults $9, children 12 and under $5.

MEDICAL EMERGENCY **Outer Cape Health Services** (508-487-9395), Harry Kemp Way. Open year-round by appointment. Call for summer walk-in clinic hours.

Lyme disease. Ticks carry this disease, which has flu-like symptoms and

EXPLORING THE DUNES
Art's Dune Tours (508-487-1950; www.artsdunetours.com), at Commercial and Standish Streets, offers daily trips mid-April to mid-November. The Costa family has expertly led tourists on these narrated, hour-long trips through the CCNS dunes since 1946. I highly recommend taking one. The GMC Suburbans stop at least once (on the beach or atop a high dune) for photos, so you can take in the panoramic views. Trips $12–16 per person. Reservations are necessary for sunset trips. Ask about sunset clambakes and sunrise trips, too.

may result in death if left untreated. Immediately and carefully remove any ticks that may have migrated from dune grasses to your body. Better yet, wear long pants, tuck pants into socks, and wear long-sleeved shirts whenever possible when hiking. Avoid hiking in grassy and overgrown areas of dense brush.

✳ To See

Listings are from east to west.

Commercial Street. Until Commercial Street was laid out in 1835, the shore-line served as the town's main thoroughfare. Because houses had been oriented toward the harbor, many had to be turned around or the "front" door had to be reconstructed to face the new street. Some houses, however, still remain oriented toward the shore.

✳ ⬙ **Provincetown Art Association & Museum** (508-487-1750; www. paam.org), 460 Commercial Street. Open noon–5 daily and 8 PM–10 PM on Friday and Saturday, late May to mid-October (plus 8 PM–10 PM daily in July and August); noon–4 or 5 on Saturday and Sunday the rest of the year. Organized in 1914 by artists to "promote education of the public in the arts, and social intercourse between artists and laymen," PAAM members have included Ambrose Webster, Milton Avery, and Marsden Hartley. One of the country's foremost small museums, its four galleries feature established and emerging artists. Selections from the permanent collection of 1,700-plus works change frequently. Special exhibitions, juried shows, and other events are sponsored throughout the year. The bookstore specializes in the local art colony. Suggested adult admission $5; children free.

MacMillan Wharf. By 1800 Provincetown was one of the country's busiest seaports; 50 years later it was second largest whaling port. By the 1880s, when cod fishing reached its peak and Provincetown boasted the Cape's largest population, MacMillan Wharf was just one of 56 wharves jutting into the harbor. (MacMillan Wharf, built in 1873, was originally called Old Colony Wharf after the railroad that met Boston packets, but was ultimately named for native son Admiral Donald MacMillan, who explored the North Pole with Admiral Robert Peary.) The town bustled with herring canning, cod curing, whaling, and fishing. Although only a few wharves are still standing, MacMillan Wharf remains true to its original purpose: Even though the fishing industry has recently suffered because of overfishing, some boats still unload their afternoon catch here. And instead of whaling ships, the wharf now is lined with whale-watching boats. The view of town from the end of the pier is expansive. And to townspeople's delight, the pier received a much-needed major overhaul in 2002 after discussions for nearly 20 years!

⬨ ⬙ **Expedition *Whydah*** (508-487-8899; www.whydah.com), 16 MacMillan Wharf. Open 10–5 daily, April to mid-October; weekends mid-October through December. This museum is devoted to chronicling the story of the *Whydah*, the only pirate ship ever salvaged. It sank 1,500 feet offshore from Wellfleet's Marconi Beach on April 26, 1717, and Cape Codder Barry Clifford discovered it in 1984. Adults $8; children 4–12, $6.

Provincetown Town Hall (www.provincetowngov.org), 260 Commercial Street. Open 8–5 daily. Constructed in 1878, the building serves as the seat of local government and community agencies. The auditorium is also used for concerts and lectures. Look for the Works Progress Administration (WPA)–era murals of farmers and fishermen by Ross Moffett and the portrait by Charles Hawthorne.

Pilgrim bas-relief, Bradford Street, behind Town Hall. Sculptor Cyrus Dalin's memorial commemorates the Mayflower Compact, which has been called the "first American act in our history." After traveling from England for almost two months, the Mayflower sat in the harbor until the compact was drawn up. No one was allowed to go ashore until he signed the document, attesting to his willingness to abide by laws. One relief memorializes the five Pilgrims who died before reaching Plymouth. (Three Pilgrims are buried near the center of town.) The other relief contains the text of the compact and the names of the 41 people who signed it.

✳ ♦ ⚲ **Pilgrim Monument** and **Provincetown Museum** (508-487-1310), High Pole Road, off Winslow Street from Bradford Street. Open 9–7 daily, July and August; 9–5 daily, April through June and September through November. Last admission is 45 minutes before closing. The 252-foot monument (the tallest all-granite U.S. monument) commemorates the Pilgrims' first landing in Provincetown on November 11, 1620, and their 5-week stay in the harbor while searching for a good place to settle. President Theodore Roosevelt laid the cornerstone in 1907, and President Taft dedicated it in 1910. Climb the 116 stairs of the monument—modeled after the Torre del Mangia in Siena, Italy—for a panoramic view of the Outer Cape. On a clear day you can see 42 miles to Boston.

One wing of the museum is devoted to early Pilgrim travails: the *Mayflower's* first landing, finding corn and fresh water, the unsuccessful search for a place to settle. The other wing contains dioramas and changing exhibits dedicated to a whaling captain's life ashore, the birth of modern theater, shipwrecks, dolls and toys, the Lower and Outer Cape, and local art. Free parking for the first 2 hours; then they start charging you. Beware: Your car will be towed if you linger or park illegally. Adults $6; children 4–12, $3.

✳ **Universalist Meetinghouse** (508-487-9344; www.oumh.org), 236 Commercial Street. Generally open 9–1 Sunday through Thursday. This 1847 Greek Revival church contains trompe l'oeil murals (by Carl Wendt, who painted similar murals for Nantucket's Unitarian Universalist Church), a Sandwich glass chandelier, and pews made with Provincetown pine. The pews are decorated with medallions carved from whales' teeth.

Pilgrim plaque, at the western end of Commercial Street. Provincetown's version of Plymouth's Rock—a plaque in the middle of a landscaped traffic circle—commemorates the Pilgrims' landing.

On the outskirts of town
Old Harbor Lifesaving Station (508-487-1256), Race Point Beach. It's best to call for hours. This 1872 structure, one of nine original Lifesaving Service stations on the Outer Cape, was floated by barge from Chatham to its present

location in 1977. The Lifesaving Service, precursor to the Coast Guard, rescued crews from ships wrecked by shallow sandbars and brutal nor'easters. The boat room contains the original equipment, but on Thursday at 6 PM (confirm the time before going), hour-long demonstrations are given using the old-fashioned techniques. "Surfmen" launch a rescue line to the wrecked ship and haul in the distressed sailors one at a time. Plaques lining the boardwalk to the museum explain how the service worked. Suggested donation $3 adults, $1 kids 16 and under. But you'll have to pay an additional $10 to park at Race Point Beach.

Dune shacks, beyond the end of Snail Road. In the dunes between Race Point and High Head in North Truro, along 2 miles of ridges and valleys, stand about 17 weather-beaten dune shacks. Constructed between 1935 and 1950 of driftwood and scavenged materials, the shacks are the subject of local legend. Over the years, notable writers and artists have called them home for weeks, months, even years: Among the tenants have been Jack Kerouac, e. e. cummings, Norman Mailer, Jackson Pollock, poet Harry Kemp, and Eugene O'Neill.

When the CCNS was created in 1961, the federal government set up 25-year or lifelong leases with squatters who were living in the shacks. (Only one of the

HARRY KEMP'S DUNE SHACK AT CAPE COD NATIONAL SEASHORE

Kim Grant

inhabitants held a clear title to the land.) Some shacks are still occupied. In 1985, Joyce Johnson, a dune dweller since the early 1970s, founded the Peaked Hill Trust to oversee some of the shacks. Members of the trust can win stays through a lottery system; write to P.O. Box 1705, Provincetown 02657, for membership information. Since Province Lands was added to the National Register of Historic Places in 1989, the maintenance and fate of most of the historic shacks have fallen to the National Park Service. At this point, policies are decided from season to season. The park service still sets aside a few shacks, though, for an artist-in-residence program.

During the summer of 2000, I won a weeklong stay in one of two shacks owned by Hazel Hawthorne Werner. It took until the fifth day to shake the first thought that came to my mind after returning to the shack from a walk: I wonder who called while I was out? Remarkable. Remarkable that the shack felt so much like home and remarkable that it was such a deeply ingrained response to being away. I wrote many other impressions but didn't produce anything approaching Cynthia Huntington's *The Salt House*, which she wrote over many, many months of living in that shack. It's well worth reading.

There are a few off-road parking spots at the end of Snail Road. Take the short woodland trail and hike up the first steep dune, then over the next two crests; the shacks will appear in the distance. You can also reach the shacks by walking east from Race Point Beach. Remember, however, that most shacks are still occupied, and people live out there for privacy, to pursue the creative process uninhibited, to contemplate in isolation.

SCENIC DRIVES You simply must drive out Race Point Road from Route 6 and around Province Lands.

✳ Outdoor Activities

AIRPLANE RIDES ✿ **Willie Air Tours** (508-487-0240; 800-443-3226), Provincetown Municipal Airport, Race Point Road, offers rides late May to early October. Gwen Bloomingdale and Barbara Gard offer 15-minute trips in a 1930 Stinson Detroiter that help you grasp how narrow and vulnerable this strip of land is. A flight costs about $60 for one person, $105 for a group of three. Purchase tickets at the airport.

BICYCLING/RENTALS Province Lands. Eight miles of hilly paved trails—around ponds, cranberry bogs, and sand dunes—wind through Province Lands' 4,000 acres. Spur trails lead to Herring Cove and Race Point Beaches (see *Green Space—Beaches*). Access is from Race Point Road near Route 6. There are parking areas at the Beech Forest Trailhead (see *Green Space—Walks*), Province Lands Visitor Center (see *Guidance*), and Race Point and Herring Cove Beaches.

Rentals. Shops are open April through October. Bike rentals cost about $3–4 hourly, $14–19 daily, $60–70 weekly, depending on what kind of bike you get. **Arnold's** (508-487-0844), 329 Commercial Street, since 1937, enjoys a prime location right in the middle of town. They have beach umbrellas and chairs to rent, too. **Galeforce Beach Market** (508-487-4849), 144 Bradford Street Extension, is on the western edge of town with free parking. **Nelson's Bike Shop** (508-487-8849), 43 Race Point Road, is located about 100 yards from the bike trails, with free parking.

BOAT EXCURSIONS/RENTALS ✑ *Viking* **Princess Cruises** (508-487-7323), MacMillan Wharf. Mid-May through October. The *Viking* offers a number of trips, including a sunset tour for $15 per person. Harbor tours (adults $10, children $6) head around one of the world's largest deepwater ports. Critter tours (adults $14, children $9) are fun, hands-on educational trips. Nature tours (adults $18, children $13) are given in conjunction with the Cape Cod Museum of Natural History (see "Brewster").

Bay Lady II (508-487-9308) and Schooner ***Hindu*** (508-487-3000), both on MacMillan Wharf. Mid-May to mid-October. These 2-hour harbor sails into Cape Cod Bay are aboard traditionally gaff-rigged schooners. Four trips daily in-season (two off-season), including a sunset trip. Adults $10–16; children under 12, $7.

Flyer's Boat Rentals (508-487-0898; www.flyerboats.com), 131A Commercial Street. Daily 8–5, May through October. Since 1965 Flyer's has been renting boats to suit your needs: Sunfish, sloop, kayak, powerboat. Sailboats cost $16–25 hourly, $50–100 daily; single kayaks cost $25 for 4 hours, $40 daily. Flyer's also offers early-bird fishing specials: For 4 hours (8 AM–noon), you can get a boat, bait, and two lines for $55. Two-hour sailing instruction (by reservation only) is also offered for $60 per person; the price for additional people is negotiable.

FISHING Surf-casting is great on Race Point Beach in the early morning or after sunset. Nonresidents are not permitted to shellfish.

EARLY-MORNING SURF-CASTING AT RACE POINT

Kim Grant

WHALE-WATCHING

Located just 8 miles from Provincetown, the fertile feeding grounds of **Stellwagen Bank** attract migrating finback and humpback whales. Although the area was designated the country's first **National Marine Sanctuary** in 1992, the government's attempts to control the ocean's intricate ecosystem don't always work out as planned. For instance, whales feed on sand lance, which thrive when herring populations are small. (Herring eat sand lance larvae.) But since the government began protecting dwindling stocks of herring, the number of sand lance larvae has decreased. Some naturalists theorize that humpbacks are heading elsewhere in search of more abundant food supplies. Whale sightings vary each season. Some summers, sightings are a dime a dozen; other times, not. Although whale-watching outfits guarantee sightings (in the form of a free voucher for another trip), you may not have another afternoon to spare. Don't wait, as Doug and Lucyna Robertson did, until the last day of your trip. As they said, "d'oh!"

Most whale-watch cruises last about 3½ hours and have an onboard naturalist. Bring a sweater (even in summer), and seasickness pills if you think you'll need them. Also, check the chamber of commerce brochure rack (see *Guidance*) or with your lodging for money-saving coupons.

Dolphin Fleet Whale Watch (508-349-1900; 800-826-9300), MacMillan Wharf. Mid-April through October. Scientists aboard the Dolphin Fleet, the best outfit in town, hail from the Center for Coastal Studies. Adults $20–22; children 7–12, $19; children under 6, free.

Portuguese Princess **Whale Watch** (508-487-2651; 800-442-3188), MacMillan Wharf. May to mid-October. Early-morning trips are a bit less expensive. Park at their lot on Shank Painter ($10 in summer, free off-season) and then walk 20 minutes into town.

Cee Jay (508-487-4330; 800-675-6724), MacMillan Wharf. From June to mid-October there are three daily departures on half-day bluefishing and fluke excursions. The third-generation crew will fillet your fish if you have a place to cook it. $30 per person.

Nelson's Bait & Tackle (508-487-0034), 43 Race Point Road. Open mid-April to mid-October. If you're not hiring a charter boat (which supplies the necessary equipment), Nelson's is the source for rod rentals, live and frozen bait, and fresh- and saltwater tackle.

See also Flyer's Boat Rentals under *Boat Excursions/Rentals.*

✔ **FOR FAMILIES Playgrounds** are located at both ends of town: at Bradford and Howland Streets (East End) and at Bradford and Nickerson Streets (West End).

HORSEBACK-RIDING INSTRUCTION ❊ **Bayberry Hollow Horse Farm** (508-487-6584), West Vine Street Extension, offers horseback-riding instruction but no trail rides.

IN-LINE SKATING Skating is off-limits on the National Seashore bike trails.

KAYAKING **Off the Coast Kayak Co.** (877-785-2925; www.offthecoastkayak.com), Whaler's Wharf. Open seasonally. These folks rent kayaks for paddling out to Long Point, in Provincetown Habor, or Pamet Harbor in Truro. They also lead tours, which might include a full-blown clambake. Four-hour rentals $25; daily $45. Tours $40–70 per person.

SAILING LESSONS See Flyer's Boat Rentals under *Boat Excursions/Rentals.*

TENNIS Town courts are located at **Motta Field** off Winslow Street.

Provincetown Tennis Club (508-487-9574), 286 Bradford Street. Open 8 AM–7 PM daily, late May to mid-October. Five clay and two hard courts are available for non-club.

Bissell's Tennis Courts (508-487-9512), Bradford Street Extension. Five clay courts and lessons are offered late May to late September.

✳ Even More Things to Do

❊ FITNESS CLUBS **Mussel Beach Health Club** (508-487-0001), 35 Bradford Street. Open daily, the club has state-of-the-art equipment, free weights, and cardiovascular equipment. Day-use fee $12; "punch card" for multiple visits (5 for $53, 10 for $85).

Provincetown Gym (508-487-2776), 81 Shank Painter Road. Open daily. Cardiovascular machines and free weights. Day-use fee $10, or six visits (which can be transferred between people) for $54. This place might be less intimidating for women.

SPECIAL PROGRAMS ❊ **Fine Arts Work Center** (508-487-9960; www.cape-codaccess.com/fineartsworkcenter), 24 Pearl Street. Open 9–5 Monday through Friday. The center was founded in 1968 by a group of writers, artists, and patrons, including Robert Motherwell, Hudson Walker, Stanley Kunitz, and Myron Stout. The intent was to provide a place for emerging artists to pursue independent work within a sympathetic community of their peers. In 1972 the center purchased Days Lumber Yard, where artists have worked in small studios since 1914. (Frank Days Jr., who had been concerned about the plight of artists, built 10 studios over his lumberyard. And Charles Hawthorne was one of the first tenants in 1914.) Writing and visual arts residencies, which include a monthly stipend and materials allowance, run October through April; the deadline for applications is February 1. Twenty candidates are chosen from a pool of about 1,000. Readings, seminars, workshops, and exhibits year-round are open to the public. There's also a summer program for creative writing and visual arts, as well as weeklong and weekend workshops in printmaking, sculpture, fiction writing, and the like.

☙ **Provincetown Museum School** (508-487-1750), 460 Commercial Street at Bangs Street. Programs early July to late August; galleries open noon–4 on weekends. Printmaking, painting, etching, monotypes, and watercolor are just some of the classes taught by notable artists at the Provincetown Art Association & Museum (PAAM). Children's classes are also offered.

Cape Cod School of Art (508-487-0101; www.capecod.net/artschool), 48 Pearl Street. Workshops June through September. This excellent program carries on Provincetown's impressionist tradition established by Charles Hawthorne in 1899, and is the first U.S. art school dedicated solely to outdoor painting, "plein air." (The CCSA was basically responsible for Provincetown developing into an art mecca.) Workshops in a variety of media, mostly held outdoors, are available for practically all ages and levels. Director Lois Griffel was a longtime student of Henry Hensche, Hawthorne's successor.

❋ **Campus Provincetown** (508-487-9666; www.campusprovincetown.org). For those who never stop learning, a consortium of cultural and scientific institutions has banded together to offer educational courses, workshops, field studies, and stage productions. Additionally, the Provincetown International Art Institute offers college-credit courses through the Cape Cod Community College. With impending state budget cuts at press time, the fate of this program was unclear.

Center for Coastal Studies (508-487-3622; www.coastalstudies.org), 105 Bradford Street. Library open to members year-round. This independent, nonprofit, membership-supported institution is dedicated to research, public education, and conservation programs for the coastal and marine environments. Among other things, researchers study endangered right whales (there are only about 300 in the world) and are working to explain the large number of whales that beach themselves between Brewster and Provincetown. They have raised important environmental questions about Boston's Outfall Pipe, which discharges treated sewage just 16 miles from Stellwagen Bank and 36 miles from Provincetown. The center is also the only East Coast organization authorized to disentangle whales trapped in fishing nets. Educational offerings include trips and lectures for Elderhostel.

❋ ☙ **Provincetown Community Center** (508-487-7097), 44 Bradford Street. In addition to a bunch of classes sponsored by the Provincetown Recreation Department and held here, the center has a weight room, karate classes for adults and children, dance, and yoga classes. Call for current schedule, offerings, and fees.

SWIMMING POOLS **Provincetown Inn** (508-487-9500), 1 Commercial Street. This outdoor, Olympic-sized pool is free and open seasonally.

See also Boatslip Beach Club under *Entertainment*.

❋ Green Space

BEACHES After you look at a map or take an airplane tour—to see the long spit of sand arching around the harbor—you won't doubt there are about 30 miles of beach within the CCNS in Provincetown.

Race Point Beach, CCNS, off Route 6. Because Race Point faces north, and, as such, it gets sun all day; it also has long breaking waves coming in off the Atlantic Ocean. Surrounded by dunes as far as the eye can see, Race Point feels as remote as it is. In spring, with binoculars, you might see whales spouting and breaching offshore. Facilities include lifeguards, showers, and rest rooms. Parking from mid-June to early September costs $10 daily (permit valid all day at any CCNS beach); entering on foot or bicycle is $3; a yearly pass is $20.

Herring Cove Beach, CCNS, at the end of Route 6. The water here is calmer and "warmer" (it's all relative, isn't it?) than at Race Point. Because the beach faces due west, lots of folks gather for spectacular sunsets. Lifeguards, showers, rest rooms, and a snack bar. Parking is the same as at Race Point (see above). Both lots fill up by 11 AM in summer; there's rarely a charge to park after 5:30 PM.

Harbor Beach is about 3.5 miles long and parallels Commercial Street. Although there is little beach at high tide, and few public access points, it's great to walk the flats at low tide.

Long Point. Long Point is easily accessible by boat in summer (see Flyer's Shuttle under *Getting Around*), although relatively few people make the effort. You'll be rewarded if you do, but don't forget to pack a picnic and plenty of water. You can walk atop the breakwater (see *Walks*), but it takes about 2 hours. **Long Point Lighthouse,** at the tip of the spit, was built in 1816, two years before a community of fishermen began to construct homes out there. By 1846

THE TRADITION OF OPEN-AIR PAINTING CLASSES BEGAN IN PROVINCETOWN AND STILL FLOURISHES HERE.

Kim Grant

there were 61 families on Long Point, all of whom returned to town during the Civil War. (Two Civil War forts were built on Long Point.) As you walk around town, notice which old houses sport a blue enamel plaque in the shape of a barge. This plaque identifies Long Point houses that were floated across the harbor on barges. (Locals call them "floaters.")

WALKS **Beech Forest Trail,** CCNS, off Race Point Road from Route 6. This sandy, 1-mile trail circles a freshwater pond before steep stairs cut through a forest of beech trees. Warblers migrating from South America pack the area from mid- to late May, but the trail is also beautiful in autumn. It's one of my all-time-favorite Cape walks.

Breakwater, at the western end of Commercial Street (at the Provincetown Inn) and Bradford Street Extension, is a mile-long jetty that serves as a footpath to the secluded Long Point beach. Even walking out partway, it's a great place to watch the tide roll in. Once you reach the beach, **Wood End Lighthouse** (1872) is to the north; **Long Point Lighthouse** is at the tip.

Hatches Harbor. From Herring Cove Beach, at the end of Route 6, walk about 10 minutes toward Race Point Light to the entrance of Hatches Harbor. There's a dike along the back of the salt marsh and tidal estuary that you can walk across.

See also Dune shacks under *To See* and Province Lands Trail under *Outdoor Activities—Bicycling/Rentals.*

✳ Lodging

If you care about where you stay, don't go to Provincetown in summer without reservations. In fact, try to reserve a condo or apartment in January for July or August. Although there are upwards of 100 places to stay, good ones fill up fast. If you must wait until the last minute, there are often vacancies midweek in July. Most places have lengthy minimum-night stays during special events and holiday weekends—again, reserve early. Rates for holiday weekends are always higher than I've reported. Since the East End tends to be quieter than the West End, I've indicated where each lodging is located, unless it's in the middle of town. All guesthouses included below welcome everyone: gay and straight. If you want to know the specific disposition of a guest-house (Is their clientele more straight than gay in summer? Are there more

men in summer than women? . . . and so on), ask the innkeepers. You won't be offending anyone. Finally, Provincetown has a limited water supply; try to conserve.

The zip code for Provincetown is 02657.

BED & BREAKFASTS/GUESTHOUSES
&. **The Brass Key** (508-487-9005; 800-842-9858; www.brasskey.com), 67 Bradford Street. Open mid-April to mid-November and holiday weekends. More like a small hotel or a luxurious private enclave—fenced in and gated—the Brass Key has catapulted Provincetown accommodations to new heights. It's elegant and sophisticated and friendly, thanks to proprietor Michael MacIntyre's expertise and his staff. All 33 rooms surrounding the enclosed pool and courtyard are completely different. A few generalizations can be made, though: Expect vaulted

PARABOLIC DUNES ON THE NATIONAL SEASHORE

Kim Grant

ceilings, working fireplaces, whirlpool baths, fancy amenities, nightly turn-down service, and antiques. Some rooms have balconies; all have access to a widow's walk and two living rooms. An expansive continental breakfast buffet is served in the country-inn-style Gatehouse. Wine and beer and cheese and crackers are offered each afternoon. Mid-June to mid-September $245–445 (5-night minimum); off-season $110-325.

🐾 ❄ **Fairbanks Inn** (508-487-0386; www.fairbanksinn.com), 90 Bradford Street. This 1770s sea captain's house, the first in town to have indoor plumbing, is a Federal-style beauty. In the 1800s it was owned by the town's wealthiest individual, David Fairbanks, who began Seamen's Bank. Today it's a restored jewel, brought up to 21st-century standards without sacrificing historical integrity. Period antiques, wood-burning fireplaces, and wide-plank floorboards comple-ment fine amenities and plush bed-ding. Although rooms in two adjacent

buildings are less historic, they are still quite desirable. In fact, there isn't a single room I'd hesitate to recom-mend. Stylish and thoughtful touches are everywhere. An expanded conti-nental breakfast is served in a wicker-filled, glassed-in porch; in the Revolutionary-era dining room; or on the quiet brick patio. Innkeeper Lynette Molnar has an expert staff (including Kay Halle) to help with this 14-room inn. $119–289 mid-June to mid-September and holidays; $65–175 off-season.

❄ **Copper Fox** (508-487-8583; www.provincetown.com/copperfox), 448 Commercial Street (East End). Innkeeper John Gagliardi worked his tail off to renovate this three-story Federal sea captain's B&B into the wonderfully relaxing hostelry that it is today. Set back from the road, the deep front lawn and covered porch offer plenty of places to relax. Inside, the sunporch and living room are a treat on inclement days. The three guest rooms and two suites have top-notch furnishings and are meticulously maintained. For longer stays, John has two apartments with kitchens and separate entrances. Expanded continental breakfast included. Mid-June to mid-September $150–189 rooms, $205 apartments; off-season $85–95 and $100, respectively.

The Red Inn (508-487-0050; 866-473-3466; www.theredinn.com), 1 Commercial Street open April through December. Soothing and sophisticated, top-rate and to-die-for, the Red Inn makes others green with envy. Not only is the waterfront location almost unequaled, but the accommodations (four rooms, two suites, and two residences) are worthy of design and comfort awards, as well. A bed of down pillows (and 600-thread -count sheets) will cradle your body as a tranquil color palette lulls your spirit. Hint: Reserve right away! This is a boutique and lifestyle hostelry, the likes of which haven't descended on Provincetown until now. Two waterfront "residences" are absolutely stunning, if you can afford them. Late June to mid-September $195–295 rooms; off-season $100–210; residences more.

❀ ✳ Inn at Cook Street (508-487-3894; 888-266-5655; www.innatcookstreet.com), 7 Cook Street (East End). Owners Paul Church and Dana Mitton operate a mixed house (gay, straight, men, women), which is just the way they like it. It's a gracious 1836 Greek Revival sea captain's house, with four rooms and two suites. They are all very tasteful and highly recommended. Pick your room based on its sleigh bed (Gable), how much sun it gets (the Hobbit Suite is very bright), or its deck access (some have a private deck). All have TV,

telephone, and air-conditioning. A hammock in the private, shady backyard is enticing, a rare amenity for Provincetown B&Bs. Continental breakfast. Mid-June to mid-September $135–175; off-season $95–130.

✳ ❀ Land's End Inn (508-487-0706; 800-276-7088; www.landsendinn.com), 22 Commercial Street (West End). Land's End has some of the best (albeit inland) ocean views in town. It's easily Provincetown's most unusual place to stay. That'll be readily apparent as you walk up the hidden path, catching glimpses of turrets and decks. (No description can really prepare you.) Now under the same ownership as the Brass Key, this place is a visual feast, chock-full of Victoriana, woodcarvings, stained glass, and Oriental rugs atop floral carpets. Built in 1904, the inn offers 16 rooms and three apartments; the tower rooms and loft suite are spectacularly situated. Most theme rooms have access to decks; some rooms sleep four. There are lots of common areas in which to relax. It's all very tranquil and attracts a very diverse clientele. Continental breakfast; on-site parking. Late June to early September $165–215 rooms, $215–495 kitchenettes and tower rooms; off-season $95–165 and $125–395, respectively.

✳ Beaconlight Guesthouse (508-487-9603; 800-696-9603; www.beaconlightguesthouse.com), 12 Winthrop Street (West End). Innkeepers Stephen Mascilo and Trevor Pinker—and their golden retrievers—have a knack for creating warm and homey surroundings. There's a palpable sense of it within the two living rooms (one with a grand piano begging to be played) and a country-style kitchen, scene of fine expanded continental breakfasts and lively conversation that extends well into the late morning. The 10 rooms are elegantly furnished and named for lighthouses; Cape Ann is particularly spacious. All have TV and VCR; some have a fireplace and separate sitting room. There are three decks (arguably the largest roof deck in town, with panoramic views), and an outdoor hot tub is on the lower deck. This is primarily a men's guesthouse. Mid-June to late September $120–265 rooms and suites; off-season $65–170.

❦ **Oxford Guesthouse** (508-487-9103; 800-456-9103; www.oxford-guesthouse.com), 8 Cottage Street (West End). Innkeepers Stephen and Trevor (of the Beaconlight, above) opened this refined English-style B&B in 1998. I particularly like their front and back decks and gardens, a great place for coffee or just hanging out. Guests will definitely appreciate the lovely living room, furnished with plump sofas and a fireplace, and might appreciate having access to an office/computer. As for the seven guest rooms (two with shared bath), they have central air-conditioning, TV and VCR, CD player, robes, and telephone. A few rooms have a gas fireplace. Specifically, Worcester has a private entrance, and the Trinity suite is a good value. An expanded continental breakfast is included, and served in an elegant but relaxed dining room. This is primarily a men's guesthouse. Mid-June through September $120–195 rooms, $210–245 suites; off-season $65–115 rooms, $145–165 suites.

❧ **Windamar House** (508-487-0599; www.provincetown.com/windamar/), 568 Commercial Street (East End). Open May through December. This circa-1840 sea captain's house has six modest rooms (two of which have private bath) and two apartments. Bette Adams, innkeeper since 1980, has filled them with antiques, local art, and coordinated fabrics and wallpapers. The small common room, where a continental breakfast is set out, has a refrigerator and TV. The most spectacular guest room overlooks the garden and grape arbor, while one large and airy apartment has cathedral ceilings and a view of the harbor. The well-manicured lawns and gardens in the backyard are an oasis. (On-site parking is, too.) Rooms: late May to mid-September $65–145, off-season $55–115. Apartments: in-season $795–895 weekly, mid-September to mid-October $695–795 weekly, off-season $95–110 nightly. No credit cards.

See also White Horse Inn under *Apartments, Cottages, & Studios*.

APARTMENTS, COTTAGES, & STUDIOS ❦ **Watermark Inn** (508-487-0165; www.watermark-inn.com), 603 Commercial Street (East End). These 10 contemporary suites are right at the water's edge. They feature triangular gable windows, skylights, modern bathrooms, spacious living areas, cable TV, and either a full kitchen or a kitchenette (two rooms have a fireplace). Sliding glass doors open onto decks, many of which are private; at high tide the water laps at the deck. A 20-minute walk from town; parking on-site. Mid-June to late September $1,150–2,350 weekly; off-season $85–170 nightly (excluding holiday weekends); discounts for some off-season stays.

❧ ❦ **White Horse Inn** (508-487-1790), 500 Commercial Street (East

End). Frank Schaefer has presided over this low-key, artsy hostelry since 1963, intent on providing clean, comfortable rooms at good prices. Six studio apartments are individually decorated with an eclectic, bohemian flair. Some are light and airy; some are dark and cozy. All defy description; even Frank has a hard time describing them to people over the phone. (On my last visit, though, he did describe one bathroom aptly as "postmodern nautical.") Suffice it to say each is a work of art in progress. Although the 12 guest rooms are basic (most with a shared bath), they are filled with local art from the last 30 years. They're a real find and are very popular with Europeans. Mid-June to early September $80–90 double ($50–80 single) rooms, $124–140 studio apartments with a 3-night minimum. Off-season $50–60 double ($40–50 single) rooms, $75–100 studios; inquire about weekly studio rates. No credit cards.

✳ ♪ **The Masthead** (508-487-0523; 800-395-5095; www.themasthead. com), 31–41 Commercial Street (West End). At the far end of the West End, about a 15-minute walk from the center of town, the Masthead offers a superb variety of well-maintained apartments, cottages, and rooms. The neatly landscaped complex, operated by the Ciluzzi family since 1959, has a boardwalk with lounge chairs and access to the 450-foot private beach below. Each cottage has a large picture window facing the water. Units, in buildings more than 100 years old, have fully equipped kitchens, low ceilings, pine paneling, and early American furnishings that are a bit dated but nonetheless charming and comfortable. Although most units can accommodate four people, one sleeps seven.

ALTHOUGH THE FISHING FLEET IS DWINDLING, BOATS STILL UNLOAD THEIR DAILY CATCH HERE.

Kim Grant

The web site has very detailed descriptions. Great for families; children under 12 stay free. Limited on-site free parking. July to mid-September $179–363 for two to four people ($86–205 rooms); off-season $95–214 ($92–130 rooms).

❄ ☃ ⚓ **Bay Shore & Chandler Houses** (508-487-9133; www.provincetown.com/bayshore), 493 Commercial Street (East End). A 15-minute walk from the center, this six-building complex boasts four beachside units clustered around landscaped grounds. (Units across the street have access to the lawn and beach.) Most of the 25 units have private deck or patio and large picture window; all have well-equipped kitchen; a few have fireplace. The traditional exteriors belie individually and newly decorated interiors. I particularly like the Chandler House units, more contemporary and bright. All of these have a fireplace and "very good" or "spectacular" views. Although this is a condo complex, managers Ann Maguire and Harriet Gordon keep standards consistent and high. They also rent two highly recommended, new units (weekly) in the West End. Mid-June to early September $1,295–1,795 weekly; off-season $85–155 nightly. Rates are for two to four people.

Capt. Jack's Wharf (508-487-1450), 73A Commercial Street (West End). Open late May to late September. On a rustic old wharf, these 16 colorfully painted bohemian apartments (condos, actually) transport you back to Provincetown's early days as an emerging art colony. Many units have whitewashed interiors, with skylights and lots of windows looking onto the harbor. Some first-floor units have narrow cracks between the planked floorboards—you can see the water beneath you! I particularly like Australia, a two-story unit with a spiral staircase and more than 1,000 square feet of space. The wharf is strewn with bistro tables, pots of flowers, and Adirondack chairs. Late June to mid-September $1,000–2,200 weekly; off-season $780–1,600 weekly, $95–230 nightly (3-night minimum). No credit cards.

See also Surfside Inn under *Motels.*

MOTELS ⚓ ✿ **Bill White's Motel** (508-487-1042; www.oncapecod. net/billwhitesmotel/), 29 Bradford Street Extension (West End). Open early May to late October. Across the street from sweeping marshes and dunes at the very end of town, this small, 12-unit, family-run motel provides arguably the best value in town. Owners Maggie and John Tinkham welcome a mixed crowd of families and couples. Rooms are simple but well maintained, and the Portuguese hospitality is warm. Rooms have one queen or two full beds and cable TV. It's 15 minutes to the beach, 20 to MacMillan Wharf; the shuttle also goes right by here. July to early September $88 for two people, $15 each additional; off-season $70 double.

✿ **Best Western Tides** (508-487-1045; 800-528-1234; www.bwprovincetown.com), 837 Commercial Street (East End). Open mid-May to mid-October. This 6-acre complex on the Provincetown-Truro line sits right on Cape Cod Bay. Most of these pleasantly upgraded motel rooms are waterfront, within a shuffle of the motel's 600-foot private beach. Ground-floor rooms open onto the beach. All rooms have a king-sized bed or two doubles and a refrigerator and coffeemaker; consider bringing or renting bikes so you can ride into town rather than drive. July and August $120–200; off-season $89–180. Children under 18 free in parent's room.

❧ **Surfside Inn** (508-487-1726; 800-421-1726; www.surfsideinn.cc), 543 Commercial Street (East End). Open mid-April through October. At four stories, this is the tallest commercial building in Provincetown. One building sits on the private harborfront beach; the other overlooks the large pool. The 87 renovated rooms have VCR, cable TV, telephone, small refrigerator, and balcony. The best accommodations are the two new apartments, which sleep four to six people and have fully equipped kitchens. On-site parking. Early July to early September $139–309; off-season $89–159; continental breakfast.

LIGHTHOUSE ❧ ✿ **Race Point Lighthouse** (508-487-9930; www.racepointlighthouse.net). Open early May to mid-October. After the Coast Guard decommissioned this light in 1972, it stood empty for more than 20 years before the nonprofit New England Lighthouse Foundation took over. Now that it's renovated, overnight stays are wonderful for families and groups. The keeper's house has three different-sized bedrooms that share 1½ baths as well as a living room. There is no electricity, but there is a propane-powered refrigerator and stove in the shared kitchen. You'll have to bring your own food. It's glorious out here—with the Atlantic Great Beach on one side and Hatches Harbor, a tidal estuary with shallow warm water, on the other.

First-time visitors tend only to come for 1 night, but those in the know come for 2 or 3. After making reservations (as early as possible), you'll arrange a meeting point so that a volunteer can drive you out to the lighthouse. $145–175 double; each additional person $25.

CAMPGROUNDS ❧ **Dune's Edge Campground** (508-487-9815; www.dunes-edge.com), off Route 6. Open May through September. One hundred wooded lots, mostly for tents, on the edge of the dunes and within earshot of the highway; $28 for two people tenting without electricity. Reservations recommended in summer and on holidays. No credit cards.

Coastal Acres Camping Court (508-487-1700; www.coastalacres.com), West Vine Street Extension. Open April through November. Wooded sites on the western edge of town; $25 for two in a tent, $37 with hook-ups.

HOSTEL **The Outermost Hostel** (508-487-4378), 28 Winslow Street. Open mid-May to mid-October. Personally, I'd rather camp in the rain than stay here. Nonetheless, for the record, this independent hostel (not affiliated with the American Youth Hostel—AYH—system) has 30 well-worn bunks in five tiny cabins, each with a bath in need of upgrading. The hostel is in a quiet area near downtown, across from a soccer field and tennis courts. $19 per person nightly.

RENTAL HOUSES AND COTTAGES **In Town Reservations** (508-487-1883; 800-677-8696; www.intownreservations.com), 4 Standish Street, represents hundreds of condos, houses, and apartments, rented on a Saturday-to-Saturday basis in-season. One-bedrooms start at $850 weekly, two-bedrooms at $2,000, and a few three-bedrooms at $3,500.

Swan Associates Real Estate (508-487-2990; www.provincetown-realty.com), 374 Commercial Street, and **Pat Shultz Real Estate** (508-487-9550; www.patshultz.com), 406 Commercial Street, have listings for weekly and longer stays in Provincetown. You might get lucky and find a two-bedroom waterfront for $1,100 weekly, but listings go up to $3,500 weekly. If you wait until June to line up a rental, you'll probably still find something, but the pickings will be slim. Call on January 2 if you can.

❀ **CANINE ACCOMMODATIONS** ❀
KC's Animal Resort (508-487-7900; www.ptownpets.com), 79 Shank Painter Road. Since so few inns and guesthouses accept pets, this kennel seemed an obvious idea to Karen and Custudio Silva Jr. in late 1998. Bring your dog on vacation with you, take her to the beach and on bike rides, drop her off overnight, and then play together again after you've had breakfast the next day. Adjacent veterinary facilities.

❋ Where to Eat

The quality of Provincetown restaurants continues to impress me. In fact, it has the greatest concentration of fine restaurants of any town on the Cape. You'll have plenty of choices to suit your budget and taste buds. Instead of listing places in order of preference (as I usually do), listings are from east to west relative to Commercial Street. The opening and closing months listed here are only a guideline. Although many places are closed certain days of the week, I generally don't mention that because it's so changeable. Better for you to call ahead than rely on information that changes so quickly. If you have your heart set on a particular place, call ahead off-season, and make reservations when you can, especially in summer.

DINING OUT ❋ ✐ ♈ **Ciro & Sal's** (508-487-6444), 4 Kiley Court at Commercial Street. Open for dinner. Opened as a coffeehouse and sandwich shop for artists in the early 1950s, this northern Italian restaurant was recently sold to longtime cook Larry Luster, who is married to Cynthia Packard (of the painting family—see *Selective Shopping*). The menu is extensive, with traditional signature dishes like veal Marsala and a nice infusion of specials like rack of veal with herbed risotto. You'll find lots of seafood, too. Upstairs, Ciro & Sal's has a nice bar, candlelight dining, and Italian opera music playing in the background. The ground-floor wine cellar is cozy, with brick and plaster walls and Chianti bottles hanging from the low rafters. Reservations recommended. Entrées $14–27.

❋ ♿ 🍴 ♈ **Mews Restaurant and Cafe** (508-487-1500), 429 Commercial Street (between Kiley and Lovetts Courts). Open for dinner nightly and Sunday brunch. When I asked our waiter what the restaurant was particularly known for, his response was immediate: "Fabulous food." After the meal it was easy to excuse his lack of humility: It's true. One of Provincetown's most sophisticated restaurants, the beachfront Mews is elegant and romantic, awash in peach tones and bleached woods. Longtime chef Laurence deFreitas offers a popular mixed seafood grill and dishes like peppercorn tuna with ginger horseradish mashed potatoes. Servers are very knowledgeable. Sauces are rich and delicious. The more casual upstairs café, with the same great water views and "American Fusion" menu, also has fancy burgers, appetizers, salads, and pasta. It's a great place for a before-dinner drink or after-dinner dessert and coffee; the Mews stocks over 120 types of vodka, the largest selection in New England. There's also entertainment in winter. Reservations recommended. Dine before sunset to better appreciate the water view. Brunch $9–15, dinner entrées $18–29.

Chester (508-487-8200), 404 Commercial Street (between Dyer and Washington Streets). Open for dinner mid-April through October. Even among the most sophisticated Cape restaurants, Chester is impressive. It made a splashy debut in 1998 and continues to reach higher and higher. The sea captain's house, with banquettes and local art, features a seasonal New American menu that changes monthly and weekly. Chester emphasizes fresh food enhanced by complex sauces. Presentation is simple and beautiful. On a recent visit, chef-owner Jay Coburn offered "soup, soup, soup," a trio of tantalizing tastes (really spoonfuls of spring). We then moved on to special cod cakes and the most sublime scallops ever harvested (paired with lobster custard). Ask for assistance pairing dishes with the intriguing, well-chosen, and moderately priced wine list. (You might want to start with their killer cosmopolitans, though.) Reservations

recommended. Entrées $19–33.

✿ ℣ **The Bistro at the Commons** (508-487-7800), 386 Commercial Street (between Law and Pearl Streets). Open for dinner April through October; for lunch daily late May to early September. Perhaps my favorite midrange eatery, The Bistro does what it does very well. This eclectic place offers wood-fired pizzas, grilled lobsters, and fancier entrées like pan-seared halibut with orange glacé and oven-roasted ravioli in a ricotta and cream walnut sauce. I particularly like the sidewalk tables (warmed by heaters late into the season), but there is a covered second-floor deck and upscale indoor dining, too. Lunch $7–15, dinner entrées $14–24.

Dancing Lobster Cafe (508-487-0900), 373 Commercial Street. Open for morning espresso (9–1) and dinner May to mid-October. Chef-owner Nils "Pepe" Berg moved to this larger location in the late 1990s and started accepting reservations. As for the food, Pepe honed his considerable skills at his family's namesake restaurant. Simple, flavorful Tuscan and Mediterranean specialties include homemade pasta with lobster fra diavolo and scallopini of veal. Entrées $16–28. Reservations recommended.

✿ **Edwige at Night** (508-487-4020), 333 Commercial Street (at Freeman Street). Open for dinner mid-May to mid-October. With sophisticated cuisine that even surpasses the lovely atmosphere, the Edwige is one of Provincetown's top places to dine. Although Edwige is a hopping breakfast place (see *Eating Out*), by night it's romantic, with subdued lighting and solicitous service. Chef Steven Frappolli's eclectic Thai and international menu—with an American flair—changes seasonally. Think fried rock shrimp cocktail served in a martini glass; Thai vegetable shrimp salad; risotto with littlenecks and fiddleheads; and Maine crabcakes. The food and presentation are fun, the staff colorful, and the salads creative. You can't go wrong here. Partner Rocco Carulli keeps the place humming. Edwige mixes a killer cosmopolitan, concocted from homemade vodkas. Entrées $18–24.

❋ ♂ & ♠ ⊻ **Napi's** (508-487-1145), 7 Freeman Street at Bradford Street. Open for lunch September through May; dinner year-round. Chef-owners Helen and Napi Van Dereck opened this unusual restaurant in 1973 and have filled it chockablock with local art, plants, stained glass, and lively objects to stir your imagination. The eclectic menu has an international flair: dishes made with Portuguese sausage (linguiça), organic salads, a large selection of vegetarian dishes, fresh fish, pasta dishes, and stir-fry. Health-conscious Napi's also accommodates no-fat and low-salt diets. A favorite of local artists, townsfolk, and the "Old Guard," Napi's is even more lively off-season. For a quick bite, you can always get cold snacks and appetizers at the bar. Reservations essential in summer. Parking on the premises; early specials. Dinner entrées $14–22.

♠ ⊻ **Front Street** (508-487-9715), 230 Commercial Street (between Gosnold and Masonic Streets). Open for dinner May through December. One of the Outer Cape's most consistent places, this bistro-style restaurant is located in the cozy brick cellar of a Victorian house. It's a convivial place, made more so by candlelight, small tables placed close together, antique booths, and local artwork. Service is provided by unobtrusive, attentive, and longtime waitstaff. Donna Aliperti, chef-owner since opening the restaurant in 1987, reigns over a kitchen creating much-lauded "Mediterranean-American fusion." The repertoire of Italian, French, and Continental dishes changes weekly, but might include rack of lamb, tea-smoked duck, and softshell crabs. Leave room for pastry (and sous-) chef Kathy Cotter's delicious finales. Front Street wins *Wine Spectator* awards for excellence. A full Italian-only menu is also served off-season. The small, popular bar is open until 1 AM. Reservations highly recommended. Entrées $13–23.

& ♠ **11 Carver** (508-487-2119), 11 Carver Street (at Bradford Street). Open for dinner April through November. For the money, this spacious bistro within the Gifford House is a good bet. Chef-owner Kelly Weiss executes an eclectic northern Italian-inspired menu: pasta with shrimp and vodka cream sauce, duck breast with green peppercorn sauce and mashed sweet potatoes, spicy tuna with watermelon relish and a coconut risotto cake. Or come for a few appetizers like grilled portobello mushrooms, steamed mussels, and crab- and lobster cakes. The menu changes seasonally. Entrées $17–25.

❋ ⊻ **Martin House** (508-487-1327), 157 Commercial Street (at Atlantic Street). Open for dinner. Year after year, after dining out oh-so-often, I can long recall my dinners here. Siblings Glen and Gary Martin preside over one of my favorite Cape restaurants, where the dining experience rises to an art form. The circa-1750 whaling captain's house is rustic colonial through and through: exposed beams, wall sconces, sloping dormers, fireplaces, low ceilings, wainscoting, and a series of small dining rooms. As for the classic New England cuisine with world influences, it's decidedly modern and complemented by well-paced service. Chef Alex Mazzocca's dishes always push the proverbial (creative) envelope. Look for innovative variations on game, Black Angus beef, roast duck, and local seafood; halibut is always popular. Oysters Claudia are particularly renowned. Life is short, save room for sublime desserts like Glen's bread pudding. In summer, meals are also served in a lovely garden. Reservations required. Gary presides over the small, convivial bar. Entrées $16–33, prix fixe $50–85.

Ⴤ ♣ **Lorraine's** (508-487-6074), 133 Commercial Street (between Pleasant and Franklin Streets). Open for dinner mid-April through October. One of my all-time favorite restaurants, this authentic Mexican hideaway serves upscale south-of-the-border dishes like carnitas enchiladas, featuring the owner's third-generation recipe for pork tenderloin with mole sauce. Vegetarians will gravitate to Estelle's Enchiladas; and for seafood with a twist, try specials like blackened sea scallops ensalada and blackened tuna soft-shell tacos. The menu tops out with paella. There is a great margarita bar (with more specialty tequilas than you can imagine) open until 12:30 AM. Entrées $15.50–25.

♣ ✑ & **Sal's Place** (508-487-1279), 99 Commercial Street (at Cottage Street). Open for dinner early May through November; long weekends in spring and fall. Reserve a waterside table on the deck covered in grapevines, and enjoy southern Italian dishes as you listen to the waves lapping at the deck pilings. There's no better to way to spend a summer evening. One of the two indoor dining rooms is classic trattoria: Chianti bottles hang from the ceilings, and red-and-white-checked cloths cover the tables. Two or three nightly specials like scampi Adriatico (grilled shrimp with squid in pesto) supplement classics like *melanzane alla parmigiana* and a 28-ounce *bistecca pizzaiola*. Service is very friendly and leisurely, portions large, and the tiramisu heavenly, thanks to longtime chef-owners Lora and Jack Papetsas (Jack has presided over the kitchen since 1964). Reservations recommended. Entrées $10–25.

The Red Inn (508-487-0050), 1 Commercial Street. Open for brunch/lunch on weekends, dinner nightly April through December. For years, locals lamented that this prime waterfront location was wasted with an unworthy restaurant. They're not sad anymore! The hottest thing for local foodies in a few years, this excellent restaurant is decked out in white linens and soothing colors. Perched on water's edge, the beautifully restored old house has sanded floors and huge picture windows, perfectly blending a contemporary aesthetic with a classic one. That about sums up the cuisine, too. The menu (executed by a former sous-chef of Julia Child) exudes finesse: herb and Dijon crusted rack of lamb, pepper-crusted filet mignon with truffle mashed potatoes, and grilled duck breast with a passion fruit maple glaze. Then there's the specialty: a big porterhouse steak! Brunch mains $7–20, dinner entrées $20–33.

EATING OUT ♠ ✳ **Fanizzi's by the Sea** (508-487-1964), 539 Commercial Street (between Hancock and Kendall Streets). Open for lunch and dinner mid-April to mid-October. If you find yourself in the East End suffering from hunger pangs and lusting for a water view, you now have a good choice. And a waterfront choice at that! Enormous portions of comfort cuisine, seafood, and Italian American dishes are served at very good prices. Try the midday fish-and-chips or burgers and the evening grilled salmon or roasted half chicken. Lunch $7–16, dinner $13–20.

♠ **Cafe Edwige** (508-487-2008), 333 Commercial Street (at Freeman Street). Open for breakfast from early May to late October. If you don't get here in the morning by 9:30 or so, expect a wait; loyal locals know a good thing when they find it. Proprietor Nancyann Meads has been here since 1974, dishing up frittatas, excellent specialty omelets (perhaps with Boursin and asparagus), fruit pancakes, homemade granola, spicy homefries, broiled flounder and eggs, and a tofu casserole. High-backed booths and small tables fill the lofty second-floor space, bright with skylights and local art. Expect strong cappuccino and a great signature poppy seed cream Danish. Dishes $5–10.

✐ **Lobster Pot** (508-487-0842), 321 Commercial Street (between Freeman and Standish Streets). Open daily for lunch and dinner April through November. This venerable waterfront institution has been under the same ownership—Joy McNulty's—since 1979. Over the years, the Lobster Pot's neon red lobster sign has been a symbol of Provincetown. Although the restaurant feels touristy and the service can be hurried, the menu features a wide selection of fresh seafood, shore dinners, and truly great clam chowder. Look for the red neon and then head down the long corridor, past the kitchens, and up the ramp. Lunch $7–13, dinner $13–19, children's dinner specials $8.

& ✳ **Post Office Café** (508-487-3892), 303 Commercial Street (between Standish and Ryder Streets). Open daily for breakfast, lunch, and dinner (closed mid-January to mid-February). This casual eatery serves sandwiches, salads, seafood platters, and lots of fried appetizers. Although the menu is a bit disappointing for a year-round establishment, the drag queens who haunt it are fun. Breakfast $4–8, dinner dishes $6–14.

♉ **Euro Cafe and Island Grill** (508-487-2505), 258 Commercial Street (between Ryder and Gosnold Streets). Open for lunch and dinner, mid-May through October. For me, the raison d'être is second-floor outdoor tables overlooking the street parade. By the looks of the bar, though, you'd be hard-pressed to believe Euro Cafe serves anything besides tropical drinks. But it does: sandwiches, light entrées, grilled and fried seafood, and a New England clambake. Lunch $7–20, dinner entrées $10–35.

♠ **Cafe Heaven** (508-487-9639), 199 Commercial Street (at Carver Street). Open for breakfast and lunch April through November; dinner June to early September. This excellent storefront eatery with high ceilings is always lively, but sometimes it just feels noisy and cramped. (Peek in and decide for yourself.) Deservedly popular for all-day breakfasts, Heaven's specialties include fluffy create-your-own omelets, sweet cornmeal scones, fluffy banana pancakes, garlicky homefries, and crunchy granola. An extensive lunchtime selection of cold salads and sandwiches reigns midday, while dinner offers create-your-own pasta dishes: Choose a pasta, maybe penne, then pair it with a sauce and add a topping like zucchini. You can expect ambitious blackboard specials, homemade desserts, and friendly service. Breakfast and lunch $5–8, dinner $10–18. No credit cards.

✱ 🐾 **Ross' Grill** (508-487-8878), 237 Commercial Street, within Whaler's Wharf. Open lunch and dinner, closed Tuesday and Wednesday during the summer. Overlooking the harbor from a second-floor vantage point, this casual American grill is a happening place, with good music, a structural steel ceiling, and an open kitchen. The menu is simple but good: arguably the best burgers in town, as well as pad Thai, jambalaya (the chef-owner is half Cajun), a raw bar, and steak *frites*. There's also an impressive list of 40 wines by the glass and a dozen international beers. Lunch $8–13, dinner entrées kept under $20.

🍷 🐾 ♿ **Bubala's By The Bay** (508-487-0773), 183 Commercial Street (at Court Street). Open for all three meals May through October. Bubala's draws crowds because of its streetside tables and indoor bayside views. Breakfast omelets are popular; lunch leans toward burgers (great) and focaccia sandwiches (messy); and dinnertime dishes include spicy fishcakes and baked Cuban cod. Piano bar. Lunch $7–12, dinner $11–23.

🐾 **Carreiro's Tip For Tops'n Restaurant** (508-487-1811), 31 Bradford Street (at Pleasant Street). Open

for all three meals, mid-March to mid-November. Owned by the Carreiros since 1967, this family-style restaurant offers good, simple food at good prices, away from the Commercial Street crowds. The name, by the way, is shorthand for "the tip of the Cape for tops in service." Breakfast specials ($5) are served until 3 PM. There are plenty of seafood and Portuguese specialties, as well as a few sandwiches ($5). Early specials ($11), dinner $10–16; parking on the premises.

TAKE-OUT 🐾 🐾 **Mojo's** (508-487-3140), Ryder Street, next to the MacMillan Wharf parking lot. Open 11–5 daily early May to mid-October. There are two important distinctions between this clam shack/fry joint and others of its type: The selection of dishes is extensive and the fried foods are light and fresh. Try almost anything and you'll not be disappointed: fried mushrooms, baskets of fried shrimp or fish, chicken tenders, subs, french fries, burgers, Mexican dishes, salads, and vegetarian sandwiches. Take your enormous portions to the beach, pier, or, if you're lucky, to one of a few outdoor tables. Dishes $3–13.

🐾 🐾 **Tofu A Go-Go!** (508-487-6237), 336 Commercial Street (at Center Street). Open for lunch April through October, and dinner mid-June to mid-September. When you're ready for some healthy food, this predominantly take-out place won't disappoint. The menu features international vegan and vegetarian dishes, great Indonesian "sauté" and traditional Japanese macrobiotic dishes. The veggie burger, which boasts 28 ingredients, comes as a sandwich by day and is dressed up with rice and veggies at dinner.

The deck above Commercial Street offers a bird's-eye view of the street scene. Lunch $7–10, dinner under $14.

⚓ ♂ ♿ **Clem & Ursie's** (508-487-2333; 508-487-2536), 85 Shank Painter Road. Open for lunch and dinner mid-April to late October. This multifaceted, postbeach hangout is dubbed the food ghetto by locals, but if you're not careful you could drop a lot of cash here. In addition to steamed lobster while you wait (to take home or to eat at outdoor picnic tables), you can have fried seafood or raw items from the raw bar. There are lots of Formica tables between the retail and take-out areas. The retail portion (with an excellent bakery—see Connie's Bakery, under *Snacks and Delis*) sells fish, homemade seafood cakes, imported cheese, homemade bread, deli sandwiches, and pastries. This very casual roadside joint is always hopping, particularly on lobster nights (Wednesday and Thursday). The hefty barbecue offerings are classic and can feed more people than you'd expect.

CAFÉS AND COFFEE **Spiritus** (508-487-2808), 190 Commercial Street (between Carver and Court Streets). Open daily 11:30 AM–2 AM, April to mid-November (from 8 AM in summer). The place to see and be seen after midnight, Spiritus is quite a scene. Most patrons come for great thin-crust pizza, munching it down slices while socializing out front. But Spiritus also has excellent coffee, espresso shakes, freshly squeezed orange juice, baked goods on summer mornings, and ice cream all day long. There are wooden booths inside for rainy days.

✳ **Joe** (508-487-6656), 148A Commercial Street (between Atlantic and Conant Streets). Consistently exceptional coffee. (There's nothing worse—well, I'm exaggerating to make a point—than finding a great cup o' joe, only to return the next day and face disappointment.) This tiny shop was so packed when it opened that one worker commented, "It was so busy I thought I was selling drugs." The beans are roasted by two women at Indigo, a small place in the tiny western Massachusetts town of Florence. There are fine pastries, too. Joe has both ends of town covered: Look for Joe in the East End at 353 Commercial Street (508-487-6868), open mid-April to late November.

♿ **Coffee Talk** (508-487-3780), 205 Commercial Street (between Carver and Masonic Streets). Open 8 AM–9 PM daily May to mid-October. This take-out coffee and pastry bar serves strong cappuccino; Seattle's Best supplies it. It also blends protein powder drinks and juice combos like Ginger Rogers—carrot, ginger, and apple. Take your coffee to the deck overlooking the harbor—preferably in the early morning when the town is still quiet.

♂ ♿ **Café Blasé** (508-487-9465), 328 Commercial Street (between Freeman and Standish Streets). Open daily 9 AM–midnight, late May to mid-September. The food is surprisingly good at this prime people-watching spot, operated by Jeff, Carl, and Kristine Hart since 1990. I can heartily recommend a few dishes: crabmeat salad (with real crabmeat) on dense French bread; smoked turkey, Swiss, and roasted red peppers with oniony potato salad; Caesar salad with grilled tuna. You'll also find inexpensive breakfasts as well as pasta dishes, burgers, and garden burgers. The biggest draw is pleasant patio dining under blue and pink umbrellas, set the café apart physically. Get a strong iced coffee (not watered down, like at some places), a streetside table, and stay for a while. Frozen drinks are popular. Dishes $10–21.

SNACKS AND DELIS Connie's Bakery (508-487-2167), 85 Shank Painter Road. Open seasonally. The magical mixture of flour, butter, and sugar (not to mention more exotic ingredients) never tasted so good. Based at Clem & Ursie's, these folks make everything from scratch. Try their challah and sourdough, cornmeal, and sesame breads. I dare you to leave Provincetown without going back for more.

Provincetown Portuguese Bakery (508-487-1803), 299 Commercial Street (between Standish and Ryder Streets). Open daily, April through October. If you haven't tried Portuguese breads and pastries, this is the place to come (short of hopping on a plane to Lisbon): *pasteis de coco*, meat pies, *pasteis de nata* (a custard tart), and *tarte de Amendoa* (almond tart). In summer the ovens are baking 24 hours a day, and the fried dough *(mallassadas)* flies out as fast as they can make it.

❊ **Adams' Pharmacy** (508-487-0069), 254 Commercial Street (at Gosnold Street). Open daily. Provincetown's oldest business in continual operation was opened in 1875 by Dr. John Crocker, who was also the first publisher of the *Advocate* newspaper. Adams' still has an old-fashioned soda fountain dispensing coffee and soda.

❊ The deli market is cornered in Provincetown. When you're in the middle of town, head to **Provincetown Cheese Market & Deli** (508-487-3032), 225 Commercial Street (at Masonic Street), purveyors of Starbucks coffee. The **Provincetown General Store** (508-487-0300), 147 Commercial Street, caters to the West End. In addition to excellent baked goods, deli sandwiches, and creative salads, they have home-cooked hot meals like mac and cheese to take away. In the East End, you'll find **Angel Foods** (508-487-6666), 467 Commercial Street. Owned by the proprietors of Cafe Heaven, this upscale deli also has gourmet cooking fixings. Too bad they couldn't make a strong cup of cappy, though, on my most recent visit. **Nelson's Market & Deli** (508-487-4335), 35 Race Point Road, can set you up with picnic fixings for your bike ride in the dunes. All are open year-round, except Nelson's.

✳ **Entertainment**

Note: Smoking is not permitted in bars or clubs.

THEATER Provincetown Repertory Theatre (508-487-0600), 260 Commercial Street. The Rep was founded in 1995 and performs to enthusiastic audiences. Catch them if you get the opportunity.

Provincetown Theatre Co./Narrowland Arts (508-487-8673), at various locations including the Schoolhouse Center and Provincetown Inn. This group, founded in 1963 to further the goals of the early-20th-century Provincetown Players, features new local playwrights and classic drama. Thanks to the David Adam Schoolman Trust, the theater company will be moving to permanent digs at 238 Bradford Street.

See also the Schoolhouse Center for Art and Design under *Selective Shopping*.

🍴 ⛵ ☀ MOVIES **New Art Cinema** (508-487-9222; www.newartcinemas. com), 214 Commercial Street. Open mid-May to mid-November. New releases are shown in two small theaters.

Whaler's Wharf (508-487-4269), 237 Commercial Street, second floor. This newer screen is also owned by New Art Cinema and may stay open year-round.

Movies at the Best Inn (508-487-1711), Route 6A at Snail Road. Year-round except January. Every night an ever-changing group of about 40 locals get together to watch a free movie and eat unlimited popcorn in the Whaler Lounge. Movies aren't first run, but they haven't made it to video yet, either.

🍸 NIGHTLIFE Provincetown's after-dark scene can get rather spicy. There's something for everyone: gay, straight, and in between. When the bars, clubs, and shows close at 1 AM, it seems like everybody ends up in front of the Provincetown Town Hall or Spiritus (see *Where to Eat—Cafés and Coffee*). It's rather extraordinary when you think about it: There can be 300 people hanging out in front of Spiritus in the middle of the night without any problems.

For a really classic, old Provincetown experience, belly up to a bar stool at the **Old Colony** or **Mayflower Café** (508-487-0121), both on Commercial Street.

☀ **Chaser's** (508-487-7200; www.chasers-bar.com), 293 Commercial Street. For karaoke head to this women's basement bar, with pool tables, darts, and a great jukebox.

In addition to some of the places below, for live music head to **Bubala's By The Bay** (see *Eating Out*) for an eclectic lineup and **Twomey's** (508-487-6500; 269 Commercial Street) for Irish music.

The Boatslip Beach Club (508-487-1669; www.boatslipresort.com), 161 Commercial Street (between Central and Atlantic Streets), which offers theme dances, is best known for its gay summertime Tea Dances (3:30–6:30 daily) on the poolside, waterfront deck. It's quite the scene for serious posing, cruising, and sweaty dancing. Open late May to mid-October. You can also rent pool chairs for $3 if you're not staying here, as long as you depart by tea time.

☀ **Atlantic House** (508-487-3821), 4 Masonic Place, more commonly referred to as the A-House, has three diverse bars: the so-called Macho Bar (a nationally known men's leather bar); the nautically decorated disco Dance Bar; and the Little Bar (more intimate, with a roaring fireplace in the off-season). No other 18th-century house sees such action. Open 365 days a year. There isn't a gay man in town who doesn't stop into the A-House in the off-season. Some credit the A-House with establishing Provincetown's "off-season" versus "closed for the season."

Pied Bar (508-487-1527; www.pied-bar.com), 193A Commercial Street (between Carver and Court Streets). Open May through October. Provincetown's waterfront women's bar hosts popular "after tea" women's tea dances beginning at 6:30. They have great DJs spinning sizzling dance music. Look for a lineup of alternative events at The Pied, which has been infused with new life recently. It's been around since 1971. There's never a cover.

Esther's (508-487-7555; www.esther-lives.com), 186 Commercial Street. Open April through December. The downstairs lobby and piano bar has live entertainment on Friday and Saturday. Otherwise look for screenings of old movies or Ab Fab nights. No cover.

Vixen Nightclub (508-487-6424), 336 Commercial Street (between Freeman and Center Streets). Open April through January. This women's bar and dance club opened in 1995 in the newly rebuilt Pilgrim House Inn; check the entertainment schedule for shows. DJs, pool tables, dancing, and house music.

❄ **Crown & Anchor** (508-487-1430; www.onlyatthecrown.com), 247 Commercial Street (between Gosnold and Masonic Streets), which suffered a devastating fire in 1998, has a new leather-and-Levi's bar, piano bar, pool tables, a disco and outdoor pool patio, popular drag shows, and cabaret acts. It draws a gay and mixed crowd. Check it out. You can't miss it: Drag queens will be strutting up and down Commercial in the late afternoon handing out flyers to their shows.

Post Office Cabaret (508-487-3892), 303 Commercial Street (between Standish and Ryder Streets). Open late May to mid-October. Although this long, narrow room has too many pew seats, it hosts big-name female impersonators like Jimmy Jones along with women comedians and singers (like Cris Williamson and Suzanne Westenhoefer). Despite the space limitations, it's a great community asset.

❄ **Governor Bradford** (508-487-9618), 312 Commercial Street (at Standish Street). To get a different but equally "real" flavor of Provincetown, stop into this townie and straight tourist tavern for a game of

PROVINCETOWN DUNES SEEM TO GO ON FOREVER.

Kim Grant

chess or backgammon or to listen to live music. From the game tables, you can watch people on the streets watching each other.

Steve's Alibi Bar & Cabaret (508-487-2890; www.stevesalibi.com), 291 Commercial Street. For drag shows where you can sneak-a-peak before committing, take a gander through the big picture windows and then head in for some libations with personality.

✳ Selective Shopping

Unlike other chapters, in which shops are arranged according to what type of merchandise they sell, they're listed here from east to west along Commercial Street. (That's because there are upwards of 300 shops on the strip.) Shops that are not on Commercial Street have been inserted in the text where you would naturally detour to them from Commercial.

Most shops are open mid-April to mid-October, although some galleries keep a shorter season (mid-June to mid-September). Many shops stay open until 11 PM in July and August, and a number of them offer sales in mid-October. Shops designated with the "off-season" icon ✳ , are usually open in winter on weekends only. Other shops that aren't "supposed" to be open year-round may open without notice in winter, depending on the weather.

Provincetown Arts (508-487-3167; www.provincetownarts.com), 650 Commercial Street, Provincetown 02567. This 150-page annual published in July is Provincetown's bible of visual arts, literature, and theater. Send $13 and they'll mail you one, or you can look for it in town.

Galleries hold Friday openings staggered between 5 PM and 10 PM, so patrons may stroll the street, catching most of the receptions. Artists are on hand to meet visitors. Most galleries change exhibits every 2 weeks.

See also Provincetown Art Association & Museum under *To See* and Fine Arts Work Center and Provincetown Museum School under *Even More Things to Do—Special Programs.*

DNA Gallery (508-487-7700), 288 Bradford Street, above the Provincetown Tennis Club. Open mid-May to mid-October. DNA's spacious gallery showcases bold work by Provincetown artists focusing on contemporary photography, and art derived from photography. DNA also holds video screenings, poetry jams, and, on Sunday evening, a reading series.

East End Gallery (508-487-4745), 491 Commercial Street. Open late May to mid-November and on sunny days in winter. Director Bunny Pearlman has an eye for art; check out what she thinks is worth checking out.

The Schoolhouse Center for Art and Design (508-487-4800), 494 Commercial Street. Located in a mid-19th-century Greek Revival schoolhouse, this new venture has rehearsal and performance space as well as two galleries. The **Driskel Gallery** features photography and fine objects; the **Silas-Kenyon Gallery** showcases contemporary art.

Berta Walker Gallery (508-487-6411), 208 Bradford Street (between Howland and Cook Streets). Open late May through October; otherwise, "often by chance and always by appointment." Walker represents Provincetown-affiliated artists of the past, present, and future. It's an excellent gallery.

William Scott Gallery (508-487-4040), 439 Commercial Street. Open May through December. This venue showcases contemporary art. The gallery represents preeminent regional artists like John Dowd and Will Klemm.

❋ **Harvey Dodd Gallery** (508-487-3329), 437 Commercial Street. Dodd has been painting and exhibiting his watercolors, pastels, and oils of Provincetown and other Cape Cod scenes since 1959. His gallery, opened in 1971, is the oldest in town.

❋ **Simie Maryles Gallery** (508-487-7878), 435 Commercial Street. Maryles's vibrant landscapes sold so well in local galleries that the artist decided to open her own shop.

❋ **Lyman-Eyer Gallery** (508-487-6300), 432 Commercial Street. An unusual array of mixed media, paintings, and photo collage.

Rice/Polak Gallery (508-487-1052), 430 Commercial Street. Open May through December. I always enjoy this gallery. Rice/Polak represents more than 100 contemporary artists working in painting, photography, assemblages, graphics, and sculpture. Biweekly exhibitions feature the work of four artists; the gallery offers art consulting, too.

Albert Merola Gallery (508-487-4424), 424 Commercial Street. Open mid-April to mid-October. You'll find very fine contemporary art here, as well as notables like Milton Avery and Michael Mazure; it's always worth dropping in.

❋ **Packard Gallery** (508-487-4690), 418 Commercial Street. Gallery director Leslie Packard showcases paintings by her sister Cynthia and her mother, Anne. In fact there are five generations of Packards who have painted in Provincetown: Anne's grandfather, Max Bohm, was an early member of the Provincetown Art Association. The gallery, by the way, is housed in a former Christian Science church, which Anne's grandmother used to attend.

❋ **Giardelli/Antonelli Studio Showroom** (508-487-3016), 417 Commercial Street. Smart and sleek women's clothing by local designers and eye-catching silver jewelry. Try not to be deterred by having to ring the buzzer for admittance.

Kudu (508-487-0546), 382 Commercial Street. Open mid-April to mid-October, weekends mid-October through December and in March. Two floors of international folk art, Oriental rugs and kilims, and tapestries and ceremonial baskets from major African tribes.

✐ ❋ **Kidstuff** (508-487-0714), 381 Commercial Street. Clothing for babies, toddlers, and preteens. The owners have another kids' shop, Littlebits (508-487-3860), at 214 Commercial Street, which is open April through December.

❋ **Turning Point** (508-487-0642), 379 Commercial Street. Chic women's clothing and subtle accessories.

Silk and Feathers (508-487-2057), 377 Commercial Street. Open April through December. Stylish women's clothing and accessories, including cool sunglasses, eyeglass frames, and watches.

❋ **Womencrafts** (508-487-2501), 376 Commercial Street. In addition to books and music, this Provincetown institution features handcrafted items made by and for women.

Wampum Etc. (508-487-0408), 371B Commercial Street. On Pepe's Wharf, this creative gold and silver jewelry is made of colorful quahog (clam) shells.

❋ **Tiffany Lamp Studio** (508-487-1101), 371 Commercial Street. Watch artisan Stephen Donnelly design, produce, and restore fanciful glass lamps.

❋ **Lasser Ceramics** (508-487-2881), 361 Commercial Street. Open seasonally. This striking stoneware (hand-painted, etched and sponged) is made in a studio in Londonderry, Vermont.

❋ **Mad Hatter** (508-487-4063), 360 Commercial Street. Don't even think of taking photos of yourself in the funny hats. If you try it, disregarding my advice and the numerous posted signs, you'll find out what I mean.

Small Pleasures (508-487-3712), 359 Commercial Street. Every shop has its niche: Here, it's antique jewelry and vintage accessories for men and women.

I Used to Be a Tree (508-487-5900), 357 Commercial Street. This "tree-mendous" little shop carries all sorts of products, gifts, and games made from wood pulp or relating somehow to gentle forest giants.

Song of Myself (508-487-5736), 349 Commercial Street. Open May through December. Brad Fowler's photographic studio is worth a visit regardless of whether you want a portrait. The walls are lined with his black-and-white work, showcasing the diversity and pride of town residents and visitors alike. In-studio portrait sitting $245, including one matted and framed print.

❋ **Shop Therapy** (508-487-9387), 346 Commercial Street. This land-

COMMERCIAL STREET IS LINED WITH DOZENS OF 20 GALLERIES.

Kim Grant

mark, psychedelic-swathed building proclaims: MONSTERS ATTACK P-TOWN. SHOP THERAPY BLAMED. Merchandise revolves around current alternative lifestyles and the retro look. It's a head shop without the dope, and it was opened in 1972 by a Vietnam vet who still owns it.

❋ **Land's End Marine Supply** (508-487-0784), 337 Commercial Street. It's amazing that this old-fashioned two-story hardware store continues to thrive; beach chairs, umbrellas, coolers, and suntan lotion.

Sunburst Leather (508-487-4624), 331 Commercial Street. Fine leather jackets, bags, wallets, and custom sandals.

❋ **Hersheldon's Leather** (508-487-9046), 317 Commercial Street. Hersh and Sheldon have a great knack for picking out just the right jacket (or briefcase) for your style and body type. I should know!

Town Camera Shop (508-487-9689), 301 Commercial Street. Overnight processing.

Bodybody Sole (508-487-9472), 315 Commercial Street. Comfortable and hip men's and women's shoes.

❋ 𝒮 **Cabot's Candy** (508-487-3550), 276 Commercial Street. The Cicero family has made its own saltwater taffy here since 1969—it's the only shop on the Lower or Outer Cape to do so. Flavors range from peanut butter to piña colada to beach plum.

𝒮 **Outer Cape Kites** (508-487-6133), Ryder Street Extension (on the beach). Open late April through October. There's no better place to fly a kite than the National Seashore dunes—no pesky telephone wires or tall trees.

❋ **Julie Heller Gallery** (508-487-2169), 2 Gosnold Street. In a little beachfront shack, Heller offers work by luminaries who established this art colony, including Milton Avery, Ross Moffett, and Charles Hawthorne.

❋ **Provincetown Bookshop** (508-487-0964), 246 Commercial Street. A good selection of children's books, Cape titles, and cookbooks; established in 1932.

Whaler's Wharf, 237 Commercial Street. After suffering a devastating fire that burned the former building to the ground, Whaler's Wharf is back and it's better than ever. This three-story open arcade is filled with artisans, shops, and a few restaurants. You're bound to find something interesting. Check out **Mema Studio & Gallery** (508-776-0712).

Pixie Dust (508-487-6600), 237 Commercial Street, at the end of Whaler's Wharf, celebrates American pop-culture kitsch. Where else will you find a *Welcome Back Kotter* lunch box or an almost life-sized Marie Osmond doll? Furniture, lamps, and vintage toys, too. Closed February.

❋ **Marine Specialties** (508-487-1730), 235 Commercial Street. One of the Cape's most unusual shops stocks an odd jumble of army-navy items in a warehouselike space: parachutes, wool blankets, candles, camel saddles, sand dollars, camping supplies, ships' salvage, and other random military surplus items. You'll undoubtedly walk out with some strange gewgaw you hadn't even thought of buying but you just couldn't pass up for the price.

𝒮 **Norma Glamp's Rubber Stamps** (508-487-1870), 212 Commercial Street. Open March through December. This shop has thousands of wacky (and not-so-wacky) rubber stamps, as well as an assortment of greeting cards and stationery supplies—on which to use your stamps.

Human Rights Campaign (HRC; 508-487-7736), 205 Commercial Street. Open April through December. For all your Human Rights Campaign T-shirt and bumper sticker needs. And if you're not a member, consider becoming one (www.hrc.org).

❊ **Century** (508-487-2332), 205 Commercial Street. Cool "gifty" stuff like martini glasses and clocks.

Don't Panic! (508-487-1280), 200 Commercial Street. Open April to late October. Hardly a run-of-the-mill T-shirt shop, this place has attitude: part shocking, part silly, but always amusing.

❊ **Impulse** (508-487-1154), 188 Commercial Street. This contemporary American crafts shop offers a large selection of kaleidoscopes, wind chimes, wood objets d'art, fragile and colorful glass creations, jewelry, and signed celebrity photos and letters.

Roots (508-487-2500), 193 Commercial Street. Beautiful accessories for the home: stained-glass lamps, kilims, handmade furniture (indoor and outdoor), antiques, ceramics, and frames.

❊ **WA** (508-487-6355), 184 Commercial Street. This Japanese-inspired oasis carries teapots, ceramics, incense, and fountains as well as offbeat specialty items such as wooden masks from Zaire and antique suitcases covered with Chinese calligraphy.

Bravo! (508-487-4700), 170 B Commercial Street. Open mid-May to mid-October. Casual and hip men's fashions.

❊ **Ruby's Fine Jewelry** (508-487-9522), 167 Commercial Street. Closed January. Co-owners Mary DeRocco and Ruby Druss's collection is an art gallery in its own right, featuring elegant and unique silver and gold designs for men and women. Particularly noteworthy are pieces that feature gorgeous Australian opals.

❊ **TJ Walton Gallery** (508-487-0170), 153 Commercial Street. Walton's large, bold canvases are a delight. She also promotes up-and-coming artists.

Tristan Gallery (508-487-3939), 148 Commercial Street. Abstract and impressionistic paintings; some photography.

Provincetown Antique Market (508-487-1115), 131 Commercial Street. Open late May through December. An engaging assortment of this and that: glass, toys, paper, books, tools, and ephemera.

✳ Special Events

Off-season, there are dozens of weekend special events geared toward single gay men, cross-dressers, lesbians, or whomever. If you want to be assured of a quieter off-season retreat, call the chamber of commerce (see *Guidance*) for an up-to-the-minute listing of events.

Early March: **Year-Rounders Festival,** Provincetown Town Hall, 260 Commercial Street. It's not what you know but whom you know at this party, which includes dinner, a talent show, and dancing.

Mid-April: **Whale-watching** begins. Seasonal shops begin to reopen. **Poetry Festival.**

Mid-May: **Cabaret Festival.**

Late May: **Memorial Day** weekend kicks off the summer season.

Early June: **A Night at the Chef's Table** (508-487-9445). An annual benefit for Provincetown's AIDS Support Group. For $77 per person, you'll get a festive, multicourse gala dinner with champagne and wine at many of the town's finest restaurants. More than 50 restaurants from Falmouth to Provincetown participate.

Mid-June: **International Film Festival** (508-487-3456; www.ptownfilm-fest.com). Special screenings, features, documentaries, international, and gay and lesbian shorts are shown at Whaler's Wharf, New Art Cimena, Schoolhouse Center for Art and Design, and Crown & Anchor. Established in 1999.

Late June: **Portuguese Festival and Blessing of the Fleet,** MacMillan Wharf. This 4-day celebration was developed to coincide with the Blessing of the Fleet (when the bishop blesses a parade of fishing boats decked out with flags and families aboard). The festival begins on the Thursday before the last Sunday of the month. Festivities include a swing-band concert, kids' fishing derby, Portuguese menus at various restaurants, a food court and bazaar on Fisherman's Wharf, parade, and competitions like lobster-pot pulls and codfish relays.

July 4: **Independence Day.** A spirited parade organized for and by the entire town and a spectacular fireworks display.

Mid-July: **Secret Garden Tour** (508-487-1750). An annual benefit for the Provincetown Art Association; quite popular.

Mid-August: **Family Week.** At this popular event, the definition of *family* is expanded to include Heather and her two mommies as well as daddy-and-poppy nuclear families.

Mid- to late August: **Fine Arts Work Center Annual Benefit Auction** (508-487-9960). A benefit for the nationally recognized fellowship program for artists and writers (see *Even More Things to Do—Special Programs*); since 1969. This is a big Art-with-a-capital-A event.

Carnival Week (508-487-2313; 800-637-8696). A weeklong gala sponsored by the Provincetown Business Guild (see *Guidance*), capped by a New Orleans Mardi Gras–style parade that's very gay and very flashy.

Early September: **AIDS Support Group's Annual Silent Auction** (508-487-9445), at Town Hall. It seems as if every artist in Provincetown donates work to this auction.

Mid-September: **Harbor Swim for Life** (508-487-3684; www.swim4life.org). A swim from Long Point to the Boatslip Beach Club to raise money for AIDS research. A "paddlers flotilla" carries close to 500 swimmers across the bay so they can swim the 1.75 miles back to town. After the swim, the Crown & Anchor holds a "Mermaid Brunch," open to the public for $5 per person. The **Festival of Happiness,** which follows it, takes place on Herring Cove Beach. In 2002, the event raised over $1 million.

The Great Provincetown Schooner Regatta (www.province-townschoonerrace.com). Two classes of sailing vessels parade along the waterfront (west to east) and then race.

Late September–early October: **Fall Arts Festival.** A 10-day gala (since the late 1980s) featuring gallery openings with artists and craftspeople, demonstrations, and open studios. Also, an ever-growing **consignment auction** of early Provincetown artists sponsored by the Provincetown Art Association & Museum (508-487-1750).

Mid-October: **Women's Week.** Reinvigorated in 2002 with gatherings geared toward women with common interests, this extravaganza features women artists and entertainers; there's always a political component to the week.

Mid- to late October: **Fantasia Fair.** This 7-day event brings crossdressers, transgender persons, transsexuals, and others to town.

Late October: **Halloween.** This is a big Provincetown event, as you might imagine, with lots of costumes and contests. The children's parade ends at the Pilgrim Monument's "Halloween Haunted Monument."

Early November: **Single Men's Weekend** (508-487-1800; 888-887-8696). Workshops, parties, and lots of other organized activities for single gay men.

Late November: **Craft Fairs,** at the Provincetown Art Association & Museum (508-487-1750). Intriguing work may be purchased directly from artists at over 60 booths. Another big fair is held at Town Hall. The fairs kick off the holiday shopping season when lots of stores have sales.

Festival of Lights (508-487-3424). Nearly 5,000 white lights (4 miles' worth) illuminate the Pilgrim Monument on Thanksgiving Eve and remain lit until early January.

Early December: **Holly Folly Festival** (www.hollyfolly.com). A annual gay and lesbian festival featuring a concert by the Boston Gay Men's Chorus, seasonally decorated house tours, street caroling, shopping galore, special holiday menus, and general gay merriment and revelry.

December 31: **First Night,** ringing in the New Year.

Martha's Vineyard

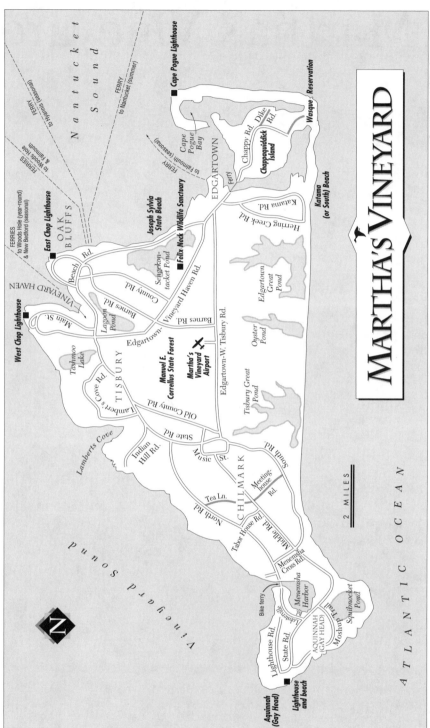

MARTHA'S VINEYARD

Paul Woodward / © The Countryman Press

Cape Pogue Lighthouse

Cape Pogue Bay

Wasque Reservation

Chappy Rd.   Dike Rd.

Chappaquiddick Island

FERRY to Falmouth (seasound)

Cape Pogue

EDGARTOWN

Ferry

Katama Rd.

Herring Creek Rd.

Katama (or South) Beach

FERRY to Nantucket (summer)

Nantucket Sound

to Hyannis (seasonal)

FERRY

to Woods Hole & Falmouth

FERRIES

Joseph Sylvia State Beach

Felix Neck Wildlife Sanctuary

Sengekontacket Pond

Edgartown Great Pond

Vineyard Haven Rd.

Barnes Rd.

County Rd.

Beach Rd.

FERRIES to Woods Hole (year-round) & New Bedford (seasonal)

East Chop Lighthouse

OAK BLUFFS

VINEYARD HAVEN

Main St.

West Chop Lighthouse

Lagoon Pond

Barnes Rd.

Edgartown–W. Tisbury Rd.

Martha's Vineyard Airport

Manuel E. Correllus State Forest

Edgartown

Tashmoo Lake

Cove Rd.

TISBURY

Lambert's Cove Rd.

Old County Rd.

State Rd.

Indian Hill Rd.

Music St.

Oyster Pond

Tisbury Great Pond

2 MILES

ATLANTIC OCEAN

Lambert's Cove

Vineyard Sound

North Rd.

Tea Ln.

CHILMARK

Meetinghouse Rd.

South Rd.

Tabor House Rd.

Middle Rd.

Menemsha Cross Rd.

Menemsha Harbor

Bike ferry

Lobsterville Rd.

Lighthouse Rd.

State Rd.

AQUINNAH (GAY HEAD)

Moshup Trail

Squibnocket Pond

Aquinnah (Gay Head)

Lighthouse and beach

N

MARTHA'S VINEYARD

Intrepid explorer Bartholomew Gosnold was the first European known to have visited Martha's Vineyard (in 1602), although Leif Eriksson may have done so earlier. Gosnold named the island for its bounty of wild grapes, but Martha's identity remains a mystery; she may have been Gosnold's daughter. The island was formally colonized in 1640, when a shipload of English settlers bound for Virginia ran short of supplies. They docked in Edgartown, found the resident Wampanoag friendly, and decided to stay.

The settlers converted the Wampanoag to Christianity with startling success, perhaps aided by the imported diseases that were killing Wampanoag by the thousands. A century after Edgartown was founded, the island's Native population had dropped from 3,000 to about 350. During that time, Vineyarders learned (from the surviving Wampanoag) how to catch whales. They also farmed in Chilmark and fished from Edgartown and Vineyard Haven.

During the American Revolution, islanders suffered extreme deprivation after British soldiers sailed into Vineyard Haven Harbor and looted homes and ships. Among their plunder were some 10,000 head of sheep and cattle from island farms. The island didn't fully recover until the 1820s, when the whaling industry took off. The Vineyard enjoyed a heyday from 1820 until the Civil War, with hundreds of whaling vessels sailing in and out of Edgartown. Whaling captains took their enormous profits from whale oil and built large Federal and Greek Revival homes all over the island. Many still stand today as gracious inns, renowned restaurants, and private homes.

After the Civil War, with the whaling industry in decline, tourism became the Vineyard's principal source of income. By 1878 the Methodist Campground of Oak Bluffs had become a popular summer resort, with 12,000 people attending annual meetings. Over the next 30 years, other travelers discovered the island and returned summer after summer to enjoy its pleasant weather, relatively warm water, excellent fishing, and comfortable yet genteel lifestyle. By the turn of the 20th century, there were 2,000 hotel rooms in Oak Bluffs alone—there aren't that many B&B or inn rooms on the entire island today! Summertime traffic was so high that a rail line was built from the Oak Bluffs ferry terminal to Katama. Daily ferry service ran from the New York Yacht Club to Gay Head (present-day Aquinnah).

Although the whaling industry rapidly declined, other sea-related businesses continued to reap healthy profits. In 1900, Vineyard Sound was one of the busiest sea-lanes in the world, second only to the English Channel. Heavy sea traffic continued until the Cape Cod Canal was completed in 1914. Tourism picked up again in the early 1970s. And when President Clinton, Hillary, and Chelsea spent summer vacations here in the mid-1990s, they created a tidal wave of national and international interest in the island.

Today the year-round population of 15,000 mushrooms in July and August to about 105,000. Grumpy year-round Vineyarders are fond of saying that the island sinks 3 inches when ferries unload their passengers.

The terms *up-island* and *down-island* are holdovers from the days when the island was populated by seafarers—as you travel west, you move up the scale of longitude. *Up-island* refers to the less developed, hilly western end, including West Tisbury, Chilmark, Menemsha, and Aquinnah. Edgartown, Oak Bluffs, and Vineyard Haven, which are the most developed towns, are all *down-island.*

Elegant Edgartown is chock-full of grand white Greek Revival ship captains' houses, with fanlights and widows' walks. Many of these private homes are clustered on North and South Water Streets, while elsewhere downtown you'll find chic shops, galleries, and restaurants.

Although it's less showy than Edgartown, Vineyard Haven maintains a year-round level of activity that Edgartown doesn't. It's the commercial center of the island, where "real" people live and work. An interesting thing has happened in recent years: Vineyard Haven has attracted better-quality shops than Edgartown. The harbor is home to more wooden boats than any other harbor of its size in New England. For an experience straight out of the 19th century, stop in at Gannon and Benjamin Boatbuilders on Beach Road; it's one of the few remaining wooden-boat rebuilding shops in the country. Literary and journalistic personalities like Bill and Rose Styron, Art Buchwald, Mike Wallace, and Diane Sawyer and husband Mike Nichols have second homes in Vineyard Haven.

Oak Bluffs today is at once charming and honky-tonk. A number of prominent African Americans have vacationed here over the years, including Spike Lee, Vernon Jordan, Dorothy West, and Charles Ogletree. In fact, Oak Bluffs has a long history of welcoming and attracting African Americans: In 1835, Wesleyan Grove was the site of the Methodist congregation's annual summer-camp meetings. The campers' small tents became family tents; then primitive, wooden, tentlike cottages; and finally, brightly painted cottages ornamented with fanciful trim. Cupolas, domes, spires, turrets, and gingerbread cutouts make for an architectural fantasyland. The whimsical, precious, and offbeat cottages are worlds away from Edgartown's traditional houses. So are Oak Bluffs' nightclubs and the baggy-pants-wearing, pierced youth.

West Tisbury is often called the Athens of the Vineyard because of its fine New England Congregational church, Town Hall, and Grange Hall. Music Street, where descendants of the island's 19th-century ship captains still live in large houses, was so named because many of these families used whaling profits to purchase pianos. Over the years, West Tisbury summer residents have included *Washington Post* owner and Katharine Graham, cartoonist Jules Feiffer, and historian David McCullough. Other A-list celebs clamoring for their place in the

ROLLING, OPEN FARMLAND TYPIFIES THE UP-ISLAND LANDSCAPE.

Vineyard sun (in Hollywood East) have included Ted Danson and Mary Steen-burgen, Film mogul Harvey Weinstein, John Cusack, and Michael J. Fox.

Chilmark is a peaceful place of rolling hills and old stone fences that outline 200-year-old farms. You'll find dozens of working farms up-island, some still operated by descendants of the island's original European settlers. Travel down North Road to Menemsha, a small (truly picturesque) village and working harbor that you may recognize as the location of the movie *Jaws*. The surrounding area is crisscrossed by miles and miles of unmarked, interconnected dirt roads, great for exploring. (Alas, many are private.) Chilmark is sparsely populated, to the tune of 850 or so year-rounders, and they aim to keep it that way. In order to limit growth they issue the island's only 3-acre-minimum building permits. Chilmark (among the 50 wealthiest towns in America; single-family homes average $1.1 million) has hosted such disparate personalities as photographer Alfred Eisenstaedt and John Belushi. (Belushi is buried on-island; "Eise's" photos are found in galleries and at his beloved retreat, the Menemsha Inn and Cottages.) Harvard Law School professor and Alan Dershowitz is a denizen of Lucy Vincent Beach, one of the island's many residents-only beaches—and a nude one at that.

Aquinnah, a must-see destination, occupies the island's western tip. (If you haven't visited the Vineyard for a while, you may know Aquinnah as Gay Head. It was renamed Aquinnah, "land under the hill," in mid-1997 by a narrow 79–76 town vote.) Of the 700 members listed on the Wampanoag Indian tribal rolls, approximately 300 still reside on the Vineyard, half in Aquinnah. Tribal legend holds that the giant Moshup created the Vineyard, taught the Wampanoag how to fish and catch whales, and remains a protector. The Wampanoag own the brilliantly colored bluffs and the face of the Clay Cliffs of Aquinnah.

Martha's Vineyard has always attracted celebrity summer visitors. But in

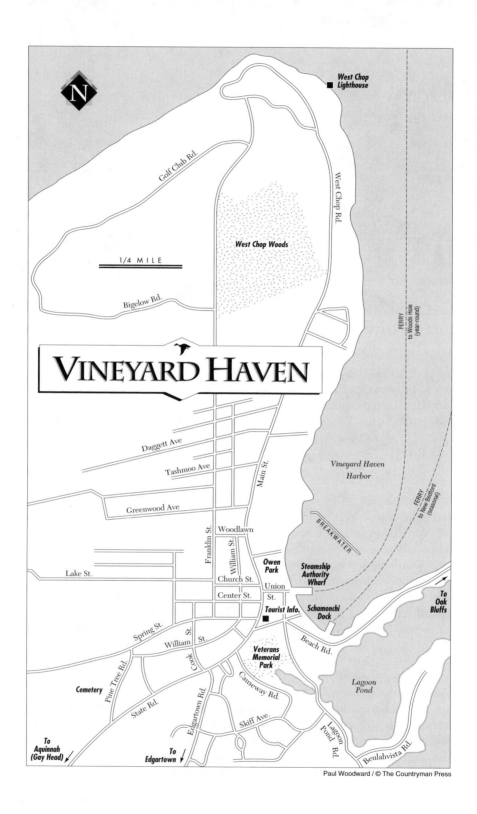

VINEYARD HAVEN

West Chop
Lighthouse

Golf Club Rd.

West Chop Rd.

West Chop Woods

1/4 MILE

Bigelow Rd.

FERRY to Woods Hole (year-round)

Daggett Ave

Tashmoo Ave

Main St.

Vineyard Haven
Harbor

FERRY to New Bedford (seasonal)

Greenwood Ave

Franklin St.

Woodlawn

William St.

BREAKWATER

Lake St.

Owen
Park

Steamship
Authority
Wharf

Church St.

Union
St.

To
Oak
Bluffs

Center St.

Tourist Info.

Schamonchi
Dock

Spring St.

William St.

Cook St.

Veterans
Memorial
Park

Beach Rd.

Pine Tree Rd.

Cemetery

Edgartown Rd.

State Rd.

Causeway Rd.

Lagoon
Pond

Skiff Ave.

Lagoon Pond Rd.

To
Aquinnah
(Gay Head)

To
Edgartown

Beulahvista Rd.

Paul Woodward / © The Countryman Press

recent years many who visited decided they wanted to own a piece of it. Beginning in the late 1980s and continuing to this day, a tremendous building boom has changed the face of the Vineyard. While the Vineyard had been a place where the well-heeled and well-off came to escape notice, today the celebrities and power brokers come as much to see and be seen. Although residents are generally unfazed by their celebrity neighbors—movie stars, authors, journalists, musicians, financial moguls—many locals and longtime visitors agree that the Vineyard is no longer the quaint, tranquil island it was prior to the mid-1980s.

Martha's Vineyard is unlike most of the rest of America; people tend to get along pretty well with one another. They work hard to maintain a sense of tolerance and community spirit. Most lengthy debates center on land use and preservation rather than on race or religion. (Of course, there are notable exceptions.) Everyone relies, to some extent, on the hectic summer season that brings in most of the island's annual income, though residents do breathe a sigh of relief when the crowds depart after mid-October.

To experience the Vineyard at its best and still have a dependable chance for good weather, plan your visit from May to mid-June or from mid-September to mid-October. From January to March, the Vineyard is truly a retreat from civilization.

GUIDANCE ❊ **Martha's Vineyard Chamber of Commerce** (508-693-0085; www.mvy.com), Beach Road, P.O. Box 1698, Vineyard Haven 02568. Open 9–5 weekdays, 10–4 weekends (except 10–2 Sunday May to September). You'll find lots of booklets, brochures, maps, and other valuable information.

❊ **Information booth** (no phone), Steamship Authority terminal, Vineyard Haven. Open 8–8 daily, late June to early September in-season; 8:30–5:30 Friday through Sunday in shoulder seasons from mid-May to mid-October.

Information booth (508-693-4266), Circuit Avenue at Lake Avenue, Oak Bluffs. Adjacent to the Flying Horses Carousel, it's open 9–5 daily, mid-May to mid-October.

❊ **Edgartown Information Center** (no phone), Church Street, Edgartown. Around the corner from the Old Whaling Church, this minor, town-sponsored center has rest rooms, a post office, and serves as a shuttle-bus stop (see *Getting Around*).

MEDIA *Vineyard Gazette* (508-627-4311; www.mvgazette.com), 34 South Summer Street. The newspaper, which first rolled off the press on May 14, 1846, is a beloved island institution. As the masthead declares, it's "A family newspaper—neutral in politics, devoted to general news, literature, morality, agriculture and amusement." Although its year-round circulation is only 14,000, the paper is mailed to island devotees in all 50 states. There's no single better way for an Explorer to get a handle on island life.

PUBLIC REST ROOMS & LAUNDROMATS In Vineyard Haven head to the top of the A&P parking lot (seasonal) and to the Steamship Authority terminal (year-round) off Water Street. In Oak Bluffs restrooms are next to the Steamship

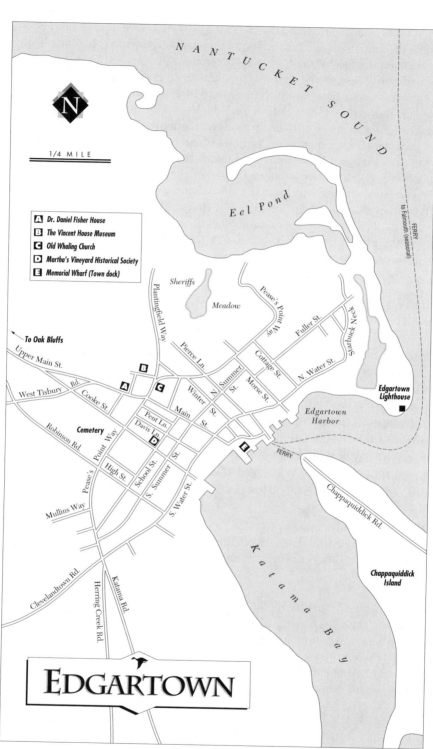

NANTUCKET SOUND

Eel Pond

1/4 MILE

N

A Dr. Daniel Fisher House
B The Vincent House Museum
C Old Whaling Church
D Martha's Vineyard Historical Society
E Memorial Wharf (Town dock)

FERRY
to Falmouth (seasonal)

Sheriffs
Meadow

Plantingfield Way

← To Oak Bluffs

Upper Main St.

West Tisbury Rd.

Cooke St.

Pierce Ln.

Pease's Point Way

Fuller St.

Cottage St.

N. Water St.

Starbuck Neck

Edgartown
Lighthouse

B

A C

Winter St.

Main St.

N. Summer St.

Summer St.

Morse St.

Edgartown
Harbor

Cemetery

Robinson Rd.

Pease's Point Way

Pent Ln.

Davis Ln.

D

High St.

School St.

S. Summer St.

E

FERRY

Mullins Way

S. Water St.

Chappaquiddick Rd.

Clevelandtown Rd.

Herring Creek Rd.

Katama Rd.

Katama Bay

Chappaquiddick
Island

EDGARTOWN

Authority terminal on Seaview Avenue; on Kennebec Avenue, one block from Circuit Avenue; and next to Our Market on Oak Bluffs Harbor. In Edgartown, they're at the visitors center (year-round) on Church Street. Facilities are also located near the parking lot for the Clay Cliffs of Aquinnah, and at Dutcher's Dock in Menemsha Harbor. In West Tisbury, rest rooms are in Grange Hall next to the Town Hall.

❊ **Airport Laundromat** (508-693-5005), off the Edgartown–West Tisbury Road.

PUBLIC LIBRARIES ✄ ⸆ ❊ Most of these libraries have story times; call ahead for opening hours and schedule vagaries:

Aquinnah (508-645-2314), State Road at Church Street.

Chilmark (508-645-3360), Chilmark Center.

Edgartown (508-627-4221), 58 North Water Street.

Oak Bluffs (508-693-9433), Circuit Avenue at Pennacook Avenue.

Vineyard Haven (508-696-4210), 200 Main Street.

West Tisbury (508-693-3366), 1042A State Road.

See also the Martha's Vineyard Historical Society under *To See*.

GETTING THERE ❊ *By boat from Woods Hole:* **The Steamship Authority** (508-477-8600 or 508-693-9130 for advance auto reservations; 508-548-3788 for day-of-sailing information from Woods Hole; 508-477-7447 for last-minute day-of-sailing reservations in summer, but don't count on getting lucky; www.island-ferry.com), Railroad Avenue, Woods Hole. The Steamship is the only company that provides daily, year-round transport—for people and autos—to Vineyard Haven and Oak Bluffs. The Vineyard is 7 miles from Woods Hole, and the trip takes 45 minutes. About 15 boats ply the waters daily year-round.

The Steamship annually carries upwards of 2 million people to the Vineyard, and they begin taking auto reservations via the web on February 1. Prior to that, mail your requests with payment to: Reservation Bureau, 509 Falmouth Road, Suite 1C, Mashpee 02649. Get your request in as close to February 1 as you can. Auto reservations are mandatory on weekends (Friday through Monday) between mid-May and early September. Otherwise, the Steamship has a "guaranteed standby policy" that states if your car is queued up by 2 PM on Tuesday, Wednesday, or Thursday in summer, you are assured of passage that day.

Round-trip tickets from mid-May to mid-October cost: $11 adults; $5.50 children 5–12; $6 bicycles; $110 autos. Off-season, auto prices drop to $68. If you are not taking your car, the Steamship Authority provides free, frequent buses between the parking lots and the ferry dock. Each bus has a bike rack that holds two bikes. Parking is about $8 per calendar day.

By boat from Falmouth: **Island Queen** (508-548-4800; www.island queen.com), Falmouth Heights Road, Falmouth. This passengers-only service (smaller and more comfortable than the Steamship Authority's boat) operates late May to mid-October and takes about 35 minutes; departures are from Falmouth Inner

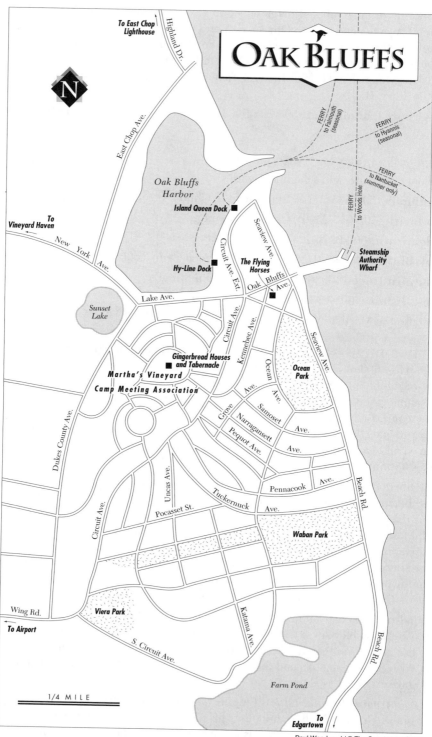

Harbor to Oak Bluffs. There is plenty of parking near the *Island Queen*'s dock ($10–12 per calendar day). Round-trip fares cost $10 adults; $5 children age 3–12; $6 bicycles.

Falmouth–Edgartown Ferry (508-548-9400), 278 Scranton Avenue, Falmouth. From late May to mid-October, this service plies the waters three times daily between Falmouth and Edgartown (Memorial Wharf). Round trip: adults $24; children 5–12, $18; bicycles $6. Parking is $12 per calendar day.

By boat from Hyannis: **Hy-Line Cruises** (508-778-2600; www.hy-linecruises. com), Ocean Street Dock, Hyannis. Passenger boats to and from Oak Bluffs from May to late October. A high-speed ferry takes 1 hour, while the traditional ferry takes almost twice as long. In May there is one morning boat daily on weekends. From late May to early June, there are three round trips daily; from early June to mid-September, there are four. If you haven't purchased advance tickets, it's wise to arrive an hour early in July and August. From mid-September through October, the schedule drops back to one trip daily. Round-trip high-speed fares: adults $58, children $41; round-trip traditional fares: adults $27, children $13.50, and bicycles $10.

By boat from New Bedford: **Martha's Vineyard Ferry *Schamonchi*** (508-997-1688; www.mvferry.com) operates passenger boats to and from Vineyard Haven from mid-May to late September. The trip takes about 1½ hours. From mid-May to mid-June and early September to mid-October, there is only one boat daily, at 9 AM. But on weekends during these periods and daily from mid-June to early September, there are three boats. Round-trip fares: $20 adults, $10 children, and $10 bicycles. Parking is $10 per calendar day. For visitors coming from the south, New Bedford is a more convenient departure point than Woods Hole. Even those driving from points north may wish to consider taking the New Bedford ferry to avoid Cape Cod Canal bridge traffic. From I-195, take exit 15 (Route 18 south) to the third set of lights, turn left, and follow signs to ferry parking.

By boat from Nantucket: **Hy-Line Cruises** (508-778-2600 in Hyannis; 508-693-0112 in Oak Bluffs; 508-228-3949 on Nantucket; www.hy-linecruises.com) offers inter-island service between Oak Bluffs and Nantucket from early June to mid-September. The trip takes 2¼ hours; three boats make the trip daily. One-way fares cost: $13.50 adults, $6.75 children age 5–12, and $6 bicycles.

See also Patriot Party Boats under *Outdoor Activities—Boat Excursions* in "Falmouth and Woods Hole."

By bus: **Bonanza Bus Lines** (800-556-3815; www.bonanzabus.com) provides daily year-round service to Woods Hole from Boston, New York, Hartford, and Providence (including T. F. Green Airport). Buses are scheduled to meet ferries, but ferries won't wait for a late bus.

Vineyard Express (508-477-8600) operates Friday afternoon through Monday morning from late June to early September. It provides a direct, nonstop connection between the MBTA/Amtrak station at I-95/Route 128 in Westwood (where you can park) and the Steamship Authority in Woods Hole. There is joint ticketing with the Steamship. An ecofriendly option for area residents, this service is also convenient for Northeast Corridor users and Amtrak Acela riders.

Kim Grant

THE FERRY *ON-TIME* MAKES THE 100-YARD DASH ACROSS EDARTOWN HARBOR TO
CHAPPAQUIDDICK

By air: With a booming increase in jet-setting visitors, it's no wonder a new terminal was built in 1999. **Cape Air** (800-352-0714; www.flycapeair.com) flies to
the Vineyard from Boston, Hyannis, Providence, Nantucket, and New Bedford.
Cape Air has joint ticketing and baggage handling between its flights and most
major airlines. **US Airways Express** (800-428-4322) offers seasonal service to
and from Boston, New York City, Philadelphia, and Washington, D.C. **Continental Express** (800-525-0280) has seasonal service between the Vineyard and
Newark, New Jersey. Delta (800-221-1212) provides service from Boston, New
York, and Nantucket.

GETTING AROUND *By car:* The infamous Five Corners is the trickiest and most
dangerous intersection on the island. It's also the first thing you'll encounter as
you disembark from the Vineyard Haven ferry terminal. If you're going to Oak
Bluffs, Katama, Edgartown, and Chappaquiddick, take the left lane. For West
Tisbury, North Tisbury, Lambert's Cove, Menemsha, Chilmark, and Aquinnah,
enter the right lane and turn right.

When making plans, consider these sample distances: Vineyard Haven to Oak
Bluffs, 3 miles; Vineyard Haven to Edgartown, 8 miles; Oak Bluffs to Edgartown, 6 miles; Vineyard Haven to Aquinnah, 18 miles.

Unfortunately, summertime traffic jams are commonplace in down-island towns.
Try to park outside of town and take shuttles into town (see below). Why would
you want to stop and crawl in a picturesque village on a vacation day?

In-season, expect to pay about $80 daily for the least expensive rental car;
$110–160 for a van; $150 for four-wheel drive; $45 for a moped. Off-season,
rates go as low as $50 daily for a car.

Before heading out, invest $2.95 in the very detailed gold-and-orange "Martha's Vineyard Road Map" produced by Edward Thomas (508-693-2059). It's an excellent, accurate resource and even lists mileage between intersections. It's available at most bookstores, drugstores, and groceries.

Note: it is illegal to pass mopeds in no-passing zones, which can sure feel like every single road up-island, when you're moving at 20 mph.

Car rental companies include **Budget Rent-a-Car** (508-693-1911; 800-527-0700), 45 Beach Road, Vineyard Haven; Circuit Avenue Extension (at the ferry dock), Oak Bluffs; 257 Edgartown Road, Edgartown; and Martha's Vineyard Airport. I've always found **Thrifty** (508-693-1959), Five Corners, Vineyard Haven, particularly helpful. For a splurge call **Vineyard Classic Cars** (508-693-5551) in Oak Bluffs and Vineyard Haven. By the way, gas is usually cheapest at the airport.

By moped: If most Vineyarders and emergency room doctors had their way, mopeds would be banned. Once you've seen the face, arms, and legs of a fellow Explorer skinned, you'll know why. Sand, mopeds, winding roads, and speed do not mix. Take a look at the mopeds you might be renting; many of their plastic hulls have been cracked from accidents. Having said that and not wanting to appear too paternalistic, here goes: Many rental agencies are located near the ferry terminals in Oak Bluffs and Vineyard Haven. **Adventure Rentals** (508-693-1959, 7 Beach Road, Vineyard Haven) and **Ride-on Mopeds** (508-693-2076, Circuit Avenue Extension, Oak Bluffs) both have mopeds. Extra training, yellow diamond road signs (at notorious intersections), and maps (with danger spots and distances between points) should help reduce casualties.

🦑 ❋ *By shuttle:* **Martha's Vineyard Transit Authority (VTA)** (508-693-9440; www.vineyardtransit.com) operates an excellent system of buses. Twelve buses travel among Vineyard Haven, Oak Bluffs, Edgartown, West Tisbury, Chilmark, Menemsha, and Aquinnah year-round. Buses seem to stop everywhere you want to go; you can also flag them down. They even have bike racks. Get a copy of the very helpful VTA map with stops and routes clearly listed. Carry it with you wherever you go. One-day pass costs $5, 3-day $10, 7-day $15. Single tickets cost $1 per town (if you go from Vineyard Haven to Edgartown, for instance, it costs $3 because you have to go through Oak Bluffs). Exact change is strongly suggested since change is given only in the form of credit vouchers for future trips.

Edgartown Park & Ride. VTA has an alternative to wrangling for a parking place in Edgartown's car-choked streets. Leave your car at The Triangle (at the corner of Edgartown–Vineyard Haven Road and Oak Bluffs Road) and ride the shuttle. Parking and rides are free.

Tisbury Park & Ride, State Road (across from Cronig's Market). Avoid the parking nightmare in Vineyard Haven and let the VTA shuttle drop you off downtown. The frequent trolleys ($1) run from mid-May to mid-October. Parking is $2, but you must purchase tickets in advance at the Cumberland Farms (at the Five Corners intersection) and Town Hall (William and Spring Streets) in Vineyard Haven or at the Chilmark Store.

South Beach Trolley (508-693-9440). Mid-June to early September. The daily trolley ($1) runs from Edgartown's information building (near the corner of Church and Main Streets) to three points at South Beach.

By bus tour: **Gay Head Sightseeing** (508-693-1555) and **M.V. Sightseeing** (508-627-8687) are operated by the same company (www.mvtour.com) and offer daily, 2½-hour tours from early May to late October. The clearly marked buses meet ferries in Vineyard Haven and Oak Bluffs. The Gay Head tour makes one stop—at the Clay Cliffs of Aquinnah—where there are small food stands, souvenir shops, public rest rooms, and a wonderful view of the cliffs and the ocean. The M.V. tour goes only to the down-island towns of Oak Bluffs and Edgartown, but it stops in Edgartown for 90 minutes. The only potential drawback: You may tire of hearing the constant running commentary about which celebrities live down which dirt roads. Adults $17, children $5.

By taxi tour: Most taxis conduct island tours for a price—$100–150 for an all-island trip, depending on the season. But you don't want to go with just anyone. I highly recommend **Jon's Taxi** (508-627-4677). Trips with Jon's assistant cost $50 per hour for two to four people and leave promptly at 9 AM. If you're lucky, you can arrange a full island tour with Jon himself; it'll cost a bit more, but it's worth it. Jon even throws in lunch at Larsen's for free.

Adam Cab (508-627-4462; 800-281-4462; www.adamcab.com) is also very good and offers tours twice daily from Edgartown at 9 AM and 1 PM from late May to early September. This 3-hour, all-island tour costs $5 per person. If you'd prefer to arrange your own itinerary, hire them for $50–75 per hour, depending on the number of people (up to seven).

⑤ *By bicycle:* Bicycling is a great way to get around, but it requires stamina if you're heading up-island (see *Outdoor Activities—Bicycling/Rentals*).

⑤ ❄ *By foot:* **Ghosts, Gossip, and Downright Scandals** (508-627-8619) is conducted by very knowledgeable folks from **Vineyard History Tours.** These excellent walking trips depart at various times and from various points in Vineyard Haven, Edgartown, and Oak Bluffs. Call ahead for the current schedule. They basically take people by appointment any time of the year, except perhaps during a nor'easter. Their special tour focusing on Edgartown's whaling days, "A-Whaling We Will Go," is also very good. All tours cost $10 per person.

HERITAGE TRAILS **Aquinnah Cultural Trail** (508-645-9265; www.wtgh.vineyard.net). For those interested in something other than beaches and shops, look for the excellent and informative map once you're on-island. It is full of interesting facts about the "first people of Noepe," place-name translations, Moshup legends, local government, and a schedule of events.

African-American Heritage Trail (508-693-4361). Tours on request late May to early September. The brainchild of a M.V. Regional High School history teacher and NAACP archivist Elaine Weintraub, this developing trail currently has 14 sites devoted to telling the story of the island's strong association with African Americans. Every town has sites, including abandoned graveyards; the home of Dorothy West, a Harlem Renaissance writer who lived on the island

and died in 1999; and a decrepit "Gospel Tabernacle" that served as a community church in the late 19th century. Pamphlets are sold in local bookstores.

MEDICAL EMERGENCY Martha's Vineyard Hospital (508-693-0410), off Beach Road, Oak Bluffs.

Lyme disease. Ticks carry this disease, which has flu-like symptoms and may result in death if left untreated. Immediately and carefully remove any ticks that may have migrated from dune grasses to your body. Better yet, wear long pants, tuck pants into socks, and wear long-sleeved shirts whenever possible when hiking. Avoid hiking in grassy and overgrown areas of dense brush.

✳ To See

In Vineyard Haven

Compass Bank (508-696-4400), Main Street. Open weekdays. This distinctive 1905 fieldstone building has lovely stained glass and great acoustics. On this site, incidentally, stood the harness shop where the Great Fire of 1883 started. The conflagration destroyed 60 buildings.

William Street. The only street in town that survived the devastating 1883 fire boasts some fine examples of Greek Revival architecture. The **Richard G. Luce House,** near the corner of William Street and Spring Street, is prime among the carefully preserved sea captains' homes. Captain Luce never lost a whaling ship or a crew member during his 30-year career, and apparently his good fortune at sea extended to life on land.

Jirah Luce House, near the corner of South Main and Main Streets. Built in 1804, this is one of the few buildings to survive the Great Fire of 1883.

Old Schoolhouse, Main Street at Colonial Lane. Built in 1839, the schoolhouse

THE WEST CHOP LIGHTHOUSE IN VINEYARD HAVEN

Kim Grant

now houses a youth sailing program, but the Liberty Pole in front of it recounts the story of three courageous girls who defied British troops.

West Chop Lighthouse, at the western end of Main Street. Built in 1817 with wood and replaced with brick in 1838, the lighthouse has been moved back from the shore twice, first in 1848 and again in 1891. Today the lighthouse is inhabited by a family from the Menemsha Coast Guard base; it's not open for touring.

Katherine Cornell Theatre/Tisbury Town Hall (508-696-4200), 51 Spring Street and William Street. This 1844 performance center features murals by Stan Murphy depicting island scenes, whaling adventures, seagulls, and Native Americans. The town offices are here, too.

In Oak Bluffs

East Chop Lighthouse (508-627-4441). Telegraph Hill, off the Vineyard Haven–Oak Bluffs Road. Open Friday from 60 minutes prior to sunset until 30 minutes after; $3. This circa-1850 lighthouse was built by Captain Silas Daggett with the financial help of prosperous fellow seafarers who wanted a better system of relaying signals from the Vineyard to Nantucket and the mainland. Up to that point, they'd used a complex system of raising arms, legs, flags, and lanterns to signal which ships were coming in. In 1875 the government purchased the lighthouse from the consortium of sea captains for $6,000, then constructed the metal structure that stands today. There are nice ocean views from here.

COLORFUL GINGERBREAD COTTAGES IN WESLEYAN GROVE, OAK BLUFFS

Kim Grant

Trinity Park Tabernacle, behind Lake, Circuit, and Dukes County Avenues. The enormous, tentlike tabernacle was built in 1879 to replace the original meeting tent used by the Methodists who met here. Today the tabernacle is one of the largest wrought-iron structures in the country. There are community sing-alongs on Wednesday evenings (at 8) in summer.

Wesleyan Grove surrounds the tabernacle, which, in turn, is encircled by rows of colorful **"gingerbread" cottages,** built during the late 19th century to replace true tents. Owners painted the tiny houses with bright colors and pastels to accentuate the

Carpenter Gothic architecture and woodwork. There are upwards of 330 cottages today, still leased from the Camp Meeting Association. Visitors are welcome to wander around the mainly Protestant (but always ecumenical) community. No bicycles are allowed in Wesleyan Grove, and quiet time is strictly observed after dark.

Union Chapel (508-693-5350), at the corner of Kennebec and Samoset Avenues. This 19th-century octagonal chapel holds interdenominational services and hosts performing arts events throughout the summer.

Cottage Museum (508-693-7784), 1 Trinity Park. Open 10–4 Monday through Saturday, mid-June to mid-October. The interior and exterior of this 1867 cottage are typical of the more than 300 tiny cottages in Wesleyan Grove. Memorabilia and photographs span the ages from 1835 to present day. Nominal admission fee.

✔ **Flying Horses Carousel** (508-693-9481), Circuit Avenue at Lake Avenue. Open daily when school is out and weekends otherwise, mid-April to mid-October (10–10 in summer). The oldest operating carousel in the country, carved in New York City in 1876, is marvelously well preserved and lovingly maintained. It was brought by barge to the island in 1884, complete with four chariots and 20 horses (with real horsehair manes). Adults visit this national historic landmark even without a child in tow to grab for the elusive brass ring. (Here's a public service announcement: A few folks every year are not returning the brass ring when they grab it and the carousel is getting precariously close to running out of them.) Rides $1, or a book of 10 for $8.

In Edgartown

🐚 ✳ **Martha's Vineyard Historical Society** (508-627-4441; www.marthasvineyardhistory.org), Cooke Street at School Street. Open 10–5 Tuesday through Saturday, mid-June to early October; 1–4 Wednesday through Friday and 10–4 Saturday, mid-October to mid-December and mid-March to mid-June; 10–5 Saturday and by appointment Wednesday through Friday mid-December to mid-March. This excellent collection is housed in several buildings. Perhaps the most interesting exhibit is the Oral History Center, which preserves the island's history through more than 250 recorded testaments from the island's older citizens. (The project was begun in 1993.) Other facilities include a fine pre–Revolutionary War house, which has undergone little renovation since the mid–19th century. Ten rooms at the Thomas Cooke House focus on various aspects of the island's history, including ethnic groups, architecture, natural history, and agriculture. The society also has a maritime gallery, historical reference library, a tryworks replica, a carriage shed that houses boats and vehicles, and a historic herb garden. The enormous original Fresnel lens from the Aquinnah Lighthouse is here, too, and it's illuminated for a few hours each night. Adults $7 in summer, $6 otherwise; children age 6–15, $4; children under 6 free.

Dr. Daniel Fisher House (508-627-8619), 99 Main Street. The island's best example of Greek Revival architecture, this 1840 house has an enclosed cupola (perhaps more correctly called a "lantern"), roof and porch balustrades, a shallow hipped roof, large windowpanes, and a portico, all exquisitely preserved. Dr.

THE DR. DANIEL FISHER HOUSE IN EDGARTOWN

Fisher was a Renaissance man: doctor, whaling magnate, banker (he founded the Martha's Vineyard National Bank), merchant, and miller. He insisted that his house be constructed with the finest materials—with Maine pine timbers soaked in lime for two years, and brass and copper nails, for instance. The house is head-quarters for the Martha's Vineyard Preservation Trust, which is charged with saving, restoring, and making self-sufficient any important island buildings that might otherwise be sold for commercial purposes or radically remodeled. Combination tours of this house with the Vincent House and Old Whaling Church (see below) are offered late May to mid-October; call for times; $8 per person.

Vincent House Museum (508-627-8619), behind the Old Whaling Church. Open noon–3 Monday through Friday, late May to mid-October. Dating to 1672, the Vineyard's oldest residence was in the same family until 1941, and was eventually given to the Preservation Trust in 1977. Reproduction and antique furniture in three rooms depicts how the residence looked in the 17th, 18th, and 19th centuries. Adults $3 ($5 per couple); $8 per person including a tour of the Dr. Fisher House and Old Whaling Church.

Old Whaling Church (508-627-4442 events; 508-627-8619 tours), 89 Main Street, at Church Street. Built in 1843, this thriving parish church also serves as a performing arts center, hosting plays, lectures, concerts, and films. Owned by the Martha's Vineyard Preservation Trust, the building originally housed the Edgartown Methodist Church and was constructed with the same techniques used to build whaling ships. Tours $8, including visits to the Dr. Fisher House and the Vincent House Museum.

North Water Street. Some of these fine Colonial, Federal, and Greek Revival houses may look familiar because many clothing companies, including Talbot's, have sent crews of models and photographers here to shoot their catalogs. Architectural detailing on these white houses trimmed in black is superb.

Edgartown Lighthouse (508-627-4441), at the end of North Water Street. The first lighthouse to direct boats into and around Edgartown Harbor was built in 1828 on a small island. Shortly after a new lighthouse replaced it in 1938, the island became connected to the "mainland" of the Vineyard by a spit of sand. Today the lighthouse is accessible by foot. You can walk to it anytime, but you are not allowed inside. Take note of the granite cobblestone foundation (dubbed the Children's Lighthouse Memorial), a tribute to children who have died. It's the first of its kind in the country.

Up-island

Mayhew Chapel and **Indian Burial Ground,** Christiantown Road, off Indian Hill Road, West Tisbury. This tiny chapel, burial ground, and memorial to the Praying Indians (who were converted to Christianity by the Reverend Mayhew Jr. in the mid-1600s) is a quiet place, owned by the Wampanoag tribe of Aquinnah.

Grange Hall (508-627-4440), State Road, West Tisbury. Open seasonally. The original Agricultural Society Barn now hosts concerts and screens old movies on Thursday night from mid-June to mid-September.

Beetlebung Corner, at the intersection of Middle, South, State, and Menemsha Cross Roads; the center of Chilmark. The intersection was named for the grove of beetlebung trees (the New England name for tupelos), which are unusual in this region. Tupelo is a very hard wood, an excellent material for making mallets (also called beetles) and the plugs (or bungs) that filled the holes in wooden casks and barrels during whale oil days.

Menemsha Harbor, at Menemsha Cross Road near Beetlebung Corner. This working fishing village is filled with small, sturdy docks and simple, weathered boathouses. Some islanders still earn a living from the boats of Menemsha's fishing fleet. For the rest of us, the harbor is a great location from which to watch the

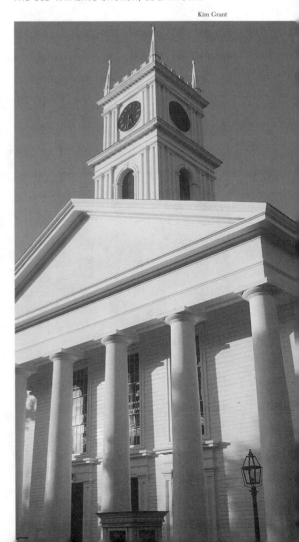

THE OLD WHALING CHURCH, EDGARTOWN

Kim Grant

CHERISHED INSTITUTION

Alley's General Store (508-693-0088), State Road, West Tisbury. Open daily. Alley's is a beloved Vineyard landmark. "Dealers in almost everything" since 1858, the store has a wide front porch where locals have gathered over the decades to discuss current events and exchange friendly gossip. In the early 1990s, though, economic conditions almost forced Alley's to close. In true island spirit, the Martha's Vineyard Preservation Trust stepped in to renovate the building and ensure its survival. Alley's continues to feel like a country store, selling everything utilitarian: housewares, mismatched cups and saucers, and locally grown produce.

ALLEY'S GENERAL STORE

Kim Grant

MENEMSHA HARBOR

setting sun. A few little shacks (shops and fast-food eateries) line the road to Dutcher's Dock.

Quitsa Overlook, off State Road. At Beetlebung Corner, bear left onto State Road, heading toward Aquinnah. After a mile or so, you'll pass over a bridge; Nashaquitsa Pond (also known as Quitsa) is on your right and Stonewall Pond is on your left. Just beyond, a spot overlooks Quitsa and Menemsha Ponds. About half a mile farther locals fill water jugs from a fresh, sweet stream that's been siphoned off to run out of a pipe. Local lore attributes various cures to the water—from stress relief, to a flu antidote, to a hangover remedy.

Aquinnah Community Baptist Church (508-693-1539), Aquinnah. Turn left at the small red schoolhouse (now the town library) across the street from the Aquinnah Town Hall, Fire Station, and Police Department. The lovely church is the country's oldest Indian Baptist church. It may have the prettiest location, too, overlooking windswept grassy dunes, stone walls, and the Atlantic Ocean.

Aquinnah Tribal Center (508-645-9265), 20 Black Brook Road, Aquinnah. Although it's only in the preliminary stages of development, the Aquinnah Cultural Center expects to have an archive, culturally relevant crafts workshops, and a fine and performing arts center that preserves documents and celebrates the local Wampanoag history, traditions, heritage, and culture.

Clay Cliffs of Aquinnah. The brilliantly colored clay cliffs, a designated national-al landmark, rise 150 feet above the shore and were formed 100 million years ago by glaciers. For a fine view of the full magnitude of this spectacular geological formation, and distant views of Noman's Land Island and the Elizabeth Islands, walk beyond the souvenir shops. A wooden boardwalk also leads to the beach, where you can appreciate the towering clay cliffs from sea level. It's important to note that the Wampanoag have lived here for more than 5,000 years and own most of this land (although most of the beach is public); only they may remove clay from the eroding cliffs.

CHAPPAQUIDDICK

Accessible via the **"Chappy ferry,"** *On-Time III* (508-627-9427), at the corner of Dock and Daggett Streets. The crossing between Edgartown and Chappy is completed in a blink of an eye. The ferry doesn't really have a schedule; it just goes when it's needed, and thus it's always "on time." Since it's the only method of transportation between the two islands, and a surprising number of people live on Chappy year-round, the ferry runs daily. Round-trip for car and driver $8; for passenger and bike, $5.

Chappaquiddick contains several lovely beaches and wildlife refuges, including the 500-acre Cape Pogue Wildlife Refuge, the 14-acre Mytoi, and the 200-acre Wasque Reservation. Unfortunately, though, the beautiful island is perhaps best known because of Dike Bridge, the scene of the drowning incident involving Senator Edward Kennedy in July 1969. To reach Dike Bridge, stay on Chappaquiddick Road after you get off the ferry until the road turns into Dike Road. When the road takes a sharp turn to the right (in about a mile), continue straight on the dirt road until you reach the bridge.

When the bridge was rebuilt in 1995, pedestrians once again had direct access to Cape Pogue, a thin ribbon of sand that stretches along the east side of Chappaquiddick and the remote Cape Pogue Lighthouse. Four-wheel-drive vehicles can use the bridge when endangered shorebirds like the piping plover are not nesting. Cape Pogue is also accessible by foot or by four-wheel-drive vehicle, over the sand of Wasque Point, several miles south of the beach.

✐ **Cape Pogue Wildlife Refuge and Wasque Reservation** (508-693-7662; www.thetrustees.org). These adjoining tracts of land on the southeastern corner of Chappaquiddick are relatively isolated, so even on summer weekends you can escape the crowds. This seaside wilderness contains huge tracts of dunes, the long and beautiful **East Beach,** cedars, salt marshes, ponds, tidal flats, and scrub brush. Overseen by the Massachusetts Trustees of Reservations, Cape Pogue (489 acres) and Wasque (200 acres) are the

Aquinnah Lighthouse (508-627-4441). This redbrick lighthouse was built in 1844 to replace a wooden lighthouse that had stood since 1799. In 1856 a powerful Fresnel lens was mounted atop the lighthouse, where it warned ships away from the perilous Aquinnah coast; it was used for almost 100 years. From late June to mid-September (on Friday, Saturday, and Sunday evenings), you can ascend the lighthouse to enjoy the sunset. It opens 90 minutes prior to sunset and closes 30 minutes after it; $3.

Moshup Beach Overlook, on the northern end of Moshup Trail and south of the parking lot for the lighthouse, off State Road. This scenic coastal road has nice views of wild, low heathlands.

group's oldest island holdings. Half of the state's scallops are harvested each autumn off the coast near the **Cape Pogue Lighthouse** (on the northern tip of the cape). The lighthouse was built in 1893 and automated in 1964. Limited East Beach parking $3; reservation entrance $3 per car, $3 per person (late May to mid-September). *Note:* It is dangerous to swim at Wasque Rip because of the forceful tide.

☙ **Three-hour natural history tours** (508-627-3599; www.thetrustees.org) of Cape Pogue are naturalist led, in an open-air four-wheel-drive vehicle, and depart from Mytoi Garden (see below). The fee is $30 for adults, $15 for children under 15. Bring binoculars and water.

☙ **Cape Pogue Lighthouse tours** (75 minutes), where you'll learn about the fascinating history of the light and the keepers who lived there, depart from Dike Bridge. Adults $15; children under 15, $6. Both trips are offered twice daily from late May to mid-October. Space is limited, so reserve early.

Mytoi (508-693-7662; www.thetrustees.org), Dike Road. Open daily sunrise to sunset. This 14-acre Japanese garden, built by Hugh Jones in 1958, has azaleas, irises, a goldfish pond, and a picturesque little bridge.

☙ **Fishing Discovery Tour** (508-627-3599; www.thetrustees.org). Late May to mid-October. Operated by the Trustees of Reservations, these 4-hour guided surf-fishing trips (two daily) drift along the Chappaquiddick shores at Wasque Point and Cape Pogue. Adults $50, children 15 and under $25. Limited to eight people per trip. Only members may take this trip, but you can purchase a temporary membership for $20 individual or $30 family.

☙ **Poucha Pond** (508-627-3599; www.thetrustees.org), Dike Bridge. Early June to early October. Members of the Trustees of Reservations may take self-guided tours; rentals $25 per half day, $35 daily. Nonmembers must first purchase an introductory family membership for $30. Boats are available 9–5 daily. Anyone can take a 2½-hour guided natural history trip. They're offered twice daily from late May to mid-October by the Trustees of Reservations; call to register.

SCENIC DRIVES Instead of making a beeline up-island, detour onto Lambert's Cove Road from State Road out of Vineyard Haven. Take North, South, or Middle Roads up-island. I particularly like cutting between the roads on Tea Lane and Meeting House Road. As you approach Aquinnah, take a left onto Moshup Trail to the lighthouse and circle back via Lighthouse Road and Lobsterville Road (but do follow Lobsterville to the very end, across the cut from Menemsha).

✴ Outdoor Activities

AIRPLANE RIDES Classic Aviators (508-627-7677), off Katama Road at the Katama Airfield, Edgartown. Open seasonally. Open-cockpit rides in a biplane or

Cessna, solo or with a friend, with or without Snoopy-like leather caps and goggles. $99 for one or two people for a 15- to 20-minute flight; $300 for 1 hour.

BERRY PICKING ♪ **Benson's Thimble Farm** (508-693-6396), off State Road, West Tisbury. Open mid-June to mid-October, the farm allows you to pick your own strawberries or raspberries and offers other farm stand goodies as well—homegrown melons, tomatoes, flowers, and other in-season produce. Children are welcome for strawberry picking, but should be over age 12 to pick raspberries because of the dangers of thorns and bees. Call for specific opening hours.

BICYCLING/RENTALS Several excellent (albeit crowded) bicycle paths connect the main towns: Vineyard Haven to Oak Bluffs, Oak Bluffs to Edgartown, Edgartown to West Tisbury, and Edgartown to South Beach via Katama Road. Because the roads from West Tisbury to Aquinnah are rather hilly, you need to be in pretty good shape to tackle the ride. A less ambitious but rewarding journey would entail taking your bike to Aquinnah and then pedaling the hilly but scenic up-island circular trail that begins at the Aquinnah Lighthouse: Take Lighthouse Road to Lobsterville Road and backtrack up Lobsterville Road to State Road to Moshup Trail. The Manuel E. Correllus State Forest (see *Green Space*), off the Edgartown–West Tisbury Road, also has several bicycle paths.

Rubel Bike Maps (www.bikemaps.com) are simply the best, most detailed maps available for those planning more than cursory cycling between down-island towns. Rubel produces a combination map that covers both the Vineyard and Nantucket ($1.95), as well as another that includes the islands, Cape Cod, and the North Shore ($4.25).

The **Martha's Vineyard Commission** also produces a free map that tells you what to expect on major routes: for instance, narrow roadways, shared with cars, gently rolling terrain, steep rolling terrain, and so on. It does not give estimated times or exact mileage, though.

Bike Ferry (508-645-3511). Weekends 9–5 from late May through June and September; daily (on demand) 8–6 from July to early September. Some people riding out to Menemsha and Aquinnah will be thrilled to know about Hugh Taylor's little ferry, which takes cyclists across Menemsha Creek (it separates the picturesque harbor from Lobsterville Beach and Aquinnah beyond). This 150-yard ferry ride saves cyclists a 7-mile bike ride. $7 round trip, $4 one way.

Dozens of shops rent bikes, including: **Strictly Bikes** (508-693-0782) near the ferry terminal on Union Street in Vineyard Haven; **Anderson Bike Rentals** (508-693-9346) next to the ferry terminal on Circuit Avenue Extension in Oak Bluffs; **R. W. Cutler Bikes** (508-627-4052) on the harborfront at 1 Main Street in Edgartown; and **Wheel Happy** (508-627-5928), 8 South Water Street in Edgartown. If you're staying up-island or you just want to begin pedaling in the center of the island, try **West Tisbury Bikes** (508-693-5495), State Road, next to Alley's General Store. Expect to pay $20–25 daily in summer for a mountain or hybrid bike. (There are 3- and 7-day rentals, too.) Most shops are open April through October; ask about delivery and pickup service.

✳ **Cycle Works** (508-693-6966), at 351 State Road in Vineyard Haven, repairs bicycles. John Stevenson and his enthusiastic and helpful crew have the largest selection of cycling equipment (for sale and rent), accessories, and parts on the island. They've been here since 1975.

BOAT EXCURSIONS/RENTALS *Vela* **Daysails** (508-560-8352; 207-359-8353 off-season), Memorial Pier next to the Chappy ferry, Edgartown. With a maximum of six people aboard, this 50-foot gaff-headed sloop can feel like a private charter without the hefty price tag. Your hosts, Havilah and Beverly Hawkins (and their two kids), live on board and are really nice folks. Snacks are provided, but you can bring your own beverages. The 2-hour sail costs $55 per person. Four departures daily.

Ayuthia (508-693-7245). This traditional 48-foot, all-teak ketch takes a maximum of eight people on afternoon sails from early May through September. BYO food and drink; $75 per person for the afternoon trip. It's an excellent choice.

Magic Carpet (508-627-2889). Departures June through September. These folks are sailors at heart. Their boat accommodates only about 18 people.

Arabella (508-645-3511), Menemsha Harbor. Captain Hugh Taylor's 50-foot catamaran sails to Cuttyhunk daily at 10:30 AM in the summer. The 6-hour sail includes a 2-hour layover on Cuttyhunk, the only public island in the chain of Elizabeth Islands, and a swim at a remote beach (tide permitting). At 6 PM Hugh offers a sunset excursion with stunning views of the Clay Cliffs of Aquinnah. Taylor, a longtime Aquinnah resident, has sailed these waters since 1970. $60 to Cuttyhunk; $50 for the 2-hour sunset cruise; kids half price for both trips; BYO food and drink.

SAILING OFF THE COAST OF MARTHA'S VINEYARD

Kim Grant

VINEYARD HAVEN'S PROTECTED HARBOR

Mad Max (508-627-7500, 627-0358 cell), in front of the Seafood Shanty restaurant, Edgartown Harbor. This 60-foot catamaran sets sail twice daily (at 2 and 6 PM) from late May through September. Tickets for the 2-hour sail, which might have upwards of 40 people on board, cost $45 adults, $35 children under 10. Captain Bob Colacray knows these waters well.

Vineyard Water Sports (508-693-8476), Dockside Marina, Oak Bluffs Harbor. Open mid-May to mid-October. One-hour, 4-hour, daily, and weekly rentals of Boston Whalers that seat five or six people.

Wind's Up! (508-693-4252 instruction; 508-693-4340 rentals), at the drawbridge on Beach Road, Vineyard Haven. Rentals and instruction mid-May to late September; retail open March through December. This full-service outfit (on-island since 1962) rents Sunfish and small catamarans and offers beginning, intermediate, and advanced instruction.

CANOEING AND KAYAKING ✔ **Martha's Vineyard Kayak** (508-693-0895; www.menemsha.com), Vineyard Haven. Late May to mid-October. Eric Carlsen will pick the right pond or protected waterway depending on your skill level,

although little experience is necessary for paddling on protected, shallow ponds. He delivers kayaks in the mornings and afternoons to about four island locations, including Edgartown Harbor ($30 for a 3- to 4-hour paddle), which affords unobstructed views of fine summer homes, and Menemsha, Squibnocket, and Quitsa Ponds ($40). Tandem kayaks have child seats, so you can bring a youngster along, too. Double kayaks also available.

Wind's Up! (508-693-4252 instruction; 508-693-4340 rentals), at the drawbridge on Beach Road, Vineyard Haven. Rentals and instruction mid-May to late September; retail open March through December. Rentals by the half and full day; private and introductory group instruction. If you're in the market to purchase a canoe or kayak, the well-priced fleet is sold at the end of each season.

৬ **Kasoon Kayak Company** (508-627-2553). Open seasonally. Guided 4-hour tours on Great Pond with instruction as well as kayak rentals. Kasoon caters to deaf and disabled folks.

❧ **Long Point Wildlife Refuge Tour** (508-693-7392; www.thetrustees.org), led by Trustees of Reservations. This is a great way to learn basic paddling techniques and about the local ecology and natural history of Long Point. The guided tours of Tisbury Great Pond, a rich ecosystem that will delight birders, are 2½ hours and cost $30 adults, $15 children 15 and under. With a maximum of 12 people per tour, reservations are recommended. Trips depart twice daily from mid-June to early September.

Chilmark Pond Preserve (508-627-7141), access just before Abel's Hill Cemetery (where, incidentally, John Belushi is buried in an unmarked grave and Lillian Hellman is buried in a marked one) on South Road, Chilmark. When you paddle across Chilmark Pond, you'll be rewarded with a small ocean beach on the south shore. This local secret (well worth the effort) is only accessed by canoe or kayak, which you must supply.

See also Cape Pogue Wildlife Refuge under the sidebar "Chappaquiddick."

FISHING Fishing is excellent from most Vineyards **beaches and bridges.** The bridge between Oak Bluffs and Edgartown is perfect for anglers. There's also a wide area that hangs over the swiftly running channel between Nantucket Sound and Sengekontacket Pond. You're most likely to catch the island's prized striped bass and bluefish before sunrise. Surf-casting is best from south-facing beaches and the beaches at Aquinnah. On Chappaquiddick, **East Beach** at Cape Pogue Wildlife Refuge and **Wasque Point** (see the sidebar "Chappaquiddick" for both) are famed for fishing.

❋ **Coop's Bait & Tackle** (508-627-3909), 147 West Tisbury Road, Edgartown. This is your basic one-stop shopping for bait, tackle, boat charters, and information on "hot spots" for catching the big ones.

Dick's Bait & Tackle (508-693-7669), 108 New York Avenue in Oak Bluffs; **Larry's Tackle Shop** (508-627-5088), across from the A&P on Upper Main Street in Edgartown; and **Capt. Porky's** (508-627-7117), Dock Street, Edgartown, rent fishing rods, tackle, and other necessary equipment. Capt. Porky's also arranges charters.

Capella (508-627-3122; 508-627-2128), Edgartown Harbor. May to late October. Captain Charlie uses light tackle, flies, and conventional means when he goes out sportfishing.

North Shore Charters (508-645-2993; www.bassnblue.com), out of Menemsha Harbor. May through October. Captain Scott McDowell takes anglers in search of bass and blues.

Fly Fishing (508-696-7551; www.saltwaterflies.com), Vineyard Haven. June to mid-November. Ken and Lori Vanderlaske specialize in shoreline, saltwater fly-fishing for stripers. Typically they take out one ($175) or two ($225) people for a 6- to 7-hour trip that usually lasts from sundown until about 1 AM.

See also Fishing Discovery Tour under the sidebar "Chappaquiddick."

✂ **FOR FAMILIES** There are so many family- and kid-friendly activities that I've interspersed them throughout this *Outdoor Activities* section. If I'd listed them under *For Families,* the other headings would have been decimated!

🍵 **The Game Room** (508-693-5163), Oak Bluffs Avenue across from the Flying Carousel. Open late May to early September. When it rains and the troops are getting restless, head for these arcade games, air hockey, skeeball, and kiddie rides.

GOLF Farm Neck Golf Course (508-693-3057 reservations), off County Road, Oak Bluffs. Open April through December. Reservations are mandatory at this stately 18-hole course, but they're only taken 2 days in advance. A challenging course, but not long.

✳ **Mink Meadows** (508-693-0600), off Franklin Street, Vineyard Haven. A fairly long, but very subtle course; more challenging than you might think.

Windfarm Golf (508-693-4842), 203 Edgartown–Vineyard Haven Road, Oak Bluffs. Open April through October and weekends in November. This driving range and practice facility will loosen you up before you drop the big bucks on the above courses. Half the tees are covered. Lessons are booked up to 4 weeks in advance.

HORSEBACK RIDING ✂ ✳ Crow Hollow Farm (508-696-4554; www.crowhollowfarm.com), New Lane, West Tisbury. Trail rides, lessons, and summer camp.

✳ **Red Pony Riding** (508-693-3788), 85 Red Pony Road, off the Edgartown–West Tisbury Road, West Tisbury. Private lessons, trails for experienced riders, and packages for B&B and riding.

✂ **Nip-n-Tuck Farm** (508-693-1449), State Road, West Tisbury. Hayrides (call to schedule one) and pony rides (offered during the summer only, daily except Sunday 3–5 PM; $3).

ICE SKATING Martha's Vineyard Arena (508-693-5329), Edgartown–Vineyard Haven Road, Oak Bluffs. Call for public skating hours. Who brings skates to the Vineyard? No one, but you can rent them here.

IN-LINE SKATING Skating is off-limits on Main Street and at the Steamship

Authority in Vineyard Haven; on Circuit Avenue in Oak Bluffs; and in downtown Edgartown.

❉ ♂ **Sports Haven** (508-696-0456; www.vineyardsportshaven.com), 5 Beach Street, Vineyard Haven. Half-day ($15), full-day ($20), or weekly rentals ($70) and free skate tours twice weekly in summer. If you're renting and new to skating, consider taking a clinic ($20) in falling, stoping, and starting; it could save your skin. If you're buying, the clinic is free.

♂ **MINI-GOLF Island Cove** (508-693-2611), State Road across from Cronig's Market, Vineyard Haven. Open daily May through September and weekends during April and October.

SAILBOARDING Wind's Up! (508-693-4252 instruction; 508-693-4340 rentals), at the drawbridge on Beach Road, Vineyard Haven. Rentals and instruction mid-May to late September; retail open March through December. Sheltered Lagoon Pond, where Wind's Up! has a facility, is a great place for beginners to learn sailboarding and sailing. The water is shallow and the instructors patient. Those more experienced can rent equipment, consult the shop's map, and head out on their own. Sailboarding is excellent all over the island, but experienced surfers should head to Menemsha, Aquinnah, and South Beach.

SAILING LESSONS ♂ **Island Sailing School** (508-627-5720; www.islandsailing.com). Basic, intermediate, and advanced instruction and racing techniques (private and group) for adults and children from Edgartown. These folks do a very good job.

See also Wind's Up! under *Boat Excursions/Rentals.*

TENNIS Public courts are located at: **Church Street** (two clay) near the corner of Franklin Street in Vineyard Haven; **Niantic Avenue** (four hard) in Oak Bluffs; **Robinson Road** (four hard) near Pease's Point Way in Edgartown; **Chilmark Community Center** (508-645-3061) on South Road at Beetlebung Corner in Chilmark (available when members are not using them); **Old County Road** (two hard) in West Tisbury.

Island Inn Country Club Tennis Courts (508-693-6574), Beach Road in Oak Bluffs. Open mid-April to mid-October. Three clay courts cost $20 per hour.

↑ ❉ **The Vineyard Fitness Club & Tennis Center** (508-696-8000; www.vineyardtenniscenter.com), 22 Airport Road, off the Edgartown–West Tisbury Road, West Tisbury. When it's raining, this full-service indoor facility arranges matches, and offers lessons, tennis camps for all ages, and ball machines.

WATERSKIING MV Parasailing (508-693-2838), Pier 44, Beach Road, Vineyard Haven. Open mid-June to mid-October. If you're over 4 years old, Mark Clarke can teach you how to water-ski, knee-board, tube, wakeboard, and parasail. If you've always wanted to learn but thought you were too klutzy, Mark is the one to teach you. He runs a safety-conscious outfit. Mark also has a shop at the Dockside Marina in Oak Bluffs for parasailing only.

❋ Even More Things to See and Do

CRAFTS, DO-IT-YOURSELF ✎ ❋ **The Melting Pot** (508-693-6768), State Road, Vineyard Haven. Use your imagination or the design catalogs to help design and paint your own pottery. Off-season, adults outnumber kids, when the atmosphere is more social or therapeutic.

❋ **FITNESS CLUB Muscle Discipline** (508-693-5096), Kennebec Avenue, Oak Bluffs. A full-service fitness facility; $18 per visit or $45 per week.

Triangle Fitness (508-627-3393), at The Triangle, Vineyard Haven–Edgartown Road, Edgartown. Open daily. Ten-use (can be shared with another person), daily, and weekly passes.

The Vineyard Fitness Center & Tennis Center (508-696-8000; www.vine-yardtenniscenter.com), off the Edgartown–West Tisbury Road, at the airport; a full-service center.

SPA TREATMENTS "Day spas" sprang up in the late 1990s. Once on-island, ask around for personal recommendations.

SPECIAL PROGRAMS ❋ **Vineyard Conservation Society** (508-693-9588; www.vineyardconservationsociety.org), Wakeman Conservation Center, Lambert's Cove Road, Tisbury. Since it was established in 1965, this nonprofit group has protected thousands of acres from commercial and residential development by engaging in conservation land acquisition and advocacy. The society also sponsors a wide range of public activities, most of them free, including the Winter Walks program, a summer environmental lecture series, educational seminars and workshops on such topics as alternative wastewater treatment and solar-powered building technology, and the annual Earth Day all-island cleanup.

✎ ❋ **Featherstone Meetinghouse for the Arts** (508-693-1850; www.feather-stonearts.org), Vineyard Haven; off Barnes Road, half a mile north of the Edgartown–Vineyard Haven Road, West Tisbury. Arts center open year-round; gallery open daily 2–5 in summer. On 18 acres donated by the Martha's Vineyard Land Bank, this former horse barn and farm has been transformed into a community art center. A dozen or so artists open their on-site studios once a week so that individuals can use their equipment and gain insight under their creative supervision (for a nominal fee). Classes change seasonally but might include woodworking, stained glass, pottery, papermaking, printmaking, weaving, and photography. Weekly summer art camps for kids, too.

WINERY Chicama Vineyards (508-693-0309; www.chicamavineyards.com), Stoney Hill Road off State Road, West Tisbury. Open January to mid-May, Saturday 1–4; late May to mid-October, Monday through Saturday 11–5 and Sunday 1–5; mid-October through December, Monday through Saturday 1–4. Tastings throughout the year; tours late May to mid-October. Despite all these hours, Chicama still counsels that "hours vary, so call ahead." When the Mathiesens planted European wine grapes here in 1971, it was the first time since colonial days that it had been done commercially in Massachusetts. Nestled in the woods of the terminal moraine left by the glaciers that formed the island, Chicama annually makes over 5,000 cases of Chardonnay, Cabernet, Merlot, and other varieties. It also makes herb vinegars, mustards, chutneys, jams, jellies, and salad dressings.

✳ Green Space

❧ Martha's Vineyard Land Bank (508-627-7141), 167 Upper Main Street, Edgartown. The Land Bank was established in 1986 in order to purchase open space with funds raised by a 2 percent tax on real estate transactions. Today there are 54 parcels of land totaling more than 2,000 acres. I highly recommend getting this organization's map prior to your visit for a current look at the Vineyard's open land. Many of the island's conservation areas—ocean beach, moors, meadows, ponds, and woods—are free for all to enjoy.

Manuel E. Correllus State Forest (508-693-2540; www.massparks.org), off the Edgartown–West Tisbury Road or Barnes Road. Comprising 5,146 acres of woodland and meadows in the center of the island, the forest's trails are used regularly by bikers, joggers, picnickers, and hikers. Park near the Barnes Road entrance.

In Oak Bluffs
Ocean Park, along Ocean Avenue. Fringed with some of Oak Bluffs's best-preserved gingerbread cottages, the park's centerpiece is a large white gazebo that serves as a bandstand for summer-evening concerts.

In and near Edgartown
❧ Felix Neck Wildlife Sanctuary (508-627-4850; www.massaudubon.org), off Edgartown–Vineyard Haven Road, Edgartown. Trails open dawn–7 PM. Visitors

A LIFEGUARD'S SURFBOARD AT THE READY ON CHAPPAQUIDDICK

Kim Grant

center open 8–4 daily June through September, and 8–4 Tuesday through Sunday, October through May. The Vineyard is populated by many species of birds that flock to the island's forests and wildlife sanctuaries. This 350-acre preserve, affiliated with the Audubon Society, has 6 miles of easy trails that traverse thick woods, open meadows of wildflowers, beaches, and salt marshes. The interpretive exhibit center has turtles, aquariums, a gift shop, and a library. Year-round activities for children and adults include guided nature walks (almost daily during summer) and bird-watching trips for novices and experts alike. Inquire about weeklong children's day camps. Adults $4, children $3, free to Audubon Society members.

See also Mytoi, Cape Pogue Wildlife Refuge and Wasque Reservation, and natural history tours under the sidebar "Chappaquiddick."

In West Tisbury and up-island

Menemsha Hills Reservation (508-693-7662; www.thetrustees.org), off North Road, Menemsha. This exceptional Trustees of Reservations property makes for a great 2-hour hike. The 3.5-mile crestline trail, part of which runs along the island's second highest point, leads down to a rocky beach. This point was used during World War II as a military lookout. No swimming allowed.

Cedar Tree Neck Sanctuary (508-693-5207), off Indian Hill Road from State Road, West Tisbury. The 300-acre sanctuary, owned and managed by the Sheriff's Meadow Foundation, has trails through bogs, fields, and forests down to the bluffs overlooking Vineyard Sound.

Long Point Wildlife Refuge (508-693-7662), off Edgartown–West Tisbury Road, West Tisbury. Open 9–5 daily, mid-June to mid-September; sunrise to sunset mid-September to mid-June. A long, bumpy, dirt road leads to a couple of mile-long trails, Long Cove Pond, and a deserted stretch of South Beach. Parking is limited at this 586-acre preserve, maintained by the Massachusetts Trustees of Reservations, so get there early. Parking: $8 per vehicle, plus $4 per person over age 18; free in winter.

Peaked Hill Reservation, off Tabor House Road from Middle or North Roads, Chilmark. Turn left on the dirt lane opposite (more or less) the town landfill and then keep taking right-hand turns until you reach the trailhead. This 93-acre Land Bank property is the highest point on the island, at a whopping 311 feet above sea level. Good for hiking, picnicking, and mountain biking, this reservation also offers vistas of Nomans Land Island, Aquinnah peninsula, and Menemsha Bight.

Waskosim's Rock Preservation, North Road, just over the Chilmark town line. At almost 200 acres, this is one of the largest and most diverse of the Land Bank properties, with great hiking, bird-watching, picnicking, and mountain biking. The Waskosim boulder marks the start of a stone wall that ran down to Menemsha Pond, separating the English and Wampanoag lands in the mid–17th century.

Allen Farm Vista, South Road, Chilmark. On the south (or the left side) about one mile beyond Beetlebung Corner as you head toward Aquinnah. Practically the entire stretch of South Road in Chilmark once looked like this striking 22-

acre field and pastureland, protected as a Land Bank property. Lucy Vincent Beach is just beyond the pond, grazing sheep, and moorlands.

Cranberry Acres, West Tisbury. This cranberry bog, on the south side of Lambert's Cove Road from Vineyard Haven, has walking trails.

Polly Hill Arboretum (508-693-9426), 809 State Road, West Tisbury. Open 7–7 late May to mid-October (otherwise sunrise to sunset), daily except Wednesday. This is a magical place. Now totaling 60 acres, this former sheep farm was brought under cultivation in order to preserve it as a native woodland by legendary horticulturist Polly Hill. The arboretum, opened to the public in 1998, is a not-for-profit sanctuary devoted to more than 1,600 native plants, many threatened by extinction. The arboretum is tranquil and beautiful from early spring well into fall. Wandering visitors will discover an extraordinary range of plants. Lecture series, too. Donations gratefully accepted: $5 adults.

Fulling Mill Brook, off South Road, about 2 miles beyond the Chilmark Cemetery, Chilmark. Hiking trails pass through 46 acres of forests, fields, and streams.

See also Featherstone Meetinghouse for the Arts under *Even More Things to See and Do—Special Programs.*

BEACHES Unlike Nantucket's, many Vineyard beaches are private, open only to homeowners or cottage renters. (By law, though, anyone has the right to fish from any beach between the high- and low-water marks. So if you want to explore where you otherwise aren't allowed, make sure you're carrying a fishing pole!) Many innkeepers, especially those in the up-island establishments, provide walk-on passes to their guests. (A much-coveted Chilmark pass will get you access to Lucy Vincent Beach off South Road, the island's prettiest. Even then, you'll still need a photo ID. And just to keep you in the loop, two other private beaches in Chilmark—Quansoo and Hancock—require a key to gain entry. If you don't summer in Chilmark, you might consider purchasing a key for a mere $120,000.) That's what they went for last time I heard. If you have to ask the price, you probably can't afford it.) The following are public beaches.

In Vineyard Haven
Lake Tashmoo (or Herring Creek), at the end of Herring Creek Road, off Daggett Avenue from Franklin Street. This small beach offers good swimming, surf-fishing, and shellfishing. No facilities; limited parking; lifeguard.

♂ **Owen Park Beach,** on the harbor just north of the ferry. Good for small children and swimming. Parking.

In West Tisbury
♂ **Lambert's Cove Beach,** off Lambert's Cove Road. Although it's restricted to town residents and inngoers in-season, you can park here off-season to enjoy one of the island's top beaches. The sand is fine and the waters calm.

In Oak Bluffs
♂ **Oak Bluffs Town Beach,** on both sides of the ferry wharf, Oak Bluffs. This calm, narrow beach is very popular with Oak Bluffs families and seasonal visitors

with small children. No facilities, although there are public rest rooms next to the ferry dock.

✤ **Joseph Sylvia State Beach,** along Beach Road between Edgartown and Oak Bluffs. The Edgartown end of this 2-mile-long barrier beach is also called Bend-in-the-Road Beach; this part of the gentle beach has lifeguards but no facilities. Park free along the roadside at the "people's beach." Good shore fishing and crabbing along the jetties, too.

In Edgartown

Lighthouse Beach, at the end of North Water Street, adjoining Fuller Street Beach. From Lighthouse Beach you can watch boats going in and out of the harbor. Rarely crowded with bathers because of seaweed, but always crowded with picture takers; gentle waves. No facilities or lifeguards. Fuller Street Beach, a favorite among college students, is a short bike ride from town and generally quiet.

Katama (or South) Beach, off Katama Road. A shuttle runs from Edgartown to this popular, 3-mile-long barrier beach which has medium to heavy surf, a strong undertow, and high dunes. Children can swim in the calm and warm salt water of Katama Bay. There are lifeguards, but not along the entire beach. Facilities at the end of Katama Road and Herring Creek Road.

PHILBIN BEACH, UP ISLAND

Kim Grant

See also Cape Pogue Wildlife Refuge and Wasque Reservation in the "Chappaquiddick" sidebar; and Long Point Wildlife Refuge, Joseph Sylvia State Beach, and Oak Bluffs, above.

Up-island

Long Point Reservation, off Waldron's Bottom Road from the Edgartown–West Tisbury Road, West Tisbury. Owned by the Trustees of Reservations, this wide beach is isolated and beautiful, with good surf. From here you can also follow nature trails to Tisbury Great Pond. Lifeguard. Limited parking, for a fee.

⚓ **Menemsha Beach,** Menemsha Harbor. This calm, gentle beach is also pebbly. Nearby rest rooms. Sunsets from here can't be beat.

⚓ **Lobsterville Beach,** off State and Lobsterville Roads, Aquinnah. This beach is popular with families because of shallow, warm water and gentle surf. Limited parking along the road. Popular for fishing, too.

Lucy Vincent Beach, off South Road, is arguably the island's nicest beach. Although it's only open to residents and Chilmark inngoers (which is reason enough to stay in Chilmark), you can enjoy the wide, cliff-backed beach off-season. The farther east you walk, the less clothing you'll see. The farther west you walk, the more trouble you'll get in, since that stretch of beach is as private as they come.

Aquinnah Beach, just south of the Clay Cliffs of Aquinnah. Take the boardwalk and path through cranberry and beach plum bushes down to the beach, about a 10-minute walk. Resist the temptation to cover yourself with mud from the cliff's clay baths; the cliffs have eroded irreparably over the past century. (If that doesn't dissuade you, perhaps the law will: It's illegal to remove or use the clay.) Instead, walk along this 5-mile beach, (called, from north to south, **Aquinnah Public Beach, Moshup** (the shuttle bus drops off here—otherwise it's a 10-minute walk from paid Aquinnah parking), **Philbin,** and **Zack's Cliffs.** The cliffs are to the north, but the beaches are wider to the south. Philbin and Zack's Cliffs beaches are reserved for residents, but if you stick close to the waterline, you might not have a problem. Zack's fronts Jacqueline Kennedy Onassis's former estate. The further south you walk, the fewer people you'll see. But those people you do see, you'll see more of—people come here specifically to sunbathe nude. It's not legal, but generally the authorities look the other way. Swimming is very good here; the surf is usually light to moderate, and the shore doesn't drop off as abruptly as it does along the island's south shore. Facilities include rest rooms and a few small fast-food shops at the head of the cliff. Parking is plentiful; $15 daily.

⚓ **Uncle Seth's Pond,** off Lambert's Cove Road. A tiny (but public), freshwater pond on the side of the road. Good for kids.

PICNICS Owen Park, off Main Street, north of the ferry dock, Vineyard Haven. This thin strip of grass runs from Main Street down to the harbor beach. It's a great vantage point for watching boats sail in and out of the harbor. You can usually get a parking space, and there are swings for the kids.

Mill Pond, West Tisbury. This wonderful place to feed ducks and swans is next to the simple, shingled West Tisbury Police Department.

✳ Lodging

With some exceptions (primarily smaller B&Bs noted by our special value ✿ symbol), it has become very expensive to stay on the Vineyard. Since the late 1990s, room rates soared well, well, well beyond the rate of inflation. Edgartown lodging is the most expensive by far. Oak Bluffs tends to draw younger visitors. Vineyard Haven and West Tisbury are the most sensibly priced towns.

Reservations, made well in advance of your visit, are imperative during July and August and on weekends from September to mid-October. The height of *high season* runs, of course, from late June to early September, but many innkeepers define high season from mid-May to mid-October. In addition, many up-island inns are booked months in advance by hundreds of bridal parties, many with no ties to the island, who want meadows, stone walls, and spectacular ocean views as the backdrop for their photographs.

So many inns require a 2- or 3-night minimum stay in summer (and 2 nights on weekends in autumn) that I have omitted it from the individual reviews. Assume it's true. Although there are quite a few year-round lodging choices, the island is incredibly quiet from January through March.

INNS Although these places serve dinner on the premises, only the really worthy ones are reviewed separately under *Where to Eat*.

In West Tisbury 02575
✳ **Lambert's Cove Country Inn** (508-693-2298; www.lambertscove-inn.com), Lambert's Cove Road. This secluded country inn, a few miles from Vineyard Haven, is a wedding reception factory for good reason: The setting couldn't be more picturesque. The farmhouse estate once belonged to an ardent horticulturist, and the impressive formal gardens are nicely preserved. A tennis court, a lush wisteria arbor surrounded by thick lilacs, an apple orchard, and ancient rock walls also grace the property. Guest rooms are scattered throughout the inn, carriage house, and converted barn. They vary considerably (and some could use freshening), but each is distinctive; ask for a full description. Some of the 15 rooms open onto sundecks; one especially comfortable room has a private greenhouse sitting room. Guests receive parking passes to nearby Lambert's Cove, one of the island's prettiest beaches. Full breakfast included. Mid-May to mid-October $185–250; off-season $90–210.

In Edgartown 02539
✳ **Charlotte Inn** (508-627-4751), South Summer Street. The Vineyard's highbrow grande dame is owned by Gery and Paula Conover, ardent Anglophiles who make frequent trips to the United Kingdom to purchase antiques. Equestrian prints, elegant armchairs, and collections of beautifully bound classic novels have turned each room a luxuriously inhabitable museum. As for more mundane needs, of the inn's 23 rooms and two suites, some have a fireplace and most have TV. The Conovers' taste for all things English reveals itself in the inn's grounds, too: ivy-edged brick sidewalks, small croquet-quality lawns, impeccable flower beds. Continental breakfast, but a full breakfast is available for an additional charge. The conservative inn boasts an excellent,

Kim Grant

NORTH WATER STREET IN EDGARTOWN

independently owned restaurant (see L'Étoile under *Dining Out*). May through October $295–750; off-season $175–550.

🌸 **Edgartown Inn** (508-627-4794; www.edgartowninn.com), 56 North Water Street. Open April through October. A hostelry since the early 1800s, the inn has hosted such notables as Daniel Webster, Nathaniel Hawthorne, and then Senator John F. Kennedy. Sandi, the inn's longtime manager, has worked hard at maintaining and upgrading the inn's 20 rooms with firm mattresses and homey antiques. The rooms are simply but nicely decorated and represent perhaps the best value in town. Bathrooms are nicely retiled. Two more modern, light and airy rooms in the Garden House have private entrances. Breakfast is additional and served in the old-fashioned, charming period dining room or on the back patio. The inn is appropriate for children 8 and older. June through September $95 with shared bath,

$125–225 with private bath; off-season $75 and $100–165, respectively. No credit cards.

❄ ⚓ **Daggett House** (508-627-4600; 800-946-3400), 59 North Water Street. This is Edgartown's only waterfront inn, and that remains the principal reason for staying. If you're not going to sit for hours on water's edge, consider staying elsewhere. The original building served as the Vineyard's first tavern in 1660, and since then has been a store, a boardinghouse for sailors, a countinghouse, and a private home. There are 31 guest rooms and suites (each with cable TV, air-conditioning, and phone) dispersed among four buildings. Each is furnished with antiques and reproductions, lace-canopy beds, and comfortable armchairs. Rooms in the main house are generally preferable to those across the street. The Secret Staircase guest room (one of the inn's best) has a "private" entrance through one of the bookcases in the dining room. Rooms in the harborside cottages have private entrances. Be aware, though, that the clanking of the Chappy ferry, which runs until late at night, bothers some people in these rooms. Breakfast is served to the public (see *Eating Out*) and available to houseguests for a fee in the remarkably authentic colonial dining room (or on the waterside patio). It's not often you get to dine in rooms like this; you are usually relegated to seeing them at arm's length in historic houses. Mid-May to mid-October $150–585; off-season $85–275.

Up-island

✒ ✆ **Inn at Blueberry Hill** (508-645-3322; 800-356-3322; www.blueberryinn.com), North Road, Chilmark 02535. Open May through October. This secluded 56-acre retreat has an intentionally exclusive feel to it without being pretentious. Miles from anything but conservation land and stone walls, it's the kind of place you won't want to leave. Completely over-hauled in 1995, the 25 soothing rooms are scattered throughout six elegantly simple buildings. All rooms have telephones and air-conditioning; cable TV is available on request. Privacy is paramount here: Most rooms have a private deck or balcony. A wide array of spa treatments are available by advance request. A very expanded continental breakfast and use of fitness facilities (heated lap pool, tennis court, aerobic and weight equipment) are included. Box lunches are offered in-season. See Theo's under *Dining Out* for specifics about the inn's excellent dinners. Mid-June to mid-September $230–275 rooms, $405 suites; off-season $161–275 rooms, $220–405 suites; inquire about cottages that accommodate a family of six; 10 percent service charge added.

✆ **Beach Plum Inn** (508-645-9454; www.beachpluminn.com), Beach Plum Lane (off North Road), Menemsha 02552. Open May through

TIME STANDS STILL ON VACATIONS, BUT ROCKING CHAIRS RARELY DO.

Kim Grant

October. Secluded amid 6 wooded acres overlooking Menemsha Harbor in the near distance, the Beach Plum has blossomed under Craig Arnold's stewardship since 1998. The 11 guest rooms are luxurious, with fine bedding, first-class bathrooms (many with deep soaking or whirlpool tubs), stylish but unpretentious furnishings, and high-quality craftsmanship. A few inn rooms have small but private balconies with harbor views, and most rooms have some sort of water view. Practical in-room amenities like umbrellas, beach chairs, playing cards, and flashlights are not overlooked, either. The four cottages are each decorated with a simple but fresh style and grace. Facilities include beach access, a croquet court, and a tennis court. Off-site health club access is also included. Because this is such a popular place for weddings, you'll find a large white lawn tent between the inn and the harbor in spring and fall. The inn also boasts very fine cuisine (see *Dining Out*). Full breakfast included. Mid-June to mid-September $250–400; off-season $200–280.

Outermost Inn (508-645-3511; www.outermostinn.com), Lighthouse Road, Aquinnah 02532. Open early May to mid-October. First things first: It's practically impossible to get a vacancy here. Hugh and Jeanne Taylor's 20-acre parcel of land has the island's second best ocean view. (The best view is just up the hill from the Aquinnah Lighthouse, where Jeanne's great-great-grandfather was born.) The inn's six rooms (one with a whirlpool, two with deck views of the lighthouse) and one suite feature natural fabrics, wool rugs, and down duvets. Subdued colors and unpainted

furniture emphasize the seaside light. Rooms are named for the wood used in each: beech, ash, hickory, and cherry. (Speaking of wood, don't miss the outdoor bar made from one long, impressive hardwood tree.) In keeping with the family's musical tradition, guitars, pianos, and other instruments are placed in the common areas. (You might get lucky and wander into an impromptu living room concert given by Hugh's brother James.) Full breakfast included. Mid-June to mid-September $260–340; off-season $210–295.

BED & BREAKFASTS

In Vineyard Haven 02568

✳ ♿ **Thorncroft Inn** (508-693-3333; 800-332-1236; www.thorncroft.com), 460 Main Street. After all these years, the Thorncroft continues to set the service gold standard. Under the care of Lynn and Karl Buder since 1980, this elegant and conservative Craftsman-style bungalow sits on a 3½-acre wooded estate (about a mile out of town). It's arguably the island's best-run inn. All 14 guest rooms are decorated with Victorian-period antiques and have plush carpeting. Amenities include thick robes, cable TV, air-conditioning, two telephone lines, and the morning paper delivered to your door. Some rooms have hot tubs or Jacuzzis-for-two; many have working (wood-burning!) fireplaces. A complimentary full country breakfast is served in the inn's two intimate dining areas, or you may opt for a continental breakfast in bed. Finally, there's afternoon tea and pastries and evening turndown service. Late June to early September $225–475; off-season $180–450.

✳ **Martha's Place B&B** (508-693-0253; www.marthasplace.com), 114

Main Street. This stately Greek Revival house twinkles seductively at night when all the interior lights are turned on. Just two blocks from the center of town, some rooms have a harbor view. All are absolutely elegant. While the house is furnished with chandeliers and Oriental carpets, the place isn't stuffy at all, thanks to down-to-earth innkeepers Richard and Martin. The first floor is given over to common space, with high ceilings and an open floor plan. Amenities include nightly turndown service, breakfast in bed (on request), and morning newspapers. Ultrafine linens, down comforters, plush towels, fancy toiletries, luxe bathrooms, and robes further the high standard of comfort. Fireplaces (with Duraflame logs) and Jacuzzis warm it year-round. Loaner bicycles and tennis racquets are available on request. An expanded continental breakfast, with excellent croissants and cinnamon rolls, is included. June through October $175–395; off-season $125–275.

❄ 🏵 **Crocker House Inn** (508-693-1151; 800-772-0206; www.crockerhouseinn.com), 12 Crocker Avenue. As one of the few inns that takes one-nighters (although I certainly suggest staying longer), the Crocker House gets my gratitude on your behalf. In 1998, when innkeepers Jynell and Jeff Kristal purchased this turn-of-the-20th-century B&B on a quiet side street near the center of town, they made the rooms lighter and brighter. Each of the eight guest rooms has a fresh summer charm, retiled bathroom, cable TV, phone, computer access, and mini-fridge items. The primo third-floor loft, tucked under the eaves with a gas fireplace and Jacuzzi, also has harbor views. Room 5 has good cross breezes and a private feeling; room 7 is larger, with a gas fireplace and strong morning sun; room 3 is good for three people traveling together and boasts a private entrance. An expanded continental breakfast, served in the small combination living/dining room (with an almost-always-on TV), is included. But many guests linger over a second cup of coffee and the newspaper on the front wraparound porch set with rockers. June through October $185–365; off-season $115–265.

❄ **Herring Run House** (508-696-7337; www.herringrunhouse.com), 419 Barnes Road. On the edge of Lagoon Pond (which has ocean access) and a few miles from Oak Bluffs and Vineyard Haven, this completely transformed old house has three guest rooms brimming with an updated aesthetic. Experienced innkeepers Louis and Katherine Costabel know what guests are looking for: de rigueur in-room amenities include feather beds, a two-person soaking tub, hardwood floors, thick bathrobes, satellite TV and VCR, and a CD player. Sunset views over the lagoon from each of the bedrooms and living room don't hurt, either. And the 35-foot deck and private beach make this place one of a kind. A full breakfast of quiche or cheese blintzes with mango and blackberry puree is included. Complimentary kayaks and bicycles, too. Mid-May to mid-October $225–285; off-season $100–200.

❄ 🏵 🐾 **Kinsman Guest House** (508-693-2311; www.kinsman.vineyard.net), 278 Main Street. Open year-round, ostensibly. Doreen Kinsman's shingled summer home is located a 10-minute walk from the center of town and a 20-minute walk to the

West Chop Lighthouse. Built in 1880 as the original manse to the church across the street, it boasts high ceilings, an elegant staircase, and a proprietor who goes out of her way to accommodate guests. It has only three guest rooms, two of which share a newly tiled bath with modern fixtures. All rooms are gussied up with Laura Ashley accents, and two have four-poster beds. Breakfast is not included, but the front porch is so inviting many people pick up something in town to enjoy here. It's also hard to beat the price: $125 June through August; $100 off-season. Pets accepted on occasion.

🐾 ✿ **Marni's House** (508-696-6198; www.marnishouse.com). Off the beaten path near the center of Vineyard Haven, Marni's is a warm and homey place, a throwback to the noncommercial era of innkeeping. It's a friendly and contemplative place, with 80 acres of conservation land abutting the property across the street. Shaded decks surround the house, and a combo living room/dining room/ kitchen is warmed by a woodstove. As for the three guest rooms, Tower has a sleeping loft, an outdoor shower, and can accommodate an extra person; Sunrise gets great morning rays and has a Jacuzzi; Treehouse features a deep Japanese soaking tub. All have private deck. May through October $150–175 nightly, $900–1,100 weekly; off-season $110–125 and $600–750, respectively. No credit cards.

In West Tisbury 02575

🌼 **The Farmhouse** (508-693-5354; www.mvy.com/farmhouse), State Road. Open May through December. Drive 10 minutes from the ferry to this unpretentious B&B, and you'll be in another world. Dating to 1810, this warm house and its longtime innkeepers—Kathleen and Volker Kaempfert—are a delight. The five

GINGERBREAD COTTAGES AND HYDRANGEAS TYPIFY OAK BLUFFS

guest rooms (four with private bath) are furnished with country antiques and down comforters. Bathrooms are newly renovated. The smallest room has a particularly unique feature: no indoor shower, but rather its own private outdoor shower! The combination living/dining room, where a decadent continental breakfast is served, features exposed beams and wide floorboards. Additional common space includes a quiet side deck. The Kaempferts are the kind of innkeepers who sit with guests at breakfast time (after they've poured your coffee). July through October $110–135; off-season $85–110.

🦟 ❄ ✐ **The House at New Lane** (508-696-7331), New Lane. Off the beaten path, this house is appealing to "real B&Bers," according to owners Ann and Bill Fielder. By that they mean the kind of guests who are happy to see family photos above the mantel and who don't need everything to be Martha-Stewart-perfect. Surrounded by acres of woods and gardens, these three large rooms share two baths. One room has a private deck and entrance. Guests also have special access to a great beach, practically worth the cost of the room alone. Full breakfast included. Children are welcome, and futons are available. $85; $20 surcharge for single-night reservations; $20 nightly for a child.

The Old Parsonage (508-696-7745), 1005 State Road. Open May through October. Fifth-generation islander Tara Whiting-Watson and her husband, David, operate this family homestead, which sweeps dramatically down to a picturesque pond near the center of West Tisbury. The 1668 house, on the National Register of Historic Places, features low ceilings and narrow doorways. The house has an incredibly rich history: The first room is said to have been built by Myles Standish's son Josiah. After staying here, you'll surely feel more attached to the island than you did prior to your arrival. Few places like this remain. The nicest accommodation is the East Room, a spacious two-room suite, but there are three other rooms as well. Continental breakfast included. Shared bath $90–100, private bath $145, suite $165.

Behind the inn is the **Davis House Gallery,** where Tara's uncle, Allen Whiting, was born, currently resides, and shows his pastoral island landscapes. His historic "barn" studio occupies a building behind the house-gallery.

❄ **The Bayberry** (508-693-1984; 800-693-9960; www.mvbayberry.vineyard.net), 49 Old Courthouse Road, North Tisbury. Off the beaten path (if there is such a thing on this island), host and expert rug hooker Rosalie Powell has been innkeeping here since 1984. Each of the five guest rooms (three with private bath) has its share of cozy, country-style furnishings. I like the first-floor room best, even though it is smaller, and even though a couple of the other rooms have large picture windows overlooking the yard. There's plenty of common space, including a homey living room with family photos, a grand piano, and a collection of glass bottles in the picture window. A full gourmet breakfast (perhaps pancakes, hash browns, and bacon) is served in front of a kitchen fireplace or on the patio. Late May to mid-October $125–190; inquire about off-season rates.

In Oak Bluffs 02557

Oak Bluffs Inn (508-693-7171; 800-955-6235; www.oakbluffsinn. com), 64 Circuit Avenue at Pequot Avenue. Open May through October. You can't miss the inn—it's the marvelously detailed pink building with an enormous third-floor cupola. It also has a great location: at the tip of Circuit, on the edge of the "campground," three blocks from a beach, and a 10-minute walk to the ferry. The friendly 30-something innkeepers, Erik and Rhonda Albert, have done a great job freshening the place up. All nine guest rooms have small but newly redone baths, air-conditioning, cottage-style bedroom sets, and views of colorful neighboring cottages from every window. An expanded continental buffet breakfast, enjoyed at individual tables, is included; guests may also eat on the wraparound porch. Families are welcome in the carriage house or the first-floor room. Mid-June to early September $175–255; off-season $130–190.

Brady's NESW Bed & Breakfast (508-693-9137; 888-693-9137; www.sunsol.com/bradys), 10 Canonicus Avenue. A 10-minute walk from the center of town and one block from the water, this has been Brady Aikens's family home since 1929; he summered here in the 1940s and opened it as a B&B in 1991. Guest rooms are named according to direction: north, east, south, or west (hence the *NESW* appellation). The summery, whitewashed rooms have wood-slat walls and are decorated in soothing colors and designer linens. West (with sunset views) is the largest and nicest room. Two rooms boast a private balcony; one has a private bath; all have a ceiling fan. Start your day with an outdoor shower, followed by a continental breakfast on the wraparound porch with rockers, and end up back here with Brady as the sun sets. (He's here at 5 PM sharp every afternoon.) The comfy living room, decorated with southwestern influences, has a large video and CD collection. May through October $132–176 (including tax); half that off-season.

Four Gables (508-696-8384; www.fourgablesmv.com), 41 New York Avenue. On the road leading into town from Vineyard Haven, Four Gables is both delightfully unusual and conventional. On one hand, it's a turn-of-the-20th-century shingled house with a wraparound porch and spacious first-floor parlor and dining room. On the other hand, it is filled with eclectic objects and art, and has contemporary porches. As for the four wonderfully spare guest rooms and one suite (perfect for a family or a longer stay, with a kitchenette), they're restful, with natural-fiber bedding, thick towels, and private balcony. Still, this is not your ordinary B&B. There is no innkeeper hovering about, and the covered porch is filled with eclectic furniture. An expanded continental breakfast is included. June through September $125–145 rooms, $195 suite; off-season $85–105 rooms, $145 suite; less in winter.

Oak House (508-693-4187; 800-245-5979; www.vineyardinns.com), at Seaview and Pequot Avenues. Open mid-May to mid-October. The shingled, gingerbread Oak House is appropriately named—there's oak everywhere, from floor to ceiling. Built in 1872, the inn is itself a finely preserved antique with a lot of Victoriana added. The glassed-in porch overlooking the beach and street is quite sunny, and the living room charming, but otherwise some may find this much oak is just dark. Nonetheless, most of the 10 rooms (2 of which are suites) have water views; all have air-conditioning. I'm partial to the third-floor rooms, with sloping ceilings. Even if your room has a private balcony, you may find yourself spending time in a rocking chair or on a swing on the large wraparound veranda. Full buffet breakfast and afternoon tea included. Early June to early September $195–250 rooms, $310–315 suites; off-season $160–190 and $220–230, respectively.

✳ ✿ **Nashua House** (508-693-0043; www.nashuahouse.com), Kennebec Avenue. Owned by the same folks who operate Zapotec Cafe (see *Eating Out*), the 1873 Nashua House has 15 breezy and simple rooms, all of which share five bathrooms. The guesthouse was completely renovated in 2000, and as a result, all its carpeted rooms are looking good. I particularly like the corner rooms (room 11 included). This guesthouse is perfectly situated in the thick of the action. Late May to early September $59–109; off-season $49–69.

✿ **Attleboro House** (508-693-4346), 42 Lake Avenue. Open mid-May through September. This authentic gingerbread cottage faces Oak Bluffs Harbor and sits on the outer perimeter of the Methodist Camp Meeting Association. It's been taking in seaside guests since 1874, and it hasn't changed much since then. In Estelle Reagan's family since the 1940s, the guesthouse has 11 simple but tidy guest rooms that share five bathrooms. (Some rooms have a sink.) Most rooms have a porch, but if yours

doesn't, there's a wraparound porch on the first floor. One suite on the third floor can accommodate six people. $75–115.

In Edgartown 02539

✳ ⅛ ✿ ✎ **Point Way Inn** (508-627-8633; 888-711-6633; www.pointway.com), 104 Main Street at Pease's Point Way. Elegantly contemporary yet stylishly informal, this 1850s sea captain's house is my favorite place to stay when I have some cash in my pocket. Owners John Glendon (a "recovering attorney") and Claudia Miller (an artist and sculptor) have a flair for creating sophisticated, soothing spaces. Claudia, in particular, approaches decor as artistic expression. White walls and recessed living room lighting set off dramatic black-and-white photos, artwork, rattan, leather, and overstuffed furnishings. Of the 13 light and airy guest rooms, all have wonderfully fresh bathrooms, white with mod accents. A fave two-room suite features two decks and a living room with pullout sofa. The garden room with a private entrance is appropriate for pets and children. Start your day with a choice of two entrées (perhaps peach crêpes or eggs) served at individual tables on handmade dishes. You borrow the complimentary guest car for a few hours; it's available on a "shared-use" basis. Then return in time for a nice tea and to enjoy the private courtyard. It's delightfully different for the Vineyard: Tall sea grasses are offset by sculptures (some by Claudia), pebbles, flagstone, and mod tables and chairs. Yet another benefit: The inn has an extra shower, so you could eke out one more day at the beach and not have to go home with sand in your swimsuit. Late May to mid-

October $300–400 rooms, $325–600 suites; off-season $150–300. Children under 12 stay free off-season; otherwise, they're $25 nightly in-season.

❊ **Hob Knob Inn** (508-627-9510; 800-696-2723; www.hobknob.com), 128 Main Street. More like a small hotel than B&B, the exclusive-feeling Hob Knob is first-rate. Renovated from top to bottom in both furnishings and philosophy (in late 1997 by Maggie White), the Hob Knob prides itself on attentive services. Just a few minutes' walk from the center of town (request a room off Main Street), this Gothic Revival house has 17 spacious guest rooms with down bedding, king-sized beds, fine antiques, and a very soothing and tasteful ambience. Additional amenities include a morning newspaper delivered to your door, cable TV, Bose radios, phones with dataports, and air-conditioning. After-noon tea and a full country breakfast, served at small tables, are included.

Or have breakfast in bed. During inclement weather, you'll appreciate the enclosed porch, a private back patio, two sitting rooms, and a front porch with rockers. Exercise hounds will appreciate the fitness room and dry sauna; massages also available. The nearby Thaxter House, a luxury rental house that accommodates eight people ($4,000–10,000 weekly), is really quite extraordinary. Mid-May through October $250–550; off-season $125–350.

❊ 🐾 **Victorian Inn** (508-627-4784; www.thevic.com), 24 South Water Street. This centrally located B&B, presided over by Stephen and Karyn Caliri since 1993, has 14 luxurious guest rooms. Some have four-poster canopy beds; many have a private porch or balcony. While I particularly like room 10, with a slanting roofline and a steady stream of sunlight, all third-floor rooms are corner chambers with harbor and chimney views.

THE POINT WAY INN'S GARDEN COURTYARD IS AN OASIS

Kim Grant

Rooms are furnished with substantial, comfortable armchairs, sofas, loveseats, fresh flowers, and desks. Steve, a very gregarious innkeeper, presides over the morning meal, serving three courses on the flower-bordered back patio or indoors at tables for two in the formal breakfast room. Although this B&B accepts children, three people are not permitted in one room. Dogs welcome off-season. Late May to mid-October $180–385; off-season call to inquire.

Tuscany Inn (508-627-5999), 22 North Water Street. Open April to mid-December. This elegant inn balances color and space with magnificent antiques, fabrics, and unusual decorative pieces. Common space includes a library (with TV), a flagstone terrace, and a plush living room with dramatic orchid sprays. Of the eight guest rooms, the least expensive are quite small, with twin beds tucked under the eaves. All enjoy fine linens; many have whirlpool bath. Breakfasts are served on the terrace or in the tiled Tuscan-style dining room with exposed kitchen. June to mid-September $200–395; off-season $100–295.

🕯 **Summer House** (508-627-4857; www.mvsummerhse.com), 96 South Summer Street. Open mid-May to mid-October. Three blocks from Main Street and a block from Edgartown Harbor, this homey and charming B&B is a welcome relief from many overdone inns. Innkeeper and retired schoolteacher Chloe Nolan offers one charming guest room (with ceiling fan) and one very large suite. Each features marvelous quilts, braided rugs, and quiet nights, as well as the benefits of a deep front yard with a tranquil garden and, my favorite, a hot-water outdoor shower. Guests

enjoy a continental buffet breakfast served in the country kitchen or on the brick terrace, both overlooking the yard. The little sunporch with rockers is comfortable, too. $175–200. No credit cards.

🕯 **The Big House** (508-627-3344; www.bighousemv.com), 20 Farm Road. Open May through October. This lofty, contemporary house is a one-of-a-kind rarity for the Vineyard. The brochure's tag lines are simple, extolling "beauty, comfort, luxury, and privacy." It couldn't be more accurate; the house has a great feel. Your hosts, Breeze Hodson and Mark Tonneson, have created a warm and relaxing space that you won't want to leave. The two rooms and one suite, painted with rich colors, are outfitted with luxe linens, plush robes, and a soothing aesthetic. The suite features a fireplace and private deck; the Tonneson room features a private entrance. Although I didn't get to see the charming and carefree cottage, I have faith in recommending it. The two-bedroom place accommodates families and up to seven people. Expanded continental breakfast served at one table. July and August $195–350; off-season $150–300; cottage $1,900 in summer, $1,400 off-season.

❋ **Jonathan Munroe House** (508-627-5536; www.menemsha.com), 100 Main Street. Although there are eight rooms, the B&B's trump card is a secluded two-story garden cottage that rents for $350 nightly from early May through October. It offers exquisite privacy and a central location.

Up-island

🐾 ❋ 🕯 **The Duck Inn** (508-645-9018), off State Road, Aquinnah 02535. This is the most unusual place to stay on the island. It's also only a 5-minute walk to Philbin Beach, one of the island's top two or three. As long as you can appreciate that the inn is a work in progress, you'll be happy here. By that I mean that while the window casings may not have trim on them yet, you may be sleeping in a sleigh bed with a silk, hand-painted, feather duvet (in my favorite room, which also boasts a balcony). Another room has a brass bed, freestanding marble basin, little balcony, and one French door to the water closet. Ask longtime proprietor Elise LeBovit for a complete description of the eclectic rooms, especially the cavelike ground-floor room. The whole open first floor is a communal-style gathering space, complete with wax-covered candle-sticks on the dining table, a central fireplace and Glenwood stove, and kilims and Native American carpets. There is a well-used game area and special breakfast table for kids, not to mention a hot tub and masseuse. A full organic breakfast is included. July to early September $105–215; off-season $100–125. Pets allowed in the "cave."

✔ COTTAGES, EFFICIENCIES, & APARTMENTS

In Oak Bluffs 02557
✔ **East Chop Harborfront Apartments** (508-696-0009), 47 East Chop Drive. Open May through October. These five very well-maintained apartments are right on the harbor, a 5-minute walk from the center of town. The one- and two-bedroom units, with full kitchens, are great for families. Units open onto private, waterfront decks. Call as early as you can; these modern apartments are very nice. July and August $1,350–1,600

weekly (Sunday to Sunday); off-season $800–1,000.

In Edgartown 02539
Winnetu Inn and Resort at South Beach (508-627-4747; 978-443-1733 reservations; www.winnetu.com), South Beach, Edgartown. Open mid-April to late November. Three miles from Edgartown and new in 2000, this 11-acre resort is great for families because of its proximity to South Beach (you can walk along a private path). Other amenities include a heated pool, putting green, tennis club, library with fireplace, ocean-view restaurant, country store, and grocery delivery service. Choose from a variety of upgraded accommodations: studios with kitchenette; one-bedroom suites with a kitchenette, combination living/dining area, and a deck or patio (sleeping a family of five); and larger suites with full kitchen. A complimentary children's program is offered mornings in-season; inquire about evening children's programs. Late June to early September $825–4,695 for a 3-night minimum stay; off-season $195–1,200 nightly. Inquire about packages at Winnetu and weekly house rentals through its associate **Mattakesett Properties** (www.mattakesett.com).

✔ **Edgartown Commons** (508-627-4671; 800-439-4671; www.edgartown-commons.com), Pease's Point Way. Open May to mid-October. These 35 efficiencies—from studios to two-bedroom apartments—are near the center of town and great for families. Most of the individually owned units are in very good condition; these are rented first. Units in the main building have high ceilings and thus feel more spacious. Many units surround the pool, but all are comfortably furnished and most feature new kitchens. Outside, there are grills, picnic tables, and a nice enclosed play area. Longtime managers Rick and Janet Bayley keep the place humming. Mid-June to early September $160–185 studio or two-room, $235–260 three- to four-room; off-season $90–110 and $140–160, respectively.

Up-island

❦ Menemsha Inn and Cottages

(508-645-2521; www.menemshainn. com), North Road, between Menemsha Cross Road and Menemsha Harbor, Menemsha 02552. Open April through October. This secluded 14-acre parcel of forest has some lovely views of Vineyard Sound, a direct wooded path to Menemsha Beach, and a friendly atmosphere. Innkeepers Kristin and Jim Travers, longtime associates of the inn, manage it with grace and warmth. Over the years (it was actually opened in 1923) it's been continually upgraded and maintained with pride. There's an emphasis on peace and quiet, rather than fussy interior decorating. The complex boasts six luxurious rooms in the carriage house (with a "great room" and fieldstone fireplace), nine smaller but bright motel-style rooms, 11 tidy housekeeping cottages, and an elegant, two-bedroom suite. Cottages have a screened-in porch, fully equipped kitchen, outdoor shower, barbecue, and wood-burning fireplace. (Maid service costs an additional $15 daily.) Walk-on passes to Lucy Vincent and Squibnocket beaches are provided. Reserve cottages in February if you can; this well-manicured place has a loyal, repeat clientele. Mid-June to late September $185–290 nightly for rooms (including

expanded continental breakfast), $1,900 weekly for one-bedroom cottages, $2,625 for two-bedroom cottages, $3,150 for waterview suite; off-season $110–165 for rooms, $1,100–1,500 weekly or $180–250 nightly for cottages. All rates are for two people; $20 per additional person. No credit cards.

See also Inn at Blueberry Hill under *Inns;* Hob Knob Inn and Jonathan Munroe House under *Bed & Breakfasts;* and Island Inn under *Hotels and Motels.*

HOTELS AND MOTELS

In Oak Bluffs 02557

🐾 ♂ ♿ **Island Inn** (508-693-2002; 800-462-0269; www.islandinn.com), Beach Road. Open April through November. If you want to avoid in-town crowds, or let the kids to run around, this is a decent choice. Situated between Oak Bluffs and Edgartown, this 7-acre resort is also within walking distance of two beaches and adjacent to Farm Neck Golf Course. In all there are 51 units with kitchenettes (in the form of studios, one- and two-bedroom suites, town houses, and a cottage) in several low-slung buildings. For a quieter stay, choose a room in the one-story buildings. Townhouse units have a fireplace, spiral staircase to the loft bedroom, and a separate bedroom. All rooms have cable TV, telephone, and air-conditioning. Facilities include three well-maintained tennis courts (a tennis pro is available in-season), swimming pool, and plenty of space to picnic and barbecue. Mid-June to early September $165–295, more for the cottage; spring and fall $75–175; $20 each additional person. Pets are accepted off-season. A larger cottage sleeps six.

SUMMERTIME AND THE LIVING'S EASY

Kim Grant

❄ 🐾 ♿ 🦞 **Surfside Motel** (508-693-2500; 800-537-3007; www.mvsurfside.com), Oak Bluffs Avenue. One of the few places open through the winter, the Surfside has above-average motel-style rooms near the ferry. The area can get a bit boisterous on summer evenings, but room rates reflect that. Each room has either a queen or two double beds, cable TV, and air-conditioning; small refrigerators and cribs are available. Corner rooms are particularly nice and spacious. Pets are welcome for an additional fee of $10 per pet per day. Mid-June to early September $150–180 rooms, $245–285 suites (up to four people); off-season $65–120 and $135–170, respectively; each additional person $20.

In Edgartown 02539
❄ 🦞 **Harbor View Hotel** (508-627-7000; 800-225-6005; www.harborview.com), 131 North Water Street.

Overlooking a lighthouse, grass-swept beach, and Chappaquiddick, the 1891 Harbor View Hotel is Edgartown's best-situated hostelry. Now managed by Wyndham Hotels and Resorts, the grande dame has 124 rooms and one- and two-bedroom suites with kitchen or kitchenette. There are tranquil harbor views from the hotel's spacious veranda and some guest rooms. Other rooms have porches overlooking the pool. Guest rooms are generally large, and appointed with wicker chairs, pecan-washed armoires, antique prints, and watercolor landscapes by local artists. Facilities include room service, swimming pool, and concierge. Because of its size, the hotel caters to large groups. Children's program in summer. June through September $325–575 rooms, $480–825 one- and two-bedroom suites; fall and spring $225–375 rooms, $280–525 suites; winter

$115–235 rooms, $285–340 suites; $20 each additional person. Children under 16 stay free in parent's room.

☌ **Harborside Inn** (508-627-4321; 800-627-4009; www.theharborside-inn.com), 3 South Water Street. Open mid-April to mid-November. This seven-building time-share condominium is one of the few waterfront (harborfront, no less!) accommodations on the island. Practically all rooms have some sort of water view; most have a porch or patio. The 90 rooms and four suites are well appointed with standard hotel-issue furnishings. Facilities include a heated pool overlooking harbor boat slips. June to early September $160–360; spring and fall rates about 40 percent less; $25 each additional person. Children under 12 stay free in parent's room. Attention sailors: Inquire about transient boat slips.

RENTAL HOUSES AND COTTAGES

Sunnyside (508-696-7682; www.marthasvineyardsunnyside.com), 45 Sunnyside Avenue. Open May through December. Franco Ferrandi's waterfront retreat on Lagoon Pond includes a main house and a studio. July and August $2,100 weekly studio (for two to three people), $4,000–8,000 weekly main house (for two to six); off-season $1,850 weekly or $200–250 nightly studio, $3,000–6,000 weekly main house.

Dozens of **real estate agencies** handle thousands of rentals, which vary from tiny cottages to luxe waterfront homes, from dismal and overpriced units to great values. Consequently, there is no way I can recommend any one agency. Your best bet is to find a rental adjacent to the owner's house. That way, you are assured of someone being able to help you if things go awry. Get a local newspaper early in the year for these advertisements.

See also Winnetu Inn and Resort at South Beach (Mattakesett Properties) under *Cottages, Efficiencies, & Apartments*.

CAMPGROUND ☘ ☌ **Martha's Vineyard Family Campground** (508-693-3772; www.campmvfc.com), 569 Edgartown Road, Vineyard Haven 02568. Open mid-May to mid-October. In addition to shaded tent and trailer sites, the campground also has rustic one- and two-room cabins that sleep five or six people ($100–110). Tents and trailers $36–40. Additional adults $10; children under 18, $3; weekly rates, too.

YOUTH HOSTEL ☘ ☌ **Manter Memorial AYH Hostel** (508-693-2665; www.usahostels.org; 800-909-4776 for in-season reservations; 617-531-0459 for reservations prior to the start of the season), Edgartown–West Tisbury Road, West Tisbury 02575. Open April to mid-November. This saltbox opened in 1955, and it remains an ideal lodging choice for cycling-oriented visitors. The hostel is at the edge of the Manuel E. Correllus State Forest (which is full of bike paths; see *Green Space*) and next to the path that runs from Edgartown to West Tisbury. Bring your own linens or rent them for the single-sex, dormitory-style bunk beds. The large kitchen is fully equipped, and the common room has a fireplace. Reservations strongly recommended, especially from mid-June to early September, when large groups frequent the hostel. Reserve by phone 2 weeks in advance. $19–22; half price for children under 14.

✳ Where to Eat

Most restaurants are open May to mid-October; some are open through Christmas; a few operate year-round. Opening and closing days vary considerably from week to week, largely dependent on the weather and number of visitors, so it's impossible to tell you reliably which days any given restaurant will be open. Always call ahead after Labor Day and before Memorial Day.

There are a few more generalizations I can make. Vineyard Haven, Tisbury, and up-island towns are "dry," so BYOB of wine or beer. (Some restaurants charge a nominal corking fee.) I've tried to note when there is a chef-owner because generally these places provide the most reliable food. Many Oak Bluffs establishments are family-oriented and casual, though there are a few sophisticated options. The dress code in Edgartown is a bit more conservative, but most places don't warrant a jacket and tie. Dining options are scarcer up-island, and require reservations well ahead of time. Otherwise, reservations are highly suggested at all *Dining Out* establishments.

DINING OUT

In Vineyard Haven

✵ ✳ **Zephrus** (508-693-3416), 9 Main Street. Open for lunch and dinner. The casual bistro is contemporary and warm, with an eclectic menu ranging from crabcakes to a large pot of steamed mussels for starters and heading to free-range roasted chicken and New York strip steak for main dishes. I particularly enjoy the seared salmon with leeks, carrots, red potatoes, and littlenecks in a saffron shellfish broth. Entrée accompaniments

change nightly, but the menu always highlights a vegetarian and pasta dish. BYOB. Lunch $9–14, dinner entrées $20–30.

✳ **Cafe Moxie** (508-693-1484), 48 Main Street. Open for lunch and dinner. (May be closed January through March.) This casually hip storefront space offers quite commendable cuisine enhanced by serious sauces. Although the chef may change from season to season, eclectic contemporary lineup, but some dishes also hint of classical overtures. Try the pan-seared scallops with butternut squash risotto cakes, or New York strip steak with mashed potatoes, or excellent grilled portobello Mushroom Napoleon. The café is also known for gourmet pizzas. BYOB. Lunch $5–12, dinner entrées $18–32.

✳ **Le Grenier** (508-693-4906), 96 Main Street. Open for dinner. Chef-owner Jean Dupon's place opened in 1979 and is consistently *magnifique*. Lyons-born, Dupon offers traditional French fare, including bouillabaisse, escargots, steak *au poivre*, and calf's brains Grenobloise. The menu is extensive, but each item is expertly prepared. As for desserts like crème caramel and banana flambé: *C'est bon*. Although the food is serious, the decor is relaxed and casual, conjuring a European indoor-garden style with twinkling lights, green-and-white accents, and hand-painted florals. Although it seems out of place at first, it's become a decidedly Vineyard institution. BYOB ; corkage fee $5. Entrées (*plats de résistance*) $21–30.

Ipanema (508-693-8383), 52 Beach Road. Open for dinner May through October. Indoor and outdoor harborfront tables are an island rarity, which is reason enough to patronize this

Brazilian-influenced restaurant. Fortunately, the unconventional menu is very good, too. Enliven your taste buds with exotic (for the Vineyard) dishes like lobster baked in pineapple or churrasco, a house specialty of roasted meats carved tableside. Entrées $20–35.

❋ ✿ **Black Dog Tavern** (508-693-9223), Beach Road Extension. Open for breakfast, lunch, and dinner daily, and Sunday brunch. Longtime Vineyarder Bob Douglas became frustrated when he couldn't find good chowder within walking distance of the harbor, so he opened this place in 1971, naming it for his dog. These days the restaurant—and its ubiquitous T-shirts—is synonymous with a Vineyard vacation. And although the portions are smaller now that Bob's son is running the place, it's a fair place to eat. (Maybe you should just buy the T-shirt?) While you'll have to wait an hour for dinner, lunch won't be much of a problem. Interior decor is simple, with pine floors, old beams, nautical signs, and shellacked wooden tables packed close together. Best of all, the shingled saltbox is cantilevered over the harbor. Fresh island fish and locally grown vegetables dominate the menu. Although the staff are often eager to hustle you out the door, don't be shy about finishing your coffee. BYOB. Light dinner meals $7–11, dinner entrées $22–27.

In Oak Bluffs
The Sweet Life Cafe (508-696-0200), 168 Circuit Avenue. Open for lunch and dinner May through December. If I could eat only one dinner on the Vineyard, it would probably be here. Indeed, with its classical gourmet menu of fresh island seafood, Sweet Life won't disappoint.

Dine with chef-owners Jackson and Mary Kenworth within the restored and airy Victorian house or outside on the twinkling garden patio. After leaving, you'll depart musing about how sweet life is, indeed! My last meal revolved around an oven-roasted halibut with roasted garlic potatoes and spring peas. The wine list is exemplary. Lunch $8–16, dinner entrées $24–38.

♈ ❋ 🍴 ✿ ♿ **Lola's Southern Seafood** (508-693-5007), Beach Road. Open for dinner, and an excellent Sunday brunch ($12–15). Chef-owner Lola Domitrovich's place is a happening, lively, unusual joint with the island's best ethnic food (in this case it's Cajun/Creole/southern). The atmosphere is a tad unusual, too: leopard-pattern napkins, brown paper tablecloths, cut-glass chandeliers, faux wrought iron, and a large multicultural mural (try to pick out Lola). Come for absolutely huge portions of seafood, BBQ ribs, a signature chicken and seafood jambalaya (or the vegan version), étouffée, and rib-eye steak. This is one place where a split-plate charge is worth it—unless you want leftovers for days. Those with more moderate wallets and appetites will appreciate the less expensive, early-evening pub menu ($11–16). Otherwise, entrées (served with buttermilk biscuits and corn bread) $20–36.

Or just come for a cosmo at the bar. Nightly bands get the joint jumpin' in summer, Wednesday through Saturday the rest of the year.

♈ **Balance** (508-696-3000), 57 Circuit Avenue. Open for dinner late May to mid-October. Co-owned by Miramax honcho Harvey Weinstein, chef Ben deForest's oh-so-hip restaurant is a

Kim Grant

BALANCE RESTAURANT

feast for the eyes as well as the palate—with its open kitchen, antique tin ceiling, and handsome bar. But it's not exactly a feast for the ears: Music and conversations bounce off the tin ceiling. Local fish and island produce are featured in Ben's "clean" cooking with sauces that don't overpower the food. The menu changes weekly. The bar, Bar None, is an equally happening scene, the only island eatery where you can get something to eat until midnight. (Try the pizzettas or fried calamari after a mojito made with sugarcane and fresh mint.) Entrées $23–35.

☿ **Tsunami** (508-696-8900), 6 Circuit Avenue. Open for lunch and dinner mid-May to mid-October. While the pan-Asian-influenced dishes fall slightly short of haute cuisine, the sushi, seared tuna, lobster Rangoon, and spring rolls are a refreshing change for the Vineyard. It's also a fun and laid-back place. Befitting its harborfront Oak Bluffs location, the converted gingerbread house is wall-to-wall windows, all the better to take in views at dusk. You can also eat at the downstairs bar, bathed in red light and lined with slouchy couches and a stylish mahogany bar. The casual and hip place is overflowing with 20- and 30-somethings and specializes in excellent sake martinis. Dinner entrées $19–35.

☙ **Jimmy Sea's Pan Pasta** (508-696-8550), 32 Kennebec Avenue. Open for dinner May to late December. Although a bit pricier now than before, this small and casual place still serves enormous portions of delicious pastas, all cooked to order and served in the pan. Chef-owner Jimmy Cipolla's intensely garlic-infused place is an even better value if you have facilities to heat up your leftovers; it's virtually impossible to eat everything you're served. Better yet, get take-out and split the dishes at home yourself. Try the mussels in white wine sauce. And note the herb garden in front—you know the seasonings are fresh. No reservations are taken, so get there early or be prepared to wait. Dishes $20–28.

In Edgartown

℣ ❈ **Atria** (508-627-5850), 137 Upper Main Street. Open for dinner. Chef-owners and partners Greer Boyle and Christian Thornton specialize in fine, elegant dining with a global flair. The food is simple and straightforward, which allows natural flavors to come through. It's a classy but casual place, with a rose garden patio raw bar, and a lighter and less expensive bar menu. (The burgers with onion rings are great, as are the shellfish spring rolls.) Fish is a big deal here. Signature dishes include rare ahi tuna tempura as a starter and pan-seared Georges Bank scallops with pancetta and white beans. The menu changes daily, but there is always a vegetarian risotto. As for dessert, try the gooey chocolate truffle cake or traditional thin pecan tart. The bar is a great place for solo diners and an even better place for a nightcap. Check out their martinis (any night) and DJ dance parties (some Saturday nights). The bar hosts live jazz, folk, and blues on many nights. Entrées $22-40.

❈ ℣ **Alchemy** (508-627-9999), 71 Main Street. Open for lunch and dinner. Chef-owners Scott and Charlotte Caskey, who had been so successful at Savoir Fare for years, have struck again in this larger and more visible space. If you're lucky, you'll get one of a few sidewalk tables. For lunch try the excellent pressed Cuban sandwich or a lobster cake BLT. Fish and seafood specialties at dinner range from seared salmon with creamed lentils, to halibut meunière with lemon, to a traditional lobster clambake for one. The wine list and wine-by-the-glass list is well chosen. Lunch $9–15, dinner entrées $25–38. Evenings, the open, rotundalike two-story bistro and bar is loud and energetic. It's a fine place for singles to nosh at the bar.

♿ **L'Étoile** (508-627-5187), South Summer Street, at the Charlotte Inn. Open nightly June through October; closed January to mid-February. You'll dine formally here in an elegant garden setting: Brick walls and a glass roof surround the conservatory dining area, filled with plants and flowers. The contemporary French cuisine, meticulously prepared and artistically presented by chef-owner Michael Brisson since 1986, is nothing short of spectacular. High expectations are always exceeded with dishes like roasted pheasant breast with sweet potato, jicama, and celery root gratin. Michael's Dover sole, rack of lamb, and étuvée of native lobster are pretty darn excellent, too. He uses local fish and produce as much as possible, and you can taste the difference. Reservations required. Men will feel more comfortable in a jacket here. Prix fixe dinner $72–78.

🍲 **Chesca's** (508-627-1234), 38 North Water Street. Open for dinner early April to late October. Chef-owner Jo Maxwell and her partner, Susan Peltier, offer more than a reliable menu of eclectic Italian-inspired seafood and pasta specials. They feature something few island restaurants do: a diverse menu where you can either eat affordably or drop a bundle. Mix and match a selection of pasta with various types of sauces. Or try a subtly roasted shrimp risotto, crabcakes, or swordfish with toasted ginger, scallion, and soy. The paella and roasted garlic and cheese ravioli are great choices, too. The atmosphere here is more low-key than at other places serving this high a caliber of food. Since reservations are accepted only for large parties, expect to wait. Entrées $15–38.

❋ **Lattanzi's** (508-627-8854), Old Post Office Square, off Main Street behind the brick courthouse. Open for dinner. Chef Albert Lattanzi and his wife, Catherine, offer sophisticated and traditional Italian cuisine in conservative but not stuffy surroundings. Tables are candlelit, covered with bistro paper and linen; the staff are professional. As for the food, it's prepared with flair: from wonderfully crusty Tuscan bread and handmade pastas to lobster and wood-grilled steaks and chops. Consider antipasti like grilled portobello mushrooms or a lovely insalate Toscana, followed by freshly caught tuna paired with a puttanesca sauce. Of course the tiramisu is great, but so is *gianduja* (flourless chocolate hazelnut cake). There is some alfresco dining. Entrées $22–38.

❋ **Square Rigger** (508-627-9968), at The Triangle. Open for dinner nightly. You can tell right away that this place is by and for locals: Patrons and servers are friendly well into September! It's a meat-and-potatoes kind of place; actually, it's a char-grilled meat, seafood, and lobster kind of place. There's nothing surprising—just good and casual, with plenty of parking and a publike atmosphere. Entrées $17–24.

Up-island

Beach Plum Inn (508-645-9454), off North Road, Menemsha. Open for breakfast and dinner, May through December. If I were going to drop a wad of cash for one romantic meal, it would be here, in a minimalist dining room devoid of distractions. The focus here is on food. Although you may have heard about the panoramic

views of Menemsha Harbor (lovely at sunset), the menu features the innovative seafood and locally grown produce of chef James McDonough. The menu changes nightly, but my recent exceptional meal included pan-seared scallops with sweet and spicy beets to start, followed by hazelnut-crusted halibut with roasted shallot whipped potatoes. No matter the accompaniment, medallions of steak Diane are always recommended. And unless you're allergic to chocolate, you'd be crazy not to order the dessert soufflé. (The chocolate quad cake ranks a close second.) Service, by the way, is friendly and low-key but professional. Order à la carte (entrées $21–39) or a four-course, prix fixe ($65 in-season, $48 off-season). BYOB; corkage $6. Reservations only.

❦ **Theo's** (508-645-3322), North Road, Chilmark, at the Inn at Blueberry Hill. Open for dinner May through October. Chef Robin Ledoux-Forte and her cooking deserve warm accolades for healthful, artful presentations and hearty portions. Served by an accommodating waitstaff, the contemporary menu emphasizes organic vegetables from the garden and local seafood. Possibilities include butternut-squash-filled ravioli and a cornmeal and herb crusted yellowtail flounder. Desserts, like a French pear tart and triple chocolate tart, will melt in your mouth. As for the atmosphere, candlelit tables and track lighting glisten off multipaned windows and cobalt glassware in a quiet country setting. If the weather is really warm, go another night, since Theo's isn't air-conditioned. BYOB. Entrées $22–38. Off-season (May and October), consider rescheduling your return ferry trip so you can enjoy

Robin's four-course rustic Sunday suppers ($31).

✍ ♿ **HomePort** (508-645-2679), North Road, Menemsha. Open for dinner mid-May to mid-October. Sunset views of Menemsha Creek are the big attraction at this local institution. It's an efficient surf-sun-and-turf kind of place, with long wooden tables and lobster cooked lots of different ways, thick swordfish, jumbo shrimp, and a raw bar. The servings are large and the clientele a bit older. Frankly, some prefer to get take-out from the back door and enjoy a view from the harbor. Reservations required. BYOB. Prix fixe $26–45.

Outermost Inn (508-645-3511), Lighthouse Road, Aquinnah. Open for dinner early May to mid-October. The inn draws patrons because it's exclusive (there are a limited number of tables) and because of dramatic sunsets over the ocean. The New American menu highlights fresh island ingredients. There are always six or seven appetizer and entrée choices, perhaps including quahog chowder and grilled free-range duck. BYOB. Reservations only; two seatings for the four-course, prix fixe dinners, $68 per person (mixers and nonalcoholic beverages are included in the price).

EATING OUT

In Vineyard Haven
❄ ✍ ♧ **Art Cliff Diner** (508-693-1224), 39 Beach Road. Open for breakfast all day and (possibly) dinner year-round. Great things come from this little shack. Although it's not much to look at and the parking is limited in summer, the buzz is resounding, the dishes stellar, and the spot brighter with each passing season. Chef-owner Gina Stanley (who was the pastry chef at Blair House, the guesthouse of the White House), a whirlwind of energy, meets and

FISHING CHARTERS DEPART FROM EDGARTOWN HARBOR.

Kim Grant

greets patrons. Look for fancy frittatas and tofu scrambles at breakfast and meat loaf for off-season dinners.

❋ **Vineyard Gourmet** (508-693-5181), 71 Main Street. This specialty food store carries picnic baskets and boxed lunches filled with the likes of smoked salmon, pâtés, and imported cheeses. Those with cooking facilities will find even more of interest. When the shop isn't too busy, call ahead and ask Helen and Diana what they've got, and have them pull something together so you can saunter right in and then be on your way. Breakfast $2–4, lunch $4–10.

Black Dog Cafe (508-696-8190), 509 State Road. Open for pastries seasonally. The Black Dog began as a cottage industry, but now it's more like an industrial complex (figuratively speaking). About a mile out of town, you no longer have to fight traffic to fork over money for Black Dog pastries. Sandwiches may or not be available by the time you read this.

In Oak Bluffs

🐾 ❋ ✐ ⚄ **Linda Jean's** (508-693-4093), 25 Circuit Avenue. Open 6 AM–8 PM daily (until 9 PM in summer). Established in 1979, this is a classic American diner without the chrome. Completely rehabbed in early 2002, the pleasant storefront eatery serves old-fashioned meals at old-fashioned prices, thanks to Lanie and Marc. Breakfast is still the best meal of the day here: Pancakes are thick but light, for instance. But the fish sandwich is quick and good, and the onion rings are crispy. Kids are happy with burgers and PB&J. And the waitstaff is friendly. What more could you ask for? If you haven't tried that famed New England "delicacy," Grape-Nut custard, this is the place to do it.

Expect a wait for breakfast even in the dead of winter! Dishes $3–12.

🍸 🐾 ❋ **Offshore Ale Co.** (508-693-2626), Kennebec Avenue. Open for lunch (except Monday and Tuesday) and dinner nightly. Not only is the food very good—crispy, wood-fired, brick-oven pizzas, hefty burgers, grilled fish, fried calamari, and beer-batter onion rings—but the place is fun, too. Each table is stocked with a mason jar full of peanuts, and patrons toss the shells onto the wood floor already covered in cedar sawdust chips. But freshly fermented beer is reason enough to frequent this dark, two-story barn—as is the homemade root beer. Check the blackboard for what's fresh from the shiny copper vats. Check out the frequent entertainment. Dishes $9–32.

✐ **Zapotec Cafe** (508-693-6800), 14 Kennebec Avenue. Open for lunch in summer, dinner May through October. This cozy place with twinkling chili pepper lights is festive and fun—as long as you're not old and stuffy. It serves huge portions of Mexican and southwestern dishes like chicken suiza in a tangy tomatillo sauce, marinated chicken with mole sauce, swordfish fajitas, and Mexican-style paella, as well as old standbys like burritos, chimichangas, and quesadillas. Flan and chocolate ganache pie are big desserts; sangria and Negro Modelo are the drinks of choice (they only have a beer and wine license); and the salsa is fresh. And they have crayons for the kids. Dinner $11–18.

🐾 ✐ ⚄ **Giordano's** (508-693-0184), 107 Circuit Avenue, at the corner of Lake Avenue. Open for lunch and dinner May through September. This classic, family-style restaurant is run by fourth-generation Giordanos, who pride themselves on serving value-packed portions. Giordano's serves some of the best fried clams on-island (head to the take-out window), along with large portions of chicken cacciatore with spaghetti, veal Parmesan, pizza, sandwiches, and fried seafood. The cocktails are also big. Dishes $8–16.

♀ ✍ **Oak Bluffs Harbor Boardwalk** (aka **The Strip**). Among the many eateries that line the boardwalk, the **Coop de Ville** (508-693-3420) has the best fry joint and raw bar. The oysters are excellent and fish-and-chips very good. Otherwise, you know the menu: seafood by the pint or quart; steamed lobster with corn; wings. With picnic tables and counters, this is a great location for fast food and people-watching. Open for lunch and dinner, mid-May to mid-October. Dishes $10–30.

♣ ♿ ✍ **Farm Neck Cafe** (508-693-3560), off County Road. Open for lunch and limited breakfasts April through November; for all three meals June through September. When I ask locals to recommend a great, inexpensive lunch place, the Farm Neck Cafe inevitably pops up. Yes, the place is crawling with golfers, but the setting is lovely—with views of long, manicured fairways. While the atmosphere is clubby, it's public and very comfortable. You can get grilled shrimp and other seafood, soups, Caesar salad, sesame chicken wrapped in a flour tortilla, a burger, or a roast beef sandwich Philly style. Listen to jazz in the evenings. Lunch dishes $6–9.

❄ **Seasons Eatery & Pub** (508-693-7129), 19 Circuit Avenue. Open for lunch and dinner. This is one of the few down-island places for a simple lobster dinner.

In Edgartown

♣ ✍ **Among the Flowers** (508-627-3233), Mayhew Lane, off North Water Street. Open for breakfast and lunch, May through October, and dinner in July and August. This small café has been under Susan and George Gamble's stewardship since 1981, and many of the staff have been here for years. Perhaps that's why this is one of the friendliest places on-island. As if that weren't enough, prices are the most reasonable in Edgartown ($5–15 for lunch, $12–22 for more upscale dinner entrées like lemon chicken and pasta). There aren't many indoor tables, but there is an outdoor patio, enclosed and heated during inclement weather. Look for excellent omelets, lobster rolls, chili, PB&J for the kids, crêpes, salads, quiches, corn chowder, and clam chowder. There are bike racks out front.

♣ ❄ ✍ ♿ ♀ **The Newes from America** (508-627-4397), Kelly Street. Open 11:30–11 daily for lunch and dinner. The food is surprisingly good for pub grub—renowned burritos, as well as burgers and sandwiches. Stick to pub mainstays and don't order anything too fancy. At about $8 per person, lunch here is one of the better island values. The atmosphere is cozy, too: exposed beams, red brick, and a wood floor. Check out the selection of microbrews. When it's cold outside, this place will warm you to the core.

Daggett House (508-627-4600), 59 North Water Street. Open for breakfast late April through October. Along with a rare setting (an outdoor waterfront patio and an atmospheric colonial interior), these folks serve a really good breakfast. Try eggs Benedict, a tomato basil omelet, crabcakes and poached eggs, or steak and eggs. Dishes $5–13.

✳ ✐ ☙ **Fernando's** (508-627-8344), Upper Main Street. Open for dinner. This casual, family-friendly Italian restaurant has positioned itself nicely with well-priced dishes made to order. Locals flock here off-season. Traditional dishes include everything from linguine with red clam sauce, to shrimp scampi, to a variety of chicken and veal dishes. Entrées $12–19.

☙ ✳ ✐ ﬕ **Main Street Diner** (508-627-9337), 65 Main Street, Old Post Office Square. Open 7 AM–9 PM (8 in the off-season). Nancy and Wayne Talley's nostalgic 1950s-style diner is a fun place for kids because there's plenty to look at—from old signs to a jukebox. As for the actual dining, you've got your basic comfort foods: eggs, pancakes, grilled cheese, meat loaf, PB&J, burgers, and some Italian. Parents won't mind the prices either: Most dishes are $6–10.

✳ ✐ **Lattanzi's Pizzeria & Gelateria** (508-627-9084), Old Post Office Square, off Main Street behind the brick courthouse. Excellent and creative (and moderately priced) pizzas from a wood-burning stone oven; homemade pastas, salads, light appetizers, family fare, and wines by the glass, too. Main dishes $10–20. Their gelateria also dishes up panini, baked goods, and deli sandwiches and, of course, authentic gelato.

♈ **Seafood Shanty** (508-627-8622), 31 Dock Street. Open for lunch and dinner seasonally. So you just want something to nibble on and drinks on the water? Head here for crabcakes or mojo shrimp and a beverage of your choice. If you can't get a table on the rooftop deck, don't bother, though.

In Vineyard Haven

✳ **Black Dog Bakery** (508-693-4786), Water Street. Open daily. At the Five Corners intersection near the Steamship Authority parking lot, the Black Dog is well positioned to accommodate the hungry hordes that arrive each day. Indeed, it is many visitors' first stop—for a cup of strong coffee and a sweet pastry, muffin, or other goodies.

✳ **BonGo** (508-693-1347), 15 Main Street. A Gen-X (and -Y) coffeehouse with excellent coffee as well as sandwiches, grilled veggie burgers, and boxed lunches from the short-order kitchen.

✐ ✳ **Louis' Café & Take Out** (508-693-3255), 350 State Road, a bit out of town. Open for lunch and dinner. With limited seating, this mostly-take-out place has cold pastas sold by the pound (baked orange-ginger chicken, sesame teriyaki noodles, and the like); a salad bar; subs and pizzas; and warm dishes like rotisserie-roasted chicken and lasagna. Dishes $5–12.

✳ **MV Bagel Authority** (508-693-4152), 82 Main Street. Breakfast bagels with eggs, deli sandwich bagels for lunch, and bagel snacks throughout the day. For the coffee fanatics among us, Seattle's Best is served here.

☙ **Sandy's Fish & Chips** (508-693-1220), State Road. Open 11–7 Tuesday through Sunday. Located next to John's Fish Market, this family-operated no-frills place has great fried fish sandwiches and fried clams. They've been offering them since the 1960s.

✳ **The Net Result** (508-693-6071; 800-394-6071), 79 Beach Road. Lobsters, shellfish, smoked fish, and bay scallops (in-season) purchased on the spot or shipped to you as a nostalgic reminder. Customers attest to the fact that it costs less to have sushi-grade Net Result seafood delivered to your door than it does to go your local market for lesser quality.

In West or North Tisbury
🌢 **Humphrey's/Vineyard Foodshop & Bakery** (508-693-1079), State Road, North Tisbury. Open mid-April to mid-November. Pick up homemade soups and enormous sandwiches made with homemade bread, and save room for their jelly- or cream-filled doughnuts, affectionately called belly bombs.

❋ **Biga** (508-693-6924), 479 State Road, West Tisbury. Open for morning pastries and light lunches. The chef here worked at the renowned Beach Plum Inn for years before giving it up for the "simple" life here.

✒ ❋ **Garcia's at Back Alley's** (508-693-8401), West Tisbury. Behind the general store, Back Alley's has sandwiches, salads, great chowder, soups, and baked goods—perfect for hungry bicyclists.

In Oak Bluffs
❋ **Mocha Mott's Good Coffee** (508-696-1922), Circuit Avenue. Open daily. This tiny, aromatic basement café is where college students meet on their day off. The rich espresso keeps me going well into the evening, and the newspapers keep me in touch.

In Edgartown
♿ ❋ **Soigné** (508-627-8489), 190 Upper Main Street. Open daily except closed for March. A connoisseur's deli just outside town, Soigné has all the makings for a gourmet picnic: the island's best take-out sandwiches,

soups, myriad cold salads, and boutique wine from around the world. Owners Ron and Diana, who have been at this since 1986, also sell "designer" pastas, pâtés, pastries, mousses, excellent clam chowder, dried fruits, imported cheeses, sauces, and select wines. It's a bit pricey, but worth every penny. By the way, something like "millions and millions" of brownies have been gobbled up here. If you're celebrating a special occasion, they make specialty cakes, too.

Espresso Love (508-627-9211), Old Post Office Square, behind the brick courthouse, Edgartown. Open daily March through December. Tucked back off Main Street, these folks make the strongest cappuccino and sweetest pastries in town. A limited selection of soups and sandwiches like Mediterranean eggplant are offered at lunch, when you can enjoy the outdoor patio.

See also Morning Glory Farm under *Farm Stands.*

Up-island
🌢 ✒ **The Galley** (508-645-9819), Menemsha. Open mid-May to mid-October. This tiny place has the best chowder on the island and great lobster rolls. Burgers and soft-serve ice cream, too.

🌢 ✒ **The Bite** (508-645-9239), Basin Road, Menemsha. Open seasonally. This tiny shack serves arguably the best fried clams on-island. Don't miss the chance to decide for yourself.

Chilmark Store (508-645-3739), State Road, near Beetlebung Corner, Chilmark. Open May through September. This general store offers great pizzas and baked goods (especially the pies) in addition to conventional general-store items. Do some people-watching from the front-porch rockers before you leave.

🐟 **Larsen's Fish Market** (508-645-2680), Dutcher's Dock, Menemsha. Open mid-April to late October. Down some oysters and cherrystones at the raw bar while you wait for your lobsters to be boiled. Or pick up some stuffed quahogs and head to the beach.

❋ **Poole's Fish** (508-645-2282), Dutcher's Dock, Menemsha. Open year-round (daily April through November). The Poole family, fish purveyors since 1946, smoke their own fish and have a small raw bar, which is convenient for appetizers while you wait for your lobsters-to-go.

Around the island

Mad Martha's has irresistible homemade ice cream and many locations in all the right places (near the ferries, on Main Streets, at the mini-golf course).

FARM STANDS Despite summer traffic, $40 dinner entrées, chichi boutiques, and a building boom, the Vineyard is an agricultural island at heart. With little effort, you'll find dozens and dozens of farms with produce so fresh you can almost taste the earth. Stop often; it will be one of the things most cherished about a Vineyard holiday.

Morning Glory Farm (508-627-9003), West Tisbury Road, Edgartown. Open late May to late November. Although their business card says ROADSIDE STAND, this is a full-fledged farm with a large rustic barnboard building. You'll find farm-fresh eggs, a great salad bar, home-baked pies and breads, and homemade jellies, including especially tasty white grape jelly.

❋ Entertainment

ARTS AND MUSIC ❋ ♪ **Vineyard Playhouse** (508-693-6450; 508-696-6300 box office; www.vineyardplayhouse.org), 24 Church Street, Vineyard Haven. This small, community-based professional theater produces well-done plays and musicals; the main stage is within a former Methodist meetinghouse. They also host many special events; keep your eyes peeled. Tickets $18–28; $18 for preview tickets on first 2 nights of each show and rush tickets (remaining unsold tickets, 10 minutes prior to curtain). Summer performances at 8 PM, Tuesday through Sunday. Look for a varied and entertaining lineup at the troupe's Tisbury Amphitheater, Tashmoo Overlook, State Road, Vineyard Haven. The playhouse also offers educational programs, theater for young audiences, summer outdoor productions, and a theater arts camp.

🐟 **The Yard** (508-645-9662, 696-6300 box office), Middle Road, near Beetlebung Corner, Chilmark. Mid-June to mid-October. Founded in 1973, this colony of performing artists in residence is always engaging and appreciated. The choreography and dance are spirited. If you have a chance to go to one of their performances, by all means go. The Yard is one of those special organizations that make the Vineyard uniquely the Vineyard.

❋ **Chamber Music Society** (508-696-8055; www.mvcmf.vineyard.net). Look for the summer series from mid-July to mid-August. Performances at 8 PM; tickets $20 in-season; $15 off-season.

Band concerts. The location alternates between Ocean Park in Oak Bluffs and Owen Park in Vineyard

Haven, but the time remains constant: Saturday evenings at 7:30 in July and August. If it's raining on the night the concert is in Oak Bluffs, head to the Tabernacle. If it's raining on the night the concert is in Vineyard Haven, you're out of luck.

Ⴧ **NIGHTLIFE** *Note:* There is no smoking in public places, including bars.

Hot Tin Roof (508-693-1137; www.mvhottinroof.com), Martha's Vineyard Airport, Edgartown. Open 8:30 PM–1:30 AM May through September. When Carly Simon opened this club back in 1979, it was the coolest island nightspot. The star-studded shack attracted the likes of Keith Richards, Jimmy Cliff, and John Belushi. Since then, it's been up and down. First, its popularity dipped; then Simon and big-name investors became affiliated with it again; then the buzz returned; then President

Clinton and Prince Andrew and Diane Sawyer hung out there; then it was for sale again; then liquor licensing almost did it in. Somehow, it remains a venerable island institution. As for the music, there is a diverse lineup of national and local R&B, reggae, and blues bands, as well as DJs (mostly Thursday through Saturday). Tickets $8–50.

❋ **The Newes from America** (508-627-4397), 23 Kelly Street, Edgartown. Open daily. This colonial-era basement tavern is atmospheric and cozy, with hand-hewn beams. The Newes features microbrews; try the specialty Rack of Beers, a sampler of five brews from the outstanding and unusual beer menu (see *Eating Out*).

❋ **Atlantic Connection** (508-693-7129), 19 Circuit Avenue, Oak Bluffs. The "AC," another hot nightclub, attracts a younger beer-drinking

THE OCEAN PARK GAZEBO IN OAK BLUFFS.

Kim Grant

crowd than does the Hot Tin Roof. Live bands, DJs, comedy, and reggae on alternate nights. It can get a bit rowdy.

❈ **Ritz Cafe** (508-693-9851), 4 Circuit Avenue, Oak Bluffs. Open daily. Locals hang out at this funky blues bar, which, according to *The Improper Bostonian,* is: "seedy," "smokin'," "scary," "disgusting," "hilarious," and "a blast."

Lampost/Rare Duck (508-693-4032; 508-693-9847 entertainment line; 508-696-9352 current events), Circuit Avenue, Oak Bluffs. On the second floor, the Lampost features dancing from mid-April to mid-October. Rare Duck, open May through September, is a frozen-drink kind of place, a smaller lounge with nightly summer entertainment.

❈ **The Wharf** (508-627-9966), Lower Main Street, Edgartown. A popular pub on the wharf.

Boathouse Bar (508-627-4320), 2 Main Street, at the Navigator, Edgartown. Open May to mid-October. Sailing types and singles stop here for outdoor cocktails, beers, and margaritas—it's just a few boat lengths from the harbor. If you must nosh (here), stick to the appetizers. Live entertainment weekends in summer.

See Lola's under *Dining Out* and Offshore Ale Co. and Farm Neck Cafe under *Eating Out,* all in Oak Bluffs, and Atria under *Dining Out* in Edgartown.

🦞 🍗 MOVIES ❈ **Capawock Movie House** (508-696-9200; 508-627-6689 show times), Main Street, Vineyard Haven. Built in 1912 but recently refurbished, the Capawock is the oldest continually operating movie theater in Massachusetts. As entertaining as movies can be, though, you may be just as entertained by conversations before the film begins: Off-season, this is a hot place to hear island gossip, real estate prices, and political scoops. You'll also pick up lots of pertinent info on where to eat and where not to go.

Strand Theater (508-696-8300; 508-627-6689 show times), Oak Bluffs Avenue, Oak Bluffs.

Island Theater (508-627-6689; 508-627-6689 show times), Circuit Avenue, Oak Bluffs.

Entertainment Cinema (508-627-8008), 65 Main Street, Edgartown. Two screens.

See also Grange Hall under *To See— Up-island.*

❊ **Selective Shopping**

ANTIQUES AND COLLECTIBLES **All Things Oriental** (508-693-8375), 123 Beach Road, Vineyard Haven. Open May through December, and by appointment. Summering on the Vineyard and shopping in the Orient sounds like a good deal. Here's a way to be in both places at once. Stop in here for a virtual trip via furniture, porcelain, jewelry, lamps, and more.

The Golden Door (508-627-7740), 18 North Summer Street, Edgartown. Open March through December, and by appointment. John Chirgwin spends half the year in Asia, leading tours and buying art. His Far East gallery is delightful; you'll find sculpture, furniture, jewelry, jade, and tribal objects.

Jane N. Slater Antiques and Collectibles (508-645-3348), Basin Road, Menemsha. Open May to mid-October. The fact that it's small and goes by the motto of "Something for Everyone" dictates that the shop be crammed with collectibles of pottery, sterling, crystal, and jewelry.

See also entries under *Home Furnishings.*

ART GALLERIES Except for the first two galleries, which are easily the most sophisticated on-island, galleries are listed below by town. For a super-complete listing of artists and galleries, look for the free and excellent *Arts Directory* available in many galleries.

✺ **Craven Gallery** (508-693-3535; 212-734-2125 in winter; www.craven-gallery.com), 459 State Road, West Tisbury. Open May through October, and always by appointment. This contemporary gallery is bursting at the seams with incredible art. Framed pieces are stacked all over the place for you to flip through, and the four little rooms are hung (literally) wall to wall with the likes of nationally acclaimed artists like Milton Avery and Edward Hopper. You'll find landscapes, watercolors and mixed media, photography and drawings. What you won't find is any schlock. Check it out; Carol Craven is to be applauded for amassing such a great collection.

✺ 🐚 **Shaw Cramer Gallery** (508-696-7323), 76 Main Street (second floor), Vineyard Haven. Nancy Shaw Cramer's exceptional contemporary crafts gallery features clay, fiber, wood, metal, and mixed media. Believe it or not, the work of about 20 to 25 islanders and 100 off-islanders is represented here. (Nancy is a tapestry weaver herself.)

✺ **Etherington Fine Art** (508-693-9696), 52 Beach Road, Vineyard Haven. Open April through Decem-

ber, or by appointment. Mary Etherington's contemporary gallery has huge picture windows that you can't ignore. Do stop in; the gallery has a very distinctive feeling. Mary represents some 30 island and nonisland artists, some of whom do abstract work.

🐚 ✺ **Craftworks** (508-693-7463), 42 Circuit Avenue, Oak Bluffs. These folks have a mixed but usually affordable selection of contemporary American crafts that's worth a look and always visually interesting. Clay, metal, glass, paper, and wood.

Firehouse Gallery (508-693-9025), at the old No. 4 Firehouse on Dukes County Avenue (off New York Avenue from the harbor), Oak Bluffs. Shows late May to early September. There's a first-floor gallery and a second floor dedicated to workshops and classes. The Martha's Vineyard Center for the Visual Arts (508-645-9671), which publishes a fine annual arts directory, has its headquarters here.

Argonauta of Martha's Vineyard (508-696-0097), 73 Circuit Avenue, Oak Bluffs. Open April through December. Adrianne Maschit and Catherine Crocket specialize in hand-painted vintage furniture, custom-painted designs, and a permanent exhibition of original artwork by local artists.

Once in a Blue Moon (508-627-9177), 22 Winter Street, Edgartown. Open April through December. This shop revels in fun and funky contemporary ceramics, textiles, mixed media, sculpture, and other objets d'art for the home.

Old Sculpin Gallery (508-627-4881), corner of Dock and Daggett Streets, Edgartown. Open mid-June

UP-ISLAND REFLECTIONS

Kim Grant

to mid-September. Operated by the nonprofit Martha's Vineyard Art Association, the building was originally Dr. Daniel Fisher's granary, then a boatbuilder's workshop. Look for the long, wide depression in the main room where boatbuilder Manuel Swartz Roberts's feet wore down the floor as he moved along his workbench during the early 20th century. Paintings and photographs of varying degrees of quality are exhibited.

❋ **Gardner-Colby Gallery** (508-627-6002), 27 North Water Street, Edgartown. Open May through December; winter weekends. Regional and national artists emphasizing Vineyard landscapes, seascapes, maritime scenes, figurative works, and still lifes are represented here.

Granary Gallery at the Red Barn Emporium (508-693-0455), Old County Road, West Tisbury. Open late May through December, and by appointment. In addition to folk art and landscape paintings, this gallery carries old and new photography. There are classic photos by the venerable photographer Alfred Eisenstaedt (who came to the island on assignment for *Life* in 1937 and vacationed here until his death in 1995), as well as contemporary photographer Alison Shaw's island scenes. Most artists represented here have some affiliation with the island.

Field Gallery and Sculpture Garden (508-693-5595), State Road, West Tisbury. Open April to late December. Tom Maley's field of joyfully dancing figures, which seem to be celebrating the surrounding beauty, is an icon of the Vineyard's cultural life. Other Vineyard artists are exhibited during summer months; receptions are held 5–7 on many Sundays in July and August.

See also Featherstone Meetinghouse

for the Arts under *Even More Things to See and Do—Special Programs.*

ARTISANS ❋ **Larry Hepler, Furniture Maker** (508-645-2578; www.lhepler.vineyard.net), 71 Main Street (upper level), Vineyard Haven. Open daily; it's a self-service kind of gallery. If you see something you like in the showroom, and there's no one there, give them a call and talk about it. Larry can and does customize most of his work, which is "handmade to hand down." He's not kidding. These fine, fine pieces have gentle curves, graceful lines, and remarkable character. Larry follows his father's advice that "it doesn't matter so much what you do as how you do it." Finishes are smoother than silk. You'll cherish a Hepler purchase.

❋ **Travis Tuck, Metal Sculptor, Studio and Gallery** (508-693-3914; www.travistuck.com), 7 Beach Street, Vineyard Haven. Tuck and his apprentices take weeks and weeks to painstakingly produce one-of-a-kind weather vane commissions (starting at $10,000—and he's booked for the next two years already!). Travis has created a very animated velociraptor for Steven Spielberg, as well as pieces for President and Senator Clinton, and a whimsical George Washington for his namesake university. You can see fine examples of his work around the island, too. Check out the weather vanes atop the new Agricultural Hall in West Tisbury (a Holstein cow); Cronig's Market on State Road (a grasshopper, as a public market symbol); the Tisbury and Edgartown Town Halls (a whale tail and whaling ship, respectively); and the *Vineyard Gazette* building (a quill pen).

Vital Signs (508-693-6057; www.vitalsignsmv.com), 67 Circuit Avenue, Oak Bluffs. Open May to mid-October and by appointment year-round. Islander Keren Tonnesen has created a primitive signature style with original block-print garments and artwork.

❋ **Chilmark Pottery** (508-693-6476), off State Road, opposite Nip-n-Tuck Farm, West Tisbury. In 1982 artist Geoffrey Borr established his studio in a weathered shingled barn where he and his staff transform thoughtfully designed, wheel-thrown creations into hand-painted pottery with distinctive seascape hues. You'll find functional mugs and goblets as well as more unusual vases and plates. He also offers classes in wheel throwing and hand building.

Martha's Vineyard Glass Works (508-693-6026; www.mvglassworks.com), State Road, West Tisbury. Open mid-May through October. Many designers share this dynamic studio, a colorfully bold visual feast where you can watch the artists and apprentices at work.

See also Davis House Gallery under The Old Parsonage, *Bed & Breakfasts—In West Tisbury.*

BOOKSTORES ✑ **Bickerton and Ripley** (508-627-8463; www.bickertonandripley.com), Main Street at South Summer Street, Edgartown. Open April through December. A charming shop with everything from travel, to local fiction, to books and activities for children.

❋ **Bunch of Grapes Bookstore** (508-693-2291; www.bunchofgrapes.com), 44 Main Street, Vineyard Haven. A larger general bookstore where browsers are welcome.

❋ **The Book Den East** (508-693-3946), 71 New York Avenue (Vineyard Haven–Oak Bluffs Road), Oak Bluffs. Open year-round (Thursday through Sunday off-season). This turn-of-the-20th-century two-story barn—complete with wood shelves, wood floors, and wood crates—is chock-full of used, rare, and out-of-print hardcovers and paperbacks. No haggling allowed. The barn has that great old-book smell, which tells me that if I look long enough, I'm going to find something I can't live without.

CLOTHING **Black Dog General Store** (508-696-8182), behind the eponymous bakery, off Water Street, Vineyard Haven. Open daily. Islanders have a love–hate relationship with this longtime icon. The Black Dog rakes in tens of thousands of dollars daily in merchandise (sweatshirts, towels, caps, and so on). If you get home and regret not buying that must-have T-shirt, you can order it from their catalog store (800-626-1991). The Black Dog has all the bases covered: There are also seasonal shops in Edgartown (South Summer Street) and Oak Bluffs (Circuit Avenue).

Sola (508-627-7715), 23 Kelly Street, Edgartown. Open May through December. Upscale but affordable, mix-and-match women's linen, wool, and cotton clothing in updated styles and colors.

The Great Put-On (508-627-5495), Dock Street at Mayhew Lane, Edgartown. Open May through October. One of the island's most fashionable clothing stores stocks an impressive selection of dressy clothing for women, more shoes for women than for men, and unisex accessories like leather backpacks, loose jackets, and sweaters.

❋ **Fleece Dreams** (508-693-6141), 3 Church Street, Tisbury. Betsy Edge makes jackets, capes, swing coats, scarves, and dresses from her own Polarfleece and velvet designs. She also works with linen, suede, rayon, and cotton.

Allen's Farm Sheep & Wool Company (508-645-9064), South Road (near Beetlebung Corner), Chilmark. Open late May to mid-October, and by appointment. You'll do your shopping "in the pastures" of one of the most beautiful spots on the island, overlooking sloping meadows crisscrossed with stone walls, with the Atlantic Ocean as a backdrop. A diet of fresh sea air and dense grass makes for thick wool, which the Allens knit and weave into beautiful scarves, shawls, sweaters, and hats.

Pandora's Box (508-645-9696), Basin Road (off North Road), Menemsha. Open May to mid-October. The emphasis here is on comfortable, contemporary women's clothing.

See also Timeless Treasures under *Home Furnishings.*

HOME FURNISHINGS ❋ **Bramhall & Dunn** (508-693-6437), 23 Main Street, Vineyard Haven. Nesting instincts are satisfied with hand-hooked rugs, picture frames, colorful ceramics, and antique furniture. All have been discovered by owners Emily Bramhall and Tharon Dunn during their annual pilgrimages to England.

Chartreuse (508-696-0500), State Road at Woodland Center, Vineyard Haven. Open May through December. Owner Deborah DeLorezo has gathered an extraordinary selection of well-priced antiques, whimsical gifts, and home furnishings from around the world.

❋ **Timeless Treasures** (508-696-7637), Main Street, Vineyard Haven. Gerda O'Rourke offers silver, hand-knit sweaters, and antique pine furniture from Ireland, to which she returns annually to shop. There are two shops across the street from each other.

❋ **Midnight Farm** (508-693-1997), 18 Water Street at Cronwell Lane, Vineyard Haven. Carly Simon's home furnishing store is located between Main Street and the ferry terminal. There are some well-chosen items here.

LeRoux (508-693-0036), Main Street, Vineyard Haven. These folks have a Main Street monopoly: They have stores devoted to shoes, clothes, kitchen items, and home goods.

Pik-Nik (508-693-1366), 99 Dukes County Avenue (off New York Avenue), Oak Bluffs. Open seasonally; by appointment in winter. Unlike any of the other shops in this category, Pik-Nik sells kitschy antiques and vintage housewares, including pottery, dishware, glassware, textiles, jewelry, and artwork from the mid–20th century. You gotta love it.

Mariposa (508-627-9332), 12 North Summer Street, Edgartown. Open April through October. Look for pottery, needlework, and carefully selected French country antiques from Provence.

JEWELRY ❋ **C. B. Stark** (508-693-2284), 53A Main Street, Vineyard Haven. Open daily. Goldsmiths Cheryl Stark and Margery Meltzer

have designed gold and silver jewelry with island motifs since 1969. Cheryl also created the original grape design that has become so popular on the island. They're "official jewelers" for the Black Dog and carry locally made wampum from quahog shells. Look for a shop in Edgartown, too.

SPECIAL SHOPS **Vineyard Lights** (508-693-2858), 39 Circuit Avenue, Oak Bluffs. Open April through December. From earthenware pottery to woven tapestries, from blown glass to jewelry, this artsy collection carries both whimsical and elegant designs by local and national craftspeople.

❋ **Paper Tiger Inc.** (508-693-8970), 29 Main Street, Vineyard Haven. This colorful and fun shop offers a great selection of fine stationery, original cards, and handmade crafts of natural and recycled materials. When other galleries close, Paper Tiger exhibits local art.

Ben & Bill's Chocolate Emporium (508-696-0008), 125 Circuit Avenue, Oak Bluffs. Open May through October. Handmade chocolates, candies, and ice cream.

Seaside Daylily Farm (508-693-3276), Great Plains Road, off Old County Road, West Tisbury. Open May to late September. These lilies are grown without the use of harmful chemicals that disrupt the ecosystem's natural balance.

Chilmark Chocolates (508-645-3013), State Road, near Beetlebung Corner, Chilmark. Open Wednesday through Sunday 11:30–5:30; closed for breaks in spring, winter, and fall. Good deeds and good products make an unbeatable combination. Not only will you love the rich and creamy truffles and mouthwatering dark and light chocolates, but you'll also appreciate that the chocolatier is committed to furthering a philosophy that all members of society should be given a chance to be productive. They hire people with disabilities to make and sell the chocolate. Try their Tashmoo Truffles or West Chomps or Squibnuggets.

✵ **Vineyard Photo** (508-627-9537), 20 Dock Street, Edgartown, and **Mosher Photo** (508-693-9430), 25 Main Street, Vineyard Haven, are both open year-round for quickie film processing. **The Wooden Tent** (508-693-2170), 1037 State Road, Tisbury, offers custom processing.

✳ Special Events

The Vineyard has hundreds and hundreds of charming—great and small—special events throughout the year. A sampling of the larger, predictable, annual events follows. Contact the chamber of commerce (508-693-0085) for specific dates, unless an

---

MUST-SEE SUMMER EVENTS

Early August: **Possible Dreams Auction,** Harborside Inn, Edgartown. Given the celebrity involvement, it's not surprising that national publicity surrounds this event. Celebrities offer to fulfill "dreams" that vary from predictable to unusual. High bidders in the past have won a tour of the *60 Minutes* studios with Mike Wallace; a sail with Walter Cronkite on his yacht; a seat at a Knicks game with Spike Lee; dinner with Lady Bird Johnson; a tour of Carnegie Hall with violinist Isaac Stern; a walking tour of the Brooklyn Bridge with historian David McCullough; a song and a peanut butter sandwich from Carly Simon; and a lesson in chutzpah at the Five Corners intersection in Vineyard Haven with Alan Dershowitz. Longtime island celebrities see the auction as their chance to give back to the Vineyard—in 2000 the auction raised more than $350,000 for Martha's Vineyard Community Services. Even adjusted for inflation, that's a far cry from the $1,000 raised in 1979 when it began and folks bid in $5 increments for the privilege of helping lobstermen set out their pots. More than 1,000 people usually attend the event. Fee.

Mid-August: **Illumination Night.** The actual date is kept secret until a week prior to the event. The evening always begins with a community sing and is followed by an Oak Bluffs resident (usually the oldest) lighting a single Japanese lantern after all the electric lights in town are turned off. Then the rest of the "camp" residents illuminate their gingerbread cottages with lanterns and candles.

Mid-August: **Agricultural Society Livestock Show & Fair** (508-693-4343). Held at the Ag Hall and Fairgrounds on State Road in West Tisbury, this is arguably the island's most beloved summer event. It's certainly one of the oldest: It began during the Civil War! Fee.

alternative phone number is listed below. For a complete listing, look for the chamber's complete event pamphlet once you get on-island.

Throughout the year: **Mountain bike rides** (508-693-4905), Grange Hall, West Tisbury, every Sunday morning, sponsored by the Vineyard Off Road Bicycle Association. Helmets and water bottle required.

Throughout the summer: **Vineyard Artisans Summer Festivals** (508-693-8989). Don't have time to pop into two dozen galleries? Then check this out. These excellent shows are held indoors and outdoors, rain or shine, weekly and biweekly at the Grange Hall in West Tisbury. Look for furniture, ceramics, book arts, fiber arts, glass, jewelry, mixed media, painting, photography, printmaking, and sculpture. Shows are held 10–2 Sundays, June through September,

and on Thursdays in July and August.

Mid-June to mid-October: **West Tisbury Farmer's Market** (508-693-8989), at Grange Hall, 2–5 Wednesday, late June to late August; and 9–noon Saturday, mid-June to mid-October.

Mid-June: **Oak Bluffs Harbor Festival** (508-693-3392). Since 1991.

Late June–early September: **Chilmark Flea Market,** Chilmark Community Church Grounds, Menemsha Cross Road, every Saturday and Wednesday 8:30–2.

July–August: **Community Sing** (508-693-0525). Singing and more at the Tabernacle, Methodist "campground," Oak Bluffs, every Wednesday at 8 PM.

Band concerts every Saturday evening, alternating between Owen Park in Vineyard Haven and Ocean Park in Oak Bluffs.

VINEYARD HAVEN HARBOR

Mid-July: **Edgartown Regatta.** Fifteen different classes of boats have been racing since the mid-1920s.

Late July: **Book Sale** (508-693-2592). A benefit since the late '50s for the West Tisbury Library, State Road.

Early August: **Edgartown House Tour** (508-627-5303). This competitive event is limited to six houses each year, and rivalries are fierce. Tea is served in the final house on the tour. Fee.

Mid-September–mid-October: **Striped Bass and Bluefish Derby.** When dozens of surf-casters begin furiously fishing from your favorite beach, you'll know it's derby time. Prizes are awarded for the largest fish caught each day, with a grand prize for the largest fish caught during the monthlong tournament. Weighing is done in Edgartown Harbor, just as it's been done every year since the mid-1950s.

Mid-September: **Tivoli Day** (508-696-7643). A lively street fair on Circuit Avenue in Oak Bluffs.

Mid-October: **Vineyard Craftsmen Art & Craft Fair** (508-693-8989), at the Edgartown School, West Tisbury Road. More than 60 crafters and artists have gathered here since the mid-1960s.

Early–mid-December: **Christmas Events** (508-693-1151). Santa arrives by ferry in Vineyard Haven; there's a chowder contest; horse and carriage rides; and "Christmas in Edgartown."

New Year's Eve: **Last Night, First Day.** An alcohol-free, family-oriented celebration. Events in Vineyard Haven and Edgartown begin at 1 PM on December 31 and end with Edgartown Harbor fireworks at 10 PM.

Nantucket

NANTUCKET

Nantucket Sound

Great Point

Great Point Light

Coskata-Coatue Wildlife Refuge

Coskata Beach

Head of the Harbor

Squam Rd.

Wauwinet Rd.

Sesachacha Pond

Sankaty Lighthouse

Polpis Rd.

Altar Rock

SIASCONSET

Milestone Cranberry Bog

'Sconset Beach

Ocean Ave.

Nantucket Harbor

Milestone Rd.

Old Tom Nevers Rd.

Nantucket Memorial Airport

Coatue Beach

Polpis Rd.

Old South Rd.

Surfside Rd.

Surfside Beach

Enlarged area

Jetties Beach

Brant Point

Cliff Rd.

Bartlett Rd.

Miacomet Ave.

Surfside Beach

Miacomet Golf Course

Miacomet Beach

Dionis Beach

Sanford Farm Ram Pasture & the Woods

Hummock Pond Rd.

Cisco Beach

Eel Point Rd.

MADAKET

Madaket Rd.

ATLANTIC OCEAN

Eel Point

Smith Point

Madaket Beach

N

3 MILES

Paul Woodward / © The Countryman Press

Brant Point

Children's Beach

Steamboat Wharf

FERRY to Woods Hole

Straight Wharf

FERRY to Hyannis & Harwichport

Easton St.

Easy St.

Washington St.

Francis St.

Lower Orange St.

S. Beach St.

N. Beach St.

S. Water St.

Whaling Museum

Tourist Info.

N. Water St.

Chamber of Commerce

Orange St.

E. York St.

Lower Pleasant St.

Peter Foulger Museum

Broad

Federal

S. Main St.

Atlantic Ave.

African Meeting House

Centre St.

India St.

Liberty St.

Hadwen House

Pleasant St.

Old Mill

Sparks Ave.

Oldest House

W. Chester St.

Main St.

Maria Mitchell Science Center

Prospect St.

N. Liberty St.

Old Gaol

Quaker Rd.

NANTUCKET

Thirty miles out to sea, Nantucket was called "that far away island" by Native Americans. Just 14 by 3.5 miles in area, Nantucket is the only place in America that is simultaneously an island, a county, and a town. In 1659 Thomas Mayhew, who had purchased Nantucket sight unseen (he was more interested in Martha's Vineyard), sold it to Tristram Coffin and eight of his friends for £30 and "two Beaver Hatts." These "original purchasers" quickly sold half shares to craftsmen whose skills they would require to build a community.

When Mayhew arrived, there were more than 3,000 Native American residents, who taught the settlers which crops to farm and how to spear whales from shore. By the early 1700s, the number of settlers had grown to more than 300, and the number of Natives had shrunk to less than 800, primarily because of disease. (The last Native descendant died on-island in 1854.)

In 1712, when Captain Hussey's sloop was blown out to sea, he harpooned the first sperm whale islanders had ever seen. For the next 150 years, whaling dominated the island's economy. The ensuing prosperity allowed the island's population to climb to 10,000. In comparison, there are also 10,000 year-rounders today.

Nantucket sea captains traveled the world to catch whales and to trade, and they brought back great fortunes. By the late 1700s, trade was booming with England, and in 1791 the *Beaver*, owned by islander William Rotch, rounded Cape Horn and forged an American trade route to the Pacific Ocean. Fortunes were also made in the Indian Ocean—hence, Nantucket's India Street.

In its heyday, Nantucket Harbor overflowed with smoke and smells from blacksmith shops, cooperages, shipyards, and candle factories. More than 100 whaling ships sailed in and out of Nantucket. But when ships grew larger, to allow for their longer voyages at sea, they couldn't get across the shallow shoals and into Nantucket Harbor. The industry began moving to Martha's Vineyard and New Bedford. At the height of the whaling industry in 1846, the "Great Fire," which began in a hat shop on Main Street, ignited whale oil at the harbor. The catastrophic blaze wiped out the harbor and one-third of the town. Although most citizens began to rebuild immediately, other adventurous and energetic souls were enticed to go west in search of gold in 1849. When kerosene replaced whale oil in the 1850s as a less expensive fuel, it was the final blow to the island's maritime economy. By 1861 there were only 2,000 people on-island.

Although tourism began soon after the Civil War and picked up with the advent of the railroad to 'Sconset, the island lay more or less in undisturbed isolation until the 1950s. Perhaps it was the sleepiness of those 100 years that ultimately preserved the island's architectural integrity and community spirit, paving the way for its resurrection. In the late 1950s and early 1960s, islander and S&H Green Stamp heir Walter Beinecke Jr. organized a revitalization of the waterfront area, replacing decrepit wharf buildings with cottages. He also declared the premise that guides tourism to this day: It is preferable to attract one tourist with $100 than 100 tourists with $1 each. In accordance with the maxim, strict zoning laws were adopted, land-conservation groups were launched, and Nantucket's upscale tourism industry began in earnest.

By the late 1990s, the well-to-do set was abandoning the Hamptons and similar enclaves for Nantucket. By 2000 it had become too popular for its own good and was placed on the list of Most Endangered Historical Places, as decreed by the National Trust for Historic Preservation. In contrast to the Vineyard's showy excess and celebrity allure, Nantucket is a restrained haven for behind-the-scenes power brokers. In the recent past, mammoth multimillion-dollar trophy houses (and to be fair, some of the more understated ones, too) have belonged to people like the Gambles of Procter & Gamble, the Du Ponts, R. H. Macy, R. J. Reynolds, Bill Blass, David Halberstam, Graham Gund, Jack Welsh, Tommy Hilfiger, John Kerry, and Russell Baker.

In 1966 Nantucket was declared a national historic landmark: It boasts more than 800 buildings constructed before 1850—the largest concentration of such

ARE YOU A "WASH-ASHORE"?

Kim Grant

buildings in the United States. The historic district is picture-perfect: paved cobblestone streets, brick sidewalks, electrified "gas" street lamps. Gray-shingled houses are nestled close together on narrow lanes, which wind as you amble beyond the downtown grid of streets. Elegant white residences are trimmed with English boxwood hedges, white picket fences, and showcase flower gardens.

With a daily summer population that swells to 55,000, today's tourist industry is about as well oiled as the whale industry once was. It's difficult to find a grain of sand or a seashell that hasn't been discovered.

Most sites in Nantucket are within a mile of the historic center—you'll probably walk more than you're accustomed to. In addition to historic houses and museums, Nantucket prides itself on offering world-class dining. Although there are little pockets of settlements around the island, the only real "destination" is 'Sconset, an utterly quaint village with rose-covered cottages. Elsewhere on the island, more than 45 percent of the island's 10,000 acres are held by conservation trusts; you'll be able to explore places where most tourists don't venture. The island boasts excellent bicycle paths and almost limitless public beaches.

Nantucket is a year-round destination. Millions of daffodils blanket the island in yellow as the earth reawakens each April. The weather in May and June is slightly less predictable than in fall, but if you hit a nice stretch, you'll probably muse that life just doesn't get any better. Gardens are brightest in May and June. Where once there were whaling ships, yachts now fill the harbor in summer. Warm ocean water and beach barbecues beckon, wild roses trail along picket fences, and many special events are staged. Come September (my favorite month on-island), the crowds recede a bit. You can swim in the still-temperate ocean by day and not have to wait for a table at your favorite restaurant at night. Skies turn crisp blue, and cranberry bogs, heathlands, and the moors blaze red, russet, and maroon. Many restaurants that close in mid-October (at the end of Columbus Day weekend) reopen for the long Thanksgiving weekend. The first three weeks of November are very quiet indeed. Before the monochrome days of winter set in, there is one last burst of activity: Nantucket Noel and Christmas Stroll (see *Special Events*). In January, February, and March you'll discover why whaling captains called the island the "little grey lady"—she is often shrouded in fog. It's a time of reflection and renewal for year-rounders and visitors alike.

GUIDANCE ✳ **Nantucket Visitor Services & Information Bureau** (508-228-0925), 25 Federal Street. Open 9–6 daily mid-April to early December, 9–5:30 Monday through Saturday off-season. In addition to information on special events and transportation schedules, the bureau maintains seasonal kiosks at Steamboat Wharf and at Straight Wharf. Whenever I stop in, I find the staff to be quite overworked. Although the bureau has information on daily guesthouse vacancies, don't wait until the last minute to locate a place to stay.

✳ **Nantucket Island Chamber of Commerce** (508-228-1700; www.nantucketchamber.org), 48 Main Street. The second-floor chamber is open 9–5 weekdays year-round. It produces a glossy book, *The Official Guide: Nantucket,* which is free on-island but costs $7 to mail in advance of your visit.

Nantucket Historical Association (508-228-1894; www.nha.org), 15 Broad

NANTUCKET, OFTEN CALLED THE "LITTLE GREY LADY," IS SHROUDED IN FOG.

Kim Grant

Street within the Peter Foulger Museum. The NHA, which owns 14 historic properties representing island life from its farming beginnings to its prosperous whaling days, is a fabulous source of historical information. Generally, NHA properties are open 10–5 Monday through Saturday and noon–5 Sunday, mid-June to early September. (Hours are shortened in winter.) Since hours change from year to year, it's best to stop in or call ahead. Most properties require a History Ticket ($15 adults, $8 children 5–14), which is valid for admission to all properties and includes a good walking tour. Purchase one at the Nantucket Whaling Museum (see *To See*).

MEDIA The venerable *Inquirer and Mirror* (www.ack.net) has been published on Thursdays since 1821.

The free weeklies *Nantucket Map & Legend* (www.mapandlegend.com) and *Yesterday's Island* (www.yesterdaysisland.com) are also useful for entertainment listings.

Two competing cable TV stations are now vying for your eyeballs. Yes, they have paid "infomercials," but they also broadcast interesting lectures and discussions and have good event information and interviews with locals. It's a great way to learn a bit more about the island. Once on-island, tune into **Channel 22** (508-228-8001, 15 Main Street, Pacific Club) and **Channel 17** (508-292-2203).

WNAN 91.1 (508-548-9600;www.cainan.org) is the NPR affiliate with local angles.

PUBLIC REST ROOMS Look for them at the Visitor Services & Information Bureau at 25 Federal Street (open year-round), and at Children's Beach (see *Green Space—Beaches*) and Straight Wharf (both open seasonally).

INTERNET ACCESS ❋ **InterNet Cafe** (508-228-9165), upstairs at 2 Union Street. Hours are variable for public use, so call ahead. If you can't leave the modern world behind, if you want to send or receive e-mail, if you need to check in with the office, this upstairs space (run by the publishers of the free weekly *Yesterday's Island*) is the place for you. $5 for 30 minutes of computer use.

ATM Short on green backs? In town, look for automatic teller machines at the Pacific National Bank (61 Main Street), The Pacific Club (15 Main Street), the Steamship Authority Terminal (Steamboat Wharf), and Nantucket Bank (2 Orange Street).

GETTING THERE With high-speed ferry service, day-tripping to Nantucket from Hyannis is more feasible than ever. Although I still recommend spending a few days on Nantucket, you are no longer shut out if you can't.

By bus: **Bonanza** (508-775-6502; 800-751-8800; www.bonanzabus.com) runs from Providence, and **Plymouth & Brockton** (508-778-9767; www.p-b.com) runs from Boston, to the Steamship Authority and Hy-Line boats. There is also **Logan Direct** (508-771-6191; www.logandirect.com) to both boats. **Peter Pan** (800-237-8747; www.peterpanbus.com) runs from New York City, Philadelphia, and Washington, D.C., to Hyannis, where you can catch the boats.

❋ *By boat from Hyannis:* **The Steamship Authority** (508-477-8600 for information and advance auto reservations; 508-771-4000 for day-of-sailing information in Hyannis; 508-228-0262 for day-of-sailing information on Nantucket; www.islandferry.com), South Street Dock, Hyannis. The Steamship, established in 1948, carries autos, people, and bikes to Steamship Wharf year-round. Make car reservations in spring for summer if you can; no reservations are needed for passengers. There are six high-season sailings daily, three off-season. Parking in Hyannis is $8–10 per calendar day, depending on the time of year. The voyage takes 2¼ hours. Round-trip fares: adults $26; children 5–12, $13 (free under age 5); bicycles $10. Cars cost a whopping $365 mid-May to mid-October, $210 off-season.

Steamship Authority's *Flying Cloud* **High Speed Passenger Boat** (508-495-3278; 508-477-8600), South Street Dock, Hyannis. Go dock-to-dock in 1 hour. The boat sails late May through December and makes five to six trips daily; $52 adults, $39 children 5–12. Reservations strongly suggested.

❋ **Hy-Line Cruises** (508-778-2600 in Hyannis; 508-228-3949 on Nantucket; 888-778-1132 for advance sales; www.hy-linecruises.com), Ocean Street Dock, Hyannis. Passengers and bicycles to Straight Wharf, early May through October. There are five summertime boats daily, one to three daily off-season. There is also a first-class lounge aboard the M/V *Great Point* if you don't mind paying $44 round trip. Otherwise, round-trip fares are adults $27; children 5–12, $13.50; bicycles $10. Parking in Hyannis is $10–15 per calendar day.

❋ **Hy-Line's** *Grey Lady II* **High Speed Passenger Boat** (508-778-0404; 800-

492-8082; www.hy-linecruises.com), Ocean Street Dock. This high-speed luxury catamaran costs a bit more but it operates year-round: $58 adults, children 12 and under $41. Reservations are strongly recommended. There are five to six boats daily, with the last one departing at 6 or 8:45 PM, depending on time of year.

By boat from Harwich: **Freedom Cruise Line** (508-432-8999; www.capecod. net/freedom), Saquatucket Harbor in Harwichport, provides daily passenger service to Nantucket, mid-May to mid-October and during the Christmas Stroll (see *Special Events*). During the summer, two of the three trips are scheduled so that you can explore Nantucket for about 6½ hours and return the same day. In spring and fall, there is only one morning boat daily. Reservations are highly recommended; make them 3 to 4 days in advance. Round-trip prices: adults $43; children 2–12, $36; bicycles $10. Free parking for day-trippers; $12 daily thereafter. The trip takes 1½ hours each way.

By boat from Martha's Vineyard: **Hy-Line Cruises** (508-778-2600 in Hyannis; 508-228-3949 on Nantucket; 508-693-0112 in Oak Bluffs, Martha's Vineyard; www.hy-linecruises.com). Three daily, inter-island departures from early June to mid-September. The trip takes 2¼ hours. (There is no inter-island car ferry.) One way: adults $13.50; children 5–12, $6.75; bicycles $10. No credit cards.

By air: **Cape Air** and **Nantucket Airlines** (508-228-7695; 800-352-0714; www. flycapeair.com) offer more than 100 daily flights direct from Boston, Hyannis, New Bedford, Providence (T. F. Green), and Martha's Vineyard. Frequent-flier coupon books for 10 one-way trips are available. Round-trip summer fares are $130 from New Bedford, $80 from Hyannis, $180–220 from Boston, $175 from Providence, and $80 from Martha's Vineyard. Don't forget to add the cost of parking. **Island Air** (508-228-7575; 800-248-7779) offers daily, year-round flights from Hyannis. Flight time is 20 minutes, and fares are competitive. **Colgan Air** (508-325-5100; 800-272-5488) offers year-round service from Nantucket to Hyannis and La Guardia, New York. **Business Express/Delta Connection** (800-345-3400) offers seasonal service to and from Boston. **US Airways Express** (800-428-4322) also flies to Nantucket from Philadelphia, Washington, D.C., and New York City.

GETTING AROUND ❧ **NRTA Shuttle** (508-228-7025). Buses daily 7 AM–11:30 PM late May through September. This is an economical and reliable way to travel to 'Sconset (two routes) and Madaket, but the schedule is too complicated to disseminate here. Pick up a route map on-island. Shuttles have a bike rack, so you can take the bus out to 'Sconset, for instance, and ride back. The Surfside and Jetties Beach buses run on a shorter season, from mid-June to early September. Tickets cost 50¢ or $1, depending on the route. Three-day ($10) and weekly ($15) passes are a smart idea; purchase them at the Visitor Services & Information Bureau (see *Guidance*), weekdays 9–2.

By car: There isn't a single traffic light in Nantucket, and Nantucketers intend to keep it that way. You don't need a car unless you're here for at least a week or unless you plan to spend most of your time in conservation areas or on outlying beaches. Even then, a four-wheel-drive vehicle is the most useful, as many of the stunning natural areas are off sandy paths. Parking is severely restricted in the historic center. Prices vary considerably; it pays to call around. Rent from **Nantucket Windmill Auto Rental** (508-228-1227; 800-228-1227), based at the airport and offering free pickup and delivery of vehicles (if they have an available driver); **Affordable Rentals** (508-228-3501; 877-235-3500), South Beach Street; and **Young's** (508-228-1151), Steamboat Wharf. **Budget** (508-228-5666; 800-527-0700) and **Hertz** (508-228-9421; 800-654-3131) are both based at the airport. The least expensive rental cars cost $90–100 daily in summer, almost half that off-season, and disappear quickly in summer.

By four-wheel drive: Nantucket is ringed by 80 miles of beach, most accessible via four-wheel drive. In addition to the above companies, try **Nantucket Jeep Rental** (508-228-1618), which delivers. Four-wheel drives are rented faster than the speed of light in summer, so you'll want to make reservations at least a month in advance of summer (as early as June for August). Expect to spend $175–220 daily in-season, $100–125 off-season.

If you get stuck in the sand, as one reader did and confessed to me, call **Harry's 24-hour Towing** (508-228-3390). Once you do call him, though, wait with your vehicle so he doesn't make the trek out to fetch you, only to find that you've been helped by a friendly local.

Contact the Police Department (508-228-1212), South Water Street, for **overland permits** required for four-wheel, oversand driving: $20–50 yearly for private vehicles. Purchase them daily mid-May to mid-October.

The Coatue–Coskata–Great Point nature area (see *Green Space*) requires a separate permit, available from the **Nantucket Conservation Foundation** (508-228-2884 information; 508-228-0006 refuge gatehouse, where permits are purchased) mid-May through October ($20 daily, $85 year-round). Off-season, pay the rangers who patrol the area. Most beaches are open to four-wheel-drive traffic, except when terns are nesting.

By taxi: Taxi fares can add up, but cabs are a useful way to get to the airport or to an outlying restaurant. Taxis usually line up on lower Main Street and at Steamboat Wharf. Flat rates are based on the destination: $16 to 'Sconset, $8–10 to the airport, and $5 within town, for instance. Rates are for one person; add $1 for each additional passenger.

By bicycle: Bicycling is the best way to get around (see *Outdoor Activities— Bicycling/Rentals*).

By moped: **Nantucket Bike Shop** (508-228-1999), Steamboat Wharf, rents scooters April through October; $40 single, $60 double, daily.

 By foot: **Nantucket Ghost Walk** (508-325-8855) departs from in front of the Atheneum (Federal and India Streets); times change seasonally. This incredibly popular tour (with upwards of 60 people walking) takes 1¾ hours and costs $15 adults, $10 teens, $5 children.

Architectural Walking Tours (508-228-1387), by the Nantucket Preservation Trust. April through November.

 By van or bus tours: **Gail's Tours** (508-257-6557), run by seventh-generation Nantucketer Gail Nickerson Johnson, offers 90-minute narrated van tours for up to 13 people. Tours leave at 10 AM, 1 PM, and 3 PM from the Visitor Services & Information Bureau on Federal Street (see *Guidance*). While Gail gives tidbits of trivia, both historic and contemporary, that will bring the island alive, she'll also tell you which celebrities and millionaires own which houses. Gail's is a unique perspective; her mother began giving tours in the mid-1950s. $13 per person; reservations advised (call in the evening).

Ara's Tours (508-228-1951), mid-April to mid-December. These late-afternoon, 3-hour barrier beach tours of Great Point (see *Green Space*) attract a lot of photographers and outdoors types; call for prices. Ara also has 90-minute island tours for $12 that make stops for photography.

☙ **Trustees of Reservations** (508-228-6799; www.thetrustees.org) offers excellent 3-hour natural history tours of Great Point from mid-May to mid-October. Tours depart at 9:30 AM and 1:30 PM and culminate with an ascent of the Great Point Lighthouse. Adults $30; children 15 and under, $15.

Barrett's Tours (508-228-0174), 20 Federal Street, and **Nantucket Island Tours** (508-228-0334), Straight Wharf, offer 60-minute narrated mini-bus tours May through October. $13 adults, $6 children.

MEDICAL EMERGENCY **Nantucket Cottage Hospital** (508-228-1200), South Prospect Street. Open 24 hours.

Lyme disease. Ticks carry this disease, which has flu-like symptoms and may result in death if left untreated. Immediately and carefully remove any ticks that may have migrated from dune grasses to your body. Better yet, wear long pants, tuck pants into socks, and wear long-sleeved shirts whenever possible when hiking. Avoid hiking in grassy and overgrown areas of dense brush.

✳ To See

ON THE HARBOR **The wharves** (from north to south). The Steamship Authority is based at **Steamboat Wharf,** but from 1881 to 1917, steam trains, which met the early steam-powered ferries and transported passengers to Surfside and 'Sconset, originated here. **Old North Wharf** is home to privately owned summer cottages. **Straight Wharf,** originally built in 1723 by Richard Macy, is a center of activity. It was completely rebuilt in the 1960s (except for the Thomas Macy Warehouse; see below) as part of a preservation effort. The wharf is home to Hy-Line, a few T-shirt and touristy shops, restaurants, a gallery, a museum, a nice pavilion area, and charter boats and sailboats. Straight Wharf was so named because folks could cart things from here "straight" up Main Street. **Old South Wharf** houses art galleries, crafts shops, and clothing shops in quaint little one-room "shacks" (see *Selective Shopping*). **Commercial Wharf,** also known as Swain's Wharf, was built in the early 1800s by Zenas Coffin.

Thomas Macy Warehouse, Straight Wharf. Built after the Great Fire of 1846, when the wharves were completely destroyed and more than 400 houses burned, the warehouse stored supplies to outfit ships. Today the Nantucket Historical Association leases the warehouse to a private art gallery. (See *Selective Shopping—Art Galleries*.)

Kim Grant

YOU'LL END UP HERE SOONER OR LATER

MAIN STREET The lower three blocks of Main Street were paved in 1837 with cobblestones, purchased in Gloucester, that proved quite useful—they kept carts laden with whale oil from sinking into the sand and dirt as they were rolled from wharves to factories. After the Great Fire swept through town, Main Street was widened considerably to prevent future fires from jumping from house to house so rapidly. In the mid-1850s Henry and Charles Coffin planted dozens of elm trees along the street, but only a few have survived disease over the years. The former drinking fountain for horses, which today spills over with flowers, has been a landmark on Lower Main since it was moved here in the early 1900s.

Pacific Club, Main Street at South Water Street. This three-story, Georgian brick building was built as a warehouse and countinghouse for shipowner William Rotch, owner of the *Beaver* and *Dartmouth,* two ships that took part in the Boston Tea Party. In 1789 it served as a U.S. Customs House. In 1861 a group of retired whaling captains purchased the building for use as a private social club, where they swapped stories and played cribbage. Descendants of these original founders carry on the tradition of the elite club.

Pacific National Bank (508-228-1917), 61 Main Street at Fair Street. This 1818, two-story, Federal-style brick building is one of only four to survive the Great Fire. It's no coincidence that the two important buildings anchoring Main Street are named "Pacific" for the fortunes reaped from the Pacific Ocean: This bank almost single-handedly financed the wealthy whaling industry. Step inside to see the handsome main room, original teller cages, and murals of the port and street scenes.

Thomas Macy House, 99 Main Street. Many think this is Nantucket's most attractive doorway, with its silver doorplate, porch railing that curves outward, and wooden fanwork. This NHA (Nantucket Historical Association) property is open to the public on special occasions.

"Three Bricks," 93, 95, and 97 Main Street. These identical Georgian mansions were built in 1836 for the three sons (all under the age of 27) of whaling-ship magnate Joseph Starbuck. Joseph retained the house titles to ensure that his sons would continue the family business. When the sons approached age 40 (firmly entrenched in the business), Joseph deeded the houses to them. One house remains in the Starbuck family; none is open to the public.

Hadwen House (508-228-1894), 96 Main Street. Taken together, 94 Main (privately owned) and 96 Main are referred to architecturally as the Two Greeks. Candle merchant William Hadwen married one of Joseph Starbuck's daughters and built the Greek Revival house (at No. 96). (Starbuck's two other daughters also ended up living across the street from their brothers—at 92 and 100 Main Street—creating a virtual Starbuck compound.) Docents point out gas chandeliers, a circular staircase, Italian marble fireplaces, silver doorknobs, and period furnishings. Don't overlook the lovely historic garden in back. The "other" Greek (No. 94) was built in the mid–19th century for Mary G. Swain, Starbuck's niece; note the Corinthian capitals supposedly modeled after the Athenian Temple of the Winds. This is another NHA property (see *Guidance* for hours and fees).

Henry Coffin House and **Charles Coffin House,** 75 and 78 Main Street. The Coffin brothers inherited their fortunes from their father's candle-making and whaling enterprises and general mercantile business. They built their houses across the street from each other, using the same carpenters and masons. Charles was a Quaker, and his Greek Revival house (No .78) has a simple roof walk and modest brown trim. Henry's late-Federal-style house (No. 75) has fancy marble trim around the front door and a cupola. Neither is open to the public.

John Wendell Barrett House, 72 Main Street. This elegant Greek Revival house features a front porch with Ionic columns and a raised basement. Barrett

PACIFIC NATIONAL BANK ANCHORS THIS CORNER OF MAIN STREET

Kim Grant

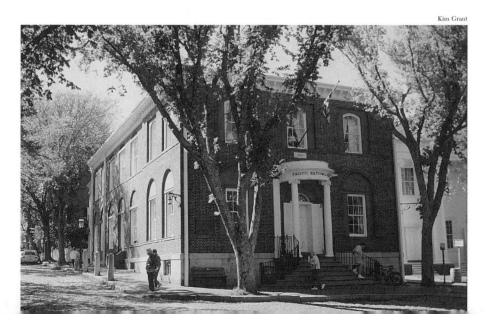

QUIET TIME

✳ ⚓ ♦ **Atheneum** (508-228-1110; www.nantucketatheneum.org), Lower India Street. Open 9:30–5 Monday, Wednesday, Friday, and Saturday; 9:30–8 Tuesday and Thursday; closed Monday off-season. This fine Greek Revival building with Ionic columns was designed by Frederick Coleman, who designed the "Two Greeks" (see Hadwen House, above). When the library and all its contents were lost in the Great Fire, donations poured in from around the country and a new building replaced it within six months. The Great Hall on the second floor has hosted such distinguished orators as Frederick Douglass, Daniel Webster, Horace Greeley, Henry David Thoreau, Ralph Waldo Emerson, and John James Audubon. (The hall seats about 100 people; there are numerous free readings and lectures here.) Maria Mitchell (see Maria Mitchell Association, below) was the first librarian. Since then there have been only five other librarians in its long history. In addition to comfortable reading rooms on both floors, the Atheneum has an excellent children's wing and a nice garden out back. Some of the more than 40,000 volumes include town newspapers dating from 1816, early New England genealogy, and ships' logs. Portraits of whaling captains grace the space, while display cases are filled with scrimshaw and other historical artifacts. This is one of the island's most special places. It's a quiet refuge from the masses in the height of summer, as well as a delightful place to spend a rainy day. Call for information about special events and story hours.

was the president of the Pacific National Bank and a wealthy whale oil merchant, but the house is best known for another reason. During the Great Fire, Barrett's wife, Lydia, refused to leave the front porch. Firefighters wanted to blow up the house in order to deprive the fire of fuel. Luckily for her, the winds shifted and further confrontation was averted. Not open to the public.

NORTH OF MAIN STREET ⚓ **Nantucket Whaling Museum** (508-228-1736), Broad Street. Open daily, late April to early October; weekends, early spring and late autumn; Saturdays in winter for a lecture and self-guided tour at 1:30. This 1846 brick building, another NHA property (see *Guidance* for hours), began as Richard Mitchell's spermaceti candle factory. (Spermaceti, by the way, is a substance found in the cavity of a sperm whale's head; it was a great source of lamp and machine oil.) Now the building houses an outstanding museum preserving Nantucket's whaling history. It's a must-see on even the shortest itinerary. Exhibits include the lens from the Sankaty Head Lighthouse; a 43-foot skeleton of a finback whale (beached in the 1960s); lightship basket and scrimshaw collections; an around-the-world map tracing the voyages of the whaling ship *Alpha;* and a reproduction tryworks, which was used to boil down whale oil on board ships. You'll also see a fully rigged whale boat, which will help you envision the treacherous "Nantucket sleigh ride": When the small boat harpooned a mammoth whale and remained connected by a rope, the boat was dragged through the waves until the whale tired. Adults $10, children $6; History Ticket with guided walking tours costs $15 adults, $8 children, $35 families.

Peter Foulger Museum (508-228-1894), 15 Broad Street. One of the island's first settlers, Peter Foulger acted as an interpreter when they purchased the island from Native Americans in 1659. Peter's daughter Abiah was Ben Franklin's mother. This NHA property has changing exhibits (see *Guidance* for hours and fees).

Centre Street was referred to as Petticoat Row during the whaling era, when men went out to sea and women were left to run the shops and businesses. It's still chock-full of fine shops.

THE NANTUCKET WHALING MUSEUM IS A TREASURE

Kim Grant

First Congregational Church (508-228-0950), 62 Centre Street. Open 10–4 Monday through Saturday, mid-June to mid-October. This church is known for its 120-foot steeple, from which there are 360-degree panoramic views of the island and ocean. On a clear day you can see from Eel Point to Great Point (see *Green Space*), and all the moors in between. Serious photographers shouldn't get too excited, though, because they'll have to shoot through dirty storm windows.

The present steeple was built in 1968; the previous one was dismantled in 1849 when it was deemed too shaky to withstand storms. The church was built with whaling money at the industry's apex in 1834. Note the things money could buy: a 600-pound brass chandelier and trompe l'oeil walls. The rear wing of the church contains the simple vestry, the oldest church building on the island (circa 1720). Since the late 1970s a special concert has been given in early July on Rose Sunday, when the church interior and island are full of blooming wild roses. Donation suggested for climbing the steeple: $2.50 adults, 50¢ children.

🌸 **Oldest House** (508-228-1894), Sunset Hill Road. Also known as the **Jethro Coffin House,** this 1686

Kim Grant

NANTUCKET'S OLDEST HOUSE DATES BACK TO 1686

home was built as a wedding present for Jethro Coffin and Mary Gardner by their parents. Peter Coffin cut and shipped timbers from his land in Exeter, New Hampshire, for the house. The marriage joined two prominent island families—the Coffins were "original purchasers" while the Gardners were "half-share men." Features include small, diamond-shaped, leaded windows, sparse period furnishings, and a huge central chimney decorated with an upside-down horseshoe. When lightning struck the house in 1987, the NHA (see *Guidance* for hours and fees) decided it was time to restore it.

Brant Point Lighthouse, off Easton Street. In 1746 the island's first "lighthouse" (and the country's second oldest, after Boston Light) guarded the harbor's northern entrance. It was rather primitive, consisting of a lantern hung on rope between two poles. The lighthouse standing today is small in size but large in symbolism. Folklore and tradition suggest that throwing two pennies overboard as you round the point at the lighthouse ensures your return. Many do, and many do. Don't pass up the chance to catch a sunset from here; it's the reason you came to Nantucket in the first place.

NEAR OR OFF UPPER MAIN STREET **Quaker Meeting House** (508-228-1894), 7 Fair Street. Open mid-June to mid-September. This small, simple building with wooden benches and 12-over-12 windows began as a Friends school in 1838. NHA property (see *Guidance* for hours); free.

Nantucket Historical Association Research Library (508-228-0722; www.nha.org), 7 Fair Street. Open to researchers 10–4 weekdays (plus additional

Saturday hours in July and August). Behind the Meeting House, this library contains Edouard A. Stackpole's collection of manuscripts, photographs, ships' logs, and other items. $5 per visit.

St. Paul's Episcopal Church (508-228-0916), 20 Fair Street. Stop in to admire this granite church's Tiffany windows.

❋ **Unitarian Universalist Church** (508-228-5466), 11 Orange Street. Open 10–4 daily, July and August; the office is also open weekday mornings the rest of the year, so you're welcome to stop in. This 1809 church, also called South Church, is known for its tall spire (quite visible at sea and a distinct part of the Nantucket "skyline"); a wonderfully illusory trompe l'oeil golden dome; and a mahogany and ivory 1831 Goodrich organ. Orange Street was once home to

GREAT POINT LIGHT TAKES EFFORT TO REACH, BUT IT'S WORTH IT

Kim Grant

more than 100 whaling captains, and for years, a town crier watched for ships (and fires) from this tower.

☙ **The Coffin School** (508-228-2505; www.eganinstitute.com), 4 Winter Street, one block off Main Street. Open 1–5 daily, late May to mid-October. The school was founded in 1827 by Admiral Sir Isaac Coffin, English baronet and a descendant of Tristram Coffin, one of the island's first settlers. It was established to provide a "good English education" for Coffin descendants. (In the early 19th century, more than half of Nantucket's children were Coffin descendants.) The impressive brick Greek Revival building now serves as home for the **Egan Institute of Maritime Studies.** It displays changing special exhibits on subjects relating to Nantucket history. A fine collection of 19th-century paintings portraying significant Nantucket events is featured, including works by Elizabeth R. Coffin, a student of Thomas Eakins. Historical lectures on the school and maritime subjects are given year-round. Admission $1.

See also Lightship Basket Museum under the sidebar "Lightship Baskets."

BEYOND UPPER MAIN STREET Hose Fire Cart House (508-228-1894), 8 Gardner Street. This small 1886 neighborhood fire station is the only one of its kind remaining on-island. As you can imagine, lots of stations were built after the Great Fire. On display are leather buckets and an old hand pumper, used more than a century ago. NHA property (see *Guidance* for hours); free.

Old Gaol (508-228-1894), 15R Vestal Street. This 1805 penal institution, built of logs bolted together with iron, was used until 1933. It had only four cells. The first incarcerated felon escaped, but others weren't so lucky. Well, perhaps they were—it's said that most of the prisoners got to sleep at home rather than on the planks that served as beds. NHA property (see *Guidance* for hours); free.

✍ ✳ **Maria Mitchell Association** (508-228-9198; www.mmo.org), 4 Vestal Street. Open 10–4 Tuesday through Saturday, June to August; call for hours September through May. Founded in 1902, the association owns five properties that celebrate the life and continue the work of Maria (pronounced mar-EYE-a) Mitchell, born on-island August 1, 1818. At age 13 Maria helped whaling captains set their navigational devices, with the aid of astronomical projections. At 18 she became the librarian at the Atheneum, where she served for the next 20 years. At 29 Mitchell was the first woman to discover a comet (which was dubbed Mitchell's comet)—from atop the Pacific National Bank, where her father (bank president and amateur astronomer) had set up an observatory. Maria was also the first woman to be admitted to the American Academy of Arts and Sciences and the first woman college professor of astronomy. (She taught at Vassar from 1865 until her death in 1888.)

The association hosts a number of children's programs that foster an appreciation of the connection between science and "beauty and poetry." Also, look for postings of special lectures and walks sponsored by the group; I've never been to one that was less than excellent. A combination ticket (available at any of the properties) costs $10 adults and $7 children 6–14, but tickets may also be purchased separately ($4 and $3, respectively).

SNUG COTTAGES ARE THE DRAW IN THIS VILLAGE.

Kim Grant

✳ ✐ **Maria Mitchell Science Library** (508-228-9219; www.mmo.org), 4 Vestal Street. Call for hours. This library, which has a children's section, houses 19th-century science books, current scientific periodicals, Maria's own papers, and natural history and astronomy books. Maria's father taught navigation by the stars in this former schoolhouse. Free.

Maria Mitchell Birthplace (508-228-2896; www.mmo.org), 1 Vestal Street. Open 10–4 Tuesday through Saturday, mid-June through August. Built in 1790, Mitchell's birthplace contains family memorabilia and the telescope she used to spot her comet. Tour the house and check out the island's only public roof walk. Adults $3, children $3.

✐ **Hinchman House** (508-228-0898; www.mmo.org), 7 Milk Street. Open 10–4 Tuesday through Saturday, mid-June through August. This natural science museum has live reptiles and preserved plant and bird specimens from the island. Inquire about nature programs and field trips for children. Adults $4, children $3.

✳ **Loines Observatory** (508-228-9273; www.mmo.org), Milk Street Extension. Open on clear Monday, Wednesday, and Friday evenings in summer (call to confirm days), when lectures and telescope viewings are held at 9 PM. It's also open year-round on Friday (8 PM). Adults $10, children $6.

✐ **Aquarium** (508-228-5387; www.mmo.org), 28 Washington Street. Open 10–4 Tuesday through Saturday, mid-June to early August; limited autumn hours until mid-October. Near the town pier, the small Aquarium has fresh- and saltwater tanks; science interns are on hand to answer questions. Popular marine-life collecting trips, for which reservations are required, are offered Tuesday through Thursday and Saturday. Adults $4, children $3.

Old Mill (508-228-1894), South Mill and Prospect Streets. Reputed to be made with salvaged wood, this 1746 Dutch-style windmill has canvas sails and a granite

'SCONSET

This charming village on the eastern shore is the island's only real "destina-tion," 7 miles from town. (Well, for the adventuresome, Great Point—see *Green Space*—is the other "destination.") The village is renowned for its tiny rose-covered cottages, all a few feet from one another. Some of the oldest are clustered on Broadway, Centre, and Shell Streets. You won't have any problem finding them since the town consists only of a post office, a liquor store, a market, and a few restaurants. Of course, 'Sconset also has its share of grand summer homes—along Ocean Avenue and Sankaty and Bax-ter Roads (on the way to Sankaty Head Lighthouse; see below). Recently, the combination of severe winter storms and the absence of offshore shoals to break incoming waves has created extreme beach erosion. Beachfront homes have been moved after several were engulfed by the sea.

Siasconset, which means "land of many bones," was probably named after a right whale was found on the beach. The 17th-century village was settled by and used as a base for fishermen in search of cod and whales. When wives began to join their husbands here in summer, the one-room shanties were expanded with additions called warts. (Perhaps early summer visitors wanted to escape the oil refineries in town, too.) When the narrow-gauge railway was built in 1884, it brought vacationing New York City actors who established a thriving actors' colony. Today 150 hardy souls live here year-round.

A few "sites" in 'Sconset include the 'Sconset Pump, an old wooden water pump dug in 1776, and the 'Sconset Union Chapel, the only place of worship in town. Despite its name, the Siasconset Casino, built in 1899 as a private tennis club, has never been used for gambling. Turn-of-the-20th-cen-tury actors used it for summer theater; movies are now shown in summer (see *Entertainment—Movies/Films*).

Sankaty Head Light, 'Sconset. Partially solar powered, this red-and-white-striped light stands on a 90-foot-high bluff at the edge of a rapidly encroaching shoreline. Its light is visible 24 miles out to sea.

stone that still grinds corn in summer. A reminder of when the island's principal activity was farming, this windmill is the only remaining of the four originals. (It's in its original location, too.) NHA property (see *Guidance* for hours and fees).

African Meeting House (508-228-9833; www.afroammuseum.org), York and Pleasant Streets. Open by appointment. Built as a church and a schoolhouse in the 1820s, when black children were barred from public school, this house is thought to be the second oldest such building in the country. Boston's Museum of Afro-American History presents cultural programming and interpretive exhibits on the history of African Americans on Nantucket. They also publish a very good pamphlet with a walking tour of the island's black heritage sites.

Moor's End, 19 Pleasant Street. This large 1830s Georgian house—the first island house made with brick—belonged to Jared Coffin. Although today it's among the island's finest, Mrs. Coffin was not satisfied with its location. She wanted to be closer to town, and so Jared built another at 29 Broad Street (see Jared Coffin House under *Lodging—Inns*). A beautiful garden lies behind the tall brick wall, but unfortunately for us, like the house, it's private.

AROUND THE ISLAND **Great Point Light,** Great Point, is accessible by four-wheel-drive vehicle, by boat, or by a difficult 5-mile (one way) trek through soft sand. A 70-foot stone structure guarded the island's northeastern tip for 166 years, until a ferocious storm destroyed it in 1984. This new one was built to withstand 20-foot waves and 240 mph winds.

Madaket. When Thomas Macy landed here in 1659, he found poor soil and didn't stay long. Today there is a large summer community and many rental houses. On the western coast, Madaket is a great place to enjoy a sunset, do some bluefishing, or get a boat repaired in the boatyard. The picturesque creek is best viewed from the little bridge to the right of the main road.

↑ ✍ **Nantucket Lifesaving Museum** (508-228-1885), 158 Polpis Road on Folger's Marsh. Open 9:30–4 daily, mid-June to mid-October. This building replicates the original 1874 Surfside Lifesaving Service station that survives today as the Nantucket Hostel (see *Lodging—Hostel*). Instead of being at water's edge, however, it's scenically situated on a salt marsh—perfect for a picnic. Dedicated to humanity's dramatic efforts against the relentless sea, this museum houses equipment used in the daring rescues of sailors stranded in their sinking offshore boats. You'll find one of four Massachusetts Humane Society lifesaving surfboats and the only surviving beachcart still used for demonstration drills. You'll also find photographs, accounts of rescues, Nantucket's three Fresnel lighthouse lenses, and artifacts from the *Andrea Doria,* which sank off Nantucket almost half a century ago. $5 adults, $2 children 6 and over.

❋ Outdoor Activities

BICYCLING/RENTALS Excellent paved, two-way bicycle paths lead to most major "destinations." If you're riding on the street, ride in the direction of traffic or you'll be fined. Or walk your bike.

Rubel Bike Maps (www.bikemaps.com) are the best, most detailed maps available for the Cape and islands. Rubel produces a combination Nantucket and Vineyard map ($1.95), as well as another that includes the islands, Cape Cod, and the North Shore ($4.25). Even though bike rental agencies give you a free map, Rubel's is worth the extra money.

Madaket Bike Path begins on Upper Main Street. This 6-mile (one-way) road takes you to the western end of Nantucket in 45 minutes. Although the route is a bit hilly and winding, it's beautiful. There are rest areas along the way and a water fountain at the halfway point, picnic tables at Long Pond (see *Green Space—Ponds*), and usually elegant swans, too.

Kim Grant

NANTUCKET LIFESAVING MUSEUM

Dionis Bike Path is a 1-mile spur trail off the Madaket Bike Path that runs to Dionis Beach. Getting to the beach has never been easier.

'Sconset (or Milestone) Bike Path begins at the rotary east of the historic district. This 7-mile (one way) route with slight inclines parallels Milestone Road; it takes about an hour to get to 'Sconset. (Visually, the ride is a bit dull.) There's a water fountain at the rotary.

Surfside Bike Path. Take Main Street to Pleasant Street and turn right onto Atlantic Avenue to Surfside Road. There are benches and water fountains along the 3.5-mile (one way) route. This flat path is very popular in summer; it takes about 20 minutes to get to the beach.

Polpis Road Path. The loop from the 'Sconset Bike Path to Polpis Road and back to town is about 16.5 miles. It's definitely worth the detour, especially in springtime when it's lined with thousands of daffodils.

Cliff Road Bike Path begins on Cliff Road from North Water Street. This 2.5-mile, slightly hilly road passes large summer homes.

With more than 3,000 rental bikes on-island, companies offer competitive rates. Average prices: $25 daily for adult bikes, $90 weekly; $15–20 daily for children's bikes; trailers, zipper strollers, and trail-a-bikes, too. Inquire about discounts for family rentals. The following shops rent bicycles: **Young's Bicycle Shop** (508-228-1151), 6 Broad Street, Steamboat Wharf; **Nantucket Bike Shop** (508-228-1999), Steamboat Wharf; and **Cook's Cycles** (508-228-0800), 6 South Beach. Young's has the longest season, but Cook's is often a bit less expensive.

See also Eco Guides under Outdoor Adventure.

BICYCLES ARE THE BEST WAY TO TOUR THE ISLAND   Kim Grant

BIRD-WATCHING Maria Mitchell Association (508-228-9198; 508-228-0898; www.mmo.org), Vestal Street, offers birding walks all over the island, mid-June to mid-September. Adults $10, children $6. Some people think that Nantucket offers the best wintertime bird watching on the East Coast. I wouldn't argue.

See also Eco Guides under *Outdoor Adventure.*

BOAT EXCURSIONS/RENTALS ✍ **Harbor Cruises *Anna W. II*** (508-228-1444), Slip 11, Straight Wharf. June to mid-October. Since 1961, the friendly knowledgeable Captain Bruce Cowan has offered trips that leave at different times of the day and on different days; call for current details and prices. Among the possible trips are: Marine Life Discovery tours (hauling traps with crabs, lobsters, eels, and fish), ice cream cruises, shoreline sight-seeing, and sunset cruises for either 60 or 90 minutes. Bring your own food and drink aboard.

Endeavor (508-228-5585), Slip 15, Straight Wharf. May through October. Captain Jim Genthner and his wife, Sue, operate a 31-foot Friendship sloop that departs on at least three daily harbor tours and a sunset cruise. Adults $22.50–35 for a 90-minute sail; $15 for a 60-minute sail. Custom sails may include pirating for children and an onboard fiddler or storyteller.

Christina (508-325-4000), Slip 1016, Straight Wharf. This 1926 mahogany catboat departs frequently for harbor and sunset sails. BYOB.

Nantucket Boat Rentals (508-325-1001), Straight Wharf, Slip 1. You don't have to be macho to handle one of these little boats that can take you across the harbor to Coatue, where you can sunbathe and picnic in relative quiet. Leave in the morning when there's less wind. Jeff has been renting runabouts and powerboats daily or weekly in-season since 1990.

✍ **Nantucket Island Community Sailing** (508-228-6600), Jetties Beach, rents Windsurfers, Sunfish, and kayaks. It also holds youth, sailboard, and sailing classes, as well as a racing class. Open for business mid- to late June through September (weather permitting).

COOKOUTS Contact the Fire Department (508-228-2324), 131 Pleasant Street, for the requisite permits for charcoal cookouts and fires on the beach. If you want to build a bonfire, speak to the chief personally.

FISHING/SHELLFISHING Permits for digging clams, mussels, and quahogs are obtained from the Marine Department and shellfish warden (508-228-7261), 34 Washington Street. Scalloping season opens October 1, after which you'll see fishermen in the harbor and off nearby shoals of Tuckernuck Island; local scallops harvested from mid-October through March are delicious.

Try your luck freshwater fishing at **Long Pond** (see *Green Space—Ponds*). Nantucket blues, which run in schools from May through October, are caught from the southern shore. Fishing isn't as good in July and August when the waters are warmer, but if that's the only time you're here, toss out a line anyway.

Mike Monte (508-228-0529), a year-round island resident, takes people surf-fishing and fly-fishing May through October. His daily trip generally goes out with "first light" at sunrise, and he has folks back in time to have breakfast with their friends and family. He'll take just one person, but no more than four. He also provides all the equipment necessary. Fishing for about 4 hours runs $140 per person.

Whitney Mitchell (508-228-2331) has taken surf-fishers to locations accessible only by four-wheel drives since 1983. Mid-June to mid-October; call for prices.

Barry Thurston's Tackle Shop (508-228-9595) at Salem and Candle Streets. Open April through late December. Yes, you need tangible commodities like bait and tackle, fillet knives, rods, and reels. But even more valuable are the fish stories, advice, and fishing gossip that Thurston's has been dishing since 1976, when the native islander opened his shop. (Barry graduated in Nantucket's 1956 high school class.) He's got the goods on where the fish are running, what time, and what they're biting on. And he's happy to give it out—usually to

LOBSTERING DON'T GET ANY FRESHER

Kim Grant

generations of repeat customers. This place appeals to the casual as well as serious angler.

Bill Fisher Tackle (508-228-2261), 14 New Lane, rents a full line of equipment, supplies daily fishing reports, and provides guide service.

Most charters in search of striped bass and bluefish are located on Straight Wharf, including *Herbert T* (508-228-6655), Slip 14, and *Just Do It Too* (508-228-7448), Slip 13. You can also call Sankaty Head Charters (508-257-9606), which takes up to three people per 4½-hour trip; tackle included. **Hal Herrick** (508-257-9606), highly recommended, is out of Madaket.

FOOTBALL Nantucket High School (508-228-7280), Surfside Road. From mid-September to mid-November, after most of the tourists have left, the smallest high school in the state suits up in anticipation of another winning season. If you want to feel like a real insider, check out one of these games with the rest of the 10,000 year-rounders, all of whom seem to show up for home games. Games on Friday and Saturday, $3 admission.

FISHING CHARTERS DEPART FROM STRAIGHT WHARF

Kim Grant

GOLF Siasconset Golf Club (508-257-6596), Milestone Road. Open late May to mid-October. This nine-hole public course, encircled by conservation land, dates to 1894.

✳ **Miacomet Golf Club** (508-325-0333), off Somerset Road. This flat, nine-hole course is owned by the Nantucket Land Bank and has views of Miacomet Pond, heathland, and the coastline. Call for tee times.

Sankaty Head Golf Club (508-257-6655), Sankaty Road, 'Sconset. Although this links-style, 18-hole course is private, the public may play from mid-April to late May and mid-October to early December. There are magnificent lighthouse views. Interestingly, this course operates the country's only caddy camp (for boys age 14–18), and it's done so since the early 1960s.

Nantucket Golf Club (508-257-8500), 250 Milestone Road (there's no sign). One of the most exclusive clubs anywhere. Many members, like gazillionaire Bill Gates, do not own property on-island, but rather jet in, play golf, and jet out. Memberships cost hundreds of thousands of dollars, plus annual dues. (The membership list is closely guarded, of course, but it has its share from the Forbes 400 Wealthiest Americans list.) The par-72, links-style course rolls with the naturally undulating landscape, within sight of Sankaty Head Light, on the moors with scrub oak and pitch pine. Generally appreciated by island conservationists, who realize that it could have been developed in less favorable ways, the 250-acre course was designed by Rees Jones.

IN-LINE SKATING Summertime skating is prohibited in town. You can skate on bike paths and at the skateboarding park at Jetties Beach; helmets and pads are required.

KAYAKING ✍ **Nantucket Kayak** (508-325-6900), Commercial Wharf. Late May to mid-October. Open 9–7 daily for roll-proof kayak and canoe rentals as well as guided tours for children and adults. Half-day kayak rental cost $30 single, $50 double; full-day cost $40 single, $60 double. It's usually calm paddling along the 8 miles of scalloped bays at Coatue. Amy, the friendly owner, is very informed.

See also Eco Guides under *Outdoor Adventure* and Nantucket Island Community Sailing under *Boat Excursions/Rentals.*

OUTDOOR ADVENTURE ❋ ✍ **Eco Guides** (508-228-1769; www.strongwings. org). John Simms offers casual, customized adventure instruction and guided group trips, for novices and experts, in birding, climbing, mountain biking, sea kayaking, snorkeling, and natural history. After settling on a trip, price, and meeting time with John, be absolutely sure that you confirm and reconfirm your trip. There is also a large youth organization geared toward year-rounders, but vacationing kids can participate, too.

SAILBOARDING **Indian Summer Sports** (508-228-3632), 6 Steamboat Wharf, rents surfboards June through August. **Force 5 Watersports** (508-228-0700), 6 Union Street, a retail surf shop with a knowledgeable staff, is a good source of information, too. Surfing is best on the southern beaches. It's open April to late December.

SCUBA DIVING ❋ **The Sunken Ship** (508-228-9226; www.sunkenship.com), Broad and South Water Streets. Perhaps because the *Andrea Doria* sank off Nantucket's treacherous shoals in July 1956, the island is a magnet for Atlantic Ocean divers. This full-service dive shop has the market cornered with charters, lessons, rentals, and even fishing referrals.

SEAL CRUISES ❋ **Shearwater Excursions** (508-228-7037; www.explorenantucket.com) has daily departures, weather permitting, to see lounging seals on the outer island of Muskeget.

See also Harbor Cruises *Anna W. II,* under *Boat Excursions/Rentals.*

TENNIS Free, public courts are located at **Jetties Beach** (see *Green Space—*

Beaches). Sign up at the Parks and Recreation Building (508-325-5334; 508-228-7213), North Beach Street, for one of six courts. Clinics and lessons are offered for adults and children.

Brant Point Racquet Club (508-228-3700), 23 Nobadeer Farm Road. Open May to mid-October. A full-service place, with nine clay courts, a pro shop, round-robins (in summer), and rentals.

Tristram's Landing Tennis Center (508-228-4588), 440 Arkansas Avenue, Madaket.

✳ Even More Things to Do

DAY SPA ✳ **Tresses & The Day Spa** (508-228-0024; www.nantucketspa.com), 117 Pleasant Street. Choose à la carte treatments—facials and skin therapies, mud or seaweed masks, salt glows, herbal body wraps, and a variety of massages—or packages with mud treatment and aromatherapy. Prices are lower off-season.

FITNESS CLUB ✳ **Nantucket Health Club** (508-228-4750), 10 Young's Way. Open daily. A full array of machines, free weights, classes, and personalized training sessions. $20 day-use fee; $125 for 10 visits.

✐ **FOR FAMILIES** **Strong Wings Summer Camp** (508-228-1769), late June to late August. This weekly action-filled day camp for kids age 5–15 has 3-day and 5-day options that might include sea kayaking, fort building, stunt-kite flying, canoeing, ghost stories, crafts, and nature exploration—depending on the age.

✳ **Nantucket Babysitters Service** (508-228-4970; www.nantucketbabysitters.com) provides parents a respite. Ronnie Sullivan-Moran assesses your needs, matches a sitter to your kids (all ages), and then sends the sitter to wherever you're staying. Services are available year-round. She'll also pick-up groceries and provide "lifestyle management" and "new home helper" services.

✳ **SPECIAL PROGRAMS** **Nantucket Island School of Design and the Arts** (508-228-9248; www.nisda.org), Wauwinet Road. Founded in 1973, the NISDA presents an extraordinary range of classes and lectures for adults, youths, and kinders, year-round. Summerlong, weeklong, or daylong classes include drawing, design, textile, folk art, floor cloth painting, puppet making, garden tours, yoga, modern dance, clay and sculpture, painting, and photography. Affiliated with Mass College of Art in Boston, the school offers college graduate and undergraduate summer sessions in a converted dairy barn. Individuals attending classes may rent the school's studios and one-bedroom cottages on the harbor.

✐ **Artist's Association of Nantucket** (508-228-0722; 508-325-5251; www.nantucketarts.org), Gardner Perry Lane. Offering seasonal workshops and classes in a variety of disciplines for adults and children year-round, the association also maintains a fine art library on Gardner Perry Lane and a gallery at 19 Washington Street (see *Selective Shopping—Art Galleries*).

◢ **Nantucket Community School** (508-228-7257), 10 Surfside Road. Offers adult-education classes and programs and camps for kids.

See also Lightship Shop under the sidebar "Lightship Baskets."

SWIMMING POOL ◢ ❋ **Nantucket Community Pool** (508-228-7262), Atlantic and Sparks Avenues. An Olympic-sized pool at the Nantucket High School is open daily for swimming; adults $7, children $5 daily; weekly rates, too. Inquire about swimming lessons, also for a fee.

❋ WINERY AND BREWERY **Nantucket Vineyard** (508-228-9235; www.nantucketvineyard.com), 5 Bartlett Farm Road, about 2.5 miles south of town off Hummock Pond Road. Open 11–6 Monday through Saturday, noon–5 Sunday in summer; then by appointment. Since vinifera grapes don't grow particularly well on Nantucket, this vineyard imports grapes for its wines. Tours and tastings are offered, as are bottles of evocatively named vintages like Nantucket Sleighride and 'Sconset Rose.

Cisco Brewers (508-325-5929; www.ciscobrewers.com), 5 Bartlett Farm Road. Open 10–6 daily except Sunday in summer; Saturday 10–5 the rest of the year. Come for a sample tasting of fresh, traditionally brewed ales, porters, stouts, and seasonal concoctions like Celebration Libation. Look for the excellent Cisco beer at island restaurants and package stores. It's more satisfying (and cheaper) than most bottles of restaurant wine.

❋ Green Space

Nantucket is renowned for the amount of open, protected land on the island. In fact, thanks to the efforts of various conservation groups, more than 45 percent of the island is protected from development. Two organizations deserve much of the credit: **Nantucket Conservation Foundation** (508-228-2884; www.nantucketconservation.com), 118 Cliff Road, open 8–4 weekdays; and the **Nantucket Land Bank** (508-228-7240; www.nantucketlandbank.org), 22 Broad Street. The Nantucket Conservation Foundation, the country's first land bank, was established in 1963 to manage open land—wetlands, moors, and grasslands. It's a private, nonprofit organization that's supported by membership contributions. Since then, the foundation has purchased or been given more than 8,600 acres on the island. Because the foundation is constantly acquiring land, call for a map of its current properties, published yearly; $4 in person. The Nantucket Land Bank was created by an act of the state legislature in 1983, granting permission to assess a 2 percent tax for all real estate and land transactions. With the tax receipts, property is purchased and kept as conservation land.

◉ **Maria Mitchell Association** (508-228-9198) leads informative nature walks around the island (see *To See*) for $10 adults, $6 children; half price for members.

Coatue–Coskata–Great Point, at the end of Wauwinet Road, accessible only by four-wheel-drive vehicle and by foot. The narrow strip of very soft sand leading to Great Point is about 5 miles long. Note the "haulover," which separates

WINDSWEPT EXPANSES INVITE DAYDREAMING

Kim Grant

the head of the harbor from the Atlantic Ocean. This stretch of sand is so narrow that fishermen would haul their boats across it instead of going all the way around the tip of Great Point. During severe storms, the ocean breaks through the haulover, effectively creating an island. (Sand is eventually redeposited by the currents.) The spit of sand known as Coatue is a series of concave bays that reach all the way to the mouth of Nantucket Harbor.

There's a wealth of things to do in this pristine preserve: birding, surf-casting, shellfishing, sunbathing, picnicking, and walking. Since the riptides are dangerous, especially near the Great Point Lighthouse (see *To See*), swimming is not recommended. These three adjacent wildlife areas, totaling more than 1,110 acres, are owned by different organizations, but that doesn't impact visitors. The Nantucket Conservation Foundation owns both Coatue and the haulover. But the world's oldest land trust, the Trustees of Reservations, also manages part of the land. Ara's Tours and the Trustees of Reservations offer tours of Great Point; see *Getting Around* for tours and for info on getting your own four-wheel-drive permits.

Eel Point, off Eel Point Road from the Madaket Bike Path (see *Outdoor Activities—Bicycling/Rentals*), about 6 miles from town. Leave your car or bicycle at the sign that reads 40TH POLE BEACH and walk the last half mile to the beach. There aren't any facilities, just unspoiled nature, good birding, surf-fishing, and a shallow sandbar. Portions of this beach are often closed to protect nesting shorebirds. For in-depth information, pick up a map and self-guided tour from the **Nantucket Conservation Foundation** (508-228-2884; www.nantucketconservation.com), 118 Cliff Road, Nantucket ($3 in person).

Sanford Farm, Ram Pasture, and the Woods, off Madaket Road. These 900-plus acres of wetlands, grasslands, and forest are owned and managed by the Nantucket Conservation Foundation and the Nantucket Land Bank. Ram Pasture and the Woods were one of the foundation's first purchases (for $625,000) in 1971. Fourteen years later, Sanford Farm was purchased for $4.4 million from Mrs. Anne Sanford's estate. A 6.5-mile (round trip) walking and biking trail goes past Hummock Pond to the ocean, affording great views of heathlands along the way. Interpretive markers identify natural and historic sites. There is also a popular 45-minute (1.6-mile) loop trail as well as the Barn Trail (1½ hours, 3 miles), which affords beautiful expansive views of the island's southern coastline.

Milestone Bog, off Milestone Road on a dirt road to the north, about 5 miles from town. When cranberries were first harvested here in 1857, there were 330 acres of bogs. Today, because of depressed prices and a worldwide cranberry glut, very few are. The land was donated to the Nantucket Conservation Foundation in 1968.

Windswept Cranberry Bog, off Polpis Road to the south. This 40-acre bog is also partially owned by the Nantucket Conservation Foundation.

BEACHES Nantucket is ringed by 50 miles of sandy shore, much of which is publicly accessible. In general, beaches on the south and east have rough surf and undertow; western and northern beaches have warmer, calmer waters. There is limited parking at most beaches; NRTA (508-228-7025) provides a special beach bus to Jetties and Surfside Beaches from mid-June to early September, and regular buses to Madaket and 'Sconset beaches.

Northern Beaches
⚓ **Children's Beach,** off South Beach Street on the harbor. A few minutes' walk from Steamboat Wharf, this is a great place for children (hence its name).

SURF-FISHING AT GREAT POINT

Kim Grant

Amenities include a lifeguard, rest rooms, a bathhouse, a playground, food, picnic tables, game tables, a bandstand, a horseshoe pit, and a grassy play area.

Brant Point, off Easton Street. A 15-minute walk from town, and overlooking the entrance to the harbor, this scenic stretch is great for boat-watching and surf-fishing. Swimming conditions aren't great: There's a strong current and a beach that drops off suddenly.

⌁ **Jetties,** off Bathing Beach Road from North Beach Road. Shuttle buses run to this popular beach—otherwise it's a 20-minute walk. (There is also a fairly large parking lot with lots of bike racks.) A great place for families because of the amenities (rest rooms, lifeguards, showers, changing rooms, snack bar, chairs for rent) and the activities (volleyball, tennis, swings, concerts, a playground, an assortment of sailboats and kayaks). Kids will enjoy the tie-dyeing clinics (508-228-7213) held here noon–1 PM on Fridays in July and August. The July 4 fireworks celebration is held here. Also a good beach for walking. Look for the skateboarding park; helmets and pads are required.

Francis Street Beach, a 5-minute walk from Main Street, at Washington and Francis Streets. This harbor beach is calm. There are kayak rentals, portable rest rooms, and a small playground.

Dionis, off Eel Point Road from the Madaket and Dionis Bike Paths (see *Outdoor Activities—Bicycling/Rentals*). Nantucket's only beach with dunes, Dionis is about 3 miles from town. The beach starts out narrow but becomes more expansive (and less populated) as you walk farther east or west. Amenities include lifeguards and a bathhouse.

WATCHING THE FERRY ARRIVE AT CHILDREN'S BEACH

Kim Grant

Southern Beaches

Surfside, off Surfside Road; large parking lot. Three miles from town and accessible by shuttle bus, this wide beach is popular with college students and families with older kids because of its proximity to town and its moderate-to-heavy surf. Rest rooms, lifeguards, showers, and a snack bar. Kite flying, surf-casting, and picnicking are popular.

Nobadeer, east of Surfside, near the airport and about 4 miles from town. There are no facilities at Nobadeer, but there is plenty of surf.

Madaket, at the end of the scenic Madaket Bike Path (see *Outdoor Activities— Bicycling/Rentals*). About 5 miles west of town (served by shuttle bus), Madaket is perhaps the most popular place to watch sunsets. This long beach has heavy surf and strong currents; there are lifeguards, portable rest rooms, and very little parking.

⌀ **Cisco,** off Hummock Pond Road from Milk Street. About 4 miles from town, this long beach is popular with surfers. There are lifeguards and surfing lessons for kids, but very little parking.

"Nude Beach," an unofficial beach, certainly, is unofficially located between Miacomet and Cisco.

Eastern Beaches

'Sconset (aka Codfish Park), at the end of the 'Sconset Bike Path; turn right at the rotary. About 7 miles from town, accessible by shuttle bus, this narrow, long beach takes a pounding by heavy surf. Seaweed lines the beach when the surf whips up. Lifeguards, playground, and very limited parking.

PONDS **Long Pond.** Take Madaket Road from town and, when you reach the HITHER CREEK sign, turn left onto a dirt road. This 64-acre Nantucket Land Bank property is great for birding. A mile-long path around the pond passes meadows and a cranberry bog.

Miacomet Pond, Miacomet Avenue (which turns into a dirt road), off Surfside Road. This long, narrow, freshwater pond next to the ocean has a sandy shore and is surrounded by grasses and heath. This Nantucket Land Bank property is a pleasant place for a picnic, and the swans and ducks make it more so.

Sesachacha Pond. Take Polpis Road to Quidnet Road. A narrow barrier beach separates the pond and ocean. There's a nice view of the Sankaty Head Lighthouse from here.

WALKS **The Moors** and **Altar Rock,** off Polpis Road, to the south, on an unmarked dirt road. When you want to get away from the summertime masses, head to the Moors (preferably at dawn or dusk, when they're most magical). From Altar Rock, the highest island point at 90 feet above sea level, there are expansive views of lowland heath, bogs, and moors. It's stunning in autumn. The Moors are also crisscrossed with trails and deeply rutted dirt roads.

Lily Pond Park, North Liberty Street. This 5-acre Nantucket Land Bank property supports lots of wildlife and plant life, but the trail is often muddy. You may find wild blackberries, grapes, or blueberries.

✳ Lodging

Although there are more than 1,100 rooms to rent (not including rental houses), consider making summertime reservations in February. Keep in mind that the historic district, while convenient, has its share of foot traffic (and boisterous socializers) late into the evening; houses are also very close together. A 10-minute walk from Straight Wharf will put you in quieter surroundings. Most lodgings require a 2- or 3-night minimum stay in-season; I indicate only minimum-night-stay policies that are extraordinary. Much to my chagrin, many places charge more for weekends than weekdays. Lastly, most places are not appropriate for small children. Unless otherwise noted, all lodging is in Nantucket 02554.

RESORTS

In town

🏊 **Cliffside Beach Club** (508-228-0618; 800-932-9645; www.cliffside-beach.com), Jefferson Avenue. Open late May to mid-October. *Stylish simplicity, understated elegance,* and *breezy beachside living* are the watchwords here. You can't get a bed closer to the beach than this: Decks sit on the beach, and a boardwalk over the sand connects the low-slung, weathered-shingle buildings. A private club when it opened in 1924, it's been in Robert Currie's family since 1958. The reception area (where a continental breakfast is set out) is large and airy, decorated with white wicker furniture, local art, and quilts hanging from the rafters. The 22 contemporary guest rooms (most with ocean views) feature outstanding woodwork, all crafted by islanders, and granite bathrooms. Five newer suites, with

outstanding views of dunes and sunsets, offer the most privacy. There are also a few luxuriously simple three-bedroom apartments. For meals, shuffle to the beachside Galley Restaurant (see *Dining Out*) walk 15 minutes into town. For exercise, use the impressive health club. Mid-June to early September $370–585 rooms and studios, $720–1,435 suites, apartments, and cottages; off-season $245–310 and $430–1,045, respectively. Add 5.3 percent service charge.

Around the island

♿ **The Wauwinet** (508-228-0145; 800-426-8718; www.wauwinet.com), Wauwinet Road, Nantucket 02584. Open May through October. When privacy and extraordinary service are of utmost concern, this Relais & Châteaux property is the place. Eight miles from town, it occupies an unparalleled location between oceanside dunes and a beach-rimmed harbor. The 25 guest rooms and five cottages feature luxurious linens and toiletries, pine armoires, Audubon prints, and sophisticated decorating touches. Public rooms are awash in chintz, trompe l'oeil, fresh flowers, and bleached woods. There's practically no reason to leave the enclave. Facilities include tennis courts, boating, mountain bicycles, croquet, a videocassette library, lobstering demonstrations, and Great Point nature trips. All are included in the room rates. Topper's (see *Dining Out*) offers outstanding dining. Enjoy as much from the breakfast menu as you'd like; it's also included. Mid-June to mid-September $390–900 rooms, $720–1,400 cottages (4 nights may be required in July and August); off-season $270–675 rooms, $545–1,200 cottages.

HOTELS **White Elephant Hotel** (508-228-2500; 800-475-2637; www.whiteelephanthotel.com), Easton Street. Open early May to late October. After a total renovation in early 2000, the sedate White Elephant is better than ever. A 10-minute walk from the center of town and on the edge of the harbor, many of the spacious 54 rooms and suites have prime water views framed by shuttered white windows. Most have a balcony or deck; many suites have a fireplace. Decor is a sophisticated blend of leather armchairs and white wicker, of crisp linens and textured, neutral fabrics, of antique prints and contemporary artwork. Bathrooms boast fine toiletries, lots of white tile, and marble counters. Common space includes a handsome library, fitness room, and broad lawns that reach a harborside dock. The harborside Brant Point Grill (see *Dining Out*) is a very nice place to lunch. June through August $410–680 (5-night minimum in July and August), suites more; off-season $280–480 rooms.

🦞 ✎ **The Beachside** (508-228-2241; 800-322-4433; www.thebeachside.com), 30 North Beach Street. Open mid-April to mid-October. Five minutes from Jetties Beach (not beachside as the name implies) and 10 minutes from town, this bilevel motel is distinctly Nantucket—quiet, tasteful, and upscale—with 92 rooms surrounding a heated pool. Some rooms have two double beds, and a few of those connect for family and friends. Many rooms feature French doors opening onto a small private patio; all have a TV and air-conditioning. General manager Mary Malavase thankfully runs a professional, tight ship. Mid-June to mid-September $240–285; off-season $130–190. Kids under age 16 free. Continental breakfast included. Shoulder-season air and ferry packages.

✎ **Harbor House** (508-228-1500; 800-475-2637; www.harborhouseack.com), South Beach Street. Open mid-April to early December. This spiffy 104-room hotel, on a quiet lane a few blocks from the center of town, consists of traditional Nantucket town houses surrounding a late-19th-century summer hotel. Gas lanterns and brick walkways connect the rooms. Townhouse rooms are spacious and nestled among small gardens or near the heated pool. July and August $325–395; off-season $125–300.

THE GRACIOUS WAUWINET

Kim Grant

STYLISH HARBORFRONT "SLOUNGING"

Kim Grant

INNS Dinner is served on the premises of these (generally) small places.

In town

Ship's Inn (508-228-0040), 13 Fair Street. Open May to early December. Beyond the bustle of Main Street, a 10-minute walk from Straight Wharf, the Ship's Inn is a largely unsung and very comfortable choice for lodging as well as fine dining (see *Dining Out*). The three-story 1831 whaling captain's house was completely restored in 1991. Its 12 large guest rooms, named for Captain Obed Starbuck's ships, all have refrigerator, telephone with voice mail, and TV. Many are bright corner rooms. Like the living room, they're large and airy, and sparsely furnished to create a summery feel. Mid-May to mid-October $235 double, $110 single with shared bath; off-season $175 and $100, respectively. Rates include continental breakfast and afternoon tea.

Woodbox Inn (508-228-0587; www.woodboxinn.com), 29 Fair Street. Open mid-June through December. Dexter Tutein's atmospheric inn and restaurant (see *Dining Out*) is located in one of the island's oldest houses, which dates to 1709. On a quiet street just beyond the densest concentration of activity and shops, the Woodbox has three rooms and six larger suites (with working fireplaces). All have period antiques. The two-bedroom suites are a good value at $305, as they can comfortably accommodate four people; they also have a living room. A rollaway cot can be added to the one-bedroom suites ($205) for an additional $25. The renowned breakfasts include wonderful popovers and egg creations. No credit cards. Rooms $185–315; 10 percent service charge added.

❄ ✿ Jared Coffin House (508-228-2400, 800-248-2405; www.jaredcoffin-house.com), 29 Broad Street. The island's first three-story house, topped with a cupola and slate roof, was built in 1845 by a wealthy shipowner for his wife. Made of brick, it was also one of the few buildings to survive the Great Fire of 1846. One year later, after Coffin's wife refused to live here, it was converted to an inn. I include it for its historical value and the large number of rooms. The 60 conventional guest rooms are located in six adjacent buildings. Rooms outside the main inn are larger, featuring colonial reproduction four-poster canopy beds, refrigerator, TV, and telephone. (Harrison Grey House rooms are the nicest.) A few rooms can accommodate children, but they are reserved quickly. More like a small hotel than an inn, the Jared Coffin employs a concierge and has two restaurants (see Jared's under *Dining Out* and the Tap Room under *Eating Out*). If you're looking for a one-night reservation, try here. May through October $125–375 double, $85–175 single; off-season packages.

Around the island

Summer House (508-257-4577; www.thesummerhouse.com), 'Sconset 02564. Open late April to late October. The brochure's photograph is almost too idyllic to believe: Honeysuckle vines and roses cover a shingled cottage with tiny windows; the double Dutch door opens to a white, skylit interior that's cozy and simple. But it's true! Dating to the 1840s, the eight enchanting cottages surround a colorful garden set with Adirondack chairs. The Munchkin-like cottages have been updated with marble Jacuzzi bathtubs, Laura Ashley fabrics, English country-pine antiques, and hand-painted borders; some have a fireplace and kitchen. All have off-season heat. Shuffle across the street to the eastern beach or to the inn's pool, nestled in the dunes just below the bluff. (Drinks and lunch are served pool- and oceanside; see *Dining Out*.) Early June to mid-September $575–925; off-season $250–550. Continental breakfast included. Add a 10 percent service charge.

In town

Pineapple Inn (508-228-9992; www.pineappleinn.com), 10 Hussey Street. Open late April to late October and Christmas Stroll weekend. The finest B&B on Nantucket, this 1838 whaling captain's house was renovated from top to bottom in 1997 by veteran innkeepers Bob and Caroline Taylor. Refined, understated elegance, sincere hospitality, and luscious breakfasts are keys to their success. Historic grace and modern conveniences coexist comfortably here. First-class touches surround you, including white marble bathrooms and custom-made four-poster beds fitted with Ralph Lauren linens and down comforters. The 12 rooms have air-conditioning, TV, and telephone with voice mail. An extensive three-course breakfast (an island rarity) is served at one convivial table or on the enclosed back patio, complete with trickling water fountain. You'll enjoy strong cappuccino, fruit compote, and a choice of oatmeal or Bircher muesli (organic oats soaked overnight in milk with dried peaches and finished with grated apples and fresh blueberries). Mid-June through September $185–325; off-season $110–175.

Union Street Inn (508-228-9222; 800-225-5116; www.unioninn.com), 7 Union Street. Open April through December. Innkeepers Ken and Deb Withrow preside over this historic hostelry (circa 1770)—one of the island's best-run B&Bs—with a sense of understated hospitality. There are a variety of rooms, many with fireplace and all with air-conditioning and TV. The two-room suite and Captain's Room (with pine-paneled wall and wing chairs in front of the fireplace) are premier, but smaller rooms aren't slighted in any way. After recent redecorating and renovating, the 12 rooms are more luxurious than ever, with fine linens, plush bathrobes, and fluffy duvets. Enjoy a full breakfast on the side patio. The art of providing attentive service remains a strong suit here. June through October $235–335 ($160 for a small room with a detached bath); off-season $140–295.

❋ **Corner House** (508-228-1530; www.cornerhousenantucket.com), 49 Centre Street. The Corner House's period restoration is true to its 1723 origins. Refined without being preten-

SUMMER GARDENS REWARD BACK STREET STROLLERS

Kim Grant

tious and comfortable without being casual, this B&B rises to the top of a places-to-stay list. Sandy and John Knox-Johnston, innkeepers since 1981, offer a variety of rooms to suit a variety of budgets. Seventeen rooms and suites, all with air-conditioning (most with TV), are scattered among three buildings. The main house—with two living rooms, a brick terrace, and an enclosed, screened porch where a nice afternoon tea is served—is filled with period English and American antiques. Even the least expensive "farmhousey" rooms on the third floor are charming, with rough plaster walls and exposed beams. Sandy offers some very attractive packages off-season. Mid-June to mid-September $155–235; off-season about $75–205.

Anchor Inn (508-228-0072; www. anchor-inn.net), 66 Centre Street. Open March to mid-December and sometimes through the winter (call first). This friendly inn has been innkeeper owned and operated since 1983. Charles and Ann Balas offer 11 guest accommodations in this historic 1806 house, the most spacious of which are corner rooms with a queen canopy bed. All have newly tiled bathrooms, telephone with voice mail, TV, hair dryer, air-conditioning, and comfortable period furnishings. One room has a private porch. The less expensive rooms are snug but inviting, under the eaves in the back of the house. A continental breakfast is served on the enclosed porch or carried to the tranquil side garden. Beach towels and ice packs are available in-season. Mid-June to mid-September $185–195; off-season $75–145.

✿ **Nantucket Landfall** (508-228-

0500; www.nantucketlandfall.com), 4 Harbor View Way. Open late April through October. This place is wonderful. With harbor views overlooking Children's Beach, the Landfall is close to town, yet far enough to be delightfully quiet. All of longtime innkeepers Gail and David More's eight whitewashed rooms have a breezy summer feel to them, thanks to billowing curtains, lots of down pillows, fine linens, and colorful quilts. A few have panoramic harbor views; one has a screened-in porch with daybed; those that don't have private porches enjoy the shared harborfront porch. The third-floor suite, suitable for longer stays, is worth every penny. The nautically inspired living room has a fireplace and library, but you'll probably end up spending most of your time on a front-porch rocker. Mid-June through September $110–250 rooms, $310 suite; off-season $95–185 rooms, $210 suite.

Martin House Inn (508-228-0678; www.nantucket.net/lodging/martinn), 61 Centre Street. Open March through December. Owner Debbie Wasil presides over this 1803 mariner's house, an elegantly comfortable and relaxed place. The side porch is decked out with white wicker; on cooler days you can curl up in front of the fire or in a window seat in the large living room. Many of the 13 guest rooms (4 with shared bath) have canopy bed, period antiques, and fireplace; all contain a welcoming decanter of sherry. Some bright third-floor singles are tucked under the eaves. A continental buffet breakfast is served at one long table, or you can take a tray table to the porch or your room. Mid-June to mid-September $125–245 double, $75–90 single

(more for the suite); off-season $80–125 double, $60–70 single.

Centerboard Guest House (508-228-9696; www.nantucket.net/lodging/centerboard), 8 Chester Street. Open April through December. A 10-minute walk from Straight Wharf, Centerboard has a generally light Victorian sensibility. The six corner rooms are romantic, with feather beds, quilts, robes, luxurious linens, and stripped woodwork. The stunning two-room suite features inlaid floors, dark woodwork, a working fireplace, plum walls, a green marble bathroom, and a pencil-post canopy bed. Two ground-floor rooms are decidedly different. One is reminiscent of a houseboat, with built-in carpentry; it sleeps four. The other has a platform bed suitable for a third person. Modern amenities like a refrigerator, TV/VCR, phone, and private bath haven't been sacrificed, though. Mid-June to mid-October $225 rooms, $325–395 suite; off-season $110 rooms, $225 suite; expanded continental breakfast included.

✳ **Nantucket Whaler Guest House** (508-228-6597; 800-462-6882; www.nantucketwhaler.com), 8 North Water Street. With the exception of a traditional 1850 Greek Revival exterior, nothing about this guesthouse is conventional. Proprietors Calli Ligelis and Randi Ott have upped the island's already considerable ante with their luxe suites and large studios, each with a private entrance and deck or patio. Furnishings are a blend of country American and English antiques; beds are dressed in linens and down comforters; towels and robes are plush; and the color palettes are soothing. Other amenities include cable TV, VCR, CD player, cordless phone (with a private number), coffeemaker, refrigerator, microwave, and toaster oven. Mid-June to mid-October $300–375 rooms, $400–575 one- and two-bedroom suites; off-season $200–300 and $325–500, respectively.

❋ ♪ **The Chestnut House** (508-228-0049; www.chestnuthouse.com), 3 Chestnut Street. Not many old-fashioned guesthouses remain, and this one has been in the Carl family since the early 1980s. Decor is busy and eclectic, with local art taking up almost every inch of wall space. (See Hawthorn House, below, for more about familial contributions to decor.) Two-room suites can sleep four people if they are good friends, or a family with children. Otherwise, for two people, they are nice and roomy. One suite is particularly quiet, and there is only one "regular" guest room. All have TV, VCR, a small refrigerator, and complimentary sherry. The free-standing cottage is more like a suite, with a Murphy bed and separate kitchen. You'll find added value in the additional bathrooms, which allow for post-beach showering and late departures. Mid-June to mid-October $170 room, $210–260 suites; off-season $85 room, $105–145 suites; includes a breakfast voucher for $9 per person per day valid at three good restaurants; cottage $325 daily for four people.

❋ **The Hawthorn House** (508-228-1468; www.hawthornhouse.com), 2 Chestnut Street. A guesthouse since the mid-1940s, this simple B&B was built in 1849, so the rooms are small. Seven of nine guest rooms are upstairs off a casual common area; two rooms share a bath. Because the B&B is in the historic district, the two ground-floor rooms can be a tad noisy in the evening. Innkeeper Mitchell Carl's family decorated the rooms: His father made the hooked rugs; his wife, Diane, made the needlepoint pillows; and his mother did some of the paintings. Mitchell is responsible for the lovely stained-glass panels. Mid-June to mid-September $160–210; off-season $85–105; includes a breakfast voucher for $9 per person per day valid at two good restaurants.

♨ ♪ **Nesbitt Inn** (508-228-0156; 508-228-2446), 21 Broad Street. Open mid-March to mid-December. Next to the boisterous Brotherhood of Thieves restaurant, the Nesbitt Inn exemplifies Nantucket's simpler lodging roots. Built in 1872 as an inn, the house has been in the same family since 1914. Many furnishings are original to the house. A favorite among Europeans, the inn's 10 double and two single rooms (which share only three baths and have in-room sinks) are Victorian in style. For inclement days, the living room has a fireplace, games, and TV. Otherwise, guests can people-watch from the front porch, relax on the back deck, and make use of the outdoor grill, refrigerator, and beach towels. Children are welcome; there's a swing set in the backyard. Late May to mid-October $85–110 double, $75 single; includes continental breakfast; 10 percent service charge added.

COTTAGES AND APARTMENTS

In town
Wharf Cottages (508-228-4620; 800-475-2637; www.wharfcottages.com), New Whale Street. Open late May to mid-October. These 22 snug cottages are fun for a change. Occupying a

unique location—jutting out on wharves in the midst of harbor activity—they have private decks, small gardens, water views, fully equipped kitchens, TV/VCRs, and daily maid service. Although the cottages are small, they're efficiently designed and crisply decorated in whites and blues. It can be noisy on the pier, but that's part of the fun of staying here. July and August $380–570 for a one-bedroom; off-season from $280.

See also The Chestnut House under *Bed & Breakfasts.*

Around the island

✎ ઠ **Wade Cottages** (508-257-6308; 212-989-6423 off-season; www.wade-cottages.com), 'Sconset 02564. Open late May to mid-October. There's nothing between the property and the ocean here except a broad lawn and an ocean bluff. Parents will appreciate the play area and swings for kids. Four rooms in the main house, where the only common space doubles as a small breakfast room, are quite modestly furnished. The other spare accommodations—a multi-bedroom suite, six apartments, and three cottages—are well equipped for the required minimum stays. Ocean views are de rigueur. The best cottage (all have a large living room) is the newest one closest to the ocean. A portion of this private estate is still used by Wade family members. July and August $630–760 for 3 nights with private bath, $365–435 for 3 nights with shared bath. Apartment and cottage rates drop about half off-season.

RENTAL HOUSES AND COTTAGES

Many islanders are opposed to the residential building boom that began in mid-1990s because the island's

THE NESBITT INN'S FRONT PORCH IS GREAT FOR PEOPLE-WATCHING

Kim Grant

infrastructure just can't handle it. Thousands of new three- and four-bedroom rental houses have been built in the last few years. According to the Nantucket Association of Real Estate Brokers, the average island home sold for about $1.3 million in 2002 ("entry level" at $700,000), but you can bet these owners don't need to rent their houses to ease mortgage payments.

Congdon & Coleman (508-325-5000; www.congdonandcoleman.com), 57 Main Street. There are thousands of one- to seven-bedroom rental houses all over the island. Expect a nice two-bedroom house to rent for an average $2,500 weekly in August. Tell the agents your requirements and they'll fax you a listing sheet with properties that match. **Jordan Associates** (508-228-4449; www.jordanre.com), 8 Federal Street, and **Nantucket Real Estate Co.** (508-228-3131), 17 North Beach Street, offer similar services.

CAMPGROUNDS Camping is not permitted.

HOSTEL ♻ ♪ **Nantucket Hostel** (508-228-0433; www.usahostels.org), 31 Western Avenue (call 617-531-0459 or enecreservations@juno.com for reservations prior to the opening date). Open mid-April to mid-October. Originally built in 1873 as the island's first lifesaving station, and now on the National Register of Historic Places, this Hostelling International hostel is 3 miles from town on Surfside Beach (see *Green Space—Beaches*) and steps from the NRTA beach shuttle, which operates June through September. Facilities include a kitchen, barbecue and picnic area,

and volleyball. Dormitory-style, gender-separated rooms accommodate about 48 people. Reservations are essential in July and August and on all weekends. $19–22 adults for HI members, $22–25 nonmembers; about half price for children under 14.

✳ Where to Eat

The dining scene here is highly evolved. Enough Nantucket diners are passionate about haute cuisine that the island supports one of the densest concentrations of fine-dining establishments in the country. And one of the most expensive: $40 entrées are commonplace even as patrons shake their heads in disbelief. Some restaurants offer less expensive, bistro-style fare in addition to their regular menu. Prices aside, many of Nantucket's 60-some restaurants would hold their own in New York or San Francisco, and repeat patrons know it: Some visitors make dinner reservations for an entire stay when they book their lodging. It's rare to be served a "bad meal" in Nantucket, but some restaurants do offer more value (note the symbol for value ♠) than others.

Unless otherwise noted, reservations are highly recommended at all *Dining Out* establishments. Additionally, you must reconfirm your reservation on the "day of" or you'll lose it, since many diners make multiple reservations and don't show up.

There are perhaps ten restaurants (not all are reviewed here) that serve the year-round community. Generally, you can assume that places are open daily late June to early September. I have not included shoulder-season hours of operation because they are

Kim Grant

WHEN DEPARTING, THROW A PENNY OVERBOARD TO ENSURE YOUR RETURN

dependent on weather, number of tourists, and owner's whim. By the way, don't pass up the opportunity to have bay scallops after mid-October (when the scalloping season begins). The experience might explain why Nantucketers are so passionate about food.

DINING OUT

In town

🏵 ♿ **American Seasons** (508-228-7111), 80 Centre Street. Open for dinner April to mid-December. *Consistency* is the watchword here; year after year, this place remains at the top of my dining list. While inspired by America's regional traditions, executive chef Michael LaScola's menu is both inviting and innovative. The ever-changing menu is broken down into: Wild West (roast duck breast with corn bread pudding), Pacific Coast (sesame-crusted tuna with a salad of artichoke and shiitakes), Down South (a pork chop with a sweet potato hash and molassses bourbon gravy), and New England (roasted halibut in a chowder of little necks and pancetta). The highlight of a recent trip was certainly the stilton and roasted pistachio ice cream appetizer. Wow! Mammoth portions of vertically presented food are balanced with savory and sweet tastes, crunchy and smooth textures. If the food weren't so good, I'd suggest simply coming for dessert: Succumb to the sampler (which changes seasonally). The candlelit bistro-style dining room features folk art murals and checkerboard tables. Entrées $24–32.

🍸 ♿ **21 Federal** (508-228-2121), 21 Federal Street. Open for dinner mid-April to mid-December. Loyal patrons return for sophisticated New and traditional American cuisine served in an elegant and reserved dining room. To some it's "pretentious"; to others it's "venerable." No matter; 21 reigns as one of the top two or three places year after year. Although the ever-changing menu highlights seafood, you might also enjoy crispy duck breast with cranberry wild rice or roast loin of pork with rosemary pear chutney. The dark-paneled bar is convivial; there is also a lighter bistro menu and garden dining. Entrées $27–37.

✳ ᵧ **Boarding House** (508-228-9622), 12 Federal Street. Open for lunch and dinner daily mid-June to mid-September, most nights off-season. Chef-owner Seth Raynor's contemporary Asian-inspired cuisine stands center stage at one of Nantucket's most consistent and superior restaurants. An award-winning wine list accompanies signature dishes (aka "BoHo Classics") like grilled lobster tails over mashed potatoes. (I'm partial to the rare-grilled yellowfin tuna.) As for atmosphere, with brick and plaster arched walls, the main dining room is cozy. At street level, there's a lively bar packed with locals and 20-something visitors; it's a real scene (especially with an extensive appetizer menu). But in good weather, the patio—surrounded by flowers and a white picket fence—is the place you'll want to be. It's common for folks to line up in summer at 4 PM for one of these seats. Lunch $14–19, dinner entrées $24–37.

ᵧ **The Pearl** (508-228-9701), 12 Federal Street. Open for dinner May through December. From the attitude to the oh-so-trendy-bar to the whole "scene," don't look now: You just might be in Miami's South Beach. Executive chef Seth Raynor (see Boarding House, above) has furthered his winning formula of coastal cuisine prepared with an Asian flair. The atmosphere and cuisine here are sophisticated, relaxing, and dramatic. (Note the onyx bar, huge fish tanks filled with brilliant fish and coral, pearl-shaped ceiling, and pale blue lighting.) Although the menu changes frequently, you can always count on creatively prepared native seafood and local fish. Patrons are particularly fond of tuna martinis (nonalcoholic)

NANTUCKET'S MAIN STREET IS PAVED WITH COBBLESTONES.

Kim Grant

and "oyster shooters": six shucked oysters served in crystal-footed shot glasses. Don't pass up the signature dessert: a decadent flourless chocolate torte with hazelnut inside and caramel sauce. (It's like a giant truffle.) Entrées $30–45; prix fixe $150, excluding beverages.

❋ **Oran Mor** (508-228-8655), 2 South Beach Street. Open daily in summer; call for off-season schedule. Chef Peter Wallace, formerly of Topper's fame (see below), has an intimate restaurant inconspicuously located over an antiques shop near the waterfront. Once you find it, you'll probably return more than once. Peter's cuisine defines *true inspiration.* His refined execution never falls short of perfection, whether he's preparing buffalo, elk, scallops, or foie gras. The lobster risotto, a transcendent signature dish, can always be requested even if it's not on the menu. It'd be downright foolhardy to bypass it. The New American menu ranges from roasted rack and grilled leg of lamb to grilled beef with potato rosti and a chanterelle demiglaze. Specials are always tempting. The Gaelic phrase *oran mor,* by the way, means "great song." Entrées $22–32.

Company of the Cauldron (508-228-4016), 7 India Street. Open for dinner late May through October and Stroll weekend (see *Special Events*); closed Monday. Peer through ivy-covered, small-paned windows and you'll see what looks like an intimate dinner party. Sure enough, since the tables are so close together, you'll probably end up talking to your neighbors before the night is over. It's a warm and inviting place, with low-beamed ceilings and plaster walls illuminated

by candlelight and wall sconces. Longtime chef-owner Al Kovalencik's New American menu is set a week in advance (www.companyofthecauldron.com). It might go something like this: fettuccine carbonara with peas and pancetta; a mesclun salad with caramelized shallot vinaigrette; ginger and herb crusted rack of lamb with blackberries and pine nut couscous; and a pear almond tart to top it all off. One or two seatings; prix fixe $48–50 per person.

❧ **Ship's Inn Restaurant** (508-228-0040), 13 Fair Street. Open for dinner May through October. Longtime chef-owner Mark Gottwald, who graduated from La Varenne in Paris and apprenticed at Le Cirque and Spago, serves California-French cuisine in a romantic, subterranean, bistro-style space. I always leave here very satisfied. Many dishes are healthful (that is, sans butter or cream) without sacrificing taste or creativity: grilled sea scallops with sorrel risotto, and seared local cod with cider and capers, for instance. Otherwise, there's the signature medallions of lobster with leeks and Sauternes. The wine list wins deserved awards. In fall, save room for a cranberry cobbler. Entrées $21–33.

♈ **Straight Wharf Restaurant** (508-228-4499), 6 Harbor Square. Open for dinner June through September. When Steve Cavagnaro took over the helm of this renowned seafood-only restaurant in 1997, he didn't miss a beat. Although considered a bit pricey, the New American dishes are well prepared and elegantly presented. Look for the likes of seafood risotto, lobster chowder, and braised halibut with crayfish and morels. Desserts are decidedly rich. In addition to a deck "sorta" overlooking the harbor (it's billed as waterfront, although it's not really) and a lofty main dining room with exposed rafters, there is a pleasantly upbeat and zippy bar. Entrées $34–38.

🅢 **Cioppino's** (508-228-4622), 20 Broad Street. Open for dinner mid-May to mid-October. Continental and New American cuisine—seafood stew, rib-eye steaks with *pommes frites* and grilled lobster tails with shrimp and pesto pasta—is featured, and cioppino is an obvious specialty. Susie and Tracy Root's dining room is quiet and the bar cozy, but in good weather the garden patio is even more tempting. My last visit, which satisfied both my wallet and senses, my meal featured baked talapa with a southwestern fruit salsa and basmati rice. Cioppino's offers an excellent "twilight dining" special ($22) and a good wine list. The key lime pie is lip-pursing tart. Lunches $9–14, dinners $19–32.

Queequeg's (508-325-09923), 6 Oak Street. Open for dinner mid-May to mid-October. New in 2001, this upscale place comes recommended by innkeeper friends. I didn't have a chance to eat here for this edition). Expect dishes as diverse as yellow Thai curried shrimp, traditional mixed grill, and Louisiana-style jambalaya. Vegetarians won't be slighted, either. The small bar is nice for before- or after-dinner drinks, as is the outdoor patio. Entrées $25–32.

🍸 **DeMarco** (508-228-1836), 9 India Street. Open for dinner mid-May to mid-October. Light northern Italian cuisine is offered in this restored sea captain's home. Downstairs has a taverny feel with a bar, wood beams, brick, and curtains, while upstairs is more airy. Start with a rich antipasto,

followed by pasta with lobster, chanterelles, sugar snap peas, chives, and cream, or a braised oxtail risotto. Fresh pasta and grilled seafood are house specialties. Don DeMarco, who has owned his namesake restaurant since 1979, has amassed an outstanding wine cellar. Entrées $28–32.

🍸 **Brant Point Grill** (508-325-1320), at the White Elephant Hotel, Easton Street. Open mid-May to late October. There's no more pleasant place to have an alfresco luncheon than this harborside terrace. (Heaters and awnings keep it warm well into autumn.) Look for smoked salmon sandwiches and mouthwatering tenderloin steak sandwiches served open faced with crispy fried onion rings. The handsome grill, with attentive service, specializes in steamed and grilled lobsters and thick, juicy Chicago-style steaks. Nothing is too fussy or overdone. The grill also makes arguably the island's silkiest vanilla bean crème brûlée. Check out the raw bar, too. As for the other bar, bartender Michael (who put 21 Federal at the top of the bar scene) draws a local crowd. He's a go-to guy. Lunch $9–16, dinner entrées $24–38.

🍸 **Ropewalk** (508-228-8886), 1 Straight Wharf. Open for lunch and dinner mid-May to mid-October. Night or day, try to get an outdoor patio table at Nantucket's only harborside (*yacht-side* might be more apt restaurant. If you can't, though, don't worry; the interior is open to sea breezes and rolling fog banks. Although the casual ambience might suggest standard seafood fare, the cuisine is really quite good and the menu extensive. Ropewalk also has an excellent raw bar and frozen drinks. Light, eclectic lunch choices include focaccia pizzas, sandwiches—a little bit of everything, really. No reservations taken. As for the bar, you can pick out the locals: They're often pitching ice (or bottle tops) at their friends passing by in boats. Lunch $11–18, dinner entrées $24–30.

Ÿ **Club Car** (508-228-1101), 1 Main Street. Open for lunch and dinner mid-May to October; also Thanksgiving and Stroll (see *Special Events*). While the kitchen has put out fabulous Continental cuisine since 1979, the menu hasn't really changed since then, either. The beef Wellington Sunday-evening specials are classic, if that's your cup of tea. It's best enjoyed in the elegant and somewhat haughty dining room, set with linen and silver. I prefer to come simply for lump crab cakes, a martini, and nightly jazz—in the only remaining club car from the narrow-gauge train that used to run between Steamboat Wharf and 'Sconset. Depending on the time of night, be prepared for yuppie sing-alongs to old Billy Joel tunes. Entrées $30–40.

Woodbox Inn Restaurant (508-228-0587), 29 Fair Street. Open for breakfast on weekends June through August, on Sundays through December; dinner most nights June through December. This 1709 house has three intimate, romantic, and candlelit dining rooms with low ceilings, dark wainscoting, and wide floorboards. Old-fashioned, classic Continental dishes like beef Wellington and rack of lamb are specialties. Popovers accompany all entrées. If you just want to enjoy the authentic atmosphere, come for breakfast (popovers). Breakfast $9.50–11.50, dinner entrées $19–32. No credit cards.

THE CLUB CAR USED TO RUN OUT TO 'SCONSET

Kim Grant

❋ **Jared's** (508-228-2400), 29 Broad Street at Centre Street. Open for breakfast and dinner May through October; breakfast year-round. Nantucket's most conservative dining room features maritime oil paintings, heavy silver table settings, and linen cloths. The all-you-can-eat seafood buffet ($27) is a bargain on Wednesday and Sunday evenings from May to mid-October. Entertainment on summer evenings. Breakfast $7–10, dinner entrées $25–35.

See also Centre Street Bistro and Black-Eyed Susans under Eating Out.

On the outskirts of town

❋ ❦ **Sfoglia** (508-325-4500), 130 Pleasant Street. Open for dinner. A mile from the center of town, this regional Italian restaurant is charmingly rustic, with mismatched table settings and the like. Look for ultra-creative and homemade pasta dishes by the husband-and-wife team of Ron and Colleen Suhanosky, both Culinary Institute of America grads, who opened the place in 2000. Entrées $22–24.

The Galley Restaurant (508-228-9641), at the end of Jefferson Avenue. Open for lunch and dinner mid-May through September. At the Cliffside Beach Club, you'll literally dine beachside, drinking in sunsets along with your cosmo. But this isn't a sand-in-your-shoes kind of place—it's elegant, bistro-style, candlelit dining under an awning on Nantucket Sound. The traditional menu features sea scallops, other local seafood, and organic greens. Jazz pianist. Entrées $29–34.

❋ ♿ **West Creek Cafe** (508-228-4943), 11 West Creek Road (between Pleasant and Orange Streets). Open for dinner. This charming and casual place is a real treat, decorated with a New American flair that complements the eclectic menu. Try the pan-seared tuna with roasted veggies and sour cream mashed potatoes. The small house has three distinct dining rooms, one of which has a fireplace that draws patrons throughout winter. Pat Tyler, who has been on-island for years (at the Boarding House and at Second Story), opened the welcoming café in 1995. Entrées $24–38.

Around the island

♿ ❦ **Topper's** (508-228-8768), 120 Wauwinet Road, Wauwinet. Open for lunch, Sunday brunch, and dinner, May through October. For a splurge, Topper's is worth every penny. The setting and service are luxurious, indulgent, and sophisticated, yet relaxed. Regional New American cuisine is matched by outstanding pairings from a French and California wine list. (Topper's consistently wins the just-about-impossible-to-win *Wine Spectator* Grand Award. And to quote myself in *National Geographic Traveler*, "Their wine pairing is unrivaled on the Eastern seaboard.") Dishes are downright sublime: tuna tartare, signature lobster and crabcakes, and Nantucket lobster navarin in a light cream sauce (another signature). Save room for rich desserts, perfect with an after-dinner cordial. A bar menu offers lighter fare, while the lunch concept is decidedly different: Choose three, four, or five selections to create your own sampler plate. Lunch is also served on the bayside porch, a lovely spot for a sunset drink, too. Topper's offers complimentary van service from town, as well as transportation aboard the *Wauwinet Lady,* which takes guests from Straight Wharf to the restaurant's private dock in-season. Jacket requested at dinner. Kudos to chef Christopher Freeman and the whole staff. Brunch $38, lunch $21–28, dinner entrées $34–56.

The Chanticleer (508-257-6231), 9 New Street, 'Sconset. Open for lunch and dinner mid-May to mid-October. The oh-so-elegant Chanticleer has won endless accolades since it opened in 1970: "Nantucket's premier dining spot;" one of the world's top 10 romantic places to dine; "one of the finest wine lists in the world, with more than 40,000 bottles in the cellar." Chef-owners Anne and Jean-Charles Berruet's exquisite classical French cuisine is served in the courtyard of a rose-covered cottage, in small dining rooms overlooking the courtyard through small-paned windows, or in the more formal main dining room with low ceilings. Local fish, local produce, and game birds are highlighted. Dining here will live on in your memory for years. Reservations required and jacket recommended. Lunch entrées $25–35, dinner entrées $35–45.

'Sconset Cafe (508-257-4008), Post Office Square at Main Street, 'Sconset. Open for all three meals in summer; lunch and dinner late in the season. This tiny place is always great. It's known for its blue cheese and bacon burger as well as chowder with herbs, but you'll also find creative salads and sandwiches at lunch. Chef-owner Rolf Nelson's dinners really shine and tend toward sophisticated New American dishes. The menu changes constantly. Chocolate Volcano Cake is a dessert specialty. No credit cards; BYOB. Reservations accepted for 6 PM seating only. Lunch $8–14, dinner entrées $20–28.

Y **Summer House** (508-257-9976), 17 Ocean Avenue, 'Sconset. Open for lunch June to early September. Ocean- and poolside light lunches of salads and sandwiches here are the epitome of a relaxed Nantucket summer. Lunch $11–25.

EATING OUT

In town

❦ ❄ **Centre Street Bistro** (508-228-8470), 29 Centre Street. Open for brunch on weekends, lunch and dinner on various nights. Chef-owners Ruth and Tim Pitts, who have been cooking on-island since 1990, have cultivated a deservedly loyal following. Perhaps it's because they serve exceedingly good food at even better prices. Their ever-evolving menu might include dishes like Thai smoked salmon taco. Or start your day with their "Nantucket Breakfast"—scrambled eggs, bacon, potato pancake, and blueberry pancake. There are only a couple of dozen seats (and a small bar) within this Mediterranean-style space, but that's fine, as people enjoy the summertime patio. No credit cards. Limited wine and beer list. Brunch and lunch $5–9, dinner $16–20.

Black-Eyed Susans (508-325-0308), 10 India Street. Open for breakfast and dinner mid-April to mid-October. This small, pine-paneled place is part bistro, part glorified lunch counter. Hip, funky (in a good way), mellow, and homey, the downscale decor belies the stylishly presented plates. The global menu changes frequently, but look for complex fish preparations and dishes like North African spiced chicken with seasonal veggies. Breakfasts run the gamut from bagels and grits to Pennsylvania Dutch pancakes and a veggie scramble with pesto (made with eggs or tofu). Breakfast averages $9, dinner entrées $18–26. No credit cards.

Y ☙ **Cambridge Street** (508-228-7109), 12 Cambridge Street. Open for dinner April through December. What a refreshing place! Hats off to proprietor Brandt Gould, who could be making tons more money by serving pricey entrées like everyone else, but would rather have a cool place where folks feel comfortable hanging out. Here's a good sign: Other restaurant workers flock here on their sole night off. This jumping place of 20-, 30-, and 40-somethings has two sections: a dark blue, barlike joint (three-deep in-season) and a section devoted solely to eating. Don't be fooled by the good selection of fresh draft beers and microbrews at the bar: Cambridge Street serves very worthy food,

too. Though it's particularly known for monster portions of Dixie-style barbecue (smoked on the premises), you can also get a whisper-thin pizza, pulled-pork sandwich, schwarma, veggie lasagna, and skewers of Tandoori-style chicken. I love this place. Look for 99¢ ribs on off-season Thursdays. Dishes $9–24.

✳ **Bluefin** (508-228-2033), 15 South Beach Street. Open for dinner. This light bistro specializes in sushi and Japanese-influenced dishes (sake-marinated halibut with a hiyashi wakame salad), but to play it safe, they also offer lobster ravioli and grilled steaks with creamy mashed potatoes. Mains $17–23.

🦞 ✳ 🍸 Y **Brotherhood of Thieves** (no phone), 23 Broad Street. Open for lunch and dinner. The 1840s former whaling tavern feels like an English pub: brick walls, beamed ceilings,

STOREFRONT RESTAURANTS AND SHOPS LINE SHADY MAIN STREET.

and few windows. It's a convivial place—helped along by an extensive coffee and drinks menu—frequented by locals chowing on chowder, burgers, cheddar cheese soup, shoestring fries (long and curly), and thick sandwiches. Open until late at night, there is live folk music most evenings in-season; otherwise the music is limited to weekends. Expect a line in summer. Dishes $9–15. No credit cards.

🦞 🍴 **Arno's 41 Main** (508-228-7001), 41 Main Street. Open for breakfast, lunch, Sunday brunch, and dinner, April to mid-December. This two-story storefront eatery is atmospheric, with hurricane lamps on the tables, high ceilings, and large canvas artwork on brick walls. Although it's been around since the early 1960s, Arno's has gained a following recently. Bountiful breakfasts feature frittatas, "bananza" pancakes, and eggs Benedict. Moderately priced lunch fare includes sandwiches, Thai peanut noodles, large portions of pasta, salads, and a few vegetarian dishes. Dinner is a bit pricier; specialties include lobster bisque, crabcakes, and scampi Florentine. Take-out; reservations recommended. Dishes $7–20.

Sushi by Yoshi (508-228-1801), 2 East Chestnut Street. Open for lunch and dinner daily, mid-April to mid-December. When you tire of eating fancy gourmet preparations, this small place offers fresh sushi and sashimi, "Aloha" rolls with yellowtail tuna from Japan, "dynamite" rolls, and noodle dishes. For dessert, consider banana tempura or green tea ice cream. Yoshi won a prize recently for pairing sushi with cranberries; see if it's on the menu. They do a brisk take-out business. Dishes $5–20.

❄ 🍴 **Tap Room** (508-228-2400), 29 Broad Street at Centre Street, in the cellar of the Jared Coffin House (see *Inns*). Open for lunch and dinner. This casual gathering spot has a cozy, publike atmosphere with dark paneling and beamed ceilings. It's best enjoyed at night or with a group of people, as many tables are close together. (The sunny garden patio ringed with flower boxes is great in warm weather.) Look for traditional New England fare like (lobster or clam) chowder, beef or salmon burgers, popular fish-and-chips, lobster rolls, and prime rib. Between-meal grazing on freshly shucked oysters or scallops wrapped in bacon is always an option. Think before ordering the rich desserts; they just might put you over the top. Lunch $6–13, dinner $14–20.

♿ ❄ 🍴 🍸 **Atlantic Cafe** (508-228-0570), 15 South Water Street. Open for lunch and dinner. The AC's lively front section is a happening place if you don't mind the boisterous pitch from the bar as the evening progresses. Earlier in the day, though, families enjoy the low-key atmosphere, large portions of pub grub, and good prices. The curly, crispy fries are good, as is the flavorful clam chowder (many say the island's best). Otherwise, stick to burgers, sandwiches, and salads. There are always lots of grazing dishes like onion rings, zucchini sticks, nachos, and wings. Dishes $7–22.

🍴 🍸 **Rose & Crown** (508-228-2595), 23 South Water Street. Open for lunch and dinner, mid-April to mid-December. This hopping place with live entertainment serves American fare—sandwiches, pastas, chicken wings, steak, and seafood—in a traditional pub atmosphere. Formerly a carriage livery, the large, barnlike

HARBORFRONT AL FRESCO DINING AT THE BRANDT POINT GRILL

room is decorated with signs from old Nantucket businesses. Two added bonuses: early specials (during summer and fall only), and kids can draw on the paper-covered tabletops. Lunch $6–12, dinner entrées $10–20.

Vincent's Restaurant (508-228-0189), 21 South Water Street. Open lunch and dinner mid-April to late October. This casual, moderately priced place is a great choice for families, with plain and fancy pasta dishes, grilled seafood, and take-out pizza. An upstairs lounge; in-season entertainment; early dinners; take-out. Lunch specials $7–12, dinner entrées $10–20.

Nantucket Lobster Trap (508-228-4200), 23 Washington Street. Open for dinner May to mid-October. If you've got a hankering for lobster, plain and simple, head to this casual eatery with barnboard walls and booths. (I only recommend the basic lobster here.) Large patio and out-door bar; delivery and take-out.

The Tavern (508-228-1266), Straight Wharf at Harbor Square. Open for lunch and dinner until late at night, mid-May to mid-October. On the edge of the marina, the outdoor tables are well positioned for people-watching, and the American food is above average. If you want a Caesar salad, chowder, a plate of fried calamari, or a drink before hopping on the ferry, this place fits the bill, too. Lunch $8–15, dinner $12–24.

On the outskirts of town

❅ **Sea Grille** (508-325-5700), 45 Sparks Avenue. Open for lunch and dinner. Despite having plenty of parking, this attractive restaurant is overlooked by nonlocals (except in the winter, when it's one of a handful open). Every kind of seafood and fish is prepared practically every way: as bouillabaisse (a specialty), grilled, blackened, steamed, fried, and raw (there's an extensive raw bar). Light meals at the bar are a good alternative. Lunch $8–16, dinner $18–29.

Around the island

🦞 ❄ ⚓ ♿ **Hutch's** (508-228-5550), Nantucket Memorial Airport. Open 6 AM–8 or 9 PM daily. Remember the television show *Wings*, which featured a tiny Nantucket airport restaurant? This is it. The Jamaican line cooks return every spring to prepare simple dishes, and the waitresses hustle like nowhere else. (Wednesday nights are reserved for killer Jamaican specials— it's a real islander thing.) Regularly scheduled dishes include fish-and-chips, meat loaf, chicken fingers, fried scallops, hot turkey sandwiches, seafood omelets. Counter, table, and take-out service. The way Hutch figures it, patrons must pass every other restaurant in town to get here, so his place has to be good. About 80 percent of his business is local. Breakfast and lunch $2–8, dinner dishes $6–14.

LIGHT FARE AND COFFEE

In town

Provisions (508-228-3258), Straight Wharf at Harbor Square. Open mid-April to early November. Even in the height of summer, when this place is cranking, they make excellent sandwiches (including one with mildly smoked turkey, stuffing, and cranberries), hearty chowders and soups, and pizza. Sandwiches are big enough to feed two people at this island institution, open since 1978. Hot and cold vegetarian dishes, too.

❄ **The Bean** (508-228-5216), 29 Centre Street. Finally, a hip place to have strong espresso; black, herbal, and green teas; specialty coffees; and baked goods. Grab a local newspaper and watch this rarefied world go by.

In winter play board games with locals and order warming soups.

⚓ **Henry's** (508-228-0123), Steamboat Wharf. Open mid-May to mid-October. Downright excellent sandwiches (including one of the best lobster sandwiches in the region), since 1969.

Even Keel (508-228-1979), 40 Main Street. Open for all three meals. The jury is out on this one—I didn't have a chance to eat here for this edition, and my innkeeper friends didn't have a handle on it yet. One thing is for sure, though: It has strong espresso. Take out, sit down in a space that doubles as an Internet café, or sit on the back patio (the best option). BYOB.

⚓ **"The Street."** The first block of Steamboat Wharf is lined with fast-food shops appreciated by families. Take-out eateries are generally open May to mid-October. You'll find a grill with chicken tenders (skip the burritos), burgers, tacos, pizza, and the like.

The Juice Bar (508-228-5799), 12 Broad Street. Open mid-April to mid-October. Yes, they offer fresh juices like carrot, lemonade, and orange, but they also make their own low-fat ice cream and nonfat yogurts, and breakfast baked goods. In fact, they make everything from scratch. I guess that's why Senator John Kerry frequents the place.

The Juice Guys (508-228-4464), 2 Easy Street. Open late May to mid-October. The original store of the guys who created Nantucket Nectars has a juice bar with fruit smoothies, and carrot and orange juice. Off-season, look for warming teas and a hot cranberry-ginger concoction.

❋ ✐ **The Soda Fountain at the Nantucket Pharmacy** (508-228-0180), 45 Main Street. This old-fashioned drugstore soda fountain, complete with swivel stools at Formica counters, offers egg creams, milk shakes, inexpensive soups, sandwiches, and New York City–style hot dogs. The lobster rolls are excellent.

Congdon's Pharmacy (508-228-0020) is similar and right next door—sorry, you'll have to decide for yourself which is better.

On the outskirts of town
Fahey & Fromagerie (508-325-5644), 49A Pleasant Street. Open April through December. Gourmands might assume they're on the Upper West Side with these treats.

❋ ✐ ✦ **Downy Flake** (508-228-4533), 18 Sparks Avenue. Open 5:30 AM–2 PM daily (except 6 AM–noon Sunday); closed March. Order justifiably famous doughnuts (there are only three kinds, but who cares?) and pancakes (but not on the same morning, please) from this island institution. Light lunches, too; $3–8.

Nantucket Bake Shop (508-228-2797), 79 Orange Street. Open daily except Sunday, April through November. Its advertisement claims more than 100 different items baked daily, including Portuguese breads, desserts, muffins, croissants, quiches, cakes, and pastries. You can take Jay and Magee Detmer's word for it; they've been baking the goodies since 1976.

Around the island
Claudette's (508-257-6622), Post Office Square at Main Street, 'Sconset. Open daily mid-May to mid-

CONGDON'S AND THE NANTUCKET PHARMACY DUKE IT OUT

Kim Grant

October. Known primarily for catering (perhaps the best catered clambakes on Nantucket), this tiny shop's raisons d'être are box lunches and lemon cake. Although there are a few indoor tables, most people take their sandwiches to the beach or ice cream to the front deck.

✳ Entertainment

MUSIC ♪ **Band concerts** (508-228-7213) are held at the Children's Beach bandstand (off South Beach Street) Thursdays and Sundays 6–7:30 PM in July and August.

Noonday concerts (508-228-5466), 11 Orange Street at the Unitarian Universalist Church, are held Thursdays in July and August. Concerts feature ensembles, soloists, and an 1831 Goodrich pipe organ. Donations.

Nantucket Musical Arts Society (508-228-1287), 62 Centre Street at the First Congregational Church, sponsors concerts with world-renowned musicians on most Tuesday evenings at 8:30 from July through September. On the night before the concert, there is a meet-the-artist event hosted at the Unitarian Universalist Church, 11 Orange Street. Ticket prices vary.

THEATER/SLIDE SHOW ✳ **Actors Theatre of Nantucket** (508-228-6325), Centre and Main Streets at the Methodist church, has staged evening and family matinees, comedies, plays, drama, and dance concerts since 1985. It's a very professional group, with occasionally smashing one-person shows and some Broadway try-outs.

✳ **Theatre Workshop of Nantucket** (508-228-4305), Bennett Hall, 62 Centre Street. In existence since 1956, this community-based group stages a variety of plays and musicals.

🎬 🎞 MOVIES/FILMS **Dreamland Theatre** (508-228-5356), 19 South Water Street, which shows seasonal first-run movies, began as a Quaker meetinghouse, was converted to the Atlantic Straw Company, and was moved to Brant Point to serve as part of a hotel before it was floated back across the harbor in 1905 on a barge.

✳ **Gaslight Theatre** (508-228-4435), 1 North Union Street, shows art films and is connected with the White Dog Cafe, where you can have a drink before or after the program.

Siasconset Casino (508-257-6661), New Street, 'Sconset, shows first-run movies in July and August. Tickets $5 per person.

🍸 NIGHTLIFE *Note:* There is no smoking in public places.

See **Brotherhood of Thieves** (live folk), **Tap Room** (live piano or guitar), and **Rose & Crown** (dancing or live bands) under *Eating Out,* and **Summer House** (live piano in 'Sconset) under *Dining Out.*

Cap'n Tobey's (508-228-0836), Straight Wharf, offers upstairs jazz.

Chicken Box (508-228-9717; www.thechickenbox.com), 14 Daves Street. Off Lower Orange Street, this divey, boxy bar and music club is very laid-back. When things quiet down in town, take a cab out to "The Box" to extend your night—if you're into pool tables and live tunes. No, you can't get chicken here, but you could in 1948 when it opened as a restaurant-club.

The Muse (508-228-1471), 44 Surfside Drive. This roadhouse has DJs, techno music, live bands (the Dave Matthews Band cut their teeth here), "air band" nights (rather like karaoke with the addition of enthusiastic, fake strumming), pool tables, table tennis, and a big-screen TV. On the shuttle circuit. Take-out pizza, too.

The Westender (508-228-5100), 326 Madaket Road. Come at sunset— along with half the rest of the island (it seems)—and down some rum-based Madaket Mysteries.

Many *Dining Out* restaurants have bars that, when diners depart for the evening, become happenin' places to socialize. Look for the ♈ symbol.

✱ Selective Shopping

❋ The principal shopping district is bordered by Main, Broad, and Centre Streets. Straight Wharf shops cater more to the middlebrow tourist market, while Old South Wharf (see below) is more upscale. About 90 percent of the shops remain open year-round, although many are open only on weekends in winter. Look for these free brochures: *Nantucket Guide to Antique Shops* and the *Guideline to Buying a Nantucket Lightship Basket. Nantucket Arts*, a glossy annual with paid advertisements found in galleries, is useful for its profiles of artists, artisans, and craftspeople.

ANTIQUES Currently Nantucket has more than 25 antiques shops. In July and August, three large annual antiques shows benefit the Nantucket Historical Association and the Nantucket schools.

Rafael Osona (508-228-3942), 21 Washington Street at the American Legion Hall, holds estate auctions on selected weekends from late May to early December. Osona auctions 18th, 19th-, and 20th-century antiques from England, Europe, and the United States.

Tonkin of Nantucket (508-228-9697), 33 Main Street. Purveyors of English and French antiques (both country and formal), brass and silver items, militaria, and marine objects. Also check out their showroom and warehouse at 587 Teasdale Circle.

Weeds (508-228-5200), 14 Centre Street. Featuring 19th-century English country home and garden furnishings, Weeds is also an exclusive dealer in Wedgwood "Nantucket" fine bone china.

Paul La Paglia (508-228-8760), 38 Centre Street. Antique prints of Nantucket, whaling, botanicals, and game fish, as well as La Paglia's own abstract impressionist oil paintings.

Nina Hellman Antiques (508-228-4677), 48 Centre Street. Nautical items, folk art, Nantucket memorabilia, and work by scrimshander Charles A. Manghis, who gives demonstrations on premises.

J Butler Collection (508-228-8429), 36 Centre Street. Open May to late October. Antiques and reproduction furnishings, collectibles, and dishware in a homey setting.

Antiques Depot (508-228-1287), 14 Easy Street. An interesting collection of furniture and fine decorative arts.

Manor House Antiques Co-operative (508-228-4335), 31½ Centre Street. Open seasonally. This basement-level shop carries porcelain, tea services, glassware, crystal, sterling, and lamps. It's the island's only multi-dealer shop.

Salt Meadows Antiques (508-228-0230), 78 Union Street. Located on the edge of town in the so-called

DESPITE NANTUCKET'S RAREFIED PRICES, SOME ASPECTS ARE DOWN-TO-EARTH.

Kim Grant

Cavendish neighborhood, this treasure trove of antiques, folk art, and crafts carries a particularly fascinating collection of copper weather vanes. They also specialize in reconditioning 100- and 150-year-old trunks.

ART GALLERIES Sailor's Valentine Gallery (508-228-2011; www.sailorsvalentinegallery.com), Lower Main Street at the Thomas Macy Warehouse (see *To See*). Open mid-April to mid-December. My favorite gallery features eclectic contemporary art and international folk art and, as the name suggests, beautiful valentines made by sailors. Don't miss the sculpture garden out back.

Artist's Association of Nantucket Gallery (508-228-0294; www.nantucketarts.org), 19 Washington Street. This cooperative of 125 artists was founded in 1945 to showcase members' work. Changing AAN member exhibits, juried shows, demonstrations, and special events conspire to make this a vital venue for the local arts scene.

Old South Wharf. Lined with small galleries, clothing stores, artisans, and a marine chandlery, Old South is located in the boat basin just beyond the A&P parking lot. Generally open mid-May to mid-October. Definitely wander over.

William Welch Gallery (508-228-0687), 14 Easy Street. Open late April to late December. Welch's renderings idyllic island scenes in watercolors, pastels, and oils.

Art Cabinet (508-325-7202), 2 Union Street. Open May to late October. If you blink as you round the corner of Union and Main Streets, you might miss this little gem of a gallery, so keep your eyes peeled. Owner Dorte Neudert showcases European contemporary artists.

The Artist's House Gallery (508-325-6422), 27 Easy Street. Open seasonally. Frederick Collord's traditional oil paintings of Cape Cod as well as Nantucket town and island scenes; giclée limited editions, too.

BOOKSTORES ✍ **Nantucket Book-works** (508-228-4000; www.nantuck-etbookworks.com), 25 Broad Street. A great shop with helpful staff. Selective travel, literature, children's books, and biographies.

Mitchell's Book Corner (508-228-1080; www.mitchellsbookcorner.com), 54 Main Street. Maritime, whaling, and naturalist books. Sit and browse titles in the small "Nantucket Room," which features all things Nantucket.

CRAFTS SHOPS Dane Gallery/Nan-tucket Glass Works (508-228-7779), 28 Centre Street. An outstanding

shop, with a dazzling array of glass sculpture by artists like shop owner Robert Dane. You'll also find lighting fixtures and custom-painted and -designed utilitarian glass blocks long favored in hip renovated industrial spaces.

Stephen Swift (508-228-0255), 34 Main Street. Beautifully handcrafted chairs, benches, beds, dressers, and other furnishings.

The Spectrum (508-228-4606), 26 Main Street. Open mid-April through December. Distinctive contemporary objects made from a wide spectrum of materials.

Erica Wilson Needle Works (508-228-9881), 25 Main Street. Featuring namesake designs by Wilson, an islander since 1958. Wilson also has a

ONE-ROOM COTTAGES ON OLD SOUTH WHARF HOUSE GALLERIES AND SHOPS.

Kim Grant

boutique in Manhattan and has penned many a title on needlepoint.

Nantucket Looms (508-228-1908), 16 Main Street. Features weavers at work on their looms and their creations.

Claire Murray (508-228-1913), 11 South Water Street. Murray came to Nantucket in the late 1970s as an innkeeper and began hooking rugs during the long winter months. She's since given up the B&B business to concentrate on designing and on opening more stores; her staff now make the rugs. She sells finished pieces as well as kits.

Four Winds Craft Guild (508-228-9623), Ray's Courts, off Fair and Main Streets. Baskets, lightship purses, scrimshaw, and marine items.

FARM PRODUCE Main Street at Federal Street. Local produce is sold from the backs of trucks daily except Sunday, May through October. It doesn't get any fresher than this.

Bartlett's Ocean View Farm & Greenhouse (508-228-9403), Bartlett's Farm Road, off Hummock Pond Road. Bartlett's boasts a 100-acre spread run by an eighth-generation islander family.

Island Herbs (508-228-9450), 2 East York Street. Open May to late October. An organic farm that specializes in fresh herbs and salad greens. Also vegetables, cut flowers, plants, and specialty foods.

SPECIAL SHOPS Sweet Inspirations (508-228-5814), 26 Centre Street. Purveyor of Nantucket Clipper Chocolates, displayed in luscious mounds in the glass cases. Of particular note are cranberry-based confections such as cranberry cheesecake truffles and chocolate-covered cranberries.

Beautiful People (508-228-2001), 13 Centre Street. Open April through December. Clothing in styles as diverse as the women who wear them.

The Fragrance Bar (508-325-4740), 5 Centre Street. A treat for the senses, this shop deals in essential oils and perfumes and looks like an old apothecary. Take a seat at the bar and let master perfumer John Harding custom-mix you an original fragrance. Gorgeous handblown glass perfume bottles, too.

L'Ile de France, The French General Store (508-228-3686), 18 Federal Street. This charming little shop features the best of France, from crockery to olive oil, from pâté to real French bread. No kidding: owners Joyce and Michel Berruet take orders and fly in fresh-baked loaves from Paris!

Bramhall & Dunn (508-228-4688), 16 Federal Street. Women's clothing, including vests and luxurious, plush scarves, as well as fine objects for the home: quilts and kilims, candlesticks, frames, glass and pottery, and lamps.

Johnston's Cashmere (508-228-5450), 4 Federal Street. Open mid-April to early January. Scottish cashmere, with a nice selection of classic women's sweaters, dresses, and scarves.

Pollack's (508-228-9940), 5 South Water Street. Open mid-April through December. The personable proprietor, Bob Pollack, stocks comfortable, fashionable clothing for men and women.

Murray's Toggery Shop (508-228-0437; www.nantucketreds.com), 62 Main Street. This shop "invented" and owns the rights to Nantucket Reds, all-cotton pants that fade to pink after numerous washings— almost as "Nantucket" as lightship baskets. This is the only shop (which, by the way, is featured in *The Preppy Handbook*) that sells the real thing, and has since 1945. They also carry high-end, name-brand sportswear lines.

Peter Beaton Hat Studio (508-228-8456), 16½ Federal Street. Open April through December. Down a little walkway, this fun little shop has finely woven straw hats. Custom fitting and trimming, of course.

The Hub (508-228-3868), at Main and Federal Streets. Get newspapers and magazines here from all over, but more than that, this is a center for

LIGHTSHIP BASKETS

Although it is thought that Nantucket's first famed baskets were made in the 1820s, they didn't get their name until a bit later. When the first lightship anchored off the Nantucket coast to aid navigation around the treacherous shallow shoals, crew members were stationed on board for months at a time. In their spare daylight hours sailors created round and oval rattan baskets using lathes and wooden molds. Stiff oak staves were steamed to make them more pliant; the bottoms were wooden. They were made to withstand the test of time. There are perhaps 20 stores and studios that sell authentic light-ship baskets, which retail for hundreds to thousands of dollars and require at least 40 hours of work to produce. Among the shops that make them and take custom orders: **Michael Kane Lightship Baskets** (508-228-1548), 18A Sparks Avenue; **Bill and Judy Sayle** (508-228-9876), 112 Washington Street Extension; and the **Lightship Shop** (508-228-4164), 20 Miacomet Avenue.

Lightship Basket Museum (508-228-1177), 49 Union Street. Open 10–5 Wednesday through Saturday, late May to mid-October. This informative little museum has re-created a workshop with simple tools that helps visitors understand the simple techniques artisans employed to make exquisite bas-kets. With baskets from the 1850s to the present, the museum certainly helps promote the art form. Adults $4, kids $2.

Lightship Shop (508-228-4164), 20 Miacomet Avenue. Although it takes years to become a pro, Donna Cifranic offers 3-day classes so you can make your own basket. Classes Tuesday through Thursday with a total of 24 hours of instruction for $350. If you want to try making them on your own, you can purchase kits and materials from Peter at the **Lightship Shop Too** (508-228-2267), Pollywog Pond. It's a long walk to the shop; take the South Loop shut-tle in summer.

Goldsmith Diana Kim England (508-228-3766), 56 Main Street, sells ele-gant gold lightship basket jewelry. **The Golden Basket** (508-228-4344), 44 Main Street, sells miniature gold versions of the renowned baskets.

island news. Lines form on summer Sunday mornings for *The New York Times.*

The Camera Shop (508-228-0101), 32 Main Street. Film and same-day processing; an extensive greeting card collection; island prints and posters.

Zero Main (508-228-4401), 0 Main Street. A women's store for classic and contemporary clothes and shoes.

David Chase (508-228-4775), 60 Main Street. Open April to mid-December. Elegant yet comfortable women's clothing and accessories.

Vanderbilt Collection (508-325-4454), 18 Federal Street. Open seasonally. An eclectic assemblage of oil paintings, glitzy handbags, sculpture, lightship baskets, and classic custom jewelry.

Hepburn (508-228-1458), 3 Salem Street. Open April through January. A chic boutique with designs for women executed in crushed velvet, satin, silk, and wool.

⚓ **The Toy Boat** (508-228-4552), Straight Wharf. An old-fashioned children's toy store selling a wooden ferryboat and dock system, rocking boats, cradles, handmade toys and puzzles, marbles, and books.

Nantucket Woodcarving (508-325-7010), 110 Orange Street. Once used to identify early sailing ships, "quarterboards" now adorn thousands of island houses. You've seen them: long and narrow carved boards, proclaiming the house's name. The price depends on letter height, number of letters, board length, and whether or not you want 23K gold leaf. A board fitting nicely over a doorway and reading KIM'S HIDEAWAY in 3½-inch painted (not gold leaf) letters, with seashell end posts, would cost about $600.

THE CENTER OF THE UNIVERSE?

Kim Grant

WREATHS Nantucket Hydrangea Wreaths (508-228-5608), at the corner of Main and Federal Streets. Islander Joanne Johnson, often aided by her son Carl, produces lovely wreaths from the back of her pickup truck during summer and well into autumn. When properly displayed and shipped, they are long lasting.

✳ Special Events

Contact the chamber of commerce (508-228-1700) for specific dates, unless an alternative phone number is listed below. Also, remember that this is just a sampling of the larger, predictable annual events. The chamber produces an excellent *Events Calendar.*

Late April: **Daffodil Festival.** In 1974 an islander donated more than a million daffodil bulbs to be planted along Nantucket's main roads. It is estimated that after years of naturalization, there are now more than 3 million of these beauties. The official kickoff weekend to celebrate spring includes a vintage-car parade to 'Sconset, a tailgate picnic in 'Sconset, house tours, and a garden-club show. This is a very big weekend.

Mid-May: **Historic Preservation Week** (508-228-1700). This celebration of Nantucket's rich local history and heritage includes discussions about preservation and educational efforts.

Wine Festival (508-228-1128). This celebration of wine includes Grand Tastings at the 'Sconset Casino, as well as winery dinners at local restaurants.

Late May: **Figawi Boat Race** (508-771-9615). Memorial Day weekend; from Nantucket to Hyannis since 1972.

Mid-June: **Nantucket Film Festival** (212-708-1278; www.nantucketfilm-festival.org). Since 1996, an intimate and important venue for new independent films and filmmakers. Screenings, Q&A seminars, staged readings, panel discussions on how screenplays become movies and on the art of writing screenplays. In 2002, the festival attracted the Farrelly brothers and Natalie Portman and included readings by Rosie Perez and Jerry Stiller.

July: **Independence Day** (508-228-7213, 228-0925). Main Street is closed off for pie- and watermelon-eating contests, dunk tank, puppets, face painting, fire-hose battles, and more. Festivities are capped off with fireworks from Jetties Beach off Norton Beach Road.

Late July/early August: **Billfish Tournament** (508-228-2299). A weeklong event on Straight Wharf since 1969.

Mid-August: **House Tour** (508-228-8968). Sponsored by the Nantucket Garden Club since 1955; pre-registration is required.

Sandcastle & Sculpture Day. Jetties Beach off Norton Beach Road, since 1974.

Mid-September: **Island Fair** (508-228-7213). At the Tom Nevers Recreation Area; a two-day event with puppet show, flea market, music, food, pumpkin weighing contest, and more.

Early October: **Nantucket Arts Festival.** This weeklong event, established in 1992, celebrates a variety of island arts, from dance to theater arts, from gallery exhibits to films, from music to literary arts.

Late November–December: **Nantucket Noel** begins the day after Thanksgiving with a Christmas-tree-lighting ceremony; live Christmas trees decorated by island schoolchildren line Main Street; special concerts and theatrical performances heighten the holiday cheer and merriment.

Early December: **Christmas Stroll.** Begun in 1973 and taking place on the first Saturday of December, the Stroll includes vintage-costumed carolers, festive store-window decorations, wreath exhibits, open houses, and a historic house tour. Marking the official "end" of tourist season, like the Daffodil Festival this is a very big event. Make lodging reservations months in advance.

INDEX